The World at a Glance

D1545454

Studies in Continental Thought

THE WORLD AT
A GLANCE

EDWARD S. CASEY

INDIANA UNIVERSITY PRESS
BLOOMINGTON AND INDIANAPOLIS

This book is a publication of

Indiana University Press
601 North Morton Street
Bloomington, IN 47404-3797 USA

http://iupress.indiana.edu

Telephone orders   800-842-6796
Fax orders   812-855-7931
Orders by e-mail   iuporder@indiana.edu

Library of Congress Cataloging-in-Publication Data

Casey, Edward S., date
The world at a glance / Edward S. Casey.
p. cm.
Includes bibliographical references and index.
ISBN-13: 978-0-253-34852-4 (cloth : alk. paper)
ISBN-13: 978-0-253-21897-1 (pbk. : alk. paper)
ISBN-10: 0-253-34852-8 (cloth : alk. paper)
ISBN-10: 0-253-21897-7 (pbk. : alk. paper)
1. Visual perception. 2. Perception.
3. Vision. I. Title.
BF241.C37 2007
121'.35—dc22   2006028119

1 2 3 4 5 12 11 10 09 08 07

To the generations who grace my family life,
each enacting the genius of the glance
in distinctive visions of what matters:

Eric Scott Casey and Cathy Gutierrez —
who look so deeply into the culture and thought
of ancient Mediterranean civilizations
and nineteenth-century spiritual practices

Erin Casey Green and Peter Green —
who understand so clearly and caringly
the complexities of being parents in a society
to which they contribute so remarkably

Samantha and Jeremy Green, my grandchildren,
who embody the gay wisdom of the glance
on their journey into a beckoning future

True philosophy consists in relearning how to look at the world.

—Maurice Merleau-Ponty,
Phenomenology of Perception

O body swayed to music, O brightening glance!
How can we know the dancer from the dance?

—W. B. Yeats, "Among School Children"

CONTENTS

ACKNOWLEDGMENTS

I wish to thank, first of all, three graduates of the doctoral program at SUNY, Stony Brook, who were present at the origin of this book: Irene Klaver, in whose congenial company I first conceived the core idea; and Fred Evans and Len Lawlor, who invited me to deliver its first public presentation. Without the initial enthusiasm of this extraordinary trio of bright minds, the book might never have seen the light of day.

I am also indebted to several more recent graduate students at Stony Brook. Tanja Staehler encouraged me at every subsequent step, bringing light into much darkness of description. Andrés Colapinto, who has a passion for clarity and a low tolerance for ambiguity, has been especially formative in the writing of the final version of this book. Emily Lee and Christopher Berndt contributed substantially at other moments in the generation of the text.

I wish to acknowledge the salutary influence of the group of psychologists and philosophers who met in recent years in Carbondale, Illinois, and in Paris, France, to examine the nature of attention and who listened patiently to my fledgling efforts to explore the attentional aspects of glancing. Among these were Anthony Steinbock, Natalie Depraz, Pierre Vermersch, Bruce Bégout, and Eugene Gendlin. Together, they formed an exemplary "équipe de travail" who were at once international and interdisciplinary.

Regarding technical questions stemming from the ancient Greek world, I have received invaluable assistance from several classicists: Peter Manchester, my colleague at Stony Brook; Meredith Hoppin of Williams College; Robert Garland of Colgate University; and especially Eric Casey of Sweet Briar College, who kept me honest regarding Greek and Latin translations and transliterations as well as suggesting invaluable sources from the classical world that deepened my appreciation of earlier theories of vision.

Professor David LaBerge of Simons Rock College informed me of recent research (including his own) on saccadic eye movements and related matters. His intervention, at the suggestion of John Compton, opened an entire world of experimental approaches to human vision.

A book such as this arises as much from indirection as from concerted focus. I have been blessed with the company of friends and colleagues who are concerned with vision in their work and their lives as a whole. Members of this extended community include David Morris, Dr. Bruce Anderson, Wes Jackson, Brian Schroeder, Bruce Wilshire, Janet Gyatso, David Abram, Betsy Behnke, Graham Parkes, D. G. Leahy, Julia Talen, Dr. Stanley Leavy, Henry Tylbor, Michael Naas, Jan Larson, Peter Atterton, Kelly Oliver, Andrew Mitchell, David Carr, Richard Bernstein, Nancy Franklin, Bonnie Karp, Ted Toadvine, Ginger Costello, and Donna Wilshire. The writings of Véronique Fóti and David Kleinberg-Levin have been of special inspiration. David Miller's approach to the glance has proven uncannily convergent with my own. Richard Kearney and Dermot Moran invited me to try out an earlier avatar of this book in a public lecture at University College, Dublin. My colleagues at Stony Brook gave direction to my ongoing work at every turn: Lorenzo Simpson, Mary Rawlinson, Eduardo Mendieta, Gary Mar, Robert Crease, Jeff Edwards, Robert Harvey, Donn Welton, Harvey Cormier, Allegra de Laurentiis, William Chittick, Sachiko Murata, Hugh Silverman, Lee Miller, David Allison, and Don Ihde. I would also like to thank James Staros, Dean of Arts and Sciences at Stony Brook, for his continuing support of my research.

My painter friends have provided a set of unique perspectives into the character of visual experience, especially as it arises in the art world: Margot McLean, Eve Ingalls, Sandy Gellis, Michelle Stuart, Wendy Gittler, Parviz Mohassel, Christina Maile, Marja Watson, Ed Horan, Gwen Gunn, Alice Hayden, and Molly McDonald. In this circle Virginia Foster stands out by her remarkable ability to put complex ideas about vision (and many other areas of life and thought) into crisp and telling words.

I wish to thank my copy editor, Karen Kodner, as well as Neill Bogan, who prepared the index.

To Mary Watkins I express my gratitude for her gifts of insight and language during the final stages of this book's completion: her glances were as discerning as they were appreciative and generously given.

I want to pay homage here to two ongoing mentors of mine: James Hillman, pathbreaking poetic delineator of the imaginal in the soul of the world; Thomas J. J. Altizer, intrepid and original theologian who discerns the apocalyptic edges of our era.

This book owes everything to the active encouragement of Dee Mortensen and Janet Rabinowitch of Indiana University Press, with whom I discussed its evolution from the very beginning. Together, and in concert with others at the Press (notably Laura MacLeod), they have brought it home to harbor.

PROLOGUE:

REGAINING THE GLANCE

I have placed you in the center of the world, so
that, from that vantage point, you may with greater
ease glance around about you on all that the world
contains.

> —Pico della Mirandola,
> *Oration on the Dignity of Man*

The eye's plain vision is a thing apart,
The vulgate of experience . . .

> —Wallace Stevens,
> "An Ordinary Evening in New Haven"

I

The world at a glance: Pico sees the creation of humans as the bringing forth of beings who can glance at all that surrounds them—at a world that solicits their look even as it evades their certain or complete knowledge.

A glance? How can something so fickle and fragile as a glance serve to distinguish creatures placed at the center of the universe (where they should enjoy the privilege of omnivision)? Is not the glance doomed to triviality and in any case prone to error? Is not Pico exaggerating if not outright confabulating?

The ancient Egyptians thought otherwise. They worshipped Osiris, god of the underworld and the judge of the dead. Osiris was cut up into a thousand pieces; only his eyes survived—and these, too, were sliced up. Many centuries later, Phoenician and Greek sailors painted eyes on the prows of their ships to guide them in their voyages: placed in that advance position, where they might help to navigate, these eyes were in effect the knowing eyes of the resurrected Osiris.[1]

The glance is a scopic scout stationed at the outposts of human perceptual experience. It discovers whole colonies of the to-be-seen world: places where sight has never before been—or if it has, it now sees differently. The glance guides the eye as it comes to know the perceived world, leading it out of more staid and settled ways of looking. This happens by actions of leaping from the zone of the familiar to the very edges of the unfamiliar, all the while taking in the intermediate stretches, and then leaping back again.

1. For the story of Osiris and his further fate, see Henri Frankfurt, *Before Philosophy* (Harmondsworth, U.K.: Penguin, 1954).

I stand at my apartment window in New York City. I have just moved in. My eye is drawn outward by the vista. I look all over the place, not step-by-step in some regular scanning action but by jumping from one point of interest to another: from the bridge at the upper left to the park at the lower right, then to the horizon where another bridge stands out. My glance swings rapidly among these various points of attachment, never resting for long anywhere, taking it all in by leaps and bounds. "All" is not here a fixed totality—not literally everything everywhere, as in the Greek conception of *to pan* (the universe, all that is)—but all as an open whole, a vista, an expanse. My glance darts in and out of this scene. In some significant sense, *I see it all:* "all that the world contains" in Pico's apt words. I see the world in a glance.

Not just this one world that is named "Upper West Side" but every world I encounter or inhabit is seen, or seeable, at a glance. That is part of the magic of this special act of seeing, for which there is no exact equivalent elsewhere in the repertoire of sight. It is no mere modification of some other, more "basic act" such as sensory perceiving.[2] It occurs in, and as part of, such perceiving itself, but it extends it—and sometimes eclipses it in an act of pure vision, as happens in mental glancing (for example, glancing into a memory).

Glancing is its own form of looking. At the same time, it contributes to other kinds of visual perception, which depend on it for its exploratory spirit, its sudden sallies into the outer fringes of the known world, as well as its adept insights into what lies close-up, right under our ethical and epistemic nose. The truth is that, inessential as glancing might seem to be, we could not do without it. Glancing is interwoven into perception at every point, indeed is indissociable from it. The most studied gaze is riddled with glances, which perforate it at every turn, letting in the fresh air of continually adventuresome looking.

None of the official epistemologies in the West consider glancing as an act worth investigating in its own right. In their sober assessments, it does not deserve separate consideration. If we consult Aristotle, Locke, Descartes, Kant, H. H. Price, D. M. Amstrong, and the many others who have written insightfully on perception overall, we will not find any serious discussion of this fugitive act. If it is mentioned at all, it is dismissed as inconsequential, as offering nothing but a sliver of what deserves closer perceptual scrutiny, typically in the guise of a prolonged gaze. A recent book that purports to be a comprehensive study of perception makes no mention of it at all.[3]

Why this neglect, if not the outright repression, of the glance? It does not

---

2. On sensory perception as the "basic act," see Edmund Husserl, *Logical Investigations.* tr. J. Findlay, ed. D. Moran (New York: Routledge, 2001), vol. 2, Fifth and Sixth Investigations. For a related, if more richly ambiguous, notion of perception as "primary," see Maurice Merleau-Ponty, "The Primacy of Perception" in *The Primacy of Perception,* tr. J. Edie (Evanston, Ill.: Northwestern University Press, 1964), pp. 12–42.

3. See A. D. Smith, *The Problem of Perception* (Cambridge, Mass.: Harvard University Press, 2002).

simply stem from the conviction that the glance is capable only of innocuous deliverances, giving us the mere aspects of things, their seemings. It also comes from the fact that the glance is incompatible with most Western paradigms of knowledge. It lacks the motive of mastery; it has no pretense to be encyclopedic or systematic (even if it can be sweeping); it does not wish to be part of a grand narrative of knowledge about the external world (it has its own *petit récit*). When I am looking out of my window in New York, I am not surveying the scene before me with some royal regard, seeking to dominate or totalize it. If I am looking for some particular building or bridge, I may scan the vista. But for the most part I am glancing all around in a playful manner, touching on this item and that and then another, in a virtual free dance of the look. Even curiosity would be too strong a motive to impute to my various acts of glancing; I am enjoying it as such and for its own sake—not for where it is going to take me later today or tomorrow. Pico's words remain apt: I am at "the center of [my] world" and from that "vantage point," I am able "with greater ease" to "glance around about [myself]." I am able to do this thanks to the gift of the glance.

Instead of bogging me down—as gazing and staring so often do—glancing alleviates my visual life. It takes place in the light, and it is brightening, sometimes soaring. When life becomes intolerably costly or demanding, when the world is too much with me, I can always glance my way out of the immediate circumstance. This solution may not be permanent (it does not pretend to be), but it does offer a crucial moment of respite, a second of solace, a liberating leap beyond what Stevens calls "the vulgate of experience" delivered by a merely "plain vision." The glance is never plain; it has no vulgate version; it is always extraordinary.

II

It is timely to turn to the glance at this historical moment. In a society of the spectacle such as ours—in which instreaming simulacra compel our looking in every hour of waking life—it is urgent to identify and valorize alternative ways of seeing: ways different from those thrust upon us in a vast video culture, where film and television prescribe what is to be seen and even when and how to see it. Indulging in these omnipresent media nonstop encourages a recourse to a mesmerized gaze as the main organ of an oculocentric culture. This is a gaze that is at once narcissistic (we see what we want to see) and stultifying (we see only what predominant channels of culture allow us to see). I shall argue that other cultures—notably those of ancient Athens and late-nineteenth-century Paris—were visuocentric without being oculocentric. They valued looking but did not insist on gazing; they left lots of room for glancing. Inspired by their example, I shall propose that the human glance furnishes a form of visual freedom that acts to undermine the hegemony of the gaze. It does so by merely playing on the surfaces of any given visual spectacle. Instead of taking the spectacle itself as ultimate, however, it inculcates an awareness that the surfaces over which it flits are surfaces *of things* (physical objects or persons) as well as of *places:* they have edges, they lead to other surfaces, finally they drop off into space. Unlike simulacra, they are never the end of the story. They are the ever-first steps of an unbridled and unmitigated looking that takes us to places we never dreamed of going.

The glance is an agent of change in the midst of the stasis induced by those established modes of seeing that favor the gaze, including inspection, scrutiny, and other forms of concerted looking. These latter have their own validity—we count on the intent gaze of the surgeon during an operation—but they cannot be taken as paradigmatic for all the ways we look. Nor should they ever be regarded as existing in strict separation from glancing: even the surgeon looks around quickly at her assistants or at an incoming tray of instruments. In the very midst of the most sober enterprise, the glance surges forth suddenly, leavening it from within and tracing its shape without. Without it, we would be lost in our looking—stuck there, limited to what we can see fixedly from a very constricted standpoint. With it, we are free to keep on looking otherwise and elsewhere.

III

In this book I show how glancing counts for much more than we may ever have imagined in earlier understandings of human perception. I shall do this without recounting the extensive history of these understandings—which often amount to misunderstandings when glancing is left out of account. Nor will I propose a new model of perception to replace traditional accounts, even if my findings on the glance will have important implications for these accounts. Instead, I shall stick to the glance itself, offering a description that will not keep the act artificially isolated from its many connections and consequences. Implicit in this same description will be a sense of what the world must be like if it allows itself to be detected by the most casual glance: it must be a world full of surprise. To be equal to that feature of the world, the glance must be an especially sensitive and singular act, capable of considerable feats of what I shall term "apperception," that is, the swift and subtle grasp of what might otherwise pass us by entirely. The glance holds in its wily regard, if only for a moment, much that would go unnoticed without its quick and sometimes quirky intervention. It is the ever-evasive trickster of vision, and as such it has eluded previous descriptions. Either it is taken for granted, or it is considered merely peripheral. This is to be expected, since part of its very character is to traffic in the sudden as well as the surprising, the simultaneous as well as the spontaneous—each of which contributes to its ability to deconstruct oculocentric models of vision.

I shall proceed in four parts. In the first, I depict the glance as it figures into everyday existence in manifold ways, in private and in public as well as in the experience of getting oriented in a new place. I also contrast the glance with the gaze in certain crucial respects. In the second part, I trace out the fate of the glance in the very different cultural and historical settings of the Athenian agora and the arcades and streets of Paris. I investigate both the unique temporality and the marked singularity of the glance, in addition to exploring the close relationship between attending to something and glancing at it. In a final part, I pursue the ingressions of the glance into the disparate areas of art, ethics, and the natural environment. The reader is advised to read the introduction and parts 1 and 2 in that order but then to range freely among the chapters that follow: these latter are forays into diverse domains of the glance-world and do not form any strict sequence. The chapter on concluding thoughts addresses delimitations of the glance in the face of the powers I have ascribed to it throughout the book.

This book carries forward an ongoing series of books that began with *Imagining: A Phenomenological Study*. In many respects, the phenomenon of the glance as I here describe it rejoins my earlier analysis of imagining in terms of such predicates as alacrity, ease of operation, and indeterminacy of content. But glancing, in contrast with imagining, is not concerned with pure possibility; it detects what is now happening to the glancer in the outer or inner world to which he or she belongs. My more recent work on place is integral to the glance, which takes us across things into the place-world of our surroundings and situates us there—for the moment at least, that is, until the next glance.

My method of proceeding in this book can be termed "paraphenomenological," for it exists alongside, literally at the limits of, traditional phenomenology. It is located on the border between the latter—which I pursue in my own informal way—and cultural studies of various particular kinds (for example, gender studies, colonial and neocolonial studies, and so on). At several points, most notably in chapters 8 and 9, I draw upon the perspective of such studies by investigating historical and social dimensions of the glance. In chapter 10, I discuss how these dimensions are ingredient in the barest acts of looking. Overall, however, I situate myself on the far edge of culturalist approaches. I draw upon them when warranted, yet for the most part I engage in a detailed descriptive account of glancing in its many nomadic maneuvers. Not unlike the glance itself, I dart back and forth between the cultural and the phenomenological, with a primary emphasis on the latter.

On this paraphenomenological basis, I do not pretend to set forth anything like a general theory of perception, much less of knowledge. Instead, I plot the trajectory of the human glance as it enters guilelessly into our daily lives: an uninvited but most welcome guest in the house of our intimate dwelling in the place-world. The least glance traverses this world with such agility that we begin to suspect that very little holds back this modest but momentous act; it comes forward alertly into the brightness of the light, yet it also brings its own light into the darkened recesses of human experience. We glance out onto the broadening world and into its distant corners; but we glance as well into our own inwardness, catching glimpses of the life that flickers within.

The World at a Glance

INTRODUCTION

TAKING IN THE WORLD
AT A GLANCE

> begin now to apprehend the edges of skeletal
> diminuendos of glancings as they ascend the
> manifest up towards its upper reaches . . .
>
> —Jorie Graham, "The Philosopher's Stone"

> More than any other philosophy, *phenomenology*,
> in the wake of Plato, was to be struck with light.
> Unable to reduce the last naïveté, the naïveté of
> the glance, it predetermined being as object.
>
> —Jacques Derrida, "Violence and Metaphysics,"
> *Writing and Difference*

> Courage slayeth also giddiness at abysses; and
> where doth man not stand at abysses? Is not seeing
> itself seeing abysses?
>
> —Friedrich Nietzsche, "The Vision and the
> Enigma," *Thus Spake Zarathustra*

I

I am no longer looking out the windows of my apartment in New York. I've turned away from the vista I was taking in, and am now seated on the couch and looking around the living room. My eye travels first to several photographs that I've put out in the central portion of my bookcase: I linger briefly on these, dusting them lightly with my look—familiar images of friends and family members, of fellow painters in Maine, and of Maurice Merleau-Ponty and Jacques Derrida. My eye moves on to the paintings on the walls, equally familiar: the monoprint by Christina Maile, two sketches by Dan Rice, and one of my own paintings. I do not scrutinize these, nor do I look at them in any particular order. I note them all, glancingly, but not as items of any inventory. My glance glides between them, careening off their surfaces. It goes on to the kitchen—the refrigerator, various glasses and bowls on the counter, a familiar frying pan on the stove. None of this happens in any systematic order (for example, shifting my glance from left to right only) or according to any general principle (paying attention only to what is useful to me at this moment). My look is adrift in the domestic scene, and is distinctly desultory in its action.

Suddenly, there is a knock on the door. This time my look is drawn to a definite object and focuses on that—on the backside of the door from which the knock issues. My glance now becomes highly intentional: it is no longer floating idly through the open space of the apartment. I stride to the door and open it. It is my friend Parviz. We exchange glances as we greet each other: the two modes of connection, visual and verbal, intermingling. My glance conveys my look, my words my greeting; both occur at once and both say in effect, "You are welcome." His glance and words in turn express the thought, "I am happy to be here." The drifting of the glance so evident in the first, quite sedentary scene has here given way to a more involved situation in which the glance has become a concerted actor in an emerging social scene. This scene opens with a bare greeting of another human being, and it continues in the form of a lively discussion on the couch—during which my friend and I look and talk back and forth in rapid succession, sometimes with the glance taking the lead, sometimes a facial expression, sometimes a verbal expression, in a rich imbroglio of emotions and perceptions, thoughts and memories.

In the midst of our conversation, we hear voices welling up from the street far below. We rush to the window and see a mass of human beings coming down 110th Street, heading west. It is the AIDS march we had planned to join! It takes only a single glance to realize what is happening. Down we go onto the street, joining the marchers as they move by rapidly. Once part of the march, we find ourselves looking around: ahead of us toward the leaders, laterally at compatriots, and even behind us espying the stragglers. Certain marchers are dressed up as comic characters, and they draw our eye immediately. Other things are more subtle, and require several successive looks: for example, a few skeptical bystanders along the parade route side by side with those who are more enthusiastic, the diverse ages and ethnicities of the marchers, the route itself as it turns off 110th Street and winds south through Riverside Park. Glancing continues throughout the march, varying from person to person: Parviz and I do not glance in the same way, nor do others we encounter: each person seems to have his or her own style of glancing, as distinctive as their own physiognomy. (So, too, do the animals encountered en route: they glance in tellingly different ways, both as different species and as individual members of those species. A German shepherd looks out alertly and on the edge of snarling, a Pekinese peers out timidly; a tomcat glances defiantly, a well-bred lady cat looks away coyly.) At the same time, the verdure of Riverside Park solicits glances at the remarkable variety of its trees, even as looks are cast down toward the Hudson River: natural prospects not readily available on 110th Street.

The march dies down. Parviz and I say goodbye: he returns to the lower West Side where he lives, and I go back to my apartment further east on 110th Street.

All of the experiences I have just undergone—beginning with the casual look about my living room and ending with the AIDS march—have lasted no more than two hours. Yet in the course of it I, along with Parviz, have glanced so often that I could not begin to count the number of times we have done so: doubtless in the thousands. And in a great variety of *ways* as well: the two of us have glanced forthrightly, furtively, slyly, accommodatingly, warmly, skeptically, receptively, inquiringly, and more. A veritable choreography of the glance has taken place, first in my apartment and then outside on the New York streets. This has happened so spontaneously that I was not conscious of it as a distinct stream of lookings; nor did I track it as such. Only in now writing about it am I aware of it as a fairly complex bit of visual history on my part and that of others. Otherwise, it is a subdued undertone, a basso continuo for the episodes I have here recounted.

What traits of glancing may we single out in the foregoing description? Beyond the capacity of the glance to take in a great deal from a delimited vantage point—as was already happening when I first looked out from the windows of my apartment—several things now stand out:

(i) the *nimbleness of the act*, bespeaking a basic bodily and cognitive aptitude or skill, so deeply ensconced in us as not to be consciously traceable in our corporeal history (when did we first start glancing?—presumably from the first moment we opened our eyes, yet we cannot recall any such moment);

(ii) the *considerable range* of glancing: from an unfocused meandering of the look as it slides off nearby surfaces to the much more attentive looking that was occasioned by the arrival of my friend Parviz, along with many intermediate acts of differing degrees of concerted focus after this;

(iii) the *marked change* that occurred when another human being became the object of my glance; something qualitatively different here arose, having to do with human presence, especially the face; something compelling that changes the destiny or trajectory of the glance itself;

(iv) a *notable thickening* that occurred when I moved from engagement in a dyadic interpersonal encounter to being in the midst of a much larger group of human beings that brought with it more kinds of glancing as well as more diversity in content;

(v) an *alteration of register* happened when I began to pay attention to the natural world that pervades Riverside Park; not only other species of animals or plants but a different kind of landscape vista ensued, seeming to call for its own separate description.

These five traits of the glance are provisional at best; they are only the first signs of something we suspect will become at once much more complicated and more subtle in any more complete accounting. Even at this early point, however, we can see that the phenomenon of glancing differs markedly from certain acts of perception held to be paradigmatic in Western epistemologies. In particular, it lacks the robustness of other forms of perceiving that reflect the full-throated grasping of perceptual particulars as straightforwardly present. This robustness consists in the full presentation of primary and secondary qualities of ordinary physical objects: their color, weight, shape, volume, and so on. These qualities form the content of standard acts of perceiving as described by Plato and Aristotle (*pistis; aisthesis*), Descartes and Hume (*perceptio;* plain "perception"), and Kant and Wittgenstein (*Anschauung;* "seeing as"). Such highly valorized acts favor the gaze over the glance, scrutiny over the passing look, knowledge over acquaintance, certainty over the indefinite.

The charm and challenge of the glance consist in its subversion of the dominant models of perception in Western philosophy. But just here you may ask: How can this stripling act, so seemingly innocent and ever young, stand up to the daunting authority of orthodox theories of vision? How can this David confront the Goliath of such theories? Without staging a *gigantomachia* ("battle of the giants"), how can we find for the glance a place that is both duly modest and multiply ramified? The glance is the slingshot of the look: at once meager in means and yet potent in effect, deceptively local in its immediate orbit and yet far-flung in its full compass. To ponder the glance is to consider the ductile strength of something whose circumscribed bodily basis—two seeing eyes—give access to a virtually undelimited domain of perception.

II

> At the same time, however, I can direct my glance
> at the perceived spatial world with its orientation.
> If I do that, the other [that is, the just perceived
> world] vanishes: And this vanishing is not a mere
> darkening, but a being pressed down to an "empty"
> presentation.
>
> —Husserl, *Phantasie,*
> *Bild-Bewusstsein, Erinnerung*

In this book I shall take a new look at the glance. The glance—not the gaze or the regard (which is Sartre's territory) or studied scrutiny (the prescribed attitude of so much of Western philosophy, from Plato to the present) or even bare contemplation (an ascetic ideal). The glance has none of the gravity of these traditionally sanctioned kinds of looking. It is a mere featherweight by comparison. Rather than petrifying things—as in the case of the Sartrian *regard*—the glance graces what it looks at, enhancing and expanding it. The glance does not make entities more entitative; rather than ballasting them with Being, it endows them with the lightness of Becoming. The spirit of gravity, which seeks to fixate and to identify, is dissipated in the mereness of a glance.

Apophansis, the urge to predicate and judge, which has held some two millennia of Western thought in thrall, is suspended in the glance. Instead of a logic of statement—of affirmation and confirmation—the glance returns us to the original and literal meaning of "apo-phansis": to *show* something *from* itself, from off its very surface. Which is precisely what the glance is uniquely capable of doing. Even the most concerted glance attends to the surface rather than piercing it and going behind it, and this is true even of a "penetrating glance." That is not to say, however, that the glance lingers on a single surface. It would not be a glance if it did. From one surface—of one thing or group of things—it is deflected to another. *The glance moves on.* Contrary to what Husserl (cited by Derrida for a quite different yet ultimately parallel purpose) claimed, the look does *not* abide.[1] At least, not if the look is a glance.

But what is the glance? What happens in it? One thing that happens is this. A glance *takes in*—it takes a lot in, namely, all kinds of surface. In so doing, it *takes us places*, all kinds of places. For places are what hold surfaces together in more or less coherent congeries, giving them a habitation if not a name: giving them a "layout."[2] If we can say of surfaces what Socrates says of shapes—namely, that they are "the limits of solids"[3]—then they are not only the surfaces of things but of places as well.

In these two regards, that is, by taking in surfaces and taking us places, a glance *takes us out of ourselves,* out of our formally defined, defensive egoic identities. It suspends these identities as surely as it dissolves the apophantic obsession with identification itself. In its egoless ecstasis, the glance refuses to succumb to the grasping that is so endemic to any settled sense of self and that is, for classical Buddhism, the essence of *samsara*, human suffering. By effecting this release, the glance can take us virtually anywhere—to almost any surface and place of the world. Indeed, it brings us to the world itself. The world at a glance: the world *in a glance.*

I said that the glance "takes *in.*" I meant this rather literally. The glance not only goes out; it comes (back) in. It is in-formative. As performative of perspectives on the world, it is informative of this same world. For it is by glancing that we learn a great deal of what we know about the world—a great deal more than official epistemologies are willing to admit. A glance reveals an entire situation, a whole scene of action. And it does so with considerable comprehensiveness and scope. Let me give some further examples:

---

1. "Contrary to the assurance that Husserl gives us a little further on, 'the look' cannot 'abide' " (Jacques Derrida, *Speech and Phenomena*, tr. D. Allison [Evanston, Ill.: Northwestern University Press, 1973], p. 104).

2. I borrow "layout" from J. J. Gibson, *The Ecological Approach to Visual Perception* (Mahwah, N.J.: Erlbaum, 1987). I return to this concept in chap. 11.

3. "Shape is that in which a solid terminates, or, more briefly, it is the limit of a solid" (Plato, *Meno* 76a).

—In being in a large city such as New York, I learn much by just glancing around at my surroundings: not only from the window of my highrise apartment or in a public march outside but in many other settings as well. A glance tells me that now I am now driving in midtown, I must be on the West Side, Soho should be coming up, and so on. I need not scrutinize the situation to pick these things up; they arise within my mere glance. (New York cabbies, it has been claimed, know where they are by the momentary feeling of wind currents, a feeling that is the kinesthetic equivalent of the glance.) It doesn't matter that the metropolis is a very complex entity; the more complex, the better suited to being known by glances: what Bertrand Russell called "knowledge by acquaintance" here assumes the form of taking in at a glance;

—or consider the very different situation of being in Montana, where the landscape is every bit as complicated as the New York cityscape; yet, just by glancing about me as I hike there, I find that I take in an enormous amount: "amount" not as an additive sum of discrete details but as a single amassed sense of the world; I perceive six or seven different types of weather in different parts of the same open sky. Even if I am driving west on Highway 90, I see the Crazy Mountains suddenly rising from the plain on my right and the Absaroka on my left; having climbed twice before in the Crazies, I recognize them instantly; but even if I do not know the Absarokas, I construe them instantly as south-central Montana mountains without pausing to scrutinize them one by one and without having to check any map. These outsize momentous Things, like the diverse weather hovering over them, are *all there in the glance*—in one or two quick looks on my part;

—or take the very different case of sexual identity: someone is walking toward me and I glance in that direction; in most such cases, I know right away whether this is a man or a woman; even in cases of cross-dressing, I can usually tell fairly soon if this is a male who is dressing as a woman, or vice versa; only if I cannot tell from a first look, do I pause—if I am interested in this question—and examine the content of my perception; but the examination itself will consist in a set of further glances at the person in question, now seen from closer up and with a more particular disambiguating purpose in mind;

—or, finally, think of the circumstance of "sizing up a situation"; this happens all the time among human beings (indeed, it happens between human beings and animals, and among animals themselves); it is effective and informative—often being all we need to understand what is going on, even if the situation is complicated (she is angry at how he treats her friend, who, however, has in certain ways provoked him); this is not to deny that some are more adept than others at quickly assessing a social situation; but virtually everyone possesses a modicum of such a skill—a skill that requires no more than a glance or two for its enactment.

Thus, in four very different circumstances—two of them involving perceived scenes and two social settings—the power of the glance is strikingly evident. In all four cases we witness a primary paradox of the glance: namely, the fact that *something so diminutive in extent and bearing can convey such far-ranging and complex insight.* What the glance takes in is vast in comparison with its own physical extent (being a mere epiphenomenon of the eye) and time of enactment (taking no more than a few seconds at best). It is as if the glance were a fulcrum, an Archimedean point of leverage, for otherwise quite demanding or massive being-in-the-world. In this respect the glance seems to be the perceptual analogue of short-term memory, which within milliseconds also takes in an enormous amount of complicated data.

The glance is the most poignant point of access, of immediate *intromission*, into the surrounding world. It is an incisive inroad into this world; it gets us there, even if we do not typically stay there after its insertion (though, in the case of disambiguation, it may insistently return there). It gets us to the surface of things, as many surfaces as we can bear—thus to as many places as we can go. These surfaces and places are not bare or brute; they are telling; they say themselves, they show themselves, to the glance that takes them in.

III

Let me say a word about how I have come to these unaccustomed thoughts, a moment of philosophical autobiography as it were. For many years I have been struck by the generally unappreciated prominence of the term *paysage* in Maurice Merleau-Ponty's *Phenomenology of Perception.* The prominence is obscured in the English translation, thanks to the fact that this term is sometimes translated as "landscape" and sometimes as "countryside." There is a passage in the *Phenomenology* that describes two men looking at the landscape—a passage that raises interesting issues concerning the commonality of perception shared by different onlookers of a given scene:

> Suppose that my friend Paul and I are looking at a landscape. . . . When I think of Paul, I do not think of a flow of private sensations indirectly related to mine through the medium of interposed signs, but of someone who has a living experience of the same world as mine, as well as the same history, and with whom I am in communication through that world and that history. . . . Paul and I "together" see this landscape, we are jointly present in it, it is the same for both of us, not only as an intelligible significance, but as a certain accent of the world's style, down to its very thisness.[4]

Already in the preface to the same book, there are a surprising number of references to *paysage.* These (and a number of later, also usually unnoticed mentions) reflect the influence of Erwin Straus's distinction between "land-

---

4. M. Merleau-Ponty, *Phenomenology of Perception,* tr. C. Smith (New York: Humanities, 1962), pp. 405–406. I further analyze this passage in more detail in my essay "Repetition and Imagination in Literature: A Reassessment" (*Yale French Studies* 52 [1975]: 249–267).

scape" and "geography."[5] The distinction is important for Merleau-Ponty because landscape provides for him an intentional correlate for the richly ambiguous act of perception he is describing throughout the *Phenomenology*. Yet, surprisingly, Merleau-Ponty nowhere singles out just what kind of perception is at stake in the experience of landscape. The answer, I would propose, is the glance.

A second clue is found in *The Visible and the Invisible*, where Merleau-Ponty (especially in the Working Notes) takes over Husserl's notion of "rays of the world" without, once again, indicating the specific intentional act for taking in such rays. Glancing, I would propose, is just such an act—as Husserl had already hinted in the importance he accorded to the idea of *Blickstrahl*, literally "ray of the look," a promising description of what happens in the glance (as we notice in the case of locutions such as "he shot her a glance": the glance as lance).[6]

Then again, I have been intrigued for a long time with Gaston Bachelard's *L'intuition de l'instant*, a neglected book whose brilliant critique of Henri Bergson's notion of duration parallels Jacques Derrida's implicit rejection of Merleau-Ponty, whose philosophical sensibilities so strikingly resemble those of Bergson. Both Bachelard and Derrida posit a form of philosophical pointillism in defiance of regnant hegemonies of continuity and synthesis. In this common project, the instant figures as a precursor to the portrayal of the glance as I construe it in this book, even if I shall prefer to use the language of "moment." Bachelard's emphasis on the compacted power of the instant—the temporal analogue of the glance—reminds one of Willem de Kooning's emphasis on the glance as essential to the evolution of his painting. De Kooning regarded an entire series of paintings done in the late 1960s as proceeding from glances he cast at the surrounding landscape in the Hudson Palisades and on Long Island as he streamed through in a car. During this same period, he wrote the following in an essay in verse form: "Each new glimpse is determined by many, / Many glimpses before, / It's this glimpse which inspires you."[7] How, I have asked myself, can such accomplished monumental paintings as those created by de Kooning in this phase of his career stem from mere glimpses? There must be much more at stake in glimpsing

5. On the distinction between landscape and geography, see Erwin Straus, *The Primary World of Senses: A Vindication of Sensory Experience*, tr. J. Needleman (Glencoe, Ill.: Free Press, 1963), pp. 318–323. For Merleau-Ponty's acknowledgment of the distinction, see *Phenomenology of Perception*, p. 287.

6. On rays of the world, see Merleau-Ponty, *The Visible and the Invisible*, tr. A. Lingis (Evanston, Ill.: Northwestern University Press, 1968), pp. 140–142, 218, 265. Concerning the *Blick* of the ego, see Husserl's *Ideas Pertaining to a Pure Phenomenology and to a Phenomenological Philosophy*, Book One, tr. F. Kersten (The Hague: Nijhoff, 1982), sections 37, 38 (hereafter referred to as *Ideas I*). For further discussion, see chap. 9.

7. Willem de Kooning, *Sketchbook I: Three Americans* (New York: New York Times, n.d.), p. 6. Reprinted in *The Collected Writings of Willem de Kooning* (New York: Hanuman, 1990), p. 177. For further discussion of de Kooning, see my *Earth-Mapping: Artists Reshaping Landscape* (Minneapolis: University of Minnesota Press, 2005), chap. 7.

(which I take to be a basic form of glancing) than I had imagined. What, then, is this stake? What makes a mere glimpse so potent, suggesting that glancing is not just a minor and indifferent perceptual act but something special in its own right?

IV

Everything durable is the gift of an instant.

—Gaston Bachelard, *L'intuition de l'instant*

In pursing such impertinent questions, let us consider certain features of the glance that at first seem to be peripheral to it: the now, the all-at-once, the here.

(a) A glance takes place in the *now;* it puts places and their surfaces together in the immediate present—or better, it *captures them* in that present. Just now the glance darts out, and it does not last longer than its own momentary operation. The glance *alights;* it does not linger. It flickers off the surfaces of what is seen, as when I glanced about my apartment. For all this, a moment suffices. This moment is not the punctiform unit of chronometric time; it is the frame for Bachelard's instant of intuition, which does not merely mark or measure time but constitutes a source of genuine novelty (Bachelard speaks, for example, of "the instant of the birth of knowledge" [*la connaissance naissante*]).[8] As the temporal basis of the glance, the moment is manifested by its diminutive duration. Indeed, if Bachelard is right, duration itself—thick, ponderous Bergsonian duration—is constituted by instants: "time is observed (*se remarque*) only in instants; duration is experienced (*sentie*) only by instants."[9] *How else* are we to take in duration except in poignant moments of intense experience? Indeed, how else is the landscape world to be grasped but in momentary incursions into this world: incursions effected by glances? Both duration and landscape—in each of which I always "already exist"[10]—are too massive to be apprehended as such: no single perception, or set of perceptions, is equal to them. At best, I glimpse this part of duration or landscape, then that part, then another—all within the arc of the whole, a whole that does not exist for me apart from the moments that give me access to it. To think that it happens otherwise in either case would require positing a special faculty of grasping them in their totality: a

8. Gaston Bachelard, *L'intuition de l'instant* (Paris: Gonthier, 1966 [Stock, 1932]), p. 6.

9. Ibid., p. 33. For further discussion of Bachelard's notion of the instant, see my essay "The Difference an Instant Makes," *Philosophy Today* 47, supp. (2003): 118–123. There I point to the creative potential of the instant when it is not construed as a mere point, e.g., a now-point. In view of this latter temptation—of which Heidegger warns us in *Being and Time*—I prefer to speak of the "moment" as a more apt expression of the temporality of the glance. See chap. 8 for further elaboration.

10. Merleau-Ponty, *Phenomenology of Perception*, p. 251.

power of synthesis that would be nothing but a deus ex machina devised to solve a problem whose solution lies ready to hand in the instant, the present moment of the now.

Crucial for our purposes is a special feature of the now most clearly articulated by Husserl: the now is a *moment of absolute flux*. It is the way such flux presents itself in the present, *as* the present. There is, as it were, a secret collusion between the now and flux—in contrast with "immanent" or "subjective" time, which is narrative and psychological in character. Thanks to this collusion, to experience the now is *at the same time* to experience more than the now. It is also to experience time in its radical mobility, its creativity, its depth, its Becoming. This is why Husserl can speak of the now as "absolute" and as "creative"—terms that Bachelard and Merleau-Ponty would welcome. The now is absolute insofar as it is not reducible to any lesser unit, and it is creative in that it always brings forth something new. In undergoing an experience now, I am at the same time experiencing myself in my deep temporality: in being in that now, I am absolutely there, I find its content captivating, and I enter into its special depths. These depths are not under or behind the surfaces I experience. As Wittgenstein said, "the depths are *on the surface*."[11] For the now is the primal form of the accessible surface of time, just as flux is the primary substance of its depth.

So too the glance is at once now and more-than-now. Now I see the Crazy Mountains, but in so seeing them I also see things that have lasted for hundreds of millions of years—I see their age on their very surface. Here the flux of Becoming is not in me but in the very thing at which I glance. It is as if the lower portion of Husserl's celebrated time diagram were tipped up and over—projected out there as a peak in the landscape rather than being kept within me as a subjective "timekeeper." (So too we can imagine Bergson's equally celebrated pyramid of time inverted to much the same effect.) The difference, of course, is that my now returns to my *own* depth, whereas the depth of the mountain's age is not mine but *its*, belonging to it alone. Of this depth I am only the witness. I do not have it within myself, nor can I (literally) incorporate it. But I can take it in nonetheless; and that's what matters most in matters of the glance. If the now implicates the durational flux of which it is an integral part, so the glance that happens in the now takes in the larger landscape to which it is directed. This indicates that, however separate the two depths (that of the mountains and my own flux) may be in principle, they coalesce in actual experience. Duration and landscape conjoin in the now of the glance.[12]

(b) In both of these cases as well, the taking-in has the character of the "*all-at-*

11. David Pears, "The Development of Wittgenstein's Philosophy" in *The New York Review of Books* vol. 12, no. 1, January 19, 1969 (available at http://www.nybooks.com/articles/11439).

12. For a more complete consideration of the peculiar temporality of the glance, see chap. 8, "Glancing Time."

once," a term I borrow from the third section of Husserl's 1905 lectures on internal time-consciousness. For Husserl, absolute flux is not merely successive (succession belongs properly to immanent time) but happens all at once (*auf einmal, zugleich*). By this, Husserl does not mean strict simultaneity: were this latter to be the case, there would be no becoming at all. Instead, the different phases of flux overlap in an amalgam of loose assimilation, such that events can be said to happen at the same time without, however, happening at the identically same instant. Analogously, my glance takes in a diversity of things and events all at once by gathering whatever is glanced at into one more or less coherent perceptual mass. *The all-around is taken in all-at-once.* This is what glancing is all about at this level of perception: I see all at once what is happening in a social scene I am part of; I perceive all at once the complex character of street life at the intersection of Sixth Avenue and Ninth Street in New York City; the Montana mountainscape gives itself to me all at once as I glance at it along a trail I'm on or (in the manner of de Kooning) through the window of a speeding car. The fact that I here switch from saying "I see" and "I perceive" to "[it] gives itself" does not matter: what counts is that a social or natural landscape is delivered to me all at once.[13]

(c) And the *here*? Here is where my body always is, and from this here I take in an indefinite number of theres in my surroundings, my literal *Umwelt.* Sound familiar? You betcha—as they say in Montana. Once more a delimited defile gives access to an astonishing richness of content: this time in terms of basic orientation. From just here I take in a very great deal of what is there. To be here is not just to be confined to a pinpointed position, my site in space; it is to be implaced in such a way as to reach out, *already,* to a world of theres (a there-world, as it were) to which I find myself multiply related. There is no such thing as being *merely here.* To believe this is to fall prey to the fallacy of simple location (in Whitehead's term). To be here at all is also to be there . . . and there . . . and there.

What is a privilege of the lived body (hence Husserl speaks of it as possessing, or better *being,* an "absolute here") is a fortiori a privilege of the glance as well. In glancing, I am conscious of glancing *from here,* the place of my bodily situ-

13. It might seem as if we are dealing with something like a good *Gestalt* here, since we also perceive such landscapes all at once. As Nietzsche already said in the *Birth of Tragedy,* "we enjoy an immediate grasp of figure (*Gestalt*); all forms speak to us; there is nothing indifferent and unnecessary"(Friedrich Nietzsche, *Birth of Tragedy,* tr. W. Kaufmann [New York: Random House, 1967], p. 34. See also Rudolph Arnheim, *Art and Visual Perception: A Psychology of the Creative Eye* [Berkeley: University of California Press, 1974], pp. 45, 46.) Merleau-Ponty's continual reversion to *Gestalt* as a paradigm for perception bespeaks much the same sense of it as something whose parts we assimilate all at once as parts of a single whole. Yet this paradigm, for all its indisputable value, has the disadvantage of implying homogeneity among the parts. The glance, however, can draw things of the greatest diversity together in an instant: this is one of its primary virtues. In short, we do not need a good Gestalt in order to glance at something, even the most complicated and diverse something, and to take it in all at once.

atedness. More exactly, I glance *from here to there* (and sometimes the converse, as when I glance at myself in the mirror and find my glance coming back to me). I take myself out of myself in order to let my here find its complement in the there-world arrayed around me; but for my glance to land over there, it must stem from the here where I am. The rapidity and ease of this glance reflect the fact that glancing, albeit a bodily act, lacks the dense corporeality of touching or walking, driving a car or hammering—or, for that matter, gazing, which often involves a comparatively fixed body posture. But it shares with them the ineluctability of the here/there dialectic.[14]

Earlier, I spoke of the now, the all-at-once, and the here as seeming to be peripheral to the glance. But we have seen that this is not so. The glance not only resembles the now and the here in certain ways—above all, in its concentrated intensity—but it actively implicates them in its own operation. A given glance cannot but occur in the now and, in so doing, draws duration and flux into its very performance; nor can it not happen here, or fail to relate to a group of pertinent theres. Moreover, every glance exhibits the structure of the all-at-once in its own manifestation. All three features are co-constituent of glancing.

Of these features, the all-at-once is the most distinctive. Whereas every perceptual act—even that of gazing—takes place in a certain now and issues from a bodily here, not every such act entails the all-at-once: many, for example, are wedded to the successiveness of their intentional objects. The glance has a unique power to take in the world *tout ensemble,* as the French say: "all together." When this gift for being comprehensive is combined with a particularly insistent now of mercurial speed, the glance emerges as something special in the array of perceptual acts. Later, I shall designate this specialness as "apperceptual" in order to underline the subtlety with which the glance enacts the now and the all-at-once in a context such as that of ethical acknowledgment.[15] For now, suffice it to say that we are on the track of what makes the glance a most distinctive act.

Our journey has only begun. Even when the three traits just discussed arise together, they do not guarantee that an act of glancing will happen. Other acts—attention, for example—possess the same three traits, albeit in variant degrees. What, then, is truly unique about glancing: what, together with the three items just discussed, makes it *glancing* and not some other act? What else characterizes the glance itself? What is its specific difference from other acts of visual perception? These are basic questions to which this book will provide answers by patiently probing the role of the glance in diverse settings.

---

14. For a more extensive account of this dialectic, and of orientation in general, see chap. 3, "Being/Becoming Oriented by the Glance."

15. On the glance as apperceptual, see especially chap. 10, "The Ethics of the Glance." As we shall see, the here is also an intrinsic part of the ethical situation, especially in the format of the face-to-face emphasized by Levinas.

V

> to strike a glancing blow
>
> —(ordinary idiom in English)

The history of the word "glance" is revealing. The four main historical usages noted in the *Oxford Dictionary of English Etymology* all correspond to senses inherent in the phenomenon as I have described it. "Gliding *off* an object struck" is the oldest usage; critical here is the "off," a word that implies a surface *off which* the gliding is done; by extension, the surface deflects an incoming entity, as in the current definition of "to glance" as "to strike a surface or object obliquely."[16] Hence: "a glancing blow," still in common parlance and capturing the outgoing intentionality of purely visual glancing. The second oldest usage, "to move rapidly," is closely akin to the factor of the glance's intrinsic speed, its quick-sightedness. Then again, to glance is "to make a flash of light," to which corresponds the way an act of glancing extends into a clearing or open space: say, into the view I beheld from my Manhattan apartment. More recently, to glance signifies "to flash a look," reminding us of the visual ray that for certain ancient Greek thinkers leaps from the eye to the object beheld—a ray with fateful consequences, as we are warned in mythological recountings such as those of Actaeon and Diana, and in Hermes's darting look.[17]

Etymologically regarded, "glance" signifies gliding or sliding off a slippery surface. Hence its origin in Old French *glacier,* "to slide, slip," also the root of the English word "glacier," whose polished surface betokens a scary glide downward to an unknown fate. It is speculated that "glance" may also derive from Old Northern French *lancher,* the source of "launch," meaning "to set in rapid motion; [or] to cause (a vessel) to move from land,"[18] that is, from the known to the unknown. Critical in both cases is the idea of the slippery slope: hence the cross-cousin *glacis,* that is, a sloping bank such as that employed in fortifications to discourage enemy advances upon battlements, as well as *glacé,* signifying "smooth and highly polished," stemming from Latin *glaciare,* "to freeze" (hence modern French *glace,* "ice," "ice cream"). Glaciers combine all these traits: slippery slopes, smooth surfaces, frozen substances; glaciers are also akin to the primary paradox of glancing in that they become something immense from a modest source such as a stream or river. In the cultural world, paintings are the

16. *Random House College Dictionary* (New York: Random House, 1968), p. 559. The historical usages are cited from the *Oxford Dictionary of English Etymology* (Oxford: Clarendon Press, 1983), p. 400; italics as in the text.

17. For more discussion of the early Greek theory of the visual ray (*opsis*), see chap. 5, "The Glance in Ancient Athens."

18. *Oxford Dictionary of English Etymology,* p. 518. On the double origin of "glance," see ibid., p. 400. Most major dictionaries agree that "glance" derives ultimately from *glacier* and that earlier forms in English include *glench, glence, glanch.*

closest correlates of the glance: here, too, smooth surfaces contain colors that have become congealed into definite shapes. De Kooning, that master of the painted glance, once called himself a "slipping glimpster."[19]

"Glance," as a verb, can mean "to allude briefly to a subject in passing."[20] Here one darts to a topic in conversation; one "touches on" the topic lightly, exhibiting that *light touch* of all glancing, conversational as well as visual. But this does not entail that glancing touches superficially, without insight; haptic lightness parallels the light of illumination, both bringing into relief something situated on the surface of what we glance at in perception or words—if not bringing it into "the brightly lit circle of perfect presentation,"[21] then at least into the space of a clarified consciousness.

This is doubtless why an extant common meaning of "glance" is "gleam."[22] By glancing, I enter into a gleaming realm. I look from the darkness of not knowing into the light of knowing: knowing things and places whose surfaces gleam sufficiently to attract my glance. I move from being *here* and *now* into the glistening horizon of being *there* and *then*—into the glint of space and duration. In merely taking a glance, I come all at once into the glitter of the world, a cosmos bedecked in its own proper cosmetics.

The rhetoric of such phrases as "at first glance" and "at a glance" as well as "a mere glance" and "a sideways glance" is of special import. As is often the case, the rhetoric mimes the phenomenon. For all four phrases—each composed of three basic English words—are diminutives that act to conceal the larger significance of glancing itself: a significance that this book, itself nothing but a series of glances at a very slippery phenomenon, seeks to bear out. Such phrases downplay what is in fact quite momentous. The rhetorical thrust is: it's only just *this*, something trivial; yet it is precisely by this initial delimitation that the larger prey is caught. In short: a game of decoy, throwing the listener or reader off the track of an insight attainable only by deconstructing the decoy: by realizing that the valuable lies concealed in the devalued. This means to abandon the straight road of the spirit of gravity, the *via regia* of sober science; it also requires leaving the primrose path of the egoic self—as well as the highway of unself-knowing despair of which Hegel speaks in the *Phenomenology of Spirit*.

The gay science of the glance proceeds otherwise. It moves ahead by means

---

19. De Kooning, *Sketchbook I: Three Americans.*

20. *Random House College Dictionary,* p. 559.

21. Edmund Husserl, *Ideas I*, section 69, p. 181. Husserl is alluding to eidetic insight.

22. "Gleam" is cited as the second or third meaning in all major dictionaries, including *Merriam-Webster* and *American Heritage* as well as *Random House* and the *Oxford English Dictionary.* Note that "glimpse," closely related to "glance," connoting faint or partial vision, derives from the same base as "glimmer," which shares with "gleam" a common origin in Middle High German *glimen*, "to shine, glow" (*Oxford Dictionary of English Etymology*, pp. 400–401). "Glint" derives from *glente*, a glimpse, look, glance. On the distinction between glimpse and glance, see the afterword.

of what Kant dismisses as mere *herumtappen:* "random groping."[23] The "swift oblique movement"[24] of a single glance glides quickly off the glabrous back of the thing or topic—the *Sache.* Glides off precisely in order to attain a more incisive insight into the *Sachen selbst,* "the things themselves." This is not unlike the way my glance steals off the surfaces of the Crazy Mountains—off those "mere appearances" (*blosse Erscheinungen* in Kant's phrase) and nevertheless sees them as a complete phenomenon. (Complete but not total, as in Cézanne's claim that a painting should be complete at every stage even if it is never finished at any.)[25]

My glance *sees* the mountains as a whole without my having to *say* anything about this whole. The apophansis happens not in statements as such but in showing off the surfaces of things or places by my mere glance. It is all a matter of *deflection,* echoed in the rhetorical force of the four ordinary English phrases I have cited, their self-deprecation mimicking the deflection of the visual ray from off the slippery surface of what we glance at. We look around in this surface even as we look at it, thus taking it in all at once. We also take it in here and now—though outside the self. The shortest way around is the most effective way home. The glance may not abide—unlike other looks, most notably the gaze—but it does deliver the special depths which only surfaces proffer. And it does so with a swift sense of surprise that should make philosophers wake up and take notice of this lambent act, which they have much too often derided and much too long neglected.

VI

I see by glimpses now.

—William Wordsworth, *The Prelude,* Book XII

If these introductory remarks have seemed unduly oculocentric, I can only plead that looking (in all its variety) remains an indispensable inroad into the surrounding world; without it, we are deeply disabled and living at a loss. This much is indisputable. Open to dispute is something quite different: namely, which forms of seeing should we choose to valorize?[26] In the West, there has been a very high valorization placed upon certain sorts of sight at the expense of others. Steady scrutiny, disciplined contemplation, eidetic insight, the "natural light": all of these have received the lion's share of attention. Different as they

23. Immanuel Kant, *Critique of Pure Reason,* tr. N. K. Smith (New York: St. Martin's, 1983), Preface to the Second Edition.

24. *Oxford Dictionary of English Etymology,* p. 400.

25. Attributed (by implication) to Cézanne by Merleau-Ponty in "Eye and Mind," tr. C. Dallery in Merleau-Ponty, *The Primacy of Perception,* ed. J. Edie (Evanston, Ill.: Northwestern University Press, 1964), p. 190.

26. On the issue of oculocentrism, which I contrast with "visuocentrism," see chap. 5.

are from one another in terms of particular practice, they share the common aim of making what we experience as definite as possible; each in its own way strives to attain "determinate presence" (*Anwesenheit* in Heidegger's word). Such presence in turn reflects prevailing hegemonies of political, social, and academic power. So powerful is the passion for locating determinate presence that there has been a rejection out of hand, often a never taking seriously, of less determinate kinds of looking. Heidegger himself discussed at least one such kind, that is, winking at someone, while Lacan explored the developmental meaning of looking at oneself in the mirror as a form of false determinacy, especially in the infantile stage of human development.[27] Merleau-Ponty has also said suggestive things about the mirror stage, and still more crucially about the crossing of looks between adults as well as in the exchange between human beings and natural things (for example, the tree that is not only seen but in a certain sense *sees us*).[28]

But no one, to my knowledge, has looked fully into the unsuspected significance of the glance. Several recent authors—most notably, Michel Foucault, Norman Bryson, Martin Jay, David Kleinberg-Levin, Gary Shapiro, Jean Starobinski, Jean-Luc Marion, and Georges Didi-Huberman—have alluded to this significance, without pursuing it further.[29] Such neglect is not surprising: the glance is all too often taken as the epitome of the shallow in human perception, something that merely flits over the *superficies*—literally the "outer face," the bare "outward appearance"—of things. Like a butterfly playing on the surface of a glacier.

My argument will be that precisely in such flitting, such ceaseless traveling among surfaces, the glance proves to be of inestimable value in coming to know

27. See Jacques Lacan, "The Mirror Stage as Formative of the Function of the I," tr. A. Sheridan (New York: Norton, 1977), pp. 1–7. For Heidegger's assessment of *winken*, see "The Nature of Language," in *On the Way to Language*, tr. P. D. Hertz (New York: Harper, 1971), pp. 95–96. Derrida has analyzed the *Augenblick* ("moment," literally "glance of the eye") as undermining pure visual presence. See his *Speech and Phenomena*, tr. D. Allison (Evanston, Ill.: Northwestern University Press, 1973), esp. chap. 5. Whereas Derrida's blink closes and cuts—makes a mark or trace—the gesture of *winken* on Heidegger's reading makes a sign *toward*, thus opens discourse (*Sprache*).

28. Merleau-Ponty, *The Visible and the Invisible*, p. 139: "I feel myself looked at by things." We shall return to this theme on several occasions, especially in chaps. 6, 7, 11, and the concluding thoughts.

29. See Michel Foucault, *The Birth of the Clinic*, tr. A. Sheridan (New York: Random House, 1975), pp. 120–122; Norman Bryson, *Vision and Painting: The Logic of the Gaze* (New Haven, Conn.: Yale University Press, 1986), pp. 121 ff.; Martin Jay, *Downcast Eyes: The Denigration of Vision in Twentieth-Century French Thought* (Berkeley: University of California Press, 1993), pp. 56–58, 81, 151, 155–156, 194; David Kleinberg-Levin, *The Philosopher's Gaze: Modernity in the Shadows of Enlightenment* (Berkeley: University of California Press, 1999), p. 336; Gary Shapiro, *Archaeologies of Vision: Foucault and Nietzsche on Seeing and Saying* (Chicago: University of Chicago Press, 2003), pp. 153–156, 161–163, 189; Jean Starobinski, *L'oeil vivant: essais* (Paris: Presses Universitaires de France, 1961), preface; Jean-Luc Marion, *La croisée du visible* (Paris: Presses Universitaires de France, 1996), pp. 15, 17; Georges Didi-Huberman, *Ce que nous voyons, ce qui nous regarde* (Paris: Minuit, 1992), esp. chap. 1 and pp. 103 ff.

the life-world in many of its primary guises. No other act of vision is capable of such subtle incursions into its surroundings. Not unlike the butterfly, by indirections we find out the world's directions—sometimes better than by conventional modes of concerted and direct visual address. In so doing, the glance bestows a special gift: it gives relief from the heavy-spirited ways of doing philosophy that have dominated the discipline since Parmenides first rose to speak of Being in the dry dust of Elea. The self-chosen yoke of philosophers has been heavy; but the burden lightens up if only we accord to the glance—and to other light-fingered phenomena of brevity and transience—a new respect and a new interest.[30]

To turn to the glance is to discover the visual equivalent of Kierkegaard's or Heidegger's "moment" (*Augenblick*)—and of what Wordsworth calls "spots of time" in *The Prelude*, a poem contemporaneous with Hegel's *Phenomenology of Spirit*. Wordsworth has this to say:

> There are in our existence spots of time,
> Which with distinct pre-eminence retain
> A vivifying virtue, whence, depressed
> By false opinion and contentious thought,
> Or aught of heavier or more deadly weight,
> In trivial occupations, and the round
> Of ordinary intercourse, our minds
> Are nourished and invisibly repaired;
> A virtue, by which pleasure is enhanced,
> That penetrates, enables us to mount,
> When high, more high, and lifts us up
> when fallen . . .[31]

Just as moments and instants in their pointed and spotty ways *cut up time,* so glances *sever space.* In this way, the oppressiveness of all that bears "heavier or more deadly weight" is relieved by the glance as well as by the now-point (*die Jetztpunkt* in Husserl's nonreductive sense). Each breaks through, and thereby undermines, the complacency of contented and continuous time and space, their heaviness and plenitude, their spirit of gravity.

But more than cutting and undermining is here at stake. The now-point is a

---

30. I should make it clear that I am not against assuming burdens, including those philosophical burdens that are challenging and productive. I here speak more of a tendency than of content: i.e., the temptation to valorize what is serious and grave at the expense of other, seemingly fanciful dimensions of human experience. When Heidegger speaks, without flinching, of "the burdensome character" of Dasein or Jaspers of the "seriousness" (*Ernst*) required to do philosophy, they fall prey to this tendency. But human existence has important, non-serious-minded modalities to be taken into account: among these, glancing is an exemplary instance of an act that—whatever it may deliver on a given occasion (it can discover quite serious matters)—is most often undertaken in a light-spirited way: e.g., in just looking around oneself. It remains the case that to write philosophically about such an activity as the glance is itself a serious enterprise, one that calls for much care and consideration.

31. William Wordsworth, *The Prelude* (version of 1805–1806), Book XII, lines 258–268.

creative source as well as a punctate entity, and the glance comprehends and connects even as it severs. It not only takes the world apart but also puts it back together again, and often both at once. Just as the moment for Heidegger and Kierkegaard allows us to retrieve an authentic relation to human temporality—a way to melt down the model of merely successive time (which Husserl called "the march of death")—so the glance enlivens our relationship to the place-world by refusing to succumb to the sclerosis of space.

The glance also enables us to cut through the cant and dogma of "false opinions and contentious thought," to traverse the dead layers of sedimented ideas, and thus to reach a lively mother lode of new possibilities of interpersonal life. A single glance suffices to detect the pathology of pretense that infects a hegemonic social scene, and with this glancing blow an entire vision of a less stratified sociality opens. The unsuspected power of the glance is nowhere better displayed than in this liberating moment in which space and time become creative companions rather than bitter antagonists. Even as a single glance insinuates itself into the very interstices of a debilitating social situation, it points to possibilities of relief and reconciliation—indeed, to a new sense of what a less divisive and more affirmative community would be like: a community composed of a genuine heterogeneity of voices. This, too, is taken in at a glance.[32]

VII

The glance is an important part of the arsenal that must be assembled in the ongoing struggle against temporocentrism, the imperialism of successive time that is the chief philosophical cancer of late modernity. Glancing restores to things and places, animals and people, their rightful due in the perceptual world. By its annealing action, the glance stitches together what falls apart under the lethal regimes of time and space. It collects and consolidates the debris of late modern and postmodern life. But it can undertake this necessary reconstructive work—aided by other agile agencies of thought and action—only on the strength of its initial discernments, its genius for quick assessments. "With one blow" (*tout d'un coup*), a glance thrusts itself into the heart of things, into the things themselves even. It is analytical before it is synthetic; it goes straight into things and people and situations. Or we should say that it goes *onto* them, gliding across their diverse surfaces, caressing them by its gentle action—rendering them all the more poignant to the glancer.

All of this happens in a thrice, in an instant wherein the now and the here commingle all at once, making space and time confluent in one gleaming moment.

Can philosophy capture, or recapture, such a moment? Can it trace out its

---

32. For the model of a "heterogeneity of voices," I am indebted to the recent work of Fred Evans, especially his remarkable forthcoming book entitled *The Multivoiced Body: Society, Communication, and the Age of Diversity.*

ever-widening circles of resonance? If so, it must go against the grain of two-and-a-half millennia of thought—the *longue durée* during which it has so often managed only to "paint its gray on gray" (Hegel). When regarded as a Royal Science, philosophy has been undertaken in the spirit of gravity: the relentless effort to find fixity wherever possible. But what if fixity (in the guise of certainty, discipline, rigor, permanence, tenacity, and so on) is not the ultimate, or even the primary, aim of philosophizing? What if there is also a "joyful wisdom" (Nietzsche) or an "archeology of the frivolous" (Derrida) to be pursued with as much right as fixity itself—and with a more creative outcome? A close look at the glance promises to contribute to such ungrave endeavors by bringing our attention to an exemplary instance of taking in the world differently.

*   *   *

This book proceeds by taking the many small steps of description that will open up vistas of reflection and thought. As so often with the glance itself, the text will move from constricted domains of the visual world to more panoramic visions: visions of what the world must be like if it is to yield itself to the glance at virtually every moment, disclosing itself as a complex palimpsest that is no mere patchwork. This world is built up from a lifetime of looking at it. I shall attempt to rebuild it in a verbal edifice which demonstrates that even the most delimited phenomenon calls for detailed characterization (and all the more so when it is so often bypassed and forgotten)—and that "the last naiveté" of which Derrida speaks is the beginning of epistemic and ethical wisdom.

It is a matter of recapturing in "the prose of the world" (Merleau-Ponty, after Hegel)—or better: in the poetry of this very prose, in concentrated concatenations of words—a lively act that animates the perceived world itself. For it is in glancing that we not only become intimately acquainted with the world at which we so casually and yet so consequentially look: we also enliven it by our very looking. The world at a glance/the world in a glance: these simple phrases point to the world we and other animals co-inhabit so deftly and delicately, so forcefully and purposefully, and yet so surprisingly.

In the end, it's all in a glance—in this singular visual act—that the world as we come to know it comes home to us.

Part 1

Approximating to the Glance

My approach to the glance will be highly descriptive. If not expressly phenom-enological—where this would mean the concerted employment of certain tech-niques (above all, bracketing what Husserl calls the "natural attitude")—my descriptions will be phenomenological in spirit. By this I mean that I will come to grips directly with the phenomenon of glancing, describing it as it presents itself in diverse contexts. I shall not stand upon ceremonial considerations of method, but will seek experiential immersion in actual instances, singling out micro-features as well as macrostructures. Far from offering a systematic survey or com-prehensive study, I shall sample particular instances of glancing without claiming that they are altogether exemplary. Proceeding in this way—jumping from in-stance to instance—will reflect the desultory life of the glance itself: *desultor* is Latin for a horseback rider who leaps from one galloping horse to another.

There are evident dangers in this deliberately offhand or informal approach. In particular, will I not end by being merely autobiographical? This is certainly a danger. But one must start somewhere, and given the fugitive character of the glance it is best to start with what is at hand, namely, one's own glancing experi-ence and that of others whom one knows well or encounters directly—in short, with a descriptive bricolage that attends to whatever and however glancing occurs in familiar surroundings. But to begin with what is readily available does not mean that one is limited to the merely random or the unrepresentative. *Every case of glancing is a valid case* (there is little, if any, mis-glancing), and by considering it carefully we can learn much as to what glancing is like elsewhere —in the lives of other people, at other times, in other places. This will occur not by extrapolating its exact mechanism—as one might from presumptively exem-plary cases—but by teasing out what Merleau-Ponty calls its "lateral univer-sality,"[1] that is to say, its manifestation in deeply similar ways in deeply different situations—where "it" is not a single thing, much less a formal essence, but rather a distinctive way of looking that will have many variant realizations.

Glancing is one of the primary ways in which we take account of the place-world in its coming forth and receding. As we shall see, glancing is multiple in form—already in our own experiences and certainly in those of others who have quite different experiences. Yet these forms are not infinitely various. There are certain constraints that all human glancers share: for example, the physical and physiological structure of the eyes, their position in the human head, the nature of light, certain material conditions of perception, various general patterns of socialization in a given culture, and so forth. These constraints do not so much limit glancing as make it possible—possible in its own free being, its diverse movement, its polyvalence of projective powers.[2] Instead of a single rigid struc-

---

1. See Maurice Merleau-Ponty, "From Mauss to Claude Lévi-Strauss," in *Signs*, tr. R. C. McCleary (Evanston, Ill.: Northwestern University Press, 1964), pp. 114–125. I return to the lateral universal in the introductory remarks to part 2.

2. I take up the theme of freedom within constraints—explicitly cultural and social con-straints—in the introduction to part 3, in chapter 10, and in the concluding thoughts.

ture, we witness a loose assemblage of traits that are distributed, laterally, across different people and different cultures: some of these traits being exhibited at one time and place, others in other settings, but only rarely all of them at once. In any case, to start from familiar experiences and to proceed by attending to what is at hand, far from being a disadvantage, may end by yielding insight not available in any objective survey, no matter how extensive. Here as elsewhere, the longest way around—the most meticulous description—may well prove to be the shortest way home.

This is not to minimize the ever-present dangers of ethnocentrism and subjectivism. In part 2, I shall address these dangers in a more forthright way by two studies of the glance in very different cultural, historical, and social settings. I will range broadly in place and time, bringing back ideas and lessons at least implicitly pertinent to one's own immediate context. Nevertheless, I believe it is best to start with the near and the known—not just as a convenient point of departure but also because it is important to begin with the experience in which one is now most fully engaged: my glancing, your glancing, the glancing of those I know well.

Let us call this approach *beginning with the first horizon*. At first and at least, we must try to grasp the glancing that is happening within the orbit of one's personal experience. This is not to deny the tendentious, and often blind, character of even the most intimately held experiences. Freud spoke of "the blindness of the seeing eye,"[3] and he did so precisely by way of self-critique: he had failed to notice certain things about hysteria that lay before his open eyes. This is the circumstance of the purloined letter: we often fail to notice the very thing that dangles right before us, much like the sought-after letter suspended from the mantelpiece in Poe's celebrated short story. We overlook the obvious. The same goes for the glances we cast all the time: they, too, lie nakedly in front of us, being part of the very frontality of our instantaneous insertion into the place-world. Only when we have come to terms with this first horizon can we savor the subtleties of the glance in other cultures: cultures that provide a *second horizon* at once more distant and more diverse. A *third horizon* is to be found in the various dimensional parameters of the glance to be taken up in parts 3 and 4: its time, its ethics, its relation to the environment, and its singularity.

Not that any of this is easy. Precisely because we glance so quickly and so spontaneously, we rarely pause to consider what glancing itself consists in. For the most part (with such notable exceptions as concerted flirtation and an angry exchange of glances), we take glancing for granted, rarely pausing to consider what is really going on when we glance at something or at somebody: What kind of activity is it? What are its goals? What are its effects? At the same time, as I have emphasized in the introduction, the glance is downplayed in comparison with more august and officially sanctioned forms of looking.

3. Sigmund Freud, *Studies in Hysteria*, in *The Standard Edition of the Complete Psychological Works*, ed. J. Strachey (London: Hogarth Press, 1953), Part IV (Psychotherapy of Hysteria).

For these two closely related reasons—its taken-for-granted status and its ongoing subordination—the glance calls for our concerted attention. We need to retrieve it for philosophical inspection so as to reflect on the spontaneous success of its operation in everyday life as well as to understand its continued neglect in Western thought. This retrieval is all the more significant in view of the intense scrutiny to which the *gaze* has been subjected in recent decades, especially in the wake of Foucault's incisive treatments of the gaze in various institutional settings such as medicine and penology. Precisely because the gaze has been so often thematized in current debates—especially in the contexts of feminism and film—it is time to take up the glance anew and on its own terms and not as the weak sibling of an ostensibly more "legitimate" or "normative" gaze, as suggested by Foucault himself as well as by Norman Bryson, Martin Jay, and Gary Shapiro.[4]

As a response to the emphasis on the gaze that has arisen in the last several decades, I shall devote chapter 4 (and the afterword) to a detailed distinction between the glance and the gaze. It will emerge from this analysis that the two visual acts are in certain basic respects epicenters of the look overall—and thus that one of them cannot be fully discerned without keeping a watchful eye on the other. Even before coming to this comparison, however, I will plunge outright into a description of the glance. In the first chapter of this part, I shall pay attention to ordinary acts of glancing as they arise in the course of an episode from everyday life. Despite this modest start, we shall soon be confronted with ethical aspects of the glance as these emerge in glancing at each other on the street. Very early on, then, we shall confront an important peculiarity of the life of the glance: despite its fleeting enactment, it is accompanied by an extensive set of ramifications, some of them interpersonal, some implicitly political, and some specifically ethical—ramifications to which we shall return in more detail later in this book. The least act of looking casts an enormous shadow.

In a second chapter, I will attend to certain of the glance traits that become evident only when viewed from up close: its miniscule motions and subtle gestures—in short, the glance laid bare in its own domain. This will constitute as it were a microphenomenology of the glance. Following this, I consider the constitutive role of the glance in orienting ourselves in place and space. In this third chapter, I trace out the ingrediency of glancing in the experience of becoming oriented in particular places as well as in the larger region of geographical space. Once again we shall witness how the slender structure of this act shows itself to be essential to the constitution of things that exceed its own immediate ambience. Not only should we "expect the unexpected"[5] (as Heracli-

4. Even these figures, with the notable exceptions of Shapiro and Bryson (who give to the glance its own distinctive "deictic" function), dispatch the glance in a bare remark or two—in effect consigning it to oblivion. For the exact references to these authors, see the introduction, footnote 29.

5. The full fragment is: "Unless you expect the unexpected you will never find [truth], for it is hard to discover and hard to attain" (Fragment #18, Diels-Kranz); translation of Philip Wheelwright in his *Heraclitus* (Princeton, N.J.: Princeton University Press, 1959), p. 20.

tus reckoned), but we should expect that the significance of the glance looms far beyond the diminutive space and time it is allotted in physical and social worlds. In each of these worlds—and in others as well—the glance proves to be far more significant than we might suspect at first: and above all in its flight from established centers of meaning and structure. In other words, the glance is powerful in its very impuissance, strong in its apparent weakness, present in its own absence.

But let us go first to the thing itself—to glancing as it arises in unrehearsed circumstances of everyday experience.

1

GETTING INTO THE GLANCE

> He who sees cannot possess the visible unless he is
> possessed by it, unless he is *of it,* unless, by prin-
> ciple, according to what is required by the articula-
> tion of the look with the things, he is one of the
> visibles, capable, by a singular reversal, of seeing
> them—he who is one of them.
>
> —Maurice Merleau-Ponty,
> *The Visible and the Invisible*

I

It is Valentine's Day in the Café Felix, a late Sunday afternoon in Ann Arbor, Michigan. Not that Valentine's Day makes much difference at the Felix, a place where people come mainly to study and write. It is a serious place, whose spirit of gravity is alleviated by the excellent coffee and the French bistro atmosphere, replete with handsome wooden paneling throughout. Alleviated, too, by the glances cast by the customers. Just by looking around, an otherwise wholly engaged person can escape the monotony and difficulty of work, however partially. A mere glance offers a moment of respite, of pause or suspension, a chance to reconsider a train of thought. At the same time, a rhythm is set whose downbeats fall in the more prolonged periods of immersion in work and whose upbeats—moments of looking up—accentuate the scene in staccato. Each person has his or her own cadence and pace, a pattern in which working and glancing alternate with each other: the one occurring by looking down at a book or a computer while the other consists in looking up and out. In this way, a circumstance emerges that draws in body and mind alike, indeed that includes character, history, and gender as well. It also draws in other people, at the limit everyone in the café; no one is exempted from the least glance. The work being done, like the conversations in which couples or groups participate, is self-absorbed; but the glance is cast freely everywhere in this packed place: it can come from anyone and alight anywhere. A resolute individualism of work and a concerted sociality of talk are complemented by an open democracy of looking.

As it is indeed Valentine's Day, a few people are intensely engaged with each other, noticeably more so than on an ordinary day in this café. Just across from my table is a couple engrossed in talk. They are very much looking at each other—especially the woman, who doesn't take her eyes off the well-dressed man, at least not while they are talking. The man, however, continually looks away, though not from any apparent lack of interest in his companion. Partly, I suspect, it is a matter of personal style, perhaps influenced by a factor of gender. Partly, too, the very intensity of the talk may call for relief—relief provided without cost by merely looking away. For the glance is cheap, being always available; one can glance away even in the most constrained of circumstances; it is not so much "ready to hand" (as is true of familiar and nearby tools) as ready to enact, without any instrumentation. Nor is any rehearsal required: the glance is not an acquired skill. Babies glance, old people glance. Everyone who sees can glance, at any age; this is part of its democracy.

This is not to deny the acquisition of sophisticated ways of looking on the part of certain classes and groups of people, including particular modes of glancing. But it remains the case that one is able to glance *in some way* on almost every occasion, short of acute blindness, complete exhaustion, or an extremely repressive circumstance.[1] Perhaps because of its very availability and general unsuppressibility, the glance is acceptable even in intimate circumstances. The fact that the elegantly dressed man keeps looking away—out at the street through the window, at the posters on the walls, at other customers—does not appear to bother his woman friend. She does not find it distracting; she allows it without complaint, not just because she is used to it but, more importantly, because for her it does not connote any disaffection. It is for the most part—with notable exceptions—an acceptable feature of interpersonal conduct, even behavior as charged as that expected in a Valentine's Day conversation. The glance is at once a momentary evasion of this conversation and an inobtrusive phase of it: a way out for him, an acceptable part for her, and noncontroversial for both.

The man at the table next to mine is now glancing at me, and I glance back at him. This spontaneous development belongs to the ongoing social ritual of the glance. The glance takes us not just *out of* a given circumstance but *into* others. Were the man to glance at me insistently and with pronounced interest, he would precipitate himself into my current life. In this case, another aspect of glancing may well come to the fore: its invasive character. Enacted intensely enough, this character can render the meekest glance intrusive: I can feel inspected, indeed attacked, by the other's look. Then I will find myself asking, Why is that man looking at me so often? What is he looking *for*?

This does not happen in the present circumstance: the anonymous customer glances at me only once or twice and then not again. I return his glances in kind, just barely glancing back. We have established contact, but the connection that

---

1. For a discussion of a situation in which glancing has effectively disappeared—that of the Musselmen in the Nazi extermination camps—see my unpublished essay, "Witnessing (in) the Holocaust: The Suppression of the Glance in Dire Circumstances" (2001).

is made is far from demanding. Here the glance occurs between two human agents unknown to each other, like a play of reflections in which the reflected image is sent straight back to the source of reflection without any further nuance. In this immediate interaction, we witness one form of the double phasing of much human glancing: glancing out/glancing back. In this case it is enacted in a pre-established social format: he glances out at me, I glance back at him. But it also occurs when I am alone in my study, when I glance out the window and sense that the world I see is somehow looking back at me. (Ultimately, we shall see that this two-beat structure is based in the overall temporality of glancing: see chapter 8.)

The couple gets up to leave. For the first time, the woman looks at me: a parting glance? Perhaps. But she remains fully engaged in being with her male friend. Her glance at me *punctuates* her visit to the café; it is not unlike a semicolon or period: indifferent in its specific content, yet useful in providing structure to a situation that might otherwise be unending, lacking the gesture of termination. She behaves like a dancer whose movement terminates in a certain posture that signifies the end of that particular phase of the dance.[2] And I, in acknowledgment of this moment of closure, glance back at her, as if to acknowledge her departure, although in a flat and unemphatic way. Were I even to smile wanly, that would establish the beginning of an articulate form of farewell that would find its way into words were it to become more complete. Instead, my glance slides off her face much as her glance brushed lightly over mine to start with. At play here is the enactment of a social contract of a certain sort: an undiscussed agreement not to look too long into the eyes of strangers, especially at the beginnings or endings of events.

My corner of the café suddenly vacant, I notice that the workers behind the counter glance at every arriving person; they are checking out what is about to happen. This is anticipatory, informative looking, not entirely unlike the kind of glancing a driver does at a busy intersection in order to see what is about to happen in the situation: who will turn next, does any pedestrian seem wayward, shall I look again at that attractive woman driver? Such glancing is instrumental in informing me of the immediate circumstance. So too with the workers at the Felix: they look to find out what is likely to happen in the next short stretch of

---

2. Lacan remarks similarly that members of the company of the Peking Opera (which he had seen recently at the time of the comment) engaged in motions whose very cessation was as critical as their enactment. Moreover, "the terminal time of the gesture's arrest" (in his phrase) has everything to do with the terminal time of the human look (*le regard*): for "the look in itself not only terminates movement but fixes it. These [Chinese] dances are always punctuated by a series of arrested moments in which the actors suspend their actions in a frozen posture (*une attitude bloquée*)" (Jacques Lacan, *Les quatre concepts fondamentaux de la psychanalyse*, Seminar XI, ed. Jacques Alain Miller [Paris: Seuil, 1973], p. 107). See the English translation: *The Four Fundamental Concepts of Psychoanalysis*, ed. J.-A. Miller, tr. A. Sheridan (New York: Norton, 1978), p. 117 (hereafter cited as "English trans." with page no.).

In what follows I refer both to the French and the English pagination, but the translations are my own.

time. Unlike the idle glancing described in earlier episodes—which are compla-
cently ensconced in the present—this kind of looking has a particular purchase
on the imminent future. If the first instances of glancing constitute glancing *in
the moment*, the second set is glancing *in view of the next moment*. There is
glancing that looks ahead as well as glancing that stays satisfied with the present—that does not seek to look further.

Glancing is not confined to the personal and interpersonal realms. It is not only
enacted but also *represented*. I look over to the opposite wall and see a framed
poster. "Café de Flore" is emblazoned on the top, and below is an address: "172,
Boulevard Saint-German—75006, PARIS." In between is a striking image of a
man depicted wearing a 50s sports jacket, holding a cigarette in his right hand and
a copy of *Le Figaro* in his left. Before him is a cup of coffee, a glass of beer, and a
bottle of red wine: rather a lot to handle at once! What is most arresting is the
man's *look*: he is glancing intently out from behind his newspaper, his eyes trained
not on me but on some third party, invisible in the poster but apparently having
enough fascination to hold his attention completely. His look is so unblinking and
steady that it is on its way to being a full-fledged gaze. But it is depicted as a
glance—as not being a lasting look—and as such is located somewhere between
meekly peeking out from behind *Le Figaro* and staring out from there. Another
ambiguity is that the poster-person is both looking for something in his own
setting—otherwise, his look would not be so deliberate—and, at the same time,
he is himself on exhibit. It is as if he wanted to be looked at himself, to be noticed
in his very looking: to be seen as well as to see, both at once. He glances out, as if
hoping to find a partner who will return his glance.

Suddenly, he seems to be looking not just at anyone, but now *straight at me*!
As if I were this wished-for partner! How can this be? How can I be looked at by
a mere two-dimensional representation, no creature of flesh and blood but
brought forth by some unknown artist's imagination? In what sense can an
altogether imaginary being look at all? A strange situation: a nonsubject looks at
me as if I, surely a subject, am nothing but the object of his look!

To make matters worse, he is looking at me searchingly: his look is not so much
inquisitive or even curious as probing and possessive, so much so that it threatens
to take hold of me. No innocent play of exchanging glances here, not even a
sliding of glances off each other's face! In fact, there is no reciprocity at all, and his
look is all the more riveting for being part of a nonmutual circumstance of one-
way looking. True, I do *look at* the poster, and the poster-man looks out at me: I
am *under his look*. But our glances *do not meet*—they never will.

Of course not, we are inclined to say: the minimum condition of the sociality
of the glance is here not satisfied. How can it be, since our looks are those of two
entirely different kinds of being? But is the matter so simple? Jacques Lacan
thinks not. He begins from the premise that the seeing I do is not on the same
level as the way in which I am seen by other entities. Other human beings and
other things see me—regard me, look at me—as if I were myself an image, even
a painting:

> In the scopic field, the look (*le regard*) is from the outside (*au-dehors*), I am looked at, that is to say, I am a painting. Here is the function that is to be found in the most intimate part of the institution of the subject in the visible. What determines me most fundamentally in the visible is the look that is outside.[3]

In what sense am I (like) a painting? I am this insofar as I, when I see, see only from a single point of view, whereas I am myself viewed from many points of view—just like an image on a canvas is. Otherwise put, "the world is an omnivoyeur."[4] And if this is the case, I might as well be a canvas—or for that matter a screen on which there is a stain at which everyone stares, as Lacan also suggests.[5] Thus, although the poster-man is casting a glance out into the strictly imaginary world of his café and is in this respect ontologically separate from me,[6] his look can seem to bear down upon me as would any look from any human source: our looks may not cross, but I sense myself being looked at "from the outside" as if I were myself somehow a poster-man on display, caught and fixed under the look of the other.

Looking further back into the Café Felix, I perceive a long mural on which two other people are represented. A woman is rolling her eyes decidedly to her left, away from the notebook in front of her and the cat climbing up on the upholstery beside her. Another woman, located perhaps thirty feet to her left on the mural, coyly and pertly peers out of a cozy corner at the far end of the same mural. They seem to be exchanging glances: the contact that eluded the poster-man is here accomplished, at least in pictorial reality. The women look at each other across an older couple and a waiter, all three of whom are depicted as in between the two glancers. It is as if these three intermediate figures do not exist at all, in any case certainly not for the two women. It is also clear that the women do not wish to be seen looking at each other. But look they do—as befits the depicted scene of the café of which they are such an integral part. Despite being ultimately decorative in status (the women are after all figures in a painting), their glancing actions at once echo and sanction the rich interplay of glancing that lies before them in the bustling life of the Café Felix.

But let us leave the pictorial world aside and return to the actual human situation. We have not begun to exhaust the possibilities in this circumstance.

---

3. Ibid., p. 98 (English trans., p. 106).

4. Ibid., p. 71 (English trans., p. 75). On this asymmetrical relation between my seeing and my being seen, see p. 69 (English trans., p. 72): "The pre-existence of the look (*le regard*) [is found in the fact that] I see only from one point, but in my existence I am looked at from everywhere."

5. "And I, if I am something in the painting, it is in the form of the screen (*écran*), which I have designated earlier as the stain (*la tache*)" (ibid., p. 90; English trans., p. 97). On the role of the stain in vision, see ibid., pp. 71–73 (English trans., pp. 74–75); on the idea of the screen, see ibid., pp. 85, 97, 99 (English trans., pp. 91, 96–97, 106–108).

6. Although the poster names the café with an actual name, "Café de Flore," and even gives its correct address, the place entailed by the image in the poster is no real place at all: it is not even represented but left entirely open as to its character.

Take, for example, the ordinary (but often quite complex) phenomenon of *glancing around* as it occurs in a place such as the Café Felix. A couple standing at the counter waiting to order coffee is about to kiss (it is Valentine's Day after all!), and just before they do so the woman glances around to see who is there—who might witness the kiss. Her look is not unduly apprehensive; it is not as if she is trying to see if anyone in particular is there to witness the kiss. It is more in the nature of a routine check to determine who might see her when she engages in such an intimate action as kissing.

Another form of glancing around is also at play. Most of those who enter the café, I observe, look over the scene as a whole as they walk into the central space. They size up the situation, yet in no concerted or systematic way; they are not looking for anyone in particular, and (unlike the poster-man) they are certainly not looking for looks nor are they (in contrast with the two mural women) already engaged in looking. They are *just looking,* and they are doing so by glancing around the café in an action of "once-over-lightly," as the English idiom revealingly puts it. Despite the fact that much if not all glancing is linked to desire—including certain powerful and even violent emotions—some glancing at least is both innocuous and innocent: it only wants to find out what is happening in a given situation, what is going on there, and little more.[7]

The aimless and harmless glancing around to which I have just pointed comes close to the looking associated with idle curiosity. But the two phenomena are not precisely the same. In the glancing around that accompanies such curiosity, I am coming from a state of boredom or nonaction and, as a consequence, I am ready to *become interested* in virtually anything that strikes my eye. I cast about idly—to this extent I am *just* looking—but I am nevertheless *curious,* which means that I will let my look rest on something that catches my attention in order to satisfy my now-aroused interest. Indeed, I see this very thing happening before me: a middle-aged man who had been looking emptily around the room spots the couple who have now (finally!) kissed and he glances at them several times in a space of a few minutes. His ennui has momentarily abated thanks to the visual spectacle before him.

Still another person is engrossed in writing—he is scribbling on a yellow pad—and he presents a related yet still different look: the *abstracted glance.* This shares with aimless glancing a nonvolitional and undirected character; but it exhibits none of the boredom of the glance from idle curiosity. The writer, who takes up the same table every day, looks at me and others in the room in a notably empty way. Even when he is looking right at me and is unquestionably *perceiving* me at the center of his vision, his glance has the peculiar property of

---

7. We shall return to the link between glancing and desire—in particular, to the bodily basis of glancing—in chap. 4. There, I shall also address the thesis of James Elkins that the phenomenon of "just looking" is to be regarded with suspicion—that it almost always harbors difficult and demanding emotions (see James Elkins, *The Object Stares Back* [New York: Simon and Schuster, 1996], chap. 1).

looking right through me. It is as if I didn't exist in his vision. He might as well be looking at a blank wall. It is not just that I am *un*interesting to him; even though I know that I form part of what he is seeing, I am out of the range of any actual interest; in contrast with the bored person looking out for something interesting, for this writer the very category of "the interesting" is suspended—at least so far as this immediate environment is concerned. His glance is wholly uninvested; he could be looking at anyone, indeed anything. This is a look that is (intentionally) *going nowhere.* Its emptiness of personal expressiveness is matched by its drifting quality, gliding from one surface to another without definite plan or purpose. Double abstraction, then: abstraction from any determinate thought or emotion and abstraction from any particular object or thing.

Glancing around can thus occur in several formats: noting who is currently looking at oneself, looking out of idle interest, and looking abstractedly. It can also happen in less overt and obvious ways that are just as frequent. One of these is the *sidewise glance.* Here one looks around by not seeming to look around. This verges on dissemblance, yet without the conscious intent that is normally part of the latter. As I walk to the restroom, I see a patron looking sidewise at the person at the next table. She keeps her head steadily in place, poised over the book she is (supposed to be) reading; but her eyes glide to the left as she glimpses her neighbor, briefly but intentionally. She is not seen glancing by this young man—just as she wishes. For the sidewise glance does not want to be witnessed; it is a glance that tries to appear not to glance at all: hence the steady position of the woman's head, directed toward the book she is ostensibly reading. Another variation on the sidewise glance is found in the glance that issues from the corners of the eyes: here, too, the eyes seem to be focused on something in the center of vision, while in fact they are glimpsing the environment from the edges of this disciplined look: a lateral looking, a *clin d'oeil* (literally, "leaning of the eye").[8] Either way, such sidewise glancing is the virtual opposite of the poster-man's look: he very much wants to be seen looking, indeed wants to make a point of this exhibition. The sidewise glance wants not to be seen seeing.

Closely related to sidewise looking is the *furtive glance.* It shares with the sidewise glance the wish not to be noticed as it is happening; indeed, it often takes place by means of an actual sidewise look. But it has the additional property of *withdrawal;* out of guilt or shame or some other motive, the furtive glance desires not just not to be observed but takes measures to obscure itself—to disappear into its own shadows. If the sidewise glance tends toward the stealthy (yet is not chagrined to be caught in the act), the furtive glance actively attempts to hide its own looking, for example, by pretending to be doing something else quite different from what it is in fact doing. This may happen not only when appearing to be buried in a book (as happened with the woman I just described) but also when gazing fixedly out a window while taking "stolen looks" at people talking in a courtyard below. The furtive look is acutely embarrassed to

---

8. For further discussion of such shifting of attention while keeping the eyes focused straight ahead, see chap. 9.

be apprehended at its own game; as soon as the glancer suspects that this is happening, he or she will look quickly down or away in an effort to appear to be giving up glancing altogether.

The sidewise glance and the furtive glance contrast with another kind of glancing around, where the issue of being seen seeing figures in a very different way. When drivers come to a four-way stop, they very often glance at each other—not in order to see the other drivers in any penetrating way but merely to grasp their basic intentions. Here one's own looking, though essential to driving safely in the situation, is indifferently disposed with respect to whether it is itself seen, and in how much detail. I simply do not care whether my own glance—cast purely for the sake of limited but pertinent information—is observed or not. There is no reason to hide this look of mine (indeed, another's perception of my glance may be useful if it picks up my intentions as a driver), yet at the same time I do not want to put it on display. Stopped at the corner and glancing around at the other cars, I am located somewhere between the poster-man (who seems desperately to want to be seen) and the furtive glancer (who does not want to be seen at all). This is hardly surprising: at the intersection, where one can pause for only a few moments before moving on, one does not have the leisure or the motive to inspect others' looks carefully nor to have one's own look studied by them in turn. One must move on; the thing that matters most is the driving, not the looking; whereas in the café one has the luxury of giving and receiving looks and sometimes actively exchanging them—and some prize precisely this visual luxury as part of the pleasure of café life.

II

This is not to say that café life is all of life. The example of the four-way stop has just taken us abruptly out of this rarified world, where we cannot linger indefinitely. Nevertheless, the Café Felix is an auspicious place for getting a first glimpse of the glance, especially glancing at fellow human beings. It is a hot-house where many such glances, familiar as well as unaccustomed, abound: a microcosm where we can experience and inspect these glances as they arise spontaneously and unself-consciously.

The scene in the Café Felix teaches us several basic lessons. The first is that whenever human beings congregate, they enter into a webwork of glances—so dense at times that there seems little escape from it . . . except by yet another glance. This is so whether those who are in such a scene are talking or not, and no matter what other action they may be engaged in: reading, writing, musing, experiencing complex emotions, just entertaining oneself with what one sees, and so on. The inclination to glance is virtually irresistible. It is a very basic activity; we do not need to try to glance or (as I have remarked) learn to glance; it is something we find ourselves doing—and doing quite skillfully. The fact is that there are very few moments when human beings are not engaged in glancing. My description of life in the Café Felix only brings to our attention something most of us have been doing for most of our lives. So much is this the case that *not* glancing is the exceptional case: the catatonic does not look up, nor does the scientist in the febrile last stages of a discovery. Such absorption occurs not only in these extreme cases, one intensely pathological and the other intensely cre- ative. The woman at the next table who was so engrossed in conversation with the well-dressed man also did not look up or out—not until she left the café. Nevertheless, she was exceptional in that scene, being the only person I noticed who was not glancing continually or at least intermittently.

A second lesson to be learned from the scene at the Café Felix is that glances exhibit a rich gamut of meaning—from the exchange of "significant looks" to so abstracted a look as to defy any imputation of determinate sense. The poster- man's look is fiercely definite in its sense and direction: we see at a glance what *his* glance signifies (that is, his wish to be seen, his hope to engage another's look). It is "intentional." The man who is writing on yellow legal pads, on the other hand, gives out a look about which I could not begin to say what it intends to say, if anything: I have no clue as to what this writer, lost in thought, is thinking about. In between are various indeterminate cases. Indeed, most glances carry with them a significant quotient of ambiguity, making it difficult to say *just what* a given glance signifies, whether by its intention or by my interpretation. Can I know for sure precisely what was meant by the quick premonitory glance of the woman who was about to kiss her lover? I cannot. I can only divine a certain range of meaning that could be designated as "checking out the scene to see who might see me kissing." But in fact she *may* have had something far more pointed in mind: "to be sure that William K. does not see me at this moment." I could not tell which was the case from my mere witnessing of her glance. Like many glances, it was not altogether telling or even fully forthcoming.

The truth is that the glance is not a highly or strictly coded gesture; its very multiplicity and plasticity are such that any effort to find or fix an exact significa- tion threatens to undermine what must remain variable and open—if the glance is to be as freely deployable as we know it to be. In Kristeva's language, a glance is a *semiotic* form of expression—one that may presume the specifically *symbolic* form found in discourse but that does not itself attain the full articulateness of verbal language.[9] To be semiotic in status is certainly to be meaningful, but it is to resist the precise parsing of meaning that is possible in the case of ordinary prose sentences. It is to achieve meaning by other means, for example, by bodily motions and rhythms—as occurs notably in the case of the glance, whose mean- ing is borne by its gestural activity, its expressive material motions. Glances possess a certain semantic density, which is ambiguous in that one cannot say for certain just what is meant in a given glance, though one knows that it is a

---

9. See Julia Kristeva, *Revolution in Poetic Language,* trans. Margaret Waller (New York: Columbia University Press, 1984). Not only is the symbolic or "thetic" presupposed in all deployment of the semiotic as its essential and ultimate horizon, but the two modes are frequently intermingled, e.g., in the paradigmatic case of poetic language where the semiotic occurs by way of self-reference of the medium to itself (as in alliteration or assonance).

signifying act: that it means *something*. Indeed, an unambiguous glance is the exceptional case—for example, the murderous look, the chilling glance, the overtly seductive look, and so forth. These latter indicate that the semiotically coded look can at times approach a symbolic status; but they can only approximate to it, since even in these instances further actions are required to pin down the precise signification: for example, an angry or threatening gesture, icy words, or an alluring ploy of seduction (such as moving closer to the other, starting an actual conversation, and so on).

We learn, thirdly, that inarticulate as many glances can be—semiotically ambiguous as they are—they nevertheless act as a powerful social bond. They are a primary mode of *Mitsein*, being-with-others in the Heideggerian expression. This is especially evident in a public space such as that of the Café Felix. If one prescinds from particular engagements of the look, one is able to grasp the organic sociality of the scene as a whole, that is to say, how all the glances taken together constitute a living vehicle of human intersubjectivity.[10] Without glances, a crucial basis of this intersubjectivity would be missing.

If there were no glances, we would have to rely much more fully on two other major ways in which to live out our relations with others: direct touch and explicit verbal language. Each of these has inherent limitations. Touching is heavily fraught with erotic overtones as well as class and gender and racial connotations. Its directness, especially when blunt, carries with it a significance that is not always appropriate or desirable in social relations. Were touch to replace the glance, it would have to be redifferentiated to perform some of the subtle tasks carried out by glances.[11] Verbal language, on the other hand, tends to be too thetic, too bound to the definiteness of its apophantic propositions to convey the semiotic density of the glance-world. Part of the game of glancing consists in not

---

10. Bernhard Waldenfels has remarked how different it is to watch a dramatic production in the company of others instead of by oneself alone—two very different experiences (see Bernhard Waldenfels, *Das Zwischenreich des Dialogs* [The Hague: M. Nijhoff, 1971]). Not only *human* intersubjectivity is at stake in the webwork of glances. Observations I made of a gorilla family at the Brookfield Zoo in Chicago revealed how much members of this family depended on glances, and the interchange of glances, in their daily lives. The dominant male, for example, was continually glancing around to see what other members of the family were doing and especially if they were getting out of line, and these others glanced back at him guardedly.

11. The converse holds too: the glance cannot replace touch without remainder. This leads into the important and vexing question of what Aristotle calls "the special senses" and their distinctive contributions. These contributions are rarely if ever interchangeable without loss: the blind person gets around in the world by a cane, yet no one supposes that this person's experience, however agile, is equivalent to that of the fully sighted person. For a discerning critique of a theory of sight that is modeled on direct contact or touch (e.g., that of Descartes in his *Dioptics*), see Maurice Merleau-Ponty, "Eye and Mind," tr. C. Dallery in *The Primacy of Perception*, tr. J. Edie (Evanston, Ill.: Northwestern University Press, 1964), section 3. In the same essay, Merleau-Ponty observes that if music is too nebulous and language too specific, vision (e.g., in its role in painting) puts us into a privileged relation to "brute being" (*être sauvage*) (see Merleau-Ponty, "Eye and Mind," pp. 159–192). To this, I would add that the glance is a privileged form of vision itself when it comes to discerning the primary features of the perceived world.

being *too* specific in implication (again with the exceptions already noted). This is not for the sake of mystery but so as to leave open edges of new and changing signification: to pinpoint the sense of a glance is often to miss its point—a point that cannot be spelled out in any simple propositional form. For much the same reason, a glance is only rarely a gesture that points unambiguously to a definite external referent. With the exception of the kind of directional, pronounced glance that signifies "it's over there" (usually accompanied with a motion of the head or hand in the same direction), a glance does not single out a designated item *for others*, that is, as having a definite meaning in the social domain. Instead, it tends to keep this domain open and flowing in such a way as to create a circuit of shared sense: I glance at you glancing at me while someone else is glancing at us both glancing at each other. And so on—sometimes to the point of exponential complexity in a social scene in which a large group of people is involved, for example, a wedding reception or a dance in which I keep numerous others in view by means of intermittent but sharply discerning looks.

Another way in which the glance is indispensable to the social fabric is found in its very availability: a trait we've met before. (Virtually) everyone can glance at (virtually) any time and in (virtually) any which way. We allude to this availability whenever we say that we can see certain things "at a glance." The same goes for the frequently used expressions, "Take a glance" and "I'll have a glance." We mean that this can be done without any special effort or preparation—that we are almost always well positioned to do this.

Social life thrives on the accessibility of actions that serve to promote this life itself. They include gestures of greeting and parting, the positioning of bodies (for example, as determined by the semiology of "proxemics"), the wearing of clothing of certain sorts, the use of emblems and badges in many societies, the way people conduct themselves at meals and at other public activities, and so on. Among these accessible actions, glancing figures prominently. It is an important solvent of social life. By the glance we get our bearings and learn those of others. It may not be the lingua franca of social life, but it is a common breath and has its own pulse and rhythm. Not only does it serve to punctuate social situations—to establish limits and boundaries—but also we take it in as if it were the very air of these situations. It has the requisite lightness and flexibility to be a main medium of intermediation between human beings, a continually accessible way of getting together and staying together.

The glance's socializing force is also due to its remarkably ramified, spread-out character. It insinuates itself into many circumstances that would otherwise be barred or closed. It not only enters into a given social situation but also opens it up from within, offering "lines of flight" to that situation, aerating it as it were, giving it breathing spaces that would not otherwise exist.[12] The ramifying power

---

12. I take "lines of flight" in the sense of Gilles Deleuze and Félix Guattari, *A Thousand Plateaus*, tr. B. Massumi (Minneapolis: University of Minnesota Press, 1987), pp. 3–4, 14–15, 88–89, 121–122. I shall return to this idea in chap. 4.

of the glance is also seen in its role in social contagion, when a single glance can touch off an entire chain of events, whether these events be celebratory—as in public commemorations—or calamitous, for example, in witch-hunts, lynchings, and other mob actions. Either way, the glance extends beyond its finite point of origin, rippling out into a much larger social world, tracing out ever new and unexpected trajectories.

III

None of this is to claim that people go to cafés just to glance or even mainly to glance. They go for other particular reasons—to read, to write, to think, to be sociable, or merely to pass time. But glance they do and very revealingly so once they are there. The fact is that there are very few glanceless moments in waking human life, just as there are very few meaningless glances.

Nor is this to say that café space can stand in for all of social space.[13] But a café is a promising place to begin to appreciate the pervasiveness of the glance in the intensely interhuman world. And it is a good place to realize not just how deeply ingredient the glance can be in a specific situation but how this happens in such a strikingly multifarious way.

It is time, however, to leave the warm embrace of Café Felix. In any case, a café offers only temporary respite from the demands of the outside world. It welcomes us into its midst on the understanding that we shall soon rejoin a more tumultuous scene. In many cities, a café gathers people of diverse interests and persuasions and provenances: businesspeople and laborers, doctors and lawyers, students and teachers, parents and children. But it brings them together only to see them leave, each person or group going to a different destination within the larger city scene. In order to get there, they must take to the streets, whether by walking or driving.

I, too, leave the café and find myself on Main Street. It is late in the day—still Valentine's Day—and I find myself making my way with scores of others in the dusk. While in the café I felt that I was in the company of people I almost knew—my glancing partners, as it were—but now I am with sheer strangers. The character of the experience changes dramatically, beginning with the way people look at each other. There are very few if any lingering looks; in fact, a lingering look would be out of place if not downright suspicious in this new circumstance: it might invite trouble or at least misinterpretation. Whatever

13. This is not to forget how important the café scene is for Sartre: Pierre's absence is acutely felt as a "neg-entity" in the café where he is sought in vain, and the waiter's *mauvaise foi* so brilliantly analyzed by Sartre occurs in the same space, whose model was doubtless the Café Dôme in Montmartre: see Jean-Paul Sartre, *Psychology of Imagination*, tr. B. Frechtman (New York: Philosophical Library, 1948) and an early passage in *Being and Nothingness* on the concept of *negatité*: see Jean-Paul Sartre, *Being and Nothingness*, tr. H. Barnes (New York: Philosophical Library; New York: Washington Square Press, 1993), p. 43.

looks there may be are only cursorily transmitted in keeping with the transient nature of the situation. In keeping, too, with the fact that bodies are in motion, rendering fixed looks very difficult to muster or maintain. The seated postures of those in the Café Felix facilitated such things as the abstracted look as well as modes of glancing around that enabled the glancer to check out an entire scene—to see who or what is there. On the street, a different circumstance obtains. Unless someone is being actively sought in a crowd of people, there are few sweeping glances that attempt to take in the whole picture. Not surprisingly: my own position is continually changing as I stride on the street, while the contents of the visual field are constantly shifting as well. I keep encountering new figures and they me—I am as new to them as they to me—in an ever-altering dialectic of interpersonal perception.

Nevertheless, glancing is an integral part of this ongoing event; it may not be as perspicuously exhibited as in the café—where virtually every bodily gesture is on display—but it is just as indispensable to the new circumstance, where it emerges from bodies in motion. And in motion *together:* here glancing must be coordinated not just mainly in space, as in the café, but now especially in time, that is, in step with the other pedestrians. The result is often a highly synchronized situation—as we realize, by contrast, whenever we inadvertently crash into someone in a crowd. This indicates that a first task of the glance on the street is *admonitory:* it warns us of oncoming bodies with which we might collide. This is a truly instrumental use of the glance—a use rarely invoked in the protected space of the café. It belongs to the moving body's perceptual reper-toire. If the stationary position of the head is more characteristic of the café—and all the more so in laboratory situations where rigorously minded psycholo-gists conduct experiments in perception—on the street, in contrast, rotational movements of the head are especially well designed to take in the complex flow of others' bodies as they impinge on one's own and stream past it.[14] This is not just a matter of sociality; it is a question of survival: glance or be knocked down![15]

At this preliminary level, it is a matter of glancing for the sake of steering one's way successfully through sidewalk traffic. There is little interest in plumb-ing others' subjectivity or finding out their motives—any more than there is at the driving intersection. My glance needs only discern the main lines of

14. For a convincing critique of psychological experiments that require a stationary head—often held in a metal stirrup—see J. J. Gibson, *The Senses Considered as Perceptual Systems* (Boston: Houghton Mifflin, 1966), pp. 194–201; *The Ecological Approach to Visual Percep-tion,* pp. 209–212. Gibson argues that, on the contrary, the paradigmatic instance of visual perception is that of the freely moving head and body, which are much more equal to the task of grasping the "information in the ambient light" that surrounds the moving body at all times.

15. There are important cultural differences at play here. The leisurely pace of walking in smaller towns in southern Europe, especially Italy and Greece, stands in striking contrast to the speed with which pedestrians on Parisian sidewalks pass each other by—virtually a form of racewalking. In the latter case, I have observed a correspondingly deft employment of the glance, which acts to anticipate the maneuvers of others at a certain distance—always just in time to avert collision.

flight assumed by the bodies of others, that is to say, their "corporeal intentionality" (Merleau-Ponty) writ large. Since this discernment happens so rapidly, my glance need not linger; indeed, it had better *not* linger, since it must also take into account the shifting hulks and hefts of other bodies bearing down upon me. There is no reason to focus on details of clothing or personality, or to interpret motives, when what matters most is safe passage.

Another closely related aspect of the street scene becomes evident in the *distant glance.* Here we catch sight not of the immediately oncoming pedestrian but of someone at a more considerable distance. Again there is no question of any significant interchange of looks—not because of the exigencies of an impending collision nor even because the other is hard to make out but rather because this is a situation of one-way looking: I am literally looking *out for* (and thus *toward*) the other who approaches me from afar. I am glancing out to see what lies ahead, both in space and time: toward where I will be in a little while. The other who walks toward me and I may not exchange glances but we do exchange places: I am moving to the approximate place he now occupies and he to mine. My primary interest lies in my getting to the place I see before me rather than in establishing contact with the figure at a distance. At this figure I glance—and keep moving on. Thus I do not expect any response from him or her, not even the return of my glance: a return that happens routinely (and for good practical reasons) in a more demanding context.

This is not to say, however, that I am always indifferent toward my fellow pedestrians. There is also an *inquisitive glance* that has its place in this same setting. In this case, something striking in the appearance of another pedestrian leads me to want to know more about this person. Could that be Ed Dimendberg over there? I ask myself, having glimpsed a tall, fashionably dressed man who reminds me of my friend, who in fact lives in Ann Arbor. The just-barely noting of others that holds for most distant glances gives way to burgeoning interest in a particular figure who is no longer just another passer-by: he stands out as a compelling presence, someone calling for further, more scrupulous glances. This circumstance includes not only those whom I recognize or those whom I find to be attractive but also those who are threatening or whom I find to be frankly puzzling at first glance: I don't yet know whether such figures are benevolent or harmless or detrimental. This uncertainty leads me to follow up on my first take. Is that really Ed? Is that woman next to him truly attractive? Is that third person in fact dangerous or just posing? The adverbs "really," "truly," and "in fact" indicate that my initial glance is not adequate; I am intrigued by what I see and must now figure out—often by still further glances—what is the case by a closer inspection.[16]

Most of the time, however, there is not sufficient time for such a follow-up, nor even the motive for it. "Proximally and for the most part" (as Heidegger says of everyday activities in general), I am hurrying on to my destination, and so are

---

16. When this follow-up becomes concerted scrutiny, we move from the glance to the gaze.

the others: we are all caught up in what Whitehead calls "the immediate rush of transition."[17] None of us has the luxury of indulging for very long in inquisitive glances, much less for following up on them. The result is not only my failure to engage the glances of others (and they mine), but a more pervasive phenomenon: the *averted glance*. It is to be observed how often people walking on streets greet each other not with open-eyed expectation (this is in fact a rare event) but with glances that have *already* turned away from the person who has been espied.

This is easily tested. Walk through virtually any crowded street and notice that the great majority of those who pass by you seem to have turned away from you by the time you come into their proximity. Even if you have spotted them—and they you—in an initial distant glance, there is a striking divergence of looks when they move into your closer vicinity, as if to say "no need to look at you further, I've already seen all that I need to see." And this is true: for purposes of passing each other by and staying on one's way, enough *has* been seen to justify averting the look. By the time oncoming others come near to me on the street, their glances are already moving elsewhere—looking ahead at new figures who approach from afar, way behind me. In general: the more successful the distant glance, the more likely the averted look.

The averted glance is not to be confused with the *downward* look. Many walkers seem to walk with their heads drawn down, eyes on the street as if to contemplate the pavement under them. This direction of the glance is less intentional than it is in aversion, which implies a semideliberate decision to look away from the other.[18] The ordinary downward look betrays more than the usual lack of interest in engaging the other; it implies a certain obliviousness, a taking oneself out of the immediate scene of glancing, as if to say, "I prefer to make my own way; I'll go it alone." It is the streetwise equivalent of the abstract look I witnessed on the part of the writer in the café. (One of the curious effects of the downward look on the street is that it releases the other person to look more intently at the downward gazer—given that there does not seem to be much risk of engaging the latter's look.)

Both the averted glance and the downward look refuse the *passing glance*. This is especially prominent in large cities, especially at rush hour, when people move by each other so rapidly. In passing glances, there is eye contact with the other, an actual exchange of the glance, even if this lasts only a few seconds or even less. The effect is that of catching the other out of the corner of one's eye. This is the converse of the situation described earlier whereby we turn away from each other at the last minute. In this case, we turn toward each other or at

---

17. Alfred North Whitehead, *Process and Reality;* corrected ed., ed. D. R. Griffin and D. Sherburne (New York: Free Press, 1978), p. 129.

18. When the downward look is more concerted, it is often an expression of a difficult emotion, as when one "hangs one's head in shame."

least take one another in. But we do this not for the sake of becoming better acquainted or learning anything in particular about the other. Nor is it necessary in a practical sense, such as to avoid running into each other. It is not inquisitive either, since it is normally accompanied with indifference. Instead, the passing glance is a matter of something quite different: confirming the other's existence and, by his or her brief look back, confirming one's own as well.

A dialectic of the singular and the universal is here at stake. By a cursory exchange of passing glances, I affirm the other's current existence as a singular fact: I am looking *just at you* and *at no one else.* At the same time, I also affirm something much more expansive in scope: I also (albeit only implicitly) affirm you as a member of the human race, as *another human being.* The singular you I support by my glance is not the autobiographically unique you—*that* I know nothing about, given that you are a stranger to me in this anonymous circumstance —but rather it is a singularity that manifests the universal of Humanity in just *this* place and at *this* time and with *this* flesh. My glance salutes Everyone in You, that is to say, You as Everyone.[19]

This remarkable, albeit rarely noted, circumstance exemplifies a strange logic that was noted in the introduction and that we shall often meet in the course of this book: something quite exiguous, seemingly trivial, shows itself to be immensely significant in its scope and effect. A narrow defile opens onto a vast vista.[20] This is the very opposite of the Law of Diminishing Returns, or any entropic phenomenon of ineluctable exhaustion. It could be called a Law of Exponential Increase, whereby the merest action leads to an expansive outcome, an augmentation of being.[21] Such augmentation holds for many phenomena of the glance, whose brevity of enactment belies its expansive presence and considerable efficacity in the visual world.

In the case before us, a meager look assures me of my existence: I am upheld in the eyes of the other. The importance of this exceeds what we might at first imagine, and can be grasped from the counterfactual circumstance: a world in which others never offered any such confirmation of my merely being there would be a disturbing place indeed. Others' passing looks at me do not prove my existence—this is not necessary, being supplied by consciousness (as Descartes would argue) or by my body (as Merleau-Ponty would insist)—but they do act to

19. On the strong but tacit collusion between the singular and the universal, see Gilles Deleuze, *Difference and Repetition,* tr. P. Patton (New York: Columbia University Press, 1990), chap. 1, esp. pp. 1, 3–5. For a more complete analysis of its role in the glance, see chap. 10 in this book, "The Ethics of the Glance," and chap. 7, "The Singularity of the Glance."

20. The "narrow defile" refers to Freud's metaphor at the beginning of chap. 3 of *The Interpretation of Dreams,* tr. J. Strachey, in J. Strachey, ed., *The Standard Edition of the Complete Psychological Works* (London: Hogarth Press, 1963), vol. 4, p. 121.

21. I borrow the phrase "augmentation of being" (*Seinszuwachs*) from Hans Gadamer, *Truth and Method* (New York: Continuum, 1989), p. 124, where it is translated "increase in being."

acknowledge it. They do so in a powerful if only tacitly expressed way. Without the confirming glances of others cast at me in passing, I would be less than myself: I would be adrift in a Sargasso Sea of generality in which my very identity, indeed my singularity, would be dissolved in a morass of indifference. By their merely glancing at me, others otherwise unknown to me offer me a garland of recognition.

To be validated by others in this way is the intersubjective equivalent of glancing at oneself in the mirror, as we so frequently do without suspecting any larger stakes. Here, too, I am confirmed by a mere look back—in this case, the literal reflection of my own looking at myself. This look, stemming from me in the most spontaneous way, is captured in the mirror, held there in such a way as to acquire a momentary existence of its own. It is as if it had become, for a brief second, the look of another who affirms my existence. Sometimes, indeed, I don't recognize myself in the mirror: can this face be mine, I ask myself? At this moment, acknowledgment ceases as I become merely the object of an alienated look, albeit my own. Another dimension opens here, closer to that of Lacan's celebrated "mirror stage," in which the emerging ego is built from a false identification with its own image, a merely fictitious and momentarily petrified version of a self that until then had been wholly fragmented and uncoordinated. According to Lacan, such identification is based on a fundamental *méconnaissance,* a failure of self-acknowledgment. For I am identifying with the projected image of myself rather than with my massive physical self; I have become my own other: in Rimbaud's famous phrase (very much on Lacan's mind), "je est un autre."[22] I am identifying with an idealized image of my own awkward, uncoordinated bodily self: an image, moreover, that exhibits right/left reversal. My ego has gotten off to a false start; it is formed in a "fictionalized direction."[23]

Whatever its dubious origins, once the ego is fully formed—once it is recognizable as my ego—a mere glance serves to acknowledge my existence. This is an acknowledgment that I desperately need in order to be the self I am, or (at the least) the self that I am in the process of becoming. In both cases, the human self is supported on the slender reed of the glance. This is so both whether the glance comes from unknown others whom I encounter as passersby on the street or whether it stems from my own glance cast at myself in the mirror. The fact that each form of glance is casually cast—each being a passing glance—belies the crucial role the glance plays in supporting my ongoing life: in affirming my existence as just *this* self, the one that sees itself or is seen by others. What is acknowledged is not any particular trait of mine; rather, it is my being a human being in the midst of my very contingency, my being an instance of the

22. Rimbaud's phrase is found in his letter to Georges Izambard, Charleville, May 13, 1871 in *Rimbaud: Complete Works, Selected Letters,* trans. Wallace Fowlie (Chicago: University of Chicago Press, 1966), p. 304. Cf. Lacan's later variation: "je me vois voir"(I see myself seeing) in *Les Quatre concepts fundamentaux de la psychanalyse,* pp. 72–73 (English trans., 80–81).

23. See Jacques Lacan, "The Mirror Stage," in *Ecrits: A Selection,* trans. B. Fink (New York: Norton, 2002), pp. 98–100.

universally human while also being an idiosyncratic self, *jemeinig* (literally, "in each case mine"[24]), myself alone and yet everyone, I in You, You in me.

This is not to deny that there is something special in the other's acknowledging me in a glance: something more decisive and dramatic than when I look at myself in the mirror. No longer is it only a matter of the recognition of my bare existing. "A glance from your eyes and my life will be yours." These words from the closing scene of Terence Malick's film *The Thin Red Line* express with poetic force the fact that if I am acknowledged by your glance I may, just then and there but also indefinitely, exist for you and become part of your life.

Thanks to the ever-deepening drama of glancing, I coexist with others and with myself. By the becoming of the glance, I am confirmed as the singular universal I know myself to be and even, on certain occasions, as an integral part of another's singular being as well.[25]

IV

One important sign that such far-reaching confirmation by the glance is far from trivial is found in the fact that it is effected by more than eyes alone. Just as what Joyce calls the "ineluctable modality of the visible"[26] occurs in several forms, so the confirming glance is capable of expressing itself in various ways. In a quite different street scene—in contemporary Galway, in Western Ireland—I was struck by an accompaniment of the glance that can be designated as the *nod of acknowledgment*. While glancing at me with their eyes only, fellow walkers in the city street displayed a characteristic motion of the head: a slight twist to the side accompanied by a rearing back that was part of an up-and-down nodding action. The effect was something more than passing recognition; it was a form of gestural address. In being the recipient of such an action, I was engaged by the other directly and more fully than by an unaccompanied glance. It was as if I had been seen as someone worthy of note. I found myself nodding back even though this was far from my usual practice. In being nodded at, I had a very distinct sense that the other was affirming me as the discrete human being I am; he or she was acknowledging me not just in my generality—as merely another passerby—but in my singularity, as just *this* person who was being encountered on the street. This is why I had the sense that I was being *addressed*—where this latter term implies that the other was on the verge of speaking to me, could very well speak to me, although this was not expected, much less required. More than

24. See Martin Heidegger, *Being and Time*, tr. J. Macquarrie and E. Robinson (New York: Harper and Row, 1962), p. 67: "We are ourselves the entities to be analyzed. The Being of any such entity is *in each case mine*" (author's italics).

25. For more on the singular universal, see the prefatory remarks to part 4 and chap. 10.

26. "Ineluctable modality of the visible: at least that if no more, thought through my eyes. Signatures of all things I am here to read" (James Joyce, *Ulysses*, ed. Hans Gabler [New York: Vintage, 1986]. p. 31). The signatures are inherently multiple.

with the usual glance, I felt fully acknowledged—just short of words of express acknowledgment.

This is a situation not of the cessation of the glance but of its extension into another gesture, the nod. A certain elderly man, dressed in an Irish black suit, certainly did glance at me on the Galway street; he was not *not* looking at me; but he was also doing something else in which the glance of his eyes was incorporated into the motion of his head. The nod, unlike the strictly ocular glance, is a movement of the whole head. As such, it involves more of the glancer's body, and for this reason it is more likely to be perceived than is the strictly visual glance—which in its speed and slightness can easily pass undetected. The functional value of this extension of the glance is evident: it makes one's acknowledgment much more salient. Later, driving back to Dublin from Dingle on a mid-sized road, I encountered a man walking on the side of the street who, with no prompting on my part, nodded back at me so vigorously that I could not overlook his gesture even had I tried. In a circumstance such as this, the nod presents itself as the amplification of the glance.

The circumstance of the nod is still more complex than this. Not only does the nod—or any other such gesture, for example, the wink—expand and fortify the standard case of glancing (with both eyes open, directed in a certain way, and so on), but it introduces a new dimension of the circumstance. For it underscores the action of glancing itself, as if to communicate that *I am now glancing at you in this circumstance.*[27] This particular message (or meta-message) can be expressed by virtually any part of the body, including the movement of the body as a whole, just as the work of the glance itself can be accomplished by senses other than the visual: in eavesdropping we can be said to hear glancingly. When a particular body part underlines the fact of glancing, it is almost as if that part has been *delegated* to do the communicative task. Another striking case of such delegation is also to be found in Ireland. When drivers pass each other on open roads—and being in open sight of each other—they will routinely lift the second finger of their right hands in acknowledgment of each other. This action is tantamount to a nod, but in this case the principals nod at each other not through the action of the head or eyes (which stay focused forward on the road) but through finger action. The finger does not itself glance, but it signals to the other driver that glancing of an apposite sort has just happened or is about to happen.[28]

We may regard the finger-nodding gesture as a case of glancing by downward displacement—to adapt Freud's formula for the formation of many fetishes.[29] Here we move down from the eyes as the primary agents to the finger as

27. I owe the gist of this last observation to Andrés Colapinto.

28. It is striking that only one finger is employed for this purpose, much as only one eye winks: as if there were an economic principle implicitly at work here.

29. See Freud, "On Fetishism," tr. J. Strachey, in *The Standard Edition of the Complete Psychological Works*, vol. 21, p. 149.

testimonial to them. The result is not a fetish, however conspicuous the ampli-fied gesture may be; instead, it is a sign of recognition effected between at least two human beings, who acknowledge each other as fellow drivers engaged in a common enterprise of steering safely. The finger-nod is a way of taking account of one another on the open road. In the end, however, this gesture cannot be considered necessary; on major highways in Ireland it does not take place; it arises only in situations of sufficient social or spatial intimacy for acknowledg-ment of some sort to seem appropriate. The "sort" in this last statement remains bodily, while the "some" allows for a distinctive variation, thanks to delegation and displacement from the eyes to another body part.

V

I walk out of my apartment in north Chicago, and begin to stroll in the nearby neighborhood. I am frankly looking for glancers, and I intend to glance freely myself. I walk for blocks, first southward on North Winchester toward the park there, then westward toward Ridge, a major avenue. These are all ordinary streets: no boulevards here! At least there are sidewalks—not to be taken for granted in modern cities—but they are mostly unpopulated. The few who are out walking on them do not "give me the time of day" (a locution that here means "do not take the time to exchange significant looks"). A tall and strapping man approaches me from down the street; we draw close, but instead of looking me in the eye he looks past me; *his look is elsewhere,* already diverted from any real engagement with my own look. Further on, having turned to my right toward Ridge, I encounter a group of teenagers who are altogether self-absorbed: at least they are looking at each other! Just beyond them, a mother pushing a pram with a baby inside crosses my path; she is not looking at my eyes but at my legs and feet to be sure there is space enough to pass on the narrow sidewalk. Only once in a walk of some thirty-five minutes do I encounter a person who is willing to exchange glances in any overt manner: this is a young man who seems to be returning from work and who, perhaps for that very reason, seems to be at comparative leisure: he, at least, can indulge in the luxury of the look! For the most part, however, I encounter very little looking that takes in the other person in a direct, eye-to-eye connection. This situation is one in which I as a pedestrian have been in effect discounted in advance, *nullified* as someone to look at. For I am experiencing here a paucity of glances exchanged and thus a situation of radically diminished looking. If glancing occurs at all, it happens as *glancing away:* so far away that one cannot even catch the first glimmering of the glance. This is not just a matter of averted or furtive, fugitive or downward glancing, much less of just glancing around; nor is it a case of glancing displaced in nods or other gestures. It is a circumstance in which the role of the glance has been still more radically curtailed—to the point of seeming to be removed from the ordinary looker's repertoire.[30]

I dwell on the vagaries of glancing on an ordinary north Chicago street to make a larger point. The reason why changes in practices of glancing are not trivial is that these practices enact an ethics of the glance that has been rarely noted or described. We have seen how crucial a mere acknowledging look is for confirming one's identity and that of others. I would even go so far as to say that we are obliged to acknowledge others by some significant look—of which glancing is a paradigmatic case—and that this acknowledgment precedes other more concrete and specific obligations.[31]

Just as all it takes is a glance to recognize a common humanity, so all it takes is a glance to offer egress from certain locked-in situations. Quite apart from the street scene just described, there are certain situations that profit greatly from a mere glance: witness the nurse who is engaged in changing a dressing, or someone in deep depression, or an artist immersed in the white heat of creative work. Even if only as offering relief from the involving character of such situations, glancing assumes a singular importance. The nurse who has been completely absorbed in her demanding task looks up and away as a means of collecting herself and opening up a certain space, not unlike an action of breathing in a suffocating circumstance. A painter glances out the window after making progress on a painting on which he has been working all afternoon: the sunset he sees offers respite and perhaps further inspiration.[32] When a depressed person unexpectedly steals a glance at someone passing by, this may be a sign of taking interest in her surroundings despite her otherwise massive withdrawal from them.

It is as if the complete absence of glancing is somehow intolerable for human beings, even for those who are highly invested in not being distracted from their current circumstance. The actual glance that is cast is remarkably efficacious as an alleviation of this situation. It may not be the case that, as Rimbaud said, "The

---

30. The fact that many of my fellow walkers in Rogers Park are African American may not be incidental. Am I being given, as a return in kind, the equivalent of the concerted ignoring and neglecting—the *scotomizing*—which *they,* in earlier segregated times and still today, experience in America? I suspect that this is sometimes the case, however tacitly it may be operative in a given instance. In south Chicago, I am told, certain militant African Americans associated with Islamic sects have an explicit policy of never acknowledging whites. Or more exactly, they will look at a white person if a street encounter occurs, but they look straight through this person—as if he or she were not there, did not exist. (I owe this report to my friend Ginger, to whose astute observations we shall return in chap. 10.)

31. To this matter we shall return in chap. 10, "The Ethics of the Glance."

32. I experienced a parallel case in the musical world. Jazz pianist and singer Mose Allison performed during one continuous set with his eyes fixed on the keyboard throughout. This was a form of concentration, almost of meditation. Despite the high degree of attention he gave to the piano, Allison would occasionally lift his eyes and glance at the bassist who played with him, not for any particular musical reason but as if to affirm his very existence as a fellow musician—and the bassist clearly noticed Allison's look, taking it in, though without returning it. Between sets, Allison would also rotate his head and look at the audience, acknowledging its presence. (Mose Allison in performance, February 20, 2000, Bird of Paradise, Ann Arbor, Michigan.)

true life lies elsewhere" (*la vraie vie est ailleurs*). But the very prospect of a disengagement, or merely of an alternative engagement, is heartening to human beings; perhaps it is even necessary to their psychic survival (and sometimes to their physical survival as well). This prospect is conveyed at once most easily and most effectively by the mere casting of a glance.

Joe Christmas, the black martyr in Faulkner's *Light in August*, is able to glance back at his persecutors just after they have castrated him; this accusatory glancing back is one action of which he could not be deprived, and (as Sartre argues) it bestows upon him the unsuspected power of making his assailants confront their scurrilous identity as torturers: putting them in their place, making them into circumscribed beings in-themselves (that is, things in effect) rather than the for-themselves that they arrogantly take themselves to be.[33] Christmas's freedom is thereby affirmed, and theirs denied, by his mere glance —a counterengagement in the very midst of a most destructive sadistic action.

The consequence of the absence of glancing becomes evident in this light. It is tantamount to the demolition of a last margin of human freedom: just to glance around is one of the easiest and yet most powerful of human actions. As we have just seen, the absence of the glance may sometimes happen on the street—where it is a matter of choice—or it may be found in the intensity of certain kinds of bodily engagement or in certain pathological mental states, about which there is very little choice. In none of these instances can its absence be sustained indefinitely; the glance beckons as a way out of an otherwise unrelieved engrossment—a way that is as accessible as the mere opening and closing of our eyes.[34] And in just looking around by means of the glance we realize a lightness of being denied to those who are altogether caught up in their own destinies at the moment, immersed in the spirit of gravity. In the very next moment, however, they too can liberate themselves. Human existence may be burdensome indeed; but it is always subject to disburdenment—if only by taking a glance at one's surroundings.[35]

VI

From the first forays of this chapter, we have seen how often the mere glance, starting as it does at the surface of things—the surface of the glancer's own body (that is, the outer surface of his or her eyes), then the surface of what is looked

---

33. For Sartre's analysis of Joe Christmas, see *Being and Nothingness*, p. 526. Medea's daughters look back at their vengeful mother, thereby causing her (unlike Christmas's murderers) to desist. See *Medea*, ll. 1040–1043. (I owe this example to Eric Casey.)

34. This claim is not restricted to physiologically functional eyes. Blind people glance in their own way: e.g., by touching or moving, and by other bodily means.

35. "A mood of elation can alleviate the manifest burden of Being; that such a mood is possible also discloses the burdensome character of Dasein, even while it alleviates the burden" (Heidegger, *Being and Time*, p. 173).

at, including that of the other's body—keeps leading us into depth, first that entailed by the epistemic confirmation of my own and others' existence and then the ethical depth at stake in the implicit imperative to acknowledge the other as singular and as a member of a common humanity. Moreover, these epistemic and ethical depths are closely related: to note the other's existence by glances is an essential prelude to recognizing the other human being as at once unique and as belonging to the species.

The glance is a basic action that clings closely to surfaces yet also goes far into the depths. If this seems paradoxical, it is only because we imagine depth to be something located apart from surface—somewhere *under* surface and independent of it. It is the very phenomenon of the glance that reminds us that (yet again in the Wittgensteinian axiom) "the depths are on the surface."[36] Or let us say that the special virtue of the glance is to bring them there—and to keep them there, too. Surfaces serve the glance in two ways. On the one hand, they afford places for the glance to alight; otherwise, it would merely dissipate, go off into the atmosphere, fizzle out. Glances adhere to surfaces as to their natural element; there is an affinity between the two to which we shall have occasion to return several times in the course of this book. On the other hand, surfaces make depths available to the glance; they make these depths accessible by *presenting* them. The glance does not have to seek depth anywhere other than on the surface on which it lands. No visual speleology is required, much less a special act of depth interpretation. The depths that are relevant to the glance lie right under the look—on the very surface of things. When I attest to another person's identity or existence, and when I acknowledge that this person shares in the same kind of generic being as I possess myself, I do so by a mere glance at the surfaces the other presents to me: those of the face I glimpse so suddenly, or the body I see so sketchily. The identity, existence, or personhood I secure in a glance is at one with the perceived flesh of the other; it is not anywhere else, and surely not in a separate spiritual realm.

Thus the glance in its alliance with surfaces is by no means superficial in its operation—as the etymological link between "surface" and "superficial" might seem to suggest.[37] At the very least, the glance finds depths on surfaces; and if it does not find them there, it imputes them to these surfaces, tracing them out. This is not to presume that all surfaces are strictly *external* surfaces. Some surfaces extend into the inner parts of a given object; they fold into it, as we see in the case of embryonic invagination and in other forms of enfoldment (including many articles of clothing, as when pockets fold into the inner parts of pants). Surfaces constitute the interiority of things as well as their outer parts. Often the

---

36. L. Wittgenstein, *Zettel*, tr. G. E. M. Auscombe and G. H. von Wright (Berkeley: University of California Press, 1967), p. 42.

37. "Surface" and "superficial" both derive from *superficies,* Latin for "surface," meaning literally "upon the face."

two kinds of surface, inner and outer, are continuous: think of how the surfaces of the lips give way to those of the throat, esophagus, and stomach. One doesn't have to *see* the esophagus or the stomach to feel its continuity with the visible lips. The inside parts are literally implicated by the outside parts in a somato-graphic whole. Their depth within the body is not separated from the outside perceptible surfaces but is at one with these surfaces. Here the depths are not so much *on* the surface—literally projected there, readable there, and so on—as they follow from it and are inwardly connected with it. To glance at the bodily surface of a human being is to sense its somatic interiority, which is not so much inferred or posited as felt and known.

There is yet another kind of surface/depth relation that is plumbed by the glance. This is not implicit but directly seen as such. I refer to the way in which we can look into another person's eyes and see an iridescent depth not present anywhere else: we see this depth at a glance, without any need to linger or probe further. Just such brief but intense looking is normally foreclosed on the street— and often in the café as well. Nevertheless, it happens fairly frequently in talking with close family, friends, and lovers. It is a mode not just of seeing the other (that is what takes place on the street) or of seeing through the other (as I have reported in certain moments of Chicago street life) but of *seeing into* the other. In fact, in looking into someone else's eyes—or our own, for that matter—we perceive a double depth in the pupil: the colored iris has a certain limited depth and the dark pupil a more profound, undeterminable depth. Taken together (and overlaid by the lens and cornea that add still another depthful dimension), they adumbrate a depth that is unique to human beings (that is, to the species; the eyes of other animals have their own quite different, distinctive depths) as well as to this individual who stands before me as I look into his or her eyes.[38] Such depth does not depend on the glance for its apprehension; it yields to other modes of looking—for example, staring into the other's eyes—but the fact that it can be detected in a glance testifies to the interpersonal perceptiveness and power of glancing.

This redoubled depth is a hallmark of the human person, at once a signal of and a way into this person—someone who is both singular and universal, an inimitable You and a generic Everyone (and someone, too, who is continually becoming other than him- or herself). Only such a person, having such depth, is capable of eliciting and sustaining an ethical relation. Moreover, the premier place that Levinas accords to the face as the source of this relation is most compellingly occupied by the eyes of that face. For the eyes deliver a depth that is neither strictly external (as would be, for example, the shallow depth of a person's cheeks, which are only "skin deep") nor wholly internal (emanating from the physiological innards of the person). No wonder that human beings

38. On the extinguishing of the fire in a dying fox's eyes, see Aldo Leopold's celebrated description in *A Sand County Almanac* (Oxford: Oxford University Press, 1949).

often feel that a person's *soul* is more manifest in their eyes than anywhere else—where "soul" is construed as the animating principle of that person's life, including his or her character and intelligence.

The ethics of acknowledgment by the glance here finds a phenomenological basis in our ongoing experiences of other people. Seeing into the depth of the person is seeing into that person's soul—not an abstract and immortal soul but soul taken as the seat of becoming that is concretely embodied in the eyes that intimate it. If the merest glance acknowledges others as embodying nonstatic, singular universals—that is, capable of becoming ever-more other to themselves (and indeed also to ourselves)—a glance into their eyes is able to apprehend persons with souls, entities worthy of respect for being who they are and for becoming what they will be.

Even though the idea of a person includes soul, a person is not a spiritual being who belongs to another world. Spiritual beings require a special kind of depth, one that is as invisible as it is intangible. This is the kind of depth that characterizes what Kant calls the Kingdom of Ends, that is, a noumenal realm that is strictly discontinuous with the phenomenal world. Spiritual beings have no surfaces, and the spiritual part of human beings is not connected with the physical part by any intermediary planes. Nor does their residence in the Kingdom of Ends entail any sense of surface. In this rarified realm, the depths cannot reside on any surface, and they are not implicated by it—nor can they be manifested by any particular bodily organ such as the eyes. According to Kant's ethics, obligation derives from somewhere beyond any possible surface, including that of the body; the categorical imperative comes from elsewhere—from pure practical reason, which is not located in any physical surface or any bodily organ. For Kant, the ethical relation is realized only in the categorical terms of the Kingdom of Ends, not in the concrete events of the phenomenal domain where bodies move, eyes dart, and looks intersect. There is action—practical action of an ethical tenor undertaken by rational subjects—but nowhere in this Kingdom is glancing to be found.

VII

The Kingdom of Ends and the Domain of Glances: somewhere between these two extremes human beings manage to relate to each other. In the Kingdom, practical reason, guided by maxims of action, operates in a transcendent realm in which self-legislation obtains. Here there is no alleviation by the look—which, like any other action of the physical human body, is for Kant a matter of incentive, of empirical interest and gain, something belonging to the phenomenal world of contingent and causal interaction. In the Domain, however, we find recognition of oneself by the looks of others, an acknowledgment that is essential to one's very personhood. The primary direction of intentionality is reversed: not from myself to others but from others back toward myself (including myself-as-other, as in the case of the mirror stage). And here as well there is a continual lightening of the spirit of gravity that afflicts most ethical situations, heavy as they are with duty and demand. This alleviation arises from the ease with which, even in a very dire circumstance, I can find a way out just by glancing around as well as from the ease with which the other's supportive look encourages me to pursue my own plans and projects.

To speak of "Kingdom" and "Domain" is to talk of two kinds of place or space, and it is in these terms that the two realms are most tellingly contrasted. The Kingdom of Ends is a form of spiritual space. I say "space" for it is a matter of a realm that is infinite, homogeneous, and isometric (where the metric is here supplied by the self-legislated laws of practical reason). These properties were attributed to physical space in the early modern era, but they were first conceived as predicates of God in the Middle Ages: it was from this religious and spiritual basis that their ascription to worldly space ensued—as can be seen most dramatically in the case of Newton, who was at once a theologian and a physicist.[39] Most important, in such space there is no room allowed for locality, that is, for the peculiarities of place, its idiosyncratic shape and history. Everything is here in equipoise, nothing is in disarray: no need to glance, indeed no need to look at all since all is known in advance. There is no room for surprise in the Kingdom. Even if the maxim on which ethical action is predicated reflects local custom and popular mores in its origin, once it is universalized it loses all trace of any such place-specific source (or so Kant would claim). For the imperative to which it gives rise *binds equally everywhere.* This entails an indifference not just to the particularities of place but also to the individual persons who inhabit given places. Person and place are affine: each is utterly individuated, each is animated by soul, and persons exist only in places.[40] They stand in contrast with spirit and space, which are universal and nonindividuated, and animated by reason or God.

The Domain of the Glance is a genuine *place:* finite and bounded, locatory and situating, heterogeneous as a medium, and nonisometric. This is no level playing field; instead, it is a field of obtrusions and protuberances, a rough surface indeed! And surface is again the key. As I have just argued, the glance thrives amid surfaces, and these surfaces are those of things and places. It is thanks to such surfaces that the peculiarities of things and places become apparent: not just their size and extent but such qualitative characteristics as color, texture, density, comparative translucency, and so on. Most important, surfaces

39. See my book *The Fate of Place: A Philosophical History* (Berkeley: University of California Press, 1997), parts 2 and 3.

40. Concerning the soul of landscape, see my *Representing Place: Landscape Painting and Maps* (Minneapolis: University of Minnesota Press, 2002), chaps. 3 and 6; and *Spirit and Soul,* 2d ed. (Putnam, Conn.: Spring Publications, 2004), esp. part 5, "Finding Soul in Place." On the relation between person and place, see Edward S. Casey, *Getting Back into Place* (Bloomington: Indiana University Press, 1993), chap. 9. Consult also George Santayana, *Persons and Places* (New York: Scribner's, 1944), esp. chap. 1, "Time, Place, and Ancestry."

determine the local topology of space, the "near sphere" in Husserl's term, "vicinity" in Descartes's word.[41] As Piaget posited, a deep level of spatiality—the first phase of spatial experience for the child—is the "topological," wherein the crucial relation is that between *neighboring regions*.[42] But this relation is not reserved for children alone; it is an important part of adult experience in the form of "the nearing of nearness" (Heidegger).[43] When the hegemony of space is crushingly dominant—as it has become in the modern world—it is just such nearing that is excluded or repressed, and with it the place-world in which propinquity matters much more than distance, touching more than testing, glancing more than observing. It was doubtless as a protest against the increasing predominance of space—evident in the thinking of city planners like Hausmann in the nineteenth century and Robert Moses in the twentieth century—that the dandy and the flâneur emerged as conspicuous reminders that the glance was still a lively option on the very streets that were becoming more of a site for traffic than a place for meeting.[44]

A place proffers proximal surfaces for apprehension and attachment. It is the privileged realm of the glance, which seeks out its most attractive or congenial surfaces (and only testily explores the most threatening ones). This is why an enclosing surface such as that provided by the walls of the Café Felix affords such opportunities for engaged glancing: not just allows it but actively solicits it, encouraging the lingering glance, the intimate glance, the caressing glance, the probing glance: each of these looking into the heart of nearness within its own region. (The fearful glance, the furtive glance, the terrified glance are the negative counterparts, which, grasping the detrimentality of a place in its very proximity, seek to evade the impending danger.)

The bond between glances and places is fast and deep. This bond reflects what they share in common: contingency, historicity, an irreplaceable tie to bodily desire and intentionality, a decided vulnerability. These shared features help to explain why we glance so often in a comparatively settled place such as a café—as if to reassure ourselves, within the circumambience of a finite enclosure, that we are not going stir-crazy! They also clarify why we glance so differently in different places and at different times. There is a striking disparity

41. On Husserl's notion of the near sphere, see Ulrich Claesges, *Edmund Husserls Theories der Raumkonstutition* (The Hague: Nijhoff, 1964), pp. 83 ff. Concerning vicinity in Descartes, see René Descartes, *Principles of Philosophy*, tr. V. R. Miller and R. P. Miller (Dordrecht: Reidel, 1983), p. 52; and my commentary in *The Fate of Place*, pp. 161, 172, 329.

42. For Piaget's theory of topological space in the child, see Jean Piaget and Bärbel Inhelder, *The Child's Conception of Space*, tr. F. J. Langdon and J. L. Lunzer (New York: Norton, 1967).

43. On the nearing of nearness, see Heidegger, "Building Dwelling Thinking," in *Poetry, Language, Thought*, tr. A. Hofstadter (New York: Harper, 1971), p. 157, and "Time and Being," in Heidegger, *Time and Being*, tr. J. Stambaugh (New York: Harper, 1969), pp. 5–15; for my treatment of this theme in Heidegger, see *The Fate of Place*, pp. 276–284.

44. I construe site as the shrunken residue of infinite space: that is, what happened to such space in the early modern period, especially in the hands of Leibniz. See *The Fate of Place*, pp. 167–179.

between glancing on north Chicago streets and on the boardwalks of Atlantic City (where people pay much more attention to each other). Different places call for different glances. Since place (unlike space) incorporates the time of its apprehension, the same street or concourse will induce varying glances at different times of the day and night. The more open and outgoing looks of the day—when these happen at all—give way to the more reticent regards of the night. A place, though recognizably the same, is not identical from one time to another, being deeply affected by altering light, season of the year, the character of who is present at a given moment, and so on. In maintaining its homogeneity and universality, space does not recognize such qualitative changes.

There is a close and continuing marriage between the glance and place. For the glance primarily seeks out what is happening within the boundaries of its own domain—within the "internal horizon"[45] that place provides. This is the case whether the glance occurs within the confines of architecture (for example, the café or the classroom) or outside the building or the city (for example, on the street, in the country): either way, the glance is most at home in the coziness of a familiar place. Glancing prospers when there are walls or buildings or hills around it: all of which supply attractive and supportive surfaces for its wayward course, its dartings and veerings. Surrounded by such surfaces, the glance can better concern itself with the peculiar character of a given place: its special contents and configurations, its conjoint motions, as well as its diverse destinies. A glance tracks the in-lines as well as the outlines of a place, its diverse denizens as well as its outlying surfaces.

This is to say that the glance thrives upon the particularities of the surfaces of places: the more irregular these surfaces, the more the glance is called into action. For it is the particular layout of surfaces that convert what would otherwise be a barren scene of space into a genuine event of place: that make a café into *this* place, the Café Felix in Ann Arbor, or the pavement of *this* street into North Winchester in Chicago or Quay Street in Galway, Ireland. The same goes for many other places: the doctor's office and the subway, the theater and the library, the outskirts of town and the hills beyond. In all of these cases, it is the configuration of surfaces that determines each to be the uniquely shaped place that it is. From within the shelter of these surfaces, we glance out into the place we are in.

When I look out into the far sphere of a landscape, I reach the limit of the glance. I am then *viewing* that landscape. Such viewing still belongs to the glance-family at its outer extremity, even if it comes very close to *gazing* at the landscape: no longer glancing at all. Here we encounter the important difference between viewing—along with such closely affiliated acts as the sweeping glance and the distant glance—and outright gazing. A given glance can look out beyond distinct boundaries, even quite remote ones, into the far sphere. Then it

---

45. This is Husserl's term: see his *Experience and Judgment*, ed. L. Landgrebe, tr. J. S. Churchill, tr. K. Ameriks (Evanston, Ill.: Northwestern University Press), pp. 360–361.

exceeds where I am stationed, the immediate place I am, and looks beyond to a region where that place begins to transform itself into another: say, viewing the Himalayas from a plateau in Tibet. I look onto the Himalaya range as an "inter-place" between the place from where I look and a place I cannot see at all, on the other side of these outsize megaliths.[46] I let my glance linger on the boundary thus presented—perhaps on the outline of the peaks at sunset: in short, the external horizon. I view this horizon, which is a zone of disappearance, at a glance, and yet I do so quite comprehensively. I take in a lot, a lot more than what could be contained in the most proximal near sphere. But the far into which I here look remains the counterpart of the near; it is nothing but the other pole of the near, its partner several times removed, the distant epicenter of the scene: it is the near no longer here but *over there,* in its own remote place.

Such glancing is at once bounded and anchored: bounded by the external horizon provided by the mountains in their encircling farness; anchored by virtue of freely adverting to the nearness of this scene despite the distance from which I am looking. Two kinds of depth are here present, that of the near sphere and that of the far sphere, both contained within the perceived surfaces of the same bounteous landscape.

But if I gaze contemplatively at the sunset that exceeds these same gargantuan mountains, letting my look merge with the uncircumscribable sky, I enter thereby into a very different experience; I begin to gaze at the scene, a very different action entailing quite another depth. In this way, I have made the transition from place to space—from the delimited domain of the glance to the unlimited kingdom of the gaze. I have left the glance-world, with its own distinctive depths and textured places, in order to move into a realm whose depth is unplumbable and that contains no places, only open spaces. I gaze into what cannot even be called a "world." For world signifies *cosmos*—an ordered whole, a Place of places, something that remains bounded and particular in its very openness. *Cosmos* is not to be confused with *universum,* an infinite Space of spaces, an unending field that is as empty of discrete places as it is of endemic qualities. Where *cosmos* is the fitting (indeed, finally the only) region in which glancing can occur, the universe is the proper realm of gazing: this is why we speak tellingly of "stargazing." The gaze calls for the kingdom of space; the glance prospers in the domain of place.

We shall return to this contrast in chapter 4. Before this, we must draw closer to the glance itself.

46. On the interplace, see my *Getting Back into Place,* pp. 162 ff.

2

COMING CLOSER TO THE GLANCE

I

So far we have been attempting to catch the glance at its own game, finding it in its spontaneous enactment in a café and on the street. But we have not yet come to terms with what the glance is *close-up*—what it consists in when considered in terms of its own constituent features. What do we do when we glance? What exactly? In this chapter I shall quite literally *ap-proximate* to the glance in an effort to discern what happens in glancing when it is seen in its own detailed working. I shall try to come face to face with the glance.

In order to gain a closer approximation to the glance, it will not suffice to glance at it. The glance will not yield its secrets to its own action. No wonder: the glance flees itself. It is exterocentric—it flies off the face of the glancer. Only rarely do we catch ourselves glancing, for example, when we have a glimpse of ourselves in the mirror or when someone else's look registers our glance and sends it back to us as it were. But the mirror petrifies the glance into an orthogonal projection—it conveys my glance back to me only as frozen into an image— and the return of my glance by another's look is highly mediated by the character of that look itself. For the most part, then, the glance escapes its own detection. It is not so much unknown to itself as *unseen to itself*: if it sees itself at all, it sees itself through a glass darkly.

In order to bring some light into this darkness, we must consider the glance in two steps: first, the locus-source of the glance itself: the eyes and, more generally, the head and human body; second, that which the glance illumines and takes in: that is, various surfaces of the surrounding world. Taken together, these two phases of the glance constitute its immediate field. Let us now take a concerted look at each of them in succession.

II

By the "locus-source" of the glance I mean those parts of the body that are engaged in the actual production of the glance, its organic infrastructures as it were. The glance centers in the eyes, but (as we have already seen in the case of the nod of recognition) it is not limited to them by any means. Ultimately, it is the whole person who glances—just as ultimately it is the whole person who is acknowledged by the glance—but at the proximal level of the concrete act it is the lived body that does the glancing.

Nevertheless, to begin with and primarily, the eyes do the glancing. It is revealing that we say that we glance not just by means of the eyes but *with them.* To glance by means of the eyes restricts the eyes to a purely instrumental role, as if their role was merely that of implementing the glance, carrying out its intentionality in a purely functional way. The eyes certainly are operational parts of our body; but instead of conceiving them as simply subordinate to these parts, we should regard them as *agents of the body.* The "with" of "glancing with the eyes" signifies their organic agency, the sense in which they have a life of their own—a life within the body's larger life, an intentionality within its more encompassing intentionality. This is doubtless why we ascribe soul to the eyes, and why we look into people's eyes when we are searching for their deeper intentions or thoughts. The eyes are telling. Instead of saying that the eyes are merely the "mirrors of the soul," that is, their passive reflection, we should rather say that the person comes to expression there, shows himself or herself in them in a uniquely revealing way.

When a person glances with his or her eyes, then, that person looks out in a most expressive manner, one that brings the entirety of the person to bear on the circumstance. No partial or superficial looking here! Instead of being "the computers of the world"[1]—the hardware for which calculative thought patterns furnish the software—the eyes are the expressors of the person, the enactors of that person's operative intentionality, the way in which the person enters most effectively into the place-world. There is no gainsaying of the eyes as the operators of the person.

The glance is one of the major ways in which the eyes operate. Thanks to it, certain intentions are realized: quickly, efficiently, and (usually) spontaneously. These intentions are not just reflections of preexisting interests already defined and formed; they include the effort to find certain things out, an effort for which the glance provides an ideal probe: a heuristic or means of discovery. The scope of the glance is considerable: it can express everything from doubt and hesitation to arrogance and confidence, along with many intermediate states such as curiosity and pruriency, alarm and concern. Whatever the exact intention expressed, however, the glance is always open to surprise, the other side of the glance as it were. Because of this openness to the new and unexpected—a theme already broached in the introduction and to which I shall return in the concluding thoughts—the glance is not just the purveyor of intentions but the expressive agent whereby these intentions exhibit themselves in the face of actual or imminent surprise.

Being open to surprise entails a maximally free eye movement, so as to let the

1. See Merleau-Ponty, "Eye and Mind," tr. C. Dallery, in *The Primacy of Perception,* ed. J. Edie (Evanston, Ill.: Northwestern University Press, 1964), pp. 159–192.

unexpected arise anywhere in the visual field. It means a wide-ranging deployment of the eyes that takes in as much as possible. This can be called the *open
glance*, which has for its mission the exploration of the full extent of the visual
field. The form it takes is an orbiting of the pupil cum iris of each eye, a motion
of circulation. But given that it is rarely enacted in any complete or systematic
form, the open glance is in fact a limit-concept. In actual practice, the motion of
the eyes is considerably restricted. This is just what we should expect: the aim of
the glance is not to apprehend the totality of any given scene but just that part of
the visual field to which it is attracted or in which it is invested.

The opposite of the fully orbiting glance is the *beady glance:* a concentrated,
straight-ahead looking that is focused on just one thing rather than on a whole
range of things. This, too, has its limit: were it to become wholly fixed in character, it would transform from a glance into a stare. This means that most cases of
glancing fit into the middle range between the open and the beady glance: they
exhibit a delimited but still actively moving pattern whose outstanding forms are
the shifty glance, the oblique glance, the idle glance, and many others. It would
beggar description to detail the motions of each of these. Some entail a right/left
eye directionality, others a vertical motion, still others a hesitant action, and yet
still others a special "jerky" movement.[2] And so on.

To consider the remarkable range of such basic glancing motions is to be
impressed with the great mobility of the eye, its high versatility. Indeed, this
versatility is unmatched in any other part of the face, with the possible exception
of the mouth (which often operates in conjunction with the glance). It is as if the
pliability and multiplicity of the glance had long since entered into active collusion with the free motion of the eyes in their sockets: ocular mobility rejoins and
reinforces the many-sidedness of the glance. So do the many microphenomena
of the pupil and iris, their subtle shifts in color, glint, and flicker. These nuanced
and continually changing presentations of the central eye—taken in conjunction
with their relation to the white of the eye—allow for the expression of minute
modulations of intention and emotion.

To make matters more complex, the collusion at play in the glance is not just
with the eyes as such! Upon closer inspection, it becomes clear that there
are also important contributions from the purlieu of the eye, most notably
the eyelids and eyebrows. Taken in conjunction with the motions and epiphenomena of the eye proper, they produce a complex and concerted total
movement in the general region of the eyes, amounting to a considerable total
expressiveness in this part of the face.

The picture is further complicated by the interaction of the eyes with other

2. This last-mentioned motion refers to a saccadic movement, in which the eye "rapidly
jumps from one briefly fixated point to another" (Martin Jay, *Downcast Eyes: The Denigration
of Vision in Twentieth-Century French Thought* [Berkeley: University of California Press,
1993], p. 7). Jay points out that Émile Javal first came up with the term based on the French
word *saccade* ("jerk") in an article in *Annales d'oculistique* in 1878. Later, in chap. 9, we shall
see that saccadic movements are much more pervasive than Javal or Jay thought.

parts of the face. These, too, get into the act: beginning with the mouth (speaking or not) but including as well the nose and ears and forehead. Sometimes these other facial features take the lead by gesturing toward or referring to the object to be glanced at; sometimes the glance initiates the action and they follow forth; sometimes there is simultaneity of enactment. The effect in any case is to amplify the resources of the glance, making it at once more expressive and more inclusive.

The amplification continues when the whole head is enlisted, as in the phenomenon of nodding with the head—a nod that, as we have seen, may take on a life of its own and even be displaced onto another bodily member such as a finger. Indeed, virtually *any* bodily member may join the glance—and even, at the limit, *become* the glance. This extension of the glance is commensurate with the prolongation of the expressive face into other parts of the body for which Levinas argues.[3] We see this prolongation in the motion of the shoulders (specifically mentioned by Levinas), a motion which can dramatize and reinforce the glance of the eyes in a gesture such as a shrug or a hunching of the shoulders. Arms and especially hands also collaborate with the glance, often being invoked for the sake of emphasis: a corporeal *under*lining by the body member. Given the expressivity of hands, there can be complex combinations with the glance that include a semideliberate undercutting of our own glance, increasing its erotic or aggressive character, or even ironizing on it from below. Even the hips and legs can enter into contention—as when we glance on the run or in beating a retreat from a difficult situation.

In the end, *we can glance with the whole body*—just as we can feel the glance or gaze of the other with the same whole body.[4] This is less surprising than it looks at first blush. The mobility and flexibility of the glance call for the maximal supportive means coming from the body, and if this support is not provided by particular bodily parts—not just by the eyes but by the mouth or hands—then it is to be expected that it will come from other parts of the body. Strictly speaking, *every* act of glancing implicates *the body as a whole*. The eyes—or head, or hands, or hips—with which we glance are not separable parts of the body but integral components of it. If each of these serves as a particular locus-source of the glance, each does so only as belonging to the lived body *totaliter.* The

---

3. See Levinas's comments on the extension of the face in *Ethics and Infinity: Conversations with Phillipe Nemo,* tr. Richard A. Cohen (Pittsburgh: Duquesne University Press, 1985), p. 85 ff., esp. this statement: "the relation with the face can surely be dominated by perception but specifically the face is what cannot be reduced to that" (p. 86). Since the face is not the literally perceived object, it can be found elsewhere than on the obverse side of the head.

4. "In a forest, I have felt many times over that it was not I who looked at the forest, some days I felt that the trees were looking at me"(André Marchand, cited by M. Merleau-Ponty, "Eye and Mind," tr. C. Dallery in *The Primacy of Perception,* p. 167). The implication here is that the painter feels himself to be seen as a whole by the forest in which he stands. See also this statement, to which we shall return: "I feel myself looked at by the things" (*The Visible and the Invisible,* tr. A. Lingis [Evanston, Ill.: Northwestern University Press, 1968], p. 139).

manyness and subtlety of the glance call not just for the extreme plasticity of the face but also for the operative intentionality of the body as an expressive whole. The range of the one is reflected in the scope of the other.

The glance at its source is not, then, just a matter of the movement of the eyes—even if these are its most conspicuous bearers—or of any other single bodily part. Just as the recognition effected by the glance acknowledges the full person of the other, so the glance itself stems from the entire republic of the glancer's own body. It comes from the concatenation of its constituent parts. This concatenation is like a complex cat's cradle of bodily gestures and motions. The strands of this crisscrossing complex stand for the plural historicities that human beings harbor at any given moment as well as for the various bodily organs and members that support the glance. Arising from this intertangled mass of history and body, the glance expresses their immanent intertwining. "There is a human body," writes Merleau-Ponty, "when, between seeing and seen, touching and touched, between one eye and another, between hand and hand, a blending of some sort takes place—when the spark is lit between sensing and sensible."[5] The glance is just such a spark, one which flies from one body part to another, and from a given body part to things in the world, thereby realizing between them a momentary but illuminating bond. Far from being a mere epiphenomenon, the glance is one of the most effective ways of keeping the body together as a single but complicated phenomenon. Thanks to its subtle and often unnoticed gestures—its continual intermediation—the glance sustains the life of the body as the active center of its place-world.

III

The glance is too revealing to be something merely superficial, but it is nevertheless something cast off the bodily surface. So far, I have been concentrating on the bodily parts—and finally the whole body—from which it stems. But the primary directionality of the glance is exterocentric: *away from the very body that is its locus-source.* To get close to the glance is not just to get close to the body from which it stems; it is to track down something that is continually falling away from this same body—that escapes it even as it issues from it, streaming off its own body of origin, flying from its own progenitive face. It is comparable to a simulacrum flung off the surface of that from which it derives. As such, the glance is intermediary in still another sense: it exists between its locus-source and the world toward which it is directed. It is quite literally *interfacial*, existing as it does between the face of the person who glances and the face of the world (*facies mundi*) at which the glance is cast.

I am taking "simulacrum" in the Epicurean sense of the word, especially as set

5. M. Merleau-Ponty, "Eye and Mind," p. 163. Note also the statement: "The body's animation is not the [mere] assemblage or juxtaposition of its parts" (ibid.).

forth in Lucretius's *De rerum natura,* according to which a simulacrum is a thin film that peels off the surface of a physical thing, thereby linking up with simulacra of other things in causal relations. But more than causal connection is at stake here. If the sense of simulacrum is extended to include Plato's notion of *phantastiké* (that is, an imaginative creation that, unlike an icon, does not depend on close formal resemblance), we can envision a quite different connotation whereby that which is cast off takes on a life of its own—heterogeneous, marginal, but also threatening. It is this sense which Deleuze emphasizes in his discussion of the simulacrum in *The Logic of Sense,* where he says expressly that "the simulacrum is not a degraded copy. It harbors a positive power."[6] Essential to this power is the speed of simulacra; Epicurus says that they are "as swift as thought," a phrase that might also apply to glances.[7] Visual simulacra in particular are more rapid-moving than the emanations that come from deep within objects. What Deleuze writes of Lucretian simulacra could be said with equal right of glances:

> Visual simulacra have two advantages over deep emanations: precisely because they detach themselves from the surface, they do not have to modify their order or their shape, and consequently [they] are representative [of the objects to whose surfaces they first belong]; on the other hand, they move with much greater velocity, since they encounter fewer obstacles.[8]

So, too, glances are representative of their agents of emission—being expressive of their intentionalities and interests—by virtue of the fact that they do not encounter many obstacles to their transmission: they sail from myself as locus-source to the other who receives them, whether this other be another person or a physical object. Nor do glances change their order or shape in relation to the same source: they remain *my* glances even as they are sent away from me. When this twofold virtue is combined with their speed, glances share with simulacra a subversive force. Just as simulacra are able to effect a "reversal of Platonism" thanks to their undoing of the model/copy relation—given that they are no longer representations in any iconic sense—so glances reverse the hegemony of the gaze (which reinstates in the world of vision the situation of a highly valorized paradigm that controls the icons that issue from it). Both simulacra and glances realize "the twilight of the idols."[9]

A glance streams off the glancer's body like a simulacrum that peels off from a Lucretian body. Each simulacrum falls fast into the void surrounding it—where

6. Gilles Deleuze, *The Logic of Sense,* tr. Mark Lester (New York: Columbia University Press, 1990), p. 262.

7. Epicurus, *Letter to Herodotus,* par. 48; cited by Deleuze in ibid., p. 363.

8. Ibid., p. 363.

9. Deleuze here is citing Nietzsche's phrase. His complete statement is: "So 'to reverse Platonism' means to make the simulacra rise and to affirm their rights among icons and copies. The problem [of simulacra] no longer has to do with the distinction Essence-Appearance or Model-Copy. This [latter] distinction operates completely within the world of representation. Rather it has to do with undertaking the subversion of this world—the 'twilight of the idols'" (ibid., p. 262).

it can collide with other simulacra. To avoid such collisions, each has its own *clinamen*, its own peculiar swerve. Just as the *clinamen* is "an originary direction for each atom" and "relates one atom to another,"[10] so the glance as uniquely emitted by each glancer swerves in traveling to what is glanced-at. In each case, it is a matter of "the heterogeneity of the diverse with itself, and also the resemblance of the diverse with itself."[11] Glances, always different from one another and hence heterogeneous, divert from their locus-source much as simulacra divert from atoms; each moves by "nomadic distributions"; yet each also bears a significant resemblance to its origin, carrying forward its traces into the realm of the other.[12]

Another ancient archetype is suggested here: the visual ray. According to certain ancient Greek theories of vision, the visual ray emanates from the eye and is met halfway by a ray stemming from the object of vision. This description fits perfectly the circumstance of exchanging glances, in which two looks intersect. But it also fits the situation in which my glance goes out to a nonhuman object and comes back to me in that basic two-beat rhythm to which I have pointed. This impersonal return glance can be considered a "ray of the world" (*Weltstrahl*): a visual ray emitted by an object (of which refraction of light would be the scientific analogue). I take the term *Weltstrahl* from Husserl, for whom it is paired with a "glancing ray" (*Blickstrahl*) that originates with the "pure ego" of the glancer.[13] We need only jettison the idea of such an ego as a "center of reference"[14] to bring us close to the Greek paradigm of two-way rays whose coordination amounts to vision—including the special kind of vision realized in

10. These are Deleuze's glosses on the Epicurean notion of the *clinamen:* see ibid., p. 269. Deleuze adds that "the *clinamen* is the original determination of the direction of the movement of the atom" (ibid.).

11. Ibid., p. 271. Deleuze italicizes "and also."

12. Resemblance is not here the formal likeness that is at stake in the model/copy relation but "is produced as the external effect of the simulacrum, inasmuch as it is built upon divergent series and makes them resonate" (ibid., p. 262). On "nomadic distributions," see ibid., p. 263 and esp. *A Thousand Plateaus,* tr. B. Massumi (Minneapolis: University of Minnesota Press, 1987), chap. 12, "Nomadology."

13. "In every wakeful *cogito* a 'glancing' ray from the pure Ego is directed upon the 'object' of the correlate of consciousness. . . ." (Husserl, *Ideas Pertaining to a Pure Phenomenology and to a Phenomenological Philosophy, First Book: General Introduction to Pure Phenomenology,* tr. W. R. Boyce Gibson [New York: Macmillan, 1951], p. 243, hereafter referred to as *Ideas I*). Cf. also ibid., pp. 257, 267, 363. On the rays of the world, see "The World of the Living Present and the Constitution of the Surrounding World External to the Organism," tr. F. Elliston and L. Langsdorf, in *Husserl: Shorter Works,* P. McCormick and F. Elliston, eds. (Notre Dame, Ind.: University of Notre Dame Press, 1981), p. 242. Merleau-Ponty comments on such rays at *The Visible and the Invisible,* pp. 218, 241, 265. At p. 241, he says that the rays of the world constitute "the gaze within which [a series of views] are all simultaneous, fruits of my I can—It is the very vision of depth." We shall return to the *Blickstrahl* in chap. 9, "Attending and Glancing," and to the Greek (and more specifically Platonic) theory of vision in chap. 5, "The Glance in Ancient Athens."

14. "The pure ego as it lives, wakeful, in the passing thought is the center of reference" (Husserl, *Ideas I,* p. 243).

the egoless glance. The glance may recognize the *other* as a person, but it stems from a pre-personal, pre-egoic stratum in myself. Even if it reflects my history and interests, it does not bespeak a coherent core self, being the very suspension of such a self. What matters most is that the glancing ray leaps from the surface of the glancer onto the surfaces of the place-world, swerving *onto* them; where it comes *from*, that is, what kind of self is at its origin, matters much less than this primary exterocentric direction. The ancient idea of visual rays captures this impersonal character of glancing vision. Indeed, the de-subjectification of the glance goes hand in hand with the de-substantialization of the glanced-at object, each being conceived instead in terms of its surface-being, each being in effect a simulacrum. This double deconstruction shows the subversive power of the glance at work in subject and object alike.[15]

IV

The cat's cradle of the glance encloses more than the cooperating organic parts of one intermeshed expressive body, and more even than the outstreaming of the glance from that body as its emitted visual ray. It incorporates the glancer into a larger body politic that includes other human beings as well as other physical things. (Indeed, if Husserl is right, it also includes other *thoughts:* I can glance mentally at the contents of my own mind, as when I catch hold of a memory or a passing fantasy.[16]) In glancing, I am immersed not just in my own rays of vision but in the rays of the world—where these rays show me that I am part of a larger social as well as perceptual world. Just as we could not keep the glance separate from the whole body, so it cannot be held apart from the whole social cum perceptual world into which it precipitates us. To glance is to "plunge into the world instead of surveying it."[17] These words of Merleau-Ponty from his early work are expanded upon in his last writings:

> The "ray of the world" is not a synthesis and not "reception," but *segregation,* i.e., implies that one is already *in the world or in being.* One carves in a being that remains in its place, of which one does not make a *synopsis*—and which is not in itself. . . .[18]

15. "Deconstruction" is of course Derrida's term, but a comparable action is at stake in *The Logic of Sense.* For the simulacrum, like the Derridean trace, "renders the order of participation, the fixity of distribution, the determination of the hierarchy impossible. . . Far from being a new foundation, it engulfs all foundations, it assures a universal breakdown (*effondrement*), but as a joyful and positive event, as an un-founding (*effondement*)" (ibid., p. 263).

16. On the mental or "noetic" glance—for Husserl, the glance of most interest—see *Ideas I,* pp. 257–258.

17. M. Merleau-Ponty, *Phenomenology of Perception,* tr. C. Smith (New York: Humanities Press, 1962), pp. 38–39.

18. Ibid., p. 242; his italics.

Similarly, the glance carves out a place in the world of which it is a part. It reaches out to that world, falls into it, not by way of synthesis or synopsis—Kant's terms for mental operations of judgment and imagination respectively—but by a segregative move of scooping out an intentional path from within what surrounds the glancer to begin with: from the place-world in which one is always already situated, from "a being that remains in its place" (*un être qui reste à sa place*).

What, then, is the proximal destination of the glance? Granting that the ultimate destination is the person in interpersonal glancing and landscape in nonpersonal looking, it is evident that in the proximity of what lies nearby the glance is directed at the visible surfaces of the perceptual and social place-world. Its plunge is into these surfaces, and its segregative action consists in their close discernment. But how does this happen?

Here we must attend to the *at-structure* of the glance. Not to be confused with what Heidegger calls the "as-structure" (which concerns the interpretation of what we understand), the at-structure refers to the way in which the glance is often a highly directed activity. When we glance, we most characteristically glance *at* that which is the object of our look, picking it out of the welter of our ongoing perceptions. This core of glancing—its accusative focus as it were—is often surrounded, and sometimes replaced, by associated kinds of glancing: glancing toward, glancing around, glancing over, and so forth. These latter bear on the *vicinity* of the glanced-at object, its immediate environs. They concern themselves with where this object is located in the overall layout of surfaces: its place-setting, as it were, a margin of nonfocal awareness.

When we glance directly *at* something, however, our look goes straight to it, whether the object of our glance is human or not. The at-structure of such glancing consists in four moments—moments that in actual experience are often melded together but that we may here distinguish as follows:

(i) *singling out:* this is the moment of decisive delineation whereby we seize upon what we glance at: we literally de-fine it for ourselves, quickly encircling it with our look; what we thus single out provides the answer to the question, "what are you glancing at?";

(ii) *taking up:* if singling out is the moment of bare noticing or apprehension, in this second moment we take up the object into our look; this is the phase of making sure that what we glance at does not vanish under our very eyes; but the facticity of grasping in the glance is of a distinctly alleviated sort compared with the grasping accomplished in sensory perception proper—a grasping that seeks to consolidate what is grasped in a decidedly possessive manner;

(iii) *taking in:* this is the receptive moment that is paired with that of taking up; I take in that at which I glance instead of keeping it at a distance—not so as to possess it but so as to let it exfoliate and resonate within me; the situation is often described by saying that we are "struck" by what we encounter in the glance, surprised by it and sometimes even amazed;

(iv) *holding:* in this moment I hold-in-eye what I behold in the glance; this amounts to a momentary pause in my looking so that I can retain that which I have just seen; it exemplifies the retentional fringe that James and Husserl both ascribe to "primary memory"; it is a matter of maintaining the glanced-at thing in view, however briefly.

This fourfold form of intervention subtends and supports the forthrightness of my glancing. Thanks to it, my glance takes me *to* the surface of the glanced-at object—right to it without the intermediation of anything but air and light. Here the "to" of direct looking reinforces the "at" of glancing proper to form a re-doubled accusative relation. Because of this relation, even the most passing glance moves me onto the surface of the object, allowing me to adhere to it, to be right there and to stay there long enough for the glance to play itself out in that place. In terms of chronometrically ordered time, this may be a very short time indeed, but it suffices for the glance in the realization of its lambent life.

V

To the surface! That is, to "where most of the action is."[19] Indeed, for the glance it is where *all* of the action is. Whatever the prominence of its locus-source and whatever its form of emission from that locus (for example, whether it goes straight to its target or swerves slightly), what matters most is where the glance finds itself going in the place-world. For the most part, it goes to the surfaces of what Husserl would call the "near sphere" of that world: where "near" does not necessarily mean next to or metrically close.[20] Whether distant or nearby in strictly spatial terms, the surfaces at which we glance are *brought near* by the glance; they are brought into lived proximity; they become part of a proximal region that I have designated as the *glance-world.* This is that part of the place-world that is comprehended by a series of linked glances. It is the near sphere (a term that designates the intimate field of full-bodied perception) as it is rendered visual in a peculiarly glancewise way. It is the robust perceptual world seen aslant, alleviated by the lightness of the glance—which, as I have

19. J. J. Gibson, *The Ecological Approach to Visual Perception* (Hillsdale, N.J.: Erlbaum, 1989), p. 23. Compare Deleuze: "Everything that happens and everything that is said happens or is said at the surface" (*The Logic of Sense,* p. 132).

20. On the concept of the near sphere or "sphere of closeness" (*Näh-sphäre*) or "core sphere" (*Kernsphäre*), see Husserl, "The World of the Living Present," pp. 248–249. Both Husserl and Heidegger distinguish between such nearness and metrically determined proximity. See, for example, Heidegger's essay "The Thing" in *Poetry, Language, Thought,* tr. A. Hofstadter (New York: Harper and Row, 1971), pp. 165–167, esp. this statement from p. 165: "The frantic abolition of all distances brings no nearness; for nearness does not consist in shortness of distance."

insisted, *alights* on the surfaces at which it looks. From a more or less coherent group of such alightings, the glance-world is constituted: not in order to last (as it must be for the gaze) but to be there, glimmering, for the glancer—to be the intermittent correlate of his or her momentary looking.

Of what kind of surface is the glance-world composed? This is not an easy question to answer, yet on its full description hangs the understanding of the glance itself when viewed up close.

It is easier to say what a glanced-at surface is *not* than what it is. First of all, it is not restricted to the faces of others in the manner of Levinas's model of the ethical relation. It is the *face of anything*, human or natural thing, artwork or animal, petite plant or monstrous mountain: anything, therefore, at which we glance. Moreover, we glance at whole sets of such surfaces as they pertain to entire groups of bodies that compose the constituents of any given glance-world, its seen scene. We glance at a *layout of surfaces*, whatever their distinctive character may be. Further, such surfaces are not different from the depths of that which they cover. They are the very appearance or presentation of these depths. Indeed, the glanced-at surface is precisely that surface which belies the usual distinction of surface and depth as two separately located levels of an object. Valéry said that "what is most deep is the skin."[21] Indeed, this is just the lesson of the most mundane glance at the human other: we apperceive the interiority of that other, his thoughts and feelings, memories and hopes, on his very sleeve, in his very flesh. The same is true for the flesh of the world with which human flesh is continuous: for it, the ancient German apothegm holds: "*Die Tiefe der Dinge ist ihre Oberfläche.*"[22] The depths are on the surface of the glance-world, complicating it yet holding it open to the least look.

Beyond these two denials—the glanced-at surface is not human only, nor is it noted apart from depth—what can we affirm about this surface in its own right? It is tempting to say that it is a portion of space: this even seems self-evident. But that is to conceive the surface here at issue in a quite abstract manner. For one thing, it is virtually redundant to claim that the glanced-at surface belongs to space; if space is defined as a universal medium (whether belonging ultimately to the physical world or to ourselves in the manner of Kant), then *every* perceptual phenomenon will be indifferently spatial, including surfaces and things, people and plants. Nothing will serve to distinguish surfaces from other items in space, much less surfaces of the sort with which we are here concerned. For another, to restrict the idea of surface to the exterior covering of physical objects is too narrow in scope—given that we can glance at whole landscapes and even (if Husserl is right) at our own thoughts. If space is too encompassing a model to

---

21. Paul Valéry paraphrased by Deleuze in *The Logic of Sense*, p. 10.

22. "The depth of things is [found in] their surface" (cited as an opening epigraph by Avrum Stroll, *Surfaces* [Minneapolis: University of Minnesota Press, 1988]). This same German proverb is reflected in Wittgenstein's statement, previously cited in chap. 1: "The depths are on the surface."

do justice to the specificity of a glanced-at surface, the outer layer of physical substances is too delimited. How shall we proceed in this impasse?

I am writing these lines in an apartment that looks out across a street onto other apartment buildings of approximately the same size and scale as my own: several three-story buildings of modest frame confront me from my window. I glance up from my computer and out toward them; I glance at the bank of buildings as a finite row of structures. The surfaces at which I glance do not present themselves to me as mere portions of some abstract space; only a Cartesian would claim that. Nor are these surfaces accruing, one by one, to separate substances (another Cartesian assumption); instead, they stream across the buildings that present themselves as one coherent group, as if wrapping this group together. Not only are the surfaces contiguous with each other, acting to collect the buildings together in one continuous mass, they give themselves to me as if they were the inner surface of a much larger, albeit tacitly perceived, structure. Suddenly I realize that this larger structure is the felt equivalent of the near sphere. My distinct sense is that I am glancing into the inside of something that positions me and the buildings opposite me as the effective epicenters of a single glance-world, within which I am free to glance at just these buildings across the way from my second-floor perch at 7529 North Winchester. The surfaces of the buildings I am looking at are the interior surfaces of this world, which (unlike infinite space) does not extend indefinitely beyond these finite epicenters. It is just big enough to enclose them—no larger and no smaller.

Now this is nothing but a *place*. The surfaces of the near sphere are those of the place of which I am part—in this case, a neighborhood place. This is not just any place but the place in which I live, itself situated in Rogers Park on the north side of Chicago. But I don't perceive the rest of Rogers Park; its surfaces are now concealed from me. The surfaces I see are those of the constituents of the place of my immediate neighborhood as it arranges itself around myself as the outward-looking perceiver, the witness of the place. When these placial surfaces coalesce with each other, they form the interior of the near sphere that is my local fate. Each time I look out at my neighborhood, and more particularly each time I glance at it, I encounter a set of surfaces that configure the near sphere in which they and I are commonly located. The merest glance brings me up against the inside of this sphere; it brings me to the nearness, the felt proximity, of my own place. Not just this, but my glance actively contributes to the nearness itself; it is not only a passive onlooker of this familiar scene but itself a participant in it: my looking joins forces with the surfaces at which it looks to form an intimate glance-world.

This is not to say, however, that we glance only into the near sphere. This may be the most frequent place to which we direct our glance in everyday life, of which neighborhood life is a leading instance. But we also look glancingly into the far sphere. A recent example spells this out. I was driving from State College, Pennsylvania to Chicago in the early winter. The highway took me through the high hills and mountains of the western part of Pennsylvania. At numerous moments, I was treated to vast vistas of distant landscape—views sometimes extending scores of miles. Since I was driving by myself, I could not pause to look intently at these intriguing views. But I could glance at them from my driver's position, taking them in briefly but tellingly. Beyond the details of each view—uniquely presented in terms of the shape of the mountains and their texture and color—I was struck by the fact that the surfaces I glimpsed exhibited a single place-logic. Instead of closing ranks together and forming the inner surface of an implicit concave sphere—as occurred on the street of my destination in Chicago—they spread out in diverse directions without being gathered together in any single unifying sphere. They *went their own way,* forming what Deleuze and Guattari call a "smooth space," that is, a space that is heterogeneous and multiple and that flows through various channels.[23] In contrast with the closely contiguous surfaces of the near sphere of the North Winchester neighborhood that seemed to move inward, here the layout of the surfaces was directed distinctly outward. Such was the diversity of these surfaces that not even the horizon could hold them together: they flowed onto and over the horizontal limit of the landscape itself. All that was able to hold them together was my glance, which swept through them and gathered them together loosely in one long-ranging look. This was still not synthesis, much less synopsis; but it did maintain together in an informal assemblage all that was manifestly disparate in the environmental outlay. I saw *all at once,* in a single glance, the outstreaming landscape. Even here, however, in this extreme instance of a far sphere, my act of glancing exhibited a fourfold structure of singling out (for example, the vistas from the land that blocked the views), taking up (in one comprehensive look), taking in (the remarkable variety before me), and holding (the complex view thereby attained). How did this differ from what I was soon going to behold in Chicago? The difference lay in the surfaces displayed: not yet those of close coadunation *within* the single vicinity of my city neighborhood but, rather, a loose confederation of regions *outside* the proximal place of my car and the highway. Just as the facades of the buildings across from my Chicago home ingress into the near sphere, constituting its inner surface, so the vistas of landscape in western Pennsylvania regressed into the far sphere, forming its outer surface. The wild places of the one contrasted with the domestic places of the other.

Despite the considerable differences between the two instances of glanced-at surfaces just explored, they share one important thing in common. This is the fact that each kind of surface counts as an integral *part of a larger whole.* In the one case, this whole is the collectivity of a neighborhood viewed from within its own domain (my place of viewing is itself part of the neighborhood viewed). In the other, the whole is the much more capacious wildscape of the western Appalachians. Where the near sphere of the former is composed of buildings constructed on a human scale, the far sphere of the latter is made up of outsize tracts of land that, instead of converging in some central near sphere, diverge

<hr>

23. On smooth space, see *A Thousand Plateaus,* pp. 410–423, 478–500.

wildly in every which way: the heterogeneity that Bergson attributed to time is here more evident in space. Nevertheless, even with such marked differences in the kind of whole at stake in each case, the relationship of the surfaces taken as parts of a whole to the whole itself is remarkably similar throughout.

The part/whole relationship shared in common is not that of piece to totality but of moment to the whole. A "piece" is a separable part of a physical whole—separable enough to exist on its own, without dependence on other pieces or on the whole itself. The bricks of which the buildings on North Winchester are made are, taken individually, pieces of these structures; they could be detached from the buildings one by one and replaced by others—and the buildings would retain their identities as total objects. Being separable and ultimately independent pieces, the bricks can be removed—and moved to a different place, where they could even become part of a different structure—and still remain identically the same substances. But parts considered as "moments" are another matter. Were one of the buildings removed from its current location on North Winchester, the character of the street, the near sphere of this neighborhood scene, would be changed drastically. Here the principle is: each moment is essential to the integrity and identity of the whole of which it is a part. In this sense, it is both integral to the whole (that is, the neighborhood cannot do without the building and still remain the same near sphere) and dependent on it (that is, the building's very identity cannot be conceived apart from its own neighborhood). This same principle is operative in my experience of western Pennsylvania as well. For if certain parts of the land were altered beyond recognition—thanks to farming or the construction of housing developments or an extensive fire—the landscape would be altered as a whole: it would never be the same again. And if the vistas I glimpse there were modified as a result of such changes in the land, the character of the far sphere as a whole would be transformed: it would become in effect another landscape, another world, at which to glance. The fields and forests I glimpse are as integral to that world as the houses I see across the street are intrinsic components of my neighborhood. And they are as dependent on this natural world as are the buildings on that neighborhood. At this level of perception—which is that of spontaneous glancing—there are no pieces, only moments of one self-appearing and self-congealing whole, and I apprehend parts *of* that whole, not its mere pieces: parts that are ingredient features of its presentation to the merest glance.[24]

24. In the foregoing discussion, to which we shall return later in this book, I am drawing on Husserl's distinction between "part" and "piece" in his Third Logical Investigation discussion of "On the Theory of Wholes and Parts," *Logical Investigations*, tr. J. N. Findlay, ed. D. Moran (New York: Routledge, 2001), section 17, pp. 28–30. For more detailed discussions, see P. M. Simons, "The Formalisation of Husserl's Theory of Wholes and Parts," in *Parts and Moments: Studies in Logic and Formal Ontology,* ed. Barry Smith, 113–159 (Vienna: Philosophia Verlag, 1982); and Robert Sokolowski, "The Logic of Parts and Wholes in Husserl's *Investigations,*" *Philosophy and Phenomenological Research*, vol. 28 (1967–1968): 537–553.

V

The epistemic importance of glancing emerges clearly from such considerations. Glancing is *the main means by which human beings come to know the surfaces of their place-worlds*. For it is in glances that human beings (and doubtless other animals) come to know these surfaces as integral parts of the things that populate places.[25] This is so whether the surfaces belong to the bodies of those human beings we meet casually in the street—surfaces of their faces and hands and of their clothing as well—or of buildings along the same street (for example, the buildings lining North Winchester in Chicago) or of vast stretches of land in the western Pennsylvania landscape. In every case and at virtually any scale, our untutored glancing takes us directly onto the surfaces of things—and thus into the heart of the place we are in.

The power of the glance is nowhere more evident than in the basic fact that in connecting us so perspicuously with surfaces we are relayed directly to the things and places of which surfaces are the integral and dependent parts and not the mere piecewise and independent components. For our look to be conveyed to a surface is also for it to be conveyed to that of which this surface is an undetachable part. A surface is the outer part *of* something; it is not a separable something in its own right; it is so much a part of the thing or place of which it is the surface that we cannot detach it and separate it out. We do focus on various features of surfaces, their color or texture or luminosity (features to which I shall return at the end of this chapter). But in doing so we remain aware, albeit subliminally, of the way in which that surface is nevertheless continuous with and constituent of its bearer, the thing or place (and often a thing-in-a-place) of which it is such an indissociable part. To glance at a surface, then, is to apprehend more than that surface—where "more" does not mean quantitatively more (the surface is coextensive with the outer limits of its body or place) but rather another *kind* of thing, that is, that which subtends the surface itself and holds it up and out to our glancing look.

We witness here the remarkable economy of the glance. Thanks to its affinity with surface, it goes straight to its object without calling for intermediaries— neither sensuous (I don't need to touch the surface at which I glance in order to have a good sense of what I am seeing) nor cognitive (no need to infer or judge

25. For a denial that surfaces are proper parts in the Husserlian sense just discussed, see P. M. Simons, "Faces, Boundaries, and Thin Layers," in *Certainty and Surface in Epistemology and Philosophical Method: Essays in Honor of Avrum Stroll*, ed. A. P. Maratinich and M. J. White (Lewston, N.Y.: Mellen Press, 1991), p. 96: surfaces "are not fictions, [but also] not parts (dependent or independent) of the bodies they bound." But Simons's view itself derives from his espousal of the thesis that surfaces are "abstractive elements" within what Whitehead calls the "extensive continuum." (For the latter, see *Process and Reality*, ed. D. R. Griffin and D. W. Sherburne [New York: Free Press, 1978], pp. 61–82.) My own sense of surface keeps them at once phenomenal and physical—thus not requiring the abstraction to which Simons and Whitehead are committed.

explicitly what I am seeing so blatantly with my own eyes). *To glance at the surface is to be at the thing or place*—to be there by a sort of "teleperception"[26] in which I am transported into its felt density. A large part of the accusative force of the "at" in the core act of glancing-at consists in this buoyant transposition of myself as glancer onto the surface of the glanced-at object.

Forceful as it is, effective as it can be, economic as it certainly is, all of this takes place effortlessly. I do not have to manipulate or penetrate what I glance at in order to come to terms with it. A bare glance suffices to take me to the "thing itself" (in Husserl's term for the ultimate object of perception; not to be confused with Kant's "thing in itself," which calls for a leap in metaphysical level). Such is its unrehearsed efficacity that it seems as if the action of the glance was guileless in its working.[27] This very guilelessness belongs to its unassuming power and allows it to play all the more freely on a given layout of surfaces.

All such epistemic finesse complements and fills out, at the level of perceptual knowledge, what we have already observed about the ethics of the glance. In both instances, a seemingly fickle and fragile action—to be ranged among the least impressive and most vulnerable forms of visual perception—exceeds our first expectations. One might have thought that there are *no* important ethical or epistemic implications of the glance. How can any such implications, heavy with history and theory, be borne by such a slender reed? But the slenderness turns out to have a competitive advantage. Just because it is so apparently marginal in its operation and effect, the glance is able to insinuate itself, like a swiftly moving Trojan horse, into the fortress of ethical and perceptual concerns. The consequential is invaded by the inconsequential, the massive by the light, the settled by the subversive, the guileful by the guileless.

A further twist is that the glancewise insertion of the human being into matters usually demanding the spirit of gravity lightens these matters themselves. The glance shows the ponderous itself to be capable of leavening, perhaps even to be itself unballasted in the end. A crucial part of being ethical is just to be recognized by the other in a glance—no more and no less. An equally important part of knowing things and places—knowing them at the level of a

---

26. "Teleperception" is Merleau-Ponty's term: see *The Visible and the Invisible*, tr. A. Lingis (Evanston, Ill.: Northwestern University Press, 1968), p. 258, where Merleau-Ponty limits its use to the image: the image I now have of Pierre in Africa is "a sort of perception—a teleperception." My memory of a perception is also a teleperception: "the sensible, the visible . . . [is] that of which I can subsequently have a teleperception" (ibid.). For a parallel but differently distributed point, see Stroll's principle that if you operate on the surface of something, then you operate on that something itself: see his *Surfaces*, pp. 21–28.

27. I say "it seems as if" the glance were guileless so as to allow for the real possibility of overdetermination by cultural and social factors, not to mention the underlay of sheer habitude and practice. Yet none of these modes of overdetermination—to take this last term *à la lettre*—is incompatible with the spontaneous directness of the glance as it is enacted on a given occasion.

tacit but basic familiarity—is to glance at them. In both cases, glancing even just once often suffices. The simplest of means gets to the heart of the matter.

Just as a mere nod of recognition takes us straightaway into the ethics of the person—being one of the least effortful yet most effective ways of acknowledging the ethical force of the human being at whom we glance—so a bare glance at the surfaces of things in their places brings us abruptly into a felt familiarity with those things and places that is no less effective for being so brief and unscheduled. Just as a narrow mountain defile may suddenly open out onto vast views, so the thin ray of the glance quickly opens up vistas we never knew were there.

No matter how extensive the vistas—and no matter how deeply the person may seem to be projected into them—the glance brings up close what is otherwise far out. Its genius is to accomplish closeness where none existed before, or none was apparent. We might say that the glance continually creates near spheres out of far spheres—where "near sphere" is taken to include both perceptual and ethical proximities. Levinas has insisted that despite the Other's exteriority to me, my ethical action is a matter of acknowledging a critical "proximity" to that Other—a closeness paradigmatically in play in the face-to-face relationship. So, too, in encountering the place-world, I must attain proximity to it if I am to be able to say that I am coming to know it—to be at least minimally familiar with it. In both cases, in attaining epistemological as well as ethical closeness, I do so by means of the surfaces that cling to things as well as to persons—constituting both and situating both within the circumambience of the place-world. These surfaces, which form the connective tissue of this primal world, are the proper objects of the glance. They are that *at which* we glance, that *whereby* we come to know things and to recognize persons, and that *with which* we enter (and keep entering) the place-world inhabited by each.

A close-up description of the glance reveals its special power to bring things and persons near within the place-world—thus to reveal dimensions of both which are otherwise inaccessible or unsuspected.

VI

It is time to address two basic questions: What do we do with the surfaces at which we glance? What do such surfaces do to us?

1. *What we do to surfaces by our glance.* Here there are two extremes to consider. (a) Minimally, we *take notice* of surfaces; our look does not linger long enough to do anything else than to graze the surface and move on. Such minimal glancing happens all the time, as we see when we glance around our immediate environment—letting our look touch on a given surface only to move on to others. With our mere glance, we dust off the surfaces of the place-world; we let these surfaces be the surfaces they are, without any effort to scrutinize them,

much less to alter them. As there is something playful about this action, it doesn't feel like an extreme; it feels like the "natural" way to glance, though we have learned how to do a great deal of it from observing parents, siblings, and peers. (b) At the other extreme, we *take measure* of what we glance at: we see how long or thick or wide the surface of something is. In this spirit, we estimate its extent—or at least its approximate extent, since the articulation of our perception in numbers or words is a quite different operation. For the time being, we rest satisfied with determining how a surface (typically, just part of it) *fits* into a larger whole, how much of that whole it takes up: say, about a half, or a third of it, or twice as long as another part, and so on. Or else we glancingly discern the shapes and sizes of what we see: this object is roughly rectangular, that is a polygon, the volume of this box is about twice that of the other. Here, too, we have to do with a spontaneous measurement that need not be exact so long as it realizes a specific, practical purpose. We are dealing with the proto-arithmetic and proto-geometry of ordinary glancing.[28]

Between the extremities of taking notice and taking measure, there is an entire spectrum of intermediate acts whereby glances encounter surfaces. On the one side, sometimes glances *careen* off surfaces, moving between them in an especially speedy way, not pausing even to take note but continually changing direction and focus. It is as if one surface were there only as a point of departure for an equally transient encounter with another surface. Here we flit every bit as much as the butterfly—yet without the equivalent of anything like a glacier on which to base our capricious movements. On the other side, glances can *fasten* on surfaces, as when we briefly lock our look on something. In this case, the at-structure of the glance possesses a punctate yet pronounced character; my attention is momentarily turned toward a surface, yet does not become stuck there: thanks to the freedom of the glance, I can always move on.

In addition, there is a host of other things we do with our glance as it lands on a surface. They are all ways of investing oneself in one's environs; what is most striking is the sheer range of glancing, which shows itself to be even more variegated than we suspected in previous chapters.[29] Thus, between the extremes of taking note and taking measure are to be found such distinguishable acts as *alighting* (where we pause for a cursory moment on a single surface,

28. Compare Avrum Stroll's notion of "the geometry of ordinary speech" (*Surfaces*, p. 4) and J. J. Gibson's idea of "a sort of applied geometry that is appropriate for the study of perception and behavior" (*The Ecological Approach to Visual Perception*, p. 33). On the proto-geometry of ordinary perception, see Edmund Husserl, "The Origin of Geometry," Appendix 6 to *The Crisis of European Sciences and Transcendental Phenomenology*, tr. D. Carr (Evanston, Ill.: Northwestern University Press, 1970), as well as section 9, "Galileo's Mathematization of Nature." In the latter text, Husserl's concern is above all with the immediate perception of shapes in the natural environment, e.g., the approximate shape of hills or rivers.

29. The forms of glancing under discussion in this section can all be considered modes of what I have designated as "glancing proper."

literally a/lighting on it in a featherweight way); *settling onto* (a more concerted form of taking notice whereby our glance pauses for a moment, lingering at least briefly); *comparing* (by which we set one surface alongside another, not in the interest of making spatial determination as such but merely with a concern for associating what would otherwise be dissociated in what lies before us; *appreciating* (that is, looking at something for the sheer pleasure of doing so, savoring it; or else because we value that something for its own sake, as when we appreciate the formal elegance of a house designed by Le Corbusier).

Laying out the conspectus of ways by which the glance connects with surfaces, we have something like this:

TAKING NOTICE <careening /// alighting // settling onto /appreciating // comparing /// fastening> **TAKING MEASURE**

This bare diagram yields in effect a functional approach to glancing: it sets out what the glance does to and with the surfaces it encounters.

2. *What surfaces do to us in our glances at them.* This is a quite different matter. No longer an issue of functional specificity, what counts now is the effect of surfaces upon us as glancers: their retro-action as it were. Rather than function, it is a question of attitude and character. Here two levels need to be distinguished: reflection and internalization.

A. *Reflection.* At this level, we have to do with the various ways in which the surfaces at which we glance affect us at *our* own bodily surface. They suffuse our skin, a notably porous surface. This is not only a sheer physical phenomenon but also affects our psychic being, our psycho-physical self. Freud said that "the ego is first and foremost a bodily ego," adding that the ego itself is formed from projections that play out on the bodily surface.[30] These projections amount to reflections—taking this latter word in Leibniz's sense of traces that embody and express a larger whole, some kind of world (including a place-world). In this sense, our body surface, our skin, *reflects* a world to an emerging self; it is the mediatrix or common ground of self and world. This is a situation of double reflection. What is happening on the surface of the skin reflects what is happening in the environing world, and these skin-events are reflected in turn in the eventual formation of the self. The reflection on the surface—what is projected there from the surrounding world—is introjected into the organism to become the nucleus of the self.

This double reflection manifests itself first of all as alterations of *attitude* on the part of the human subject. By "attitude" I mean the psycho-physical equiva-

---

30. The citation is from Sigmund Freud, *The Ego and the Id* (*Standard Edition of the Complete Psychological Works*, ed. J. Strachey [London: Hogarth, 1961], vol. 19, p. 27). The claim concerning projections onto a surface is found at ibid. The resemblance of this model to the Lacanian notion of the mirror-based formation of the self is striking.

lent of "posture" in a strictly bodily sense. It is a stance taken toward things that expresses how these same things have affected us. Rather than being something we do to things, an attitude betrays how things have done something to us: hence its characteristic way of being both directed (toward something) and sedimented (within ourselves). Let me comment briefly on six cases in point, arranged in the form of a loose series:

(i) *indifference:* In this attitude the glanced-at object fails to move us; we confront it and are directed to it, yet it does not interest us, leading us to a resultant suspension of epistemic concern; this is not intentional or studied indifference but the true indifference in which the content of our glance leaves us cognitively cold: we "couldn't care less"; here *not being moved* by surrounding surfaces is itself a limit case of what surfaces do to us.

(ii) *boredom:* In contrast with indifference, in boredom I care enough to search out surfaces for their possible interest; this is because I once had an interest in them, but they did not deliver anything striking enough to engage me then, and as a direct result I *became* bored; but this boredom can be dissipated by discovering something striking after all in the same surfaces, something that will fulfill my "empty intention" (Husserl).

(iii) *interest:* This is itself a complex attitude whose presence or absence has much to do with the constitution of other attitudes, as we have just seen; it has its own range, starting from mere titillation and continuing to intense involvement (evident in concerted efforts at follow-through); but the core of interest manifests itself in the situation in which surfaces have just enough attractiveness to gain my attention, being neither too attenuated nor too overwhelming; thus the root meaning of the term: "inter-esse," literally "being-between," implying a momentary equilibrium between the attractive surface and my interested glance at it.

(iv) *concern:* Where interest is content to dally on the surface that attracts it, a concernful glance exhibits an active care for the state or fate of the attractive surface; for example, in the sudden perception of environmental distress, causing us to be concerned; concern carries with it an edge of wanting to *do* something about the glanced-at situation, whether to alter or sustain it—if not to make a decisive difference in it, then to "deal" with it significantly (hence Heidegger links concern [*Besorgen*] with Dasein's "being-alongside the ready-to-hand").[31]

(v) *delight/aversion:* We are delighted by various prospects that not merely interest us but which we find extremely attractive, so much so that we wish to affirm their existence by our very glance; this is still an attitude, since we adopt it characteristically in relation to certain kinds of things and count on it continually: I am delighted to see paintings in certain galleries or art museums; my stance is one of looking forward to this experience; I take an expansive pleasure in glancing at the surfaces of paintings; this comes close to appreciation, but the emphasis is not

31. See Heidegger, *Being and Time,* p. 237. See also pp. 157, 169. Care, in contrast with concern, has to do with making a whole out of Dasein's dispersed dealings—a whole that is the basis for Dasein's authenticity. See ibid., section 41, pp. 235–241: "Dasein's Being as Care."

on evaluation but on being moved emotionally, not in order to do anything about the circumstance but just to bask in the enjoyment itself; all this is the effective converse of aversion, in which my look turns away.

(vi) *astonishment:* This is an attitude toward the deeply unexpected suddenly happening on the surface of things; we are never fully prepared for it, but we can adopt a posture of being open to the astonishing when and if it occurs—a posture that in turn reflects the fact that we have been astonished before and now realize that the environing world can present to us astonishing events, toward which we can be either receptive or resistant.[32]

These six attitudinal avatars of the glance are related internally by an increasing investment of attention and an augmenting willingness to be moved by a given surfacial phenomenon. Schematically:

INDIFFERENCE> /// boredom

// interest/concern //

delight/aversion /// <**ASTONISHMENT**

These are not merely disparate attitudes whose relationship is limited to expressing degrees of comparatively intense cognitive or emotional investment (or, likewise, comparatively unintense dysphoria). They are all expressions of a single, quite basic attitude: *surprise.* As I have stressed in the introduction, surprise is the constant companion of the glance; in particular, it subtends the attitudinal variety just discussed. Whenever we glance, we are subject to surprise. It is not so much that the glance *prepares us* for being surprised (that would be yet another functional aspect of the glance) as that it *holds us in readiness* for it.[33] At a prereflective level, the glance is already open to the surprising, apt for its reception ("apt" and "attitude" are related words). The glance stands ready to register the novelty of surfaces, noting their incongruity (that is, in terms of their density, texture, or support). This literal pre-paredness allows us to engage in the attitudinal response of surprise—where "response," not to be confused with mere "reaction," is the coherent sign of a readiness to act.

In surprise, we respond to the incongruous surface of things, the way in which they stand out in our experience, leading us to take note. "Sur/prise" signifies "taking hold/on—where the "on" (*sur* in French) is equivalent to *upon.* To be surprised is to let things take hold of us: to let them come upon us, even to let

32. For further treatment of astonishment and related states, especially surprise and wonder, see chap. 6, "The Sudden, the Surprising, and the Wondrous: With Walter Benjamin on the Streets of Paris."

33. The expression "holds us in readiness" is meant to reflect Roman Ingarden's notion of *Parathaltung:* see *The Literary Work of Art,* tr. G. G. Grabowicz (Evanston, Ill.: Northwestern University Press, 1973), pp. 265–267, 330, 339, 372.

them overcome us momentarily (this is not to be confused with being altogether overwhelmed: in surprise we *allow* the overcoming to happen, in contrast with a trauma that takes us over involuntarily). Surprise is letting the unexpected happen to us. It is an acknowledgment that surfaces harbor something not yet known, and it is not surprising that "sur/face" parses out comparably to "sur/prise." In both cases, what matters most is that *something is held upon something else:* surprise upon expectation, surface upon object, both upon attitudinal complacency. In glancing, we stand ready to experience surprise at any point— upon any surface of anything we may happen to witness.

B. *Internalization.* In this case, we move to another level: from attitude to character—at once profoundly rooted in the person and manifesting that person to others. Character is something that presents itself at and on the surface: we often read a person's character at a glance, for instance, in a single action of heroic self-sacrifice. Indeed, we can even glimpse character in the wrinkles on a person's face, just as we can perceive the effects of an earlier trauma in a person's hesitant or phobic gestures.[34] Character is in fact an exemplary instance of the principle we keep on encountering: here, indeed, the depth is found at the surface, the very surface at which we glance.[35]

More than attitude is astir in character, as we see in the fact that although character gives rise to attitude the opposite is rarely the case. Moreover, where attitude can be arbitrary or at least occasion-bound, character never is. How to account for this difference? Here we need to take the notion of reflection one step further. Not only is there projection of the world onto our skin, followed by the introjection of this first reflection into attitude, but also now an internalization of this double reflection. By "internalization" I mean the sedimentation within us of glancing experiences of surfaces—not just in a comparatively settled way (this much holds for an introjected and habitual attitude) but in an enduring manner that outlasts considerable vicissitudes. The character that results is the ongoing manifestation of our personhood, the way we are consistently a certain sort of person even in the most varied of circumstances.

This is a dramatic and consequential way in which surfaces act on us. They do so by *in-fluencing* us, flowing into us from the surfaces of the world (including the surfaces at stake in the actions and gestures of persons important in our early education). Our character represents the primary way in which we let ourselves be influenced by the configurations of the surficial world—not just letting them "get under our skin," as we say revealingly, but *keeping them there.* This is an "under" that remains part of the skin itself; it is the underside of the same skin that supports our public self-presentation. Instead of inserting ourselves into the

---

34. On the importance of wrinkles as manifesting character, see James Hillman, *The Force of Character: And the Lasting Life* (New York: Ballantine, 1999), p. 17.

35. By stating this, I do not mean to deny the many cases in which character shows itself only slowly over time—in many contributing and confirming actions, as tested by these actions.

surfaces of the place-world—as we do in the acting out of attitude—we allow these surfaces to *in*sinuate themselves into us, to become what we call the "bases" of our character and (in the case of an already formed character) to reinforce it from below. Instead of simulacra flowing off from the surface—as on the Epicurean model[36]—the surface itself flows into the depth of character. What the surface does to us is to engender characterological depths.

What happens between surface and depth—granting that they are linked by internalization? A crucial clue comes again from Freud: character is "the precipitate of abandoned object-choices and contains the history of these choices."[37] In other words, character arises from the demise of lapsed relationships; it is their legacy, that which fills the void left by the lapsing of love in its many forms. The internalization of these relationships is not merely their introjective reflection but amounts to the creation of a commemorative vehicle within the internalizing subject. This vehicle is the carrier of character, which (albeit unbeknownst to the subject) is built upon the internal presence of the lost other: reflection is deepened by reinstatement. Character allows the other to survive inside us—not merely as encrypted but as assimilated into ourselves, having a second life within us as transformed into our character.[38] Not only is the void filled but a presence is erected inside us that adds an indispensable dimension to our lives: a character that incorporates the edges of the other, yet in a way that has been made our own. The surfaces of the other have become our own depth—a depth that re-surfaces in characterologically conditioned action.

By the same token, the person has been endowed with a means of effective entry into the social and historical world. Character brings the person to bear in the domain of interpersonal life rather than remaining isolated and self-enclosed. The person emerges into the scene of extended activity, thereby gaining access to the place-world, thanks to character as the indispensable third term between person and place. Character thus conceived is the internalization of the perceived and enacted surfaces of the other—surfaces we grasp in glances and touch in grasping—along with their memorialization in a sedimentation that is the effective basis of an actional re-presencing.

What, finally, do surfaces do *for us*? Beyond the fact that they afford many

---

36. It is the Epicurean model that Platonism opposes: "It is a question [in Platonism] of assuring the triumph of the copies over simulacra, of repressing simulacra, keeping them completely submerged, preventing them from climbing to the surface, and 'insinuating themselves' everywhere" (Deleuze, *The Logic of Sense*, p. 257).

37. Freud, *The Ego and the Id*, p. 30.

38. In this last sentence, I am extending Freud's original paradigm in *The Ego and the Id* in the direction sketched by Nicholas Abraham and Maria Torok in their distinction between "incorporation" (i.e., whereby the other is encrypted, unchanged, inside us as a foreign presence) and "interiorization" (by which the other is fully assimilated to us, no longer being a distinguishable presence). See their text *Le Verbier de l'homme aux loups* (Paris: Flammarion, 1999), including the remarkable preface by Jacques Derrida entitled "Fors."

kinds of behavior—not just perception but actions of many kinds (building, farming, photographing, and so on)[39]—their impingement is reflected, indeed doubly reflected, in the generation of attitudes that express an array of coherent responses, above all that of surprise. At another level, surfaces go right down to the depths of our own person, influencing us from within and instituting character as the active and ongoing aftermath, the historical trace, of their effective internalization. Our personal being is augmented from the absence and loss of other persons in a compensatory gain that is unique in the destiny of the glance and that shows, once again, the glance to be anything but superficial.

VII

Let us consider the relationship between glances and surfaces for a last time. To begin with, we need to remind ourselves of what we already know in everyday perception: surface is all-pervasive, especially in the domain of glancing that is the focus of this book. To glance is to glance at a surface—of something, situated somewhere. There is no getting around surfaces, which confront us at every pass. As they are the outer limits of objects of every kind, so the glance is the outer limit of looking: from its vanguard position, the glance goes out of the organism to encounter the surfaces of its immediate environment. Glances and surfaces meet in the middle—in the near sphere of looking that constitutes the glance-world.

It is striking that despite their immense importance (it can be argued that surfaces are, along with a medium and substances, the essential constituents of every terrestrial environment),[40] there are only two basic kinds of surface—those of things and places—and only a handful of traits for any particular surface.

(i) *Surfaces of things.* Under "things" I am including persons as well as other animate beings and inanimate things. In Gibson's terminology, these count as "detached objects," that is to say, objects with "a layout of surfaces completely surrounded by the medium."[41] This means that each such object is entirely

39. On the "affordances" offered by ordinary objects of perception, see J. J. Gibson, *The Ecological Approach to Visual Perception*, pp. 127–143, esp. this statement: "Within limits, the human animal can alter the affordances of the environment but is still the creature of his or her situation" (p. 143).

40. For this ontology of the earthly environment, see ibid., chap. 2. Instead of conceiving the terrestrial environment as "a physical world consisting of bodies in space," this environment "is better described in terms of a *medium, substances,* and the *surfaces* that separate them" (ibid., p. 16; his italics).

41. Ibid., p. 34. Gibson italicizes "by." He adds that a detached object is "the inverse of a complete enclosure. . . . This is not a limiting case, for it is realized in all objects that are moving or are movable. Animate bodies, animals, are detached objects in this sense, however much they may otherwise differ from inanimate bodies. The criterion is that the detached object can be moved without breaking or rupturing the continuity of any surface" (ibid.).

enveloped by a single continuous surface, whatever the complications of its exact topology. This complete surface is the outer integument of the object. In the case of the human being, it is the skin, which is no less an enveloping surface for being an organ in a medical sense. By "continuous" I do not mean without differences in composition, curvature, color, or texture. The outside of a house is an all-enveloping surface even though it may be composed of such different things as grey roof shingles, aluminum siding, a brick chimney, wooden doors, and so on. Taken together, these various substances constitute a single layout of surfaces that surround the house completely. However variegated in material composition and however roughly conjoined, they are no less its outer sheath than is the smooth and delicate skin of a baby—an envelope that has its own subtleties of color and texture.

Taken as the all-encompassing cover, the surface of a single thing always faces outward toward us as its percipients.[42] Its inner structure as such, being concealed, does not matter to those who apprehend its outward surface. What does matter is that the exterior surface of a detached object is the perfect prey of the glance: the sheer exposure of such a surface, serving as the outpost of the object, calls for the outward-leaping look of the glance. Between these two exteriorities, a spontaneous alliance is sealed.

(ii) *Surfaces of places*. Here we have to do with a very different surfacial situation. It is no longer a question of a single continuous integument of an object detached from other objects and their common environment. No single object is definitive of the surfaces of a place (even if a given object may dominate that place, for example, the copper column in the Place Vendôme). Instead, various objects contribute their surfaces to a complex congeries for which there is no one continuous covering. The layout of surfaces is diverse not just in color or texture but, more importantly, in terms of underlying points of attachment: this surface belongs to a tree, that to a rock, a third to a person sitting on the rock, a fourth to a flower springing from the ground, a fifth to the ground itself, and so on. The result is not a mere "heap," that is, a wholly unordered set of objects. There is tacit order in the fact that all of these objects, with their respective surfaces, together compose a coherent place. The place itself is a form of "partial enclosure."[43] But in contrast with Aristotle's idea that a place is a

---

42. "The surfaces of a detached object all face outward, not inward" (ibid.). This is certainly true, but it overlooks the inner faces of the concave near-sphere that most immediately surrounds the glancer.

43. "A *partial enclosure* is a layout of surfaces that only partly encloses the medium" (ibid., p. 34; his italics). Strangely, Gibson does not relate partial enclosure to place, which he conceives as "a location in the environment"—in particular as "located by its inclusion in a larger place" and such as not to have to possess "sharp boundaries" (ibid.). Part of the fascination with Christo's "wrappings" has to do with the fact that he provides a single cover for a set of things, which, as diverse members of a given place or thing, possess no directly contiguous surface: e.g., the hills of Marin County, the parts of the Brandenburg Gate in Berlin.

strict and complete container—being coextensive with the outer limits of the objects in that place[44]—the notion of partial enclosure allows us to concede to place its own indeterminacy: it has no precise limits, it is filled with gaps between objects, there is room for a commixture of quite different elements (in the above example: earth, air, wood, flesh, and so forth). Being more than a mere location, a place presents its own world, its place-world. But the indefiniteness of this world, its felt and perceived amorphousness, does not mean that it escapes perception—that it vanishes into the void, as happens in the darkness of unilluminated night. It retains enough coherence to count as the content of perception.

This coherence of place construed as a partial enclosure is exemplified in its presentation of surfaces. This presentation is idiosyncratic and peculiar in each case. Place-worlds are never the same. Even the same set of detached objects alters placewise with changes in weather, season, atmosphere, and so on—and as we alter ourselves qua percipients. We can return to the same site, whose edges are rigid enough not to show the effects of the elements or whose perception does not reflect our own vagaries.[45] But a place-world is unique upon each experience of it. How is this so?

It is due primarily to the fact that the surfaces of that place are so intricately interrelated that a change in one surface or group of surfaces affects all the others in that place—indeed, modulates the identity of the place itself. So, too, a slightly different way of grasping the place, of taking it into our ken, will modify its manifestation to us. Thus, however coherent a given place may be—thanks to its boundaries and its constituent objects—its intersurfacial situation is such that its perceptual presentation is continually changing. Just as it does not possess one unbroken outer lining, so it does not possess one unbroken identity. In this delicate and highly contingent scene, the glance has a very special role to play: only an act with its celerity (its darting slant, quick insertion, and rapid removal) as well as its comprehensive power is able to deal with the complexity and changeableness operative here. The imbroglio of surfaces concatenated in any given place constitutes the ultimate cat's cradle of perception, and the glance alone is able to address the subtle interplay of the multifarious surfaces of that place.

(iii) *Surface Qualities.* At a more discrete level, surfaces present themselves to us in terms of various, quite special qualities, with each of which glances readily connect. These include not only Locke's classical primary qualities (solidity, duration, motion, form, size, position, and so forth) and secondary qualities (such as color) but others as well. So extensive is the range of qualities at stake here that the very basis of Locke's distinction—namely, that primary qualities are located in external objects and secondary qualities in us—comes into ques-

44. See *Physics,* Book IV, ch. 4.

45. For this sense of site, see my *Getting Back into Place: Toward a Renewed Understanding of the Place-World* (Bloomington: Indiana University Press, 1993), pp. 258–260, 267–270.

tion. Instead, we must say that *all such qualities are located in the surfaces of things and places:* surfaces that are accessible to the alembic of the glance. They configurate and specify surfaces, preparing them as it were for the glance's distilling action, an action that seeks to discern surface qualities in a comparatively pure state. (By "comparatively pure state," I mean independently of being concerned with how, and even whether, these qualities inhere in the underlying objects they qualify. This kind of concern arises when we realize that we can sometimes perceive an object without perceiving its surface as such—for example, flashes of lightning, shadows, Venus, rainbows, the sun—and, conversely, a surface without an attached object, for example, a flayed skin, something illuminated at night such that we see only its sheer texture, the equator regarded as a great circle bisecting the earth into northern and southern hemispheres.[46])

Glances direct themselves not just to the surfaces of things and places but, more particularly, to the aspects or qualities of these surfaces that draw attention. These aspects/qualities are an integral part of the at-structure of the glance: we very much look *at them* when we glance at something. Moreover, we glance at something *in their terms.* Thus we see an apple *as deep red,* the exterior of that house *as aluminum-sided,* your face *as flushed,* this computer *as dark and metallic,* that chair *as soft,* and so forth. This is not the interpretative as-structure singled out by Heidegger and Wittgenstein—according to which we see something as some *kind* of thing (for example, that fast-moving object in the semidarkness as a car, that drawing as a duck or a rabbit)—but the much more qualitative "as" of something *as specified in such and such a way:* as presented in a very particular manner. I say "very particular" since it is not just a matter of grasping something as, say, colored or even as "red" but as red in a quite distinctive way with regard to its value as well as its hue.

The glance is able to take in this nuanced specificity at once and without hesitation. In fact, it is better prepared to perform successfully at this extremely particular level—its own pointed probe gearing into the particular quality at which it is directed—than at the level of the identificatory as-structure. In this latter instance, the glance shows itself to be as fallible as any other mode of perception: I can mistakenly identify a hulking shape at which I glance at dusk as

---

46. I borrow several of these intriguing examples from Avrum Stroll's discussion of surface/object anomalies in his *Surfaces,* pp. 32–36, 75 ff. For Stroll, a surface is a boundary that takes two forms, physical ("P-Surface") and abstract ("A-Surface"). An equator is an example of an A-Surface, as would be the surface of any pure geometric object. He traces the idea of A-Surface back to Leonardo da Vinci's description of a sheer interface between two contiguous objects: see ibid., pp. 40–46. (For a discerning critical treatment of Stroll's position, along with an advocacy of surfaces as abstract yet also as "thin layers with divisible bulk," see Peter Simons, "Faces, Boundaries, and Thin Layers," p. 96.) In my own discussion, I have left aside abstract surfaces. My primary concern in this book is with glancing as a mode of human perception that is enacted by the lived body; hence my concern is mainly with the P-Surfaces that impinge upon this body.

a young calf whereas it is in fact an outsize dog, or a person walking toward me as "Dick" whereas it is in fact Tom, or even an entire town glimpsed from a certain distance as "Fairfield" while in truth it is Vallejo. Epistemic error arises most often when our glance bears on kinds of things or places, but much less often when it is focused on the given qualities of a given surface—qualities that it almost always takes in truly.

What are these qualities? Here I single out the four most salient among them:

shape: This helps to disambiguate quite decisively what we look at on most occasions (the exceptions are precisely those just mentioned that bear on the identity of the perceived object); the natural geometry of the glance picks out the shape of something as the outer limit of its surface, a limit that is definitive for the thing—not as a kind of thing but as *just this* thing rather than another; also, as this thing vis-à-vis its visual background, that is, as a "contrastive term";[47] thus I glance at a table in a room I enter for the first time and immediately note the approximately rectangular shape of its top despite the perspectival distortions that convert it into a lozenge-shape, and I see it as set over against the rug and floor on which it stands: both of which properties help me to see the table not just as *a table* but specifically as *this table;* any such shape as I here see suggests possibilities not only for ocular delectation but also for inhabitation and use.[48]

texture: In many ways, this is the single most important quality of any surface, and helps to distinguish one surface from another in definitive ways: we see things as hairy, smooth, tufted, wavy, serrated, and so on; each of these is a structure of a surface and specifies the pattern of that surface, its way of being thicker than a sheer geometric plane (which has no texture at all[49]); but this is no metric thickness, only a felt density with its own configurational properties of fineness or coarseness, striation or bluntness, curvature, and so forth; being *felt,* it calls for the hand to touch; but no literal hand has to reach out to recognize the specific texturality: the glancing eye is capable of taking over this task in a phantom touching operation, the collusion of hand and eye being as close as it is efficacious;[50] most importantly, the texture of a given sur-

47. I borrow this term from Stroll, for whom *all* surface terms are contrastive: see ibid., p. 36. This seems an extreme claim, especially with regard to such qualities as color or texture. Even if it is true that "surfaces do not in general exist independently [of their objects]" (ibid.), this does not make their experience or description necessarily contrastive in character.

48. "Differently shaped enclosures [e.g., as the room in which a table is located] afford different possibilities of inhabiting them. And differently shaped solids afford different possibilities for behavior and manipulation. Man, the great manipulator, exploits these latter possibilities to the utmost degree" (Gibson, *The Ecological Approach to Visual Perception,* p. 29).

49. "A perfectly homogeneous and perfectly smooth surface is an abstract limiting case" (ibid., p. 28). This is, again, a case of an A-Surface in Stroll's terminology.

50. On this close collusion of the ocular and the tactile, see Merleau-Ponty, "Eye and Mind," p. 161: the painter has "no other technique than what his eyes and hands discover in seeing and painting." See also my remarks in chap. 12, this volume.

face (what Gibson calls its "layout texture") is crucial for coming to know what that surface is like and how it manifests the object it covers: "the texture in each case specifies what the substance is, what the surface is made of, its composition."[51]

color: The composition of a surface brings together several qualities, most importantly texture with color; indeed, "surface color is inseparably connected with surface texture";[52] this is a two-way relationship: different textures present different colors, while a given color is always the color of some particular texture (that is, there are no pure unattached colors in nature); thus what we take in at a glance is not color or texture as separate features but the two together in a mutually qualifying dyad: two for the price of one!; the color we glancingly grasp in tandem with texture is itself specified in turn in terms of value (degree of whiteness/blackness) as well as hue (color as chromatic or tinted: green, red, blue, and so on); sometimes as well, there is symbolic specificity in a given color (red standing for anger, deep blue for melancholy, and so forth), which we also catch in a glance.

illumination: Color is a matter of "spectral reflectance"[53] whereby light is reflected in certain precise ratios from a surface illuminated by incident light; but the illumination can be apperceived on its own terms, as when we glance at the way sunlight strikes a given surface; since incident light comes from a certain prevailing direction—normally defined by the position of the sun—the relationship between the position of a surface and that direction is critical here; at any given moment, other surfaces of the same object will be differently illuminated, and at different moments of the day the same surface will be diversely illuminated;[54] the result is a continually changing illumination of any given set of surfaces, including a diminution to a minimal state at night; these changes are at once gradual (except when intervening objects intrude, for example, other objects that obstruct the instreaming light) and compatible with an approximate constancy of perceived color, texture, and shape—as if these latter were somehow compensatory for the vicissitudes of illumination; but in every case the glance is more than equal to the task of

51. Gibson, *The Ecological Approach to Visual Perception,* p. 28.

52. Ibid., p. 31. Gibson's technical definition of "composition" is precisely color + texture: "The color and texture of a surface together specify the *composition* of the substance, what it is made of" (ibid.; his italics).

53. "Spectral reflectance" refers to the fact that a given surface distributes ratios of the reflectance of different wavelengths of incident light in characteristic patterns that we apprehend as colors. See ibid., pp. 30–31 and especially Gibson's earlier treatment in *The Senses Considered as Perceptual Systems* (Boston: Houghton Mifflin, 1966), chap. 10.

54. "There is always a 'prevailing' illumination, a direction at which the incident light is strongest. A surface facing the prevailing illumination will be more highly illuminated than a surface not facing it. This principle means that the different adjacent faces of the environment will be differently illuminated at any given time of day. But it also means that the faces under high illumination early in the day will be under low illumination late in the day" (Gibson, *The Ecological Approach to Visual Perception,* p. 29).

following these vicissitudes, indeed it anticipates many of them by looking ahead to certain oncoming changes of illumination (for example, as happens when we glance at the passing landscape while we drive through it at sunset); and it anticipates as well the altering luminosity that occurs when the same light reaches different objects, whose various material constitutions entail different ways in which incident light is absorbed and reflected.

There are other phenomenal properties of surfaces that are of special significance to the glance: luminosity (the capacity to emit light and not just to receive it, as with illumination), porosity (the state of perforation of a given surface), viscosity (resistance to flow), voluminosity (partly dependent on outer shape but also on girth), opacity (degree of transparency), and various sorts of smoothness, hardness, and homogeneity of physical construction.[55] It would be too taxing to pursue each of these with regard to their connection with the glance. Suffice it to say that each is a further specification of the surfaces at which we glance, each being an inherent feature *of* such surfaces. Moreover, there is an intimate and ongoing collaboration between all such features in the case of a given surface: the way daylight illuminates the fur of polar bears differs dramatically from the way it illuminates the ice on which these same bears stand, or the parka in which I am clothed as I watch the same bears on the same ice. The ice itself is homogeneous and hard and smooth in certain ways, virtually impervious, and so on, and in each of these ways too it interacts differentially with the four factors I have just singled out. What matters is that each feature affords to the glance new opportunities for its full deployment as its engages with surfaces of many kinds, while each also makes a difference to the glance in terms of such concrete parameters as the character of surprise, the directionality and pace of perception, and the familiarity we gain and maintain with a given thing or place.

VIII

To come close to the glance is to find ourselves chock-a-block with two basic sorts of thing: our own body (especially our face but also, finally, our entire body) and places and things (including people). From this situation issue two modes of proximity, one on the glancer's side of things and the other on the side of things themselves. Despite all the manifest differences between these two sides— stretched as they are between the poles of Agent and World—they share an immersion in surfaces, which draw and bind them together in complex and sometimes convoluted ways.

We have seen that in the situation of the glance, *everything figures as a surface*. To begin with, I glance at the local surfaces of my immediate environment

---

55. Gibson claims that there are precisely seven such ways of classifying surfaces: see ibid., p. 31. Surprisingly, he does not include porosity, voluminosity, or viscosity in his list.

—those belonging to the diverse detached objects that populate this environment and find their places in it.[56] If I glance further afield—say, at the sun above me—I bring that celestial object into the near sphere of my own perception; and even if this fiery, gaseous object does not have a simple, continuous physical surface, I take it to have some significant surface when I glance at it: I see it as a disk with a visible whitish-gold surface.[57] In either instance, I glance out from my own bodily bearing, stationary or moving; and this body offers to me yet another set of surfaces. These latter, which subtend the act of glancing with their sub rosa presence, are crucial to the full situation of glancing. Without their at least subliminal support, I would be a disembodied glancer—thus no glancer at all.

The glance brings together both sets of surfaces, those of things (along with the places they inhabit) and those of my body. Without the glance as their connective Hermetic intermediary, they would be in effect two disconnected, heterogeneous series of surfaces: a world-series and a self-series, linked respectively to the disparate poles of Agent and World. The glance is their instantaneous go-between. Between these divergent series, the glance darts back and forth as adroitly as Hermes. It acts as a displaced agent of perception: as the delegate of "the natural self of perception" (in Merleau-Ponty's phrase) that extrudes itself into the domain of detached objects and embedded places. The outstreaming of the glance—which I have compared to the Epicurean simulacrum and to a visual ray—joins forces with the flung-down protuberances of the surrounding world, and in particular their flayed-out external surfaces. One form of outwardness rejoins another. What else but a glance could tie together so effectively my body, scattered things, and cohesive places—in one loose but coherent bundle? What better than this extrusive act could link the intrusion of my body with the obtrusion of things?

In this chapter I have been tracing the way the glance operates in filigree form, its detailed endoskeleton as it were. The search has been for the glance writ small. But this smallness of structure—small compared with the momentous objects of astronomic observation or of the metaphysical gaze—has proven to be all the more efficacious for being so seemingly fragile and fickle. The glance insinuates itself not just into the niches of the perceptual world, where it

---

56. These things and places belong in turn to the near sphere, which has its own implicit inner surfaces within a concave structure that has a hyperbolic geometric structure. On hyperbolic curvature, and its remarkable representation in Van Gogh's painting, see Patrick Heelan, *Visual Space as Variable and Task Oriented: A Study of Van Gogh's "Modern" Use of Scientific Perspective*, http://www.georgetown.edu/faculty/heelanp/Jcs_vgrev.htm

57. I am here disputing Stroll's claim that the sun (among several other such objects) is something I see that does *not* have a surface. It may not *have* a surface in any usual sense—given its gaseous fulgurations—but it *appears* to have one when I glance at it: and this is all that matters when the glance is at stake. See Stroll's discussion at *Surfaces*, pp. 32–36, where my objection applies *mutatis mutandis* to his other examples, most notably shadows and clouds and the planet Venus.

finds hooks waiting for it onto which to hang its effluences, but also into the densest regions of the glancer's own body and his or her personal and interpersonal history. Hence its subtle presence in such overdetermined dimensions as attitude and character—a porous presence that lightens their felt density from within. The minimum of means shows itself once more to be capable of maximum effect, whether in regard to one's own person, other persons, or things in the immediate environment.

In the paradoxical play of the glance, which combines minimal motion with maximal effect, we witness an exemplification of the part/whole relation that we considered when reflecting on surfaces as dependent "parts" and integral "moments" of whole objects. By attending closely to the part—construing the glance as a significant avatar of vision in its full scope—we stand to learn something important about the whole. Despite its ambitious scope and serious intent, visual perception divulges an aspect of the fleeting, an element of quicksilver that it owes to the glance; even when glancing is not occurring explicitly (and such moments are admittedly rare), its alleviating trace is felt. The most sober experimental scientist glances around the laboratory continually, just as he or she constantly glances at the configuration of the detailed instrumentation of the experiment itself. Even if such mobility of the look is not recognized in standard philosophies of science, its role remains undeniable and of inestimable value. It serves to leaven the gaze of the scientist. What is kept marginal in official accounts of scientific discovery has proved to be of far more central significance than these accounts allow. This reversal of role, this subversion of expectation, is altogether characteristic of the glimmering of the glance.

To describe the glance as the mediatrix of disparate surfaces is an exercise in peri-phenomenology—a phenomenology of the *around,* a willingness to pursue the capillaries that animate the surfaces of things, places, and persons. Rather than opening up the dominant veins of vision, I have been staying on or near the skin of the seeing organism: just where depths are most likely to be found. The closest way around, the way of skin and surface, proves to be the most effective way home when it comes to describing the vicissitudes of the glance.

We shall continue to stay close to the surface in taking the next step in this part. This time, however, we shall attend to the ways in which the glance figures into our basic orientation in the place-world.

3

BEING/BECOMING ORIENTED BY THE GLANCE

In a landscape we always get to one place from
another place. . . . In the landscape I am
somewhere.

—Erwin Straus, *The Primary World of the Senses*

Where are we at all? and whenabouts in the name
of space?

—James Joyce, *Finnegans Wake*

For we do not know where is the darkness or the
dawn nor where goes beneath the earth the sun that
gives light to mortals nor where it arises.

—Homer, Odyssey, Book 10

We do not fully understand the process of orientation.

—J. J. Gibson, *The Perception of the Visual
World*

I

I am back in a city that is mostly new to me—I have been here only three times
before and then just briefly each time. Normally, I am quite good at getting
oriented in new places; my friends even praise me for this ability. But now I am
perplexed: here in Ann Arbor I am quite confused. I don't seem to know where I
am at any given moment. Or more exactly, I know where I am only in the most
proximal sense: I am in this particular house, or at this equally particular address, or on a corner at the intersection of two streets clearly designated by
lucidly lettered signs. I even know—roughly—what part of town I'm in: on the
"edge" of "downtown." I know all this; it is manifest, unproblematic. Yet I am
still not oriented.

I don't know, for example, in which direction east lies. I cannot say to myself or to anyone else what I usually announce without hesitation: "East, oh that's over there." The same is true for the other cardinal directions, about which I am just as clueless. I am continually surprised to find the sun setting in a certain place; or rising from another: I wouldn't have guessed *that* part of the sky is the region where the sun would settle down; or that other part is where it would come up. In between sunrise and sunset, I am also perplexed at the way the shadows fall when the sun is out: something seems awry here, something out of kilter.

Some tell me that the cause of this lack of orientation—which turns out to be a frequent phenomenon for newcomers to this city—is the fact that certain major streets depart from the grid plan that otherwise dominates the layout of the town. Such streets as Washtenaw and Packard do not proceed in any predictable, rectilinear manner but cut across the regular grid pattern diagonally, not unlike Broadway in New York City. I am sure this explanation is right when it comes to driving in Ann Arbor: to drive on streets such as these is to veer, imperceptibly but significantly, off one's presumed straightforward course. I know this phenomenon from comparable circumstances elsewhere in which a winding road can throw off one's sense of direction or location even though one is barely aware that the aberration is occurring: one had thought one knew where one was going until, suddenly, the perception of an unexpected landmark makes it clear that one does not know at all.

But this explanation does not console me. My sense of lack of orientation in Ann Arbor is more basic than merely getting off the course when driving. Whether I am driving or not—indeed, equally in *both* cases—I am at a loss as to my implacement in the larger landscape. Besides its practical inconvenience (I cannot now follow directions that involve references to the cardinal directions), this unoriented state is embarrassing to me personally. After all, I come from the Midwest and know my way around many comparable towns in this region of America. Why not here too? I should be able to see my way around with all this open sky! And, after all, the streets are *mostly* perpendicular: should that not suffice to orient me despite a few vagrant roads? What is going on here?

Notice, to begin with, that my immediate orientation—my sense of where I am in terms of the particular locus I am at—is unproblematic even in the midst of the larger lack of orientation. A major reason why this is so is found in the easy availability of the glance. In order to gain a first, minimal level of orientation, all I need to do is to glance at what closely surrounds me. For instance, I glance around the house where I am a guest and already see several signs of familiarity even though I have been a guest here for just a few days. When I arise on the third morning of my stay, a glance is enough to tell me that I am indeed still in this same house, here and nowhere else. So, too, when I leave the house, I notice at the corner the street signs, situated perpendicular to each other, that say unambiguously "First Street" and "Koch." Such is my faith in them that I need only glimpse them to know that I stand at a very determinate spot in the Ann Arbor street plan. If I pivot around and look back at the house, the number of its address, "305," indicates with an equally crisp clarity just where on First Street this house is set.

Somewhat more ambiguous and not supported by any such locatory signs is my sense of the region of the city I am in. Even so, I am fairly well oriented in this domain. Partly on the basis of remembering that I was driven here quite directly from downtown (it was only a matter of a few blocks) and partly from the view I now have of the city center and the university from the front yard of the house I am visiting, I am able to tell unhesitatingly that I am close to the downtown, indeed on its edge in a small residential suburb. For all of this too, glancing suffices. It may not be *necessary*—I can draw upon other resources in determining just where I am: visual memories, the word of a passerby, my friend who tells me in detail where I am—but *it is sufficient in each case*. All I need to do is to glance in the right way to find out where I am in the proximal place of my immediate near sphere.

My confidence is undermined, however, when I recall suddenly that this suburb in which I am now located belongs to what is known as "the West Side." My facility in locating where I am comes to an abrupt stop as I realize that I have no idea what "west" means in this locution. West of where? Presumably of the downtown. But I don't really know *where* the downtown itself is located in the larger city that is named "Ann Arbor."

None of the accessible precision of orientation in the near sphere—in each phase of which my glancing look plays a decisive role—is on hand to help me figure out where I am in the far sphere. For all of my certainty in knowing where I am right *here* (here in this house, on this street, in this suburb), I am adrift in the more encompassing space of the city as a whole, neighboring towns, and the environing landscape: all those things far out *there*. My sense of being lost is not due merely to lacking a map or a compass. These things would certainly help, but until I can actually employ them—or until, over time, I become much better acquainted with the city—I must fall back on my immediately available resources: what I am able to do in my current bodily state (with its acquired abilities and tendencies) and in my actual state of mind (with its existing interests, thoughts, intentions, and so on).

When I appraise these personal resources, I become aware that my sense of being stranded in space derives from two notable lacks. First of all, I realize that I lack any stock of adequate memories: memories able to act as a basis for orientation in the far sphere. These memories are of two sorts: "mental maps" and habitual body memories.[1] A mental map is a schematic representation of a place in the form of a set of features that, were they to become explicit, would constitute a diagram of that place; for the most part, these features are implicitly

---

1. On habitual body memories, see my *Remembering* (Bloomington: Indiana University Press, 1987), 149–153, 163–164; and my article "Habitual Body and Memory in Merleau-Ponty," *Man and World* (fall 1984). On cognitive maps, see Peter Gould and Rodney White, *Mental Maps* (Baltimore: Penguin, 1974).

held in mind. A habitual body memory organizes movements of my body in ways regulated by the past history of being in a particular place. Both of these bases of orientation are tacit and exist more in action or practice than in thematic thought. I draw on them spontaneously instead of selecting them deliberately. Or more exactly, they are drawn out of me by the very circumstance of getting oriented. In particular, both depend on being in an already familiar situation that calls for their operation at a subliminal level. Once elicited in this un-calculating fashion, they guide my bodily actions, orienting them in assured and reliable ways. Without such mental maps and bodily habitudes, I lack a pre-reflective fund on which I can count—precisely not my current situation in Ann Arbor.

A second major lack is the glance—the glance in its orientational capacity. When I am unoriented, *I don't even know where to glance;* or more exactly, *I don't know how to glance to find out what I need to know.* The ease of glancing so evident at the first level of orientation—where already recognizable local signs (for example, the interior of the house, nearby street signs) assist me—is no longer present. At the level of the far sphere, my glance seems blocked or curtailed; it cannot attain its usual visual victories. In part, this new lack is the direct result of the first lack. Without any subtending foundation in habitual body memories or cognitive maps, I lack the grounds on which glancing can act to guide me. Thus my inability to employ the glance for orientational purposes reflects the fact that I don't know *from where* to glance—on what bodily or cognitive basis. The "from where" precedes the "know where"; both are presup-posed in *knowing how* to glance. "Know-how"—of which what we call savoir-faire is a more settled and sophisticated modality—is nonpropositional knowl-edge (where propositional knowledge is "knowledge that" in Ryle's language).[2] Knowing how (to do, say, or think X) is knowing that exists primarily in its enactment and only secondarily in representation. Such know-how is active in the efficacy of mental maps and bodily habitudes; it is also active in the glancing that builds on these as its material a priori conditions. If I don't know how even to glance to see where I am, I am almost certainly deficient in pertinent bodily and mental experiences that reflect my having been here before on a number of occasions (just how many will vary from situation to situation, and will depend on local geography, urban design, my present state of mind, my orientational aptitude, and so on). It follows that I will lack the basis for becoming oriented in spaces that are remote from my present location.

It is as if the precedence of appropriate mental mappings and bodily habi-tudes constitutes the depth of which glancing merely gilds the surface—or so it would seem. However: *caveat superficies!* The surface here at stake is a mo-mentous and not a trivial surface: it is a surface that makes all the differ-ence, including an important difference to its own depth. The glance certainly

2. See Gilbert Ryle, *The Concept of Mind* (London: Hutchinson University Library, 1949) and my discussion of remembering-how and remembering-that in *Remembering,* pp. 53–60.

builds on the depths of body and mind as these precede current orientation. But it has a life of its own.

II

The nonsuperficial life of the glance is demonstrated by the fact that, even when one is in a new situation for which there is no already existing, specific habitual/cognitive background, one's glance plays a crucial role in orientation, that of *probing the environment for orientational cues.* This is my very circumstance in Ann Arbor. Not having been here long enough or often enough to lay down a secure basis of body memories or schematic mappings, I anxiously probe the near and far environs for telling signs. I find such signs readily in the near sphere—precisely where the apposite memories and mappings are already beginning to form (thanks to the mere fact that I am now becoming familiar with my immediate surroundings). But I do not find them in the more remote regions of the circumstance. Here—or rather, *there*—I am clueless twice over: without memorial or mapping supports, I am also not presented with ready-to-hand, disambiguating clues. Precisely in this double impasse, I am led to scour the scene with a probatory glance. I look all over the place for telltale signs of where I am vis-à-vis the larger scene. In my state of geographic destitution, I have only a few resources: walking around, talking to residents, consulting a map, and glancing. Of these options, the most readily available is the glance. For I can always glance out from where I stand—even if I do not know just where I do stand. But what kind of glancing will here help me out?

The glancing now at stake is a species of its own. It is neither glancing intently *at*—which presumes that the object is already targeted and that I wish to bear down on it—nor is it just glancing *around:* a much more casual and open-ended act. The glancing in which I need to engage involves a keen *searching out* of my environs, given that I am greedy for geographical guidance. Such a glance is not a move of last resort—when all else has failed—but a step of first resource: it is out there first, in advance of my ignorance, in the vanguard position. It takes account of, indeed it is a direct response to, my lack of previous knowledge—not a mere reaction to it, but a move that copes creatively with my unoriented state.

I say "unoriented," not "disoriented." The distinction is not trivial in the present context. To be *disoriented* is to be genuinely lost in the landscape: confused, turned around, not knowing where to go at all. This is what happens when we are lost in dark and dense woods, having lost sight of all trail markers. To be *unoriented* is not to know where I am—not yet. This does not mean that I am *lost;* it just means that I cannot specify my whereabouts, nearby or farther away. I am, for the moment, unknowledgeable as to these whereabouts. This is, by and large, my situation in Ann Arbor at the stage I have just described: I lack orientation in the city at large. But the circumstance is more complex than this; here as elsewhere, there may be a mixture of the two states and not simply one or the other. With regard to my near sphere, I am already oriented—oriented sufficiently for me not to have to complain of being either unoriented or disoriented. But with respect to the far sphere, I am in fact both unoriented insofar as I am simply ignorant of the disposition of the larger setting and disoriented inasmuch as I am quite confused as to the cardinal directions that superintend this setting (which way is west?). Disorientation entails unorientation, but not the other way around.

At the same time, we need to respect another, still more crucial set of distinctions, this time between two series of terms. On the one hand, there is a natural alliance between disorientation, the far sphere, and space; on the other, there is an equal but different affinity between unorientation, the near sphere, and place.

(i) *We are disoriented in space.* Only in the expansiveness of space are we genuinely dis-oriented, that is to say, lost, confused as to our bearings. We don't say that we're *lost in place,* or even disoriented in place (with one exception to be noted below). But we do say with unerring accuracy that we are "lost in space." Since the far sphere is constituted by the loose display of things in space—that is, their layout in the aptly named "environ-ment," that is, that which ultimately *surrounds* us—it is sufficiently roomy and complex to get lost in. Only if the woods in which we are disoriented are big enough will we feel truly lost there. Even were we to feel momentarily confused as to which way to go in a small copse, just knowing that we're in such an intimate setting precludes the special panic of being lost there: "eventually," we say to reassure ourselves, "there will be a way out." We are unoriented but not disoriented. The panic of disorientation comes from knowing (or even just suspecting) that the *selva oscura* (dark wood) goes on and on without apparent end—that whichever way we walk we may get only more lost, less able to find an exit. The "far" of the far sphere here earns its name: we feel far from home, far from knowing how to get home. It is a situation not just of not knowing which particular path to take but of a sense of increasing confusion. Literally so: we are "fused with" our surroundings and have lost not only the right route but also ourselves as well-directed bodies.

(ii) *We are unoriented in place.* Places are the pre-given units of the near sphere; they constitute its content and they make up its texture. Just because they are comparatively definite—though not subject to exact definition!—places are by their very nature orienting. Short of finding conspicuous "landmarks" to guide us in space, we count on what we might call "place-marks," that is, places taken as orientational markers.[3] Think of the way in which the merest

---

3. Landmarks are conspicuous not only by size but also because of their established historicity. Place-marks have no such shared history; they are locatory signs of significance to individual inhabitants of a place.

house serves to orient us on a given street: for example, a dark green house with a modern addition in the back that is perched prominently at the intersection of First Street and Moseley. When I walk into Ann Arbor, this is a first way-station on the route (and the last on my return). To spot it in my near sphere is to know that I am "on the way." It marks a stage of the route and it beckons me to go beyond: it is at once an indicator and an adumbrator. The near sphere is studded with such place-marks: not only houses, but trees and telephone poles, streets and corners, bushes and shops. Even if lacking the salience of landmarks, these act to assure orientation in my immediate surroundings: I need only glance at them to gain a sense of where I am. Their modest appearance calls for no further scrutiny—only the merest look to confirm that I am oriented by their familiar presence.

Even short of such place-marks acting as easily recognizable orientational signs, I *always know my way around my neighborhood to some significant degree.* It is a place within which I am acquainted to some extent. I know what is just underfoot as I stand or walk—or just overhead, or just by my side. We are here on the near side of the near sphere, in its most intimate quarters as well as in the immediate ambit of our lived body. This proximal zone is composed of the absolute here of the lived body along with what we might call the "by-places" in which that body stands or into which it steps or through which it walks: for example, nooks, corners, sidewalks, the street itself. Together, the absolute here and the by-places make up one epicenter of the near sphere, that which I occupy myself at any given moment; the other epicenter is formed from the full-fledged places that surround me, including those that serve as place-marks. What I have been calling the "place-world" is in effect the combination of proximal by-places with middle-range·distinct places (for example, houses, parks, whole cities)— and sometimes also more remote places that have been drawn into my perceptual or actional orbit from the far sphere. Such a world is equivalent to what Merleau-Ponty calls a "field of experience": "When I wonder what the something or the world or the material thing is, I am not yet the pure spectator who, by the act of ideation, I am to become; I am a *field of experience.*"[4]

It is just because *I am* this field or world—I am not other than it, not opposed to it, as if it were another country ("country" as a stretch of land lying before me derives from *contra,* "opposite," "against")—that I can count on being oriented in it at a deep level of familiarity. For I am the body whose absolute here locates me in just this place and not some other. This is why I am so rarely disoriented in place; I am already the very field in which orientation takes place; I am myself part of its place-world. I have my bearings there long before the predicament of disorientation can arise.

4. Maurice Merleau-Ponty, *The Visible and the Invisible,* tr. A. Lingis (Evanston, Ill.: Northwestern University Press, 1968), p. 149; my italics.

There are two ways in which human beings are unoriented. One is to be a pure spectator, someone who *cannot* be oriented because of being bodiless, thus having no effective here and no correlative place. (Examples would include the Cartesian *cogito*, the impersonal observer, and Kant's transcendental ego.) The other is to be myself, that is, the impure glancer who is both here (absolutely) and there (in relation to the by-places and places of my near sphere). I am unoriented at this level inasmuch as orientation is not yet an issue for me. Thanks to my always being absolutely *here*, I am *located*, securely so, but I am not yet *oriented*; I am pre-oriented as it were. Orientation beyond location requires a relationship both to the passing by-places of my immediate world and to the particular places of my environment—say, to that dark green house over there and ultimately to the city in which it is set (and still more ultimately to the course of the sun and the outlying landscape). Short of all this—and I am *always* situated on the short side of things to some significant extent—I am anchored in the absolute here; I am located "just here" in my near sphere but not yet fully related to all that is "over there": that is, to my entire place-world, composed of my near sphere and (at the limit) the contiguous far sphere.

There is one exceptional and revealing circumstance that calls for mention here: a concussion or other trauma in which I lose consciousness. When I am still unconscious, I am unoriented in a yet stronger sense: I am outside the domain in which orientation is an issue of any kind. Not because I have no body but because I am so much at one with the massive facticity of my unconscious body that orientation is not in question at all. While still "out," I am out of touch with my own here and any of the by-places that encircle and subtend it, and thus all the more out of relationship with the discrete loci of my place-world. But once I "come to," I come to an awareness of being disoriented vis-à-vis both the by-places and the determinate places that circle around me: I don't know where I am in relation to them. Here disorientation occurs not with regard to space but already within the place-world and its near sphere.

The reason for this special disorientation is not difficult to discern: coming from a position of zero-implacement when I am stunned, I find any relationship with place, even a previously familiar one, bewildering. It is as if I am suddenly in a dark and unknown wood—as "be-wilder" connotes. This disoriented state recedes as soon as I re-habituate myself to my place-world; habitual body memories return, sedimented mental maps come back into operation, and I am "back on track"—back to a position where I can be both unoriented (that is, within the near sphere that is the felt and seen inner surface of the place-world) *and* oriented (in relation to the more expansive layout of things within the near and far spheres alike).

A case such as concussion demonstrates the extreme fragility of orientation— how it can be lost in a thrice. This thrice occurs in the merest pratfall (in which we suddenly find ourselves flat on our back after slipping on something under- foot) as well as in the most severe stroke (in which we may permanently lose our orientational powers).[5] At the same time, however, orientation is a remarkably robust power—again, both in ordinary experience (where we say confidently. "once oriented, always oriented") and in an extreme medical state (place orientation is one of the last things to degenerate in certain forms of advanced Korsakoff syndrome: the unfortunate "HM," though unable to recollect his past or to acquire new memories, could nevertheless navigate successfully through the complex corridors of his hospital).[6] The loss of orientation shows us at our most precarious as well as our most resilient.

It is also true that disorientation can sometimes be delightful—as when we find ourselves thoroughly enjoying drifting in a vibrant city scene, not knowing just where we are, "lost in the crowd" in Rio or in Soho on a summer night.

All of this—disorientation as well as orientation, delight along with panic— rides on a glance.

III

Getting oriented, for all its importance in our lives, is slow in coming to pass. This was evident in my own experiences of becoming oriented in Ann Arbor: after being in this city for several short visits, a total of some seven or eight days, I was still not oriented with regard to cardinal directions and the overall layout of the town. I could get around locally, within the precincts of the neighborhood where I was staying. But I was baffled when someone asked me to meet him at the "North Campus." I was able to follow his detailed directions as to how to drive over there. But this was only because I could easily follow the sequence of turns and notice the landmarks he had told me about; I moved correctly through successive near spheres, from one set of places to another, yet with no sense of what general direction I was taking or of how the North Campus, once reached, related to the downtown area. I found my way in place, but I was lost in the larger space.

The very next day, I was parking my car on a hill that leads to the downtown. It was a very bright afternoon, and I paused to enjoy the sunshine. Since the sun was now in a certain quadrant of the sky—to my left as I faced downhill—I realized that it must have traversed the sky from a position to my right. This corresponded to my perception of the sun's rising earlier that day on the horizon in the same right-hand sector of the sky. That must be east, I quickly concluded, and if so the sun is now heading west. Although I felt confident concerning this determination of cardinal directionality, I realized just as quickly that the *North*

5. See the cases studied by Oliver Sacks in *The Man Who Mistook His Wife for a Hat and Other Neurological Tales* (New York: Summit Books, 1985).

6. See the case of "HM" as reported by Brenda Milner, ed., *Hemispheric Specialization and Interaction* (Cambridge, Mass.: MIT University Press, 1975).

Campus I had visited the day before was *not* where "north" should be on the basis of this experience. Indeed, the campus in question lay distinctly "south" according to my newly acquired directional schema: for I remember driving toward the downtown on a street roughly parallel with the street I was now on— and that I then took my direction to be southward—mistakenly so. Like the Chinese emperor, I seemed to be facing south—and yet this was supposed to be the way to get to the North Campus! Not even the emperor himself could have wrought such a reversal of basic directionality!

There is an important lesson lurking in both of these everyday incidents: getting fully oriented is a decidedly piecemeal process. Sometimes it is a matter of negotiating a small part of a larger puzzle—how to drive to North Campus without knowing what "North" means—and sometimes it concerns something more momentous, as when I figured out how the sun traverses the town as a whole. In the former case, I did not expect any further outcome; I was happy to have reached my destination, with no aspirations toward the solution of a more extended problem of orientation. In the latter case, however, I had high hopes. I thought that once I had become clear as to the cardinal directions as they were traced by the sun's motion I would become thereby, instantly, more knowledge-able of Ann Arbor's overall layout—and thus of my own spatial relationship with this city. No such luck! As we have just seen, I was in a quandary with regard to how the city is disposed in space, for example, how the North Campus relates to the downtown area. To resolve one orientational question, no matter how im-portant it may be, is not necessarily to *achieve orientation*. Indeed, in this particular instance, I was even more perplexed than before, since the very name "North Campus" (designating a place I had actually found and visited) had become problematic: north of what? A coherent place in itself, its relation with other parts of the campus and the downtown region was thrown into confusion.

In these early encounters with a new town (I had never been in this city before these recent visits), I had thus gleaned various visual shards that did not fit together to form one coherent whole. I had learned how to walk about the neighborhood on the West Side where I was staying, and I knew my way to the downtown and parts of the adjoining university campus: but I couldn't make sense of how the North Campus related to this campus or the adjoining town. In fact, my breakthrough in learning the course of the sun indicated that the West Side should be *north* of the downtown and the North Campus should lie to its *south*!

Double confusion, double disorientation. Even though glancing had proven effective in regard to location and orientation in the near sphere (by allowing me to pick out and then to recognize various by-places and certain determinate places), when I ventured further out glancing seemed to have reached its limit. Look as I might, so long as I was not fully oriented I could not escape my plight by any such direct action. In the larger setting, a glance did not suffice—not yet.

IV

Orientation often occurs: by "little cat steps," *tâtonnements* as the French like to say. My own situation in Ann Arbor was no exception. In that middle-sized Midwestern city, I was wandering in the wilderness of partial perceptions. The moves of demi-orientation in which I was caught up were promising but not sufficient to give me the sense of being well oriented. However, I was confident that with time I would achieve adequate orientation. Part of living in a place is becoming oriented there: it "goes with the landscape." My frustration came from the fact that I was not planning to live in this place; I was only an occasional visitor, yet one who had stayed just long enough to feel acutely the lack of orientation in the city at large.

Puzzling over this lack—something that happens rarely to me—I recalled a map of Michigan that I had used in driving to Ann Arbor for the first time. I didn't have the physical map in front of me, but its image suddenly came back to mind: or rather, that part of it that showed Highway 94 running just below Ann Arbor in cartographic space. To be "below" a given location on any standard Western map is to be *south* of that location. Pondering this schematic but certain fact—I trusted the mapmaker, Rand McNally, even if I did not trust myself—I realized the error of my ways in a moment of unexpected insight. Suddenly everything "fell into place," as the telling phrase goes. It all made sense—even my own misunderstanding.

When I stood in the late afternoon on that hill leading into downtown Ann Arbor, I thought I was facing south when I looked downhill because of the mistaken assumption that south was below me and between east and west as these latter are defined by the rising and setting sun. But after recalling the map, I knew in cartographic fact that south was precisely the opposite direction—*behind* me as I stood on the hill—and I also knew that I was looking north when I looked from the hill into the downtown. And this direction is precisely that in which the North Campus is supposed to lie. I had aligned myself correctly with true north—north by north—at last! Here is how the situation looks in diagrammatic form:

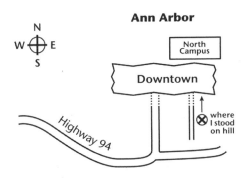

Now it had become clear that I had misinterpreted facing north (as I truly was) as facing south, restricting my guiding cues to the rising and the setting of the sun. In relation to the axis established by this rising/setting, the directions of north and south seem arbitrary: as if I could decide for myself, or let the emperor decide for me. In fact, this matter is not arbitrary. If the sun rises on my right as I observe its rising, then I am facing north and south is behind me. Since I failed to reflect on this fact, I became confused and needed an additional clue in the form of the remembered map.

But there is a further twist: the cartographic image was not corrective in and by itself. It had to be related to my present circumstance in some quite concrete way for it to be as disambiguating as it became. In my own case, this was provided by another memory: that of driving into Ann Arbor from Highway 94 along a route that took me straight into the heart of the city. This route is parallel to the street on which I stood when I was so confused by the implications of the sun's various perceived directionality. Thus I knew, by instantaneous inference, that "south" must lie behind me: in the direction from which I came when I first entered the city from the highway. It followed, by another effortless inference, that "north" has to lie ahead of me: down the hill, into the city, and then to the North Campus. I may not be the emperor of what I survey, but I have attained a mild version of what Chinese Buddhists like to call "sudden enlightenment." Or, if not enlightenment, then sudden alignment: the right solution arose only when I could correctly align the cardinal axis of north/south with existing and known locations in the larger landscape—in this case, highways and streets, buildings and an entire part of campus, as they impinge on and structure the city of Ann Arbor, Michigan.

In happy confirmation of my newfound enlightenment, only a few hours after I had managed to realign myself in the manner just described, I received a telephone call from my friend Matt. He called to give me directions to his place for dinner. "You take Liberty Street to the west, and then you turn south at Soule Street. It's on the West Side." "Fine," I said confidently, "no problem—I can certainly find my way to your place." I had arrived in town: I had become oriented in Ann Arbor.

V

Despite the buoyancy experienced in my sudden discovery, getting to this point had been notably circuitous. It took a number of twists and turns before I was finally on track. Such vicissitudes had not been necessary in the near sphere: there, I was at home almost from the beginning, whether at the proximal level of the absolute here (with its closely associated by-places) or in regard to particular places of my immediate neighborhood. There is no reason to falter in such familiar parts of the place-world; either I am oriented or simply un-oriented there, but only rarely dis-oriented. Orientation in the far sphere is another matter; here I can be deeply lost, thoroughly disoriented. And for the most trivial of reasons, it seems: an unthinking reversal of south with north and a failure to remember that I had first come into Ann Arbor from the south. Had either of these missteps not occurred, I might not have become disoriented in the first place.

More important for present purposes is to note how the glance figures at every stage of this narrative of orientation. Although it served me well in my close environs—helping me to identify and recognize items in my near sphere—it did not suffice to get me out of my predicament in regard to the larger layout of the city. Nevertheless, in one form or another it was active throughout my process of getting oriented. Let me indicate how this is so by distinguishing seven forms of glancing that were actively at play in various stages of my orientational experiences in Ann Arbor.[7]

(i) *The empty glance.* Even at the height of my confusion, I never stopped glancing. If anything, I glanced even more frequently and fervently than ever, searching out signs in the environing world. Yet, for the most part, I found nothing that was helpful. My glancing fell fallow.

(ii) *The insufficient glance.* The only stable indicators at which I found myself glancing in my geographic distress were the initial and terminal positions of the sun; these did reliably stake out east and west for me, and for this reason I thought they would guide me to full orientation. But my glance at the sun's rising and setting led me to a false confidence in regard to the north versus south distinction. In and by itself, it was insufficient, since it takes the further *thought* that "if the sun rises on my right I am looking north" to gain correct orientation on the basis of my initial glance. My glance at the solar situation was necessary but not sufficient.

(iii) *The mental glance.* In this important act, the cogitating ego looks about its own mental bric-a-brac for certain contents that satisfy its intentional interests therein.[8] In the above narrative, it was a mere mental glance at a remembered map that took me out of my orientational impasse. I *glanced in memory* at a part of this map that was capable of clarifying my current state of confusion. Instead of glancing at a perceptual thing or an environing place, I glanced at an image that arose unbidden yet was most welcome in the circumstance.

(iv) *The checking-out glance.* Of course, I could not remember the map as effectively as I did unless I had first of all perceived this map. Such perception is itself constituted by a particular way of looking at the map—

7. I call these "forms of glancing" in order to make it clear that they are not the basic *modes* of glancing I distinguish in the afterword.

8. For further treatment of Husserl on the *geistige Blick*, see chap. 9, "Attending and Glancing."

"checking it out." This occurs in and by glancing. Sometimes, especially when we are lost, we gaze at maps, but for the most part we glance at them, taking them to be schematized digests of geographical information. My mental glance in memory was just such an action of checking-out, realized in a memorial modality.

(v) *The discovering glance.* Once the crucial cue had come from the memorial glance, I could glance back out at my surrounding world with new eyes. I could now tell, at a glance, that everything lying further down the hill and in the town and beyond lay in a northward direction. My glance pursued this correct directionality by resituating the very same things at which I had looked mistakenly before my sudden realization. Once a solid sense of north was in place, I could quickly discern the proper relative position of everything that lay on the north/south axis.

(vi) *The re-orienting glance.* Closely related to the discovering glance is the glance by which I reoriented myself by reading what had formerly appeared as "south" as in fact "north"—and vice versa. This amounts to a special act of glancing, one that relocates and realigns what had been falsely located and misaligned in earlier lookings. It sees certain perceptual facts in a new geographical light. It takes them to be the same (they have not changed in inherent identity, structure, texture, color, and so on) and yet as different (that is, differently situated in terms of the four great world quadrants: in this case, interpreted as lying in the north rather than in the south quadrants).

(vii) *The confirmatory glance.* Once I have been (quite literally) *turned around* in my convictions, converted as it were, I am able to glance around me with increased ease and confidence. Having become oriented in the larger landscape, I need not glance desperately for hidden cues or disambiguating facts. Instead, without even trying I find confirmatory cues and facts everywhere I look. My whole world has gained a sense of secure orientation; and I with it. Both are seen in a different light. I can afford to glance in a continually confirmatory way, with the distinct implication that I now know where I stand.

Driving over to Matt's house on Soule Street that evening, I did not have to fret about where I was going in the far sphere. For the far sphere had now become contiguous with the near sphere, the two domains having lost the detachment from each other whereby I could be oriented in one but disoriented in the other. Now my glance glided from one to the other without sensing any significant gap between them. No longer a matter of space versus place, these two formerly truncated spheres have become part of a single, coherent place-world: two continuous domains within it. I do not have to distinguish—as formerly I was forced to do—between the disorienting and perplexing layout of

Ann Arbor as a whole and the less problematic experience of Ann Arbor viewed close-up. Thanks to this propitious development, I can content myself with the merest glances at street signs and other place-marks farther afield (for example, distant buildings and trees, the city horizon, and so forth), with no residual anxiety as to where I am going in directional space. These confirmatory glances suffice to tell me that I am oriented in such a space.

On my way to my friend's house, everything I pass stays the same, all remains in place; yet all has also changed. A subtle *renversement* has occurred, a reversal that is reflected in the differential employment of my glance. This latter is no longer bifurcated in its operation between the easy accessibility of what is close to it and the difficulty of grasping what lies far from it. Now I can glance back and forth from the near to the far and back again in one sweeping look. My glance swings between realigned and resituated stabilities—between the familiar houses and streets in the local neighborhood and the parts of the city I glimpse in the distance. All of these are perceived as belonging to the same place-world, which is differentiated only by nuances of delicate directional difference.

I am no longer geographically schizoid: partly found and partly lost. I have found myself, I know where I am, in this city.

VI

What does *being (and not just becoming) oriented* really mean? Earlier, I suggested one basis for orientation: the buildup of habitual body memories and the formation of adequate mental maps. This buildup and formation would occur if I lingered longer in Ann Arbor and began to live there on a more continuous basis. For they are the slow sedimentation that undergirds the securing of orientation as something I can count on without additional help—in particular, without recourse to assistance from external evidence or cartographic signs of the sort that saved the day in my early orientational confusion. Both body memories and cognitive maps are wholly internalized presences in my orientational system; they are not third but first terms, part of my ongoing geographic repertoire.[9] Yet even when such sedimentation has been laid down fully—when I need not count on a fortuitous recollection to steer me out of trouble—the glance has an important role to play in detecting the cues that will activate these deep-seated agencies of ongoing orientation.

Another aspect of settled orientation, as I have just hinted, is the reconnection of far sphere and near sphere. An important part of my experience of disorientation stemmed from the very disjunction between these two spheres: my being very much at home in one and quite lost in the other. But how can I be

9. A distinct recollective memory of a map has not yet been assimilated to this apparatus; in the foregoing example, I consulted an image instead of drawing on what I knew pre-reflectively in the form of already-operative geographic know-how.

so sure of myself locally—just here, underfoot, and in my immediate neighborhood—and yet so very unsure of myself outside this familiar ambience? I cannot
generalize my local knowledge to the more extensive landscape of the town; for
the latter exists on a different plane from the former, it is of a different order: as
the German language suggests in speaking of *auskennen,* "getting to know your
way around," where the prefix *aus-* underlines the fact that one must go *out* of
one's local ambience in order to get acquainted with the broader scene.

Seen in this new light, the task of orientation is not just to lay down the right
habitual responses but to bring together two otherwise alienated orders—to
allow them to become contiguous realities that (as we shall see shortly) even
invade each other. That these orders belong together ultimately is indicated in
the very language of "near sphere" and "far sphere," complementary terms that
rejoin each other across their very differences: indeed, they actively call for each
other (no near without far, and vice versa, according to a basic place-logic).
Their relationship is better expressed in still other terms: it is that between *the
place of local landscape* and *the space of perceived geography.* I here adapt
nomenclature from Erwin Straus, who distinguishes between "sensing" as an
immediate bodily insertion into the lived world and "perceiving" as an object-
oriented grasp of things taken to be steadily positioned in an objective matrix of
space. Mapping is normally of items in such space; hence there is a collusion
between geography (especially in its cartographic representations) and perception, just as there is between the lived landscape (which I prefer to call the
"place-world") and sensing. As Straus puts it:

> Sensory space stands to perceptual space as landscape to geography. Perceptual
> space is geographical space. . . . In a landscape we are enclosed by a horizon; no
> matter how far we go, the horizon constantly goes with us. Geographical space has
> no horizon.[10]

Straus here points to a crucial feature of the geographical space in which I got
lost in Ann Arbor. Although I could perceive certain horizons as I stood on a hill
in that city—they were part of the city experienced as landscape in Straus's sense
of the word—they were irrelevant to my sense of lostness. For I was lost with
respect to where "south" and "north" were located, that is, cardinal directions
that are horizonless by their very nature and that organize an indefinitely extended and wide-open plane of space.[11] In being disoriented, I did not know

10. Erwin Straus, *The Primary World of Senses: A Vindication of Sensory Experience,* tr.
J. Needleman (Glencoe, Ill.: Free Press, 1963), pp. 318–319. Straus adds, "In a landscape we
always get to one place from another place; each location is determined only by its relation to
the neighboring place within the circle of visibility" (ibid.). This is very close to my earlier
description of moving in a neighborhood from place to place. Straus employs "landscape" for
what I have been calling the "near sphere," whereas I have linked landscape to the more
encompassing region of a town or countryside.

11. Andrés Colapinto observes that even if cardinal directions do not have horizons as such

how the town of Ann Arbor fit into this plane, that is, how the town was situated with regard to cardinal directionality.[12] It was as if the entire geographic dimension—the level of cardinal directions and maps—had been lifted from the local landscape and detached from its place-world (including the horizons that encircle this world). I knew where I was at the level of sensing (that is, my absolute here encircled by various by-places; my local place), but I did not know where I was at the level of perceiving. My sensing body had been deprived of my perceiving self, my landscape of its geography, my place-world of organized positions in space.[13] I may have known my way in place, but I was dis-organized in space. The "dis-" of "disorientation" and "disorganization"—a prefix deriving from Latin and French roots meaning "apart," "asunder," "removed"— expresses precisely this predicament of being disconnected from my perceived (and not merely sensed) surroundings.

Orientation amounts to a reconnection with these more ultimate surroundings. If the reconnection cannot be done directly—that is, by glancing at the already available cues in the sensed and perceived environment—then I must have recourse to special assistance such as the memory of the map of Michigan that came suddenly to my aid. A map is a close ally of geographical space, being its cartographic representation.[14] Maps allow us to coordinate otherwise disparate pieces of perceptual and geographical knowledge; they put the separate locations that are the object of such knowledge *onto the same plane of represen-*

---

there are felt *thresholds* between them, e.g., between south and southwest (e-mail communication, June 2004).

12. In fact, the lack of horizon figures at *two* stages of being lost: in being lost in a dark forest I lack a literally perceived horizon by which I can see my way out, hence my confinement to my immediate place (where I am *not* lost); but in being lost in the wide-open space of Ann Arbor, no horizons can guide me—only something as abstract as cardinal directions. Straus's description here accords with my earlier account: "In twilight, darkness, or fog I am still in the landscape. My present location is still determined by the next adjacent location; I can still move. But I no longer know *where* I am" (*The Primary World of Senses,* p. 319; his italics). In other words, "in the landscape I am *somewhere*"(ibid., p. 321; my italics), but I do not know *just where;* the latter is determined by perceptual/geographic space as this comes to be mapped.

13. By "organized positions in space" I refer to the way in which geographic space is always a matter of strictly coordinated locations on an ideal plane—locations that are determined in relation to each other within the larger arc provided by cardinal directions. As Straus puts it: "Geographical space is closed [i.e., is horizonless] and is therefore in its entire structure transparent. Every place in such a space is determined by its position with respect to the whole and ultimately by its relation to the null-point of the co-ordinate system by which this space obtains its order. Geographical space is systematized" (ibid., p. 319). Cardinal direction contributes centrally to this systematization.

14. As Straus adds, "in such space locations can be found and defined by construction [in maps], and gaps and intervening spaces bridged [again in maps]" (ibid., p. 319). Thus I can trace on a map a route that bridges the intervening gaps, including rugged landscape that would be difficult to traverse on foot.

tation. No wonder, then, that maps are so powerful as a means of aligning the previously unaligned: they literally *line up* what is otherwise disconnected at the level of sensed places.[15]

Of course, my disparate and sometimes incongruous local knowledge may become aligned by other means. A local resident may "set me straight"—that is, give to me in words a disambiguating account that is the equivalent of the straight lines that constitute maps. Not only pictorial imagination but language "fosters order."[16] More exactly, words (for example, in the form of narratives) facilitate the reconnection of two diremptive orders, that of sensing and perceiving, landscape and geography, as well as the near sphere and far sphere. Or, alternatively, I can achieve alignment merely by lingering in the region, slowly accumulating cues until I can reliably recognize the points of connection between proximal and distal worlds. (As the Chinese Buddhists also say, Enlightenment can be "gradual" as well as sudden.) Whichever way works for me, the effect is the same: namely, the reunification of disconnected levels. The crux of orientation, its felt pivot, is the re-linking of experiential levels that were unconjoined in the state of unorientation or that have become drastically disjoined in the course of disorientation. (I say "crux" and "pivot" because it is only *after* this turning point—from a state of confusion or lack of connection to a state of clarification and continuity—that the internalized sedimentations of correct orientation come to form within the geographical subject.)

Instead of speaking of the coincidence of two levels or orders—this would be to dissolve their very difference—we should rather say that in successful orientation one order *enters into the other* to the point that we no longer feel them as discontinuous from each other: as happened when I drove so confidently over to Matt's. This can happen in either of two ways. On the one hand, landscape can be said to ingress into geography: my absolute here ties me into an extended geographic there—for example, when I witness an enormous vista that opens out before me as I stand on a cliff. On the other hand, we can just as well say that in effective orientation geography insinuates itself into landscape: for example, when towering mountains obtrude into my near sphere. Either way, "the spatiotemporal order of distance (*Ferne*) is not separable from the particularity of my living experience."[17] *Die Ferne* can also be translated as "farness," and its invocation by Straus in this context only reinforces my own view that the relationship between the far sphere and the near sphere is very much at stake in orientation.

---

15. Not that places need to be aligned; for nonmapping purposes, their discontinuity can even be a distinct virtue; the need for alignment occurs only when what we learn from places is inadequate to orient us in larger spaces: then geography and cartography serve as essential supplements to local knowledge. (On local knowledge, see Clifford Geertz, *Local Knowledge: Further Essays in Interpretive Anthropology* [New York: Basic Books, 1983].)

16. Straus, *The Primary World of Senses*, p. 317.

17. Ibid., p. 391. Cf. also: "The geographic difference becomes transformed into landscape proximity" (ibid., p. xiii).

No longer can we hold these spheres apart—any more than we can keep separate landscape and geography, sensing and perceiving. For only when the far has
been brought into the domain of the near—and vice versa—do we experience
orientation as an accomplished fact.

VII

I do not mean to suggest that the model I have been developing has removed
all the mystery from orientation. The truth of the matter is captured by J. J.
Gibson in one of the epigraphs to this chapter: "we do not fully understand the
process of orientation."[18] Even in the example on which I have been dwelling
there remain unresolved aspects. One of these is the persistence of my mistaken
view as to the relative location of north versus south. Why did I continue to
believe that the downtown of Ann Arbor and even the so-called "North Campus" lay to the south of me as I looked at the city from a position that was in
fact located to its south? Only the day before, I had driven downtown on a street
parallel to that on which I stood perplexed—and was convinced that I was
going south. I have admitted that I cannot fathom why I engaged in this reversal
of direction in the first place, nor can I account for its tenacity. (In fact, a shadow
of the erroneous belief haunted me for several days even after my moment
of geographic illumination; the mistake kept returning as if to tempt me.)
Probably nothing short of a psychoanalysis of previous orientational situations would reveal the answer to these perplexing questions: perplexing precisely because there seems to be no good reason for my persisting systematic
misapprehension.

There is another unclarified mystery: why were north and south so easily
reversed in my mistaken thinking? It was not accidental, I suspect, that my
confusion bore on their proper implacement in the larger cosmic scene. East
and west are not subject to any comparable confusion. Thanks to the manifest
trajectory of the sun every day from east to west, I am presented with irrecusable evidence of where east lies and west is found, at least early and late in
each day. Indeed, this is just what "east" means at the level of ordinary experience: *where the sun rises*, and "west" *where the sun sets*. Unless I am in northern
Finland in winter, or so smogged out that I cannot detect the sun's progression, I
will always know where east and west—and thus their axial connection—lie in
any given landscape. Perhaps this is why the very word "orientation" has *east*
buried in it: the Orient is at the heart of all direction-finding and bearing-taking
on our planet precisely because of the sun's consistent daily arising—in the east.
"Orient" derives from Latin *oriens*, rising, rising sun; ultimately from *oriri*, to

18. J. J. Gibson, *The Perception of the Visual World* (Boston: Houghton Mifflin, 1950),
p. 229.

arise, appear, be born. "East" stems from *awes-*, to shine; and it was early on associated with the goddess of dawn, Aurora in Latin, Eos in Greek. East is where day dawns, born and reborn reliably from the perceptible horizon. No wonder that every orientational activity refers back, eventually, to this unassailable fact—and no wonder that, as a corollary, so many churches and temples in the West face east, toward the Holy Land. Equally irrecusable is the fate of the sun as it sinks into the western horizon. The conjunction of the rising and the setting belongs to the horizonal structure of that ultimate place-world we call "the earth."

But north and south know no such certainty—at least not during the day. At night, the north star, Polaris, does offer guidance, though in no obvious way; a certain knowledge of astronomy is required to identify Polaris and its northerly position—whereas no such special knowledge is called for in the case of the sun, whose positions and course are manifest for all to see. It is also true that we can determine north by a magnetic compass. But in daytime and without such mechanical assistance, we possess *no inherent cue, immanent in the perceptual world itself, that enables us to distinguish north from south.* Lacking such direct evidence, I must *infer* the directions of north and south from what I already know: for example, from familiar landmarks already known in their alignment with the north/south axis or from a perceived or remembered map. Or from my already existing knowledge of the east-west axis itself. In this latter case, I must first establish the sun's trajectory from east to west, most decisively at sunrise or shortly after and at (or close to) sunset, assuming a mostly unclouded day. Once this trajectory is known—and here a glance indeed suffices—I infer immediately that north lies to the left and south to the right (if I am facing the sun's rising) and the reverse for the sun's setting.

Even here, however, I am subject to a moment of ambiguity, notably around noon. At this moment, I cannot say unequivocally where east lies—hence where west is, and as a consequence where north and south are to be found. It is not clear whether the sun is moving toward or beyond its zenith. I am visually stymied: hence my impression that the sun stands still at "high noon." Further looking is called for, either in a series of glances or in one continuous gaze (normally precluded by the sun's unbearable brightness). However the determination of the sun's exact position happens—tracking changing shadows on the ground is another option—it *cannot occur in a single glance at the sun itself.* I may see *where* it is in the sky (that is, in what general sector), but I cannot tell if it is before or after noon on the basis of one quick look. Further assistance is required—perhaps by checking my watch, remembering the sun's previous positions that same morning, or noting when no shadows are cast—but such recourse takes me away from looking at the sun itself. Here we reach a distinct limit in the deliverance of a given glance, which is otherwise so diversely effective in the complex process of becoming oriented on earth.

VIII

Despite these limitations of the glance at certain moments in the establishment of orientation and in the correction of disorientation, its range and role remain rich in our general situatedness in the place-world. It is a primary means by which the landscape world gets to be known in the first place. This is due to its deep affinity with the faces and shapes of that world. The glimmering of the glance rejoins the scintillating surfaces of every thing and every place, and of both in any given region. These surfaces flash and mutate before our very eyes, and our agile glance is uniquely capable of following them and staying with them—if only for the most cursory moment. The -scape of "landscape" connotes the shape of things, places, and regions; it also signifies their collective or gathered character, as in the related suffix "-ship" (and its variant, "-skip": "landscape" first arose in English as "landskip"). By glancing, we take in collocations of shapes, sets of surfaces. We glance off one surface only to glance at another. The glancing game is fast and complex at this level. Sometimes the glance pursues a single feature; sometimes it jumps nervously from one feature to another.[19] Either way, the glance is in constant motion, and is thus able to keep up with the incessantly changing appearances of things, their flickering lambencies. In coming to terms with these things and the places and regions they are in, the glance guides our sensing bodies into their vicinity.

But the glance can also settle onto things and their features in a somewhat more protracted manner, and when it does it is operating at the level of perception in Straus's sense—inhabiting a plane where individuated entities call for glancing of a different kind, a glancing that respects their very stability, yet still stops short of gazing. Indeed, the Strausian schema, invoked to clarify the situation of orientation, also helps us to reconsider the full range of the glance as it is ingredient in getting oriented. This range is made up of three distinguishable levels:

I. *The free glance.* This is the glance at the most intimate sensory level: the glance in its dartings and dashings amid surfaces—glancing around. We are here at the level of the absolute here and its associated by-places, along with the determinate places that bedeck the near sphere. In each of these

19. These two basic motions of the glance correspond to two fundamental eye movements, those that "drift" and those that are "saccadic" (i.e., jerky). As Gibson puts it: "The eyes of a traveller seated on the right-hand side of a moving train makes an endless series of drifts to the right and jerks to the left. The drifts are known as *pursuit movements,* and their function is to maintain the image of a selected moving spot or object at the center of the retina. The jerks are the type known as *saccadic movements,* the general function of which is to establish a new fixation, and they occur in the act of scanning the environment, in reading, and between the fixed pursuit movements just described" (Gibson, *The Perception of the Visual World,* p. 126; his italics). We shall return to saccadic movements in a more critical vein in chap. 9.

closely connected arenas, the glance moves like Mercury among the local denizens of the place-world. Unconstrained by the regularities and rigors of substance and space, the glance gets us situated in this primal order of things-in-places. It is the apperceptive sentinel of the lived body as this body finds its way step by step, look by look in the immediate landscape. In this landscape scene, I am indeed *somewhere,* even if this "where" is not yet the *stabilitas loci* of geographic orientation. I am glancing—moving and looking—among the flowing surfaces of my spontaneous existence. Such freely mobile glancing is often accompanied by a felt dimension, at once haptic and muscular, a "visual kinesthesis"[20] in which my lived body *finds out where it is going as it moves*—and as it feels itself to move. In this visual-and-felt motion through the rapids of the proximal place-world, I find myself glancing around with alert quickness. My glances here act as the sensitive tentacles of my living-moving body, its silent monitors. They glide over the sensuous surfaces of this closest region of the near sphere, this deeply pre-reflective region of my immersion in the life-world.

II. *The bound glance.* But the glance is not only the spontaneous tracker of the shifting shapes of the directly sensed landscape world. It is vigilant in a second way that is especially pertinent to orientation: it notices the inherent features, the set traits, of the very objects whose surfaces it has pursued so intimately at the first level. Now it deals with determinate presences, whole objects, "things with fixed and inalterable properties."[21] It is bound to these things: bound to be directed toward them and to take note of them. Such things exist on the plane of perception proper. Glancing *around* cedes to glancing *at:* looking accusatively at things in the environment, whether they be close by or far away. These things need not be stationary; they can very well be in motion: other humans and animals, cars, clouds, indeed the sun itself as it moves from east to west. What matters is not the motion (or lack thereof) of perceptual objects but a certain consistency that allows them to act as orientational markers (for example, landmarks, place-marks, and so on). My glance here attempts to take in a more complete object, not only its frontal surface but as many surfaces as possible—as if to confirm that this is indeed a three-dimensional thing. In glancing, I see surfaces as surfaces *of* the things they enclose and qualify so diversely; and my glancing grasps the places these things are in. My glance is bound to this entire drama of surfaces-of-things-in-places. It moves among the robust particulars in my immediate locus, out into the environing near sphere, and even further out into the remotely located entities of the far sphere.

This is not to say that the glance at this new level is merely secondary, much less degenerate, compared to its action at the first level. What happens in bound glancing is as essential to orientation as the freewheeling

20. This is Gibson's term: see ibid., pp. 224–225.
21. Straus, *The Primary World of Senses,* p. 317.

vagaries of free glancing: for we need to take account of the comparatively stable features of our environment as much as the fluid ones if we are to be able to know our way in place and to find our way in space. In Ann Arbor, I needed to apperceive the city seen from a certain distance and the sky looming overhead as well as to experience the propinquity of my close environs. Glancing in both kinds of setting—freely in one, bound in the other—proved to be a necessary prelude to getting oriented in the more encompassing domain of the city itself.[22]

III. *The geographic glance.* In this case the proper domain of glancing is not the thing or place per se—these are what concern the bound glance—nor the surface as such (the proper correlate of the free glance) but the full layout of things and places in a region. Let us call such a layout the "planomenon."[23] It subtends the presentation of things and places on its surface; but this is a surface that is not like the surface that clings to a particular thing or place as its boundary or outer edge: that is, the surface largely at stake in the last chapter. Rather, this is *the surface of a region and ultimately of the earth*—the region of regions and the proper object of geography (*geo-*derives from the Greek *gé*, "earth"). The geographic glance sweeps over the earth's surface in whatever guise the planomenon may present itself: as seen from high above (from a mountain or an airplane), as set forth in a panoramic landscape vista, or in an aerial photograph. In each of these instances, the comprehensive character of the glance, its special ability to take in so much with such slender means, comes to the fore. It is a matter of literal out-look: of *looking out* onto the earth's surface in one continuous glancing action. It is also a matter of literal survey: of *looking over* a significant stretch of the earth's surface. Just as this surface lives up to its name by being a "face upon" the earth, so the survey that takes it in is a looking down *upon* this same surface: either directly or by means of representations of this same surface.

"Geography" is not a matter of looking alone; it also implies a *tracing* of the earth via its root in *graphein*, to trace or write. The fascination with photograph-ing landscape views has much to do with recording them in exact images by means of an exact inscription. Much the same interest in inscription is evident in our use of maps. Human beings create and look at maps not just for utilitarian

22. I should make it clear that the free/bound distinction is never absolute but always a matter of degree: I am never utterly free insofar as my glance is delimited by the structure of the surfaces at which I look, and I am never wholly bound insofar as I can always shift my attention from one determinate object to another. Moreover, the geographic glance, to be discussed next, has both free and bound elements: it is bound to the phenomenon as its proper object, yet it is taken up freely.

23. I borrow this term from Deleuze and Guattari, who use it to describe the "plane of consistency" in *A Thousand Plateaus*, tr. B. Massumi (Minneapolis: University of Minnesota Press, 1987), pp. 70–73, 144–145, 251–252, 258–259, 266–277, 270–271.

purposes—for example, to help them get from Chicago to Ann Arbor—but as compelling images of the earth's surface: as compelling as landscape paintings and in many ways complementary to the latter.[24] This suggests that the earth's surface is not just any *superficies;* in human spatial experience, it is an ultimate phenomenon, the basic planomenon. We do not have to go far to seek the reason for this phenomenon: this is the only surface that does not move in tandem with the movement of particular things and places. As Husserl, parodying Galileo, said: "the earth does not move—perhaps I may even say that it is at rest."[25] The earth does not move relative to my own living-moving body or vis-à-vis other animate or inanimate bodies. Its outer edge, the terrestrial crust on which plants grow and we walk, enjoys a certain felt ultimacy. No wonder human beings are so drawn to capturing it in cartographic or photographic images. For these images make available to human vision parts of the earth's surface (and what lies on it) that any given person, in his or her delimited experience, does not know from free or bound glancing. They provide us with views (often highly abstracted) of what lies beyond the horizons of our local landscapes. This is why geographic space proper—that which is endemic to maps in particular—is indeed "horizonless" in Straus's word: "geographic space has no horizon."[26] Were this not the case, a map would not be able to depict such faraway places: places far beyond the far sphere (which remains within the domain of direct sensing and perceiving, albeit at its remote edge). Even more comprehensively than a photograph, a map traces out these places, displaying them on a graphically delineated surface for our panoramic viewing. The modular unit of such viewing is the geographic glance. When this glance directs itself at a map or photograph, looking and tracing converge.

Geographic glancing verges closely on gazing. Each is comprehensive in intent; each eschews horizons in favor of spatial spread that goes beyond anything that is limited to the local landscape—a spread that constitutes a region (or its equivalent). Both seek the most complete and undistorted views of their subject matter. Each takes a distance from that subject matter in order to grasp it more synoptically. What Foucault says of the medical gaze could seemingly be said just as well of the geographic glance:

> The gaze implies an open field, and its essential activity is of the successive order of reading; it records and totalizes; it gradually reconstitutes immanent organizations; it spreads out over a world. . . .[27]

24. For further on cartographic representation vis-à-vis landscape painting, see my *Representing Landscape: Landscape Painting and Maps* (Minneapolis: University of Minnesota Press, 2002), esp. chaps. 7, 8, 12.

25. E. Husserl, "Foundational Investigations of the Phenomenological Origin of the Spatiality of Nature," tr. F. Kersten, in *Husserl: Shorter Works*, P. McCormick & F. Elliston, eds. (Notre Dame, Ind.: University of Notre Dame Press, 1981), p. 225.

26. Strauss, *The Primary World of Senses*, p. 319.

27. Michel Foucault, *The Birth of the Clinic*, tr. A. M. Sheridan Smith (New York: Vintage, 1975), p. 121.

But in the end we must distinguish any such gaze from the specifically geographic glance. The medical gaze is tied to language, so that the world over which it is spread "is already the world of language; and that is why it is spontaneously related to hearing and speech."[28] The geographic glance may take in symbolism—for example, the emblems and keys to maps—but its natural medium is the imagistic content of maps or the perceptual givenness of landscape, neither of which is symbolically mediated. And its basic action in relation to such properly presentational planomena is not successive but simultaneous: the geographic glance attempts to take in the entire presentation all at once (whether at the level of unaided perception or the image), yet without organizing it systematically, much less totalizing it. It is a distinctive version of what I have called the "sweeping glance."

Such a glance does indeed engage an "open field"—of which Merleau-Ponty's idea of "field of experience" is an instance—but it does so differently from any gaze, since it sweeps back and forth across that field, playing itself out from one end to the other. Unlike a scrutinizing gaze, it does not "burn things to their furthest truth,"[29] but rather it is content to savor the surfaces of things and in particular the surface of the earth. It scans this latter surface not in order to be systematic or total but so as to draw from it a synoptic survey, a representative (but not necessarily representational) sample, and in any case something that is an integral part of the complete whole.[30] It moves over the earth on display, whether this display occurs in an actually perceived landscape or in an imagistic presentation of it.[31]

28. Ibid. The medical situation is more complicated than Foucault allows. Its basic actions are not confined to gazing. Foucault himself cites an early-nineteenth-century medical text that says: "Since everything, or nearly everything, in medicine is dependent on a glance or a happy instinct, certainties are to be found in the sensations of the artist himself rather than in the principles of the art" (Cabanis, *Coup d'oeil sur les Révolutions et la Réforme de la médicine,* 1804; cited by Foucault in *The Birth of the Clinic,* p. 121). Paradoxically, what Foucault says of "the clinical gaze" could be said of free or bound glancing: "The clinical gaze is not that of an intellectual eye that is able to perceive the unalterable purity of essences beneath phenomena. It is a gaze of the concrete sensibility, a gaze that travels from body to body, and whose trajectory is situated in the space of sensible manifestation"(ibid., p. 120). Furthermore, Foucault's reduction of the glance to the pointed look—"the glance goes straight to its object" (ibid., p. 121)—excludes forms of glancing (e.g., the geographic glance) that are not so focused and that sweep out capacious regions of looking.

29. Ibid., p. 120.

30. Again, Foucault's effort to delimit the glance from the gaze leads him to overlook aspects of the glance itself: in this case, scanning. He says: "The glance . . . does not scan a field: it strikes at one point, which is central or decisive" (ibid., p.121). When the glance is seen in its full panoply, we realize that it is able to do certain of the things that might be otherwise ascribed to the gaze—without becoming a gaze itself. See the afterword of this book for further discussion of this matter.

31. The scope of glancing, whether in medicine or elsewhere, is considerable. We glance at a photograph of a fetus—which puts that most interior of beings on display—much as we glance at the display of that most external of things, the earth, in photographs, maps, and panoramic vistas. For an account of the way in which modern medical technology puts the fetus in the

IX

The three kinds of glance just discussed are all at stake in being and becoming oriented. Indeed, each is essential, for each is required at its own level of orientation. We glance freely as we stand or move in local places specified by the *surfaces* of the concrete things in these places; we glance in a bounded way when our look fastens on particular things and places regarded as *objects* of perception; and we glance geographically when we take in *vistas* of open landscape (or when we look at photographs or maps of vast tracts of the earth's surface). Not only is each mode of glancing at play in the process of getting oriented; but the first two modes are intricately intertwined with each other in this process. Even when we are ensconced in a local landscape, sensing our way there, we may single out certain things in that immediate environment and *perceive* them in Straus's strong sense: even here, some things are consistent or stable enough to be properly perceived, that is, to be objects of the bound glance. On the other hand, at the level of perception not all is determinate and full-bodied; our bound looking may be laced by free glancing. Just as far sphere and near sphere conjoin in orientation without losing their eidetic difference, so free and bound glancing (which are linked to sensing and perceiving respectively) are intertangled in the experience of getting oriented in new surroundings—or reoriented in old ones.

Moreover, the geographical glance is not confined to the isolation of the study or the quietude of the map room. While I was staying in Ann Arbor, I would sometimes plan a foray into the surrounding area and consult a map of the city— or try to remember such a map. Either way, a representation of the geographic space of the city region was brought to bear in the vicinity of better-known places. It oriented me in that larger region as surely as my body does: but where my body situated me securely in *this* place, in this spot of the earth's surface, the map took me beyond this place to other places that I might visit but that are out of view from the house in which I was a visitor. Situated beyond my far sphere—which is still within the horizon of the visible, its outermost portion as it were—these other places are locatable only in the much more capacious space depicted on the map of the region: from *here,* I can find them *only there,* even though once I reach them they will become for me concrete places of another local landscape. Any such regional space is a portion of the earth's

---

display of public space, see Barbara Duden, *Disembodying Women: Perspectives on Pregnancy and the Unborn,* tr. Lee Hoinacki (Cambridge: Harvard University Press, 1993). Duden singles out the glance in contrast with the camera, which "does not see. My glance is a human act only when I see a substance that I interpret as something meaningful . . . human sight is an art that must be learned, but it can be aided by technique" (ibid., p. 15). In this light, we can say that maps and photographs alike aid the glance but do not replace it. Both function as imagistic presentations and not as representations in any strict sense. (See the glossary and chap. 10 of *Representing Place* for further treatment of the distinction between presentations and representations. For a discussion of image and glance, see chap. 12 in this volume.)

surface, and as I approach it my geographic glance glides over it, scanning its planometric layout.

Regarded not only as a representation—where issues of accuracy are paramount—a map is also a presentation that offers itself to me as an image of a part of the known earth. In relation to that part (bio-region, nation, continent, ocean), a map is not a "universally objective medium"[32] but, rather, a cartographic image, a distinctive scenography of the earth's surface. The paper surface of a drawn or reproduced map is isomorphic with the surface of the earth, once we take account of distortions introduced by various methods of projection. The result is a horizonless redescription of the earth's surface that orients me when I wish to travel to parts of that surface that exceed the particular place in which I am now located. I am indeed somewhere in the landscape, but I don't know where I am in the larger region to which I belong until I consult a map or its equivalent.[33] Such consulting can occur as gazing—that is, when I slowly scrutinize a given map—but it most often takes place by means of glances.

Consulting maps may thus overcome the restrictions of my most proximal experience. At the same time, such informative geographic looking, whether it occurs by gazing or glancing, can be accompanied by acts of bound or free glancing. I glance freely at a map when I take the merest casual look at it (for example, while I am driving in a car and can afford only a glimpse for safety's sake) or when I note its sensuous surface by the palpation of my look. At the same time, I can look at a map in a bounded manner, as when I regard it as a perceptual object in its own right: as finely engraved, as a beautiful artifact, and so on. Both free and bound glancing can thus collaborate with the geographic glancing of concerted cartographic consultation: even at such a comparatively abstract level, there is intermingling of all three modes of glancing, often in quick succession.

Becoming oriented is a matter of getting the right medley of glances to concatenate and to guide me to where I want to go—even (and precisely) as I am not there yet, but still here in this particular place and at sea in the outstretching of space. Whether I am simply unoriented (not yet oriented or concussively removed from any orientation) or disoriented (distracted and confused with regard to the larger parameters of my visual field), I require glancing to bring me to where I want to be—with the sole exception of being stymied at high noon. Such glancing can take one of several forms, or more likely it will involve their collaborative combination; however they configurate, these forms are essential to my gaining orientation within the horizons of my near and far spheres—that is, in my current place-world—as well as in the more extensive geographic world

32. Strauss, *The Primary World of Senses*, p. 316. For Straus, such a medium is required by perception in his strict sense, which rejoins Kant's idea of space as a formal a priori intuition that is both universal and necessary.

33. I say the "equivalent" of a map, since I can figure out my location in a region by way of an aerial photograph or by the verbal descriptions given to me by a knowledgeable friend—i.e., by images or words that take on locatory geographic functions.

that lies beyond the horizons of my sensing and perceiving. My concrete and spontaneous glancing spans the difference between particular place-worlds and more extensive geographic worlds. Without being able to glance in the three manners I have identified, I would not know fully where I am, much less where I am going to be.

X

So far we have been concerned mainly with vicissitudes in the process by which we get oriented in the places of landscape and the spaces of geography. I have described how this happens in one extended but exemplary case. By saying "get oriented," I do not mean to imply that once we have become oriented we are out of the woods for good; orientation is fragile enough to be undermined at any moment. In driving out of Ann Arbor at the end of my last trip there, I was suddenly tempted to turn left onto Highway 94 in order to get back to Chicago; in fact, this would have led me to Detroit, in the very opposite direction! I had assumed that to head to this major highway from Ann Arbor was to go north from the downtown of the city instead of south, the correct direction. Only when I remembered the latter fact did I realize that I had to bear right at the junction of the highway in order to return to Chicago. The mistaken view was quickly expelled, but it had intervened quite stealthily to mislead me at a crucial moment. (Perhaps this is why we must rely so extensively on road signs at such junctures—signs that I had ignored in this particular case.)

But let us take *becoming oriented* as something established, albeit always subject to the incursions of misdirection. One major descriptive task remains: to consider what *being oriented* means: not just how we gain orientation but what we do with it once it has been achieved. What does *orientation* really signify, assuming that we no longer need to rely on memories or maps—or, for that matter, compasses, clocks, and other paraphernalia—but can count on our own unassisted knowledge?

Being oriented means at least three major things: knowing how to find your way; knowing where you are; and being at home in the place-world. In each case, we shall see that the glance has a major role to play.

A. *Knowing how to find your way.* To be oriented is not just a matter of knowing where you are located in geographic space. It is also knowing how to find your way between places—above all, from the place where you are at the moment to the place where you want to go. This is a very distinctive form of knowing-how. It is not savoir-faire, which signifies sophisticated and (typically) socially conscious knowledge. If anything, it is a matter of *connaître-faire*—to coin a compound verb in French that would mean "knowing how to do" and, in particular, knowing how to find your way about at the primal level of bare acquaintance. When I "know my way about town," I am engaging in such knowing. This is not propositional knowledge ("knowing that") about the details of a given landscape. It is knowledge that exists primarily in the actual enactment (the *doing*) of moving over and through the local landscape, guiding myself or being guided by familiar sights. In the city, this is knowing how to navigate and negotiate the streets; in the country, it is knowing how to get around by paths, trails, and other informally instituted routes.[34]

Such orientational know-how is rarely limited to acquaintance with just *one* street or path. Normally, it extends to knowing an entire nexus of routes that reticulate a given place or region: that is, knowing *alternative* ways to get to my destination from where I am now located. In Ann Arbor, if I am to get to the State Movie Theater from the western part of town, I can get there via Liberty or Washington or William streets—or by a combination of these as they connect via various cross-streets. Part of knowing how to get to the State Movie Theater is knowing how to reach it by several possible routes, not just one only. This multiple-track know-how does not consist exclusively in mentally entertained propositions; it is held just as much, indeed often much more, in the lived body that knows its way around without recourse to such propositional content; this is why I need not pause to *think* how to get to my destination by a different route: I know this alternative route in my muscles and bones, which guide me to it on their own spontaneous accord.

The emphasis of this account differs from Wittgenstein's: "[A] map will show different roads which lead through the same country and of which we could take any one at all, but not two."[35] Wittgenstein here contrasts the manifoldness of the map—which shows all known connecting routes—with the reality of having to take one route, finally, to reach one's destination. Geographic space (here, of a cartographic sort) is juxtaposed with the actualities of getting from X to Y by some single route. But in the lived world of moving in the landscape there is no such sharp dichotomy. Here, I am always in the midst of several possible routes and not confined to taking just one: at least not until I have decided which one I want to follow. Wittgenstein focuses upon the exclusivity of the choice: I can only take one route at a time. This is certainly true, but in experiential fact I am in a more complex and open-ended situation. One route may be most efficient, or most familiar, or most beautiful; but I am still able to take others—short of being forced by circumstance to take just one.[36] The reasons for choosing to take a particular

---

34. I say that such knowing is "primarily" enactive or performative; even if it *could* also be expressed in propositional form, it exists mainly and most effectively in guiding bodily movements without having to formulate it in particular propositions.

35. Ludwig Wittgenstein, from a Cambridge lecture of 1933–1934. Cited in a lecture by Manfred Frank at SUNY Stony Brook, New York, November 1998.

36. Wittgenstein does not deny such multiplicity of choice; but he subordinates it to the singleness effected by my decision to take just one route instead of others. My own account emphasizes the multiplicity experienced at the moment of decision.

route (when I can indeed choose) are various: external conditions (William Street is cleared of snow, but Liberty is not; and there is roadwork on Washington) or my own subjective condition (I am tired of walking on William) or aesthetic inclination (Washington is the most pleasing to traverse)—or I may take one of the routes from a motive of "elegant variation" (in H. H. Fowler's term) or out of sheer whimsy. Whatever the precise reason, however, the important fact is that the several ways of getting to the State Movie Theater are all available to me when I start my brief journey, and they are part of what I know in being able to find my way to this building.

Finding my way is not only a function of external obstacles (which, taken together, constitute the "coefficient of adversity" in Bachelard's phrase) or personal advantages and interests. It also reflects the structure of the routes themselves—their own contribution to finding my way. Sometimes this contribution amounts to gentle guidance: as in the case of dimly demarcated country paths that only adumbrate the way to walk, ceding to me virtually every important decision on how to proceed. But sometimes the guidance amounts to being directed: driving on Highway 94, I must respect its shape and extent precisely, on pain of driving off the road. The signs it posts specify and supplement its physical form. The highway and its signage constrain me to drive in a certain way—at a certain general speed, at a certain distance from other cars, and so on—while escorting me forward along the route. At this extreme, finding my way consists in following a preordained route. At the other extreme, I find my way by forging my own path, as when I pick my way gingerly across a rankly overgrown field or grope through a dimly lit forest, barely able to discern my way and with no signs to point the way.[37]

Whatever the kind and degree of the guidance, the route I choose to take offers many opportunities for glancing. The mere fact that it is a route at all means that it affords disclosures *along the way of the way itself.* Not having to be preoccupied with questions of navigation, I am able to look about more freely and to pay attention to whatever I encounter. As the Germans might say, *Fahren ist Erfahren:* "to travel is to find out." Part of finding my way is finding out what is to be found en route. The more my route is reliably underfoot (or under my car), the less constrained is my look and the more I am free to glance out from the route itself to discover what lies before or around me.

Such glancing out is the fortuitous result, the gift, of knowing how to find my way—and even more so of having found it. In the latter case, I am liberated to look around openly at my environs (literally, what is around me at any given time), being able to *appreciate* what surrounds me as I make my

---

37. It remains, however, that I almost never engage in what Kant calls "random groping" (*herumtappen*), that is, the cognitive counterpart of wholly arbitrary motions of my body in place; even when disoriented and lost, I still attempt to find my way with comparatively orderly movements, trying to eliminate those that are unnecessary or repetitive.

way: not just to notice it (as I must do in some minimal fashion in finding my way to start with) but to find in it things of interest and value. What I have been calling "by-places" are here importantly supplemented: no longer confined to what is proximal to my body, they now reach into all the boundaries and margins of the routes I take. These include shops, houses, and parks—or even the barest bit of lawn bordering a sidewalk—as I walk about a city. They also include the bushes, trees, and fields that surround a trail in the countryside. All such boundary phenomena are at once *beside* me ("by-places" in the strict sense) and *between* my route (with its things and places) and the more remote regions of the city or country.

Once on the route, I am free to discover, by merely glancing, what populates the by-places, places, and regions of my perambulation and travel. These passing items festoon—and sometimes also threaten—my route. They stand out and solicit my glance, which responds more effectively to the degree that I know my way: to find my way is to find them out. This is why the appropriate mode of glancing is a free, unbound glancing *out* (of which glancing around and glancing about are variations). I glance out to discover what beckons to be found out.

Being oriented is knowing how to find my way along particular routes, and it entails knowing several ways to get somewhere. But knowing how to find my way by various routes—and in various conditions, including different moods—is not just knowing how to get from one place to another. It is also putting myself in a position to discover and appreciate the by-places and regions that cluster around and about the route I am taking. Finding my way is finding out what is on the way—and sometimes just beyond.

B. *Knowing where you are.* Having found one's way is that aspect of being oriented that superintends motion in the place-world, giving to that motion the assurance it needs so as not to lose its way. But being oriented also involves knowing where you are—for example, knowing whether you are moving or not, en route or standing still, on a regular road or on the rudest unmarked path. At any moment, anywhere on any route, we can ask ourselves: Where am I? Not how did I get here, or where am I going, but *where am I now*? Or, in Joyce's wording, "Where are we at all?" This is the most basic single question of orientation. How do we begin to answer it?

One way *not* to answer it is to assume that this question is asking for anything like definite position—for example, geographic location or any other version of "simple location" in the early modern sense criticized so effectively by Whitehead.[38] This is to abstract from my felt locus: how it feels to be

---

38. See Alfred North Whitehead, *Science and the Modern World* (New York: Macmillan, 1962), pp. 72, 84, 98, 132, 224. For a comparable characterization, see Merleau-Ponty's claim that, for early modern thought, "every point of space is and is thought to be right where it is—one here, another there; space is the evidence of the 'where'" (Maurice Merleau-Ponty, "Eye and Mind," tr. C. Dallery, in *The Primacy of Perception*, ed. J. Edie [Evanston, Ill.: Northwestern University Press, 1964], p. 173).

where I am. It is to take myself out of place in order to determine precisely where my place is—just where it is in geographic space or, more vastly, in world-space. It is to reduce being here to being at an indifferent spot in space. On the other hand, I am not simply *here* either: to confine consideration to a pinpointed position having no significant environs is equally mistaken. Instead of too much abstraction, this is to invoke too much concretion. It is true that I am always *at* a place, *with* it and *in* it, but this implacement is so deeply immanent in a surrounding place-world as to resist reduction to a here-point that is analogous to the now-point in time.

Where I am is somewhere between infinite space and the sheer here: between unlimited expanse and the unextended point. It is not *everywhere*—as in Whitehead's own view that "in a certain sense, everything is everywhere at all times"[39]—and it is not just *anywhere* either. Nor is it exactly halfway between open space and the here-point. None of these ways of conceiving location captures the distinctive sense of being situated in a particular place; they de-situate this situation. At the very least, we must be able to say that I am *somewhere*—somewhere in relation to the near and far spheres of my current place-world. Straus is right: "In the landscape I am somewhere."[40] Not only do I "always get to one place from another,"[41] but I am *someplace* there at all times. What kind of a place is this?

The someplace is the minimal kind of place in which I can exist—yet a place whose structure is shared by all other places. This structure consists in *an intricate dialectic of here and there, which together constitute the matrix of the where.* Whenever I am located in a place, I am embroiled in the tensional arc of a here/there bipolarity that, rather than dividing my location, constitutes its inner armature.[42] The "here" at stake is no longer punctiform or self-absorbed; it is relative to the various "theres" that draw it out, forming with each one of these a dyad of intimate relationship. I am not just right here, as if at a sheer point, much less over there at another point; rather, I am always *here in relation to there,* a primary there recognized as such that is determined by the specific project in which I am engaged, as well as in relation to other, auxiliary or secondary theres that help to fill out my place-world. An instance of the first kind of there is the post office to which I repair

39. Whitehead, *Science and the Modern World,* p. 133. See the remarkably similar statement by Merleau-Ponty: "we are everywhere all at once" ("Eye and Mind," p. 187).

40. Straus, *The Primary World of Senses,* p. 321.

41. Ibid., p. 319.

42. On the tensional arc, see my *Getting Back into Place: Toward a Renewed Understanding of the Place-World* (Bloomington: Indiana University Press, 1993), pp. 55, 185. The following analysis builds on my treatment of the here/there structure in this earlier book while modifying it slightly. Nancy touches on a similar phenomenon when he writes that "the 'there' is the spacing of the tension, of the ex-tension" (Jean-Luc Nancy, "The Surprise of the Event," in his *Being Singular Plural,* tr. R. D. Richardson and A. E. O'Byrne [Stanford: Stanford University Press, 2000], p. 173).

if my project is to mail packages; the second kind would be present in the various intermediate locations by which I pass in getting to the post office in question. Each there, whether primary or secondary, is located in turn either in the near sphere or in the far sphere of the same world. When I glance freely, I glance *from here to there*—and often back again—within the compass of these intertwined spheres.

We are getting *somewhere*—by getting to the "where" of somewhere itself. To be somewhere is to be located betwixt here and there, in the area where they intersect. The complex location, the bi-location, arising from this intersection is my *whereabouts.* In the word "whereabouts" we can hear two things: "*about* where," that is, approximately somewhere rather than metrically or punctually positioned;[43] but also "where *about,*" that is, in the encirclement of any here by its corresponding theres as they are featured in the double domain of the near and the far. To be in the whereabouts of something is to be in its vicinity. It is to find it as encompassing me, whether nearby or faraway. My whereabouts surround me, and they are always about where I think they are.

It is a striking fact that there is no answering term "whenabouts"—despite Joyce's effort to create this latter word by means of an oxymoron: "Whenabouts in the name of space." Its only analogue in human experience is *duration* in Bergson's sense of a nonchronometric time in which I find myself continually immersed, in contrast with a clock-time that is removed from durational immanence and that gives me the temporal equivalent of positioning in space. Nevertheless, every here (as Hegel insisted) comes accompanied by its own now, and the combination of the two only deepens my sense of being oriented in the place-world—especially when this orientation is filled out by thens that specify the temporality of the theres that belong to every here.

I am somewhere when I am able to recognize and identify my whereabouts. Then my experienced here/now links up with a series of theres and thens that provide the spatiotemporal superstructure of every event of being oriented in the place-world. The result is that I am indeed some/where in my immediate landscape—always some/place there. Such whereness, such implacement, is indefinitely distributed in the "some" shared by the terms "somewhere" and "someplace": *some* signifying not several (for example, as in "some things") but something really situated (as "in some place"). The somewhere and the someplace, the two slopes of any whereabouts, are at once the condition and the result of orientation: the condition insofar as there would be no orientation without them, the result inasmuch as they articulate what is

---

43. This corresponds to the dictionary definition of "whereabouts" as "about where . . . the approximate location of someone or something" (*American Heritage Dictionary*). Curiously, the word can be either singular or plural, thereby reflecting the singularity of the "here" in conjunction with the plurality of "theres" to which it is almost always linked.

often blurred or tacit in orientation itself. They are held—better, stitched—together by glances that pick out particular by-places, places and regions that make up the content of my whereabouts at any given moment of time.

C. *Being at home in the world.* To be oriented is to be at home in the world. This does not mean that one is then perfectly relaxed and in a known domicile. One can be oriented somewhere and still be apprehensive or uneasy in certain regards: I am at the right place, say a homeless shelter, but I still am not certain whether I will eat tonight or with whom I will have to share a makeshift bed. Being at home in the world should not be confused with experiences of comfort or certainty. If I am oriented, I am at home to some significant degree, but I am not necessarily in my own home—or any home at all.

The most important single trait of being at home in the world is being *familiar* with that world—a place-world in which I am oriented. To be familiar is not just to know how to get somewhere, and not only to know where one is once there, but to find the place of something with which one is already acquainted to some degree. This acquaintance may consist merely in being able to say: I recognize just this particular piece of furniture or that painting or that wall color. But I can find familiar a place I have never visited before, either because it has been described to me extensively by someone else or because it is a type of place with which I am already acquainted. Familiarity does not require literal acquaintance with a literal place—only the sense that the place in question is within my ken and is not dissonant with my current state of orientation. (We signify this open possibility when we say that we "find X familiar." We may not have encountered it as such on a particular previous occasion, but it nevertheless reminds us of *some* prior experiences.)

"Familiar" is a linguistic cousin of the word "family" (via Latin *familiar*)—thus implying a mutually supportive social world. Hence its natural alliance with "home." But once again we must not be too literal. Just as "home" is not limited to the place where one's family of origin dwelled, so "family" itself exceeds one's kin. It includes any group of beings who together constitute a domestic environment. A neighborhood or a workplace can very well serve as a family, and one can find home in many places (not excluding desolate and isolated places). What ties together the familiar with the homelike is an ancient root of "family": *famulus*, Latin for servant or attendant. That with which I am familiar, in its full extension, is neither my actual home nor my genealogical family but what *attends me*.

Attendance is crucially constitutive of the familiarity that accompanies orientation. In being oriented, I am at home in the world in such a way that this world is my attendant. By this I mean three things.

(i) First, my place-world *attends to me:* it pays attention to my presence (literally so, if other humans are involved; but in other ways as well: the forest looks at me as much as I look at the forest). It is as if the other denizens of the place I am in cannot help but notice that I am in their midst. I in turn attend to them in their very familiarity.

(ii) These same entities *have regard for me;* I count on *their* perception and witnessing; my presence makes a difference to them, however diminutive this difference may in fact be. The regard here at stake is two-way, for I have regard for the other denizens just as they have for me. Indeed, my looking is not complete without theirs: one requires the other. As Georges Didi-Huberman puts it, "That which we see counts—lives—in our eyes only by that which looks back at us."[44] The resulting circle of regard is an extension of what Heidegger calls the "care-structure," a feature of all being-in-the-world; but where for Heidegger the caring stems primarily from a human being or Dasein, in the familiarity of an oriented world it comes just as much from the non-Dasein members of that world.

(iii) A third aspect of attendance is found in the way in which the fellow inhabitants of my place-world not merely take notice of me or have regard for me but *actively solicit me to look at them.* They draw me out precisely because they are so familiar; things less familiar to me would not be so effective in this respect since I would regard them with indifference or suspicion. The citizens of the place-world—nonhuman as well as human—solicit those who are at home in it. By "solicit" I have in mind such things as luring me to enter further into this world, asking me to linger longer there, warning me of an impending crisis, and so on. In each of these ways, the members of the place-world, my familiars, prove solicitous, acting to move me ("solicit" means in origin "to move as a whole"). In our familiarity with these diverse members we are open to being moved by them—to being the targets of their earnest solicitation.

Each of these three modes of attendance—by which the familiarity of being at home in the world is enacted and reinforced—is accomplished by acts of glancing: "a glimpse," says James Elkins, "is the glance of an object—it is the way an object glances at us."[45] Attending to something is most swiftly and often most effectively achieved by glances, whether these be my own or those of things that surround me. So, too, the regard that passes back and forth between myself and the occupants of my place is effected by an exchange of glances from both sides: to "re-gard" means literally "to look back" or "to look again." Moreover, solicitation is concretely conveyed by a glance or its felt equivalent: I am solicited not just by how the place-world looks but also by how it looks *at me*, that is, by how it

44. "Ce que nous voyons ne vaut—ne vit—que par ce qui nous regarde" (Georges Didi-Huberman, *Ce que nous voyons, ce qui nous regarde* [Paris:Éditions de Minuit, 1999], p. 9).
45. James Elkins, *The Object Stares Back: On the Nature of Seeing* (New York: Harvest, 1996), p. 207. The relationship between attending and glancing is discussed at length in chap. 9.

draws me out by its look. Every glance in such a world is at once a glance out and a glance back. Not only things but their surfaces glance out at me; their peculiar reflectance makes me pause and constitutes an invitation to do or think something differently. Things and their surfaces are the active ambassadors of the place-world.

Being at home in this world by dint of this triple play of attendant glances spells out and sustains my familiarity with it. To at-tend and to be at-tended (to) in such an interplay of looks is to be in a world in which glancing-at is fostered, along with glancing-around: both of these basic forms of glancing help me to find my way there and finally to be there. Thanks to this continually reinforced familiarity, I am able to extend my place-knowledge beyond what I would know were I to be entangled in an exclusively interhuman exchange of glances. Once oriented and thus at home in the world—acquainted with it and, still more effectively, familiar with it—I am in a position to find out new things about it and to appreciate it anew. I am better able to see *what awaits me there:* awaits my ever-renewed glance, gives me glances I did not anticipate, and allows me to give new glances back.

Thanks to the intimate domain of the familiar, my being at home in the world is not merely habitual, repetitive, or predictable. Instead of being merely routine, to be oriented in places in which I feel at home is a matter of a continually reopening attendance of things upon me and I upon them. In this co-attendance is to be found what I did not expect: the quotient of the new over the renewed, the spontaneous over the habitual—and, at the same time, the different within the same, the unknown within the known, the unfamiliar within the familiar itself.

XI

Something else is at play in being oriented in all three forms just examined: knowing how to find my way, knowing where I am, and being at home in the world. To be oriented in any of these ways stems from a peculiar process of *double-tracking*—indeed, a triple double-tracking. I have in mind the fact that when we are oriented, this happens at three levels, each dyadically structured: landscape/geography, near sphere/far sphere, here/there.

(a) *landscape/geography.* In the absence of particular obstacles, we are aware of where we stand vis-à-vis both the landscape in Straus's sense of the term (that is, the immediate arena of bodily sensing and movement) *and* the geographic whole made up of perceptual objects and their spatiotemporal medium (of which maps are efforts at explicit representation). On the one hand, I experience the world underfoot and overhead as well as by my side: in short, the environing place-world in its physiognomic character. But I also experience the same world regarded geographically—that is, as part of a larger whole, typically a city or an entire region. As I have argued, this geographic world is by no means incompatible with the landscape world but can enter into it; and this ingression is what allows me to keep track of both at once: to grasp where I am in regard to each at any given moment. It is as if my consciousness had at least two streams parallel to each other and yet also overlapping, thereby enabling me to be aware of them as a twosome whose members are at once distinguishable and together.

(b) *near sphere/far sphere*. We are also conscious in tandem of where we are situated in regard to the near and far spheres, bringing these latter into each other's close company—as already begins to happen in becoming oriented. By the time we are well oriented, the matrix of the somewhere and the someplace has knit together near and far places, if not into a seamless whole then into a coherent collocation of such places. Even when I am in the midst of this intimate intercalation, I am able to keep my eye both on what is near to me and on what is farther away: to see them in their differences even as they are united in my experience. I keep track of each sphere on its own *and* of both at once. To be oriented in the place-world requires the inclusion of both spheres as doubly tracked in their very convergence.

(c) *here/there*. Even the here and the there are tracked twice. Despite the close enmeshment of their tensional arc—each here calling for its own set of primary and secondary theres, and vice versa—the oriented subject is at all times able to distinguish them, to put each in its place. Nevertheless, there could be no sense of being *here* without an awareness of the apposite *theres* with which it is associated (and again the reverse). I know myself to be here (not as a pinpointed position but as concretely *where* my body now is) at the same time that I know myself to be over there in my perception or desire, interest or history. I know myself to be situated in relation to both simultaneously—the two poles of my proximal place-world being at once distinct and continuous.

Subtending all three forms of double-tracking is the glance, which dashes back and forth between the members of each pair of terms. I glance from my landscape world to the more encompassing geographic world and back again, taking in both at once by a distinctive double movement. Similarly, I conjoin the near and far spheres by my glance even as I hold them apart by the same glancing action: I *see* them to be different even as I know them both to belong to the same visual field. So, too, it is my glance that anneals the brittle bipolarity of here/there even as it discerns their distinctness. In every instance, then, the glance is a primary agent for determining difference within sameness—in short, for the double-tracking that is an indispensable component of being oriented in the place-world.

Just why is the glance so effective here? The connection between the members of each pair is not just something we cognize: only abstractly, at the level of the concept, can we say that we know that the here and there, near and far,

landscape and geography are members of the same dyad. In practice, the particular conjunctions are ever new, since the specific way in which the here or the
far of a given landscape appears differs from circumstance to circumstance,
even from one moment to the next. Only the glance has the requisite agility and
alertness to link the respective members of a dyad as paired, and to do so "in
the twinkling of an eye." The gaze is too laborious, too plodding, to accomplish
this task.

Closely associated with such thrice-realized double-tracking by the darting
glance is the experience of gaining our *bearings*. "To get your bearings" means
becoming geared into the environing world, anchored there bodily, fitting into its
existing structurations by means of an ongoing engagement in double-tracking.[46]
Thanks to this engagement, I am stably situated with regard to the relation
between landscape and geography, near and far, here and there. But getting
one's bearings also connotes becoming grounded with respect to various landmarks, place-marks, and other orientational signs in the surrounding world.
Here I refer not just to a single disambiguating factor—for example, a particular
street sign at a given intersection—but to a multiplicity of things that stud the
surrounding landscape and act as so many indicators of where I am or where I am
going: billboards, whole buildings and massive hills, a sunset. These fill out the
orientational scene and give to it a fund of relevant information that supplements
what I glean from the other clues on which I so often rely (for example, cartographic maps, mental maps, place memories, and so on).

The common phrase "taking your bearings" means to determine your position by taking into account all the relevant locatory signs: the configuration of
certain stars, a series of landmarks, printed atlases, general geographical lore
(including narratives of the region), and much more. We take our bearings by
taking in as much information as is available at the time; we "triangulate" our
position by reference to three or more pertinent items in our current perception; we bear out our relation to the landscape by discerning which among its
plethora of placial clues are most relevant. The discernment is accomplished by
the glance in its capacity of glancing out—leaping out to the diverse locational
indicators around us so as to find our bearings in their midst. Beyond double-
tracking, the glance takes us swiftly and surely to these various markers. If it is
the body that gears us into the place-world, it is the glance that takes the
bearings of this world and thereby tells us where we stand within its encompassing but sometimes deeply ambiguous embrace.

The broad orientational significance of double-tracking and of getting our
bearings, both consummated by the glance, is never more appreciated than
when we are in a circumstance in which we lose access to them. This very
circumstance occurred as I was returning to Chicago from Ann Arbor later that
same night. I had been moving along Highway 94 quite well—believing I was

---

46. Merleau-Ponty says explicitly that "the body is our anchorage in the world" (*Phenomenology of Perception,* tr. C. Wilson [London: Routledge, 2002], p. 167).

making good time to Chicago—when suddenly a dense fog moved in, blown off the surface of Lake Michigan, along whose southeastern edge I was then driving. The density was such that I could not see more than thirty feet in front of my car, which seemed to be entirely enclosed in its insistent presence.

As I set out from Ann Arbor (despite the momentary confusion that occurred as I was first turning onto Highway 94), I had been gloating in my having become oriented in that city—finally. But here I was disoriented again, now in a more dangerous modality. I could still make out the painted white lines between the lanes—barely—but beyond this and the palpable sense that my car was traveling over the concrete highway itself, I could not see anything further. I was beginning to imagine the worst: going over the edge of the highway into a ravine, straying into the oncoming lane.

In short, I could not glance out effectively; I could only glance in—into the inscrutable depths of the fog that swirled about me. My outlook had become a considerably constricted in-look. My place-world had shrunken to the inside of my car and the interiority of the fog bank that surrounded it. Where was I at all in space? This was not so much unorientation (I still had the highway to orient me in some minimal way: at least it was leading in the right direction) or even disorientation (which connotes a confusion as to just where I am in geographical space) as *dys-orientation:* a deeply dysfunctional relationship to orientation, an immersion in the environing world so complete that I could not see my way out of it, much less through it.

The immediate effect of this fogbound state was to eliminate any effective double-tracking on my part. I could not keep one eye on my situation in the local landscape and the other on my situation in the larger geographic world, for the latter was now altogether occluded. Nor could I make any meaningful distinction between near sphere and far sphere: the far had not entered into the near (as happens when I am successfully oriented) but had disappeared from view. By the same token, I could not take my bearings: not just because my usual ability to double-track myself in several ways had been suspended but because, more importantly, the galaxy of supplementary locational signs was no longer visible. The claustrophobic sense I felt was due not only to the closely confining fog but also to the conspicuous absence of indicators as to where I was in relation to what lay beyond the bare strip of highway to which I was so desperately clinging. There was nothing to gear into—nothing beyond the indeterminate and dimly illumined fog swirling about me. There was no there there.

My usual orientational resources were lacking in this nightmarish circumstance: not just double-tracking and knowing how to take my bearings but also my sense of being at home in the world: no matter how well acquainted I had become previously with the ground over which Highway 94 moves, I could not feel at home there any longer. On the contrary, I was very much at sea on this very ground! No longer was there a secure sense of familiar surroundings: there was nothing to which I could attend except the measureless inner surface of the fog, and the fog itself possessed no features that could attend to me. This double in-attention reflected the fact that there were no discrete items *at* which I or anyone could glance. Instead, a blur of glancing ahead and around—looking that was on the verge of becoming a hypnotic gaze—had taken the place of the accusative and attentive focus of glancing at.

In this perplexing circumstance, my prior confidence that I knew how to find my way to Chicago was undermined, since I knew that I could lose my way at any moment—for example, were I to turn off the highway inadvertently onto a sideroad—and, in the end, I could not say that I knew where I was. I was certainly *in the fog*, but *where* was I in it? Where was I anyway, in what place? Indeed, *where* was the fog itself—where did it begin and end? These disturbing questions kept coming at me as I made my way through the fog—which put me in the unhappy situation of feeling that I was no-place in no-space. Instead of being in a known place that ensues from effective double-tracking, I was enveloped in a lostness that did not know its own name: I was not lost in the usual sense (I knew I was *somewhere* between Ann Arbor and Chicago) but lost within the found—or at least, lost within what could be found once again.

Just as becoming oriented in a strange place can be strenuous, so being oriented is precarious. In a matter of minutes, orientation can be wiped out, with no assurance of its return. In my own case, it did return—albeit very slowly. After almost two excruciating hours, I suddenly spotted the moon drifting just above the fog, which looked dead black beneath it. The moon did not orient me, but it was a relief to behold it: at least there was *something* that managed to escape this blasted fog! Then, a half-hour later, the fog bank thinned out and began to lift, just as I was entering Chicago, whose brilliant night-lights were never more welcome. These lights restored an entire layer of locatory signs, whose absence I had felt so acutely back in Michigan and eastern Illinois. I felt re-oriented by their mere presence—in one stroke they proffered to me a larger and brighter place-world, a city-world that embraced with open arms the lonely and exhausted traveler.

In coming to Chicago from Ann Arbor, I passed from dysorientation to orientation just as earlier I had moved from unorientation and disorientation to orientation in Ann Arbor itself. Oriented twice over, I was ready to consider something else—something new and different.

XII

This something else is the *surprising*, the last gift of orientation and its final fruit. To be oriented is to be in a position to be surprised. We here return to my claim in the introduction that the surprising belongs intrinsically to the experience of glancing. In fact, we have been edging toward the surprising at several points in this chapter. I have said that in being oriented I become open to such things as discovery and appreciation, the unexpected and the unfamiliar and the unknown. Just because I *am* oriented—and no longer coping with the challenge and confusion of *becoming* oriented—I am able to glance out in new ways, and thus to be ready for surprise, even to embrace it eagerly.

The better implaced I am, the more fully I am oriented, the more my glance is able to travel without undue constraints from its immediate environment. The glance, essential to the process of becoming oriented in its free and bound and geographic guises, is now liberated to carry out a more extensive project of being in touch with the world. Indeed, the very anchorage of orientation releases the glance to be receptive in new ways that are no longer of mainly functional significance in the establishment of orientation. Such receptive world-openness is tantamount to being open to the real possibility of being surprised.

The situation is this: now that I know where I am, now that I have found my way, now that I am at home in the world, I am able to exercise my glance for nonpractical purposes. I can release it from any spirit of gravity that may have slowed down or shadowed over its employment. Now I can release it to the alleviated spirit of being receptive to surprise. The surprising buoys up the glance with its gift of the unanticipated, its leap into the unknown, its sudden-ness of event. As Nancy says, "the surprise is that the leap . . . surprises itself."[47] Surprising itself, the event toward which I leap surprises me as its witness. The invocation of the leap signifies that I am not burdened down by the demands of getting oriented in strange surroundings.

As the "-prise" part of the word "surprise" signifies (*prise* means "take" in French), when I glance freely outward I am *taken by surprise*. But as the "sur-" prefix connotes (*sur* means "over" or "upon"), I am also *overtaken by it*: that is to say, exceeded or surpassed.[48] Like a truck on Highway 94 that overtakes me on the left, surprise passes me by from every side. But to be overtaken thus is not simply to be *overcome*. Were the latter to be the case, I would be set back into disorientation once again—or worse yet, into dysorientation, as when fog over-came me on my return trip to Chicago. Instead, in being surprised I am sur-passed by what I had not expected, yet not in such a way as to lose my bearings, much less my way (as is more likely to occur in astonishment or trauma). I remain oriented, I stay in place even as I am overtaken, but I allow myself to be discombobulated by what I had not expected. Indeed, it is precisely because I am so securely oriented that I can let this upset happen. *I let myself be taken over by surprise itself:* I let myself leap toward it even as it moves toward me.

The surprising delivered by my glance is the ambiguous but powerful com-bination of my *letting something happen*—a free act, always within my volition—and *something happening to me*, something outside my control. My stake in this is at once active (that is, in getting oriented in the first place) and receptive (in

---

47. Nancy, "The Surprise of the Event," p. 173. Nancy also states that "surprise is nothing except the leap right at being (*à même l'être*)" (p. 172). Nancy here carries forward the earlier description of the leap by Kierkegaard and Heidegger.

48. See Nancy's comments on surprise as involving a factor of "unexpected arrival" (*sur-venue:* literally, "coming up"): ibid., p. 168 and translator's footnote 9.

allowing myself to be taken over by the surprising once I am oriented). It is both of these while avoiding the extremes of possessiveness and passivity. Toward the surprising captured by my glance I am not in the least possessive, since my aim is not to seize it and master it but just to take it in. But I am not merely passive toward surprise either, as if my role were merely to register it. The receptivity here in question is also something different from letting myself be instructed by my environs, looked at by its denizens, or even solicited by them. Instead of these actions—each of which is an important ingredient in becoming oriented—I am *gripped* by the surprising. To be gripped connotes a constructive combination of activity and receptivity: I am grip*ped*, that is, taken over, but it is myself who lets such gripping happen. I let it happen insofar as I am open to being moved—emotionally "struck"—by the unexpected: by what I could neither fully anticipate nor fully understand once it occurs.

Although I can be surprised by aspects of things and even though surprise is conveyed to the glance by the surfaces of things and places, what is finally most surprising is the very happening, the *taking place* that I witness. I let this happening grip me; I let it be an *event*. Such an event is not just something that occurs indifferently; it is an occurrence that has enough bite or poignancy to attract my attention and to grip my glance. An e-vent (literally, an "out-come") is something that *stands out* in my experience. Hence it is able to engage my glancing out: one *out* connects with the other. This is why an event, strictly speaking, is always surprising: "the event surprises or else it is not an event."[49] It surprises me as exceeding my glance even as it evokes it. The event at which I glance—noting its aspects and surfaces (for example, its comparative speed, its felt force, its visual configuration)—is outside what I have thought I would find; but it is not entirely beyond my ken; its outer edge, its spatiotemporal happening in a particular place, joins up with the outer edge of my looking; the two edges conjoin; the event comes out to meet me in the action of the glance I cast toward it.

The character of the surprising that I encounter in the glance vacillates between two extremes. On the one hand, it can be just the "pleasantly surprising," that is to say, the mildly titillating or merely distracting: but this does not take me over, there is nothing to grip me here. On the other hand, the surprising can approach the shocking. Taken in its full force, this would indeed overwhelm me, chasing the glance away and calling instead for intense scrutiny (that is, a form of gazing)—or outright flight. In most instances, however, the surprising leaps out at me but stops short of shock even as it exceeds the merely diverting. It indi-

---

49. Nancy, "The Surprise of the Event," p. 167. See also ibid., p. 174: "there is an event, a surprise." Nancy, on whose notion of event (ultimately inspired by Heidegger's *Ereignis*) I here draw, is less convincing with regard to the perception of events as surprising. He places this perception under the heading of a "pure vision" that is more reminiscent of the gaze than the glance, despite his own insistence that such vision has to do with the sudden (it occurs "in a flash" [p. 174]; on the sudden, see p. 163) and is "outside itself" (p. 174). On pure vision, see p. 174; on the surprise inherent in thinking, see p. 175.

cates to me that a certain course of action—the course of complacency, of self-satisfied stultification—will have to be altered from here on. After being surprised, I can't go on glancing in the older manner, as if nothing had happened.

The surprising event of which I take notice is now taking me *out of my way:* say, suddenly encountering an old friend in a place where I did not expect to encounter him. His appearance does not take me so far out of my way as to disorient me, much less to induce dysorientation, but still I am "de-routed": I am put off the track, the double-track, of my previous orientation. I am momentarily be-wildered (as *se dérouté* connotes in French)—dazzled if not disturbed. In being surprised by seeing my friend just here, I am being open to what does not fit my expectations about this place. Something different, something new, has happened.[50] But it is not so different, or so new, as to *keep* me off the track: only the "absolutely surprising," the consternating, would do this.[51] Moved as I am by suddenly seeing my friend and disconcerted as I may be by this unanticipated event, I do not lose my stride because of it: I greet him and begin to talk with him. I remain rooted in the place-world to which I have become oriented by my earlier glances. To be momentarily displaced by surprise is not to lose my route altogether, much less to become seriously lost. It is to stay oriented, even if I am now taking a momentary detour. It is to persist in the place-world, albeit moving through it differently than I would have thought I would before being surprised.

To be surprised when glancing is to experience a subtle difference in the visual world. This is not a difference that makes all the difference in subsequent perception. But it may make a significant difference with regard to orientation. This is so in two ways. On the one hand, it may act to confirm the rightness of my present orientation: in which case, it will induce the confirmatory glances of which I spoke earlier. If I am surprised to see hills on the highway in Michigan, this exceptional perception does not undermine my general impression—gleaned from much glancing en route—that the state is nonetheless mostly flat. On the other hand, the difference that surprise makes may act to re-orient me—to convince me that I need to find new ways to be (or to get) somewhere. Not because the surprising event I encounter has taken away my prior orientation: this latter remains as a condition of surprise itself; but because new directions and new possibilities have been opened up in my place-world. As Hamlet says, "There are more things in heaven and earth, Horatio, than are dreamt of in your philosophy."[52] Indeed—and this *more* is often delivered by the glance as it encounters the surprising. From the glance, acting as a touchstone, new ways of doing something as seemingly ethereal as philosophy itself can take their rise.

---

50. Nancy denies the relevance of the new to the surprising; surprise "is not some newness of Being that would be surprising in comparison to the Being that is already given Being" (ibid., p. 171). But if it is true that the surprising cannot be reduced to novelty alone, the new does characterize it in many cases.

51. On "absolute surprise" as "the nonpresence of the coming to presence," see ibid., p. 172.

52. Shakespeare, *Hamlet*, Act One, scene five, ll. 186–187.

XII

Proceeding in this chapter from a circumstance of disorientation in the city—
and from a look at the unorientation that often precedes this—while considering
later a case of dysorientation on the highway, I have examined how we become
oriented in place and in space: how this is achieved, with what direct means of
our own, and by way of what external assistance. This has allowed us to investigate in turn the state of being oriented itself, especially in terms of its three
major modes: knowing how to find your way, knowing where you are, and feeling
at home in the world. When these modes are fully achieved, we are brought to
the brink of the surprising as it emerges at the edge of events and things we
encounter, or by letting ourselves be gripped by what the world offers to us.
Surprise takes this moment of excess (excessive in relation to the demands and
necessities of orientation itself) one step further: to be surprised is to let ourselves be influenced by the extraordinary within the ordinary.

If extraordinary enough, the surprising content of our glances may lead us to
consider, and then to take, new orientational stances in the place-world. When I
meet an inspiring person whose exemplary behavior takes me by surprise, I may
well consider changing my orientation to suit this new circumstance: perhaps by
undertaking a new course of study, or by painting or writing in untried ways, or
by altering the way I conduct myself ethically or politically. If I take this kind of
lead from surprise, I may even find myself entering a new phase of my life, re-
orienting myself not only in place or space but at a different level with its own
rigors and requirements, on the way to an altogether different sense of what
being oriented means—where and how and with regard to what.

In all of this, along the way and at every stage, the glance plays an indispensable if largely neglected role. It does so in one or more of its major forms of free,
bound, and geographic glancing—forms that are ingredient in becoming and in
remaining oriented. Glancing spans the differences between landscape and
geography, near and far spheres, and the here and there. It is the moving force in
the double-tracking that each of these binary pairs entails. It also figures into
orientation in many other ways: as the glancing-at of concerted perception, the
glancing-around that establishes both my immediate place as well as more extensive geographic layouts, and the glancing-out that allows me to transcend my
current confinements and to take in the surprising itself. When I am in the midst
of getting oriented in a new situation, I glance back and forth, down and about,
over and around, in and out. I glance every which way in an effort to get my
bearings. And when I have become stably oriented, I continue to glance in every
accessible direction—to keep my bearings and to maintain a steady stance in the
place-world even in the most confusing circumstances, and to be receptive to
new encounters with the surprising.

Glancing is never far from the central scene of orientation, and it is actively
present even in the outskirts. Thanks to its alert polyformity and its remarkably
skillful means, it does not fail to disclose those surfaces of the place-world that

will serve to situate us in its midst, all the while letting us stay open to surprise in the same midst. To glance is essential to being and becoming oriented in unfamiliar places—and re-oriented in still other places. Glancing is where a great deal of the action is to be found, whether this action be that of seeking and initiating orientation or that of confirming and deepening it. It is an indissociable part of the very event of orientation itself, taking us into the place-world in ever more subtle and significant ways.

4

THE HEGEMONY OF THE GAZE

> The alterity that disturbs order cannot be reduced
> to the difference visible to the gaze that compares
> and therefore synchronizes the same and the other.
>
> —Emmanuel Levinas, "Phenomenon and
> Enigma"

Among ways of looking at the surrounding world, two stand out as especially significant. These are gazing and glancing, the two great modes of human looking—where this latter is to be construed as the basic form of visual perception or "seeing." Looking itself is modally neutral, and as such it is specified into glancing, gazing, and still other modes, each of which has its own set of realizations, its own taxonomy. But gazing and glancing are of special significance in the domain of vision; together, they represent the two ends of an entire axis that extends from steady, continuous looking to darting and discontinuous seeing. This is not the only axis that counts—others include looking in the service of other acts ("instrumental seeing," for example, for the sake of survival), visionary looking (for instance, messianic, religious, and so forth), looking in specific contexts (such as artistic life, social life, and more)—but it constitutes an indispensable dimension of human experience, since it has everything to do with just how our look is invested in the various place-worlds we inhabit. It may linger within one of these worlds, or it may move restlessly among them—or somehow manage to do both. With gazing and glancing, then, we have to do with quite central ways of being in the visual world.

I

When I gaze at something, I allow my look to linger—to caress the surface of what I'm looking at, or else to plumb its depths patiently. Gazing is taking in the world at one's own pace; it is open-eyed, literally unblinking, as if I were swimming in the ocean of the world with my eyes open. And I keep them open throughout; there is a duration proper to the gaze: a sense of a certain leisure, of having sufficient time in which to accomplish my aim. That aim can be various; I gaze for many reasons and to many different effects. But each episode of gazing is comparatively unhurried: indeed, I cannot gaze at high speed. It is thanks to this very property—which can be frustrating when I am under pressure—that the gaze is valued so highly in certain philosophical or scientific contexts that prize the very gravitas of the gaze, its sloe-eyed character, its conscientious inhabitation of an object or event.

We gaze in many ways. We concentrate (a concerted gazing in the midst of distractions), we gape (when we see something so extraordinary that our mouth falls open), we ogle (gazing by an ostentatious engagement of the eyes). But I shall restrict consideration here to the following five major modes of gazing.

contemplating: In contemplating something, I look with a "soft" focus (where "focus" implies a concerted looking); the action is open and patient—even to the point of being meditative, either in a technical sense of "meditative practice" (where one gazes at a fixed point in space) or in an informal sense of "being in a meditative mood." As the "con-" of "contemplative" signifies, I am *with* what I contemplate; I am sitting (or standing) with it, in its very presence; I am not trying to alter it, to master it, or even to study it. My gaze is invested in the act of contemplation itself, not in its object; what matters most is the investment I am making; yet this investment is nonurgent. My eyes are open—not so as to discover any hidden structure but so as to bathe in the atmosphere, the "medium" (as both Levinas and Gibson call the elemental matrix in which substances and their surfaces appear).

scrutinizing: When my look becomes more focused, it singles out a distinct object (or set of objects: a scene). Now I am looking *for* something, whether this be a mere detail or an overall structure; I am no longer content to be engrossed in the sheer looking (as contemplating often is) but want to *find* something in particular—something that inheres in the object or scene. In order to accomplish this, I must invest my energies in the looking itself, not for the pleasure of merely looking (as is frequently the case with contemplating) but for the sake of detecting and holding fast to what I am scrutinizing; an element of visual fixation is here present.

scanning: Closely related to scrutiny is scanning, a systematic deployment of the gaze. Now I direct my look over a privileged set of surfaces so as not to let anything relevant escape my look—relevant, that is, to my basic visual search. In this case, I may seek technological assistance, for example, in the form of binoculars or a telescope; these prosthetic devices extend the range or the detail of my scanning operation; but I must still *direct them* by my own visual intentionality: in scanning, I am the active operator—much more so than in contemplating, when I am characteristically dependent on some detail in the place-world.

staring: This is a still more focused form of gazing; I stare *at* something, where the "at" indicates the delimited and specific character of that at which I stare; the stared-at object is almost always a human being or event, and it is this because of some outstanding or unusual feature of a person or action: something in particular inspires my stare, usually something incongruous, "odd," eccentric. In its very intensity, the stare answers to what Husserl calls the "obtrusion" of things in my environment: I wouldn't stare unless something had obtruded upon my attention and drew my gaze straight to it—and kept it there.[1]

glaring: When the stare becomes still more intense, it becomes a glare; but now the state of the subject is more constitutive than is the object: a glare almost always evinces hostility to some degree; not only have I been led to look by something untoward, but this very untowardness bothers me: I cannot accept it with equanimity; I feel the need to *look back,* not just to vent my frustration but to get back at that which has irritated me; hence the characteristic accompanying gestures of the glare: furrowed brows, beady eyes; overall, there is an effort to dominate the other by my look: to make it clear who is in control in any real (or imagined) contest of looks.

From this schematic survey we can see that gazing is not so much a single sort of looking as an entire *way* of looking that has several species, each of which is distinct yet all of which share certain basic features: unhurriedness, open-eyedness, a tendency to focus and to fixate (albeit less completely so in the case of contemplation), and an interest in getting at the structure or essence of something. Two things above all are important in every type of gazing: *taking in* and *getting at the depth.* A gaze aspires to take in—not just to apprehend but to internalize— what it is engaged with. Its concern is not with noticing as such, much less with altering its content in any way. To gaze at something is to immerse oneself in it to such a degree that this something becomes part of one's ongoing perceptual history: a resource for one's subsequent looking. At the same time, gazing is getting into the depth of the gazed-at. If it takes something into oneself in the interiorization just mentioned, it also takes itself into the interior of the same something. Thus it combines two modes of interiority, that within (or coincident with) oneself and that without (identical with the depths of the content or scene). To gaze is to conjoin the incoming with the outgoing; hence its remarkable range, not only in terms of its plural forms but in view of the scope of its content: the gaze is not just perceptual but interpersonal, historical, political, social, and religious. In the end, the gaze manages to go just about everywhere that human interests may wish to go, acting as a conduit for these interests.

No wonder the gaze has been so attractive to religious thinkers and scientists, who have vested interests in taking the world in as well as in looking into its depths. But it has been even more seductive to philosophers. A recent book by

---

1. In the concluding thoughts, I contrast "stare" with "gaze" as if they were different acts; but this is only to say that if we insist on contrasting them, the two modes of vision can be regarded as separable; but in the current context, where I am not seeking contrast but assimilation, staring can be regarded as one of several kinds of gazing.

David Michael Levin has the revealing title: *The Philosopher's Gaze.*[2] Levin demonstrates the paradigmatic position of the gaze in Western philosophy from the very beginning to the present day. Philosophy is said by Aristotle to begin in "wondering" (*thaumazein*), of which the gaze is the natural accompaniment. To wonder at something is to stand before it in open-eyed amazement; it is to take it in fully and freely—free of prejudice and presupposition.[3] Husserl, at the other end of the history of philosophy, requires "presuppositionlessness" (*Vorausetzungslosigkeit*) as the starting point of philosophy: this, too, calls for a certain gazing into the heart of things—into their "essence" (*Wesen*) in Husserl's preferred term—freed from the prejudices of the "natural attitude" that closes down upon the gaze, constraining it to a "squint,"[4] that is, the very opposite of the gaze. What Husserl calls "essential intuition" (*Wesensschau*) is the methodologically sanctioned equivalent of the gaze, which triumphs over the myopia of the natural attitude. In such intuition, one looks essences straight in the face, without the fetters of naturalistic interpretations, that is to say, without "the prejudice in favor of an objective world," as Merleau-Ponty puts it.[5] The aim of phenomenological method is to gaze unblinkingly into the way things are—into their necessary structures, that without which they would not be what they are.

One could not look so forthrightly without the proper illumination in which to see—without an open, lighted area. This is what Husserl calls "the sharply illuminated circle of perfect givenness" and Heidegger "the Open" or "the Clearing."[6] One cannot gaze properly in flickering light or in the semidarkness. One needs steady light and lots of it if the gaze is to pursue its task of concerted looking into the heart of things. J. J. Gibson has famously proposed that information is "in the light"[7]—that is, the circumambient light that surrounds us in daylight or in artificial light at other times. By the same token, the essences sought by Husserl (and much earlier by Aristotle) are available to philosophical examination only in the light: the clarified light of consciousness (or of active

---

2. The full title is *The Philosopher's Gaze: Modernity and the Shadows of Enlightenment* (Berkeley: University of California Press, 1999).

3. For further treatment of wonder, see chap. 6, part 3.

4. On the squint, see M. Heidegger, *Being and Time*, tr. J. Macquarrie and E. Robinson (New York: Harper and Row, 1962), p. 175: "When irrationalism, as the counterplay of rationalism, talks about the things to which rationalism is blind, it does so only with a squint." For presuppositionlessness, see Edmund Husserl, Prolegomena to the *Logical Investigations*, tr. J. N. Findlay (New York: Humanities Press, 1970), vol. 1.

5. See Maurice Merleau-Ponty, *Phenomenology of Perception*, tr. C. Smith (New York: Humanities Press, 1962), p. 6.

6. Husserl's phrase is found at *Ideas Pertaining to a Pure Phenomenology and to a Phenomenological Philosophy: First Book: General Introduction to a Pure Phenomenology*, tr. F. Kersten (The Hague: Nijhoff, 1982), p. 157 (hereafter referred to as *Ideas I*). Heidegger's ideas of the Open and Clearing are found in many places, first of all in *Being and Time*, p. 171, and later, for example, in "Conversation on a Country Path," in *Discourse on Thinking*, tr. J. M. Anderson and E. H. Freund (New York: Harper and Row, 1966), p. 74.

7. See J. J. Gibson, *The Ecological Approach to Visual Perception* (Hillsdale, N.J.: Erlbaum, 1979), chap. 14, "The Theory of Information Pickup and its Consequences."

intellect in Aristotle's case). The natural attitude closes down on the light required for clear intuition, and its suspension is meant to make such light available for essential insight. *The gaze thrives in light,* which is its very medium. "To
open oneself to the gaze," says Levinas, is "to inundate it with light."[8] But
the issue is not just quantity of light—whereby more light should entail more
insight—but the right kind of light: that which facilitates and supports philosophical (and other sorts of) intuition.[9] This is not confined to physical light, that
is, to the effects of photons; it can be the light provided by language (as Heidegger emphasizes) or by human action (as Aristotle and Kant would both insist) or
by the visual environment (as Gibson maintains). "Light" signifies a sustaining
medium that clears a space for lucid thinking.

There can be no doubt that the gaze and its illuminative matrix provide the
most characteristic scene for philosophical reflection. Paradigmatic instances
abound. When Rembrandt painted *Aristotle Contemplating the Bust of Homer,*
he showed the Stagirite gazing at the head of Homer in a redoubled glow of
light: the literal illumination of a study in which the statue was placed and that
very different light furnished by the language of the blind bard. Rembrandt
painted this exemplary work in the middle of the seventeenth century—at the
very time when, and in the same country where, Descartes was first fashioning
philosophy in its modern guise. For all of his logical and geometrical rigor,
Descartes relied on the "natural light" as the ultimate source of philosophical
insight; such light is anything but naturalistic: it is the nonphysical light in which
reason understands in a definitive way the nature of space, the existence of God,
the character of thought, and matters of like importance.

Switch the scene to the middle of the twentieth century and one finds equally
regnant the primacy of the gaze in Sartre's early work, *Being and Nothingness.*
There, human relations are dominated by the gaze: *le regard,* the objectifying
look that makes the other person a being-for-me, and I a mere visual object for
her. My own outgoing consciousness is spontaneous and free from any such
petrification, but when it gazes at another human being—who as for-herself is
just as free as I—it endows that other with a carapace of characteristics, a
sclerotized presence that is foreign to freedom. As human beings gaze at each
other, a progressive perceptual fixation sets in. Not essences or insights but

---

8. The full statement is: "The infinite is a withdrawal like a farewell which is signified not by
opening oneself to the gaze to inundate it with light, but in being extinguished in the incognito
in the face that faces" ("Phenomenon and Enigma," in Emmanuel Levinas, *Collected Philosophical Papers,* tr. A. Lingis [Dordrecht: Nijhoff, 1987], p. 72). Compare Lacan: "In what
presents itself to me as the space of light, that which is gaze (*regard*) is always some play of light
and opacity." Also: "It is by the gaze that I enter into the light, and it is from the gaze that I
receive the effect of light" (Jacques Lacan, *Les quatre concepts fondamentaux de la psychanalyse,* ed. J.-A. Miller [Paris: Seuil, 1973], pp. 89–90 and 98).

9. There are precise parallels in science: the brightly lit laboratory, the clear space of
theorizing, the open field of critique and falsifiability, and the like.

delimited identities are gleaned by the gaze in the light of intersubjective relations.[10] "Hell is other people" precisely to the extent that I have objectified others—and they me—in the blinding light of the gaze. Each gazer adopts the mask of Medusa vis-à-vis the looked-at other.

The light of the gaze is blinding in both senses of the word: blinding as inundating ("all over the place"), but blinding also as making oneself blind to that which one is looking at in the eye of the gaze. In this way the opening of vision on which the gaze is predicated and promulgated in Western thought turns into closure—a closing down on the very openness that is its much-vaunted virtue. We enter here the "shadows of enlightenment" of which Levin speaks in the wake of Horkheimer, Adorno, and Benjamin.

The insightfulness of the gaze, the powers of its patient probing of the world of essence, comes with a price—indeed, three sorts of price that threaten the neutrality implied in saying, "I'm just gazing." First, its open-eyed stance conceals from itself the fact that one's gazing eyes are taking in only certain sorts of evidence to the exclusion of others. Under the banner of being open to whatever presents itself in intuition—albeit "only within the limits in which it is presented there"[11]—one is in fact restricted in what is seen: for "the limits of the giving" are often far more stringent than one had imagined. Sartre's model of gazing, for example, recognizes clearly the fossilized aspects of others, their tendency to fall into fixed patterns; but it is at the same time blind to their unpredictable generosities, their capacity to change in the very midst of their sameness, their power to be genuinely *other* to my very gaze, not just beings for-others but beings who exist outside the usual parameters of my perception.

Second, not only is there such closure *within* the Open of gazing itself but there is closure *before* the act has even taken place. I refer to the preselection of evidence—to the literal sense of "pre-judice" highlighted by Gadamer in *Truth and Method*. On the basis of the habitual fore-structure sedimented from one's entire life-history, one has already decided as to what will count as evidence, indeed even as to what will count as visible, as worthy of being seen at all: "ce qui vaut d'être regardé" in René Char's phrase.[12] I am already closed in my very

10. Levinas criticizes Sartre thus: "In Sartre the phenomenon of the other was still considered, as in all Western ontology, to be a modality of unity and fusion, that is, a reduction of the other to the categories of the same. This is described by Sartre as a teleological project to unite and totalize the for-itself and the in-itself, the self and the other-than-self. It is here that my fundamental philosophical disagreement with Sartre lay" (cited in Richard Kearney, *Dialogues with Contemporary Continental Thinkers: The Phenomenological Heritage* [Manchester: University of Manchester Press, 1984], p. 53).

11. See Husserl, *Ideas I*, p. 44. The full statement of "the Principle of All Principles" is that *"everything originally . . . offered to us in 'intuition' is to be accepted simply as what it is presented as being,* but also *only within the limits in which it is presented there"* (his italics).

12. Char's full statement is: "Si l'homme ne fermait pas *souverainement* les yeux il finirait par ne plus voir ce qui vaut d'être regardé" (his italics; cited by Lysane Fauvel in her essay "A Blind-Spot of the Sovereign Eye: On the Gaze in Merleau-Ponty and Lacan"). Earlier in the

openness. Third, contributing to this closure is the ineluctable *interpretation* I give to what I have just taken in by the gaze: indeed, interpretation after interpretation, often without any consciousness of my own interpretive activity. In such unself-aware activity, I twist what I have seen to suit my cognitive or personal, social or political satisfaction, all the while believing that the world just comes this way—that it is thus "laid out" (as *Aus-legung*, the German word for "interpretation," literally implies). No wonder I am so unaware of my own interpretive thrusts: *any* interpretation is tendentious in the context of the gaze, whose self-professed innocence it is felt to sully and spoil. It is like the shadow that consumes the light even as the light is shining forth; it defeats illumination at its own game.

In these three ways, then, the gaze proves problematic. For the Open into which it looks so intently is closed from within regarding what is admitted into its bright circle, closed from before its own opening, and closed from without by the force of the ways we construe it. All of these forms of foreclosure—which collude among themselves to the point where it is often difficult to distinguish between them—arise in the very midst of the manifest virtues of the gaze: its conscientious attentiveness, its patience, its highly inflected thoughtfulness, its aversion to drawing hasty conclusions. These are considerable philosophical (and religious and scientific) virtues whose value I would not want to gainsay. But they act to conceal the foreclosures to which I have just pointed, thereby undermining the proclaimed openness of the gaze itself.

Another such foreclosure is found in the fact that the gaze, for all its putative fullness and completeness, in fact curtails the role of the lived body in its own enactment. When I gaze in the manner recommended by philosophers or scientists—for example, when I scrutinize and scan something—the last thing of which I take account is my body. As I turn toward the light, I turn away from the organism that makes gazing itself possible in the first place: my body in the panoply of its perceptual powers. Just as I distance myself from the other in the Sartrian *regard*, so I distance myself from myself in the course of the gaze. In the one case, alienation from the other (and vice versa) results; in the other, alienation of myself from myself: self-alienation in the form of disembodiment.

We shall have occasion to return to the body, but there is another front on which we find a comparable duplicity at play. Not only is it "difficult for the gaze to limit itself to ascertaining appearances,"[13] but (as we have seen earlier) it seeks to get to the *depth* of things: to what lies *under* the manifest content of

---

same sentence I refer to Heidegger's notion of the *Vorstrukter* of knowledge—which was very influential in turn on Gadamer's model of "pre-judicial" knowing. See also *Being and Time*, pp. 192–195 and *Truth and Method* (New York: Seabury, 1975), pp. 245–274.

13. Jean Starobinski, *The Living Eye*, tr. A. Goldhammer (Cambridge, Mass.: Harvard University Press, 1989), p. 3. Starobinski adds: "By its very nature it must ask for more [than appearances]" (ibid.). Depth for Starobinski is understood as "the passion for the hidden" (ibid., p. 1).

what is seen by its means. It not only takes place in the Open; it opens up this Open in its depths, its infrastructures, its *bathos*. Descartes's natural light allows the philosopher's gaze to grasp the hidden mathematical substructures of physical extension—substructures not evident on the visible sleeve of things. Sartre's theory of interpersonal vision, following Freud *malgré lui,* shows the perverse underbelly of human relations, their sadistic and masochistic roots that are often inaccessible to the very subjects of these relations. Husserl's essences have to be laid bare once the incrustations of the natural attitude—its "garb of ideas" (*Ideenkleid*)—have been removed to let the light of the phenomenologist's gaze shine upon them.[14]

These various appeals to depth are often self-serving or at least self-supporting: just because essential structures come to us concealed thinkers consider themselves justified in employing a special philosophical method to get at them—a method prescribed by someone who is convinced that only by proposing a new procedure in philosophy or science will the truth of things become unconcealed. Moreover, it is not at all certain that gazing takes us into the depths of a given phenomenon to begin with. We do speak of "gazing into the depths"; but if this is to occur effectively, these depths must become accessible—on some surface, somewhere. Let us agree that, at the least, the depths sought by philosophers and scientists—and doubtless also by the religiously minded—must find their way to some significant plane of presentation if they are to be apprehended by any human look, whether this be a gaze or a glance. "The surface," as Gibson remarks, "is where most of the action is."[15]

II

The glance has a genius for surfaces. It takes pleasure in cavorting and circulating on their presence—in playing off them and playing on them. What light is for the gaze, surfaces are for the glance: they are its privileged medium. Although the deeper truth sought by the gaze must finally locate a surface to accomplish its mission, the way is often arduous, requiring a "hermeneutics of suspicion" (Ricoeur). The glance, in contrast, goes to surfaces outright as to its natural element. Even when it doesn't fasten on them as such, the merest glance finds in surfaces the proper arena for its enactment and does not seek (because it does not need) to go elsewhere to flourish. This is so whether the glance pauses momentarily on a given surface, or glides off it onto another surface. Either way, the scene of glancing is what Gibson designates as the "layout" of the visual environment: "the persisting arrangement of surfaces relative to one another

---

14. For the idea of the "garb of ideas," see E. Husserl, *The Crisis of European Sciences and Transcendental Phenomenology,* tr. David Carr (Evanston, Ill.: Northwestern University Press: 1970), "The Mathematization of Nature," section H.

15. Gibson, *The Ecological Approach to Visual Perception,* p. 23.

and to the ground."[16] The glance alights on surfaces, finding its way freely in their midst—not unlike a hummingbird flitting among the delicate surfaces of flowers in bloom. The glance is a literally superficial activity, and that is its very strength.

It follows that glancing is not well suited to plumb depths. Unlike the gaze, it does not even pretend to go into the depth below the surface. It stays on the surface as in its own habitat. It has nowhere else to go. It lives within the layout of the surface-world. If it is true that (as Gibson also claims) "the perception of layout takes the place of the perception of depth or space in traditional terminology,"[17] then this is all the more conspicuously true in the case of the glance. The glance does not need depth or space since it flourishes in the midst of surfaces and their layout. This layout may indicate depth or adumbrated space. But the glance is under no obligation to pursue that which is indicated or adumbrated; it suffices for it to attend to the perceived surfaces of the world, and it is quite content to do so. If nothing more is called for (to connect with a surface is to link up with a central feature of the perceived world), nothing less is expected (glances must attach to *something* if they are not to be utterly ephemeral, even if this something is as nonsubstantial as a surface).

A surface that is glanced at is a *part* of an object—part of a person, material thing, or event. The glance can be considered literally superficial (that is, a matter of being "on/the face," *sur* + *facies*, of something), but surfaces themselves are not superficial. They are attached—usually permanently—to that of which they are the surface; and they frequently give access to its very depth, thereby guaranteeing that this depth is not detached from what is perceptible but is at one with it. They are often the *only* point of access to what lies beneath them—the only way *into* the interior.

To be *part of* something is to be an integral feature of it; it is not just to be *a* part in the manner of a *piece,* which is detachable in principle and separately identifiable. Articles of clothing contribute to my sartorial identity, my style of dressing; but each article is a separate piece of that repertoire, and can be detached from the rest—as well as from my lived body. But the trunk of my body is not detachable from this body: were it to be removed, my body itself would change its basic identity (assuming that I survived). Thus my trunk is an integral part of my physical being. It belongs to this being and is part of it: where the "of" designates an objective genitive relation of intrinsic belonging.

When I glance at the surface of something, I am looking at what belongs to that something as a constituent part, not just as an adventitious piece of it. This is perhaps most evident when I look at a landscape scene—thus at part of the surface of the earth. As I drive through western Pennsylvania on Highway 80,

---

16. Ibid., p. 307. Finally, all is surface, even the ground: "The ground is the basic persisting surface of the environment. It is the surface of support, the terrain, the earth extending out to the horizon" (ibid.; Gibson underlines "ground").

17. Ibid.

for example, I glimpse patches of distant landscape. Each of these patches belongs to the earth of that region; each is a part *of* the region, beholden to it as well as constitutive of it. In Husserl's terms, it is a "moment" of the landscape: indissociable from it, integral to its full identity.[18] Even when—in a very different situation—I glance at a sweater or a hat worn by a passer-by, I am still viewing something that *qua surface* belongs intrinsically to the article of clothing itself, even if this article is merely a piece of attire and easily dissociable from the person wearing it. When the glance goes to the surface—as it almost always does—it goes to something that pertains essentially to the thing of which it is a surface.[19]

The glance has it both ways. On the one hand, it lands *on* the surface, the outermost external feature of something. On the other hand, it grasps this surface as integrally related to the thing whose surface it is. In the first case, the surface is distinguishable (though it remains inseparable) from that whose surface it forms: we sense that we are experiencing surface as such. In the second, we feel that we are experiencing surface as inseparable from depth as a dimension of the full-bodied object—a depth somehow shared by the perceived thing and the surface itself. In this latter case, we sense that the surface with which we connect brings with it the *rest* of the object, since the part of this object we apprehend is grasped as (and only as) continuous with a more encompassing whole.

At the same time, the surfaces and objects (including persons and events) we attain by glancing themselves belong to places, ultimately to entire place-worlds. I shall return to this point, on which I have touched before; but for now suffice it to say that if the pertinent surfaces at which we glance are parts of (in the strong sense of "parts") the objects or persons or events to which they pertain—if they are constituent moments of them or are in legion with them—they are also parts of (in the same strong sense) the places to which they also belong: ultimately, to the place-worlds that form their most encompassing context. This became evident in the case of orientation as discussed in the last chapter.

In gazing, by contrast, we are engaged neither with surfaces per se nor with other integral parts of objects—nor, therefore, with the places to which both of these features point.[20] Instead, we are more apt to look into the depths of

18. For Husserl's "merology," see his Third Logical Investigation in his *Logical Investigations,* tr. J. N. Findlay, ed. D. Moran (New York: Routledge, 2001), vol. 2, Third Investigation ("On the Theory of Wholes and Parts"), section 17, pp. 28–30. There, detachable "piece" (*Stück*) is contrasted with "part" (*Teil*) and "moment" (*Moment*) in much the same way as I am here comparing "*a* part" with "part *of.*" I have drawn upon this distinction in chap. 2, and will return to it in chap. 7.

19. This is so even when the surface I glimpse is such that it can be removed at certain times: e.g., the detachable hood of a coat that can be altogether detached in clement weather. When I perceive the hood, I grasp something that belongs to the coat as such, even if it need not be literally attached to the coat at any given time. The surface of the detachable part is still the surface of a larger whole to which that part belongs integrally, not as a merely adventitious add-on.

20. In a later section, we shall encounter an exception in which certain gazes do concern surfaces—but not for their own sake, as is almost always the case with glances.

something after first noticing it. Such depths are *not* on the surface; they are both distinguishable *and* separable from the surface that rises above and beyond them. Moreover, the gaze tends to grasp its object as a whole, not just a part of it. We gaze at the thing in its entirety: taking as much of it in as we can, all the way in. The gaze's distinctive receptivity (signified by its open-eyedness, its patience) means that the full-bodied object (or person or event) is likely to become its content: *this object in its depth dimension,* though not, significantly, as continuous with a larger place-world where it is located. It is as if gazing at a single object or event sufficed to satisfy the looking—which, unlike the restless glance, rarely moves on to a larger locatory matrix. Indeed, it is precisely because of this whole-bodied visuality, this focus on phenomena in their very discreteness, that the gaze is so favored in philosophical and scientific investigations—both of which like to be in a position to claim that they deal with concreta in their well-rounded dimensionality, their most robust format. Taking up this position, however, is no guarantee of impartial or complete results; if anything, as I have argued, such theoretical ambitions make these investigations more, not less, vulnerable to tendentiously prejudicial readings of the object domains that they explore so thoroughly.

III

It is time to take up a more direct and definitive confrontation between gazing and glancing, taken as the two palmary kinds of looking. I shall do so under two headings: (1) The Sobriety of the Gaze; and (2) The Subversiveness of the Glance.

1. *The Sobriety of the Gaze.* To engage in gazing in any concerted way (and gazing is nothing if not concerted) is to enter into "the spirit of gravity" in Nietzsche's celebrated phrase. Living under this regime, I refuse levity and assume instead the burdens of the world, accepting all that bears down upon me, trying to give to it its due weight. In other terms, I approach things in their *determinate presence.* This latter phrase is a translation of Heidegger's word *Anwesenheit,* which signifies the metaphysical rigidity into which Western ways of conceiving Being have been cast since Plato.[21] When things are considered as determinately present, our understanding of them is confined to settled schemata of conception, for example, as mere instantiations of Forms in the case of Plato, as substances in the case of Aristotle, as representations in Descartes and Kant, and as Will to Power in Nietzsche's own case.

This is not only a matter of debate among philosophers but also reaches into everyday life. Whenever I take something into my gaze, I bring it there as having just this sort of presence or as able to gain it in the course of gazing itself. The

21. *Anwesenheit,* determinate presence, already occurs in the introduction to Heidegger, *Being and Time,* pp. 46–48.

interest of the gaze lies in encountering what is determinate or at least determinable: what can be taken seriously as *just this* thing or *just that* idea. Even contemplating, whose object is the most indeterminate of all forms of gazing, still concerns what is definite enough to dwell on for a considerable period of time—definite enough to *take seriously*. And that is just the point: the gaze is allied with the spirit of gravity precisely because it takes its contents so seriously. It invests them with theoretical dignity. It presumes that these same contents (things, ideas, and so on) have depths worth plumbing, holding that in these depths the truth of what is gazed-at resides—there and nowhere else.

The gravity of gazing is also exhibited in its unremitting "quest for certainty" (in John Dewey's phrase). This quest is pursued in three major ways. First, by a concern for incorrigible *evidence*—evidence so certain that it cannot be controverted. Husserl called such evidence "apodictic," that is to say, necessary to the very identity of something (such that, without it, that something could not be what it is). Second, by a passion for *objectivity:* that is, nonpersonal knowledge of the gazed-at object as beheld from a neutral position, "the view from nowhere." The gaze would like to take up that very view, so that it could deliver the objective truth about what it takes in. Third, by a rigorous adhesion to *consistency* in procedure, modes of inference and reasoning, and so on: that is, anything having to do with the way that evidence is gathered and interpreted—and objectivity established. If the gaze is not always directly involved in the pursuit of such consistency, it is the constant ally of such a pursuit. For it lends its sanction and support to what purports to be consistent. This is an instance of the confirming gaze, which builds upon the inaugural gaze that establishes evidence in the first place. The gaze is active at every stage in the quest for certainty.

Also contributing to the sobriety of the gaze is its affirmation of the status quo. It seeks to be the witness of the way things are as measured by how they were at some prior point: the status quo is a direct function of the *status quo ante*. In this spirit, the gaze does not contest the "rules of the game" but, on the contrary, takes pleasure in their continual reenactment. Its interest is not in how things should be or might be otherwise but in how they stand and do not change. Here, too, gravity is at stake: the gravitas of the same rather than the *celeritas* of the different. The same is reduced to repetition of the identical—rather than the kind of repetition that makes a difference, as on Kierkegaard's or Heidegger's or Deleuze's conceptions.[22]

In all of this, the gaze contributes powerfully to keeping one's overall outlook steady. The spirit of gravity is a spirit of constancy. It calls for continual vigilance concerning the same: keeping the same in sight so that it does not stray far from

---

22. See Soren Kierkegaard, *Repetition*, available in *Fear and Trembling and Repetition*, tr. J. Hong and K. Hong (Princeton, N.J.: Princeton University Press: 1983); Gilles Deleuze, *Difference and Repetition*, tr. Paul Patton (New York: Columbia University Press, 1995), chap. 2; and Martin Heidegger, *Being and Time*, pp. 437–439. On a more generous reading of the same, it includes the different—as Heidegger insists in his late seminar, "Identity and Difference."

one's look. It is not accidental that we speak of "stargazing." Stars are the most constant objects in the sky: the slowest-moving and the least-changing. They represent a paradigm for the steadiness of the gaze in its sober attentiveness. The gaze plays a game of the same, and for this reason it calls for an unchanging posture: in gazing, the eyes and the head, indeed often the entire body, is held steady. The status quo in content (if this content is not the stars, then it is something comparably steadfast) is matched by a comparable status quo of the gazing body.

In each of these ways—above all, in its obsession with certainty and the same—the gaze shows itself to be the essence of sobriety. It is the visual enactment of the spirit of gravity. Its look is heavy-lidded and dry-eyed: heavy with the serious matters that weigh it down, dry in its austere devotion to evidence and objectivity and consistency. These epistemic ideals call not for an ethical optics, much less a spiritual optics, but for an optics of the uncorrected gaze, the unflinching eye, the unblinking look.[23] These embody the sobriety of the gaze— its single most pervasive and revealing trait.

2. *The Subversiveness of the Glance.* In counterpoint to the tempered character of the gaze, the glance shows itself to be distinctly subversive, and this in several ways. Not that it directly contests the sober truth—this would be to make it much more concerted and scheming than it is—but it spontaneously subverts the sober spirit. It gets under the skin of the spirit of gravity: it is guilelessly "subversive," given that it "turns/from below" and thus "turns upside down" (as *subvertere* means in Latin). How does this happen?

It happens first of all by its very *celeritas:* its rapidity, the fact that it darts and dashes all over. Precisely because the glance never lingers long on any one surface, it does not become invested with its object; it moves on too quickly for this to happen. The glance is too wayward for serious preoccupation. It is too restless to rest—too actively curious, or else too impatient, to be bogged down by what is weighty, however significant it may be. The glance does not stand on ceremony. It is already off and running: ahead of other forms of visual lookings and ahead of itself as well. Instead of staring the present down, it lives off the oncoming edge of the future. Its mode of lived time is protentional; its existential temporality is the ahead-of-itself.[24]

Thanks to its restlessly nomadic way of life, the glance does not thrive in the

---

23. On ethical optics, see Levinas's statement that "ethics is an optics" (*Totality and Infinity: An Essay on Exteriority,* tr. A. Lingis [The Hague: Nijhoff, 1979], p. 23; cf. also p. 29) and his qualification of this in terms of a "spiritual optics" (ibid., p. 78). By these claims Levinas means that we see other persons *through* ethics—that is, through the lens of the ethical relation we have to them.

24. "Protentional" is Husserl's term for the forward fringe of time-consciousness; the "ahead-of-itself" is Heidegger's expression for the primacy of the future in Dasein's authentic relationship to temporality. For further treatment of these matters, see chap. 8, "Glancing Time."

company of determinate presence. Its true life is where the burdens of the present are absent. The present promises evidence and objectivity: that which can be seen straight off, without diversions or complications. The glance is devious by comparison, always looking away from the present into what lies ahead. Taking little interest in evidence and even less in objectivity, it does not pretend to consistency either. It is too agitated and uneasy to want to find, much less to stay with, unassailable evidence. It cannot stay put long enough to occupy the "view from nowhere," the bird's-eye view of objective perception. Its view is the view from *anywhere*—anywhere in its flight, its cursory course of action.

The glance dis-establishes what is perceptually (and ultimately socially) established. Even as it stays on the surface, it gets under the official and officious skin of the epistemic establishment, which favors the gaze as a matter of principle. It does this not by overt rebellion or by a concerted plan of action but by its own gentle form of guerilla warfare, its own nomadic maneuvers on the periphery of the state apparatus, in its own smooth space.[25] There is nothing regulated, nothing normal, nothing striated here: no adherence to a grid. In the life of the glance, everything is aslant and akimbo, splayed out as the glancing eye moves in an unregulated and seemingly arbitrary fashion—with no upright posture or steady stance to draw things back together; no rectitude. Everything is in disarray, all is disrupted, everything is disintricated from everything else, dismembered: the situation is Dionysian. The bane of sober procedure, the tiny, tottering glance is the true revolutionary of the perceptual world.

Where the gaze is obedient to what fascinates it—following it faithfully at every turn, closely attuned to its content—the glance is never simply subservient to its subject matter. It is too distractible to be docile. Just as it does not stand on ceremony, so it is no respecter of persons. The bourgeoisie value of respectability —lampooned so mercilessly in Sartre's *La nausée* in the guise of official portraits of local dignitaries at whom one is expected to gaze respectfully—is here inverted. Anything goes in the glance: anything can be looked at, no matter what its social standing or economic value. There are no intrinsically more, or less, valuable things to be observed. The radical democracy (if not the anarchy) of the glance is such that in a thrice it can look away—and thus abolish from view—what one is *supposed* to admire. Once I am in a museum, no one can control my glance: the portraits are hastily dismissed "in a glance" as I rush on to more interesting works. Indeed, I don't even need to be in a museum to take in works of art freely and effectively in a glance. Just looking at artworks in books and catalogues allows me to construct a genuine museum without walls—in

25. I borrow these various terms from the chapter on "nomadology" in Gilles Deleuze and Félix Guattari, *A Thousand Plateaus: Capitalism and Schizophrenia*, tr. Brian Massumi (Minneapolis: University of Minnesota Press, 1987). Concerning "smooth space," see my discussion in *The Fate of Place* (Berkeley: University of California Press, 1997), chap. 10, and my essay "Smooth Spaces and Rough-Edged Places: The Hidden History of Place," *Review of Metaphysics* 52 (1998): 392–405.

Malraux's sense, whereby photographs of artworks have replaced the works themselves.[26]

The glance is subversive not just in its spontaneous but efficacious anti-establishmentarianism. It subverts in a positive way as well: by its experimentalism. To glance is to explore the environing world by sampling its surfaces. For this reason, they are paradigmatic instances of "probe-heads" in Deleuze and Guattari's suggestive term: glances like probe-heads "dismantle [fixed] strata in their wake, break through the walls of significance, [and] pour out of the holds of subjectivity."[27] A probe-head (*tête-chercheuse:* literally, a guidance device) leads off from the face in its socially determined format, its "faciality." So too the glance "flies off the face"—not entirely unlike the film (*eidolon*) cast off from the surface of things according to Lucretius. In this outstreaming probative activity, the glance leaves behind for a brief moment the fixed features and settled traits that the face has inherited from its social milieu. Above all, it leaves behind the gaze, the officially sanctioned look of the régime in power. Indeed, it undoes the gaze at its own game: despite its brevity, a glance can look more acutely and probingly than does a gaze, especially if this latter becomes obsessed with its subject matter to the point of fixation.

The glance, then, is a probe. It is experimental in its pro-action. It tries things out in advance by looking ahead of the face from which it extrudes. It is probative in the sense of testing out, "proving" (but precisely *not* proving in the sense of "establishing to be objectively true"). The glance as probative lives up to its ancient root: *proba* is Late Latin for "examination." By glancing we investigate the layout of surfaces in our immediate environment; we get close to these surfaces, so close as to be virtually at one with them: our look plays on them, so intimately as to learn from them in ways that are genuinely unique.[28]

But the glance is too restless to stay with any one set of surfaces. The glance keeps moving on. Always taking in new surfaces, it discovers novel approaches and directions. The probatory glance is protentional in its extended explorations of the surfaces of things as these surfaces unfold at the edge of the oncoming future. The glance is *pro-visional:* it sees ahead, albeit in a tentative and uncertain manner, by trying out new pathways. At the same time, glances build up "provisions" in the form of a repertoire of lookings, a vocabulary of seen surfaces, a syntax of visual configurations.

26. See André Malraux, *The Voices of Silence,* tr. Stuart Gilbert (Princeton, N.J.: Princeton University Press, 1978). For further discussion, see below, chap. 12.

27. Deleuze and Guattari, *A Thousand Plateaus,* p. 190. Probe-heads also "fell trees in favor of veritable rhizomes, and steer the flows down lines of positive deterritorialization or creative flight" (ibid.). Cf. also p. 301: "a deterritorialization of faces and landscapes, in favor of probe-heads whose lines no longer outline a form or form a contour, and whose colors no longer lay out a landscape."

28. To probe is "to examine or investigate penetratingly; delve into" (*Random House Dictionary of the English Language* [Boston: Houghton Mifflin, 1976], p. 1043). If this is so, the glance probes in a peculiar way: it delves by staying on the surface itself.

Moreover, if it is true that a social formation is defined by what escapes it—by "lines of flight" that traverse it and not just by its "contradictions" (in a Marxist sense)—then the glance as probe-head is a privileged vehicle for such lines of flight.[29] Or let us say outright that a glance is itself a line of flight, it traces a trajectory by its playful ingression into the layout of surfaces. Thanks to being such an effective *ligne de fuite,* the glance is liberative—freeing human subjects from the spirit of gravity that bogs them down by making them beholden to laid-down sedimentations and stratified structures. The glance, in short, puts us on probation from the long and heavy sentence effected by the gaze.

IV

This is not to say, however, that the glance is something simply cast out from the face randomly and irresponsibly, without reference to the human being who is its source. The subversive glance includes more than its extroversion. The line of flight that it follows—that it *is*—does not simply terminate among the surfaces it probes so provisionally and yet so perspicaciously. The glance is never entirely detached from the subject who casts it. Even as it explores the layout of its place-world, caressing its sinuous surfaces, the glance remains attached to the glancer. The full action of the glance includes not just glancing out but glancing back—this in keeping with a double-beat rhythm which was mentioned in the introduction and to which we shall have occasion to return.[30]

Indeed, this very feature of the glance, its anchorage in the human subject, also serves to distinguish it from the gaze. The latter detaches itself more completely from its own condition of enactment. The "sovereign look" that epitomizes the gaze is that of a self-transcending intentionality that buries itself in the object or scene onto which it gazes. This is the look of "Christ Pantocrater"—who looks on fiercely at the idiotic play of mere mortals. It is also the much milder look of the *Mona Lisa,* who gazes serenely out at us in detachment from the landscape glimpsed distantly behind her and from the invisible earth below her. Such a look looks out but does not look back. Its line of flight is fully invested in what it sees before it, without regard to its own concrete implacement in space and time.

The glance is decisively different. It goes out only to come back. It is dispossessive only to repossess (but not possessively!). It dismantles so as to reincorporate (though not literally!). This is the paradox of its very subversiveness, which is not limited to the shaking up of external rigidities—as in its capacity to *épater les bourgeosie*—but involving a return to the subject who emits it, unsettling it in

29. See Deleuze and Guattari, *A Thousand Plateaus,* p. 90: "a social field is defined less by its conflicts and contradictions than by the lines of flight running through it." Cf. also p. 216: "From the viewpoint of micropolitics, a society is defined by its lines of flight, which are molecular. There is always something that flows or flees, that escapes the binary organizations, the resonance apparatus, and the overcoding machine."

30. See chap. 8, "Glancing Time."

turn. Displacement without is accompanied by displacement within. The subversion effected by the glance is thus twofold: both by way of im-plication (that is, folding of the outgoing look into the object) and of re-implication (re-enfolding this look back into the subject). The glance flies off the face of the subject in a first moment of "de-facialization" or "de-territorialization" in Deleuze and Guattari's special terms: here is the glance as probe-head, as protentional and provisional. But in a second moment there is a re-facing or re-territorializing that brings it back to the subject: a move inimical to the exterio-centrist thrust, the lines of flight, advocated by the authors of *A Thousand Plateaus*. For the glance is *tethered to the very subject from which it proceeds.* Unlike the gaze, it is never entirely deracinated from the human subject, whom it continues to illuminate even as it flees.

This illumination, however, is of a subject who has been transformed by the flight of the glance itself. To return to the exact same subject would be merely to reinstate the self-identical—another form of the metaphysics of determinate presence, now in the guise of a self-assertion of the constant subject of the gaze. Here Levinas's critique of the Odyssean return to the Same out of nostalgia—the same country, the same subject—is most pertinent.[31] Whatever the power of this attraction (and it is finally the same as that of the metaphysics of presence, in relation to which nostalgic return is merely one historically configured exemplar), it must be resisted. On this point, Levinas concurs with Deleuze and Guattari. But this does not have to mean—as the latter two authors insist—that the subject is to be given up altogether: that the line of flight takes one exclusively "toward the realms of the asignifying, asubjective, and faceless."[32] On the contrary, the example of the glance teaches us just the opposite: it demonstrates that the flight from the self-same subject, the sober subject of the gaze, is not only compatible with a move back to the subject but that it is all the more subversive for being so.

For the subversion effected by the glance is at once a subversion of established settings *and* a subversion of the subject who is engaged in these same settings: of the gazer as well as the gazed-at. In glancing out, the seeing subject undermines the antecedently settled world by refusing to become fixated on any single surface or group of surfaces. In receiving the glance back, this subject refuses to affirm itself as a single self-identical being; the glance does not go back to the same but to a continually different subject: the subject who has glanced and been changed in the moment, the *Augenblick,* of glancing itself. Changed not only in becoming de-facialized in the sense of *A Thousand Plateaus*—that is, in dropping the white mask cum black holes of standard

31. See Emmanuel Levinas, "The Trace of the Other," section one (in Levinas, *Collected Philosophical Papers*).

32. Deleuze and Guattari, *A Thousand Plateaus*, p. 187. The basic move that I here question is contained in this sentence: "Dismantling the face is the same as breaking through the wall of the signifier and getting out of the black hole of subjectivity" (ibid., p. 188).

Western socialization—but in losing face in still more radical ways. Sometimes this happens by realizing the *monstrosity* of one's own face: "The face, what a horror!"[33] Sometimes it consists in not being able to recognize one's face *as one's own:* the swing out from the self can be so extreme that one cannot swing back to anything self-reassuringly the same. Even in the course of ordinary glancing one risks becoming a monstrous nonpresence unknown to oneself.

V

The most telling subversion of the glance is therefore of the subject who glances. This subject is subverted because of the irresolvable tension of the circumstance: the glance comes *from* and returns *to* a subject, yet goes *beyond* that same subject. It comes from the subject as does any intentional act, whether this be thinking or imagining, remembering or perceiving. But it comes from not just in the sense of deriving from—that is, as a matter of psychic genealogy—but as being *flung from* the subject, thrown out from him or her: glances are "cast" outward, they are not demurely poised or cautiously positioned. Far from it! They dart out like so many arrows—with no common target—and they dart back just as aimlessly.

Where the gaze consolidates its gains, the glance acts to dispel and disconnect. "All it knows is dispersal," says Norman Bryson, who underlines its "flickering ungovernable mobility."[34] Because of this mobility, the glance never settles for solidity, preferring to alter course at every opportunity. In particular, it never settles for a single *site*, a fixed point of attachment. The gaze seeks site and holds onto it; it is a primary agent of territorialization: one gazes with pleasure over territory that is laid out before one—there to be seen, to be conquered and possessed, or to be painted. The glance takes no such satisfaction; it "can never be sated."[35] This is to say that the glance is an agent of displacement. Doubly so:

33. Ibid., p. 190. In italics in the text. I have added the exclamation mark. For Deleuze and Guattari, however, this descriptive claim is merely part of their general project of defacialization: "[The face] is naturally a lunar landscape, with its pores, matters, bright colors, whiteness, and holes" (ibid.). Yet their further characterization seems to take it out of the human/social realm and closer to my sense of the unrecognizable subject of the glance: "there is no need for a close-up to make it inhuman; it is naturally a close-up, and naturally inhuman, a monstrous hood" (ibid.).

34. Norman Bryson, *Vision and Painting: The Logic of the Gaze* (New Haven, Conn.: Yale University Press, 1983), pp. 122, 121. I am indebted to Bryson's discussion of "The Gaze and the Glance," the title of chap. 5 of his book, even as I differ from him on certain key points.

35. Ibid., p. 121. The full sentence is: "however avid for total possession, the Glance can never be sated." On my reading, however, the glance normally lacks precisely such possessiveness. It may be greedy to *see*, but not to own—to make one's own. Compare Starobinski's statement, "A magical wish, never entirely fulfilled yet never discouraged, accompanies each of our glances: to seize, to undress, to petrify, to penetrate: to fascinate" (*The Living Eye*, p. 4). But I do not agree that the glance seeks to petrify: that is the province of the gaze. Conversely, I

not seeking the security of site in the world around it, it moves rapidly from place to place, finding no privileged surface on which to alight. And it fails to find site within as well. The glance gives the lie to Saint Augustine's counsel: "Go back into yourself, for truth dwells in the inner man."[36] The inner self is evacuated by the glance: not just emptied but made abyssal. A scene of continual displacement—thanks to the rapid emission of glances at every waking moment. This is why the glancer is so monstrously unrecognizable to herself: in the continual advance of the glance, any shred of selfhood is rendered otiose. Not only is the face flayed by the glance—its surface torn off, as it were—but the subject of the face is itself dismantled. The horror is that after the dispersal of the glance there is no coherent self left. Between glances, any such self is suspended. The glance deconstructs its own subjectivity by giving it no site to inhabit, no entitlement to existence, no substrate on which to count.

It is the subject, then, that is most deeply subverted in the sharp-edged action of the glance. Instead of being "thrown under" one's experience—as *sub-jectum* literally implies—its abyssal status means that this experience has become baseless. It has no perdurance: not in a self and not in space or time. As continually dis-placing itself, going wherever the glance goes, the glancing subject lacks *stabilitas loci.* But it also lacks *stabilitas temporalis.*

This latter claim requires demonstration, especially since we normally presume that all human actions, perceptual or otherwise, take place in a secure matrix of time. As Bryson argues, there is an at least apparent affiliation between the glance and the present—in contrast with the gaze, which is tied to the aorist tense of the historian: the impersonal and disembodied past of completion that makes no reference to the narrator.[37] In contrast with this fixation on the past as finished and as independent of the historian-narrator, the glance implicates the subject in temporal deixis, that is, an essential reference to the subject's sense of time in the present as the indispensable pivot of certain basic temporal relations (for example, yesterday, sooner, some time ago, and so on: all of which arise only

---

cannot concur with Starobinski that "the gaze [*le regard*] is never satisfied" (ibid.). The Swiss critic is able to claim this only because of his general thesis that "sight [of any kind] opens all space to desire, but desire is not satisfied with seeing. Visible space attests to both my power to discover and my powerlessness to attain" (ibid.). Only if desire is posited as a human constant at the basis of all vision can the glance and the gaze be assimilated to each other as equally nonsatisfying; but the descriptive truth is that the gaze is often satisfied with what it has fixed upon—as Starobinski himself acknowledges: the gaze "is willing to give up the faculty of immediate perception in exchange for the gift of *fixing* more permanently whatever flees its grasp" (ibid., p. 3; his italics).

36. Saint Augustine, *de vera Religione* 39, no. 72. Cited by Husserl in the conclusion to his *Cartesian Meditations,* tr. D. Cairns (Nijhoff: The Hague, 1950).

37. "The aorist presents an action which came to completion at a certain time before the utterance; and it describes that action without involvement or engagement on the part of the speaker recounting the action . . . . The deictic tenses (the present, and all compounds of the present) by contrast create and refer to their own perspective" (Bryson, *Vision and Painting,* p. 88).

in relation to the present). Moreover, this present is that of *durée réelle* in Bergson's meaning: a lived-through time that prolongs the present from something merely pinpointed to a process of undergoing that is ineluctably bodily: "Against the Gaze, the Glance proposes desire, proposes the body, in the *durée* of its practical activity."[38] The invocation of the body and desire is certainly right and welcome—we shall return to it just below—but Bryson is off the mark with regard to the temporality of the glance.

The appropriate unit of the glance is that of the self-dismantling *instant,* not duration. Duration implies a continuity of temporal phases that is more appropriate to the gaze, which in Starobinski's words "does not exhaust itself immediately [but] involves perseverance, doggedness, as if animated by the hope of adding to its discovery or reconquering what is about to escape."[39] Such durational detention is foreign to the glance, which proceeds instead by the outright disruption of temporal continuity. When I glance here, and then quickly after over there, and then somewhere else again—all in a matter of the briefest moments—I do not constitute a continuum of *durée réelle.* On the contrary: I undercut all temporal continua, just as I undo all spatial homogeneities. I leap from one instant to the next in saccadic (again, "jerky") leaps of attention that unravel any fabric of continuity. Indeed, Bryson himself (in the wake of Gombrich) emphasizes just such saccadic movements: "the disjointed rhythm of the retinal field."[40] This is the very rhythm of the glance in its instantaneous flights and perches in the stream of experience—that is to say, in the durational present from which it so quickly departs and to which it equally rapidly returns.

38. Ibid., p. 122. Here Bryson departs from Starobinski's general claim that all seeing is desiring (see n. 31 above).

39. Starobinski, *The Living Eye,* pp. 2–3. For Starobinski, the durational character of the gaze is ultimately based on its "impatient energy" that "lies in wait, hoping that a moving form will come to a standstill or that a figure at rest will reveal a slight tremor" (ibid., p. 3). Even such impatience requires a *durée* that is inimical to the glance, which does not lie in wait but springs forth immediately, darting to its object.

40. Bryson, *Vision and Painting,* p. 122. See also p. 121: "The material construction of the eye permits only one area of the image to clarify at each moment, while its acute mobility precludes regularity of scansion." This is in keeping with the fact that deixis bears both on spatial as well as temporal aspects of the speaker's position (cf. ibid., p. 88). However, Bryson reveals the flawed character of his view of the time of the glance, when he speaks of "a protracted, *fragmented durée* of viewing, which labors to build an eventually total scheme of the image and to apprehend the composition *im Augenblick,* but which cannot achieve this scheme through the limited empirical means at its disposal" (ibid.). On the one hand, duration is precisely that which *cannot* be "fragmented" without ceasing to be duration, as Bergson stresses in *Time and Free Will.* On the other hand, the glance proceeds from one *Augenblick* to another, and yet is perfectly able to take in a "total scheme of the image": that is part of its (admittedly surprising) comprehensiveness. E. H. Gombrich first pointed to the jerky, discontinuous "saccadic" movements of the eye as it looks at paintings in his *Art and Illusion: A Study in the Psychology of Pictorial Representation* (Princeton, N.J.: Princeton University Press, 1960). We shall return to the perception of paintings in chap. 12, "Glancing at the Image in Photography and Painting."

The glance is subversive of the subject who counts on the continuities and homogeneities of space and time alike in order to be a perduring self. The glance is, in Bryson's own image, a trickster figure whose irregular and instantaneous motions belie any persisting selfhood underlying experience.[41] Indeed, experience itself, far from being a sheer stream, is so thoroughly traversed and retraversed by the glance's peregrinations, its constant deterritorializations, that we cannot count on it as a continuing substrate. The deconstruction effected by the glance's subversion of the subject goes *all the way down.*

All the way down *to the body*, the "natural subject of perception."[42] The body? Surely the body is that from which the glance decisively *departs.* Does not the glance leave the body behind from the very start by its rapid adversions to whatever attracts it? Is the glance not the body's most immediate and most effective means of self-transcendence? Does not its line of flight fly straight away from the obdurate mass of the body—as surely as Hermes's fleet-footedness moves away from any habitual locus on the earth? (Lines of flight meet only at crossroads, of which Hermes was the recognized master in ancient Greece: that is to say, at the very places where the body must choose to move itself in a definite direction.) Is not glancing a matter of de-corporealization as much as of de-territorialization? Is this not already signified in Deleuze and Guattari's invocation of de-facialization?

Nevertheless, despite one's first impression—wherein the body seems to be a merely marginal presence for the glance—the glance is deeply ensconced in the carnal. It may well be the case that the body's apparent marginality vis-à-vis the glance gives to the body an unsuspected power as "the hidden term on whose disavowal the whole system depends."[43] But the body is not only marginal; it is a powerful if subterranean determinant of the glance itself. If glancing is a form of deixis (as on Bryson's hypothesis), then it will ineluctably involve the body in its operations. For deixis of any kind is "utterance in carnal form and points back directly (*deikonei*) to the body of the speaker."[44] It does so by establishing this body as irrecusably *here,* that is, as the source of the glance and the locus to which it returns. In Greek, the grammatical form called "deictic iota" intensifies an adverbial expression of location, so that *outos* or "this" becomes *outosi,* which

41. "For as long as the dream of an instantaneous and timeless painting—the Essential Copy [i.e., the ideal of the Gaze]—rules in the art of the West, the Glance takes on the role of saboteur, trickster, for the Glance is not simply intermingled with the Gaze, as it is with the Byzantine or the high-deixis image, but is separated out, repressed" (Bryson, *Vision and Painting,* p. 121). For excellent recent treatments of the figure of the trickster, see Glen Mazis, *Trickster, Magician, and Grieving Man: Reconnecting Men with Earth* (Santa Fe: Bear and Co. Press, 1994), and Lewis Hyde, *Trickster Makes This World; Mischief, Myth, and Art* (New York: Farrar, Straus and Giroux, 1998).

42. "The body is a natural self and, as it were, the subject of perception" (Merleau-Ponty, *Phenomenology of Perception,* p. 206).

43. Bryson, *Vision and Painting,* p. 121.

44. Ibid., p. 88.

can be translated as "this one right here."[45] So too the glance is a look that originates right here—in the locale of the looking face—and that comes back from the there of the glanced-at surface to this same here in a more intense form, ready to glance again. As Starobinski remarks, "everything recommences *here.*"[46] The body itself is an "absolute here," again in Husserl's striking phrase; but such uncompromised hereness does not mean that the body is a simple substance, much less a simple location. The here to which return is made is only a springboard for further glancing, not the core of the corporeal subject. As I have insisted, the subject of the here—hence the here itself—is changed by the return. "Here" signifies *from here*: from here and here alone, future lookings as repeated relookings or re-gards will arise.[47] "Quick now, here now, always," says the Bird in "The Waste Land," as if describing the lively and ever-changing incarnations of the glance.

The glance is incarnate in a second sense: as an expression of desire. If it is true that (in Starobinski's ocular axiom) "sight opens all space to desire,"[48] then the glance is the first expression of desire, its most spontaneous representative. In glancing, not only do I *follow* my preexisting desire; I also *guide* it onward and outward in space and time; I extend it to surfaces that it would not reach were it to remain contained and unexpressed within me. The glance is at once the creature of bodily desire and its most active proponent: as Bryson suggests, it literally "pro-poses" desire: sets it forth, risks it, exposes it, shows it. (*Deiknumi,* the verbal root of *deixis,* means "to show," "point out.") It "teleguides"[49] our desiring body in certain directions rather than others by orienting it toward satisfaction; it indicates what we need to do—what subsequent bodily motions we have to take—if we are to realize our own desire; it even points to ways in which our body must ally itself with other bodies in particular social situations if the mutuality of desire, its interpersonal exchange, is to be attained. The glance traces out the intentionality of desire, and for this reason Lacan can speak of "the privilege of the glance in the function of desire."[50]

---

45. I am grateful to Eric Casey for this point about Greek grammar.

46. Starobinski, *The Living Eye*, p. 5; his italics.

47. "French resorts to the word *regard,* whose root originally referred not to the act of seeing [merely] but to expectation, concern, watchfulness, consideration, and safeguard, made emphatic by the addition of a prefix expressing redoubling or return. *Regarder* is a movement that aims to recapture, *reprendre sous garde* [to place in safekeeping *once again*]" (Starobinski, *The Living Eye*, p. 2; my italics).

48. Ibid., p. 4. The full sentence is: "Sight opens all space to desire, but desire is not satisfied with seeing."

49. "Teleguides" is Lacan's expression; though applied by him to the look or the gaze (*le regard*), in fact it fits the glance better: "We see thus here that the gaze operates in a certain descent, doubtless the descent of desire, but how to say this? The subject is not wholly responsible for it, he is teleguided (*téléguidé*)" (Lacan, *Les quatre concepts fondamentaux de la psychanalyse,* p. 105).

50. Ibid., p. 80: "We can grasp this privilege of the [glance] (*le regard*) in the function of desire in flowing through the length of the veins as it were in which the domain of vision has

Thus the body is deeply implicated in the glance at every turn, thanks to the action of deixis and the pursuit of desire. This continual incarnation is the very converse of the situation occasioned by the gaze, which "bears within it a strange power of separation."[51] This is a separation above all from the lived body of the gazer. The thrust of the gaze is not just *away* from the body—this much is true of the first beat of the glance—but it is a matter of taking itself altogether *out of the body:* of becoming extra-corporeal. This is why the gaze so often seeks the supernatural realm in a "second sight" that exceeds whatever stems from the natural world. But even when confined to this world, the gaze has a genius for losing itself, for disincarnating itself in the object that fascinates it. It is not only the case that "unique, discontinuous, discarnate bodies move in spatial apart-ness, under the gaze of the Other"[52] but that the gaze is itself disembodied: it has repressed the bodily basis of its own looking. "The extremity of the gaze," as Starobinski adds, "is already something more than gaze, and pursues its aim in the act whereby vision renounces and sacrifices itself."[53] What it renounces and sacrifices is mainly its own body: the body from which it starts but to which it does not return.

VI

The detachment of the gaze from its corporeal fundament, far from weaken-ing its status in the eyes of many Western thinkers, has only strengthened its estimation. It is just because the gazer is convinced that his or her body is irrelevant—or in any case subordinate—to the enactment of gazing itself that the gaze has been so highly valorized. For the body is regarded as something confus-ing and degrading, a matter of downward drift undermining the visionary state to which the gaze aspires. When subjected to the "indiscretion and dispersion" of bodily states—to "carnal curiosity" and "natural extravagance"[54]—the gaze fails in its mission to attain a sublimated sight that may surely require the body as its point of origin but that must just as surely leave it if it is to realize its full potential and the high seriousness that is its due. The glance, in comparison, is considered by the same thinkers as a mere spontaneous gesture of the body and thus ineluctably linked to its fate: as fickle as the body's appetites, as blind as its instincts, as insatiable as its desire. The conclusion can only be that glancing is incapable of attaining philosophical or scientific truth; lacking the spirit of true gravity, it is bound to a life of perpetual errancy in the false gravity of flesh. Where the gaze finds and fixes, the glance undoes and dissolves.

---

been integrated into the field of desire." In view of the link between the glance and bodily desire, I have inserted "glance" as a more appropriate translation of *le regard* here than "gaze."

51. Starobinski, *The Living Eye*, p. 9.
52. Bryson, *Vision and Painting*, p. 117.
53. Starobinski, *The Living Eye*, p. 5.
54. All three phrases are from ibid., p. 5.

The hegemony of the gaze over the glance—the two poles between which this chapter has moved—is everywhere to be seen. In philosophy first of all: in Plato's promotion of the eidetic at the expense of the corporeal by recourse to a rarified act of *noesis* (relayed by Aristotle in the form of "active intellect"), in Descartes's invocation of a self-authenticating and disembodied *cogito* and of the *lumen naturale* of reason, in Kant's appeal to categorial understanding and to formal intuition, and in Husserl's early insistence on attaining eidetic insight (*Wesensschau*) by means of a phenomenological method that makes no reference to the bodily state of the investigator. Each of these four archetypal Western philosophers privileges the august and steady gaze over the merely hasty glance, seen as nothing more than what Kant called disdainfully "random groping" (*herumtappen*). For them—and for most of the philosophical tradition of which they are the pillars—the glance (along with such allies as the glimpse, the peek, the bare view) is only marginal. Even if it is true that (as Bryson insists) its disavowal is required for the prosperity and power of the gaze itself—repression depending on the continuing attraction of the repressed term—it is no less the case that the glance is regarded as *deserving marginalization and calling for repression.* And this is precisely because of its unseverable tie to the clamorous desires of the body, the tumultuous sea of its ever-shifting emotional life.

It is not only in philosophy that the predominance of the gaze is to be found. The same predominance is to be found in other fields. Bryson's *Vision and Painting* is devoted to demonstrating that "the Logic of the Gaze" (the subtitle of the book) triumphs over the illogic of the glance from Zeuxis onward: the continual effort to hide the traces of the process of painting under the veneer of sheer naturalism or realism is at one with the repression of the body that leaves these marks. In contrast, early Chinese painting of the Northern Sung era prizes the contingent effects of the painter's bodily motions:

> Painting in [Northern Sung–era] China is predicated on the acknowledgement and indeed the cultivation of deictic markers. . . [An explicit aim is] "the building of structure through brushwork"; and in terms of its classical subject-matter, Chinese painting has always selected forms that permit a maximum of integrity and visibility to the constitutive strokes of the brush: foliage, bamboo, the ridges of boulder and mountain formations . . . landscape is certainly the subject, but equally the subject is the work of the brush in "real time" and as [an] extension of the painter's own body . . . . The work of production is constantly displayed in the wake of its traces; in this tradition the body of labour is on constant display.[55]

In decided contrast, Western painting from Zeuxis to Mondrian attempts to remove all remnants of the painter's bodily gestures from the finished work and to present this work as a frozen moment of sheer contemplation, that of the "Founding Perception" of the painter's world:

55. Bryson, *Vision and Painting*, pp. 89–90. Bryson extends this tradition to Japanese painting after Sesshu.

Suppression of deixis in the West operates by abstracting from the physical process of painting and [from] viewing a valorized moment when the eye contemplates the world alone, in severance from the material body of labour. . . . In the Founding Perception, the gaze of the painter arrests the flux of phenomena, contemplates the visual field from a vantage-point outside the mobility of duration, in an eternal moment of disclosed presence . . . [such] vision as it is presented to the viewer is that of the Gaze victorious over the Glance, vision disembodied, vision decarnalized.[56]

Finding in Titian's *Bacchus and Ariadne* the "technical zenith" of such a conception of painting—in which "everything that was in rhythm is arrested and everything that had been mobile is petrified"[57]—Bryson argues that the triumph of the gaze in Western painting is at one with the suppression of the painter's body (and, by implication, the viewer's body as well): thus of the glance as the body's most characteristic gesture in the realm of visual experience.[58] The perennial popularity of the panoramic landscape scene is further evidence of the priority given to the gaze in Western art.[59] Bryson's argument helps us to realize that this priority is bought at the price of abandoning the body: panoramas certainly exist in ancient Chinese and Japanese painting, but they are conveyed by deliberately self-displaying brushwork that keeps the painter's body part of the painted scene itself. Not until Cézanne and Van Gogh, de Kooning and Pollock, Gorki and Mitchell, will this body be fully integrated into Western art, along with the glance as its active outpost.

Comparable cases can be made for the hegemony of the gaze in still other fields: in literature, for example, where the omniscient gaze of the author and/or narrator commands every significant view. Starobinski claims that French writers from Corneille and Racine to Rousseau and Stendahl all have recourse to the gaze as "the living link between the person and the world, between self and others."[60] Although each author treats the dialectic of glance and gaze differently, in the end the gaze triumphs as the primary means of pursuing a hidden and fascinating reality—"a reality temporarily dissimulated yet within the grasp of anyone who knows how to force it out of hiding and compel its

56. Ibid., pp. 94–95. On Zeuxis as paradigmatic for the early obsession with realistic painting —and with trompe l'oeil in particular—see Lacan, *Les quatre concepts fundamentaux de la psychanalyse*, pp. 95, 102.

57. Ibid., p. 96.

58. "The logic of the Gaze is therefore subject to two great laws: the body (of the painter, for the viewer) is reduced to a single point, the *macula* of the retinal surface; and the moment of the Gaze (for the painter, for the viewer) is placed outside duration. Spatially and temporally, the act of viewing is constructed as the removal of the dimensions of space and time, as the disappearance of the body: the construction of an *acies mentis*, the punctual viewing subject" (ibid., p. 96).

59. On the significance of panoramic painting, see Edward S. Casey, *Representing Place: Landscape Painting and Maps*, pp. 7–10, 18, 24–25, 65–66.

60. Starobinski, *The Living Eye*, p. 6.

presence."[61] The underlining of "presence" reminds us of the ultimate stakes in the game of the gaze: namely, the determinate presence that has controlled so much of Western metaphysics from its inception and that calls for the sovereign gaze as a comparably commanding visual action. In the case of modern French literature, it follows that "what [is] needed, accordingly, [is] to retrace the history of a gaze lured by desire from discovery to discovery."[62] Here, too, there is a powerful temptation to succumb to the exigencies of "the panoramic gaze."[63] Only when the renegade writer questions the primacy of this gaze is the glance legitimized: for example, in Henry James's *Portrait of a Lady* and in many of Samuel Beckett's works in which the most exiguous glance becomes the pivot of the plot. The mere fact that the role of the glance is so rarely thematized bespeaks its suppressed situation in Western literature.

We could continue to document the hegemony of the gaze in Western life: for example, in the case of the "medical gaze" so strikingly presented by Foucault in *The Birth of the Clinic.* But this is hardly necessary since Western life itself, especially in the modern and postmodern eras, is so deeply dependent on the valorizing of the gaze: it is so integral to the very fabric of this life that it could not survive without it. No wonder, then, that the glance becomes so subversive: given the situation, this, too, could not be otherwise. As Foucault puts it:

> The gaze implies an open field, and its essential activity is of the successive order of reading; it records and totalizes; it gradually reconstitutes immanent organizations; it spreads out over a world . . . . [The glance] is essentially demystifying. If it strikes in its violent rectitude, it is in order to shatter, to lift, to release appearance . . . [it] can take in [only] the fragment, the collage, and [is] unable to participate in the unitary mysteries of reason.[64]

Bryson is more succinct in his rendition of the dichotomy between gaze and glance: "vision is portrayed under two aspects, one vigilant, masterful, 'spiritual,' and the other subversive, random, disorderly."[65] Once a master term has been identified and lionized as much as has the gaze—regarded as an exclusive source of truth and insight—any alternative becomes ipso facto a merely subordinate term whose very life is derivative from the prevailing figure. It is cast as renegade—as untrustworthy and unreliable, as incapable of attain-

61. Ibid.; his italics.

62. Ibid.

63. Ibid., p. 12. For Starobinski, however, this term refers primarily to the *critic's* temptation to take into account the entire context of a literary work, "the whole picture" (p. 13). But the critic would not be so tempted were the work not already panoramic in tendency.

64. Michel Foucault, *The Birth of the Clinic,* tr. A. Sheridan (New York: Random House, 1975), pp. 121–122.

65. Bryson, *Vision and Painting,* p. 93. Bryson is talking specifically of how vision is discussed in English and in French, but his point holds more generally—as does his assessment of the differential destiny of the Gaze and the Glance in painting.

ing serious truth, as whimsical and trivial in any claims it may make. Such is the fate of the glance.

VII

In fact, the circumstance is more complicated than is indicated by the dichotomizing and hierarchizing to which the gaze and the glance have been so often subjected in the West. Exceptions may not "prove the rule," but they remain of undeniable significance. At the very least, they remind us that the field of visual perception cannot be partitioned in some neat and everlasting manner. This is not just because of the uncontainable proliferation of modes and species (which means that no definitive taxonomy will ever prevail) but because the poles themselves, presumably the most distinct and independent terms of all, intermingle and cross over in certain crucial ways.

The predominance of the gaze, though powerfully present in virtually every domain of Western life, is not without complications, some of which are introduced by the glance, its presumptive antitype—and this despite its marginality, indeed, *from* its very marginality. To begin with, let us note that not all gazing is imperious, much less tyrannical. The contemplative gaze, for example, does not fiercely totalize but calmly takes in its surroundings: active here is a receptive look, one that does not tyrannize in the name of objective truth. Its aim is more to appreciate than to classify or restructure the visual field. This kind of gaze is far from the epistemically ambitious, overriding look that is the ideal of the philosophers to whom I have referred and, indeed, of many scientists. It is allied with still other sorts of nontendentious gazing: for example, the admiring gaze or the mutually respectful gaze. When the poet says "Look at me only, with thine eyes," he is referring to the loving gaze—a special kind of erotic look whose concupiscent edge is not greedy or demanding. (In this situation, paradoxically, the glance is more likely to be possessive in expressing the immediacy of desire.)

There is also the "reflexive gaze" as Starobinski calls it: this is the open look by which I return to the world of ordinary experience, bringing to bear a fund of prior reflection. Even if the impulse of much gazing is to leave the surfaces of this world behind and to look elsewhere—typically in the depths or heights of some domain of experience—there is a wish to return in certain cases: to clarify and to illuminate, to reappreciate and to reconnect what has been left. This is not the quasi-automatic return of the glance that happens in virtually *every* case of this act: that is, the second beat of glancing-back. Instead, it is an occasional but highly insightful form of looking that embraces the very experience that has been surpassed in the first, sublimatory action of the gaze: "If a little reflection takes us away from the sensible world, a more demanding philosophy brings us back—as if, having braved the limits of the horizon and traversed the void, the gaze had no alternative but to return to immediate evidence. . . . [Here we encounter] the idea of recommencing knowledge with a wisdom that, under the protection of the *reflexive* gaze, trusts in the senses and in the world the senses reveal."[66] Here the gaze goes against its own proclivity for seeking presence in the supra-sensible realm. This can go to the extreme of preferring surface to depth. If it is usually the case that the gaze is "irresistibly drawn into the vertiginous void that forms in the object of fascination"—that is, to say, into the depths of that object—it is also sometimes the case that the same gaze will seek to "shake off the bewildering fascination with depths in order to rediscover the shimmering reflections that play on the water's surface."[67] This is the same *jeu des reflets* that draws the glancing eye to the surfaces of things. But where the glance darts there first of all—and typically stays there, however fitfully—the gaze only comes there following its enchantment with depth, with "the hidden [that] is the other side of a presence," or else after its disenchantment.[68]

There is still another form of gaze that falls outside the totalizing tendencies of the standard Western model. This is the gaze of the world back at *us*, a *speculum mundi* in the literal sense of "the world's look." Instead of our embracing the world in the panoramic possessiveness of the epistemophiliac gaze, now the world turns back to regard us. In Merleau-Ponty's vocabulary, this is a "chiasmatic" circumstance in which a reversal of normal expectations occurs: the looker becomes the looked-at, the looked-at the looker. Not just reversal but intertwining (*entrelacs*) is here at stake: an interleaving of visible and invisible, self and world, gaze and its object—all of these brought together in the "flesh of the world." As Merleau-Ponty says in *The Visible and the Invisible:* "I feel myself looked at by things."[69]

There is a remarkable moment in *The Four Fundamental Concepts of Psychoanalysis* when Lacan, inspired by the recent, posthumous publication of *The Visible and the Invisible,* begins to explore much the same motif in psychoanalytic terms. Lacan distinguishes rigorously between the "eye," that is, the physiological organ that belongs to the perceiving person, and the "gaze" (*le regard*), which, far from emanating from the eye, looks at the person from *somewhere else* (and not necessarily from another person, as in the case of the Sartrian *regard* that freezes and petrifies me). Notably in dreams and in paintings, "the gaze shows itself" (*le regard se montre*).[70] In a dream, *I* do not look at

66. *The Living Eye,* pp. 5–6; his italics.
67. The first phrase is from ibid., p. 2; the second is from p. 3.
68. Ibid., p. 1: "Le caché est l'autre côté d'une présence."
69. Maurice Merleau-Ponty, *The Visible and the Invisible,* tr. A. Lingis (Evanston, Ill.: Northwestern University Press, 1968), p. 139. The full statement is: "The vision [the seer] exercises, he also undergoes from the things, such that, as many painters have said, I feel myself looked at by the things, my activity is equally passivity." On p. 134, Merleau-Ponty says that "As soon as I see, it is necessary that the vision . . . be doubled with a complementary vision or with another vision: myself seen from without." Comparable themes are to be found in "Eye and Mind," section 2.
70. For the radical "schism" (*la shize*) between the eye and the gaze, which is reminiscent of Merleau-Ponty's distinction between the "pure gaze" and the "gaze of our eyes" (see n. 76), see *Les quatre concepts fondamentaux de la psychanalyse,* pp. 70–71, esp. this statement on p. 70:

what I dream but am myself regarded or witnessed by the dream scene.[71] In a famous dream analyzed by Freud near the end of *The Interpretation of Dreams*,[72] the child whose body has in fact caught fire by accident while his father dozes cries out in the dream: "Father, can't you see, I'm burning!"[73] The boy was looking at his father in alarm in the dream dreamt by this same father. Similarly, in Hans Holbein's "The Ambassadors," an anamorphic skull looks out at the viewer, arresting him by its gruesome admonitory gaze.[74] More generally, Lacan holds that whatever takes the position of the *objet a,* that is, the constitutive gap or lack signified by the missing phallus, is constantly gazing at the human subject from its displaced and separated locus in the field of desire: "the *objet a* in the field of the visible is the gaze . . . in the scopic field, the gaze is outside, I am gazed at."[75]

One need not follow Lacan all the way into the arcanum of his theory of desire to realize that he is making a crucial point: the gaze is not bound to human subjectivity (above all, not to the egological self) but may stem from pre-egological or even prehuman aspects of the visual field. The seat of the gaze is "outside" (*au-dehors*) the subject—in which case, it need not become the agent of the all-too-human appetite for the mastery brought by knowledge: an appetite appeased, if never satiated, by the gaze in its institutionalized realizations. Only the eye (and the ego, formed from the eye's vision of itself in the mirror) is truly appetitive and epistemophiliac.[76]

"Eye and gaze: such is for us the schism in which is manifested the drive at the level of the scopic field"; for a critique of Sartre's view, see pp. 79–80; on *speculum mundi,* p. 71; and for the dream as a psychic phenomenon in which "*ça montre*"—with a pun on *ça* as referring to the unconscious as well as simply "that"—see p. 72: "In the waking state, there is elision of the gaze, elision of the fact that not only does it gaze (*ça regarde*) but it *manifests* (*ça montre*). In the field of the dream, on the contrary, that which characterizes the images is the fact that *it manifests (ça montre).*" For an insightful discussion of Lacan on the gaze, see Barbara Freedman, *Staging the Gaze: Postmodernism, Psychoanalysis, and Shakespearean Comedy* (Ithaca, N.Y.: Cornell University Press, 1991), pp. 61–66, 69–72.

71. "Our position in a dream is, in the end, to be emphatically he who does not see" (Lacan, *Les quatre concepts fundamentaux de la psychanalyse,* p. 72).

72. Freud, *The Standard Edition of the Complete Psychological Works,* vol. 5, pp. 509 ff.

73. For Lacan's remarks on this celebrated dream, see *Les quatre concepts fundamentaux de la psychanalyse,* pp. 58, 68.

74. For Lacan's analysis of "The Ambassadors," see ibid., pp. 80–83.

75. Ibid., pp. 97–98. Lacan continues: "That which determines me most deeply in the visible is the gaze that is outside. . . . From which it follows that the gaze is the instrument by which light is incarnated and by which . . . I am *photo-graphed*" (ibid., p. 98; his italics; see also pp. 70, 90). It would be of interest to compare this remark to the view of J. J. Gibson that we are surrounded by information in the ambient light (see Gibson, *The Ecological Approach to Visual Perception,* chap. 2). Concerning the theme of separation and castration anxiety aroused by the prospect of a missing phallus, see *Les quatre concepts fundamentaux de la psychanalyse,* p. 78 and esp. p. 108: "the subject is strictly speaking determined by the separation itself determined by the cut effected by the *a,* that is, the fascination introduced by the gaze."

76. "In what does this giving-to-see (*donner-à-voir*) satisfy something—if not in the fact that

Just as the gaze shows itself to be capable not just of variation but of consider-able complication and even reversal of role, so the glance also manifests a diversity of avatars (as I describe in more detail in the afterword). Take the fact that not all glances are merely playful, innocent, or benign—as one might sus-pect when contrasting the fickleness of the glance with the sobriety of the gaze, as I have myself done earlier in this chapter. Indeed, there is a whole series of dark glances that, even if not exhibiting the spirit of gravity, nevertheless weigh heavily on the human soul. So, too, there are self-undermining glances: glances that turn away from their intended target out of shame, self-denigration, self-consciousness, or guilt. Another set of looks from the dark side includes sus-picious glances, spiteful glances, resentful glances, hateful glances, withering glances. Virtually every culture has some version of the *mal occhio*, the "evil eye."[77] Valéry exclaims: "How many children there would be if glances could impregnate! How many dead if looks could kill!"[78] If the glance is allied with desire, it is also affiliated with aggression—as we say when we talk of someone as having "daggers in his eyes." The drive-basis of the glance runs deep: it engages Thanatos as well as Eros. The more these drives are acknowledged, the less likely is it that there are any entirely innocent glances—glances that can be regarded as "just looking."[79]

Moreover, the glance can be deeply complicitous and conniving: as occurs when two people "exchange significant looks" (for which the Germans have invented a special word: *Blickwechsel*). A great deal of scheming and plotting happens in such exchange, often accompanied by subtle gestures like winking or raising one's eyebrows. Further, much prejudicial perception happens in a glance, as when one passes summary judgment on another person just because of their skin color, their lack of dexterity, their gender, their way of dressing, and so on. The glance, far from being merely receptive on such occasions, is direly judgmental: it puts people in their place in the most peremptory way. This kind of literal pre-judice is often the most entrenched and thus the most difficult to eradicate. Being so embedded in perception itself, deeply prejudiced sub-jects are barely aware of the extent and effect of their damaging glancing. This is

---

there is an appetite of the eye for he who gazes? This appetite of the eye which we attempt to nourish constitutes the value of painting's charm" (ibid., p. 105).

77. Lacan claims that the evil eye is universal and predominates over the "good eye," which is much more rare and occurs only in the form of the "prophylactic eye." See his discussion at ibid., p. 105: "The true function of the organ of the eye [is] the voracious eye, which is the evil eye. If one thinks of the universality of the function of the evil eye, it is striking that there is nowhere any trace of a good eye, an eye that blesses." Lacan attributes the evil eye to a "separative power" that is closely related to envy: see pp. 105–106. On the exceptional, pro-phylactic eye, see Lacan's conversational interchange with Françoise Wahl, ibid., p. 108. I return to the negativities of the glance in the concluding thoughts to this book.

78. Paul Valéry, as cited by Starobinski in *The Living Eye*, p. 4.

79. On the extreme unlikelihood of a merely innocent "just looking," see the chapter of this title in James Elkins, *The Object Stares Back* (New York: Simon and Schuster, 1996), passim.

the very opposite of the glare or stare, modes of gazing in which a self-conscious posture of angry looking is taken. But it is no less aggressive in tone and detrimental in outcome. At such moments, the glance rejoins the gaze, and one may even reinforce the other in a dangerous dialectic of looking: as when one glancingly discovers an object of loathing, then gapes fixedly at that same object, only to glance away and then back again. Others can join in this game of hateful glancings cum gazings, creating an overtly hostile environment from which there is little escape—except for the (often humiliated) party or parties to leave the scene, thereby emptying the highly charged field of interpersonal perception.[80]

<h1 style="text-align:center">VIII</h1>

I do not want to leave the impression that the complications and interlacings to which I have just pointed mean that the glance and the gaze are easily assimilable—or that they are in the end equal partners, fellows in the flesh having the same ultimate valence and purport. Instead, I want to suggest in closing this chapter that when the glance and the gaze are set beside one another the former is a *primus inter pares.* How is this so?

Consider the experience of looking at a painting—or for that matter, at a distant landscape or a tall building. In a meditative and receptive mood, one can enter into a prolonged gaze at the painting or landscape or building. This is a gaze in the full-fledged sense of uninterrupted and even serene looking, open-eyed and open-minded. One is captivated and fascinated by what one is gazing at, and is not even tempted to be distracted from one's visual investment in that object. Yet even here, when one is attentive to the circumstance, one notices that one's eyes are in fact constantly changing direction, being diverted (if not distracted) many times in a given stretch of looking. In short, one is engaging in quick eye movements, even if one may be quite unaware of this while engaged in gazing proper. I seem to be engrossed in Picasso's *Guernica,* but in fact my look is darting all over this enormous and moving canvas; or I think that I am "sunk in the landscape," whereas I am looking all over the place (though not systematically: that would be scanning); or I am taken up by my immersion in beholding the Sears Tower in Chicago, yet I am also and at the same time noticing a myriad details in this building: the way it tapers, the form of its windows, the twin towers on top, and more. What Bryson says of perceiving a

---

80. This is not to mention the fact that, even apart from such emotionally overdetermined circumstances, there are other areas of overlap between glancing and gazing. The ogle, though a type of gaze, resembles the glance in its brevity and lack of fixity. Viewing, a form of glancing, is not unlike gazing, especially in its contemplative mode. This is not to endorse a continuum between the two kinds of act overall; but it is to suggest that we cannot keep them altogether apart—that *les extrêmes se touchent* here as elsewhere in human experience. Again: see afterword for a more complete discussion.

painting is true of these other instances as well: "As the eye traverses the canvas, the path of its movement is irregular, unpredictable, and intermittent."[81] In all three cases, *I glance as I gaze; I am glancing in my gazing.*

The reverse cannot happen: the two acts can collaborate closely (as in their frequent collusion in social settings), but I cannot gaze *while* glancing. The gaze spells the death of the glance; but the glance can insinuate itself into the interstices of the gaze, becoming part of its perceptual infrastructure as it were. The same is true regarding other members of the gaze family: I can glance *in* staring, glaring, scrutinizing, scanning, contemplating, and so forth. But I cannot gaze in glimpsing, peeking, peering, or even viewing. Something about the gaze—the trump card of its sobriety as it were—discourages its fusion with the glance. Something about the glance—its very mercuriality, its penchant for change and difference—allows it to join forces with the gaze.

Despite the historical and cultural hegemony of the gaze, the glance has phenomenological priority in the end: or rather, in the beginning, at the very moment in which the gaze arises from the micro-movements of the look. Its subversive potential gives it an edge that is not just based on its tricksterish ways, the levity that mocks the spirit of gravity. It is also found in the fact that the glance is able to work its way into the gaze *from within:* it subverts by insinuating itself into the midst of the act of gazing itself. This sabotage is more effective than any direct external confrontation in which the gaze, with its extensive historical and institutional support, will always triumph. The power of the glance is that of *underdetermination:* undoing the gaze at its own game, showing that it cannot maintain its own power without the help of rapid glances that stitch together the fabric of the gazed-at object. Without such help, this fabric would not only fall apart; it would not be perceived as coherent cloth to begin with. This is not to say that the stitching effected by the glance is the result of the sober sewing of regular rows by means of disciplined, scansional looking; instead, such glancewise stitching is the unregulated creation of the cloth as one fabric of many colors: a rhapsody of sight. ("Rhapsody" means originally "stitching together.")

The more-than-equal status of the glance has everything to do, then, with its subterranean working, its unsuspected role as a subtle and tacit form of "going under" (*untergehen* in Nietzsche's sense). The glance goes under the gaze and thereby takes precedence over it. It steals a march on the gaze from within. It is the gaze's other—not because it is overtly opposed to it but because it works to ends different from the official tasks of the gaze as sanctioned by social and political forces beyond the control of either. It accomplishes these ends all the more effectively for being concealed within the gaze, hidden in the very heart of its operation.

The glance is the force of becoming in the field of vision. It may not *prevail* in

81. Bryson, *Vision and Painting*, p. 121. I return to the role of glancing in the perception of painting in chap. 12.

this field: that is the more likely fate of the gaze in its worldly (and otherworldly) ambitions. But if it does not prevail, this is not a simple defeat for the glance, since prevailing is not one of its goals in the first place. The glance aims to intercede and insinuate, not to direct and dominate. Even if it does not triumph over the gaze, the glance manages to *precede* and *pervade* it. In this double action lies its uncelebrated victory over the gaze. The glance precedes in that it takes the interstitial steps that build up the gaze in all its ostentatious strength; and it pervades in that no phase of the gaze, no moment of it, is not full of glances.

Indeed, the glance precedes not only the gaze but all other visual acts; it is their probe-head, their secret agent. And it pervades them as well: nowhere in visual perception is glancing of some sort not going on. To start with in the gaze, but also in every other kind of looking. *No seeing without glancing:* this is a proposition we must bear out in various ways in subsequent parts of this book.

Part 2

Glancing Earlier and Farther Afield

So far in this book we have been immersed in the singular worlds of individual subjects who are situated in the contemporary moment—subjects who glance here and now for the most part. It is time to return to the glance's prior implacement in larger structures of history and culture—going "farther field" in the sense of uncovering its own overdetermining forces, examining how it takes its place on the open stage of geography and history, how it arises in the marketplace—the marketplace both of interpersonal interaction and of ideas that are embedded in that interaction. In this spirit, we shall turn *without,* looking farther back in time and out into space than we have gone so far. It is a matter of gaining a new purchase on the glance by taking up a stance of literally *outlooking.* We shall be on the lookout for factors previously neglected—factors of history and culture as these pervade different eras and styles of vision.

Glancing occurs not only in time but also in space—for example, in the midst of an open landscape. But it also arises in the close confines of the place-world. These confines (for example, houses, cafés, streets, sidewalks) are not independent of the particular culture and society within which a given act of glancing takes place, nor of the historical time in which it occurs. Whereas geographic space is universal in its scope—or at least purports to be, given its homogeneous constitution and isotropic directionality—the place-world in which we do most of our glancing is irrecusably specific in origin and scope. This world is always the world as experienced by a certain set of people at a certain place and time, and not just by me as an individual glancer; it is constituted by the intimate intermeshing of groups of persons and their surrounding spatial situations.[1] Since any group of humans—to be a coherent group at all—must share various cultural conventions, the place they co-inhabit will also embody these conventions. Such a place will embody them directly: as is evident in the striking differences between the circular layout and thatched dwellings of a contemporary Bororo village in Brazil and the rectangular marble stoas and temples of the Athenian agora as it existed in the fifth century B.C.[2] The enclosedness of circular structures, at once fostering and reflecting close community and family life, here contrasts with the formal porches of the stoas (ideal for peripatetic discussion) and the rows of columns around the temples (reinforcing the exclusivity of the sacred space within). Even the tholos, the one circular building

1. Equally, a place-world is a habitat of groups of animals and plants; but that is another story. Humans and other natural entities—including inanimate things—occupy layouts of places, some of which intersect with human places and others of which are entirely independent of them. See my *Getting Back into Place: Toward a New Understanding of the Place-World* (Bloomington: Indiana University Press, 1993), part 4, "Wild Places."

2. On the layout of the Bororo village, see Joseph Rykwert, *The Idea of a Town: The Anthropology of Urban Form in Rome, Italy and the Ancient World* (Princeton, N.J.: Princeton University Press, 1976), pp. 169–171. Rykwert also discusses the Athenian agora in ibid., chap. 1. For a more complete study of the agora, see the discussion in section III below.

permitted in the agora, was meant for political debate and voting—not for confidentiality or personal sharing.

In other ways of being in public places, the impact of culture is less overtly manifest yet no less telling. These would include the ways people walk in public, their modes of greeting—and their forms of glancing at each other. Sometimes, walking is regulated in highly specific ways, as when Cistercian monks are permitted to walk only in a certain direction and at certain times of day around the enclosed cloister of their monastery. In Italy and Spain, the evening promenade—in which citizens parade up and down the main street of town in the early evening—is delimited as to time and place. In both cases, different as they are, glances are exchanged on a routinely delivered, socially scheduled basis. In the monastery, we may presume that the glances are quite circumspect, while in evening promenades in Italy and Spain they are comparatively vivacious, expressing intense interest in how other people present themselves at the time. These variations in glancing behavior are due to cultural differences that run deep. They reflect two different ways of comporting oneself in one's customary place-world: one of them devotional and reverential, the other concerned with interpersonal recognition and social status in a local community.

To glance in a given place-world is not just to glance in that world but *in terms of it*. It is to act on certain cultural commitments that have already been made, tacitly or explicitly, at some earlier moment in personal and collective history. Thanks to these commitments, glancing behavior often reaches far back into time, for example, to the founding of the austere Cistercian Order in France in A.D. 1098, or to repeated social practices of southern European towns as these have evolved from an undatable point of origin. A given glancer also embodies social and class differences as well as decisive gender-specific, racial, and ethnic identities. All such cultural, historical, and social determinations run deep in the glancer's body; indeed, they reach right down to the base of her eyeballs and to the tips of her fingers and the soles of her feet. The consequence is that there is no entirely individual glancing, no glancing that is simply mine or yours. As singular as it is in style of execution and in the instant of enactment, it is also, at the same time, collective in character: shared with others (or stemming from them), if not precisely *in time* then *over time*—over the slow evolution of customary behavior adopted by generations across entire epochs of history. This behavior is precipitated into the least gesture, including the barest glance, of someone belonging to a contemporary generation.

To say that every glance is overdetermined in this manner is not to say, however, that every glance is predictable and nothing but a creature of the history of its generation. On the contrary: in the very midst of its historical matrix, a glance retains a margin of free motion that allows it to be responsive to every new situation—where "responsive" is not reducible to being merely reactive and "new situation" signifies what is always the case. Even on the most familiar daily promenade, different configurations of passersby occur—the same people will be differently dressed, in different moods, aware of a current economic crisis, and so on—just as in the discipline of the cloister there are slight variations in perambulation that call out different modes of glancing, despite the fact that the same persons make the same rounds day in and day out (and their predecessors may have repeated these rounds for generations). A saving remnant of ocular liberty exists even in the most compelling circumstance as we have seen in the case of Joe Christmas, who glances back at his torturers even as they castrate him. This glance may not embody the absolute freedom of the for-itself that Sartre ascribes to it, but it does represent an edge of free action in the face of duress. In the most coercive circumstance, just when one would have expected it to do something expectable and programmable, the glance evades the expectation, undoes the program. The glance surprises us by its openness to surprise itself. Its very inconspicuousness gives it the advantage of the entering wedge, allowing it to be all the more effectively infiltrative of the most recalcitrant regions of the place-world.[3]

In part, this extraordinary but subtle liberty is due to the anatomy of the eye itself—especially its rapidly shifting action, which allows it to move unhindered through the field of vision, much more so than other bodily parts and organs within their respective domains. The ears do not naturally move on their own, much less rotate: we must turn the whole head to alter their relative positions. The same goes for the nose. Indeed, it is significantly more difficult to move the body as a whole—the seat of our sensorium—than merely to move our eyes in their sockets. The only organs of comparable versatility are the mouth and the hands, and as if in recognition of this fact they often extend, emphasize, and modulate what the eyes are already engaged in.[4]

Anatomy and physiology conspire with the interests and intentionalities of the human subject to effect a creative compromise of *free action within strict bounds.* One form of determination—anatomico-physiological—helps the human subject to act freely within another form of determination, cultural/historical/social. Enframed by these two modes of determination, the glance realizes a moment of embodied freedom, a margin of corporeal liberty. It is as if the body's own materiality was the vehicle for the liberation of this same body

3. To be "effectively infiltrative" is not necessarily to be *efficacious* in each case. The glance may fail of its purpose—Joe Christmas dies from his wounds, despite his defiant looking-back at his tormenters—yet concerning it we can at least say that it has moved freely in a densely determined situation. For Sartre's treatment of the passage in *Light in August,* see Jean-Paul Sartre, *Being and Nothingness: A Phenomenological Essay in Ontology,* tr. H. Barnes (New York: Washington Square Press, 1966), pp. 525–528, esp. this passage: "this explosion of the Other's look in the world of the sadist causes the goal and meaning of sadism to collapse. The sadist discovers that it was *that freedom* which he wished to enslave, and at the same time he realizes the futility of his efforts" (pp. 526–527; his italics).

4. See my detailed discussion of attention in chap. 9, I shall return to the import of ocular rotation for the freedom of the glance in the concluding thoughts.

from a subjected state in which it would merely carry out social imperatives and honor cultural constraints. The mobile eye, acting as the agent of the glance, releases us from the crushing weight of these imperatives and constraints. At least it does so momentarily. It lets us look where we will—indeed, to look or not to look in the first place—and thereby to realize a freedom of in-determination.[5]

Despite this crucial redeeming moment of freedom in glancing, the glance itself remains culturally, historically, and socially saturated. Glancing looks are encoded and enacted within these broad parameters. These parameters—which extend to our entire interhuman life—have everything to do with what we allow ourselves (or, alternately, are allowed) to look at in the first place, including such things as the eyes of others, other parts of their bodies, their own expressions of sociality, their links to the environment, and so forth. Such parameters also bear on how we glance, the manner and mode, the style and form. They frequently prohibit the prolongation of the glance into a stare, which can have socially dangerous or devastating consequences: as is manifest on a New York subway. (On the other hand, the erotic glance can be sustained without any such deleterious consequences. Alma Mahler remarks in her diary, for example, "We exchanged a voluptuous glance—for a long, wonderful moment—regardless of onlookers. Such a glance can be stunningly sensual."[6]) At the limit, cultural or social restrictions may prohibit the barest act of glancing, for example, between "untouchables" and other castes in India or between blacks and whites in the Old South, even if such prohibitions are often breached. The same forces also influence other ways we glance: with our eyes wide open or partly closed, with or without hand gestures, in certain clothes, through glasses or a veil, and so on. These concomitant gestures of the glance form its living exoskeleton and are deeply imbued with sociocultural determinations.

In part 1, I was for the most part speaking in my own voice in the initial descriptions of the glance. This same voice incorporates and reflects my culture and society of origin, and doubtless my being male and white; these categorial

---

5. Freedom of in-determination is not to be confused with a nondetermined state of being; it is a freedom to act in the very midst of causal and historical determinations. Thus it is also not to be equated with anything like a freedom of the will (which requires a separate voluntary action), much less a freedom of perfection (whereby my free act lets me attain a state of perfection, e.g., the good in some ideal sense). The simplest and yet quite radical act of the in-determination of glancing occurs when we voluntarily let our eyes close, thereby eliminating the visual world at one stroke. As Robert Garland notes, sight "is the one sense we can obliterate—within the twinkling of an eye and the one [sense], therefore, that we most effectively control, either by averting or closing the eyes" (Robert Garland, "Sight and Insight: The Eye as Sensory Organ," unpublished manuscript, Colgate University, circa 1998, p. 2). For further discussion of the freedom of in-determination, see the concluding thoughts to this book.

6. From Alma Mahler-Werfel, *Diaries 1898–1902*, tr. A. Beaumont (Ithaca, N.Y.: Cornell University Press, 1999), as cited in the review of this book by John Simon, "Serial Muse," *New York Times*, April 17, 1999, p. 15. Garland states, "How we see is also a reflection of culture . . . . What the mind sees is not necessarily what is [objectively] there but what the mind *supposes* might be there" ("Sight and Insight," p. 2; his italics).

determinants do not invalidate my findings, but they do delimit their scope.[7] For this reason alone, one has to look to cultures and societies other than one's own. This is not for the sake of some putative objectivity or formal universality but so as to add nuance and depth to one's own descriptions as well as to remind oneself that cultural, social, and historical dimensions make an important difference in our construal of how we ourselves glance, what we glance at, and with what means we glance. Just as there is no innocent eye, so there is no pristine account of the eye's actions—not even of its most spontaneous performances, for which the glance is paradigmatic. The most idiosyncratic first-person account is ineluctably third-person in origin and range. The singularity of the glance is itself a product of nonsingular forces that predetermine, yet do not cause, the emergence of a given glance.

In an effort to acknowledge such nonsingular dimensions of the glance, I shall consider in this new part two quite disparate circumstances of glancing, those found in ancient Greece and in late-nineteenth-century Paris, offering characterizations of each that will highlight their specialness as well as their commonalities with other acts of glancing that occur elsewhere and at other times. Above all, I shall direct my attention to what is extraordinary within the ordinary life of the glance in Athens and Paris: to what stands out in the midst of everyday enactments in these contrastive place-worlds.

These two places (and times) are chosen not just because of their disparity but because each is especially instructive with regard to certain aspects of glancing that the highly focused accounts given in parts 1 and 3 are not suited to pursue. My aim is not to give a comprehensive account of the role of glancing, much less of vision generally, in the two situations I shall examine. Instead, I employ cultural, literary, and philosophical analysis to investigate the differential destiny of glancing in each instance. My contention is not that these situations are to be presumed paradigmatic for understanding the glance elsewhere and elsewhen but that, nevertheless, they allow us to savor special aspects of the glance that, distinctive as they are in their cultural instantiations, illuminate the place of glancing in many other, quite disparate situations.[8] Features such as the inherent bidirectionality of the glance, its arrow-like launching and its gleaming quality, its close affinity with wonder—to name just four features to be encoun-

---

7. For a subtle analysis of the incorporation of other voices into one's own, see Fred Evans, *The Multivoiced Body: Society, Communication, and the Age of Diversity* (forthcoming), esp. chap. 7.

8. Once again, we approach the idea of the "lateral universal" in Merleau-Ponty's sense of the term. See Maurice Merleau-Ponty, "From Mauss to Lévi-Strauss," in *Signs*, tr. R. C. McCleary (Evanston, Ill.: Northwestern University Press, 1964), p. 120: "no longer the overarching universal of a strictly objective method, but a sort of lateral universal which [involves the] incessant testing of the self through the other person and the other person through the self." On the combination of the singular with the universal, see Gilles Deleuze, *Difference and Repetition*, tr. P. Patton (New York: Columbia University Press, 1994), chap. 1. I return to this link in chap. 10.

tered in this part—can be found anywhere, in any society, albeit in variant guises and with differential emphasis and effect. To recognize such features is important not just because it brings them to our attention to begin with but also because it alerts us to parallel presences in other settings—altered as these presences may be in detail. To accomplish such recognition, however, we must undertake a close analysis of the settings in which they stood out in their saliency.

5

THE GLANCE IN ANCIENT ATHENS

> And that which first came to the city of Ilium,
> call it a dream of calm
> and the wind dying,
> the loveliness and luxury of much gold,
> the melting shafts of the eyes' glances,
> the blossom that breaks the heart with longing.
>
> —Aeschylus, *Agamemnon*

> Sharp is the eye of the gods to see everything.
>
> —fragment of anonymous Greek tragedian,
> preserved in Stobaeus, *Eklogai* 1.3.16

> Let me only glance where you are.
>
> —Sappho, "Invocation to Aphrodite"

> The Greeks were, as we say, "visual," "people of the
> eye" (*Augenmenschen*). They grasped the world pri-
> marily by the eye, and therefore they paid attention
> to looking and the look.
>
> —Martin Heidegger, *Parmenides*

I

"Oculocentrism" is a phenomenon that cannot be confined to the early modern era in the West—the era in which Michel Foucault so discerningly detected
its presence in the institutions of medicine, pedagogy, and penology. He demonstrated compellingly that in these institutions, the gaze, as the basis of oculocentric paradigms, is strongly favored, indeed legitimated and sanctioned at
every turn: for example, the medical gaze or the gaze of the guards in the
Panopticon (along with the internalization of this gaze in the unhappy prisoners
held there, resulting in a sense of continual surveillance) or the supervision of
hapless students seated in straight rows in the classroom. But the gaze is also
valorized in other ancient cultures, for example, in Mesopotamia: in the *Enuma
Elish* Marduk is depicted scanning Tiamat's slaughtered body in a concerted act

of gazing. In these various instances, certain attributes of the gaze are stressed: its penetrating power, its undaunted and forthright character, above all its collusion with institutional power. When these attributes conjoin in a consistent pattern of looking, the result is oculocentrism.

Privileging vision over the other senses is more the rule than the exception in almost every epoch of Western history.[1] This privilege has its earliest fully documented manifestation in ancient Greek civilization. What is extraordinary about the Greek case is that the emphasis on vision found there includes both the gaze and the glance. Moreover, for the early Greeks the gaze is by no means predominant when it comes to matters of vision. Precisely because of this circumstance, the charge of oculocentrism is here complicated, if not misapplied, insofar as the term "oculocentric" entails the primacy of the gaze, especially in the form of fixated or focused looking such as scrutiny and (putatively) neutral observation. On the other hand, the Greeks of the eighth to the fourth centuries B.C. were unquestionably "visuocentric," by which I mean the privileging of vision over the other senses, without any commitment to the priority of the gaze over the glance. As Aristotle says expressly in the opening paragraph of his *Metaphysics*:

> All men by nature desire to know. An indication of this is the delight we take in our senses; for even apart from their usefulness they are loved for themselves; and above all others the sense of sight. For not only with a view to action, but even when we are not going to do anything, we prefer it (one might say) to everything else. The reason is that this, most of all the senses, makes us know and brings to light many differences between things.[2]

To be visuocentric in this manner—to rank vision highest not dogmatically or tendentiously but for a particular reason: namely, its ability to make distinctions —is not necessarily to be oculocentric: not if this latter implies prioritizing the gaze over the glance and other supposedly capricious or menial acts of seeing. Visuocentrism, in whatever form it occurs, means recognizing that vision is especially well adapted to perceiving things at a distance and to determining depth; that it is remarkably easy to employ (just open your eyes and look!); that it is closely coordinated with handling, walking, and other basic human activities (thanks mainly to its position in front of the head); that it is discriminating (as Aristotle holds) in regard to particular features of any given perceived thing; and that it is very skilled at figuring out such things as movement, speed, trajectory, and so on. In all of these ways, vision proves to be central, indeed, indispensable,

---

1. A notable and well-documented contrast with oculocentrism is found in the unabashedly audiocentric people of Papua New Guinea. See Steven Feld, *Sound and Sentiment: Birds, Weeping, Poetics, and Song in Kaluli Expression* (Philadelphia: University of Pennsylvania Press, 1987).

2. Aristotle, *Metaphysics*, tr. W. D. Ross, in *The Works of Aristotle* (Oxford: Clarendon Press, 1928, 2d ed.), Book A, 980a–980b. For a brief but pointed account of the Greek valorization of vision, especially in terms of the tension between "speculation" and "observation," see Martin Jay, *Downcast Eyes: The Denigration of Vision in Twentieth-Century French Thought* (Berkeley: University of California Press, 1993), pp. 21–31.

to human sensory experience. I would maintain that visuocentrism as I have just specified it is not an exaggerated view of the human condition but is often characteristic of this condition at the level of sensing.

The ancient Greeks embraced visuocentrism in the context of a model of knowledge that was resolutely hierarchical. As exemplified by the celebrated analogy of the Divided Line as proposed in Plato's *Republic,* the highest objects of knowledge are also the most invariant, that is, the Forms. As one moves upward on the scalar schema in a veritable "ascent to the absolute,"[3] one finds increasingly fixed and abstract items: from fleeting shadows to sturdy perceptual objects, then from mathematical entities to metaphysical Forms. If Plato had been unremittingly oculocentric in his thinking, he would have insisted on correspondingly determinate kinds of looking (for example, gazing, scrutinizing, and so forth) as essential to, indeed increasingly employed in, the ascent itself. As we shall see, such insistences are not absent from Plato's account, but he also leaves open a significant place for glancing at every stage, including the last and most exalted stage.

The prisoners in the cave glance at the shadows before them: in this case at least, one might have expected as much in view of the flickering nature of the shadows cast by puppets dangled before a fire on the parapet behind the prisoners. But the glance is ingredient in each later stage as well, albeit in different ways: first, in the bedazzlement caused by the bright rays of the sun as the prisoners emerge from the cave (gazing in an open-eyed way would be tantamount to being blinded);[4] then, in the glimpsing of the hypothetically posited "mathematicals" that have diagrammatic if not actual being (they lack the substantiality that would call for mental gazing); and finally, in the noetic vision of the Forms themselves, which possess their own dazzling properties, taken as analogous to solar radiation: at such august and ultimate presences the knower is best advised to glance, not to look steadily.[5] In the Seventh Letter, moreover, Plato suggests that the link between *nous* (mind) and *eidé* (Forms) is best conceived on the analogy of "sparks" that fly from the knower to the known: "when, suddenly, like a blaze kindled by a leaping spark, [knowledge] is generated in the soul and at once becomes self-sustaining."[6] Such noetic sparks are

3. See J. N. Findlay, *Ascent to the Absolute* (London: Allen and Unwin, 1970).

4. Compare also the fate of Semele, the mother of Dionysus, who in seeing Zeus face to face is incinerated on the spot. (I thank Meredith Hoppin for suggesting this analogy.)

5. I am here drawing on passages in the *Republic,* Books 6 and 7, concerning the analogy of the Good with the sun, the Divided Line, and the Allegory of the Cave. This is not to mention that the craftsman discussed in Book 10 must look back and forth between the Forms and the object he is fashioning—and the artist, working at third remove from the Forms, must glance among the latter, the physical object, and the work of art. (I owe this last observation to Michael Naas.)

6. Plato, Seventh Letter, tr. L. A. Post, in *Plato: Collected Dialogues,* ed. E. Hamilton and H. Cairns (New York: Pantheon, 1963), p. 1589.

vehicles of the glance; their quickly intermittent flashing calls for, and at the same time emblematizes, the glance's own darting, discontinuous character.

This affinity between the glance and the supreme objects of knowledge is no anomaly, as an oculocentric perspective would have to hold; its affirmation is precisely what we should expect in a visuocentric culture that is sensitive to nuanced differences between varieties of vision and is not wedded to the supremacy of one major kind of seeing such as the gaze (and, more particularly, to a single kind of gazing such as beholding or contemplating). For what better than glancing in its inherent fugitiveness could withstand the austerity and fierce presence of the Forms, those archetypal exemplars of what Heidegger calls "determinate presence" (*Anwesenheit*)?[7] To gaze unblinkingly at the Forms —as at their empirical instantiations displayed in the dazzling sunlight—is to risk losing sight of them in their sheer brilliance, indeed *losing sight* altogether, becoming blinded by this same brilliance.[8] Only a subtle mode of vision like the glance, which as a matter of course no sooner looks than it blinks and *looks away,* can tolerate such an intensely illuminated scene. At the same time, the glance alone, thanks to its extreme agility, has the capacity to insinuate itself deftly into the eidetic or mathematical or perceptual matter at hand—to create intimate inroads into otherwise impenetrable physical and metaphysical presences. To stare at such presences open-eyedly and in the spirit of gravity is to risk losing them altogether: better to get acquainted by the indirection of glancing. Going roundabout is once more the best way to get home. The alliance between the glance and noetic presence in particular runs deep—even as it plays itself out on the surface.

The ancient Greeks, and most notably Plato, were the first in the West to appreciate and explore this apparently paradoxical, yet quite effective, relationship. In it, we witness the stealthy ability of the glance to join up with more formidable forces. This is a combination we shall encounter later in the very different context of ethics, where quick discernment combines with efficacy in inaugurating (and sometimes sustaining) ethical actions.[9] In the epistemological realm at stake in the middle Books of the *Republic,* there is a comparable conjunction of these two quite different potencies. Given a chance, the glance gives a remarkably subtle reading of any given phenomenon—literally, anything under the sun—by detecting the infrastructure of the perceptual object across otherwise distracting "rays of the world" (in Husserl's apt expression, already noted in the introduction and discussed more fully in chapter 9). It sees between these dazzling rays, as it were, alighting on the thing itself. When its object has metaphysical and no longer exclusively physical status, the glance is no less able

7. On determinate presence, see again the introduction to Martin Heidegger, *Being and Time,* tr. J. Macquarrie and E. Robinson (New York: Harper, 1962), pp. 47–48.

8. For a discerning discussion of being blinded by looking straight into the sun, see James Elkins, *The Object Stares Back: On the Nature of Seeing* (New York: Harcourt Brace, 1996), pp. 12, 87, 103–105, 106, 107.

9. See chap. 10.

to touch upon the Form to which it gives sinuous but skillful access. Thanks to this ingression into the visible and invisible worlds alike, the glance proves to be unusually skillful in its epistemological finesse. It goes straight to objects from (and through) shadows, and it goes equally straight to Forms from (and through) perceptual particulars and mathematical objects. The glance is no more deterred by robust objects than by eidetic formalities in helping the knower to reach certain epistemic goals.

Neither the state of ignorance (exemplified in the shadow world within the cave) nor the threat of blindness (epitomized in the egress from the cave and the ascent to the Forms) can deter the glance from making a major contribution to the project of coming to know the world; it is at the vanguard of the inquiring subject who thrusts himself/herself into the midst of things to be known. It is a matter of the *glance-ahead* that transforms the prospective knower into the knowing looker. To glance ahead is to enter the domain of the knowable from a position in the not-yet-known. In the case of the Divided Line, one glances forward beyond spurious shadows, then looks with equal forwardness into the brightness of the perceptual day-world, and from there leaps ahead into mathematical structures and the finality of Forms.

Just as sparks fly forth from flint struck with a metallic object, so knowledge flares up from an encounter with those things at which the glance looks ahead with incomparable nuance and incontestable power. "What the primary Beauty in bodies really is," said Plotinus at a later moment, "is something which we become aware of even at the first glance."[10]

II

As I have emphasized in the preceding remarks to this part, every glance is overdetermined. Beyond specific cultural determinations such as a certain accepted model of acquiring knowledge (for example, that which we have just considered in Plato's case), there are other determining factors like time of day, climate, and weather. We glance differently on different days and at different times of day: at high noon, we avert the glance if the reflectance of what we are

10. Plotinus, *Enneads*, tr. H. Armstrong (Cambridge, Mass.: Harvard University Press, 1966), I.6.2. Plotinus elaborates on this point: "What prevents the soul, when she is in the upper world, from knowing the object of knowledge at once, be the object of knowledge one thing [e.g., a Form] or many [e.g., mathematical structures]? Certainly nothing prevents her from that, because she is simple, possessed of simple knowledge, knowing the one thing, be it simple or compound, at once, *like the eyesight which sees a whole face at once*, although the face is compounded of many parts, while the eyesight perceives it as being one and not many. *So does the soul when she sees a compound thing of many parts know it all at once simultaneously*, not part by part." (Plotinus, *Theologia*, tr. Geoffrey Lewis, ed. P. Henry and H. R. Schwyzer, *Plotini Opera* [Paris: Desclé de Brouwer, 1959], vol. 2, ch. 2, ll. 19–24; translator's emphasis). Such simultaneous seeing is best accomplished by the glance.

looking at is too bright to bear; at dusk, we may let the glance linger over its object, in keeping with the quiescent mood of a pensive moment; outside at midnight, our glance may come close to a squint as we try to make out what is around us. So, too, the glance may vary with differences in weather: the ambit of my glance is more restricted in stormy weather and may be confined to the secure ground just under my feet if a gale is blowing, while on a warm and clear day I will be tempted to glance as far afield as the landscape permits. Season matters too: if I am plodding through heavy, unplowed snow, I am less given to glancing in a wide-circuited way, whereas in spring and summer I enjoy looking out as openly and broadly as possible. Not that any of these various factors is definitive: no more than in the case of cultural and social factors is it a matter of a strict, much less total, determination. Climactic and seasonal conditions are just that: *conditions* for action, not simple causes of it. In Gibson's term, they *afford* action; they enable certain things to happen instead of forcing them to occur. Among these actions is that of the glance, which is influenced by the partic- ular settings in which it finds itself and yet is not completely determined by them. It is literally *over*-determined by their presence: determined from above (or from below, or from the side) without being compelled from within or caused from without. But this amounts to saying that it is underdetermined in the end: room is always left for leeway in the exact form that glancing takes on the ground.

A case in point is the particular *landscape* in which a concrete act of glancing takes place. Landscape is the proffered surface of the place-world as this latter presents itself to us on any given occasion. It is a double-edged phenomenon: on the near side of objective space (thus always intimately accessible to us in contrast with the comparative remoteness of such space), it is on the far side of the body (regarded as the natural subject of perception, before whom a land- scape displays itself).[11] Landscapes, including seascapes and cityscapes, provide both the given circumstance (that is, wherein we stand) and the circumam- bience (wherein we move and look out) within which glancing arises. We look out into a landscape as into the milieu in which we are concretely situated; it is a scene of orientation construed as adumbrating wherein we are placed—in what region, what part of the place-world, which portion of world-space. No wonder, then, that glancing occurs differentially in its midst. A vast landscape scene such as that presented by the Himalayas as seen from the high plateau of southern Tibet will draw the glance into its own farthest reaches; it will elicit its circum- spective powers, by which it moves back and forth across the larger landscape and its far horizon. Other landscapes precipitate other kinds of glancing: in a narrow canyon of the Colorado River my glance will be correspondingly re- stricted, in keeping with the overarching and closely concatenated natural struc- tures of that place: I am torn between looking straight down into the river that

---

11. "The body is a natural self and, as it were, the subject of perception" (M. Merleau-Ponty, *Phenomenology of Perception*, tr. Colin Smith [New York: Humanities Press, 1962], p. 206).

roils around me and straight up into the surrounding cliffs. This experience rejoins that of being in the cavernous architectural canyons of midtown Manhattan, where I must attend both to what is immediately underfoot as well as to what soars high overhead.[12]

III

How different is the cityscape of midtown Manhattan from the ancient Athenian agora! The agora as it existed from the fifth to the second centuries B.C. was a very open place (as *forum,* the Latin equivalent of the term "agora," literally implies: it is related to *foris*, "outside"). Here the built environment solicits wide-eyed and open-minded glances. Unlike midtown Manhattan, the buildings do not tower over the open space, choking off any longer view. Instead, they are mainly of modest scale and are situated at irregular intervals throughout the agora itself.[13] Paths between them are equally irregular, some narrow (just footpaths), some wider (for example, the route of the Panathenaic procession). Walking these paths, one can see considerable distances— onto the Acropolis in one direction, toward the mountains in another.

On this agoric arena, ordered in its very sprawl, everything conspired to elicit and valorize the mobile glance among the citizens of ancient Athens. If the built environment here set the stage for open-ended walking and looking and talking, so did the climatic conditions in which they flourished. These conditions were characteristically bright and dry and clear, amounting to the climatic equivalent of what Heidegger would call a *Lichtung,* an Open or Clearing that encourages the free exchange of glances and their rapid modulation into other forms of looking. "The light in which stood the landscape and things that surrounded the life of the Greeks," say Hans Blumenberg, "gave to everything a clarity and (in terms of optics alone) unquestionable presence that left room for doubt regarding the accessibility of nature to man only late and only as a result of thought's experience with itself."[14] Under such a bright sky and in the ambience of such

12. For a dramatic description of traveling down the Colorado River, see the classic description of John Wesley Powell, *The Exploration of the Colorado River* (Chicago: University of Chicago Press, 1957). Artists such as Georgia O'Keefe and John Marin, both primarily landscape painters, capture this deep analogy between Manhattan and the canyons of the Southwest. I discuss the relation between cityscape and landscape in my unpublished essay, "The Experience of Place, Space, and Site in Urban Life" (circa 2002).

13. For detailed plans of the Athenian agora at several important historical moments, see the discussion and drawings in John Camp, *Athenian Agora: Excavations in the Heart of Classical Athens* (New York: Thames and Hudson, 1992). See also Homer A. Thompson and R. E. Wycherley, *The Agora of Athens: The History, Shape, and Uses of an Ancient City Center* (Princeton, N.J.: American School of Classical Studies at Athens, 1972).

14. Hans Blumenberg, *The Legitimacy of the Modern World,* tr. R. M. Wallace (Cambridge: Harvard University Press, 1983), p. 243. Translation slightly modified.

radiant buildings (many of them constructed from gleaming white marble), the glance was not only brightening but *brightened.* It was in its element—its atmospheric as well as architectural element. Upon this propitious elemental basis, it entered into the concrete contexts of ordinary discourse, political deliberation, and chance encounters.

It is no accident that Aristotle chose as the leading example of "chance" (*tuché*) the encounter of two people whose paths intersect suddenly in the agora as each goes about his separate task of doing errands.[15] Agoric space lends itself to the fortuitous meetings of those who have no intention of seeking or finding the very person whom they so precipitously meet. Nor is it any accident that the very word "agora" is etymologically affine with *ageirein,* "to gather together," as well as with *agorazein,* "to frequent the marketplace."[16] To meet in the marketplace, especially in an accessible and brightly lit place such as the ancient agora, is to facilitate the interchange of glances by which individuals acknowledge each other as fellow citizens of the same polis. Even if these glances arise from chance encounters, they are necessary to a robust political life: as Edward E. Cohen remarks, "The ability to identify one another at a glance is, for Aristotle, the essence of the traditional polis."[17]

Contrast this with contemporary American ways of shopping: getting to stores in sealed cars that allow no looks of genuine recognition, parking these vehicles in purely linear fashion, and entering stores where others are for the most part strangers. The walking is from car to store and back; the looking is largely limited to the inspection of goods rather than the acknowledgment of other persons; and talking is often absent altogether. Nowhere is there the kind of open civic intercourse that constitutes the life of the polis in ancient Greece—an interaction in which open-eyed looking is an integral part.

The recurrent recognition of one another by members of a Greek polis was facilitated by the architecture of the agoric buildings: whether structured as a circle (as in the *tholos,* where a minimum of seventeen citizens met every day and night, fully in each other's looks) or as a rectangle (as in the outer structure of the *bouleutérion,* whose vertically arranged seating for fully 500 people maximized possibilities of witnessing those who spoke and noticing how others pres-

15. See Aristotle, *Physics,* Book II, 195b40–196a5.

16. Furthermore, *agoreuein* means to speak (especially in a public assembly), while the word *agoreutérion* signifies a place for speaking. Similarly, the earliest meaning of *agora* is a place of assembly. For more on *agora,* see the entry in P. Chantraine, ed., *Dictionnaire Etymologique de la langue grecque* (Paris: Klincksieck, 1999). (I owe these refinements to Meredith Hoppin.)

17. Edward E. Cohen, "A Modern Myth: Classical Athens as a Face-to-Face Society," *Common Sense* 6, no. 1 (spring 1997): 101. Aristotle's claim is at *Politics,* 1327a1–1327a2. It is an open question whether Athens was in fact small enough to allow for this face-to-face glancing. Isocrates claimed that as a result of Athens's "great size and the large number of its inhabitants," the inhabitants were not "cognizable at a glance (*eusunoptos*)" (cited at ibid.). But *in the agora* direct glancing among the citizens was certainly happening, given its delimited size (i.e., approximately 200m × 200m).

ent voted).[18] The glancing that was so favored outside these buildings by climate and landscape was thus further facilitated within these same buildings, where, shielded from sun and weather, chance encounters were replaced by officially scheduled meetings. In both settings, the glance figured as a primary medium of the exchange of looks that is the core of communication and discussion.

Whether in the amplitude of the agora or in the strictly self-enclosed *tholos*— or in such intermediate spaces as the *theatron*, which favored peripheral vision —the glance was not restricted to detection and observation, noticing and inspecting. It also accompanied the conversations that were so crucial to daily life in the agora. But more than accompaniment was in play. Socratic dialogues (many of which took place in the agora) were exemplary of a circumstance in which the self-certainties of the interlocutors were dissolved under relentless questioning. Such "cross-examination" (*elenchos*) can be considered the word-wise equivalent of the glance in its inquisitive and penetrating powers. A Socratic dialogue often opens with the verbal analogue of the glance—the bare gesture of situating that performs in language what the glance accomplishes in vision. The *Republic*, for example, opens with these words of Socrates:

> I walked down to the Piraeus yesterday with Glaucon, the son of Ariston, to make my prayers to the goddess. As this was the first celebration of her festival, I wished also to see how the ceremony would be conducted . . . we were leaving to go back to the city [that is, Athens], when from some way off Polemarchus, the son of Cephalus, caught sight of us starting homewards and sent his slave running to ask us to wait for him. The boy caught my garment from behind and gave me the message. I turned around and asked where his master was. There, he answered; coming up behind. Please wait.[19]

Much as the glance pins down the respective positions of two people who pass each other by (or who are seated near each other in an auditorium or theater), here place and event in the dialogue are established by actual glances (for example, when Polemarchus "caught sight" of Socrates and Glaucon), as well as by the various expressions that intimate the presence of glances: "I turned around," and even the locative adverb "there."

As it happens, a major festival in honor of Athena was called the Panathenaea, whose route (as I have mentioned) directly traversed the agora. The *Republic* opens with a chance encounter, much as often happened in the Athenian agora. Once Socrates and Glaucon have settled in Polemarchus's home along with several other guests, Socrates asks a series of questions that expose the epistemic

---

18. In the *bouleutérion*, "the space which concentrated attention on the [speaker's] voice also created a regime of visual surveillance: because of the raked seating, councilors could be easily identified as to how they voted" (Richard Sennett, *Flesh and Stone: The Body and the City in Western Civilization* [New York: Norton, 1994], p. 57). In other words, in such settings one could *tell at a glance* what one's fellow citizens were up to.

19. *The Republic of Plato*, tr. F. M. Cornford (Oxford: Clarendon Press, 1941), Book I, 327a– 327b4. The very first word of the *Republic* is *katebén*, which prefigures the descent into the cave as described in the opening of Book 7.

arrogance of his interlocutors—a classical instance of the Socratic *elenchos* of engaged disputation. These questions act to undermine such arrogance in much the same way in which a withering glance can deflate social arrogance.[20] Doubtless accompanied by sharp glances in its original format, the dialogue consists in a deflation of putative claims to knowledge by means of verbal parries that effect glancing blows to one's conversational partners.

Just as one acquires knowledge by a succession of ever-more discerning glances, so one is disabused of false belief and shadowy images—of *doxa* and *eikones*—by various verbal thrusts and parries that are the linguistic equivalent of glances which place the smug self-certainties of others into question. Remarkably, both the discreditation of misleading images and incorrect beliefs and the attainment of knowledge are portrayed in the movement of a single dialogue such as the *Republic*—in a lingering conversation that is as much a drama of glances as a debate in words. Not surprisingly: face-to-face encounter, as Levinas would insist, is as much verbal as visual.[21] It is both at once: the face of the Other is not just seen by me but speaks to me in phatic discourse that, like the glance itself, addresses me and puts me on the spot and asks me to distinguish what seems to be the case (that is, imagination, belief) from what is truly the case (that is, knowledge). Only in dialogue can this happen: left to my own devices, unquestioned by the Other, I lapse into arrogance—or else I fall into the well of ignorance, as surely as did Thales when he stared at the stars in his solitary philosophical musings. In active conversation with others, I draw myself out of this well—another kind of cave—by a genuinely dialectical exchange of glances and words, acting as emissaries of the look and the voice respectively that together set the stage for philosophical and other kinds of community.

IV

Given these propitious circumstances—cultural and climatic, seasonal and social, architectural and disputational—it comes as no surprise to learn that the ancient Greeks had a rich repertoire of words for glancing and still more for vision

20. As I suggested in the introduction, "glance" itself is etymologically affine with "lance." The Latin word *arrogare* means "to claim for oneself." It is striking that the intense encounter between Socrates and the insolently arrogant Thrasymachus opens with a precautionary glance on the part of Socrates: "And I, when I heard [Thrasymachus], was dismayed, and looking upon him was filled with fear, and I believe that if I had not looked at him before he did at me I should have lost my voice. But as it is, at the very moment when he began to be exasperated by the course of the argument, I glanced at him first, so that I became capable of answering him" (*Republic* 336d –336e; tr. Paul Shorey, in *Plato: Collected Dialogues*, p. 586). I owe this reference to Michael Naas.

21. For Levinas's assessment of the face-to-face relation, see his *Totality and Infinity*, tr. Alphonso Lingis (Pittsburgh: Duquesne University Press, 1969), pp. 79–82.

in general. As Bruno Snell says, "to begin with there was no one verb to refer to the function of sight as such, but . . . there were several verbs each designating a specific type of vision."[22] This was especially true for such early epic poets as Homer and for lyric poets of the archaic period like Anacreon of Teos or Archilochus. For them, the glance was prized in its own right—long before the gaze came to dominate philosophical discourse. Proof of this is found in the sheer proliferation of verbs for glancing to be found in Homer alone: *paptainein,* "to dart a glance in anxiety or terror"; *athrein,* "to glance all-inclusively, to spy out"; *derkesthai,* "to flash a glance in the manner of a snake"; *laein,* "to grasp intensely in a glance"; *skeptesthai,* "to glance in a focused, snatching way"; *dokeuein,* "to glance in a hidden way, as in watching a prey before killing it"; *dokein,* "to look at in a tentative manner, that is, with regard to how things seem."[23]

The larger issue raised by these differentiated and highly expressive verbs for glancing concerns the *source of the glance.* Is this source within the glancing subject (as most of the words just cited seem to imply) or is it to be found in the illuminative display of the surrounding world, in its sheer appearing? The former source is suggested by the way in which verbs for glancing are sometimes linked with *noos,* "mind," as when Andromache, "darting glances about (*papténasa*), stood on the wall, and she grasped him [Hector] with her *noos* [*noésen*]."[24] There is a "hidden spot within"[25] from which the darting glance stems— an "obscured inner experience" in contrast with a "clear outer one."[26] The latter source is indicated by a series of other words, mostly nouns and collected under the most generic word for appearing, *phainesthai:* for example, *éelios,* "the sun"; *seléné,* "the moon; bright light, blaze, flash (as in flash of lightning)"; *augé,* "ray, beam, light of the eyes, gleam on the surface of bright objects, sheen"; *selas,* "gleam, glare, beam"; *lampros,* "bright, radiant"(related to *lampein,* "to flash forth"); and in particular *phaos,* "light, especially sunlight": as in this phrase from Homer, "the sun whose light is the sharpest looks [out] for itself" (*Iliad,*

22. Bruno Snell, *The Discovery of the Mind: The Greek Origins of European Thought,* tr. T. G. Rosenmeyer (Cambridge, Mass.: Harvard University Press, 1953), p. 4. He adds: "the activity [of sight] is at first understood in terms of its conspicuous modes, of the various attitudes and sentiments connected with it, and it is a long time before speech begins to address itself to the essential function of this activity" (ibid., p. 7).

23. For this list of terms and their approximate meanings, as well as certain corresponding noun forms in the next paragraph, I draw on the comprehensive discussion of Raymond A. Prier, *Thauma Idesthai: The Phenomenology of Sight and Appearance in Archaic Greek* (Tallahassee: Florida State University Press, 1989), chap. 1, "Sight and Cite: The Vocabulary of Sight and Appearance in Homer." Prier himself draws on Snell's seminal discussion in *The Discovery of the Mind,* e.g., concerning the verbs *paptainein* and *derkesthai.* (For a detailed discussion of these latter, see *The Discovery of the Mind,* pp. 2–4.)

24. *Odyssey,* Book 19, l. 552; as cited by Prier in *Thauma Idesthai,* p. 26.

25. "From the hidden spot within, a glance is thrown that must, if not impeded, somehow comprehend the diverse phenomena without" (ibid., p. 28).

26. Ibid.

Book 14, ll. 344–345). The sun glances at us as much as we glance at it. This is only to be expected if it is indeed the case that, as Heidegger suggests, *phainesthai* ("to show itself") is derived from *phainein* ("to bring to the light of day") and is intimately related to *phós* ("light": the contracted Attic form of *phaos*), thereby intimating that the source of all appearing (and thus the basis of all glancing) is to be found in the light of the sun.[27]

If both of these sources, one located in the subject and the other external to it, are indeed valid ontogenetic origins of the glance, indeed of the very light that makes it possible, we are faced with an antinomy, that is, two assertions each of which can be shown to be true (separately) but which together appear to be incompatible. The two assertions can be juxtaposed thus: the glance originates in the subject; the glance comes from the external world. How can *both* be true? Yet if both *are* true, this is tantamount in turn to saying that light derives from subjective as well as cosmic sources, given that the fate of the glance and light are inextricably intermingled in the ancient Greek conception of the world. At one level, the antinomy reflects the Greek theories of visual perception, accord-ing to which rays of light (*augai* and more specifically *opseis,* that is, visual rays with a strictly linear path) issue both from the perceiver—"extramission"—and from an external source (that is, the "intromissionist" model). Aristotle and the ancient atomists (for example, Democritus, Epicurus, Lucretius) held the sec-ond view—whereby corpuscular emanations come from the surfaces of things to the eye of the perceiver—while the first view was endorsed by the Pythagoreans as well as by Euclid and Ptolemy.[28] To this ancient debate we shall return. But for now let us only note it raises the general question as to what respective contributions the glancer and the glanced-at object make to the perceptual situation. On the one hand, it is true that a person glances out from within her own resources: her own visual habits (*hexeis*), her beliefs (*doxai*), her history, her culture. These endemic factors not only help to determine what she will glance at but make its very operation possible. On the other hand, one always glances in the presence (and in the terms) of light that is given from outside oneself. This latter light can be conceived as deific in origin (the sun as a god, "Helios": an idea that goes back to the time of Akhenaten in the second millennium B.C.) or as a circumambient physical presence. Either way, the glancing subject assumes a receptive stance toward such instreaming light instead of being the source of

27. See Heidegger, *Being and Time,* p. 51. For a critique of Heidegger's etymologizing on this very point, however, see Prier, *Thauma Idesthai,* p. 280, n. 70.

28. On these two models of vision, see Gérard Simon, *Le regard: l'être et l'apparence dans l'optique de l'antiquité* (Paris: Seuil, 1988). Richard Powers has this to say: "Two inimical theories vied to explain the mystery of vision. Euclid, Ptolemy and other mathematicians demonstrated that light necessarily traveled from the eye to the observed object [i.e., the extramissionist view]. Aristotle and the atomists assumed the reverse [i.e., the intromissionist view]. Both theories were complete and internally consistent, with no way to arbitrate between them" (Richard Powers, "Wide Open Eyes," *New York Times Magazine,* April 18, 1999, p. 82).

light herself (as are male heroes as Hector and Priam Diomedes, and especially Achilles, in the *Iliad*).

The question becomes: do we have to choose between these two theories of light (with their respective models of the glance) as if they were altogether exclusive options? Despite the apparent antinomy, a closer look at any given glancing situation reveals commixtures of what *both* theories and models would ascribe to it. The disjunction is not final; the presumption that it is reflects our own modernist incapacity to grasp a much more complex interaction than any such exclusivist paradigm allows. In this interaction, there is a dense dialectic of the two poles of analysis, a dialectic that is exhibited in several closely paired sets of terms:

—*seeming/appearing:* The mere seeming that obtains in the epistemic act of *dokein* (which connotes both subjectivity and uncertainty: a matter of mere belief) is intimately intercalated with the sheer unrefusable brilliance of *phainesthai*, the scintillating appearing that is in no way subjective nor about which anyone can be uncertain. "The sun also rises" is a proposition that captures the quintessence of indubitable appearing; hence Homer's preoccupation with dawn (*eós*), to which there are at least thirty-six references in the *Iliad* and the *Odyssey*. "To look upon the light of the sun (*phaos éelioio*)" means "to live." Diomedes appeals to Athena to save him from the man who has wounded him and who now boasts that Diomedes "cannot live to look much longer on the shining sunlight."[29] But any instance of phainesthetic appearance brings with it a justified belief that surpasses mere conjecture; to be alive at all is to be able to witness the sun's shining: this we cannot doubt. Just as guessing here yields to knowledge, so seeming is replaced by genuine appearing: the sun does not just *seem* to someone to rise at dawn, it truly does rise up in our awakening vision at that time.

—*this versus other/that:* The subjective purview of the glance is a "this," that is, something closely related to my own body/mind; but the glance is always also directed at an "other/that," its noematic object as it were. The seeming/ appearing differentiation is parallel to this same distinction; closely related is the way in which the linear character of the eye's visual ray (*opsis*), *this* ray, opens onto an entire visual scene, *that* world; so too the action of espying is closely correlated with *what* I espy, the singularity of one rejoining the particularity of the other. In short, "this side" is not simply "opposed to the experience of the other/that [side]"[30] but is deeply imbricated with it. During the

29. *Iliad*, Book Five, l. 120. For this same equation see also Book Eighteen, l. 61, 442; Book Twenty-Four, l. 558; *Odyssey*, Book Four, l. 833; Book Ten, l. 498, etc. The striking liaison between living and witnessing the sun was pointed out to me in conversation by Robert Garland of Colgate University, Department of Classics.

30. This is Prier's claim at *Thauma Idesthai*, p. 41. In this paragraph, I am drawing on Prier's terms, especially "this vs. other/that," which are organizing principles for his entire analysis of archaic poetry.

night before battle at Troy, the stars "appear clear for themselves" (*phainet' ariprepea*) while the moon sends out its beams (*phaeiné seléné*). At the same time, the Trojan campfires "appeared for themselves" (*pura phaineto*).[31] The use of the middle-voice *phainesthai* in both cases allows *this* campfire light to be the correlate of *that* celestial nightlight. Both kinds of light appear for themselves, yet are linked by the imbrication of each in the other.

—*inner/outer light:* The intromissionist and extramissionist theories of vision both distinguish inner from outer light, as if such forms of light were wholly separate from each other. But certain literary episodes of glancing do not yield to any such separation. In these, a glance goes out from a human or god only to mix with light from an external source: for example, Hector's looking at Achilles's shield, which sends light back by refraction, the two illuminative sources thereby merging. Citing two passages in the *Odyssey*, Raymond Prier remarks:

> In both passages it would appear that a powerful "gaze," that is, direction of light, emanating from the clusters of the stars, approximates, or is identified with, the glance that the viewer himself uses to grasp the cosmos in its entirety. Both passages reveal a strong bond between the inner, but intentionally outwardly directed, force of sight and an "other/that" that generates a geometric structuring of the cosmos.[32]

Inner and outer, like this and other/that, belong together as distinguishable but ultimately inseparable members of the same pair. This bond is marked in English by the phrase "glancing out," which connotes that a looking that begins inside the human subject has for its destiny to seek and illuminate that which is outside this same subject. Such looking momentarily surpasses the subjectivity of its own origin while nevertheless depending on it: every looking subject is always already inverted in something beyond the looking itself.

—*recognizing/recognized*: This is the phenomenon that I emphasized in chapter 1 in the text of Homer—that is, recognizing the other by means of the glance, often accomplished by the other's recognition of me. Achilles recognizes Athena in a celebrated passage from the *Iliad*: "Straightaway he recognized Pallas Athena, and terribly suddenly were her eyes seen to appear."[33] Recognition of the other for the ancient Greeks was thought to depend on the light of appearing that streams not from the eyes of the recognizer but from those of *the one who is recognized*. One doesn't primarily recognize the other in her or his body, much less in terms of character, but from the peculiar light that beams from the other's eyes. This light is seen by some but not by others: Athena is recognized by Odysseus but not by Telemachus: "for in no way do

---

31. *Iliad*, Book Eight, ll. 555–561, as reported by Prier, *Thauma Idesthai*, p. 57.

32. Prier, *Thauma Idesthai*, p. 38. Prier, who sometimes fails to distinguish between gaze and glance, here rightly puts the former word in double quotes. He adds that "it is, of course, the inherent inner and outer order of light and sight that makes possible the mythical experience of astrology"(ibid.).

33. *Iliad*, Book One, ll. 199–200. Prier's translation as given at *Thauma Idesthai*, p. 57.

the gods appear clearly to all."[34] Indeed, Odysseus himself is by no means recognized by everyone, and a considerable part of his celebrated "cunning" (*métis*) consists in his cleverness in evading recognition by others.[35] In contrast with the evening promenade to which I have referred, where many human beings take pride in letting themselves appear to each other in blatant display, in the world of Homer recognizing the other and being recognized by that same other is a constricted affair, limited to certain persons only and then to what they will allow in the way of being recognized. The issue is not that of a common humanity, of singularities conjoined with all others, but of a singularity in legion with selected others only: certain citizens or certain gods. Face-to-face recognition of each by all is replaced by partial recognition of some by a chosen few.[36] Nevertheless, this delimitation in no way undermines the fact that when recognition happens it happens in a flash—I recognize the other's recognizing me—and with a certainty that is a matter of genuine appearing into which seeming has been subsumed.[37]

These dyadic terms, then, mitigate the initial disparity between the two sources of the glance—one within the subject and the other outside in the world—as well as that between the intromissionist and extramissionist theories of light that favor these respective sources in their differences. What matters most is the ability of glancing itself to bridge the gap: whether coming from the human subject or from nature or the gods, its gleaming action dissolves, or at least suspends, disparities. The glance takes in the glittering light of the Greek landscape and returns it in kind. One kind of scintillating surface—that of the sun, the stars, or the shield—merges with another such surface: that belonging to the eye of the beholder (including the eye of the gods). The glancing out that issues from the eye's own *opsis* rejoins the incoming gleaming that stems from the bright world of pure appearance. Together, the two forms of glancing con-

---

34. *Odyssey,* Book Sixteen, ll. 159–64, in Prier's version as cited at *Thauma Idesthai,* p. 62. At *Iliad,* Book One, ll. 197–199 Athena again "appears for herself to him alone."

35. "At the opening of the last half of the *Odyssey* the question is *not so much who recognizes Odysseus as what and when he (anér) will allow himself to be recognized*" (Prier, *Thauma Idesthai,* p. 181; his emphasis). For an extended rumination on *métis,* see Marcel Détienne, *Cunning Intelligence in Greek Culture and Society,* tr. J. Lloyd (Chicago: University of Chicago Press, 1991).

36. For a critique of Athens as a face-to-face society, see Edward E. Cohen, "A Modern Myth," pp. 101 ff. in a section whose title is "'Not Knowing One Another in Athens.'" Cohen's argument is based partly on the comparatively large size of Athens and partly on the homogeneous appearance of most of the population.

37. The appearing at stake in recognition may be aural as well as visual. Just as Levinas insists that the face of the Other presents itself to us not only visually but in speech, so the *phainesthai* of human others is synaesthetic: they are heard as well as seen. Otherwise put, there is an auditory equivalent of the glance of recognition, a sudden hearing that is parallel to sudden seeing. For the etymological relationship between *phainesthai* and *phanai* ("to speak"), see H. Frisk, *Griechisches etymologische Wörterbuch* (Heidelberg: Carl Winter, 1970), article under *phainó.*

stitute an amalgam that acts to deconstruct binary pairs such as self/other, inside/outside, and this/that, showing that each member of each pair is deeply linked with the other member of that same pair. All such supposedly separate terms meet in the intermediate space shared by seeming and appearing—an interplace that is continually lit up by acts of mutual recognition.

V

But what of the glances of the gods? Ancient Greek literature—epic and lyric poetry alike—forces us to face up to a circumstance in which glances are given and received not just among humans as members of the same species, or even among different living species (for example, domesticated animals and humans), but among entities of entirely different sorts, that is, deific and human respectively. The difficulty here is not just whether there can be any communication between two such very different kinds of being, but bears on the extremely one-sided situation that would obtain in this instance: one-sided because the gods would retain the power of looking, given their superior force and intelligence. They alone can look at us, and human beings are consigned to existing under their "watchful gaze" (*opsis*)—a mode of continual surveillance that is not reciprocated. As Hesiod says in *Works and Days:*

> There are immortals near to men who mark [those] who oppress each other by crooked dooms, recking not of the gods' watchful gaze; for upon the nurturing earth are thrice ten thousand immortals, Zeus' guardians over mortal men, who watch over their dooms and their wicked deeds, being clad in mist and going everyway on the earth.[38]

Zeus himself, father of the gods, is explicitly depicted in Homer as a being "of broad vision," thus "all-seeing" (*panoptés*).[39] His own watchful gaze is the archetype for that of all the other gods. This is not surprisingly so in view of the fact that Zeus is the ultimate sky-god; like an eagle, he can spot anything that is happening on earth below him. He literally "oversees" the deeds of mortals: he sees everything they do, whereas they can only rarely detect his presence (for example, in the thunderbolts he throws when he is angry, like so many angry looks). And when he is not looking on from above, his many minions are viewing mortals from nearby—from within the mist that conceals them from us. A one-way scene of looking in short!

Zeus is in effect an enormous sky-eye; or let us say that, by his presence, the sky itself becomes a gigantic eye. "The eye of Zeus," adds Hesiod, "sees all and

---

38. Hesiod, *Works and Days*, ll. 249–255. Cited in Raffaele Pettazzoni, *The All-Knowing God: Researches into Early Religion and Culture*, tr. J. H. Rose (London: Methuen, 1956), p. 146.

39. See *Odyssey*, Book Fourteen, l. 82.

understands all."[40] Hence the association of Zeus with the sun, the daytime celestial eye. But there are many other eyes in the heavens: the moon is called "the eye of evening" by Pindar, "the eye of night" by Aeschylus.[41] Attributed to Plato is this epigram: "You gaze at the stars, my Star; would that I were Heaven, that I might look at you with many eyes!"[42] The stars are conceived as eyes by the Greeks and Romans: in Plautus's *Rudens* the stars are distant eyes at night that come down to earth during the day to wander invisibly among humans: here is the source of the "thrice ten thousand" spies to whom Hesiod alludes. Diké, the daughter of Zeus by Themis and the goddess of Justice, is thought of as an eye who sees all that happens, even in the dark.[43]

Ancient Greek writers even posited one god who embodies the very property of many-eyedness: Argos. Ovid attributes 100 eyes to him, Aeschylus 10,000, and others simply "many."[44] Argos is always on the lookout; he never sleeps, or if he does, only some of his multiple eyes close while the others remain open. Most strikingly, Argos has eyes all over his body, and vases depict his flesh filled with eye-structures everywhere. His nickname was "Panoptés," the very word we have seen applied to Zeus himself. He is also shown as having two faces, one looking forward and the other backward like Janus, each with its own set of eyes: clearly, all these eyes allow him to be bidirectional in his looking. At any given moment, he can look both ways at once: something no mortal can claim to do.

In fact, to be a god at all, in any form, is to be capable of omnivision. One fragment simply states: "God (*theos*) is present everywhere and beholds all things."[45] This looks ahead to later Christian conceptions of God as omnipotent (*pankratés*) as well as omnivoyant. This is visuocentrism writ large—as large as the universe itself. It is composed of gazes and glances alike. Gods can do both from their eminent domain, even if the gods' celebrated celerity is better expressed by glancing than by gazing.

The power of the gods' glances is not confined to what their many eyes and looks can accomplish. The arrows of Apollo and especially those of Eros (that is, Cupid in his Greek guise) can be construed as materializations of the glance, its embodiment in something literally sharp: as sharp as a pointed glance that finds its object in the surface it seeks. The aerodynamic and ballistic virtues of arrows share with glances their capacity to transmit themselves quickly over long distances and to reach targets swiftly. Bergson compares arrows to shrapnel that finds its deadly way into human flesh; both possess an "indivisible mobility."[46] So

40. Hesiod, *Works and Days*, l. 267; Pettazzoni translation.

41. Pindar, *Olympian Odes*, 3.20; Aeschylus, *Seven Against Thebes*, l. 390.

42. *Greek Anthology*, Book Seven, poem 669; tr. J. M. Edmonds, revised by John M. Cooper in his *Plato: Complete Works*, ed. J. Cooper (Indianapolis: Hackett, 1997), p. 1743.

43. I take the reference to Plautus and to Diké from the translator's note to Hesiod, *Works and Days*, l. 267; Pettazzoni translation, pp. 146–147.

44. See Ovid, *Metamorphoses*, Book One, l. 625; Aeschylus, *Prometheus*, l. 569, l. 678.

45. Cited by Pettazzoni as fragment 480 (Hesiod, *Works and Days*; Pettazzoni translation).

46. "As the shrapnel, bursting before it falls to the ground, covers the explosive zone with an

too glances are arrows of looking that are shot out with a velocity that cannot be divided into quantifiable units. As such, they often take the place of explicit communication in words, which can be considered as missiles sent between human beings and sometimes between human beings and gods.[47]

The analogy between arrows and glances, and words and glances, hints at something of more general significance. It testifies to the special virtue of the glance to overcome barriers because of the facility and speed with which it flies, arrowlike, through the *air*—which is, along with light, the privileged medium of vision. Zeus himself was sometimes identified with air, when this latter was regarded as a means of knowledge and not only as a medium for the transmission of light. After all, air is everywhere, just as is the vigilant look of Zeus: "there is no place where Air is not, and being everywhere, he [that is, Zeus, here identified with Air] must know all things, who is with all."[48] The glance, even in its most ordinary avatars, is Zeus-like in its capacity to go everywhere and to traverse the most resistant obstacles. It flies across considerable distances to alight on its chosen object. Like winged words, it also flies across equally considerable differences among class and culture, gender and species, the human and the nonhuman. As is becoming increasingly evident, the glance is the great mediatrix of vision; it is the most effective means by which we catch sight even of the most obscure and transient of phenomena, including the most evanescent surfaces. Its swiftness and sureness recall the Greek gods in their resolute rapidity —not just Zeus or Apollo or Athena or Argos but also Hermes, whose swift sandals were legendary for the speed with which they propelled him across the most forbidding boundaries: Hermes is a god of borders and crossroads, and he is a messenger of the gods, the ultimate mediator between gods and humans. His mercurial movements, in their streamlined power, enact the equivalent of the glance.

It is revealing that the Greek gods—those bodiless and supernal beings— exemplify particular traits of the down-to-earth glance: not only do they manifest such things as love of vision and swift and decisive movement, they put them on concrete display. By illustrating such traits in emphatic and exaggerated forms, they help us to appreciate more fully our own human versions of them:

---

indivisible danger, so the arrow which goes from A to B displays with a single stroke, although over a certain extent of duration, its indivisible mobility" (Henri Bergson, *Creative Evolution,* tr. A. Mitchell [Lanham, Md.: University Press of America, 1983], p. 309).

47. In one striking passage in the *Iliad,* Chryses addresses himself to Apollo to "let your arrows make the Danaans pay for my tears shed." To this entreaty is added the simple sentence: "So he spoke in prayer, and Phoebus Apollo heard him" (*Iliad,* Book One, ll. 42–43). This could be interpreted as Chryses's wish that Apollo *notice* the Danaans' iniquities by glances that act as arrows of accusation as well as punishment, along with Apollo's acknowledgment of this plea in the form of hearing it. In this case, arrows/glances and words rejoin and reinforce each other.

48. Philemón, fragment 91. Diogenes of Apollonia thought of air (*aér*) as possessing intelligence and thus as the proper element for Zeus's omniscience. See the discussion of Pettazzoni (Hesiod, *Works and Days*; Pettazzoni translation, pp. 153–154).

how intensely we can glance and to what powerful effect, how prominent our eyes are in this very intensity, how swiftly we succeed in reaching the object of the glance, how we cleave the air in so doing, how much like an arrow our glance can be, how often it gleams.[49]

VI

Another instructive case in point is that of the erotic glance—the glance induced by Eros as well as the glance coming from the god of love himself. The glance of Eros is as fast-moving as that of Hermes, though its purpose is quite different: no longer communication but the expression of amorous intentions. As Ibycus, the archaic sixth-century B.C. poet, tells us, Eros has a "quick chariot" from which his seductive glances stem:

> Once again love [Eros] darts me
> A melting glance from under
> Dark eyelids, again looking at me meltingly with his
> eyes under dark eyelids.[50]

This poem articulates the searing force of the erotic glance, its dark power to destroy as well as to lure: the glance of Eros, astride his "quick chariot," makes its recipient "tremble," precipitating the latter into "the inescapable nets of Aphrodite."[51] As Sappho testifies, "Eros shook my heart like a wind and storm falling upon oak trees."[52] Eros renders stupefied the person at whom he glances. Archilochus of Paros, the earliest-known lyric poet, already points to this predicament: "Here I lie mournful with desire."[53] This is not to mention the blindness of love: the capacity of the erotic glance to close off and render invisible:

> Such is the passion for love that has twisted
> its way beneath my heartstrings
> and closed deep mist across my eyes
> stealing the soft heart from inside my body . . .[54]

49. On the gleaming of the gods, consider these words from the *Homeric Hymn to Apollo:* "it is Phoebus Apollo who plucks the lyre, stepping high and beautifully, while around him a radiance emanates from the gleaming of his feet and his well-spun glistening chiton" (*Homeric Hymn to Apollo*, ll. 203–204; Lonsdale translation). It is as if each part of Apollo, even his clothing, were a mode of glancing in its gleaming action.

50. Ibycus of Rhegium; translated by A. M. Miller as fragment 287 in A. M. Miller, ed., *Greek Lyrics: An Anthology in Translation* (Indianapolis: Hackett, 1996), p. 98. The Greek word here is *derkomenos*.

51. These words and phrases are also from the same fragment of Ibycus.

52. Sappho of Lesbos; adapted from Lattimore's translation (in R. Lattimore, ed., *Greek Lyrics*, 2d ed. [Chicago: University of Chicago Press, 1960]) by Meredith Hoppin, to whom I am indebted for a number of the texts cited in this section of the chapter.

53. Archilochus of Paros; fragment 24, tr. R. Lattimore, in R. Lattimore, ed., *Greek Lyrics*, p. 5.

54. Archilochus of Paros; fragment 26 in ibid. "Deep mist" implies blindness; it is in deep mist that the "thrice ten thousand" gods observe human beings' foibles.

No wonder the erotic glance may lead to an averted glance in response, as if in anticipation of the upset to which it may give rise. "My Thracian filly," asks Anacreon of Teos, "why do you look at me askance?"[55] The direct glancing-at of unrestrained passionate love here occasions an act of glancing-askance, as the Greek participle *blepousa* (in conjunction with the adverb *loxon*)—also translatable as "looking from the corner of the eye"—signifies.

This is not to deny that the erotic glance also has a gentle edge. One of Bacchylides's odes proclaims: "With gentle eyes the Delian-born son of Leto the deep-girdled glanced upon [Eros]; and many the wreaths of flowers on Alexidámos were tossed there in the plain of Kirrha."[56] There is also a bashful, modest form of glancing that can be an integral part of erotic experience, as is expressed in this couplet by Praxilla of Sicyon:

> Girl of the lovely glance, looking out through the window,
> your face is virgin; lower down you are a married woman.[57]

Here the glance is literally framed, as if to curb its complex potential, allowing the virginal face to shine through the conventional frame of marriage. Instead of going straight to its target, or darting out from a speeding chariot, in this case the glance of love has lowered its ambition—not to avoid the other's glance altogether but because it embodies a nonthreatening, innocent love that is the visual equivalent of a soft touch that takes hold of its object nonpossessively.[58]

The window through which the girl with the lovely glance looks is the architectural analogue to the *veil*, crucial to the pursuit of Eros in ancient Greece. Penelope "holds her veil up on either side of her face" when approached by her suitors; in contrast, Medea is depicted as "holding her veil aside" as a sign of giving way to Jason's seductions.[59] The veil is the carapace of the glance, its outer

---

55. Anacreon of Teos; fragment 417, tr. A. M. Miller, in A. M. Miller, ed., *Greek Lyrics*. Another translation: "Thracian filly, why do you look at me from the corner of your eye, and flee stubbornly from me?" (tr. D. A. Campbell, in D. A. Campbell, ed., *Greek Lyric* (Cambridge, Mass.: Harvard University Press, 1988; Loeb edition), vol. 2. *Blepein* means more generally "to look at," but it includes the case of glancing-at. For another expression meaning "to look askance," there is the Homeric phase *hypodra idón* (as at *Iliad*, Book One, l. 148).

56. Bacchylides, Ode 11 (for Alexidamos of Metapontion), R. Lattimore translation in R. Lattimore, ed., *Greek Lyrics*.

57. Praxilla of Sicyon; fragment 2 in R. Lattimore's translation in his *Greek Lyrics*, p. 49.

58. "Greek notions of vision, hearing, and smelling involve touching, physical contact by means of rays, sound as a kind of airy or smoky substance. . . . Glance as a kind of touching, akin to 'catching a whiff' of something? 'Catching sight' of something? 'Taking hold' of something? 'Glancing at' something? English avoids direct objects in these phrases, making use instead of prepositional phrases (whiff *of*, glance *at* or off *of*). Similarly in Greek, many verbs denoting touch or perception either can or must take the genitive case rather than the accusative" (Meredith Hoppin, private communication, November 5, 1997; I am grateful to Professor Meredith Hoppin of Williams College, Massachusetts, for her comments upon two drafts of this chapter and to Professor Eric Casey of Sweet Briar College, Virginia, for many indispensable remarks).

59. The citation from the *Odyssey* is from Book Sixteen, l. 416 (repeated at Book Eighteen, l. 210); Medea is thus described in Apollonius Rhodius, *Argonautica*, ed. R. C. Seaton (Oxford: Oxford University Press, 1900), Book Three, ll. 444–445. Both citations are from Anne Carson,

garment as it were. It allows the glancer to retreat from public space—to be less than fully revealed, though still visible in that one's eyes peer out above the veil. Or one glances *through* a semitransparent veil that covers one's entire face. The veil—shown prominently on Greek vases that portray heterosexual love—is itself a metaphor of the erotics of the glance. Such visual erotics is in certain respects the very converse of Zeus's panopticism: the sky god sees all, and the avid lover wants to see all too; but the beloved is more invested in fleeing the erotic glance (or meeting it coyly or modestly) than in being its direct target. The game of the glance is not the possessive one of grasping outright the sought-for other—that way lies the gaze (as is connoted in the "watchful gaze" that accompanies acts of omnivoyance)—but instead the game of pursuit and flight. As Anne Carson puts it:

> The moment of ideal desire on which vase-painters as well as poets are inclined to focus is not the moment of the *coup de foudre*, not the moment when the beloved's arms open to the lover, not the moment when the two unite in happiness. What is pictured is the moment when the beloved turns and runs. The verbs *pheugein* ("to flee") and *diókein* ("to pursue") are a fixed item in the technical erotic vocabulary of the poets, several of whom admit that they prefer pursuit to capture. . . . Erotic scenes on vases offer clear evidence that eros deferred or obstructed, rather than eros triumphant, is the favored subject.[60]

We are here at the opposite extreme from the aggressively projected lookings of Eros—his glances as lances hurled in a one-way power trip. We are in the presence, instead, of a two-way situation of chasing after and being chased. If the uninhibited erotic glance *turns toward* the beloved as the intended object, the beloved himself or herself *turns away* from these invasive yet exciting looks, these bittersweet glances. The turning away can be accomplished by literally turning around and running away or by adopting a physical veil, as well as by reshaping one's glance in various ways: "veiling" it by looking askance in the manner of the Thracian girl, or casting one's head down coyly, or letting one's eyelids express *aidós*, a comely "shamefastness" (in Carson's translation) that is part of the subtle game of erotic interchange. In this latter case, the glance is present by its very absence: the withheld glance is *looking* nonetheless: "the proverbial residence of *aidós* upon sensitive eyelids is a way of saying that *aidós* exploits the power of the glance by withholding it."[61] Not only does one see

---

Eros the Bittersweet: An Essay (Princeton, N.J.: Princeton University Press, 1986), p. 22. I am indebted to Carson for much that follows in this and the next several paragraphs. In the *Iliad*, when Andromache hears of Hector's death, she tosses down her wedding veil to the ground. Homer uses the word *krédemnon* for "veil"—a word that elsewhere means "the battlements that crown a city's walls" (see *Iliad*, Book 22, l. 470).

60. Anne Carson, *Eros the Bittersweet*, pp. 20–21. On the general importance of the flight/ pursuit situation in ancient Greece, see Christiane Sourvinou-Inwood, *"Reading" Greek Culture: Texts and Images, Rituals and Myths* (Oxford: Oxford University Press, 1991), as well as Stephen Lonsdale, *Dance and Ritual Play in Ancient Greece* (Baltimore: Johns Hopkins University Press, 1993). Meredith Hoppin remarks that "the mixture of resistance and compliance [on Greek vases] is in itself glance-like" (comment in conversation of May, 2001).

61. Carson, *Eros the Bittersweet*, p. 21. Carson adds: "and also that one must watch one's

something even under the heaviest veil, however dimly, *one glances in not looking out.* Such is the subtlety of the glance in the play of love that it can be more effective when withdrawn from visibility—appearing in disappearing—than when it is perfectly manifest as given or received.

The early Greek awareness of the complex erotics of the glance allows us to realize both the focused force of this kind of looking—its virtual violence, the darkness under the lids—and its diffusive diminution in gentler avatars, veiled and self-veiled looking, glancing away and withheld glancing. Where the erotic force is a matter of the direct unleashing of the glance like an arrow shot outward through limpid air, the diminution bears on the indirection of the glance, its reverberating in the delicate mirror-game of love. If the most salient image of the first epicenter of Eros is that of the arrow shot through space—the radiant space of desire[62] or imagination—the most striking instance of the other epicenter is found in a hall of mirrors. In the latter place, one can glance at another person to whom one is attracted without being seen to do so by that same other; yet that other still feels looked at in this collusive and indirect way. Kallimachos had said that Eros is a "bypassing game that lies available, for it knows only to pursue what flees."[63] The film *Last Year at Marienbad* explores just such a game of glances that pass each other by, and a comparable scene of visual indirection has been described thus by Thomas Nagel:

> Suppose a man and a woman, whom we may call Romeo and Juliet, are at opposite ends of a cocktail lounge, with many mirrors on the walls which permit unobserved observation, and even mutual unobserved observation. Each of them is sipping a martini and studying other people in the mirrors. At some point Romeo notices Juliet. He is moved, somehow, by the softness of her hair and the diffidence with which she sips her martini and this arouses him sexually. . . . Juliet now senses Romeo in another mirror on the opposite wall, though neither of them yet knows that he is seen by the other . . . cleverly calculating the line of her [look] without actually looking her in the eyes, he realizes that [her look] is directed at him through the mirror on the opposite wall. . . . But there is a further step . . . Juliet now senses that he senses her. This puts Romeo in a position to notice, and be aroused by, her arousal at being sensed by him. He senses that she senses that he senses her. This is still another level of arousal. . . . If both are alone [that is, without a commitment to partners who are present], they will presumably turn to look at each other directly, and the proceedings will continue on another plane.[64]

I cite this long passage not just to indicate the lengths to which the exchange of looks will go in the preparatory stages of erotic attraction—especially in unobserved glances abetted by mirrors—but more importantly to underline that

---

feet to avoid the misstep called *hybris*" (ibid.). Carson is commenting on the following fragment: "*aidós* dwells upon the eyelids of sensitive people as does *hybris* upon the insensitive. A wise man would know this" (ibid.).

62. "A space must be maintained or desire ends" (ibid., p. 26).

63. Kallimachos, *Epigrammata*, 31.5–31.6. Cited by Carson at ibid., p. 20.

64. Thomas Nagel, "Sexual Perversion," in Nagel's *Mortal Questions* (Cambridge: Cambridge University Press, 1979), pp. 45–46.

amatory glancing flourishes, today as in ancient Greek, in a scene of indirect-
ness. In both eras, *bypassing is the name of the game:* to pass by the other in
sidewise glancing, to look *toward* but not *at* him or her, allows for a safe space of
desire (safe because one is not yet seen by the other and can always choose not
to pursue this barely glimpsed phantom person), a visual haven both for oneself
and for the other (since the other is also free not to engage further in this
incipient interchange). The price that is paid for direct and unobstructed looking is often a one-sided situation in which the looker dominates the person
looked at—instituting a visual hegemony in which the glance of just looking is
transformed into a gaze of surveillance: in short, visuocentrism becomes oculocentrism. The most valid form of such directness is found in recognition, or in
the ethics that arises from confronting the "nudity" of the face: it is just here that
Levinas makes a decisive contribution. In contrast, the virtue of indirect and
bypassing glancing is the prospect it proffers of a deferred two-sided visual
exchange that has little or nothing to do with the ethical in the interhuman
realm. Zeus can look at me (and everyone else) without my being able to look
back at him with any comparable omniscience or omnipotence; the situation is
on the verge of sadism: those who torture others reinstate the Zeusian hegemony —if not in visual terms per se, then in an alternative sensory equivalent.[65]
Another kind of one-sided looking, less sadistic, is that effected by the ring of
Gyges, which renders its bearer invisible and yet able to witness the other.[66] But
if I am engaged in amorous pursuit by looking in a less monovalent way (whether
by recourse to flight on foot, to various veils, to downcast eyes, to engagement
with a hall of mirrors, or to withholding the glance altogether), I and the other
can exchange places in the course of the game: the pursuer can become the
pursued; the latter can shoot arrows of desire back at the pursuer, who can in
turn cast his or her eyes down, veil him or herself, withhold the glance; or else
the pursued can initiate a mirror-game of looks back and forth in a hall of
mirrors.[67] If erotic desire is indeed bittersweet, as Sappho claims—"Eros once
again limb-loosener whirls me sweetbitter"[68]—it is similarly ambivalent in its
enactment: literally two-sided, twice valid in its pursuit or its reception.

65. A striking painting of torture at the Museum of the Art Institute of Chicago shows the
victim both naked and blindfolded as his torturers prepare to go about their grisly business:
Interrogations II, by Leon Golub, 1980–1981.

66. The ring of Gyges is discussed by Plato in the *Republic* at Book II, 359c–360d. The
ethical consequences of the ring are discussed by Levinas in *Totality and Infinity,* pp. 60, 90,
173. See also Tanja Staehler, "Getting Under the Skin: Platonic Myths in Levinas," unpublished manuscript, 2004.

67. I say "can" in all these instances in order to indicate that *in principle* the two parties can
exchange positions; *in fact,* in a given society at a given time, such exchange may not be
possible.

68. This is Anne Carson's translation of Sappho's fragment, which reads in full: "Eros once
again limb-loosener whirls me / sweetbitter, impossible to fight off, creature stealing up" (*Eros
the Bittersweet,* p. 3). For further commentary on this poem, see the chapters entitled "Bittersweet" and "Read Me the Bit Again."

VII

Pervading all, suffusing everything, is *light*. Despite this fact—as evident in ordinary life as it is to scientific theory—light is not one of the five ancient elements. The Greeks considered it to be a form of fire, but fire purified to such an extent that it does not burn: the gods made "such fire as had the property not of burning, but of providing a gentle light, proper to day."[69] If daylight is fire, it is fire that has lost its most elemental, pyric power. Since all elements require light in which to appear—certainly air and aether but also earth and water and fire itself—light is a condition for the exhibition of elementality rather than an element itself.[70] It is also a condition of vision, requisite for its coming into being. Without light, we certainly could not see—not just not see *far* or see *well* but not see *at all*. The ancient Greeks were perfectly aware of this, and accordingly devised scientific models to account for light, two of which we have already encountered: intromission and extramission. But we have also seen that these two models, construed as competitive, constitute an antinomical impasse from which we had to extricate ourselves.

Plato was already concerned with finding a way out of this impasse: indeed, he was preoccupied by it. His *Timaeus* in effect proposed that *both* models were valid, though neither completely so. The intromissionist view—whereby light enters the eye from without—is at least partly true: if you need to be convinced, just look at the refulgent sun on a bright day. Its rays will find their way to your eyes even if you turn away—and even if you cover your eyes with a cloth. But the extramissionist account is equally tempting in view of the fact that the activity, position, and condition of my eyes makes a crucial difference in what I see: as George Berkeley was to emphasize many centuries later. Extramitted rays also help to explain other visual phenomena: for example, why I see less of an object as I approach it, or why the more distantly points appear on an elevated plane the more they seem to be located lower on this plane.[71] No wonder that the extramissionist model was the most widely embraced paradigm of light's source and transmission in the ancient world, first appearing among the Pythagoreans (especially Alcmaeon of Croton) and the Atomists (for example, Democritus) and being endorsed, as already remarked, by such later thinkers as Euclid and

69. Plato, *Timaeus*, 45b; tr. A. E. Taylor, in *A Commentary on Plato's Timaeus* (Oxford: Clarendon Press, 1928), p. 277.

70. Thus Aristotle maintains that light is "that state of a transparent medium in which transparency is actualized" (David C. Lindberg, *Theories of Vision From Al-Kindi to Kepler* [Chicago: University of Chicago Press, 1976], p. 8). As a state of a medium, light cannot be itself an element or, for that matter, a substance. It is more of an epiphenomenon than a phenomenon in its own right. Thus Aristotle analogizes light to "the color of what is transparent" (*De Anima*, tr. J. A. Smith, in R. McKeon, ed., *The Basic Works of Aristotle* (New York: Random House, 1941), 418b12–418b13).

71. I owe these examples to Wilbur R. Knorr, article on "Optics," in *Oxford Classical Dictionary*, S. Hornblower and A. Spawforth (New York: Oxford University Press, 1996), p. 1070.

Ptolemy: "the eye obviously has fire within," said Theophrastus, "for when one is struck [this fire] flashes out."[72]

Plato proposed a creative compromise that would resolve the dilemma into which previous Greek theories of vision had precipitated themselves: how can light originate equally within the eye *and* from the world? According to Plato, a thin ray of gentle fire emanates outward through the cornea, which is impervious (*puknos*: literally, "dense") to all but such "fine" (*manos*) emissions: "they made the fire within us which is akin to [sunlight] flow in a fine stream through the eyes, having first compacted the whole, and more particularly the middle of the eye so as to be smooth and dense."[73] This nonburning stream issues from the eye in an outgoing visual ray (again: *opsis*) and combines with the ambient daylight of the surrounding world, thereby forming a smooth and continuous cone that extends from the eye to the object seen: a "sympathetic chain" in effect.[74] The light outside the seeing subject comes primarily from the sun's rays but also from reflecting surfaces and from local fire sources (for example, candles, campfires, and so on). All such external light constitutes a flux or flow that is given shape by visual rays, thereby forming a temporary but effective "body" that is capable of transmitting the motion of things seen:

> Accordingly, whenever there is daylight round about, the [eye's] visual current issues forth, like to like, and coalesces with it [that is, daylight] and is formed into a single homogeneous body in a direct line with the eyes, in whatever quarter the stream issuing from within strikes upon any object it encounters outside. So the whole [body thus formed], because of its homogeneity, is similarly affected and passes on the motions of anything it comes in contact with or that comes into contact with it, throughout the whole body, to the soul, and thus causes the sensation we call seeing.[75]

The homoiomeric principle of like to like—of ancient vintage in Greek thought and active at other points in the cosmogony of the *Timaeus*—here draws the visual fire of the eye into close collusion with surrounding daylight in the generation of a visual field that connects eye with world. As one recent commentator puts it, the emphasis in the above passage is "not [simply] on the emission of an effluence from both the eye and the object of vision, but on the formation of a

72. Theophrastus commenting on Alcmaeon's theory; cited by Lindberg, *Theories of Vision From Al-Kindi to Kepler,* p. 4. For an excellent account of the Arabic version of the same ancient debate, see Lindberg's essay "The Intromission-Extramission Controversy in Islamic Visual Theory: Al-Kindi versus Avicenna," in *Studies in Perception: Interrelations in the History of Philosophy and Science,* ed. P. K. Machamer and R. G. Turnbull (Columbus: Ohio State University Press, 1978), pp. 137–159.

73. Plato, *Timaeus,* 45b; tr. Taylor. The channels of the eye are so fine that they cannot be filled with water or any other element—only fire qua light can permeate them.

74. The phrase "sympathetic chain" is F. M. Cornford's in his *Plato's Cosmology: The Timaeus of Plato Translated with a Running Commentary* (Indianapolis: Hackett, 1957), p. 153, n. 1.

75. Plato, *Timaeus* 45b–45d; tr. F. M. Cornford, in *Plato's Cosmology* (New York: Harcourt, Brace, 1937), pp. 152–153.

body, through the coalescence of visual rays and daylight, which serves as a material intermediary between the visible object and the eye."[76]

This nuanced model of vision defies any simple separation into intromissionism (which gives all the credit to incoming light) and extramissionism (making the human subject the sole source of vision). Instead, subject and sun, eye and world contribute equally in the formation of the intermediary body, shaped as a cone or chain or cylindrical "pencil" that is necessary for vision. Only through this composite body can the visual ray reach the illuminated world: we do not see in the dark precisely because no such effective vehicle can arise in the absence of sunlight. Likewise, only as coursing back over the same body will effluences from visible objects reach us, thereby giving rise to "sensations" that are felt in body and soul alike.

Plato's model is as ingenious as it is empirically false. It is ingenious as a compromise between two major competing models that were formerly considered exclusive of each other. Now both have a place in the new version. But the model is false as an actual description of how vision arises. Aristotle noted: "In general it is unreasonable to suppose that seeing occurs by something issuing from the eye; [or] that the ray of vision reaches as far as the stars, or goes to a certain point and there coalesces with the object. . . . It would be better to suppose that coalescence occurs in the very heart of the eye."[77] These doubts proved to be prophetic, since it is assumed by modern medicine that the primary action of vision is indeed "in the very heart of the eye," where light (on a renewed intromissionist model) interacts with the physiology of the retina and the optic nerve to convey visual information to the brain.

Nevertheless, Plato had a point. If we read his model metaphorically rather than literally, it proposes something quite important and quite true. This is that vision—all kinds of looking, including the glance—combines two quite different ingredients. On the one hand, there is the *givenness of light,* the massive facticity of its pervasion and suffusion of all exposed surfaces in the place-world. Not only is there "information in the light" (in J. J. Gibson's apposite phrase), but light itself is an irrecusable source of vision, its material condition of possibility as it were. It is at once irreplaceable (no artificial light, no matter how extensive,

---

76. David C. Lindberg, *Theories of Vision from Al-Kindi to Kepler,* p. 5. The result is that vision does not result from the direct encounter between the visual ray and sunlight—as on misleading simpler interpretations such as A. E. Taylor's in his *Commentary on Plato's Timaeus*—but rather from the encounter between the homogeneous body just described and effluences from the object (e.g., the "whiteness" that gives rise to the perception of color): i.e.: "from an encounter between the emanation from the object and the 'single homogeneous body' already formed by coalescence of the ocular emanation and daylight" (Lindberg, *Theories of Vision from Al-Kindi to Kepler,* p. 6). If Lindberg is right, there are three and not two relevant items in the generation of vision (i.e., beyond the seer's body and the sun): the visual ray proper, the homogeneous body formed from the combination of this ray with ambient sunlight, and effluences from the object seen.

77. Aristotle, *De sensu et sensibilia,* tr. W. S. Hett, in *On the Soul, Parva Naturalia, On Breath* (Cambridge, Mass.: Harvard University Press, 1936), Book Two, 438a26–438a29.

will ever take its place entirely) and transcendent (that is, to the perceiving subject). Surely this is what Plato himself intended to imply by his choice of the sun as an exemplar of the Good: both the sun (that is, the dominant object in the daytime sky) and the Good (the highest Form) give light [foresight and insight respectively] and yet they are not simple objects of ordinary perception:

> It was the Sun, then, that I meant when I spoke of that offspring which the Good has created in the visible world, to stand there in the same relation to vision and visible things as that which the Good itself bears in the intelligible world to intelligence and to intelligible objects [that is, Forms].[78]

It is the fourth century B.C. by the time Plato says this, and he does not hesitate to replace Zeus with the sun as an ultimate cosmic entity: "And of all the divinities in the skies is there one whose light, above all the rest, is responsible for making our eyes see perfectly and making objects perfectly visible?"[79] Even if Plato still believed that the celestial bodies are immortal living creatures—as is evident in the phrase "all the divinities in the skies"—he is unmistakably thinking of the physical sun in the latter part of the indented passage just quoted. The worship of Helios, the sun as god, has given way to heliocentrism—the subordination of all sublunar things to the sun, toward which they ineluctably turn in bodily motions, growth, perception, and thought.

On the other hand, Plato's model in the *Timaeus* also acknowledges the distinctive contribution of these sublunar entities. These latter, and most notably human beings, are not just passive recipients, mere registrants of sunlight and its effects. They play an active role in making vision happen: the emanation of the visual ray from the eye can be construed as the perceiver's contribution to the intermediate body of sight. As the very idea of a peculiarly "fine" fire suggests, however, we should interpret this contribution to the formation of such a body less than literally—as is also suggested in the language of a "single homogeneous body," since no such body is to be found in the natural world itself.[80] Instead, it incorporates all that perceivers lend by way of their intentions, volitions, emotions—their "mind" in the rich sense of *noos* that we have seen to underlie the glance.[81] It also collects the influences that derive from the percipient's culture and history: influences so deeply embedded as to be scarcely

78. Plato, *Republic*, tr. F. M. Cornford (New York: Oxford University Press, 1945), Book Six, 507b–507c.

79. Ibid., 507a.

80. Sappho invokes a similar idea of a thin fire (*lepton pur*) in an erotic context: see poem 31, ll. 9–10.

81. There appears to be a deep etymological link between *noos* or *nous* ("mind") and *nostos* ("return"), via the root *nes-*, "return to life and light." This suggests that light always returns to the mind that comprehends an illuminated world. See Douglas Frame, *The Myth of Return in Early Greek Epic* (New Haven, Conn.: Yale University Press, 1978), pp. 29–31. I should make it clear that the model of the mind's contributions to vision is my own and not Plato's. But it is in the spirit of Platonic thought, and in my view represents a plausible extension of it.

visible. All such psychical contributions from the side of the subject may not generate a literal visual ray, or form part of a physical cone or pencil of light, but the ray and the cone/pencil exemplify in physical terms what is happening psychically and culturally. On the one hand, they embody the *concentration* and the *directedness* that are the hallmarks of the subject's contribution. On the other, the various cultural and social influences—their literal "in-flux"—must consolidate and come to a focus in the psyche if they are to be effectively deployed in the formation of an intermediate body. And they must also coalesce with this body if they are to find application or expression there. Even if they do not themselves form a cone or cylinder, they must at least find a suitable vehicle, a "body," if they are to put their intentionalities into actual practice: to bring them to bear in that practice.

It follows that the psychical factor is not limited to the *last* moment of perception, when sensation arises in the soul. It is already actively at work in the earliest stages of vision, an integral part of the generation of sight, inherent in the visual fire, part of the eye's own work. We witness here an exemplary instance in which the psychical and the physical, despite their very different points of origin (in the subject and in culture versus the natural world) join forces in the coordinated construction of what Freud would call an "intermediate common entity."[82] In other words, the respective contributions of the "rays of the world" and "mental rays" (to employ a distinction of Husserl's that parallels that between the sun's rays and the eye's visual ray) *meet in the middle*—in the coalescent cone, the intermediate body, wherein "sight" itself takes place.[83] This bivalent, middle-range body is the truth of vision—not the scientific truth sought by Aristotle, Al-Kindi, Alhazen, Kepler, Newton, and Helmholtz but the experiential truth of ordinary seeing. It is the same truth we encountered earlier when we were driven to search for terms that bridge the otherwise separated members of divisive pairs such as inner versus outer, this versus other/that, and seeming versus appearing. There, too, the truth of the matter lay in the middle path, for example, in the power of recognition to link otherwise disparate terms. Now we rediscover the same truth at the level of optics—of vision as the complex outcome of the subtle interplay between the seeing subject and the seen object, the body and the culture of this subject, and all this within the context of the circumambient light.

82. This is Freud's phrase for the compromise formation of dreams that are formed by condensation. See his *Interpretation of Dreams*, tr. J. Strachey, in *The Standard Edition of the Complete Psychological Works*, ed. J. Strachey (London: Hogarth Press, 1953), vol. 5, chap. 6, "The Dream-Work."

83. Husserl had himself insisted that *noesis* and *noema*, terms he adapted from Platonic *nous*, must conjoin in the noematic nucleus that is the core of the intentional object of perception. See Edmund Husserl, *Ideas Pertaining to a Pure Phenomenology and to a Phenomenological Philosophy: First Book*, tr. F. Kersten (Dordrecht: Kluwer, 1983), chaps. 3 and 4. For Husserl's treatment of visual rays, see chap. 9.

VIII

The same psychical (if not physical) logic applies to the glance, another ambivalent avatar of vision whose own binary structure calls for a different kind of intermediacy. Just as the cone or cylinder of vision merges internally derived visual rays with external light (primarily that stemming from the sun but also that given off from reflectant and self-luminous objects), so the glance combines two comparable moments: that of the *outgoing* with the *incoming*. The first moment includes all the ways in which the glance moves out from the subject who casts it—out from its eye most evidently but also (as belonging to an overall corporeal intentionality) out from its skin, its clothing, its hands, and other body parts. Indeed, the glance moves so far out from the eye itself as to threaten the unity of the perceiving body: it is a feature of a "fragmented body" (*corps morcellé* in Lacan's term).[84] The second moment encompasses all that comes toward and into the seeing subject: not just direct and reflected light as such but all that the glancing subject takes in: above all, the surfaces by which such particular aspects of things as color, shape, size, and texture are presented, along with the complex configurations of objects that make up entire states of affairs. In the first moment, the glancing subject is actively *engaged*—bringing to bear influences of many kinds, including those of personal, social, and cultural history as well as ethnicity and gender. In the second, the same complexly configured subject shows itself to be remarkably *receptive,* being open to that which comes from without (including certain things in whose formation this same subject may have played an active role).

The two moments become perspicuous in the two facets of Eros: first as coming in from without when one is "smitten" in love—the moment of Cupid's arrow, the *coup de foudre*—and then as concealed within the modesty and gentleness of a retracted, veiled state. Just as both sides of Eros are realized in specific forms of glancing, so glancing of many kinds—aggressive as well as erotic, inquisitive as well as skeptical—exhibits both an outgoing and incoming aspect. (Gazing, in contrast, stultifies the situation by attempting to fill in the discrepancies between the two sides, attempting to dissolve the outgoing in the incoming, as if the subject were a mute witness of the one phenomenon that is allowed to count: the object of the gaze.)

To acknowledge the twofold nature of the glance is to call for a third term no less than in the Platonic theory of vision. Curiously, the glance's own *tertium quid* is suggested by a neglected feature of Plato's solution to the antinomy

---

84. It is a revealing fact that Homer frequently considers the "body" not as a single substance but as a loose alliance of limbs; similarly, the glance disaggregates the body in its capacity for issuing from various body parts and for focusing on them in turn: "Instead of 'body' Homer says 'limbs'" (Snell, *The Discovery of the Mind*, p. 5). It was not until the fifth century B.C. that "body" was regarded as a singular entity to be designated by the technical term *sóma*. Before that, the word refers alternately to the dead body (as in Homer) or to the living body (as in Hesiod and the lyric poets).

posed by his predecessors. This is the fact that the cone of vision is in effect an extended sense organ not just of sight but of *touch*. Stretching between the eye and the object seen, it reaches out to this object and touches it. Recall the end of the passage from the *Timaeus* cited above: "So the whole, because of its homogeneity, is similarly affected and passes on the motions of anything it comes in *contact with* or that comes into *contact with it*, throughout the whole body [i.e., of the cone], to the soul" (emphasis added). The intermediate entity of vision operates by contact. As A. E. Taylor comments:

> Light is thus a kind of extended touch or contact at a distance. E.g., what happens when I see a mountain ten miles away is this. The light issuing from my eye has for the time been fused into one homogeneous body with light "reflected" from the mountain. This temporary ten-mile-long extension of my body is "like," homogeneous throughout, and therefore the sensation due to its contact with the mountain is transmitted along its whole length . . . from the mountain at one end to my organism at the other.[85]

However absurd this model may seem to be—to Aristotle, the prospect of the homogeneous body reaching not just to a mountain ten miles away but "as far as the stars" constitutes a reductio ad absurdum; to Cornford, equally absurd is the idea that this intermediate body amounts to an extension of my own body that is "sensitive throughout"[86]—still it may be construed in a less literal way and fruitfully applied to the glance. Then it would signify that the glance in its fully mediated state, that is, taking account of both its outgoing and incoming moments, includes an essential element of tactility. Touch, that is, touching and being touched, would mediate these otherwise disconnected moments.

Lest you respond that this is piling Pelion on Ossa—placing one mystery on top of another—let me indicate two reasons for staying with this model. First of all, every time we glance we are aware of the action of glancing itself; we have a kinesthetic consciousness of its muscular movement, however subtle and marginal it may be. I take such kinesthesis to be an essential supplement to the fact that in normal circumstances we do not *see* our own glance (only in an elaborate mirrored situation such as that depicted by Nagel do we glimpse ourselves glancing). The Greeks also questioned whether we see our own visual rays, or for that matter those of others: "Why," asks Alexander of Aphrodisias, "do we *not* see each other's visual rays?"[87] Just because we do not *perceive* visual rays

---

85. A. E. Taylor, *A Commentary on Plato's Timaeus*, p. 278.

86. F. M. Cornford, *Plato's Cosmology: The Timaeus of Plato*, p. 153, n. 1: "What is transmitted along this sympathetic chain is *motion* partly originated by qualitative changes in the object. . . . This motion reaches the bodily organ and causes qualitative changes there, which when they penetrate to the soul (but not before) are called 'sensations'. There is no ground for Taylor's notion of a pencil of light, a temporary extension of my body which may be miles long and 'is *sensitive throughout*', and so transmits *sensation* from one extremity to the other'" (Cornford's italics; the passages cited are from Taylor, *A Commentary on Plato's Timaeus*, p. 278).

87. Alexander of Aphrodisias, *De Anima*, 128, sec. 10; in his *Praeter Commentaria Scripta*

proceeding from ourselves or from others, there must be an alternative way of sensing such rays if we can be said to sense them at all. This alternative is found in the kinesthetic awareness that we are indeed looking out into the world via the glance. As you glance out at something, you will notice the way your whole eye is felt to move in its socket as well as inside its eyelids, which feel the motion from within. This internally generated and consciously felt kinesthesia accompanies every glance, even if in different ways in each instance. We glance *in* this self-touching action as well as *by means* of it—an action that is itself an instance of the more pervasive phenomenon of the complex intertwining of the touching with the touched as this occurs in many bodily registers: what was a problem for Aristotle (how can the same body touch itself touching?) becomes a paradigm for an entire way of regarding the living-moving body, indeed for the general relationship between the visible and the invisible.[88]

Second, kinesthesia is not confined to self-touching but reflects contact with the world at large. Like the glance itself, it reaches out into this world. This becomes evident in a basic action such as that of walking. In walking, our kinesthesias (and there are always several of them) extend outward onto the path over which we move and into the surrounding landscape. Berkeley had already suspected as much in his theory of vision, according to which the eye estimates the distance of an object in the visual field by projecting (that is, feeling in advance) the concrete bodily motions by means of which one would traverse the open stretch between one's current position and the object in question. What presents itself as an explicitly visual circumstance is at least equally a kinesthetic one: without a sense of the felt motions, including an imagined sense, the distance could not be accurately determined.[89]

Berkeley is pointing to what we can call "visual kinesthesia." This is a far more

---

Minora, ed. J. Bruns (Berlin: N.p., 1887); as cited by Charles Mugler, *Dictionnaire historique de la terminologie optique des grecs: douze siècles de dialogues avec la lumière* (Paris: Klincksieck, 1964), p. 295; my italics. For further treatment of touch, see Michael N. Nagler, *Spontaneity and Tradition: A Study in the Oral Art of Homer* (Berkeley: University of California Press, 1974).

88. "The Aristotle illusion"—whereby two crossed fingers of a single human hand produce confusing sensations of relative location—is cited by Merleau-Ponty in his *Phenomenology of Perception*, tr. C. Smith (New York: Humanities Press, 1962), pp. 237–238. Merleau-Ponty returns to the question in *The Visible and the Invisible*, tr. A. Lingis (Evanston, Ill.: Northwestern University Press, 1968), where the facticity of the touching/touched aspects of the body inspires general formulations of a chiasmatic relation of the body to itself and of the visible with the invisible: see esp. chap. 4 ("The Intertwining—The Chiasm") and in certain working notes (e.g., "Blindness [*punctum caecum*] of the consciousness," "Flesh of the world— Flesh of the body—Being," "Touching—touching oneself— —seeing—seeing oneself— —the body, the flesh as *Self*" [notes May 1960]; "Chiasm— —Reversibility" [note of November 16, 1960]).

89. For a much more complete statement of Berkeley's theory of distance and depth, see his *Essay Toward a New Theory of Vision* in George Berkeley, *Philosophical Works*, ed. M. R. Ayers (London: Dent, 1975), pp. 1–60, and Margaret Atherton, *Berkeley's Revolution in Vision* (Ithaca, N.Y.: Cornell University Press, 1990).

pervasive phenomenon than we might think at first. As a matter of fact, instances of pure seeing—perforce pure glancing—are the exception rather than the rule (a rule that is taken for granted in oculocentrism, which privileges pure looking). Rarely indeed do we engage in sheer vision, detached from any other sensory-bodily activity and the world in which it takes place. The same goes for "just looking," which is not only suffused with culture and desire—with *nomos* and *eros*—but is also accompanied by parts of the body other than the eye alone. No less than the glancing eye—and in close association with it—these parts put us in touch with the world at which we look. Here we encounter not the fragmented but the *concerted* body, the body that pulls itself together around vision, giving to this latter an ongoing basso profundo support from below: from the hands, the feet, the viscera, the trunk, the arms, the legs, indeed from the very earth on which we stand or walk. Even looking in the mirror has a tactile aspect.[90]

Seeing ramifies itself in many ways—thanks to our polysensuous bodies, which offer multiple inroads into the surrounding place-world. The same holds for glancing. Even when seated, we make use of our mobile head, adjusting its position to suit the glance; and in so doing we feel its transposition kinesthetically, just as we also feel the orbiting of the eyes located in this same head. We also glance while on the move, above all when we are walking. In this latter circumstance, glancing acts in close concert with our moving legs: the two actions realize a complex commixture of coordinated motions in which sometimes the glancing, sometimes the walking, takes the lead—and sometimes they act in perfect synchrony.

IX

Let us return to the agora, going back to that sunlit scene of high Athenian culture where citizens exchanged glances and greetings as they perambulated around the polygonal plaza. Earlier, I stressed the architecture and the light of this scene, as well as the clarity of mind and transparency of speech attained there; I also mentioned the chance encounters in which the glance plays such a prominent part. But there is another factor in any such circumstance that has risen to prominence in the last few pages: the lived body that supports the glance and carries its work forward in various ways—being its bearer as it were. The glance is of and into the brightness of the day—and into the scintillation of ideas as well—but it is continually ballasted by the body that underlies it as its constant companion. This body, *my* body, helps to hold the glance together; it subtends its two major moments of going out and coming in; it keeps the

90. "Memory seems to be to perception what the image reflected in the mirror is to the object [placed] in front of it. The object [seen in the mirror] *can be touched as well as seen;* acts on us as well as we on it; is pregnant with possible actions; it is actual" (Henri Bergson, "False Recognition," in *Mind-Energy*, tr. H. W. Carr [New York: Holt, 1920], p. 165; my emphasis).

enterprise continually and diversely alive, and gives to the opening of the glance a corporeal density and depth. Yeats had it right: "O body swayed to music, O brightening glance! How can we know the dancer from the dance?"[91] It is as if the shadows of the cave in Plato's primal allegory had been subsumed into the bodies of the prisoners, who have now been set free finally to move as well as talk, but only by incorporating the cave's legacy, its dark domain compacted into the body of the person who believes and (ultimately) knows: a person who must step over his own shadow to glimpse the Forms.

Only when not moving at all, standing stock still, is the liberated soul tempted to *gaze* at perceptual and noetic objects: then this visual modality is favored; in the words of the *Republic:* "when its gaze is fixed upon an object irradiated by truth and reality, the soul gains understanding and knowledge and is manifestly in possession of intelligence."[92] But for the most part, as Plato himself admits, every ordinary soul "looks toward that twilight world of things that come into existence and pass away, its sight [becomes] dim, and it has only opinions and beliefs which shift to and fro."[93] This is to say that everyday souls, *our* souls, are absorbed in a game of delimited glancing, bearing the shadows of ignorance into a less than fully illuminated world. Every such soul is bearing witness to the heft and opacity of its own body, and all the more so when it is moving—when its primary parts must coordinate to give to the glance the corporeal basis it has to have to be as free as it can be.

The shadows are not only those of a primitive cognitive state, for example, the debased reflections that characterize the first stage of the Divided Line. They are borne forward from an earlier time in Greece as well: they are shadows of the archaic notion of sight itself, still seething under the elegant tunic that covers the later Athenian citizen's athletic body. Here we return to the time of Homer, when verbs of seeing were so heterogeneous as to defy any easy assimilation under a single process, much less a single theory, of vision. We return to a marked visuocentric emphasis that is not reducible to the blinders of oculocentrism: for we have to do with the recognition of manifold forms of looking that do not defer to the gaze as the exemplary case.

Bruno Snell has emphasized that there is no single all-encompassing word for "sight" in the archaic, pre-Periclean world. Instead, there is a variety of verbs and verbal expressions for seeing—including all of those for glancing reviewed in section IV above, in addition to several others such as *theasthai* ("to look with one's mouth open, to gape") and *leussein*, "to see something bright, to let one's eye travel."[94] Each verb picks out a mode of concretely corporeal looking, with

---

91. W. B. Yeats, "Among School Children," in W. B. Yeats, *The Poems*, ed. R. J. Finneaan (New York: Macmillan, 1989), p. 217.

92. *Republic* 508a; tr. Cornford.

93. Ibid., 508b.

94. This latter verb is especially pertinent for our purposes: letting one's eye travel is to act in a manner that is mimetic with the traveling of one's own body in walking. See Snell, *The Discovery of the Mind*, p. 3. Snell concludes that "to begin with there was no one verb to refer to the function of sight as such" (ibid., p. 4).

the result that "the verbs of the early period . . . take their cue from the palpable aspects, the external qualifications, of the act of seeing, while later on it is the essential function itself, the operation common to every glance, which determines the content of the verb."[95] By "palpable aspects" Snell means such actions as handling, reaching, hearing, smelling—and walking.

"Later on," two or three centuries later in the classical period of Periclean Athens, only two members of the rich harvest of diverse Homeric verbs for looking survived as part of common usage: *blepein,* meaning both "to look at" and "to glance," a verb we have encountered in the words we have cited from Anacreon of Teos: "Thracian filly, why do you glance at me askance?"; and *theórein,* which derives from *theóros,* " spectator," as when a citizen was dispatched to another town to observe the quality of their theatrical performances: the words "theory" and "theater" are first cousins. From its spectatorial base, *theórein* took on connotations of contemplation, sheer seeing as it were, "the objective essence of sight."[96] Shedding earlier attitudinal and emotional senses it had when it connoted engaged viewing, it came to signify "an intensification of the normal and essential function of the eyes."[97] The normal, once instituted, entails *normalization,* that is to say, a socially sanctioned, officially endorsed right way of doing something: Latin *norma* means "carpenter's square," "rule," "pattern," "precept." Still more deeply embedded in "normal" is Greek *nomos:* the established institution of custom and law, state regulation, and more generally "orthodoxy" (that is, belief in the right, the straight, the correct, the upright).

When the very idea of vision is beholden to the normal and the orthodox—the presumptively right way to see—the gaze triumphs over the glance. For the gaze in its various modalities (scrutinizing, staring, and so on) is the agent or ally of

95. Ibid., p. 4. See the statement of principle that "in comparatively primitive speech abstractions are as yet undeveloped, while immediate sense perceptions furnish it with a wealth of concrete symbols which seem strange to a more sophisticated tongue" (ibid., p. 1). Snell also points out that the very variety of such verbs of seeing reflect another principle, namely, that "seeing is determined by the object and the attending sentiment" (ibid., p. 4)—an object that is itself intrinsically multiple.

96. "It goes without saying that even in Homer men used their eyes 'to see', i.e., to receive optical impressions. But apparently they took no decisive interest in what we justly regard as the basic function, the objective essence, of sight" (ibid., p. 5). The increasing usage of *theórein* signified the rise of such interest in the sheer functioning of sight. On the rich origin of *theórein,* see especially David Michael Levin, *The Opening of Vision: Nihilism and the Postmodern Situation* (New York: Routledge, 1988), pp. 99 ff. Levin cites Heidegger's notion that the root of the modern, objectivist sense of theory is found in the fact that already in Greek "theory" refers to "the outward look, the aspect, in which something shows itself" and that "*theórein* is . . . to look attentively on the outward appearance wherein what presences becomes visible and, through such sight—seeing—to linger with it" (Martin Heidegger, "Science and Reflection," tr. W. Lovitt, *The Question Concerning Technology and Other Essays,* ed. W. Lovitt [New York: Harper and Row, 1977], p. 163). Gadamer points out that a *theóros* is someone who is appointed to be a spectator at a religious festival. See H.-G. Gadamer, *Truth and Method,* 2d ed., tr. S. Weinsheimer and D. G. Marshall (New York: Continuum, 2004), p. 122.

97. Snell, *The Discovery of the Mind,* p. 4.

institutionalized life: as exemplified in the rigid straight-ahead look of soldiers in parade position, or of those who officiate on state occasions. The gaze has the support of the state and its institutions (legal, military, penal, educational, medical). In this direction lies Plato as the philosopher of the state, the *politeia* ("Republic"). This is the Plato who does not hesitate to proclaim the primacy of the gaze—that is, that look which is *"fixed* upon an object irradiated by truth and reality"—and to consider anything as capricious as a bare glance to belong to the realm of images (*eikasia*). Indeed, the gaze is geared to the hegemony of the Forms: upright being calls for right looking. As such, it superintends all other forms of looking, including the glance, which is thereby reduced to a mere minion of the gaze, or else thought to be nothing but a failed or stunted form of it. Thus the seeds are sown in fifth-century Athens for the increasing primacy of the gaze in theoretical accounts of vision, and from there to the flourishing of oculocentrism in the West.

But at another level, that of everyday experience and ongoing practices in a given place and time, the glance proves rebarbative to the subordinating moves I have just outlined. The very "academicians"(that is, members of Plato's Academy) who touted the supremacy of the gaze in theory glanced at each other daily in the agora and in the porches of the stoas that lined it. They glanced around, continually, with their bodies in full peripatetic motion, walking through the porches and crisscrossing the agora, running up against other moving bodies in dispersed aleatory rhythms. Nothing could normalize such truly tychic encounters. Nor could any law or regulation, custom or institution altogether suppress the glancing that "let[s] one's eye travel." Short of detaining people in prison, not even the most repressive laws can bar the nomadology of the wandering eye that accompanies the unregulated walk of a person with arms akimbo, legs loosened, the moving body as palpable in its perambulation as it is perceptive in its unleashed look.[98]

98. The ultimate root of *nomos* is *nem-*, as in *nemein,* which signified the distribution of livestock in pastures, their scattering into smooth space: another case of dispersion. The nomad escapes the Law of the State, its gates and limits, while observing a deterritorialized Logos of the Earth. On this derivation of *nomos,* see Emmanuel Laroche, *Histoire de la racine "Nem" en grec ancien* (Paris: Kliencksieck, 1949). Deleuze and Guattari, to whom I owe this reference, elaborate on the *nem-* root by linking it to the nomadic distribution of animals in deterritorialized smooth space: *"to take to pasture (nemó)* refers not to a parceling out but to a scattering, to a repartition of animals" (G. Deleuze and F. Guattari, *A Thousand Plateaus*, tr. B. Massumi [Minneapolis: University of Minnesota Press, 1987], p. 557; their emphasis). In ancient Greek, the root *nem*-gave rise to two words, both spelled *nomos,* that differed only in accent. *Nomos* with the accent on the last syllable meant a pasture or field; when accented on the first syllable, *nomos* meant usage, custom, or law. Euripides in the *Bacchae,* for example, exploits this ambiguity by depicting Dionysus as someone who violates Theban *nomos* (i.e., law) by taking women out of the city and up onto a *nomos* (i.e., open field). (I owe this example to Eric Casey.) I am taking Logos here in Heidegger's sense of the term: a loose assemblage or gathering of scattered parts—not the Logos that became logic in Aristotle's formal sense. The latter is nomothetic in the later, strictly law-bound sense of *nomos.* (See Heidegger's essay "Logos," in *Poetry Language Thought,* tr. A. Hofstadter [New York: Harper, 1971].)

Just as Plato's own rigorous model of vision was mitigated by a recognition of touch, so his fierce nomocentrism could not altogether eliminate the role of glancing in the acquisition of knowledge. As I proposed at the beginning of this chapter, glancing is operative at every successive level in the process of this acquisition—from the cave to the first emergence into sunlight (that is, from ignorance to belief) and from mathematical insight to the intuition of Forms (thus from a hypothetical to a categorial mode of knowing). Throughout, and even in the most austere epistemic contexts, glancing is at play, leavening the spirit of seriousness that attends the ascent to the absolute and lightening the burden of disciplined hierarchical learning.

Not even Plato, the first self-proclaimed logocrat in the West, could keep the glance out of play. Nor can post-Platonists: which means practically every later philosopher. Just as Plato could not suppress glancing as an indispensable inroad into the "ineluctable modalities of the visible," so we cannot rule it out either—try as we might in an Age of the World Picture (a *Weltbild* in which there is once again no official room for the glance but only for representations of determinate presences) and of Enframement (for which glancing is irrelevant in the domain of standing reserve).[99]

Homer (and other early archaic poets) may have had the first word, but Plato by no means had the last in the ongoing struggle between the glance and the gaze, those bipolar extremes of human vision.

The glance itself leads us to question the very model of first and last words, as well as the idea of extremities of vision. For the merest glance loosens the stranglehold of the sternest gaze. Whatever the pretensions of this latter, it cannot finally withstand the cunning and wit of glancing, its *métis*-inspired methods and mercurial motions, its protean powers. To glance anywhere, at any time, is to launch a foray in the life-world of looking, and there is never a last such look. This was already the case in the brilliant high culture that arose in the luminous space of the Athenian agora—just as it is still so even now, in and through the shimmer of the simulacra that populate the postmodern world of the spectacle.

---

99. See Martin Heidegger, "The Age of the World Picture" and "The Question Concerning Technology," in *The Question Concerning Technology and Other Essays.* For further discussion of the model of *Weltbild* and of the era of representationalism, see my *Representing Place in Landscape Painting and Maps* (Minneapolis: University of Minnesota Press, 2003), concluding thoughts.

6

THE SUDDEN, THE SURPRISING, AND THE WONDROUS

WITH WALTER BENJAMIN ON THE STREETS OF PARIS

> Unless you expect the unexpected, you will never find [truth], for it is hard to discover and hard to attain.
>
> —Heraclitus, fragment #18

> The emotion named Wonder is . . . more than simple Novelty. One degree beyond novelty is surprise, or the shock of what is both novel and unexpected. There is in surprise an element of contradiction and conflict, which, if acute, would of itself be painful; most surprises, however, give merely a neutral excitement of different degrees of intensity. . . . Wonder contains surprise, attended with a new and distinct effect, the effect of contemplating something that rises far above common experience, which elevates us with the feeling of superiority.
>
> —Alexander Bain, *The Emotions and the Will*

I

It is a long way from the bright and dusty agora of ancient Athens to the clean-swept boulevards of late-nineteenth-century Paris—not only in time (approximately 2,500 years) but also in space: from the eastern edge of Europe to one of its westernmost parts. There is a world, a place-world, of difference between an emerging civilization, at once awkward and wayward (though emerging with brilliant éclat), and a late capitalist society that has settled into prosperity and high culture, building on an earlier era of hegemony in Europe and of global empire. Public discourse and elaborate civic ceremonies were prominent in the former case, commercialism and sophistication in the latter; municipal and religious buildings of classical proportions contrast with flowing, monumental Third Republic architecture; the smallish but densely configured place of the agora could not be more different from the elegant and elongated Hausmannian boulevards that contained crowds of shoppers. In the one case, vistas opened out toward the elevated mesa of the Acropolis and the low-lying marshes of the Kerameikos (the local cemetery); while in the other, endless cityscapes stretched in every direction; in Athens, aristocratic classes and helots mixed in the marketplace, whereas in Paris the pavements bustled with members of the haute bourgeoisie and the working class. The set of contrasts could be continued—given that there are considerable differences in place and culture, language and economy, building types and kinds of landscape, class structure and forms of political life.

And yet in each case we encounter a glancer's world, in which animated actions of glancing cut across cultural, historical, and social differences. It is doubtless true that these differences are deeply sedimented in certain inflections of looking—bolder in certain regards, more cautious in others—and even amount to very different styles of glancing: after all, one will glance differently from behind a veil in a Middle Eastern street than when brazenly walking through an American shopping mall! But glance one will, veiled or not, no matter what the setting, no matter who else is present (and even if no one is present at all). There is no visual world, in any cultural and social setting, that does not constitute a lively matrix for glancing of virtually every kind, whether stemming from isolated subjects or from those who are in close communication with others. As I argued in my opening remarks to this part, glancing realizes a certain freedom of in-determination; even as it incorporates the specific historical milieu from which it springs, it remains free to move and rove in its own idiosyncratic way, leaping from one surface to another, whether in Athens or Paris, Damascus or Saint Paul. To glance is to look all over the place, whatever the place may be like, however it is disposed, wherever it exists. I glance at you; you glance at the dog in the street; your child who is barely capable of object permanence glances at her kitten; and the computer addict, seeming to stare at his screen without reprieve, in fact glances all over the screen and his study in an open dance of the look.

Between the aleatory and unconstrained on the one hand and the stylized and culturally conditioned on the other is a middle realm where very special phenomena arise. In this realm—where most human beings live most of the time— the idiosyncratic and the stereotypical interact in a continually changing commixture, exhibiting sometimes more of the fixed and foreseen (for example, the knowing glance, the look that puts you down) and sometimes more of the unexpected and unforeseeable (for example, the suddenly suspicious look, the inspired gesture of an action artist). In this same central domain are to be found conspicuous features of glancing that are more evident in certain cultures and times than in others. We have encountered some of these features in Athenian culture in the form of a certain heliotropism (in keeping with the corresponding epistemic hierarchy), the valorizing of casual encounters in the agora, discussions that strike glance-like blows, and so on. Such features can be called *salients* of glancing. In principle, they can occur in any setting, no matter how diverse; but certain historical and social, geographical and political factors favor their more prominent appearance in some settings more than in others. These settings at once precipitate and sustain their appearing, thereby helping to make them focal features of a given circumstance wherein they play a formative role.

Hence my strategy in this part: to bring out as clearly as possible certain salients of glancing that arise in two very different historical and cultural circumstances. As ever, no attempt is made to be comprehensive, either across cultures or within a given culture. But the salients I shall describe—ultimately, three in each instance (see the coda for a summary discussion)—are nevertheless important dimensions of glancing that are all too easily neglected if the kind of analysis I here pursue is not undertaken: dimensions that, despite their manifest specificity of appearance, point to more general lessons about the fate of glancing in any culture and at any time.

II

When we glance, we do so with characteristic celerity: there is no slow glancing, just as there is no rapid scrutinizing. To glance means to look quickly—as is underlined by such descriptive phrases as "to steal a look" (wherein I look hastily) and "to catch her glance" (whereby the speed of my glance has to match hers if it is truly to catch it as in a net). Glancing also signifies—with very rare exceptions—that what it captures in its visual net is *sudden* in its appearance and that, by the same token, it is *surprising.* Casting the most casual glance delivers something that, to some certain degree, "takes us by surprise." It does so insofar as we did not expect it; our habitual ways of looking did not anticipate what has so quickly arisen—not just in details but also, sometimes, with respect to the very types of things or events that arise. Thus I am surprised not just by the features of the face that suddenly comes before me when I thought I was engaging in a leisurely view of an open landscape or a busy street scene but, even more significantly, by the fact that it is a *face* that I now see and not a hill or a building. The scope of surprise is considerable, ranging from the modest to the dramatic.

The sudden and the surprising that draw my glance do not always occur together in our experience: something familiar can appear suddenly, or else something strange may reveal itself only by steps. But when they do conjoin in a glance as they so often do, we are moved—"struck." This is not to say that we are overwhelmed, much less that we suffer dismay or shock. We may certainly be startled; but the discomfort is likely to be moderate, as in the parallel case of an imagination whose most extreme exercise (for example, conjuring up ghosts) is nonetheless felt to take place within tolerable bounds. It remains that in most glancing we do encounter the unexpected and the exceptional; we are continually subject to surprise—and a surprise that occurs in the guise of the sudden.

The sudden is rarely discussed as a significant philosophical category. The exceptions can be counted on one hand: Parmenides, Plato, Descartes, Kierkegaard, Heidegger. The first three are especially notable since each is committed to a philosophy that proclaims Being, or Reason, triumphant over Becoming (to which the sudden would certainly seem to belong). Parmenides, the first philosopher of Being and someone who so much disdained Becoming as to declare it a form of Non-Being, turned to the sudden when the question arose as to how to characterize the transition between rest and motion: the transition cannot be piecemeal, for then rest would phase into motion, or motion would invade rest, rendering the very distinction between these categories otiose. As Plato presents it: "For a thing doesn't change from rest while rest continues, or from motion while motion continues."[1] Instead of a continuous movement from one to the other—instead of gradually becoming one from the other—in the case of the sudden there is an altogether abrupt moment of change: a moment that is only equivocally in time. The sudden is literally *atopon,* "without place," thus "strange" (as *atopon* also signifies). It is a matter of a transition that is at once instantaneous and unexpected: both of which are connoted by the word *to exaiphnés,* "the sudden." Here is the crucial conversation that, as reported by Plato, introduces the sudden for the first time into the Western philosophical vocabulary:

> "there is no time in which something can, simultaneously, be neither in motion or at rest."—"Yes, you're quite right."—"Yet surely it also doesn't change without changing."—"Hardly."—"So when does it change? For it does not change while it is in rest or in motion, or while it is in time."—"Yes, you're quite right."—"Is there, then, this queer thing (*atopon*) in which it might be, just when it changes?"—"What queer thing?"—"[The sudden] (*to exaiphnés*). [The sudden] seems to signify something such that changing occurs from it to each of two states. . . . this queer creature [the sudden] lurks between motion and rest—being in no time at all—and . . . in changing, [the One, regarded as both resting and moving] changes at an instant, and when it changes . . . just then it would be neither in motion nor at rest."[2]

Here the sudden signifies the strange situation where the One, the paradigm of motionless rest, changes "at an instant"—changes from rest to motion, or vice

1. Plato, *Parmenides* 155d, in the translation of M. L. Gill and P. Ryan in *Plato: Complete Works,* ed. J. Cooper (Indianapolis: Hackett, 1997). I am indebted to Peter Manchester for pointing out to me this passage and commenting on its significance; he also brought to my attention the passage from Kierkegaard cited below.

2. Ibid., 156c–156e. I have replaced "the instant" with "the sudden" in this citation.

versa. This cannot take up any determinate stretch of time, for then it would be either in motion or at rest *for that time;* instead, it occurs in a timeless moment that can only present itself suddenly: *ex-aiphnés,* literally "outside of showing." This is a "now" that cannot be reduced to the present, for this latter is a phase of time allied to a past and future in a continuum of time. It is a radical moment indeed—a break in time rather than a part of time, yet somehow holding out the prospect of the three temporal dimensions: as Peter Manchester remarks, " 'now' is 'when' there 'are' 'past/present/future.' "[3] It is a moment that, lacking temporal breadth, can only be encountered in the unexpected emergence of an event that we experience *as suddenly happening.*

For Kierkegaard and Heidegger, the sudden occurs as the Moment, the *Augenblick*—not a timeless instant but an open moment in which the temporal and the eternal conjoin (as Kierkegaard maintained) or in which decisiveness occurs (as Heidegger holds in *Being and Time*). The moment may not be a stretch of *time*—Heidegger rigorously distinguishes between time and temporality—but it is a valid temporal modality in which the sudden arises, unbidden yet with incisive presence: "that Present which is held in authentic temporality and which thus is authentic itself, we call 'the moment of vision' (*der Augenblick*)."[4] Such a moment, not to be confused with any mere now (which belongs to time, not to temporality), is not merely a caesura between rest and motion but has its own "ecstatic" structure; it is "a rapture which is held in resoluteness."[5] Kierkegaard takes Plato/Parmenides to task for rendering the moment as "a silent atomistic abstraction, which, however, is not explained by ignoring it."[6] Instead, *in the moment* time and eternity conjoin concretely—and suddenly. Such suddenness is not merely nugatory, it is not just not being in time, or "a halt in the now,"[7] but it is a way in which the eternal ingresses, for a passing but portentous moment, into human experience.

Just as the sudden is only of exceptional interest to philosophers, so too the surprising is rarely seen as philosophically interesting. This is only to be expected in the light of philosophers' proclivity for what Nietzsche calls "the spirit of gravity" and Jaspers the attitude of *Ernst,* "utter seriousness." Such seriousness discourages sensitivity to the surprising. It calls for continuous attention to what is directly and irrecusably before one—whether things in the perceptual realm or ideas in one's own mind. When it is genuinely serious, this attention is

3. Peter Manchester in email correspondence (January 29, 2001).

4. Martin Heidegger, *Being and Time,* tr. J. Macquarrie and E. Robinson (New York: Harper, 1962), p. 387. Heidegger italicizes "Present," "authentic," and "moment of vision."

5. Ibid., p. 387; Heidegger italicizes "held." On the now as "belonging to time as within-time-ness (*Innerzeitigkeit*)," see p. 388. Overall, "temporality" (*Zeitlichkeit*) belongs to Dasein and thus to being-in-the-world, while "time" and "within-time-ness" belong to the present-at-hand.

6. Soren Kierkegaard, *The Concept of Anxiety,* tr. R. Thomte and A. B. Anderson (Princeton, N.J.: Princeton University Press, 1980), p. 83.

7. Ibid., p. 84.

all-consuming and does not leave room for the surprising; if the surprising arises nonetheless, it is regarded as an intrusion or a distraction—in short, a matter of regret, to be suppressed or surpassed.

Despite a powerful temptation to dismiss the surprising as of merely trivial significance, it is noteworthy that at least two thinkers have accorded it a privileged place in the philosophical pantheon. One is Heraclitus: as the exergue to this chapter indicates, the unexpected is not considered to be extraneous but to be something that comes as a surprise from within the very expectedness that precedes it. Such emergence of the unexpected is philosophically valid to the precise extent that it teaches us an important lesson about universal flux, wherein the stream of becoming always brings with it unanticipated flotsam and jetsam.

Descartes takes exception to this positive attitude toward the surprising. For him it is all too likely to be allied with wonder, and when wonder happens suddenly as well we are likely to enter into "astonishment"—which threatens to immobilize the knower and to limit his perception to just one aspect of what is to be known; and "this can never be other than bad."[8] For this reason, we must liberate ourselves from that very "inclination to wonder" that "makes us disposed to acquire scientific knowledge" in the first place.[9] It may be good that we are born with some such inclination—or we might not seek scientific knowledge at all—but "after acquiring such knowledge we must attempt to free ourselves from this inclination as much as possible."[10] Why? Because what matters is that we pursue this knowledge with the right kind of sober attention in the appropriately serious mood:

> For we may easily make good its absence [that is, of wonder] through that special state of reflection and attention which our will can always impose upon our understanding when we judge the matter before us to be worth serious consideration.[11]

Here the classical paradigm of concerted scrutiny undertaken in the spirit of gravity leaves little room for receptivity to the surprising. When we are carried away by surprise, we are too inclined to seek the novel for its own sake: which is to guarantee superficiality of knowledge. Either our attention becomes constricted to "the first image of the objects before us without acquiring any further knowledge about them"[12] or (as a result) we form a habit whereby we fixate only on such an image to the neglect of deeper knowledge. Either way, we are in danger of becoming the craven subjects of "blind curiosity," that is, subjects

---

8. René Descartes, *The Passions of the Soul*, tr. J. Cottingham, in J. Cottingham, R. Stoothoff, and D. Murdoch, eds., *The Philosophical Writings of Descartes* (Cambridge: Cambridge University Press, 1985), vol. 1, p. 353. Wonder arises with "the sudden and unexpected arrival of the impression which changes the movement of the [animal] spirits" (ibid., p. 354).

9. The phrases in this sentence are from ibid., p. 355.

10. Ibid.

11. Ibid.

12. Ibid.

"who seek out rarities simply in order to wonder at them and not in order to know them."[13] Here wonder and knowledge are antithetical to each other, with surprise regarded as the accomplice of wonder.

And yet Descartes is in the end ambivalent about surprise, and in this he is emblematically modern in spirit. Despite its dangerous alliance with wonder, considered by itself surprise is "a special state of attention and reflection"[14] that is not present in any of the other six major passions of the soul. Moreover, if surprise is altogether lacking we will never be moved to the point of passion of any kind.[15] Surprise, we might say, is an elixir of the emotions as well as a first spur to knowledge. It animates affects, and it offers a fillip to the generation of knowledge. Moreover, it takes us out of ingrained epistemic habits by its alertness to the unexpected, encouraging us to become more open to what we do not (yet) know, thus conscious of the shortcomings in our epistemic expectations. For surprise is uniquely well equipped to signal to us "unusual and extraordinary objects"[16] that our extant knowledge has not foreseen.

Descartes expressly links surprise with the sudden. For an impression to be maximally surprising to us, it should arrive suddenly. Wonder itself is defined as "a sudden surprise of the soul."[17] Surprise is the inner motor of wonder precisely because it arises suddenly, without warning. Moreover, the effect of surprise is intensified by the sudden. The fact that their collusion reaches a high pitch in the case of wonder—especially as it veers toward astonishment—does not invalidate the same collaboration in more responsible epistemic contexts. In these contexts, surprise can seize hold of us *all at once*—so suddenly that it shakes us out of our cognitive complacency. For this reason, Descartes cannot afford to ignore the combination of surprise and the sudden as it emerges more broadly in the philosophical and scientific inquiries he himself pursued and recommends to his readers. Yet he fails to single out this emergence.

Even more importantly, Descartes overlooked one phenomenon in which the sudden and the surprising are allied in everyday life. This is in ordinary glancing, where the alliance is even more active and accessible than it is in concerted research. It arises in virtually every glance we take—when we see, all at once, what we had not expected to see, what is different from what we already knew, what takes us in a different direction than we had intended to go. In its sudden surprisingness, a single glance delivers a "first image" of evidence and insight that puts previously held knowledge and belief in a new light. Without requiring any special setting—whether scientific laboratory or philosophical study—the merest glance delivers the surprising and the sudden in one fell swoop.

13. Ibid., p. 356.
14. Ibid., p. 355.
15. See ibid., p. 350: "If the object before us has no characteristics that surprise us, we are not moved by it at all and we consider it without passion." On p. 353 he adds that surprise "normally occurs in and augments all [of the passions]."
16. Ibid., p. 353.
17. Ibid.

III

Walter Benjamin was keenly aware of this fact, and he investigated it in his *Arcades Project*, where he sought the fate of the sudden and the surprising as these were delivered in glances cast while walking on the streets of Paris. His fascination with life in the Paris arcades and in the grand boulevards outside them led him to consider closely how citizens of Paris in the late nineteenth century experienced city life, including how they looked around them in the course of that life.

The *Project* is an extraordinary treasure trove of documents and insights, many of which bear on the intimate tie between the glance and the sudden and surprising. In most of the remainder of this chapter, I shall trace out this part of Benjamin's itinerary, focusing on his account of street life in Paris, with an emphasis on how the sudden and the surprising arise in acts of glancing in this particular place.

For Benjamin, streets and other material constructions of a given society are not merely physical works but highly revealing symptoms of a collective consciousness and an equally collective unconscious. In contrast with Freud's fascination with psychoneurotic symptoms of individuals with a dynamic personal unconscious, Benjamin sought public and social expressions of a historical past that is to be unearthed by a new form of cultural analysis. As with Freud, however, Benjamin argues that we cannot rest content with the manifest phenomenon but must look beneath it for the hidden roots of what is puzzling or problematic on the surface. In Freud's case, free associations to the manifest image of the dream uncover repressed wishes stemming ultimately from childhood; for Benjamin, a method of "literary montage"—that is, something like a culturally informed free association—allows the pertinent past to be revealed in a flash, in "the now of recognizability (*das Jetzt der Erkennbarkeit*)."[18] In each instance, there is an adverting to an inaccessible past in order to illuminate the present. Freud spoke fondly of his "predilection for the prehistoric," whether in the individual or in the earliest epochs of civilization, while Benjamin sought what he called "primal history" (*Urgeschichte*).[19] None of these underlying kinds of ur-history is available to ordinary daylight consciousness; each requires

18. For this phrase, see Walter Benjamin, *The Arcades Project*, tr. H. Eiland and K. Mc-Laughlin (Cambridge, Mass.: Harvard University Press, 1999), p. 486. We shall return to it below. Not that Benjamin was uninterested in childhood: "Every childhood achieves something great and irreplaceable for humanity" (p. 461), and he explicitly links "memory, childhood, and dream" (ibid.). For the flâneur, every street leads back and down into a past which "always remains the time of a childhood" (ibid., p. 416). But there is no systematic return to childhood for the crucial clues to adult behavior. The phrase "literary montage" is at ibid., p. 460. We shall return to the question of montage at the end of this chapter.

19. "Primal history" occurs at ibid., p. 4. Freud's phrase occurs in a letter to Fliess dated January 30, 1899, included in *The Complete Letters of Sigmund Freud to Wilhelm Fliess, 1887–1904*, tr. Jeffrey Moussaieff Masson (Cambridge, Mass.: Harvard University Press, 1985), p. 342.

a special sort of excavation; and each shows itself to have been characteristically hopeful in origin, whether as wishful or as utopian. In Freud's parlance, the child's "basic wishes" derive from the "primal scenes" of early life that bear on desire in relation to gender and sexual formation; for Benjamin, it is a matter of a deep past in which the fundamental wish is for a classless society. As Benjamin puts it in his "Exposé of 1935":

> Corresponding to the form of the new means of production, which in the beginning is still ruled by the form of the old (Marx), are images in the collective consciousness in which the old and the new interpenetrate. These images are wish images; in them the collective seeks both to overcome and to transfigure the immaturity of the social product and the inadequacies in the social organization of production. At the same time, what emerges in these wish images is the resolute effort to distance oneself from all that is antiquated—which includes, however, the recent past. These tendencies deflect the imagination (which is given impetus by the new) back upon the primal past. In the dream in which each epoch entertains images of its successor, the latter appears wedded to elements of primal history (*Urgeschichte*)—that is, to elements of a classless society. And the experiences of such a society—as stored in the unconscious of the collective—engender, through interpenetration with what is new, the utopia that has left its trace in a thousand configurations of life, from enduring edifices to passing fashions.[20]

Despite the striking use of familiar terms like "wish images," "dream," and "unconscious," Benjamin's departure from Freud becomes apparent in a passage such as this. For each of these quasi-technical terms has a resolutely *collective* status in Benjamin. Whereas Freud can say unblinkingly that "dreams are completely egoistical,"[21] Benjamin insists on the social and intersubjective character of all of the "elements of primal history." For Freud, primal history is that of the individual (that is, in his or her childhood) or that of the entire species (regarded as a super-individual). For Benjamin, primal history is that of a particular collective group that has its own social structure and history, its own dynamics and dialectics.

Benjamin departs from Freud not only with regard to the collective status of the subject of history but also as to the *implacement* of that subject: its cultural location as well as its physical "whereabouts." A stray remark from Benjamin's "Exposé of 1939" is revealing in this regard: "construction plays the role of the subconscious."[22] For Freud the unconscious is ruled by the "primary processes" of condensation, displacement, and symbolization; these processes construct the manifest dream out of a complex concatenation of instinctual urges, memories, and events of the previous day (*Tagesreste*), but the construction remains entirely psychical and the result is a dream accessible only to the dreamer, both as an experience and in its ultimate meaning. Benjamin has in mind something

---

20. "Exposé of 1935," in Benjamin, *The Arcades Project*, pp. 4–5.
21. Sigmund Freud, *The Interpretation of Dreams*, tr. J. Strachey, in the *Standard Edition of the Complete Psychological Works* (London: Hogarth, 1953), vol. 5, p. 358.
22. "Exposé of 1939," *The Arcades Project*, p. 16.

else again: "construction" as social formation as well as physical construction, both of which are revealed paradigmatically in the vanishing arcades of the late nineteenth century in Europe. The collective consciousness and the collective unconscious alike express themselves in the customary actions of a given historical era (for example, in modes of fashion) but also in the buildings and other architectural works of that era. It is in these actions and works that the collectivity of the era expresses itself and finds its fit formulation—at least as much as in particular artistic expressions, in diaries, or in dreams: all the products of highly individual and individuated labor.

If this is so, it behooves the cultural critic or social analyst to take to the streets—or at least to track those who inhabit or haunt streets. Not only the library and the consulting room, those privileged interiors of nineteenth-century thought and experience, but the whole outside metropolitan world with complexes of buildings and labyrinths of streets constitute the exploratorium of Benjamin's long-pursued fascination with arcades. The street scene rather than the dream scene is the focus of his remarkable project.

Benjamin turns back to the nineteenth century, then, not just from the despairing sense that genuine wonder is no longer possible in a time of rising Fascism. He does so from a quite positive sense that he will gain insight not otherwise available: the step back is a step forward. He also hopes that a new sense of wonder may come from this step back and that it will emerge by stepping out onto the streets of Paris, thereby getting back into stride with those who strolled along the boulevards of that great city. Freud left the confined space of his consulting room only to walk around the *Ringstrasse* of Vienna at midday—as a momentary relief from his detailed and laborious descent into the underworld of his patients' unconscious minds. Benjamin, in contrast, closely followed the perambulations of the flâneur around Paris—a walker in the city who is not taking a break from work but who finds primary inspiration in the walk itself and what it reveals. Here, too, there is descent into the underworld. Benjamin cites Virgil in an epigraph to Convolute C: "Easy the way that leads into Avernus [that is, the entrance to the underworld]."[23] Freud had famously cited Virgil in the opening epigraph to the *Interpretation of Dreams:* "Flectere si nequeo superos, Acheronta movebo" (if I cannot change the higher powers, I will move the infernal regions). But for Freud the concerted journey into the underworld can only take place in the consulting room, while in Benjamin's view it is something that happens all the time in city life:

> One knew of places in ancient Greece where the way led down into the underworld. Our waking existence likewise is a land which, at certain hidden points, leads down into the underworld—a land full of inconspicuous places from which dreams arise. All day long, suspecting nothing, we pass them by, but no sooner has sleep come than we are eagerly groping our way back to lose ourselves in the dark corridors.[24]

23. *The Arcades Project*, p. 82; from Virgil, *The Aeneid*, Book 6, line 126, in the translation of Allen Mandelbaum (Berkeley: University of California Press, 1982).
24. Ibid., p. 875.

The "hidden points" leading into the underworld are not vexing neurotic symptoms with hidden meanings but, instead, such literally hidden channels as sewers and catacombs in a vast city such as Paris. This becomes clear in another passage from the *Arcades Project:*

> The street conducts the flâneur into a vanished time. For him, every street is precipitous. It leads downward—if not to the mythical Mothers, then into a past that can be all the more spellbinding because it is not his own, not private. Nevertheless, it always remains the time of a childhood.[25]

The Avernian past in question is that of the history of a people, who leave traces of their existence in subterranean places. If that now-vanished existence is "a time of childhood," it is a collective childhood in relation to the metropolitan present. Its primary form of survival is spatial rather than temporal: it is found in the remnants of earlier forms—artifacts and rituals—of dwelling in the city. These constitute a dense underground world beneath the pavement on which the flâneur promenades: "In the asphalt over which he passes, his steps awaken a surprising resonance. The gaslight that streams down on the paving stones throws an equivocal light on this double ground."[26] The ground is redoubled: it is both literal pavement and the underworld below it. Surprise rises in the streets—from their capacity for offering a foothold to the walker while sheltering a deeper ground underneath that is the nonpersonal past, the collective space, of the people who formerly occupied that place. This is why Benjamin liked to cite the following statement of Daniel Halévy, prefacing it with the words "maxim of the flâneur": "In our standardized and uniform world, it is *right here, deep below the surface,* that we must go."[27] The depths at stake are not only buried beneath the surface but also, at the same time, they are "right here," at this very place where the flâneur is walking: on the pavement, over the sewer, near the catacomb. Down here below.

The nineteenth century is not only a period of intense historicism but also a time when the unsuspected cultural and social significance of spatial structures was beginning to be taken seriously. These structures were not only seen with the voyeuristic eyes of the flâneur regarded as a "scout in the marketplace"[28] but also felt first of all underfoot, in an intense draw downward into the chthonian depths of the city. If it is true that "space winks at the flâneur,"[29] then it does so from the mute pavement beneath his walking feet.

---

25. Ibid., p. 416. "The Mothers" (*die Mütter*) is Goethe's phrase from *Faust.*

26. Ibid.

27. Ibid., p. 444; my italics. This is cited from Daniel Halévy's *Pays parisiens* (Paris: N.p., 1932), p. 153.

28. "The flâneur plays the role of scout in the marketplace. As such, he is also the explorer of the crowd" (ibid., p. 21). On the flâneur as an observer, see ibid., p. 417 and esp. p. 427: "The flâneur is the observer of the marketplace. . . . He is a spy for the capitalists, on assignment in the realm of consumers."

29. Ibid., p. 418.

IV

The flâneur walks the streets of the metropolis—paradigmatically Paris.[30] He walks on the exposed surface of the city, its manifest image, its very face: "There, we may say, everything is face."[31] Not face in any strict Levinasian ethical sense—which would stop the walker in his tracks so as to deal with the uncompromisable demands of the Other—but the impersonal urban face of anonymous multitudes, the face of "the crowd" (in Kierkegaard's term). The flâneur takes the city at face value. Which does not mean to take it as something superficial but to experience the city's variegated, condensed, expressive significance for the person who has eyes to see and feet to feel. Gliding from surface to surface—where "surface" can mean the physical surface of pavement as well as the socially inscribed surfaces of other walkers—the flâneur looks for clues, signs, winks. Or rather *blinks*, as is stated in this remarkable passage:

> A look at the ambiguity of the arcades: their abundance of mirrors, which fabulously amplifies the spaces and makes orientation more difficult. For although this mirror world may have many aspects, indeed infinitely many, it remains ambiguous, double-edged. *It blinks:* it is always this one—and never nothing—out of which another immediately arises. The space that transforms itself does so in the bosom of nothingness. It is like an equivocal wink coming from nirvana.[32]

The narrow lanes of the classical arcades—along which the display windows mirror each other in "double-edged" fashion—induce a situation in which the flâneur not only looks at the buildings and crowds through which he moves but also they, in turn, return his look. There is a dialectic of looking at play in this situation—a "whispering of looks" (*Blickwispern*), of gazes and especially of glances (of which blinking and winking are close cousins). Not only does the casual walker look out with his vagrant, versatile eyes but the denizens of the street (human beings as well as built places) look back, much as one windowpane mirrors back to another its own image. Benjamin continues:

> The whispering of looks fills the arcades. There is nothing here that does not, where one least expects it, open a fugitive eye (*ein kurzes Auge*), blinking it shut again; but if you look more closely, it is gone. To the whispering of these looks, the space lends its echo.[33]

At stake here is not only the exchange of looks between animate and inanimate beings but also a factor of surprise: the fugitive eye of mirrors as of other human

---

30. "Paris created the type of the flâneur. What is remarkable is that it wasn't Rome" (ibid., p. 417).

31. Ibid., p. 418. Benjamin adds: "Each thing has the degree of bodily presence that allows it to be searched—as one searches a face—for such traits to appear. Under these conditions even a sentence (to say nothing of the single word) puts on a face, and this face resembles that of the sentence standing opposed to it" (ibid.).

32. Ibid., p. 542; my italics.

33. Ibid., p. 542.

beings opens "where one least expects it," with the result that the spectator of this scene of interchange can only "stop short in some surprise."[34] It is as if the very space traversed by the crisscrossing looks is itself amazed at what is happening to it, and the flâneur as witness reflects this ramified mirror-play of looking—mirrors the mirroring in his or her surprise at this extraordinary visual event in the very midst of ordinary commercial life.

The exchange of images in such a situation is not only surprising but sudden in its occurrence. And it is the former as accompanied by the latter; the exchange is virtually simultaneous: just as one shop window is reflected immediately in another, so the flâneur's look is returned at once from what he looks at. All of this happens so quickly that Benjamin imagines the visual space to ask itself: "Now what can possibly have overcome me?" To which the flâneur retorts: "What, indeed, can possibly have come over you?"[35] To these two questions comes the same crucial response: "We stop short in some surprise."[36] This translates "*Wir stutzen*," where *stutzen* can also can mean "to be startled" or "to be puzzled"—and to "wonder."

Wonder, then, arises from the unexpected and, in particular, from the conjunction of the sudden and the surprising. Dismissed by Descartes as excessive in the face of scientific and philosophical probity, wonder arises unrehearsed and nontraumatically in the cozy corridors of the nineteenth-century arcade. But this is a wonder far from philosophical or scientific. It is closer to *wondering at* than to anything like amazement, much less astonishment. As the "at" signifies, it is more focused and less diffuse than these latter. It is being struck by a singular spectacle, caught up in its specific energy, moved by the particularities of the scene itself. Above all, it is wondering at the remarkable fact that one's look is reciprocated just where one expects it least.

The reciprocated look is also an important theme for Merleau-Ponty, who in discussing the "fundamental narcissism of all vision" comments that when I am immersed in a given perceptual field "I feel myself looked at by the things."[37] Then my situation is "not to see in the outside, as the others see it, the contour of the body one inhabits, but especially to be seen by the outside, to exist within it, to emigrate into it, to be seduced, captivated, alienated by the phantom, so that the seer and the visible reciprocate one another and we no longer know which sees and which is seen."[38] Strikingly, Merleau-Ponty reverts to reciprocal images in mirrors—each reflecting the other—at this very point: "a Visibility," as well as "a Tangible in itself," emerge between the perceiver and the perceived that

34. Ibid., p. 542.
35. Ibid.
36. Ibid.
37. Maurice Merleau-Ponty, *The Visible and the Invisible*, tr. A. Lingis (Evanston, Ill.: Northwestern University Press, 1968), p. 139.
38. Ibid.

belongs, strictly speaking, to neither one separately: "as upon two mirrors facing one another where two indefinite series of images set in one another arise which belong really to neither of the two surfaces, since each is only the rejoinder of the other, and which therefore form a couple, a couple more real than either of them [taken separately]."[39]

Such double-sided, reciprocated looking occurs in many contexts. One of these, far from the city, is wilderness: Merleau-Ponty liked to cite many painters' conviction that "things look at them," for example, trees in a forest.[40] Another is the realm of the unconscious conceived as an Other who looks back at our constricted egological self: inspired by Merleau-Ponty, Lacan has explored the psycho-logic of this intrapsychic looking.[41] Between the natural Other and the psychical Other is the still-different otherness of the city—the scene of the street, at once othered and othering. If the unconscious is, vis-à-vis waking life, a different "scene of action" (*Schauplatz:* in Fechner's term favored by Freud),[42] the street is another scene of action altogether, a very different place of manifestation (as *Schau/platz* literally signifies). If in all three cases there is reciprocal looking—and equally mutual feeling or touching, as Merleau-Ponty insists and Benjamin implies[43]—what sets the street scene apart, what is distinctively different about it?

What sets the street apart is *reciprocal inhabitation.* By this I mean the way in which a given street is experienced—paradigmatically by the flâneur but also by many other citizens—both as an open landscape *and* as a special kind of inner space. This is an insistent subtheme of the Arcades project. To start with, "Parisians make the street an interior . . . [a] domestic interior."[44] Benjamin does not

---

39. Ibid.

40. In a claim I have had occasion to cite in chap. 2, Merleau-Ponty says: "Many painters have said that things look at them. As André Marchand says, after Klee: 'In a forest, I have felt many times over that it was not I who looked at the forest. Some days I felt that the trees were looking at me'" (Maurice Merleau-Ponty, "Eye and Mind," tr. C. Dallery, in *The Primacy of Perception,* ed. J. Edie [Evanston, Ill.: Northwestern University Press, 1964], p. 167). I shall return to this sense of being witnessed by nonhuman others in the concluding thoughts.

41. See "Of the Gaze as *Objet petit a,*" in Jacques Lacan, *The Four Fundamental Concepts of Psychoanalysis,* tr. A. Sheridan (New York: Norton, 1977), pp. 67–121.

42. "[For Fechner] *the scene of action of dreams is different from that of waking ideational life*" (*The Interpretation of Dreams,* p. 81; his italics; cf. also p. 574).

43. "There is vision, touch, when a certain visible, a certain tangible, turns back upon the whole of the visible, the whole of the tangible, of which it is a part, or when suddenly it finds itself *surrounded* by them, or when between it and them, and through their commerce, is formed a Visibility, a Tangible in itself, which belong properly neither to the body qua fact nor to the world qua fact" (Merleau-Ponty, *The Visible and the Invisible,* p. 139; his italics). Benjamin implies the reciprocity of feet and pavement in the city in his careful descriptions of walking on the asphalt of Parisian sidewalks: e.g., his citation of Alexis Martin's "Physiologie de l'asphalte" in *The Arcades Project,* p. 421, which speaks of how poets, stockbrokers, and old men with canes all feel the asphalt underfoot differently.

44. *The Arcades Project,* pp. 421–422.

mean merely that city streets become familiar places for those who habitually traverse them. They contain elements that are reminiscent of rooms in houses:

> Streets are the dwelling place of the collective. The collective is an eternally unquiet, eternally agitated being that—in the space between the building fronts— experiences, learns, understands, and invents as much as individuals do within the privacy of their own four walls. For this collective, glossy enameled shop signs are a wall decoration as good as, if not better than, an oil painting in the drawing room of a bourgeois; walls with their "Post No Bills" are its writing desk, newspaper stands its libraries, mailboxes its bronze busts, benches its bedroom furniture, and the café terrace is the balcony from which it looks down on its household. The section of railing where road workers hang their jackets is the vestibule, and the gateway which leads from the row of courtyards out into the open is the long corridor that daunts the bourgeois, being for the courtyards the entry to the chambers of the city. Among these latter, the arcade was the drawing room. More than anywhere else, the street reveals itself in the arcade as the furnished and familiar interior of the masses.[45]

There is displacement and transformation going on in this striking observation. The individual is displaced into the collective, which becomes the city subject capable of experience and knowledge usually ascribed only to isolated individuals. In turn, the street—that is, a primary locus of inhabitation for this collective subject—is transformed into a room: an open space for perambulation becomes a cozy place for the collective. To what end? To show that streets are not indifferent to what happens in them, mere places of passage. Instead, they are active scenes of inhabitation and movement, filled with dynamic bodies having diverse intentionalities. At the same time, they are receptacles of memories and imaginations: collective memories that rise from the primal history of the city (and especially a particular region of that city) and imaginations that constitute entire shared phantasmagorias (evident in the flâneur's grandiose conviction that he can "read from faces the profession, the ancestry, the character"[46]).

To contain—to house—such rich collective experience calls for something like a room. "Room," a linguistic cousin of German *Raum* ("space"), signifies a crucial third term between space and place that keeps on showing up in the history of philosophy, albeit rarely thematized there.[47] A room is less confining than a place—if "place" is taken to mean that which immediately surrounds something: *topos* in Aristotle's sense of the space occupied by a given physical thing—but not as amorphous and unending as space. A room expands or contracts in keeping with its content. Thus construed, a room describes life on densely inhabited streets: their very roominess can be felt as confining when

45. Ibid., p. 423.
46. Ibid., p. 429. For a more general statement of phantasmagorias of city life, see "Exposé of 1939," ibid., pp. 14–15.
47. For remarks on the importance of "room" in this generic sense, see *The Fate of Place: A Philosophical History* (Berkeley: University of California Press, 1997), pp. 87, 122–124, 166, 252, 257–258, 261, 274, 282, 313, 330.

overbearing buildings loom on both sides of a small city block, or it can extend outward along open boulevards to a whole region of a city—or even to the entire city itself. But at each level, a fitting space, a sense of accommodating room, acts to encompass the variety of pertinent contents—contents such as those mentioned by Benjamin: shop signs, posters, mailboxes, benches, café terraces, courtyards, whole arcades. Each of these corresponds to parts of imagined rooms: for example, wall decorations, oil paintings, bronze busts, vestibules, corridors, drawing rooms. In each case, the felt roomfulness of a street matches its projected (or, alternately, introjected) contents by providing adequate architectural shelter. It bears out the *in* of "inhabitation," that is, being customarily located in-between various built places (apartment buildings, shops, and so on).

Benjamin's imaginary transformation also works in reverse: a single room in an actual house can be the scene of an imaginary walk. "So the flâneur goes for a walk in his room":[48] these words precede the recounting of a tale Benjamin borrows from Kierkegaard, a story of a child who was encouraged to take a voyage with his father in his own room: "Off they went, then, right out the front entrance, out to a neighboring estate or to the seashore, or simply *through the streets,* exactly as Johannes [that is, the boy] would have wished. . . . While they strolled in this way up and down the floor of his room, his father told him of all they saw. They greeted other pedestrians; passing wagons made a din around them. . . ."[49] This is a *voyage autour de ma chambre*—to cite the title of a book that describes mental voyages undertaken by a prisoner in his cell during the French Revolution.[50]

For Benjamin, however, it is the first transformation that is most notable. In particular, arcades are exemplary instances of streets that have become interior rooms. Thanks to their comparatively modest scale—arcades were in effect minimalls—the "streets" that ran through them lacked the enormity of expansive grand boulevards; they were more like lanes or mews than the streamlined streets of contemporary urban or suburban life. Normally, a glass roof arched over the central lane, and storefronts were so intimately appointed that they were more like cabinets than separate businesses. A contemporary observer said in 1828 that "the shops resemble closets."[51] The effect was that of an extended, diversely structured room—or, at the limit, a labyrinthine rooming-house. Just as room in general is situated between space and place, so an arcade is a middle-range architectural phenomenon whose overall extent falls midway between a single room in an apartment and the larger space of the city as a whole.[52]

48. *The Arcades Project*, p. 421.

49. Ibid.; my italics.

50. This is the title of a book by Xavier de Maistre published in 1794.

51. Cited by Benjamin at *The Arcades Project*, p. 422, from *Nouveaux Tableaux de Paris, ou Observations sur les moeurs et usages des Parisiens au commencement du XIXe siècle* (Paris: N.p., 1828), vol. 1, p. 34.

52. For a moving documentation of the few arcades that remain in Paris, see Graham Parkes's DVD, *The Paris Arcades: Projecting Walter Benjamin* (2005).

An arcade has a fitting scale for the flâneur, whose close visual observation, occasional hesitation, and sensitive overhearing call for a space neither too large nor too small—a "near sphere," in Husserl's term.[53] It is also a space in which to glance openly, though on an intimate scale: to look from one display to another, from one window to the next, just as one might glance freely at the diverse contents of a richly decorated living room. The intense mirror-play of the arcade—the windows of one shop reflecting those of another—is matched by the play of the flâneur's glance, which darts between the surfaces of arcade shops; once back on the boulevard, the flâneur glances more broadly at things and people, buildings and vehicles. The scale becomes correspondingly larger, the pace of his walking picks up, and his glances become more sweeping: more a matter of glancing out than glancing in.

The more we think in this direction, the closer we come to the forthright *promeneur*, for whom boulevards are the exclusive walkways and who openly strides, often without looking around in his or her headlong movement. This is especially true for those engaging in socially sanctioned promenades of the sort to which I pointed in the opening to this part, where the emphasis is on synchronized walking in step with others. But promenading can also signify "meandering capriciously," and is described as such by Baudelaire in an essay in *L'Art romantique*.[54] It emerges not only in the city but also in nature. The latter situation is described by Rousseau in *Les rêveries du promeneur solitaire*, where he writes that "these hours of solitude and meditation are the only ones in the day when I am completely myself and my own master, with nothing to distract or hinder me, the only ones when I can truly say that I am what nature meant me to be."[55] What "nature meant me to be" is to live in, to move through, and to meditate in the natural landscape; much the same sense of active walking is found in Thoreau's essay, "Walking." For both, the paradigmatic case is that of walking in nature.

Walking in an urban scene may lack landscape—with the notable exception of perambulating in great parks such as the Bois de Boulogne or Central Park— but it does take place in a "cityscape"[56] that is the equivalent of natural landscape. Benjamin does not fail to note this extended dimension of street move-

---

53. On the near sphere, see esp. chap. 3 above. Concerning the flâneur's observation, see *The Arcades Project*, pp. 427, 453, 454; on his overhearing, p. 431 (but note pp. 433, 447 for Simmel's emphasis on seeing as privileged in the city); on hesitating, p. 425.

54. See the essay, "Marceline Desbordes-Valmore," as cited by Benjamin in *The Arcades Project*, p. 442, where the phrase "meandering capriciously" occurs—apparently taken from Baudelaire.

55. Jean-Jacques Rousseau, *Les Rêveries du promeneur solitaire* (Paris: N.p., 1926), p. 15; cited by Benjamin at *The Arcades Project*, p. 453.

56. Referring to a passage from Proust that I shall analyze below, Benjamin says that "this passage shows very clearly how the old Romantic sentiment for landscape dissolves and a new Romantic conception of landscape emerges—of landscape that seems, rather, to be a cityscape (*Stadtschaft*)" (ibid., p. 420).

ment. Citing Karl Gutzkow's statement, "It is wonderful that in Paris itself one can actually wander through countryside," he remarks:

> The other side of the motif is thus touched on. For if flânerie can transform Paris into one great interior—a house whose rooms are the *quartiers,* no less clearly demarcated by thresholds than are real rooms—then, on the other hand, the city can appear to someone walking through it to be without thresholds: *a landscape in the round.*[57]

"Landscape" here does not signify natural prospects such as those provided by parks but is instead a term that answers to "room" when the "thresholds" that are so important for any given room (such as walls, doorways, windows) are opened out to allow for more capacious viewing, more panoramic scenes: as when walking along the Champs Elysées or the Rue de Rivoli. Revealed here is a perceptual world viewed "in the round" (*in der Runde*)—that is to say, without the usual foreclosures of the look that delimit the sense of openness sought in unconstrained promenading.

In the end, Benjamin considers slower-paced walking through arcades and open strolling on boulevards to be two dimensions of flânerie, one of which is more hesitant and tentative and the other actively exploratory of the larger cityscape ("a werewolf restlessly roaming a social wilderness"[58]):

> Landscape—that, in fact, is what Paris becomes for the flâneur. Or, more precisely: the city splits for him into its dialectical poles. It opens up to him as a landscape, even as it closes around him as a room.[59]

Here room and landscape are explicitly juxtaposed as extremes that do not, however, exist in isolation from each other. As poles that are dialectically related, they are always in touch; indeed, they are necessary to each other's existence. Just as there is no perception of objects without the direct or indirect enclosure of a horizon within which they are co-implaced, so the closed-in, roomlike intimacy of the arcades actively calls for the open, landscapelike vistas of the great boulevards that also made up the Parisian cityscape in the post-Haussmannian period.[60]

---

57. *The Arcades Project,* p. 422; my italics. Gutzkow is cited from his *Briefe aus Paris* (Leipzig: N.p., 1842).

58. *The Arcades Project,* p. 418; with reference to Edgar Allan Poe's "The Man of the Crowd."

59. Ibid., p. 417. Cf. Merleau-Ponty's similar remark (in a very different context): "For example, I see the next-door house from a certain angle, but it would be seen differently from the right bank of the Seine, or from the inside, or again from an aeroplane: the house *itself* is none of these appearances" (Maurice Merleau-Ponty, *Phenomenology of Perception,* tr. Colin Smith [New York: Routledge, 1962], p. 67; his italics).

60. On Haussmann and his influence on Paris, see Convolute E, "Haussmannization, Barricade Fighting," *The Arcades Project,* pp. 120–149. Benjamin is largely critical of Haussmann's redesigning of Paris, but he would not deny the essential complementarity between the experience of the Arcades and that of the boulevards to which I am here pointing. This complementarity continues to structure many cityscapes, e.g., that of the midtown of Manhattan in contrast with Soho and Greenwich Village.

V

Indeed, this inherent complementarity of two basic dimensions of city life is itself implicated in three other, still more generic coordinations. The first has just been mentioned: the thing with its horizon or, more technically, the internal horizon of the thing (its adumbrational aspects) along with its external horizon (which encompasses a group of things). The second coordination is that between the near sphere and the far sphere as first explored in chapters 2 and 3: the closed circle of items in proximity to each other and to their viewer in contrast with the open space in which they co-inhere and that extends outward endlessly into the distance. Still more pertinent in the present context is a third form of coordination: the close connection of time and place within a given event such as walking, perceiving, or speaking. Benjamin is especially struck at how in cities remote times and places become concurrent: "We know that, in the course of flânerie, far-off times and places interpenetrate the landscape and the present moment."[61] These *Länder- und Zeitenfernen* (that is, distances of lands and times) combine in the double event of "landscape" (*Landschaft*)—that is, the most complete spatial unit—and the "present moment" (*Augenblick*), that is to say, the most intensely felt temporal phase. Primal history comes to bear at just this moment, as do the labyrinthine aspects of the city (its underground as well as its outskirts) along with its many panoramic views.[62]

The result of this complex coordination of aspects and dimensions is the *dialectical image*: this image, manifest in spatial structures, is overdetermined historically insofar as the past forcibly invades the present—becoming more real than it had been when it first happened.[63] *Eindringen*, the German verb translated as "interpenetrate" in the citation just given, also means "to enter forcibly." The past is complicit with the present at every point: hence the axiomatic claim that "everything new it could hope for turns out to be a reality that has always been present."[64] Going from present to past allows for the leisure of writing history; but the present itself is always already invaded by the past, especially the primal past of formative events. This means that the city is not only a perceived

<hr />

61. *The Arcades Project*, p. 419.

62. On the city as a labyrinth, see ibid., pp. 519, 523, and esp. p. 429: "The city is the realization of that ancient dream of humanity, the labyrinth. It is a reality to which the flâneur, without knowing it, devotes himself." To this labyrinthine, remote aspect of the city answers the "linguistic cosmos" of the many streets situated over the labyrinth: see ibid., p. 522. Concerning the panoramic dimension of the city, see Convolute Q, "Panorama," ibid., pp. 527 ff., esp. p. 527 on the great multiplicity of -ramas.

63. "In regard to [historical] perception, one could speak of the increasing concentration (integration) of reality, such that everything past (in its time) can acquire a higher grade of actuality than it had in the moment of its existing. How it marks itself as higher actuality is determined by the image as which and in which it is comprehended. And this dialectical penetration (*Durchdringung*) and actualization of former contexts puts the truth of all present action to the test" (ibid., p. 392).

64. "Exposé of 1939," in ibid., p. 15.

landscape of spatially situated things but also a "storied landscape"[65] that represents the intimate interfusion, the interpenetration, of space and time in an event that happens in the present moment and at a given place.

The pivot around which these various basic dyads—thing/horizon, near sphere/far sphere, remote time/faraway place, past/present—is the *body:* in the case before us, the moving, walking body of the flâneur. Interpenetration of all these kinds (and still others[66]) is effected not just *by* but *through* this body, whether it is active in arcades or on boulevards. Its mode of moving, its pace and direction, its very posture as well as its ongoing perceptions—all these are the effective basis of being on the streets in nineteenth-century Paris. The lived-moving body is the mediatrix of such streetwise existence. Nevertheless, Benjamin rarely specifies the corporeal component of the flâneur's experience.[67] Why is this? Doubtless because of Benjamin's emphasis on the historicity of metropolitan life as well as on its social and political parameters. Yet these parameters, along with historicity itself, are nothing if not bodily; indeed, they would be nothing were they not to have bodily enactments. This is not to say that they are *only* bodily; but it is to say that the corporeal subject is always at stake in urban experience—beginning with the rudimentary action of walking on the streets. It is the ambulatory body that is surprised and struck by the happening of the sudden in the city. Still more importantly for our purposes, it is this body that notices the sudden in its surprise, and it does so paradigmatically in the glance.

If it is the case that "the city is the properly sacred ground of flânerie,"[68] the body is the vehicle that moves over that ground: the vessel that sanctifies it. And if "the city can appear to someone walking through it to be without thresholds: a landscape in the round," this is only because the "someone walking" is a someone who engages in the bodily activity of perambulation. For Parisians to inhabit their streets in the concrete and diverse ways so effectively described by Benjamin himself, they must do so as embodied beings—beings whose primal history is as much in their bodies as in the city through which they move. If "Parisians make the street an interior," this interiorization can only happen through their active embodiment. The *Urgeschichte* is as much in the bones and organs and muscles (and the corresponding body memories) as in the

65. "Even before Lefeuve, who described Paris 'street by street, house by house', there were numerous works that depicted this storied landscape as backdrop for the dreaming idler" (ibid., p. 417).

66. For the interpenetration of street and house, see ibid., p. 423; of images by the past, p. 518.

67. An exception occurs just after the passage on "far-off times and places [that] interpenetrate the landscape and the present moment": "When the authentically intoxicated phase of this condition announces itself, the blood is pounding in the veins of the happy flâneur, his heart ticks like a clock, and inwardly as well as outwardly things go on as we would imagine them to do in one of those 'mechanical pictures [of movement]' which in the nineteenth century (and of course earlier, too) enjoyed great popularity. . . ." (ibid., p. 419–420).

68. Ibid., pp. 420–421.

buildings and catacombs of the metropolis, its streets and sidewalks. The deeply
diachronous character of this primal history—not to be confused with a written history that aims at coherent narrative—is at once pre-reflective and pre-
egological.[69]

To hold that the pertinent historical subject is collective and not individual—
given that "the streets are the dwelling place of the collective"—does not mean
that this subject is any less corporeal in character; indeed, the collectively constituted body politic is all the more dependent on the habitual bodily behaviors
that are constitutive of street life in any metropolis: for example, in terms of
basic orientation as well as styles of walking. The small streets within arcades
become "the furnished and familiar interior of the masses" only on the basis of
a socially inscribed bodily experience.[70] Knowing how to get around in such
streets as on the boulevards is at once collective and bodily: and one because of
the other.

Only by means of bodily experience and its associated memories can we tell
the basic difference between "street," "way," and "labyrinth" in Benjamin's
important distinction. Only a body can discern the difference between these
fundamental routes:

> "Street," to be understood, must be profiled against the older term "way." With
> respect to their mythological natures, the two words are entirely distinct. The way
> brings with it the terrors of wandering, some reverberations of which must have
> struck the leaders of nomadic tribes. In the incalculable turnings and resolutions of
> the way, there is even today, for the solitary wanderer, a detectable trace of the
> power of ancient directives over wandering hordes. But the person who travels a
> street, it would seem, has no need of any waywise guiding hand. It is not in
> wandering that man takes to the street, but rather in submitting to the monoto-
> nous, fascinating, constantly unrolling band of asphalt. The synthesis of these twin
> terrors, however—monotonous wandering—is represented in the labyrinth.[71]

Outlined here are two basic ways by which the body moves in space. On the one
hand, we engage in a quasi-nomadic wandering (for example, in a trailless
wilderness area) that calls upon a freely moving body to negotiate "the incalculable turnings and resolutions of the way"—where "way" signifies an open path
rather than a settled route. On the other hand, we walk the streets of a modern
metropolis in a perambulation that, in the manner of the flâneur, follows the
pavement underfoot even as the eye wanders freely. At the limit—that of the

69. For the diachronous (or "anachronous") character of human existence at the pre-
egological level, see Emmanuel Levinas, *Otherwise Than Being: Or Beyond Essence*, tr. A.
Lingis (Pittsburgh: Duquesne University Press, 1998), pp. 9–10, 13, 24, 52, 57, 80, 154–155.
We are not so far from Levinas as it might seem when we recall that on the street (as cited
earlier from Benjamin), "everything is face."

70. I have written on the bodily basis of collective memory in my essay: "Is Social Memory
Something Cognitive or Something Else?" (forthcoming, to appear in a volume published by
the Sage Foundation).

71. *The Arcades Project*, p. 519.

maze or labyrinth—we do both, following an established or imposed route, yet wandering when we become lost, including lost in looking (for example, not knowing where to look for visual clues). Body is integral to all three forms of negotiating the place-world, way and street and labyrinth, path and route and maze. There is no motion in space, no path through place, except in and by the body of the walker who looks out and around as he moves.[72]

VI

Just as the concept of landscape is capacious enough to include city and country, outright striding and more cautious walking, remote vista and close-up view, so it also allows for the various crossovers discussed in the last few sections: looker and looked-at, street and room, interior and exterior, walking outside and walking inside, being lost in a maze, and so on. In the midst of a landscape, walking can be "aimless," yet also involve "felt knowledge."[73] Its basic action sustains the walker who is a paradoxical combination of the hidden and the revealed—seen by others even as his inner thought may be concealed—feeling "everywhere at home"[74] even as he walks in new and unknown space.

The flâneur, that paradigmatic walker of the late modern epoch, is a threshold figure of a decidedly Janus-faced cast—always looking forward and back at once: pursuing a project of pure observation on the streets while being drawn down into the labyrinthine underworld under his feet ("Easy the way that leads into Avernus"); pursuing the near future in the very undertow of the primal past in which he is caught up—and both in an irrecusable, refulgent present; creating a path as well as following a street; and moving between street and residence, indeed between room and landscape itself. The flâneur is bi-directional at the sensory level as well; primarily visual, he is also closely attuned to what he happens to hear on his sojourns: "his eyes open, his ear ready, searching for something entirely different from what the crowd gathers to see."[75] This search

72. I have explored in more detail the differences between "way" or "path" on the one hand and "route" (of which "street" is an important variant) in my *Earth-Mapping: Artists Reshaping Landscape* (Minneapolis: University of Minnesota Press, 2005), chaps. 1 and 4.

73. On the flâneur as walking "aimlessly," yet as involving "felt knowledge," see *The Arcades Project*, p. 417.

74. "For the perfect flâneur . . . it is an immense joy to set up house in the heart of the multitude, amid the ebb and flow. . . . To be away from home, yet to feel oneself everywhere at home; to see the world, to be at the center of the world, yet to remain hidden from the world" (Baudelaire, "Le Peintre de la vie moderne," in *L'Art romantique*, as cited by Benjamin, *The Arcades Project*, p. 443). For the flâneur as hidden/revealed, see ibid., p. 420. Another paradox is that the flâneur is a combination of magic and money: see ibid., p. xii (translators' introduction). For further discussion of walking and home, see my *Getting Back into Place: Toward a Renewed Understanding of the Place-World* (Bloomington: Indiana University Press, 1993), part 3.

75. *The Arcades Project*, p. 453.

is itself paradoxical; it is not the simple pursuit of a definite goal, it is not a particular project; for the flâneur's very leisure is his work, his avocation his vocation.[76]

No wonder that the first epigraph to the Convolute on the flâneur in *The Arcades Project* is this: "A landscape haunts, intense as opium."[77] Only a landscape can encompass all the paradoxical and Janusian aspects of the flâneur, including the various reversals to which he (equally she, in the rarer cases of female flâneurs) is subject or of which he or she is the witness. As Erwin Straus says, "To be fully in the landscape we must sacrifice, as far as possible, all temporal, spatial, and objective precision."[78] In a landscape setting, the vaguely sensed triumphs over the exactly perceived, accustomed dichotomies dissolve; blinks and winks, rather than fully articulate signs and words, become the primary means of communication, phantasmagorias flourish, and in general the indeterminate takes precedence over the determinate. In Merleau-Ponty's words, "obscurity spreads to the perceived world in its entirety."[79]

This is a circumstance where (in Benjamin's own descriptive terms) aura triumphs over trace, colportage/collection/montage over serial ordering, and the simultaneous over the successive. In the remainder of this part of the chapter, I shall consider each of these contrasts in relation to the glance as that act which, more than any other, delivers surprise in the face of the sudden as it is encountered in city life.

Aura versus Trace

The aura is the resonance of the past as it is borne forward into the living present—temporally distant from the present wherein it appears, yet reverberating there in its literal absence. It is the unique being of something that, however much it ramifies into the present, appears to be out of reach. An exemplary case of aura is to be found in Benjamin's own experience of arcades that were built in the nineteenth century, his vivid sense of their original presence, at once remote from the present moment and yet still quite accessible to the ordinary shopper in the early decades of the twentieth century. Aura connotes the ongoing duration of something, its perdurance into the present even as its origin belongs to the distant past. In experiencing the aura of something, we sense "its presence in time and space, its unique existence at the place where it happens to be,"[80] yet only as stemming from a primal past that is removed from

76. "Basic to flânerie, among other things, is the idea that the fruits of idleness are more precious than the fruits of labor" (ibid., p. 453).

77. Mallarmé, "Autrefois, en marge d'un Baudelaire," in *Divagations*, cited at *The Arcades Project*, p. 416.

78. Erwin Straus, *The Primary World of Senses*, tr. J. Needleman (Glencoe, Ill.: Free Press, 1963), p. 324.

79. Merleau-Ponty, *Phenomenology of Perception*, p. 199.

80. Walter Benjamin, "The Work of Art in the Age of Mechanical Reproduction," in *Illuminations*, p. 220.

the present. It is aura that disappears in "the age of mechanical reproduction," in which every exemplar comes clean-shaven and without allusion to the past of its creation, its source in ritual and its subsequent history, in short its tradition; thus a mechanized reproduction of an artwork, such as a photograph of it, deprives it of its uniqueness and authenticity, its "authority."[81]

Aura is felt by Proust, for example, when he experiences railway stations as "tragic places," resonating with their own past and full of nostalgia and mystery. The Gare Saint-Lazare is "one of those vast, glass-roofed sheds . . . which extended over the rent bowels of the city one of those bleak and boundless skies, heavy with an accumulation of dramatic menaces, like certain skies painted with an almost Parisian modernity by Mantegna or Veronese, beneath which could be accomplished only some solemn and tremendous act, such as a departure by train or the Elevation of the Cross."[82] The aura is felt in the penumbral way in which the sky as painted by these two Italian Renaissance painters seems to inhabit the sky as perceived through the smoky glass roof of the late-modern Parisian train station: this dramatic background, wholly historical and merely suggested, is present for Proust in its very absence.

A trace, in contrast with an aura, imports the past right into the present—brings it into our proximity rather than keeping it at a remote distance. Benjamin puts the distinction in this way:

> The trace is appearance of a nearness, however far removed the thing that left it behind may be. The aura is appearance of a distance, however close the thing that calls it forth. In the trace, we gain possession of the thing; in the aura it takes possession of us.[83]

A trace is a mark by means of which we can interpret and understand the past. The dream image or psychoneurotic symptom is a trace in this sense, since it is an imprint (however distorted it has become) of a pathogenic or traumatic past: a past that we can repossess only by dint of concerted techniques of interpretation. Benjamin cites a Roman inscription that can be translated this way: "We leave an imprint each time we enter into a history."[84] This imprint allows others to grasp what we did in our own time; remaining in its physicality, it carries this

---

81. "The authenticity of a thing is the essence of all that is transmissible from its beginning, ranging from its substantive duration to its testimony to the history which it has experienced. . . . And what is really jeopardized when the historical testimony is affected is the authority of the object" (ibid., p. 221). The central claim is that "that which withers in the age of mechanical reproduction is the aura of the work of art" (ibid.).

82. Cited at *The Arcades Project*, p. 561, from Proust, *A l'ombre des jeunes filles en fleurs* (Paris: Flammarion, 1987). One is reminded of De Chirico's celebrated painting from the same period in which Proust was writing this passage, *Gare Montparnasse or the Melancholy of Departure* (1914).

83. Ibid., p. 447.

84. Cited as the epigraph to Convolute P, "The Streets of Paris," in *The Arcades Project*, p. 516.

doing over into a future time of interpretation and understanding, making it available to others whom we cannot know.

The aura is not a physical thing but something that surrounds a thing, conveying to us a sense of how far the past is from us even as it lingers in this penumbral format. In this very lingering, however, it has special powers in the present. In particular, it has that "surprising resonance" that is awakened by the footsteps of the flâneur "in the asphalt over which he passes."[85] Precisely in its capacity to surprise us, it takes possession of us. Where a trace puzzles us by its encrypted character (for example, in hieroglyphic inscriptions in a language we do not know) and thus calls for acts of interpretation, an aura captivates us by the way in which it delivers the past to us at once and in whole cloth. Remote as this past is, it does not call for interpretation: for it is a matter of the very image of the past, its "presentation" (*Darstellung*). Instead of puzzling us, it surprises us—takes us over. And it surprises us all the more when it takes us over suddenly, as in the rapid perception, in a glance, of the skies brooding over an immense railroad station, or when we pass through other, more modest such stations that proffer to us the essence of a town: Abilene, Smithtown, Wuppertal. The signs that announce these places to us are not mere traces of a buried past; the images we grasp (that is, in the form of "views") resonate with an aura that stems from their respective pasts, their local traditions, their dense histories. Rather than taking control over them as we attempt to do in figuring out traces, they pervade and seize us by their atmospheric presence.

At this moment, we are on the edge of wonder, especially when we are sensitive to the mystery of how a past we never knew personally has become accessible to us in the present. This, too, we take in at a glance, which moves quickly from sheer surprise to the verge of wonder—as if the former were the harbinger of the latter. The surprise occasioned by the perception of aura, by its sheer survival, precipitates a state of wonder that extends beyond the immediate givens of what we experience.

Colportage/Collection/Montage versus Serial Ordering

"*Colportage*" is the uniquely Parisian phenomenon of selling books and pamphlets in a tray that is slung around one's neck (*col*). Benjamin sees it as emblematic of street life, in which diverse items are co-perceived all at once by the flâneur: they are taken in at one glance. The same is true of seeing things together in a room, that is, the domestic equivalent of the street, as we have seen. Colportage covers both situations:

> The "colportage phenomenon of space" is the flâneur's basic experience. Inasmuch as this phenomenon also—from another angle—shows itself in the mid-nineteenth-century interior, it may not be amiss to suppose that the heyday of

85. Ibid., p. 417.

flânerie occurs in this same period. Thanks to this phenomenon, everything potentially taking place in this one single room is perceived simultaneously. Everything
winks at the flâneur.[86]

The winking is due to another aspect of colportage—one closely associated
with aura. I refer to the ambiguous or equivocal light in which things are co-
presented in a street or a room. Earlier, we considered this sentence: "The
gaslight that streams down on the paving stones throws an equivocal light on this
double ground."[87] Then, we focused on the double ground—the street at one
level and then the sewers and the catacombs lying underneath. Here let us take
note of the character of the light over the street: in its shimmering, it is the
physical equivalent of aura. In the dimly lit and suggestive scene that results,
liminal phenomena such as winking and other such allusive activities are more
likely to arise. Benjamin cites Odilon Redon in this connection: "The sense of
mystery comes from remaining always in the equivocal, with double and triple
perspectives, or inklings of perspective (images within images) . . . . All things
[are thus] more suggestive just because they do appear [as equivocal]."[88] It is
just such a situation that elicits the experience of wonder.

Collection is an important term for Benjamin in his Arcades project. As things
come to be displayed—and accumulating their manifest presence is at the heart
of collecting—they are set out for the delectation of the collector as well as those
to whom the collection is being shown. A collection on display is in effect a
colportage of the objects collected: it is not accidental that it is often arranged in
trays—not unlike the offerings of the original colporteur. But collection is distinguished from colportage proper by three traits. First, collecting is a largely
tactile experience, in which one touches or more exactly "fingers" the collected
items: "Collectors are beings with tactile instincts. . . . The flâneur [is] optical,
the collector tactile."[89] Second, the collector brings order out of disorder: the
objects in their primary state are dispersed, often in random places (for example, in the case of rocks to be collected); once collected, they are ordered in
terms determined by the science and/or taste of the time, yet always by reference to the disorder from which they came.[90] Third, collecting involves a factor
of possession and ownership, which are closely "allied with the tactile":[91] a

86. Ibid., pp. 418–419.
87. Ibid., p. 416.
88. Cited at ibid., p. 429.
89. Ibid., pp. 206–207. But in a fragment soon after, Benjamin emphasizes that, at the same
time, the collector has a "'disinterested' contemplation" that can be compared to "the gaze of
the great physiognomist" (ibid.).
90. "There is in the life of a collector a dialectical tension between the poles of order and
disorder" (Walter Benjamin, "Unpacking My Library: A Talk about Book Collecting," in *Illuminations*, p. 60).
91. *The Arcades Project*, p. 206. Benjamin is doubtless building on the etymology of the
German *haben* ("to have") in the Latin *habere* ("to have, to hold").

collection of objects is something one holds onto. But what is held onto is not simply the objects themselves, arrayed in a display case; at a deeper level, it is "the pathos of nearness"[92] that is operative in a collection. Nearness, as we have seen, is an intrinsic aspect of aura. The items of a collection bring into the proximity of the collector's private space the distance of their own past—their idiosyncratic and nonreproducible histories.

It is striking that Benjamin talks of collected things in terms very similar to those with which he describes works of art: both bring to our present awareness the ineffaceable marks of their making and subsequent history. The collector, as Benjamin says in "Unpacking My Library," has "a relationship to objects which does not emphasize their functional, utilitarian value—that is, their usefulness—but studies and loves them as the scene, the stage, of their fate."[93] This fate is what they have undergone over time, their convoluted destiny in the hands of previous owners and/or collectors; this fate, their primal history, entails a form of temporal distance that is savored as such: "One has only to watch a collector handle the objects in his glass case. As he holds them in his hands, he seems to be seeing through them into their distant past as though inspired."[94] Collecting capitalizes on this crucial action of bringing things with their auratic distance into the present moment, and in a given place, a literal "showplace." Benjamin elucidates this action in another passage from the Arcades project:

> The true method of making things present is to represent them in our space (not to represent ourselves in their space). (The collector does just this, and so does the anecdote.) Thus represented, the things allow no mediating construction from out of "large contexts." The same method applies, in essence, to the consideration of great things from the past—the cathedral of Chartres, the temple of Paestum— when, that is, a favorable prospect presents itself: the method of receiving the things into our space. We don't displace our being into theirs; they step into our life.[95]

Such ordering, touching, and owning—each experienced under the heading of felt nearness—might seem to exclude the unknown and the unexpected. On the contrary! Not only do collected objects enter into our lives but their collocation in a display case allows for many surprises that would not occur were they to be arranged in some simple sequential order of creation or use: "It must be kept in

92. Ibid., p. 545.

93. "Unpacking My Library," *Illuminations,* p. 60.

94. Ibid., p. 61. Cf. the comparable passage in *The Arcades Project:* "It suffices to observe just one collector as he handles the items in his showcase. No sooner does he hold them in his hand than he appears inspired by them and seems to look through them into their distance, like an augur" (*The Arcades Project,* p. 207). Distance also obtains for the natural landscape, which brings its own aura: "If, while resting on a summer afternoon, you follow with your eyes a mountain range on the horizon or a branch which casts its shadow over you, you experience the aura of those mountains, of that branch" ("The Work of Art in the Age of Mechanical Reproduction," *Illuminations,* pp. 222–223).

95. *The Arcades Project,* p. 206.

mind that, for the collector, the world is present, and indeed ordered, in each of his objects. Ordered, however, according to a surprising and, for the profane understanding, incomprehensible connection."[96] The effect is that of a "magic encyclopedia," full of unanticipatable turns, thereby intensifying the aura of the collected objects.[97] Collecting may even occasion "shocks" of disconcerted perception—shocks that were for Baudelaire integral to his experience as a flâneur in contact with the masses of Paris.[98] Just as these masses present themselves in tumultuous scenes of quasi-synchronous space for the poet-flâneur, so the items laid out tidily in a collection case conceal a deeper disorder that, once grasped, may shock the viewer. Hence the *striking* character of the collection, especially for the collector himself or herself:

> If, let us say, we were to live vis-à-vis some things more calmly and vis-à-vis others more rapidly, according to a different rhythm, there would be nothing "subsistent" for us, but instead everything would happen right before our eyes; everything would strike us. But this is the way things are for the great collector. They strike him.[99]

This strikingness is akin to the way in which a dream so often strikes us as delivering to us something we didn't expect—something surprising that can be quite shocking at times. This factor of surprise in the mode of the striking or shocking is common to dreams, collecting, and walking through Parisian arcades.[100]

When the organizing principles of colportage and collecting are carried over into film or writing, the result is *montage*. This is precisely Benjamin's own procedure in the Arcades project, which mimics colportage on the streets and

96. Ibid., p. 207.

97. "The period, the region, the craftsmanship, the former ownership—for a true collector the whole background of an item adds up to a magic encyclopedia whose quintessence is the fate of his object" ("Unpacking my Library," *Illuminations,* p. 60; cf. p. 207 of *The Arcades Project:* "All of these—the 'objective' data together with the other [nonobjective aspects]—come together, for the true collector, in every single one of his possessions, to form a whole magic encyclopedia, a world order, whose outline is the fate of his object" [Benjamin underlines "fate"]).

98. On the sense of shock in Baudelaire, see Benjamin's essay, "On Some Motifs in Baudelaire," in *Illuminations,* esp. p. 165: "the close connection in Baudelaire between the figure of shock and contact with the metropolitan masses." Cf. also *The Arcades Project,* p. 383: "In Baudelaire's theory of art, the motif of shock . . . is operative wherever Baudelaire appropriates Poe's theory concerning the importance of surprise in the work of art."

99. *The Arcades Project,* p. 205. Benjamin adds: "How he himself pursues and encounters them, what changes in the ensemble of items are effected by a newly supervening item—all this shows him [that] his affairs [are] in constant flux" (ibid.).

100. "Here, the Paris arcades are examined as though they were properties in the hands of a collector. (At bottom, we may say, the collector lives a piece of dream life. For in the dream, too, the rhythm of perception and experience is altered in such a way that everything—even the seemingly most neutral—comes to strike us; everything concerns us. In order to understand the arcades from the ground up, we sink them into the deepest stratum of the dream: we speak of them as though they had struck us.)" (ibid., pp. 205–206)

collection in a room. For Benjamin, montage consists in the juxtaposition of citations from authors he has read, his own comments on these citations, and his independently authored statements—all assembled into *Konvoluten*, a word whose prefix connotes the "togetherness" at stake throughout. *Konvolut* is definable as "bundle, roll, scroll."[101] In each such instance, the same rule of reading obtains: namely, that the items referred to by the written text are gathered together in the same manuscript or set of manuscripts. Moreover, just as one scans at once the things displayed by the collector or the colporteur, or takes in everything on a film screen, so the reader peruses the written texts of the convolute, taking them in all at once. Hence Benjamin can proclaim, "This work [i.e., the Arcades project] has to develop to the highest degree the art of citing without quotation marks. Its theory is intimately related to that of montage."[102] To cite without quotation marks induces a special sense of intimacy while also producing a sense of unimpeded textual flow. Above all, it is to present the text as a manifest image—something to be *shown* rather than to be deciphered:

> Method of this project: literary montage. I needn't *say* anything. Merely show. I shall purloin no valuables, appropriate no ingenious formulations. But the rags, the refuse—these I will not inventory but allow, in the only way possible, to come into their own: by making use of them.[103]

When items are genuinely *shown*, they are set forth in such a way that they can be read in any order: backwards as well as forwards, or by discontinuous 'random walk'. The exact order doesn't matter. Contrast this freedom of movement —parallel to that of the flâneur who can crisscross the city at his will—with another method of textual composition, that of strict serial order. In this latter case, items are presented in such a way that there is only one right way in which to read them: from beginning to end, left to right, up to down, etc.

Serial order organizes most texts—perhaps even the majority—in many world civilizations. In contrast, sheer co-presentation is restricted to such things as scrolls setting forth an unfolding landscape painting or albums of reproduced paintings (in which the images on opposite pages are juxtaposed). Benjamin undermines seriality by his method of montage. It is as if his own extension of the metaphor of landscape to the city were amplified still further—now to texts in which the city itself is described. Not only does the city "open up to [the flâneur] as a landscape,"[104] but the Arcades project as a whole opens up to the reader as a densely co-inhabited bookscape of citations and comments and statements in which one can start or stop at any given point, that is to say, browse at full leisure.

---

101. Karl Wildhagen, *The New Wildhagen Dictionary* (Chicago: Follett, 1965).

102. *The Arcades Project*, p. 458.

103. Ibid., p. 460; his italics. Compare the epigraph to Convolute S ("Painting, Jugendstil, Novelty"): "To create history with the very detritus of history" (cited from Remy de Gourmont, *Le Ime Livre des masques*, at ibid., p. 543).

104. Ibid., p. 417.

In montage as in collection and colportage, there is a strong factor of surprise. The surprise comes less from the appearance of an unexpected image or word—as happens so often in serially ordered phenomena, when the succeeding items remain unknown because out of sight—than from the very juxtaposition of images or words with each other. The surprise arises from the Gestalt they realize together rather than from the sudden appearance of newly perceived individual items. Hence the affinity between the Arcades project and surrealism: we are reminded not just of Louis Aragon's *Le paysan de Paris* (1926)—which is set in arcades of the 1920s—but of the basic Lautreamontian principle of placing together two or more things normally disconnected from each other: the sewing machine with the umbrella on the operating table, the octopus with the gauze of silk.[105] Whether presented together in a painting or in a group of words, such collocations are instances of "a surprising and, for the profane understanding, incomprehensible connection."[106]

Such co-presented items are also fit subjects for the glance, which is uniquely well suited to sweep through a single complex scene of presentation, taking it all in at once. This is as true for the contemporary reader of *The Arcades Project* as it was for the flâneur on the streets of nineteenth-century Paris; for each, glancing is a privileged mode of vision that links reading this kind of text and walking in that particular way. When I glance at a page, I encounter it all at once; when I glance along the street on which I walk, I take in people and buildings in one fell swoop. In both cases, I effect a special form of visual montage, a colportage of images that is as comprehensive as it is manifest. I make my own collection of these images on the spot: in this place, with this glance.

Simultaneous versus Successive

Medieval philosophers were accustomed to saying that God views the world *totum simul,* "all together" or "all at once." An approximation to this God's-eye view is available to human beings in selected contexts—those in which the simultaneity of what is perceived or thought or remembered is the primary spatiotemporal parameter. This parameter obtains in the case of collection, colportage, and montage: we grasp the contents of the collector's showcase all at once, we see the offering of printed materials in the colporteur's tray in one brief look, and we take in each page of Benjamin's own text as a single coherent whole.[107] The simultaneities in question are, respectively, the array of collected objects in their showcase, the books together in the tray, the statements on a

---

105. Bringing together the two topics of this sentence is this fragment of Benjamin's: "The arcades as milieu of Lautréamont" (ibid., p. 847).

106. Ibid., p. 201; cited earlier.

107. In the case of an entire convolute, there is only, strictly speaking, quasi-simultaneity: we treat the group of associated texts as if it formed one whole, to be scanned together. The quasi-simultaneity extends to the entire book when we consider that the various convolutes are themselves given in no particular order.

given page. Each such experience would be undermined, indeed destroyed, were we to focus on a past disentangled from the present moment of perception —as might an archeologist or a historian who was pursuing traces of past events. And the same experiences would be further undercut if we were to regard the items of the collector's showcase or the colporteur's tray as if each were a separate offering, or if we kept various parts of a given montage apart from one another.

The same principle of composition obtains in all three cases we have just been considering: this is *simultaneity of presentation*. As Benjamin himself muses, "Say something about the method of composition itself: how everything one is thinking at a specific moment in time must at all costs be incorporated into the project then at hand. Assume that the intensity of the project is thereby attested, or that one's thoughts, from the very beginning, bear this project within them as their telos."[108] The "intensity" here aimed at is best achieved by a convergent generation of thoughts, which conjoin in the composition of a given text.

In fact, two kinds of simultaneity are here at stake. The first of these is mere *synchrony*, that which happens at the very same moment; this is characteristic of modern technology, especially in the form of machinic production where speed is at stake. Benjamin cites Marx in this connection: "Each detail machine supplies raw material to the machine next in order; and since they are *all working at the same time*, the product is always going through the various stages of its fabrication, and is also constantly in a state of transition from one phase to another."[109] Notice that such machinic simultaneity is not inconsistent with diachrony or successiveness in time ("the machine next in order," "a state of transition from one phase to another"). The same is true for the panoramic paintings that were so popular in mid-nineteenth-century America: each such painting is a single continuous work, yet we can only view it successively (for example, by perambulating a platform built around it, or by putting the panoramic vista itself into motion).[110] But we also need to recognize a second and richer sense of simultaneity: an *expansive simultaneity* in which both synchronic and diachronic moments (each taken in its narrow sense) are expressly included, along with other things that do not fit perfectly onto either of these two formally determined axes. The leading instance of such inclusive simultaneity is precisely the dialectical image, which cannot be reduced to the utter simplicity of the bare

---

108. Ibid., p. 456.

109. Cited from *Das Kapital*, vol. 1, 344, at ibid., p. 394; my italics.

110. For Benjamin's treatment of panorama, see *The Arcades Project*, Convolute Q, "Panorama," esp. p. 527 (on the multiplicity of "-ramas") and p. 532, where the panorama is positively valorized as analogous to what happens "in seeing the true city—the city indoors [i.e., in an arcade]." Concerning panoramas in America, see J. F. McDermott, *The Lost Panorama of the Mississippi* (Chicago: University of Chicago Press, 1958) and Barbara Novak, *Art and Nature: American Landscape and Painting, 1825–1875* (Oxford: Oxford University Press, 1980), pp. 20–27, and my discussion in *Representing Place: Landscape Painting and Maps* (Minneapolis: University of Minnesota Press, 2002), pp. 7–10, 18, 24–25, 65–66.

instant. In such an image, past and present coexist in one complex whole—not as static components but as dynamic elements in a state of active interfusion. Through such an image, indeed in it, the past is threaded; or in Benjamin's own analogy, the past is the wind that sets the sails of the present into motion.[111]

This more ample notion of simultaneity points us to a more capacious sense of the "present moment" itself. For only such a moment is capable of bearing the past into the present even as it allows us still to distinguish them. As such, it combines the focus and suddenness of the *Augenblick* with the dark heritage of the primal past that flickers in its aura. This is the moment in which the dialectical image itself arises. On the one hand, such an image "is an image that emerges *suddenly*, in a flash."[112] Yet, on the other hand, as Benjamin adds immediately, "What has been is to be held fast—as an image flashing up in the now of its recognizability."[113] To be *held fast* (*festzuhalten*) requires that the moment in which the past comes to inhere has to have sufficient breadth to offer a grip; without this breadth, for example, in the case of a sheer instant, this past would slip away without effect or notice.

In a dialectical image, there is not only the brief illumination of the now, its "lightning flash," but "the darkness of the lived moment" (*das Dunkel des gelebten Augenblicks*).[114] Both are needed if the present moment is to be at once sudden and surprising, as well as the basis for a new sense of wonder that is not subject to Descartes's critique. Taken together, both the illumination and the darkness constitute the dialectical image in its unique forcefulness: such an image is "that wherein what has been comes together in a flash with the now to form a constellation."[115] And both factors—the darkness of what "has been" and the light of the "now" with which it conjoins in a "flash"—are needed if we are to achieve awakening in and by such an image.

"Awakening" (*Erweckung*; compare also *Erwachen*) is an awakening to wonder. Such wonder itself has two dimensions, both closely related to the two aspects of the "present time" (*Jetztzeit*) just distinguished: the instant and the now. Awakening being is both "punctuated and intermittent" *and* something gradually acquired: "a graduated process that goes on in the life of the individual as in the life of generations."[116] We have to do here with another form of capa-

---

111. "What matters for the dialectician is to have the wind of history in his sails. Thinking means for him: setting the sails. What is important is *how* they are set. Words are his sails. The way they are set makes them into concepts" (*The Arcades Project*, p. 473; his italics).

112. Ibid.; my italics.

113. Ibid.

114. The second phrase occurs at ibid., p. 393; the first in this passage: "In the fields with which we are concerned, knowledge comes only in lightning flashes" (ibid., p. 456).

115. Ibid., p. 462. Benjamin adds: "This is dialectics at a standstill—where this latter does not entail mere lack of motion but an intensive pause or halt in which something further can unexpectedly arise" (ibid.).

116. The phrase "punctuated and intermittent" appears at ibid., p. 392; the full clause is from p. 388.

cious simultaneity. There is the sudden "flash of awakened consciousness,"[117] but there is also, equally, something slower or thicker—something akin to the gradual amassment and consolidation of memories: "remembering and awakening are most intimately related."[118] If what Benjamin calls "dialectical reversal" (which is closely related to the earlier forms of reversal I have discussed) is never gradual and is like awakening precipitously from a dream, on the other hand for the dream itself to be remembered a more patient process is required: "to pass through and carry out *what has been* in remembering the dream!"[119]

Once again, then, "what has been" (*das Gewesenes*) darkens and thickens what would otherwise be merely instantaneous as a narrowly synchronic slice of time, broadening out the latter to rejoin the former; from this very interplay, awakening arises: "there is a not-yet conscious knowledge of what has been: its advancement (*Förderung*) has the structure of awakening."[120] One awakens from the darkness of what has been, and in a flash (a flash that is not an instant but an ample present moment): "while the relation of the present to the past is a purely temporal, continuous one [that is, in the lapsing of the "now" into the "then"], the relation of what-has-been to the now is dialectical: [it] is not progression but image, suddenly emergent."[121] The "now of recognizability" itself reflects this same bilaterality, since recognition is a form of memory which often occurs precipitously: it is a matter, once more, of "an image flashing up in the now of recognizability."[122] This image is none other than the dialectical image.

In constituting this expanded now, in this enriched present moment of the dialectical image, space and time—what Benjamin calls "spacetime" (*Zeitraum*) —are found for wonder.[123] Benjamin discovers a fitting mythical expression for such a moment in the *Iliad:* "The imminent awakening (*das kommende Erwachen*) is poised, like the wooden horse of the Greeks, in the Troy of dreams."[124] Such awakening is not confined to this extraordinary moment in the

---

117. Ibid., p. 388.

118. Ibid., p. 389. Benjamin even ventures to say that "awakening is the great exemplar of memory" (ibid.).

119. Ibid., p. 389; his italics. It is significant that in the same passage Benjamin gives credit to the Chinese for having "found, in their fairy tales and novels, a highly pregnant expression" for "the dialectical schematism at the core of this process" (ibid.). This observation bears on the Chinese distinction between two forms of Buddhist enlightenment to which I have referred just above.

120. Ibid., p. 389. As the translators of the *Arcades Project* make clear, *Förderung* implies "drawing up" or "hauling to the surface" in the context of mining (see ibid., n. 4, p. 983).

121. Ibid., p. 462.

122. Ibid., p. 473.

123. On "space-time," see ibid., p. 389: "The nineteenth century [experienced] a spacetime (*Zeitraum*), a dreamtime (*Zeit-traum*) in which the individual consciousness more and more secures itself in reflecting, while the collective consciousness sinks into ever deeper sleep." For a related but finally different concept of "time-space" (*Zeit-Raum*) as well the "free play of space and time" (*Zeit-Spiel-Raum*), see Heidegger, *Contributions to Philosophy,* sections 160, 238–242.

124. *The Arcades Project,* p. 392.

mythos of the ancient Greeks; it is to be found *now*, in any given place and in the contemporary moment—there where surprise joins with the sudden, and sometimes with the striking and shocking, to generate what is wondrous. To cite more fully a passage quoted earlier: "In our standardized and uniform world, it is right here, deep below the surface, that we must go. Estrangement and surprise, the most thrilling exoticism, are all close by."[125]

And the special wonder is that it is by a close consideration of late-nineteenth-century Paris—that quintessentially modern city—that we gain insight into the twentieth and twenty-first centuries in the multifarious enclaves of their increasingly global culture. It is right there, in that place, that we can glimpse the character of places to come, that we can go under the surface of the present—down here below—so as to encounter the depths of the past and bring them back in such a way as to illuminate present and future places. It is a matter of drawing the primal past of city life back onto the surface of our current consciousness, reawakening it to the wondrous in the flash of a renewed now of recognition. Coming back to us suddenly and with distinct surprise, such a sense of wonder is not only "the mark of the philosopher"[126] as Plato thought, and it is not just the beginning of philosophy (as Aristotle emphasized), but is also an experience to be had by walking the streets of Paris, or any other metropolis, in the manner of the flâneur or his postmodern successor: perambulating at our own pace, looking around at our own leisure, and thereby taking in the whole scene—the city and the people gathered in one complex visual spectacle—all at once and in a single sweeping glance. Such a spectacle is cause for wonder.

VII

The compresence of time and space at stake in the last section—above all, the idea of an expanded simultaneity that is the pivot of their creative conjunction—provides a fecund field for glancing. So far, I have only hinted at the explicitly visual dimensions of this field; it is time now to spell them out in more detail as they affect the gaze as well as the glance.

In the case of collections, the array of items on shelves or in glass cases fosters both gazing and glancing. The orderliness that is manifest in the alignment of these items, each spaced apart at a certain distance suitable to the size and proper order of the collected objects, invites their scrutiny in sequence along a row or track. A concerted gaze fixes on each item in succession, pursuing a decidedly serial course: first, this form of agate, then another; then geodes of various sorts; finally, igneous rocks, and so on. Although it is possible to gaze at a

---

125. Ibid., p. 444.

126. "The sense of wonder is the mark of the philosopher" (Plato, *Theatetus* 155 d; this is the translation of F. M. Cornford in Cornford's *Plato's Theory of Knowledge* [London: Routledge and Kegan Paul, 1935]), p. 43.

collection as a whole, this is discouraged by the very circumstance, since such an effort will not yield the kind of focus that is the goal of gazing. Here we witness a ready alliance between gazing and sequential time: on the one hand, the gazer pauses for more than a curt moment in considering each item; on the other hand, he or she moves on resolutely to the next item in the series. This is especially the case in what I have just called the "concerted gaze," wherein the motive is to become acquainted with every member of a set of items whose linear display induces (though it cannot force) the gaze to proceed *seriatim*.

In contrast, the very same collection evokes glancing at the same group of items. The spread-out presentation, the relatively uniform plane of display, and the comparative clarity of its illumination encourage glancing at two basic levels: first, that of seeing the collection in its entirety, for which the sweeping glance is so apt (what is pointless for the gaze is very much to the point for glancing); second, that of divagating among the items in a species of visual vagabondage—that is, the nomadic looking for which the glance is a privileged vehicle. Either way, looking draws upon an ampliative simultaneity that subtends and makes possible both sorts of glancing.

The situation in colportage is still more facilitative of glancing and correspondingly ill-suited for gazing: it would be inappropriate indeed to stare at items that are hanging from the colporteur's neck! Even as these things are set out before the potential purchaser, they call for the deftness of the glance, which picks out what things are to be more closely looked at. Only at this point is gazing called for in the careful examination of certain items. In fact, what we call "browsing" is itself a combination of gazing and glancing: the latter spotting the book or piece of clothing or jewelry in the first place, the former supervening to have a closer look. A miniature dialectic of the two kinds of looking is set up—a back and forth between gazing and glancing that "takes its time" rather than happening in the single moment that is the favored temporal mode of the dialectical image. Nevertheless, even here we encounter an expanded simultaneity that is the material condition of possibility for gazing and glancing alike. In looking at the colporteur's goods, there is *distentio animi*, "distention of soul" in Saint Augustine's celebrated phrase—an opening of time in which there is time for many kinds of looking, including both gazing and glancing.

We are here led to another instructive contrast, that between action and situation. Colportage is an action of presentation—that is, an action of offering for sale books and pamphlets carried in a cloth bag slung around the neck—and it asks for an equally active visual response such as the glance to match its own constantly changing character as the colporteur moves and shifts his body and the load it bears. In contrast, a collection is an already constituted and thus a static site, the result of earlier actions rather than an action itself. As such, it lends itself to concerted gazing at the fixed set of items it sets forth—often arranged in rows and sometimes literally glued in place. In each case, both gazing and glancing can arise; but one will be favored over the other, depending on whether the visual scene amounts to a settled situation (encouraging the gaze) or elicits a further bodily action (typically accompanied by glancing).

Montage is closer to situation than to action. However active the composer of a given montage may have been in its creation, as presented to the viewer a given montage is *something already assembled for the eye's delectation.* Like the collection, it is notable for having both single displays (such as the page, the painting, the film image) and a succession of such displays. Hence it invites the gaze when the viewer wishes to remain with a given appearance, to stay on the same page for a while, or to arrest a video scene at a certain shot by "pausing" it. But unlike the collection—which is typically pre-organized in terms of certain systemic principles—montage displays a liberty of arrangement that, not being invested in serial order, can be composed of imaginative juxtapositions of incongruent items in the same presentation, as in Dada and Surrealist works: for example, paintings by Miro or Dali or films such as *L'age d'or* or *Le chien andalou.* Or, preeminently, Walter Benjamin's own text in *The Arcades Project,* each page of which presents a welter of textual and intertextual passages, true to the German and French words for "arcades": *Passagen, passages.* It is as if the Benjaminian convolute were a place for the reader's eye to amble, glancing all the way—much as the flâneur glances back and forth at the various shop windows in the arcade through which he is strolling. The displays in these windows change every few days, not unlike the changes that occur page to page, passage to passage, in the Benjaminian palimpsest of texts that is fittingly entitled *Passagen-Werk.*[127]

It is the special virtue of montage to surprise us at every turn—at every turn of the page we make, every painting or film image we see. The surprise prepares the ground for an experience of wonder. I have already singled out a number of occasions when the surprising, suddenly appearing, leads to wonderment on the viewer's part. Although the surprising can arise in any context, including collection and colportage, it is much more likely to characterize experiences of montage, especially when this latter is set up in a deliberately nonconsecutive manner or, all the more so, in a crazy-quilt fashion. Surprising scenarios of these sorts call for the glance. The key is again the factor of suddenness. When something arising suddenly takes us by surprise, we are led to look at it quickly—to take it into account as soon as possible. For the most part, we do this by glancing. (I say "for the most part," since we also react in other, more visceral ways: for example, by squirming, flinching, grimacing, and so on.) In the circumstance, and thanks very much to its celerity and comparative effortlessness, the glance comes to our aid: hence our spontaneous recourse to it. We apperceive thereby what is happening *all at once*—whatever strikes us in our local environment—and we do so *at once*, without hesitation.

The circumstance is more complex when we make a triage between the sudden, the surprising, and the wondrous. If these three terms are set side by side for purposes of comparison, we cannot help but notice that the sudden is

---

127. For close studies of this palimpsest, see Susan Buck-Morss, *The Dialectics of Seeing: Walter Benjamin and the Arcades Project* (Cambridge, Mass.: MIT Press, 1989) and Pierre Missac, *Walter Benjamin's Passages,* tr. S. W. Nicholson (Cambridge, Mass.: MIT Press, 1995).

the specific instigator of the glance, its precipitating cause, often happening outside of consciousness; the surprising characterizes the content of what has appeared suddenly in relation to our expectations on any given occasion. If the sudden catches us "by surprise," nevertheless surprise itself exists in the intimate interface between what appears and our response to it. The sudden and the surprising accrue to two phases of the glance respectively, its befalling us from seemingly nowhere and then its being apprehended, attended to. In contrast to both of these phases, the wondrous is more like an atmosphere or diffuse setting. As such, it calls for glancing and gazing alike: glancing in its first moment of appearing, gazing insofar as we linger with it, staying on its surface rather than gliding off it. The Greek word *thaumazein* signifies both being wonderstruck (that is, the moment of the glance: of primary apperception) and being in awe (the time of the gaze, most notably the philosophical gaze of disciplined looking). Both are required for full visual wonderment to occur: the glance that takes note, the gaze that lingers.

Only in an expanded simultaneity can two such divergent kinds of looking collude so intensely that we can barely distinguish them in the experience of wonder itself: an experience that *overtakes* us, and more massively so than the sudden or the surprising. As a result, the wondrous has the potential for transforming us. The same collusion obtains in the more mundane instances of colportage, collection, and montage—each of which offers opportunities for subtle commixtures of gazing and glancing, arising in a closely concatenated way. The two kinds of looking are felt to be inseparable in experience even if they are distinguishable upon analysis—analysis of the very sort that I have undertaken in this book. If philosophy begins in wonder, it also consists (as Aristotle asserts) in "making distinctions," a procedure of "division" (*diairesis*) or "differentiation" (*diapherein*). Indeed, philosophical wonder itself can arise from the making of distinctions that are all too often glossed over, or buried, in the course of everyday life. One primary such wonder is the phenomenological fact that temporal simultaneity can be amplified beyond sheer synchrony to include the diverse phenomena that Benjamin has brought to our attention. Each of these phenomena requires an expanded simultaneity, whether it presents itself suddenly, surprisingly, or wondrously—or whether it calls for gazing or glancing taken separately or for their close collaboration.

VIII

I am seated in the Saurin Parke Café on West 110th Street in Manhattan. It is situated on the southernmost edge of Harlem, near the northwest corner of Central Park. The clientele is much more diverse than it was in the Café Felix; ethnically, racially, socioeconomically, and with regard to age and sexual orientation. Unlike my Ann Arbor hangout, here no reference to Parisian cafés is to be found. From within—there is no outside seating in this place—I am cozily ensconced, intent upon writing. Nevertheless, in the very midst of this immersion, I find myself glancing and being glanced at: seemingly a harmless but in fact a most telling activity. The glancing arises as if another attentional track has been added to my writing, supplementing it like a group of grace notes. (Were my glancing to become more engaged, I would doubtless become distracted: the line between these states is easily trespassed.) Two parallel activities here coexist, one handwork, the other eyework—whose twain will never meet: except in the rare case where I am writing about what I am currently experiencing. As is in fact happening at the present moment.

A young Latin American woman is reading the Sunday *New York Times*. Every so often, she raises her eyes from the paper and looks over my way. On several of these ocular swings, our glances cross, as if lightly touching each other—as if our projected bodies had reached out and just barely grazed one another. These are not erotic or seductive actions. Our manner of looking makes this clear: there is no genuine engagement, no looking *into* the other's eyes, no effort to fathom the intention or thought of the other. Still, in the moment of interchange itself there is an amplified simultaneity: a now that is more than a synchronous slice, an ever so slightly distended intertanglement of looks. The glancing taking place here, despite the difference in setting, is closely related to the glancing that occurs in the three exemplary instances I have examined from the Arcades project—that is, collection, colportage, and montage—each of which also flourishes from an open present. In another respect, too, there is overlap: the young woman is not only looking at *me,* as I might narcissistically hope or imagine; she is also looking around the entire interior of the café, looking at others, at the walls, at the furniture. This traveling glance is both quickly accomplished and yet comprehensive: it takes in a lot within very little time. The augmented moment is here set in a temporal-spatial nexus that is at once time-taking and space-searching. Only a glance could navigate this complex nexus so skillfully and with so little conscious volition or expenditure of effort.

Suddenly, two young women walk into the café. They eye me at my table, trying to figure out if I am about to leave. In that probative moment, our eyes meet, and somehow I manage to convey to them in my glance back that I am here to stay—without saying a word, or making any other gesture. My message, a response to their tacit inquiry, is all in my eyes, there and nowhere else. The women have posed an unarticulated yet pointed question: will you be leaving soon? I have responded immediately, in the very next blink of the eye. An utterly visual conversation has taken place. After the women find an empty table for themselves, we continue to stay in eye contact, as if to continue the conversation, even though the primary topic has been addressed. From now on, glances shoot back and forth at their own leisurely pace, constituting their own casual rhythm—more regular than that adopted with the *Times* reader, yet just as insouciant. Our visual relationship devolves into an open series of passing looks.

This otherwise banal episode shows the civilizing force of vision directly at work in a distinctly nonpossessive transmission of glances that seeks nothing in particular yet gratefully receives confirmation from the other's response. Thus is realized the interpersonal acknowledgment I first singled out in part 1 of this book; embodying a delimited democracy of the glance, it is emblematic of the ethics of glancing to be discussed in chapter 10. My café companions and I could not be more different bodily or ethnically, yet on the basis of a certain "equality in diversity,"[128] we form a *société intime* of local lookers. The equality is located in the looking—in our quite spontaneous, untutored exchange.

Not that all is always well in the domain of the glance. I do not mean to be cavalier, much less meliorisitic, in my assertion of visual democracy. Other scenarios can arise. On the same occasion I have just described, people passing by on the street outside sometimes glared into the café with a mixture of curiosity and resentment, as if to say: What is going on in there? You look like you're enjoying some pretty special privilege just sitting at your tables! These passersby looked hard-pressed and, probably, exhausted from a long day of work (or so I imagined: they might also have been unemployed). Here was a very different circumstance, one of asymmetrical looking. Persons on the street shot looks into the dark interior of the café, not singling out any particular person there but exuding a certain disdain toward all. Nor did anyone inside look back: the nonresponse was as expressive as the question implicitly posed. Nothing headed toward dialogue was going to happen here! In this momentary encounter there was nothing even remotely democratic. On the contrary, the situation was lopsided and unreciprocal: no gestures that might open a conversation were proffered by either side, whereas it was perfectly possible that I and my comrades inside the café might have begun to talk at some point. In its lack of reciprocated looking, this was a social nonstarter—to say the least.

In another episode later the same afternoon, two women were engaged in a tutorial situation. A Chinese woman was teaching her native language to an Anglo woman intent upon learning this challenging tongue. Although the Chinese woman was seated just opposite me, never once did she lift her eyes and look at me even for a glance. It was not that she *withheld* any such looking; she simply did not look at all in my direction. I was in effect passed over, unacknowledged. It was as if I did not exist for her. I was nothing but a visual nullity, a *negatité* (a not-being) as Sartre puts it.[129] This was no tragedy for me, but it was felt and registered. Had I pursued the matter further, I might have

---

128. This phrase is from Vandana Shiva, *Staying Alive: Women, Ecology, and Development* (London: Zed, 1989), p. 5: "the interdependence and complementarity of the separate male and female domains of work is the characteristic mode, based on diversity, not inequality. Maldevelopment militates against this equality in diversity." See also Shiva's "Development, Ecology and Women" in *Healing the Wounds: The Promise of Ecofeminism,* ed. Judith Plant (Philadelphia: New Society Publishers, 1989), p. 83 where she writes that "maldevelopment militates against this equality in diversity."

129. On *negatité,* see Jean-Paul Sartre, *Being and Nothingness,* tr. H. Barnes (New York: Washington Square Press, 1966), pp. 56–66.

begun to doubt myself in some painful way: am I so unappealing or so uninteresting that this woman (who was meanwhile glancing at others in the café even as she overlooked me) would not lend me her merest look? Am I a visual eyesore, a repulsive force in her visual field? Fortunately, on this occasion, I did not indulge in any such thoughts; but I did feel unacknowledged as a member of the petite polity of the glance that so often makes up life in a café.

Two upbeat and two downbeat visual circumstances, all four set in a single scene of glancing. Doubtless other avatars of the glance figured in such a scene; some of these have already been described in chapter 1: the amorous glance, the furtive look, the glance of inanimate objects (for example, that of the poster-man in the Café Felix). At that early point, I was not attuned to the negative dialectic of the glance. The more complete truth is that, despite their apparent innocence, many glancings are shadowed by something else of darker, or at least denser, purport. Each of the four episodes I have just described arose spontaneously, but this is not to say they all *came free,* with no problem to ponder or price to pay. It is as if the equivalent of the *sous-sol,* the underground that subtends the sidewalks of Paris on Benjamin's portentous reading, is always lurking somewhere under the glistening of the glance—wherever it emerges, in whichever city and in whatever time. We here encounter a deep ambivalence of the glance—its two-sidedness, one side illuminated and the other lost in shadow— that extends previous paradoxicalities of this diminutive but finally undiminishable act.[130]

130. I wish to thank Tanja Staehler for fruitful discussions of themes in an earlier draft of this chapter, and Andrés Colapinto for his acute reading of a later version.

CODA

If the glance as such has not always been in thematic focus in part 2, this is only because I have emphasized certain *salients* to which the glance itself gives us access. These are the manifest structures of its circumambience: they indicate what the glance *leads to*, where it takes us. Glance salients are what stand out in a given cultural or natural setting, not only in the sense of being literally conspicuous in that setting but also as formative of its very appearance.

In chapter 5, we witnessed at least three prominent salients. The first was that of *gleaming*, especially evident in the solarism of ancient Greek culture: its continual exposure to light (at once a matter of landscape, climate, and architecture), a distinctive heliocentrism in models of knowledge (that is, in the analogy between the sun and the Good in the *Republic*), and a proclivity for discussion in the light of day, in the porches of the stoa and in other open spaces of the Athenian agora. Equally important, however, was the ancient belief in the visual ray, the *opsis* that streams forth from the eye to meet incoming rays of daylight—thus forming a homogeneous field, an intermediate body, wherein things come to appearance. The hypothesis of this ray was not just an artifact of early scientific thought in Empedocles and Democritus; it also reflects a pervasive phenomenological fact: the gleaming of the eye that is conspicuous in virtually any context. As Wittgenstein remarks two-and-a-half millennia later:

> We do not see the human eye as a receiver, it appears not to let anything in, but to send something out. The ear receives; the eye looks. (It casts glances, it flashes, radiates, gleams.) One can terrify with one's eyes, not with one's ear or nose. When you see the eye you see something going out from it. You see the look in the eye.[1]

Here the single salient of gleaming—which in Greece was the basis for an ongoing debate concerning the character and genesis of visual perception—is described in a way that could be confirmed in almost any imaginable interchange between humans (and probably also between animals), and in any era (even though it is more prominent in certain forms of sociality than in others: for example, among lovers).

A second salient at play in the first chapter of this part was the *chance encounter*. A public place like the Athenian agora facilitated such an encounter, especially in a culture that was almost entirely pedestrian. Aristotle's original descrip-

1. Ludwig Wittgenstein, *Zettel,* ed. G. E. M. Anscombe and G. H. von Wright, tr. G. E. M. Anscombe (Oxford: Blackwell, 1967), p. 40. The parenthetical words in German are: "Es wirft Blicke, es blitzt, strahlt, leuchtet." *Strahl,* the noun form of *strahlen,* is ordinarily translated as "ray."

tion (to which I have already alluded) rings true still today in those Western countries where walking is increasingly rare:

> Consider, for example, the case of someone who chanced to come into the city square [that is, the agora] and met someone he wanted to meet but had not expected to find there.[2]

For our purposes, what is most striking about the chance encounter is its combination of the sudden and the surprising: for example, in the element of coincidence at stake in meeting someone one had wanted to see but did not think would be in the place where one happened to walk. Had one gone to the public square expressly to meet a friend who was known to be there, one would not have encountered him by chance but by intention.[3] In the case of an encounter by chance, one is genuinely surprised to find one's friend in the agora—a surprise that here takes the form of his sudden appearance. This is a bivalent phenomenon that is likely to occur in any circumstance in which people walk freely in public spaces, including the streets and boulevards of Paris many centuries later or those of Manhattan today. That is why I was able to emphasize the sudden/surprising dyad in Walter Benjamin's descriptions of the flâneur's peregrinations. But the glancing any walker does in any landscape—rural as well as urban—always has the potential of showing up something unexpected and quickly arising. For every landscape or cityscape has opaque edges around or behind which the unexpected other is lurking: a friend, an enemy, a debtor, a lover.

Finally, the early Athenian world engendered a sense of *proto-community* realized in the exchange of glances. This is a salient whose full significance may not be evident at first, when there seems to be an innocent offering and return of spontaneous looks: as at the Saurin Parke Café that afternoon in New York. Yet this gentle and unscheduled reciprocity, when widespread across an entire culture, is capable of creating a subtle but powerful social bond: that is, the formation of a dyad (or polyad, if more than two people are involved) that is a first form of human community—just as it is also a primal ethical moment in which I and the other acknowledge each other as concrete singular universals. I have cited Edward E. Cohen in his groundbreaking essay on Athens as a face-to-face

---

2. Aristotle, *Physics*, Book II, ch. 4, 195b40–196a4; in Aristotle, *Physics*, tr. R. Waterfield (Oxford: Oxford University Press, 1996), p. 42. Aristotle goes on to question whether chance itself is a genuine "cause" in the circumstance: isn't the true cause in the situation as described the man's "wanting to go and do business in the square"? (ibid., 196a 4–5).

3. Referring to a comparable example of someone encountering a person who owes him money, Aristotle remarks that "we say that he [the lucky walker] chanced to come, but if he had chosen to be there and had come for this purpose, or if he always or usually went there when he was in the process of collecting money, we would not ascribe his coming to chance. Clearly, then, chance is a coincidental cause in the sphere of events which have some purpose and are subject to choice" (*Physics*, Book II, chap. 5, 197a2–197a6; Hussey translation).

society. He adds, "In a society that is not easily 'cognizable', the citizens cannot 'know one another', and there is no possibility of personalized participation in decision making and office holding, the essential element of a 'true' polis."[4] By "cognizable," Cohen means *recognizable in a glance,* and this in a certain vicinity that allows for glances to be exchanged in the proximity that an agora provides. Since *polis* signifies a minimal political community, the Greek example allows us to realize that merely taking in others by a glance—with or without an exchange of words—is a critical first step in getting just such a community under way. We are not speaking of a social contract here, but of a continually renewed experience in which community is formed and re-formed, confirmed and reconfirmed. This experience, consisting in the bare interlocking of looks, counts as a social salient.

We can also discern three comparable but quite different salients from the discussions just offered in chapter 6: aura, way, and wonder. In the case of *aura,* we have to do with the way in which the past can haunt the present yet reside there precisely in its temporal remoteness: not held in a determinate trace but suffused around a scene as a dimension that is at once intimate and distant. Even though aura lacks the definite shape of an object or event, it is accessible in a single glance—in the "now of recognizability." At the same time, it embeds the present in a primal past, thereby creating a dialectical image that exceeds any deliverance of the present alone: it subtends this present, coming at it from below as it were (for example, from underneath the streets of Paris in the form of the catacombs and sewers and other substructures that are sensed but not known in detail by the passing pedestrian). This salient allows us to appreciate how the glance is not restricted to taking in the present as sheer immediacy; rather, thanks to aura, the glance can note temporal and spatial depths on or just under the very surface of what it apperceives.

By the same token, the flâneur's glance allows him to make his *way* in a space that exceeds the cartographic locus of his moving body. For way is not reducible to route; it possesses an "openness of the open" (Heidegger) that characterizes the glance itself. The flâneur glances not only back and to his side as he moves at his own pace on city sidewalks but also *ahead,* as if his very glance breaks open a path he might—yet need not—take. The glance is a way-finder; it makes its own way in urban space (as well as in walking through natural landscapes). "Way" is another salient of the glance-world: it characterizes a direction of movement that is at once oriented and yet capable of significant variation. When the flâneur sets out on his daily round, he does not know exactly which course he will take; he has only a schematic sense of where he might go: a sense that is subject to continual revision.[5]

---

4. Edward E. Cohen, "A Modern Myth: Classical Athens as a Face-to-Face Society," *Common Sense* 6, no. 1 (spring 1997): 101.

5. Compare Thoreau's practice of spinning his body around before his afternoon walk in order to determine in which direction he would set out. See Henry David Thoreau, "Walking,"

Thanks to aura and way, the walker opens himself not just to surprise and the sudden but to *wonder.* For the wondrous can arise even from such modest experiences as being disconcerted or startled—and not only from being "astonished" in Descartes's sense or from such dark states of mind as "amazement" (Benjamin) and "startled dismay" (Heidegger): any of these can precipitate wonder, often from a threshold of excess or trauma. Wonder is more directly affiliated with what Heidegger calls "deep awe," a properly philosophical emotion whose ancestor is the Greek term *thauma,* "wonder." As Plato says, "philosophy indeed has no other origin, and he was a good genealogist who made Iris the daughter of Thaumas."[6] Iris or "rainbow" is connected etymologically with *legein* (via *eirein:* to engage in heated discussion) and thus with dialectic.[7] The rainbow is a paradigmatic case of a natural phenomenon that shimmers and gleams at its surface—indeed, is *all surface*—and that, given its highly evanescent character, can often only be glanced at. So, too, the wondrous is something we glimpse in a brief moment of transient appearance: Juno appearing from a cloud. Both aura and way are fit places to find the wondrous. No wonder, then, that wonderment is so important in Benjamin's Arcades project, which demonstrates how the marvelous arises in the very midst of the quotidian.

The six salients I have just identified are deeply affine with each other. Linking them all is the *indeterminate,* a kind of "super-salient." It is striking that Aristotle makes indeterminacy the most basic dimension of the circumstance of chance, intrinsic to its very causality: "The things which act as causes of chance events are bound, therefore, to be indeterminate. That is why chance too is taken to be indeterminate and opaque to people. . . ."[8] We can say as much of what gleams (in the eye or in the world) and of the interpersonal encounter that constitutes the decisive moment of proto-community; both are characterized by ambiguity of meaning or significance. So, too, are aura and way and wonder, each embodying the indeterminate in a uniquely powerful way: aura as intrinsically vague in its very presentation, way as the not-yet-determined, and wonder as what escapes and challenges established philosophical concepts by its very elusiveness. All such indeterminacies, despite their diversity and scope, are taken in at a glance. For the glance has a gift for discerning and exploring the indeterminate—for finding it meaningful and not merely chaotic, formative and not just formless. As Merleau-Ponty says, "we must recognize the indeterminate as a positive phenomenon."[9] It grasps as emerging into salience that which lacks

---

in Ralph Waldo Emerson, *Nature* / Henry David Thoreau, *Walking* (Boston: Beacon Press, 1991), p. 86: "I turn round and round irresolute sometimes for a quarter of an hour, until I decide, for a thousandth time, that I will walk into the southwest or west."

6. Plato, *Theatetus,* 155d (in the translation of F. M. Cornford in F. M. Cornford, *Plato's Theory of Knowledge* [London: Routledge and Kegan Paul, 1935]).

7. This is Cornford's interpretation at *Plato's Theory of Knowledge,* p. 43, n.

8. Aristotle, *Physics,* Book II, chap. 5, 197a8–197a10.

9. Maurice Merleau-Ponty, *Phenomenology of Perception,* tr. C. Smith (New York: Humanities Press, 1958), p. 6.

rigid definition or a fixed limit. In contrast, the gaze seeks out determinate visual phenomena and if it does not find them, it attempts to pin down the indeterminate itself—to fix it and delimit it, indeed to reduce it to something having a more definite shape.

As much as body and light, earth and world, the six salients here at stake serve to highlight and structure the very medium of the glance, to orient it at a quite basic level. The glance gleans the saliencies of any given visual field, appreciates them as such, and prospers from their indeterminate presence. The narrow defile in which it is enacted (it takes place exclusively between pairs of eyelids) opens onto a very broad vista: that of the place-world in its ramified and rhizomatic complexity, its continual expansion outward, its indefinite range and undelimited scope.

Part 3

Getting Inside the Glance

In this part, we will *move within ourselves* by restricting our focus to certain intimate aspects of the glance. These aspects contrast with the more overt features to which glancing also gives access: for example, the natural environment and the interpersonal scene of the ethical to which we shall come. Before this, we must reckon with the more interior reaches of the glance—reaches we have so far held at bay. It is time to get further inside the glance, and we shall do so by examining three inner dimensions of glancing: its characteristic singularity, its special relationship to temporality, and its close alliance with attention. This is to extend and deepen the work we began in part 1, where we discerned certain evident and everyday structures of the glance in contrast with the gaze. In this new part, we shall go further inside the glance, pursuing it into the finer meshes of the human subject: time, singularity, and attention. We shall seek several substructures of the glance, subtle aspects such as quick eye movements, the cut of the instant, sheer singularity.

What do these facets of glancing have to do with each other? They are closely related despite their apparent diversity. Time, for example, is enacted in a present moment that is as much singular as singularizing. Moreover, time links attention with singularity within the same present moment. When we attend to something, we do so not just in the present but *as* the present—as the focal temporal modality of the attentional field. To attend is to concentrate on what is happening just before us—just now, though not *as* "the now." When the attending is done by means of the glance (and I shall argue that this is far from a contingent affair), then the present is delivered to us in momentary crosscuts into the stream of time. In this way, the glance singularizes time itself, providing a vehicle in the moment of presentational awareness. In this moment, we experience a spontaneous self-display, the appearance of something at its very surface: just here, just now, nowhere and nowhen else, altogether at once. As the proper unit of the time we experience, the present moment is the temporal modality in which we glance at something singular as well as the singular unit of our own attentional action.

Thanks to the structure of this temporality, attention and singularity closely complement each other. In attending to something, I move my conscious focus to it along with its immediate environs; I invest my current interest in the item to which I attend, with varying degrees of intensity. In this way I begin to appreciate the item in its unique presentational being—in its singularity: what makes it just *this* item and no other. I attend to it *as* singular; the more focused my attending, the more sheer the singularity. The glance plays a central role in realizing this positive correlation. This is not surprising, for the glance is an indispensable organ of attention, and it has a decided gift for sensing the singular. It is the skillful spy of singularity, seeking it out and identifying it decisively and with finesse. Although I shall discuss attention and singularity separately in what follows, it should be kept in mind that the glance is the basis of their very contiguity, at once conjoining them and yet also serving to distinguish them. Making both possible is the moment in which they occur.

By these closely related means—time, attention, and singularity—we gain inroads into the interiority of the glance-world, its way of delivering itself to us from within our own experience. This experience, being that of a human subject, is deeply imbued with cultural and social history, but in the case of the three-dimensional modalities under description in this part the direct effects of this history are selectively suspended. This is not to deny that there are always differential incursions of the cultural and the social into every ongoing experience. That to which we attend in the first place, for example, may well reflect interests stemming from certain cultural constraints: as when we do not look straight at the sexual parts of the body of someone whom we encounter on the street. But we may still *glance* at these forbidden regions—if only to glance away immediately. The constraint against staring at them may be potent, but it is not altogether determinative: we always have the choice to look otherwise than the way we have been taught. The same is true of singularity, whose uniqueness does not prevent it from being imbued with social and cultural, historical and political parameters.

My experience of time itself is subject to differential effects of local and global culture—for example, in the form of calendrical and other institutional structures, such as my sense of how much time is properly left for a given event to end. Still, the moment of time in which we attend to the singular brings with it an element of the pristine that can never be the mere product of prior learning and knowledge, or the simple reflection of a preexisting framework. In the end, the three directions at stake in this new part of the book are mine to savor. They not only point to the inner sides of otherwise public or social events, but they also deliver the very mineness of these events, the way they arise within my experience of glancing as the felt sense of that experience itself.

Despite the intertwinement to which I have just pointed, it is at this stage of the book that the reader should begin to pick and choose according to his or her own interests. The following three chapters—and those of the next part as well—can certainly be read in sequence. But each is a more or less self-contained whole and can be read separately and for its own sake. Each represents a foray into particular kinds and ways, sources and contexts of glancing. Making no claim to comprehensiveness, they are efforts to fathom the multifariousness of the glance in certain of its most characteristic and compelling patterns of presentation.

7

THE SINGULARITY OF
THE GLANCE

The world always arises suddenly each time according to a decidedly local turn [of events].

—Jean-Luc Nancy, *Being Singular Plural*

. . . so singular in each particular . . .

—Shakespeare, *The Winter's Tale*

I

In this opening chapter I bring together two seemingly disparate topics. Just as the glance is rarely singled out in standard studies of visual perception, still less attention has been given to the conjunction of the glance and singularity: their affinity for each other, their complementarity, indeed their mutual enhancement. I shall explore the unsuspected but deep connection between them, aiming to cast light on each by considering both together.

Singularity can be said to be that aspect of any entity or event that determines it as incomparably itself, so radically so that it cannot be subsumed under a concept as if it were a mere particular case of that concept; at the same time, it is not something reducible to the actuality of substance (Aristotle) or to sheer existence (Kierkegaard). The singular defies categorization as a member of a species or genus, and it also resists characterization in terms of certain settled properties or traits. Nevertheless, the singular is not the utterly individual, a wholly idiosyncratic item; it has an intrinsic and internal bond with the universal insofar as this latter is not confined to a fixed conceptual content but is itself open-ended. As Deleuze states, singularity is "opposed to the particular subsumed under laws [but is allied with] a universal opposed to the generalities which give rise to laws."[1] The challenge for us is to determine how the glance

1. Gilles Deleuze, *Difference and Repetition*, tr. P. Patton (New York: Columbia University Press, 1994), p. 5. For Deleuze, the alliance in question can occur only as mediated by a radical conception of repetition: "if repetition exists, it expresses at once a singularity opposed to the

256

gives access to such singularity cum universality. We shall witness this access most strikingly in the situation of acknowledging another human being as at once singular and a member of the universal designated "human being"—a situation first encountered in chapter 1 and that we shall further analyze in the context of the ethical dimensions of the glance (see chapter 10). In the current chapter, I will first focus on the singularity that is at stake in the delimited setting of ordinary visual perception—after which, I shall make a preliminary foray into the conjunction of glance and singularity in the interpersonal sphere.

The glance sustains a dense dialectic with singularity: itself a radically singular act, it takes us to singularities in what lies before and around us that are not otherwise available. Its own singularity allows it to link up with the singularities of that which it encounters. The glance takes singularity, already potent in its own case, to new levels: the level of the visual world and of social and political life. Singularity gains a visual avatar, a vizier of vision as it were, in the action of the glance, which can be considered the most poignant form of singularization in the realms of sensory and intersubjective experience. We might say that the glance singularizes singularity itself by being at once its most efficacious empowerment and its most forceful embodiment in the visual sphere.

To begin with, I shall examine specifically visual singularity, moving from this to a consideration of the intimate relationship between glancing and the surface of things (a theme first explored in chapter 2 and to which we shall return in chapter 11). After this, I take up implications for being-with-one-another in the social world. At all three levels of analysis, the dialectic between singularity and the glance will be at stake.

II

When we glance at the visual world, we pick out three main kinds of singularity: *singularity of feature, region, and character.* In the case of *featural singularity*, the glance discerns a given aspect of something in the immediate environment: say, a certain green now illuminated by the late afternoon sun in the lawn below me as I write these words in Wuppertal, Germany. I spot this green even though I am not looking for it; it is as if it presents itself to my visual delectation. I certainly recognize it as "green"; but I (who know something about color names) do not categorize it as any particular green, any distinct species of green. As glanced-at, it gives itself to me as *just this* green, this and no

general, a universality opposed to the particular" (ibid., p. 2). In a study of the glance, however, the role of repetition cannot be taken for granted; at the most, it exists in the limited form of the "two-beat" rhythm I shall analyze in chap. 8; but it certainly does not figure in the full-fledged positivity at stake in Deleuze's discussion, of which a representative statement is this: "The repetition of a work of art is like a singularity without concept" (ibid., p. 1). For Deleuze, repetition generates, or is the condition for, singularity; for me, singularity is coeval with the glance, each highlighting the presence of the other.

other—indeed, not even this *versus* another (for that would presume a comparative move that is foreign to the glance). What matters, the very matter of the glance, is the strict singularity, the sheer *this*, and in the case before us: *this very green*. Hegel would doubtless judge such a bare "this" (*Dies*) to be an abstract "universal" (*Allegemeines*), yet we have to do here with something utterly concrete, not to be sure a concrete universal, but with what Husserl calls a *concretum*.[2]

Belonging to this concreteness is its situatedness. The green I have spotted is located just where I saw it, *there and nowhere else*. Were it to change location, it would not be the same color; part of its singularity is its unique locality. But to be located at all it has to assume a minimal shape, that of a "patch." Yet the shape of this patch, its "outline" as it were, is also its own: were this to change (as it does below me just now, given that the slant of the sun's rays is ever-changing, thereby producing continually differing shapes),[3] I would be given a different patch. In that case, it is indeed tempting to compare the new patch with its predecessor. But nothing requires this—nothing in the next glance that has fastened on the successor patch. It might as well be an altogether new content of a new glance . . . except that the power of primary memory, its fateful "sinking down" (*Absinken*), does lay down into the new apperception a fading profile of the first patch. This profile is itself glimpsed in what Husserl designates as a properly "mental glance" (*geistige Blick*). I see from within the content of the new perceptual glance (that is, the grasp of Patch #2) a dimmed-down image of Patch #1, a penumbral presence that enriches the new perception while also rendering it more coherent as a member of a just-beginning series of experiences. But even with this new complication, we still have to do with singularity: the subjacent outline of Patch #1 as it sinks down into Patch #2 is itself unique, its vagueness not to be confused with generality.[4]

Just as we have seen that a single glanced-at feature is accompanied by other associated features (color-with-illumination-with-shape-with-location, and so

---

2. "A concretum is obviously an eidetic singularity because species and genera . . . are non-self-sufficient on principle. *Eidetic singularities* are divided into *abstract* and *concrete*" (Edmund Husserl, *Ideas Pertaining to Pure Phenomenology and to a Phenomenological Philosophy*, First Book, tr. F. Kersten [Nijhoff: The Hague, 1982], p. 30; his italics; hereafter referred to as *Ideas I*).

3. It also generates new sizes, the two being essentially correlated: indeed, when I glance a few minutes later, one patch has ceded place to another, with its own unique color, lighting, size, and shape.

4. Is there comparison at work here as the two patches become aligned with each other, as one reader (Andrés Colapinto) suspects? If so, it is quite tacit and is certainly not a separate act (as when we determine two things, e.g., colors, patches, etc., to be "alike" or "similar"). I prefer to think of the older patch as *blending* into the newer by a form of subtle infusion in which the identity of the first patch is not retained—as it would have to be in a case of outright comparison—but melts down into the presentation of the second patch as a form of internal penumbra, of dim "in-line" as we might call it. All of this is implied on my reading of Husserl's original concept of "sinking-down."

on), so our ongoing glance is not restricted to the features of a given visual object. We usually glance at *several things at once.* Each such "thing" (object, patch, side) has its own features, but taken together with other things a new level of the singular content of the glance reveals itself. This is a level that Husserl would designate as the fit subject matter of a "polythetical" (or better "poly-rayed") look.[5] We *com*prehend several things as component parts of a single situation, as connected by certain lateral relations, for example, forms of congruence or noncongruence, modes of composition, kinds of implacement, over-all texture, and so forth. At this level we encounter what I shall call *regional singularity.*

Looking into the lawn, I also perceived *other greens* along with the green I first singled out for discussion: these did not just coexist with the highly lit light green that caught my eye at first but were co-constituents of the same perceptual scene, parts of its wholeness (again in Husserl's strong sense of integral "parts" that are not mere "pieces"). The various greens, different as they are in hue and value, constitute so many different patches; glimpsed together, they make up a single green scene, that of the backyard below the balcony on which I am precariously perched as I write. I glance at them not as a distinct set (that is, as if they were perfectly distinguishable members of a collection) but as forming a totality of their own, a "variously-greenly-colored-stretch-of-space"—in other words, a "region." This group of greens, taken as this more or less coherent congeries of patches, has its own singular status—so much so that experienced landscape painters despair of ever doing justice to them in their colorific disparity.[6]

The remarkable thing is that my mere glance suffices, in its casual and un-troubled way, to take in the patches of greens, their co-relations, and their differentiated but common location. The configuration of all this, no matter how complex, calls for a comparably complex attention on the part of my look wherein its various "gleams" (in Wittgenstein's term: see below) prove to be adequate to the many aspects of the scene at which I glance: aspects that have their own glitter of reflective and refractive return in the form of "world rays" (*Weltstrahlen,* in Husserl's late locution).[7] Thanks to the convergence of the two sets of rays—those stemming from my eyes and those from the scene these eyes behold—I experience regional as well as featural singularity. It is as if Plato was justified, phenomenologically if not scientifically, in his proposal that vision consists in the convergence of intromitted and extromitted rays in a common space.

My opening set of glances bore on singularities that are inherently muta-tional—that change not just between my several looks but even within a single

5. On polythetic looking, see *Ideas I*, sections 118–119, pp. 283–287.

6. I owe this observation to the painter Dan Rice.

7. On instances of "world rays," see Edmund Husserl, "The World of the Living Present and the Constitution of the Surrounding World External to the Organism," tr. F. A. Elliston and L. Langsdorf, in P. McCormick and F. A. Elliston, eds., *Husserl: Shorter Works* (South Bend, Ind.: University of Notre Dame Press, 1981), p. 242.

look: as when a passing cloud suddenly takes away the bright illumination of the patch of grass that first caught my glance. *Under* this look, feature *a,* "brightly lit," was replaced by feature *b,* "dully illuminated."[8] The presentation of featural and regional singularity is not only intrinsically heterogeneous in content but continually altering in its panoply of properties. Perhaps this is why Kant referred to it as *blosse Erscheinung,* that is, "mere appearance," but there is nothing "mere" or "just" here. We have to do with a veritable ocean of qualities and traits, powers and forces—with a richly varied sensuous display, with "multitudinous seas incarnadine" (Shakespeare). In the case of an actually perceived sea, each feature, each wave, has its own shape, while at the same time changing with every passing moment. Any given wave (in its shape, density, and other qualities) is no less singular for altering, indeed disappearing, so often and so quickly. This shows that featural singularity has temporal as well as spatial dimensions, for it is wholly consonant with the evanescence displayed in the protean, shape-shifting sea-world—a world that elicits the glance in its own shifting stances. Doubtless this is why Leibniz, imagining himself *au bord de la mer,* posited an "apperceptional" level of experience, that of his celebrated *petites perceptions* that continually modulate. We may consider such microperceptions to be the receptive substructures of the glance and the basis of its power to insinuate itself subtly into the surrounding visual world.

The same analysis holds for whole groups of waves gathered by a common shape or location or illumination. Looking out at a sea, I see more or less coherent areas, not just individual waves but entire stretches of roiling water subtending these same waves and embracing them as a group. These, too, I grasp in a glance: as possessing their own properly regional singularity, in which the predominant traits are relational rather than ensconced in each individual member. Just as the various distinctive patches of green I saw below me in Wuppertal together made up a given singular region, so in the more complex vista of the sea I witness several singular regions in continually changing juxtaposition—the darkly portentous patch of the deep I spot over there diverging sharply from a much lighter area lying to its left and farther out. Nowhere is there simple identity (it is impossible, for example, entirely to isolate a given wave from its successors); everywhere there is sheer singularity, and it is there right in the midst of a highly interfused scene. Rather than saying with Goethe *öd' und leer ist das Meer* ("desolate and empty is the sea"), we should say rather that the sea before me is brimming with unbridled interchange, full of interinvolved aspects, and never not in continual exchange of motion.

So intertangled and so full, indeed, that we cannot help but move—indeed, we are always already moving—to singularity of still another order, a third level of singularity, beyond featural and regional, which we can call the *character* of

---

8. This change, despite its suddenness, is more complex than I here indicate: the value of the color of the grass, even its exact hue, can change at the same time and for the same reason; so does its perceived texture.

things, their concatenations, and their co-locations. By "character" I mean something close to style, or manner of presentation; this is the "how" at stake in the German word *Darstellung* ("presentation"), its *dar-* or "there," what makes something distinctive as a single whole. Character is a recognitory mark, and is more lasting than any merely passing sense of unity, since it persists through the many changes in featural and regional singularities that make up the course of perceptual and apperceptual experience. It adheres to things, places, and regions alike (just as it inheres in persons in a different but parallel sense of the term).

Consider the sea again: in addition to its miniscule units, its uncountable and ever-vanishing waves and their loose collections into regions, I also see the sea itself as a single whole: *this one sea.* The multitudinous has become one, albeit very complex. I take it in *all at once*, and I do so with my mere glance—though in fact it is no more "mere" than are the appearances that make up the experiential manifold for Kant. For the power of the glance consists in its ability to detect and to savor the character of the entire presentation before it, the diffuse singularity that characterizes each manifold as a whole. In addition to its decisive ability to pick out highly differentiated features and their regional co-inherence, the glance is able to sweep across an entire seascape. In this comprehensive action it shows itself to be equal to a complicated task indeed: capturing the distinctive style, the unique configuration, of the complete seascape.

The characteral singularity that is the correlate of the sweeping glance lasts in the way that the full face of the sea lasts as I look at it, or walk or run along it. Its character as this very sea persists through the time of looking at or walking along it—or, for that matter, hearing or touching, imagining or remembering it (wherein I glance at it mentally), or for that matter writing about it in poetry: "She sang beyond the genius of the sea . . . and when she sang, the sea, whatever self it had, became the self that was her song."[9] Such temporal persisting is to be contrasted with the retentional profiling that occurs at the level of featural singularity: there, a dim outline, a postperceptual phantom, of the previously perceived color (or other feature) glimmers within the next perception; here, another kind of apperceptual mass inhabits the depths of each successive glance. This inhabitation is neither momentary (as in the cut of the instantaneous glance) nor fading (as with the sinking-down of primary memory). It is ongoing, lasting throughout the scanning effected by the glance. It allows the unmitigated presence of the sea—as of a mountain, or the sky: any outsize thing, any immense part of the world—to become an ingredient within the thinnest glance. It takes the sea as a whole within itself, and keeps it there as a mute and abiding force.[10]

9. From Wallace Stevens, "The Idea of Order at Key West" (Wallace Stevens, *Collected Poetry and Prose* [New York: Library of America, 1997], pp. 105–106).

10. No wonder Leibniz could regard the apperception of the sea as paradigmatic for understanding monads, which take in the whole universe from their own point of view—their own glance. This is not to deny that, at another level of analysis, the sea and its singular character are also preconditions of the very glance that incorporates them.

This abidingness within the glance, slowing it down from below, allows the character of a given seascape (or landscape or skyscape or, for that matter, cityscape) to emerge with special salience. Character comes out within the expanse of the glance. This character is the way a place, region, or thing consistently presents itself in the how of its appearing in and to the glance—an appearing still farther yet from the merely mere, the barely *blosse*, indeed irreplaceable in giving a sense of what is unique about that place, region, or thing. Character in this sense is singular indeed, for it pervades the entity taken in by the glance: pervades it utterly, not being excluded from any part, however modest or marginal. It is at once *extensive*—indeed, co-extensive with the entire spatio-temporality of what I sweep into my glance—and *intensive* as taken into that same glance as its inner content. By the same token, it is the character of *just that entity*: thus it appears *throughout it* and yet *in it alone*. Character imbues all that we glance at in a certain moment, that and nothing else. It is all we see. It is seized all at once, *totum simul*—there to be seen, here to be held, now to be grasped.

If featural singularity is the content of the glance in its pinpointing power, and if the singularity of a region is grasped in the spontaneous grouping of features in their common locus, the character of that region as of the larger landscape in which it is set is delivered to the glance in its sweeping across the entire presented scene in which the world appears to us at any given moment. In this way, content and character, feature and region, thing and place—each in its own specific singularity—enter into the embrace of the glance: an embrace that is at once ingoing and outgoing, taking in and giving back, narrowing down and opening up.

This embrace is finally that of the glance and singularity themselves: the glance as a singular and singularizing act, singularity as the tri-level spectacle that, already singular on its own terms, is singled out and specified by the glance. The yard below me, like the sea before me, is uniquely configured in its sheer self-presentation; but being given *to me* as its apperceptual and perceptual witness, each becomes singular twice-over, a "twice" that happens all at once: singular *in itself* and singular *for me*, being "in-itself- for-me" (to adapt a formula of Merleau-Ponty's), therefore singular both ways, bi-singular as it were.[11]

---

11. "We must discover the origin of the object at the very center of our experience; we must describe the emergence of being and we must understand how, paradoxically, there is *for us* an *in-itself*" (Maurice Merleau-Ponty, *The Phenomenology of Perception,* tr. C. Smith with F. Williams and D. Guerrière [New York: Routledge, 2001], p. 83; his italics). Also, I should add that nothing changes in principle, at this level of analysis, if I am taking in the sea in the company of others on the same beach. But the matter will change when I and these others exchange glances among ourselves, turning away from the sea so as to look at each other: no longer looking out alone or with others but at these others themselves and they at us: this is the situation upon which I shall touch later in this chapter and more fully in chap. 10 and the concluding thoughts. For Merleau-Ponty's treatment of shared looking, see the passage in ibid., pp. 471 ff.

III

Just *where* do the glance and singularity conjoin? Where do they take place together? The answer is straightforward: on *surfaces*. This may seem unlikely after our discussion of such seemingly elemental "things" as grass and water. Yet in every case, including that of the most elemental, it is the surface of such items that is at stake. As we have seen at several reprises, the glance thrives upon surfaces, settling on them as if they were its proper home. Every glance goes to some surface, often to several at once. Instead of penetrating the surface of that to which it is directed, my glance falls on it, touches it briefly, and darts away. It dusts it. This basic action of the glance is peculiar to it. Other kinds of looking linger on the surface in order to examine it more exhaustively; some try to get behind it to another, concealed layer; and some question it for its deeper meaning. The glance can certainly be inquisitive; it may be looking *for* something; but it does not possess the requisite patience, nor does it have the right resources, to undertake sustained inquiries. Whatever it learns from the content or configuration of a given surface, it learns at a single stroke, after which it moves on . . . to another surface. A glance that stays on a given surface is no longer a glance; it has become a look, a gaze, and finally a stare.[12]

A paradigmatic surface for glancing is a mirror, whose analysis we here pick up again. As we have seen, a mirror returns our look to us instantaneously: it gives us back our own image of ourselves glancing into its reflective surface. In most cases, this is all we want and need: we wish only to catch a glimpse of ourselves, to see how we look *in the mirror,* not because it is a complete or definitive image but precisely because it is just the kind of passing image that others catch of us in the course of everyday life—an "impression" of what we look like. In other words, the surface of the mirror conveys back to us how our own facial (or other bodily) surface appears to us and thus, despite differences of position or perspective, to others as well. It is a matter of transference: from one surface to another, from my surface as *origo* to that of the mirror, and from the latter to a possible look on the other's part. Throughout, the agent of transference is the glance, mine and (by projection) others'. My glance is the intentional agent that takes me from the anatomical confinement of my own eyes—in an outgoing moment in which (as it seems) a visual ray streams forth—to the refractive surface of the mirror, which beams back to me, via a mimetic return ray, an image of myself (and also usually my immediate context) which my eyes take in as they look at this image. Each of these moments, the one productive

12. "We say: it's impolite to stare. We don't say: it's impolite to listen, it's impolite to smell, it's impolite to taste" (Robert Kelly, "Notes on Brakhage," *Chicago Review* 47:4, 48:1 [2001–2002]: 167). We also don't say it's impolite to glance—except in the rare situation where glancing is felt to be intrusive or inappropriate: e.g., when someone is undressing who does not want to be seen doing so. Otherwise, the lightness of the glance alleviates it of the responsibility entailed by steady looking in which it can be held more fully accountable for what it sees and how it sees.

and the other reproductive, belong to the same speedy action of glancing: they are its opening and closing phases, which (as we know from the last chapter) are not separated by any significant temporal interval but occur together in one open stretch of simultaneities.

Even when I am not looking at a mirror surface, a glance suffices to tell what kind of thing I am looking at and what its primary predicates are. In this case, the rebounding ray bears an impression not of my own surface but of the surface of something else—of which it affords me a glimpse.[13] It tells me just enough to let me know the singularity of these predicates as they qualify this surface, their featural singularity, the singularity of the immediate region to which the glanced-at thing belongs, along with the overall character of the scene inhabited by this same thing. All of this is noted in a thrice, and yet with considerable discernment.

Whether reflective or not, then, a surface allows my glance to capture just enough of its qualities, relations, and overall situation to let me know what kind of surface it is, including what kind of thing the surface itself belongs to. Surfaces of many kinds provide for the glance the apposite support for the ongoing project of glancing—a "wherein" (a *Worin* in Heidegger's term[14]) onto which it can fasten itself, however momentarily, and still gain, at a single stroke, what it seeks to find or recognize in that surface. Surfaces hold in place the singularities that stud the field of perception like so many upholstery buttons.[15]

A given surface is of double relevance to singularity. It is itself singular in its own configuration, being the surface of *just this* thing or group of things; it is its, or their, unique support, that which underlies it or them in a more or less continuous and coherent way. But a surface is also that which surrounds. On spotting a given surface, one knows right away that it is the specially suited sheath or skin for whatever one is noticing: nothing else can fit better, or more intimately. Indeed, it fits so closely that it is less a cover or integument than an undetachable part that is at one with the depths under it: depths that rise to their own surface.

The surface is the sole mediator between a given thing (a substance or group of substances, an event, a seascape, and so on) and the medium provided by air or light or atmosphere: it is "the interface between a substance and [a] me-

13. In keeping with the discussions in part 1 and the afterword, I here take "glimpse" to be the specific content returned by a given glance, that which it captures: a portion of the glanced-at thing. At other moments in this book I bow to common parlance and use "glimpse" and "glance" more or less interchangeably.

14. On the "wherein" see Martin Heidegger, *Being and Time,* tr. J. Macquarrie and E. Robinson (New York: Harper, 1962), pp. 53–54, 93–94, 106–107, 111, and esp. p. 119: "this 'wherein' [i.e., of understanding] is the phenomenon of the world" (all in italics).

15. I borrow the metaphor of upholstery buttons from Lacan, who analogizes psychoneurotic symptoms to *points de capiton* that hold or pin down unconscious and repressed meaning. I should add that this holding is a making, in keeping with the root of the word "surface" in *superficies:* literally, a "making upon (something)." It is a question of making room for singularities that are held down upon a surface.

dium."[16] Where a thing is self-enclosed and has its own mode of thickness (material or otherwise), the medium is wholly dispersed through any given place or situation, spreading to every corner of it. *A surface attaches a thing to its place in the midst of a medium.* It is the outer limit of the thing, and at the same time the zone where the diffusion of the medium is arrested. A surface is an "interplace," as I like to call it: the immediate place of a thing situated within the more capacious place in which that same thing is set. Thanks to this double implacement, a surface is a presentational manifold in which various singularities come to our attention as residing *on* it and being *of* it.[17]

Where a thing (or event, place, or person) is particular, a medium is general. The surface is the singularity that effectively mediates between these otherwise disparate domains of the visual world, putting them in touch with each other, bringing the particular and the general together in one layout of appearances. Rather than being a merely passive reflective surface (as the model of the mirror too readily suggests), the surface is an active force: it *singularizes* thing and medium, both at once. On the one hand, it allows a diffuse medium to bear on a particular thing or event or place, condensing the medium at (or on) the surface itself: for example, light in relation to the patch of grass of my first example— light that was otherwise indifferently circumambient and spread evenly through the optic array.[18] Thanks to the receptive surface of the grass, light (that is, sunlight) had a home on that surface, however momentary this domicile may have been; it came to a certain concentration and intensity there not evident elsewhere in the garden scene before me.[19] On the other hand, the same surface singularizes the thing of which it is the surface, in this case the grass spread below me. More exactly, it is the *becoming singular* of that thing, the way the thing presents itself to the glance as *just this thing* and *no other.* Taken in itself, as a particular substance, it is not yet singular; were it to be reducible to determinate properties such as volume or weight or size (or to being nothing but their

16. See J. J. Gibson, "What Is Involved in Surface Perception?" in *Reasons for Realism,* E. Reed and R. Jones, eds. (Hillsdale, N.J.: Erlbaum, 1982), p. 111. See also Gibson's statement that the environment "consists of a medium, substances, and the surfaces that separate the substances from the medium" (*The Ecological Approach to Visual Perception,* p. 307).

17. For this reason, Gibson calls the visual world, or more strictly the visual environment, a "layout of surfaces." We shall return to this latter concept, first introduced in chapter 2, in chap. 11.

18. I do not here distinguish light from a medium, even though I am aware that they are not strictly identical in optical theory. As *experienced,* however, light serves as a medium of illumination; and in this same capacity, it presents itself as evenly distributed, even though it has a source and differing degrees of brightness. (I thank Andrés Colapinto for his remarks on this point.)

19. In the same spirit, we also speak of the "surface of the wind," its outer edge as it moves across a prairie. As Levinas remarks: "The element has no forms containing it; it is content without form. Or rather, it has but a side: the surface of the sea and of the field, the edge of the wind; the medium upon which this side takes form is not composed of things. It unfolds in its own dimension: depth" (Emmanuel Levinas, *Totality and Infinity,* tr. A. Lingis [Pittsburgh: Duquesne University Press, 1969], p. 131).

bearer), it would be simply one substance among other such substances—green grass amid more grass, sea water in more sea. Once invested with its own surface, however, what as material substance is merely a particular subsumable under a genus ("grass," "sea") becomes unrepeatably unique: this very patch of grass, that special stretch of sea—"singular in [the case of] each particular."

Nothing is lost by the doubly singularizing action of the surface; the particularity of substance remains, as does the generality of the medium: indeed, these are necessary to the circumstance in its environing three-dimensionality. But each is transformed, each gains something essential otherwise lacking. A scene that would fall apart into separate things positioned in pure space—in short, the Cartesian world-picture—is consolidated by the singularizing activity of surface, which holds together even as it renders unique. Surface thus construed is not just itself a singularity (that is, something having its own structure and traits, for example, the polished and reflective power of a mirror-surface), but it singularizes that *of which* it is the surface (the thing) as well as that *in and through which* it is the surface (the medium). It also singularizes that *for which* it is the surface: the glance, whose own singularity as a visual act is at once confirmed and enhanced by being presented with a singular surface to which to adhere: confirmed, since such a surface is its proper object; enhanced, since the same surface calls the glance to be ever more subtle in its entrainment on it. More so than any other part of perception, *surfaces connect;* they provide what Giordano Bruno called "the link of links" for all that inhabits a life-world: places and people, things and events, apperceptions and glances.

Itself singular in its intrinsic powers and properties, singularizing in relation to substance and medium, the surface also *sets forth* given singularities. First of all, any fully constituted surface *bears* singularities on its face, holding them up for detection by the glance. In this capacity, it must have a certain material consistency or density that allows it to support certain configurations. It has to possess just enough rigor to bear the singularities that it presents to vision. It need not be perfectly solid or impenetrable but only firm enough to carry out this presentation: that of blades in the case of the green grass, of water in the instance of the roiling sea. In other words, it has to have *the right ratio of rigidity*—a ratio itself determined by the relationship, in any given circumstance, of medium and substance. Further, a surface *displays* the singularities it supports. Without such display, a surface would fail at its own mission, which is to show itself and its contents as singular. We would be saddled with a self-defeating surface that fails to present what belongs to it—that conceals its own contents. Even in the most ordinary surface, all is on display, nothing is unavailable, everything is evident. It is evident to the glance as its partner in vision, even if it is not evident for those kinds of vision that are looking for layers not now visible: as happens when we sleuth for something hidden or interpret something symptomatic by reference to concealed or repressed forces.

The featural, regional, and characteral singularities discussed earlier are precisely what surfaces bear and present to the glance. These fill out the glance and satisfy it, delivering themselves to it in their own unique ways. They do so even when thing or medium act to obscure that which is manifest on the surface: the thing hiding something inside itself, the medium clouding perception with its dim translucency. But the box that conceals a box within it still presents its own outer surface as capable of such concealment, and the fog that sets in over the sea does not eliminate its surface but leads it to come forward in other ways (for example, by its sound, its smell, the sense of its presence near us). The surface as such is designed to display itself and its contents; it is a being of transparency even if it may at times fall into obscurity; left to its own devices, it gives itself to the glance. If it is indeed true that (as Deleuze claims) we must "liberate the singularities of the surface,"[20] we need only add that this is happening all the time: that is to say, every time we glance.[21] In the end, it is the glance more than any other act of vision that liberates the several sorts of singularity that accrue to a seen surface and that we see abounding there.

IV

Among visual surfaces are those of the faces and bodies of other human beings. If I have neglected such surfaces thus far in this chapter, this is not because they are less important, or because we must first understand the glance in nonhuman perceptual situations before understanding it in human ones. On the contrary: I agree with Jean-Luc Nancy, who proclaims (contra Heidegger) that *all* Being is being with-one-another, and that the with-structure of our existence is first and foremost.[22] The glance contributes powerfully to this very structure and is essential to its massive presence in human (and doubtless other

20. Gilles Deleuze, *The Logic of Sense*, tr. M. Lester with C. Stivale, ed. C. V. Boundas (New York: Columbia University Press, 1990), p. 141.

21. Deleuze links singularity with universality—a move I have not pursued in my emphasis on the ineluctable specificity of what each surface delivers. As Deleuze puts it: "Generality, as generality of the particular, thus stands opposed to repetition as universality of the singular" (Deleuze, *Difference and Repetition*, p. 1). And he ties surface in turn to the "plane of consistency" and the "planomenon," which are vaster in scale than the discrete phenomena on which I have focused. (On planomenon and the plane of consistency, see especially Gilles Deleuze and Félix Guattari, *A Thousand Plateaus*, tr. B. Massumi [Minneapolis: University of Minneapolis Press, 1987], pp. 21, 50, 56, 70–73, 251–252, 266–272, 422–423.) If my scope has been more modest, this has been in the effort to find for the glance an appropriate perch, a place for it to land ever so lightly—while yielding perspicuous insights into the very differences and heterogeneities, the "Dispars," which Deleuze aims to promote in the face of that preoccupation with the identical and the same that have characterized so much of Western thought.

22. "If Being is being-with, then it is, in its being-with, the 'with' that constitutes Being; the with is not simply an addition" (Jean-Luc Nancy, *Being Singular Plural*, tr. R. D. Richardson and A. O'Byrne [Stanford: Stanford University Press, 2000], p. 30. Cf. also p. 70: "Being-with is constitutive of Being, and it is [constitutive] for the totality of beings." For Heidegger's more restricted view of being-with (*Mitrein*), see *Being and Time*, sections 26–27.

animal) lives. Following Nancy's lead, I shall here give only the briefest indication as to how this is so, reserving for chapters 10 and 11 a more complete
treatment.

Nancy rarely discusses the glance as such, but his descriptions of human
interaction are very suggestive for our purposes. In *Being Singular Plural* he
says that when we are with others, they offer to us "silhouettes that are both
imprecise and singularized, faint outlines of voices, patterns of comportment,
sketches of affects."[23] He insists on the ingredient of the "instant" in interpersonal encounters, and of the role of contiguity therein.[24] The sudden is made
integral to these interinvolvements, as is the role of what he calls "touches of
meaning."[25] Overall, the redemption of "everyday" human intercourse is on the
agenda as is the centrality of the "between" and the "simultaneous."[26] I regard
each of the items I have just noted as integral to the glance—and the glance
to them.

Singularity is also at stake in Nancy's analysis. Consider one of his seemingly
casual—yet altogether telling—observations:

> From faces to voices, gestures, attitudes, dress, and conduct, whatever the "typi-
> cal" traits are, everyone distinguishes himself by a sort of sudden and headlong
> precipitation where the strangeness of a singularity is concentrated. Without this
> precipitation there would be, quite simply, no "someone." And there would be no
> more interest or hospitality, desire or disgust, no matter who or what it might
> be for.[27]

Human singularity, then, presents itself in forms of bodily conduct that are at
once sudden and strange. We grasp the other person's idiosyncratic style in a
thrice: all at once.How does this happen? I suggest that it is primarily by the
glance. In its power to alight on surfaces and to grasp various kinds of singularity
thereon, the glance is a primary agent of discernment in human relations. Before anything else—often before words have been exchanged—it sends itself
into the between of human beings, into their very being with-one-another,
grasping their strange being and sudden appearances, touching the other not
with any concrete hand but with spontaneous vision, thereby attaining the other
as "*each time* one."[28] The interpersonal glance has a light touch indeed; it does
not so much grasp (as might a gaze) as barely graze upon the other; this is why it

23. *Being Singular Plural*, p. 7.
24. On the instant, see ibid., p. 4, 32–33; on contiguity, pp. 5–6. For further on the instant,
see chap. 8 below.
25. See ibid., p. 6.
26. On the everyday, see ibid., pp. 9 ff.; on the between, pp. 5 ff.; on the simultaneous,
pp. 38, 99.
27. Ibid., p. 8.
28. "The being-other of the origin is not the alterity of an 'other-than-the-world.' . . . This
'other', this 'lower case other', is 'one' among many insofar as they are many; it is *each one,* and
it is *each time* one, one *among* them, one among all and one *among* us all" (ibid., p. 11; his
italics).

is so well suited for discerning such ghostly demi-presences as profiles and outlines, the "faint outlines" of the other. More than any other single act, it goes "right up to" (*à même*) this same other, instantly traversing any intermediate space, physical or social, at once, without standing on ceremony—indeed, without standing at all but moving with frictionless velocity, across the space of the between as rapidly as does the visual ray that escorts it to the other and back. Speed and politics: speed *as* politics: recalling Aristotle's observation that in a polis citizens must be able to glance at one another—to give each other the "once over."[29]

V

This suggests that there is an alliance between the spontaneity of the glance and the fact that other human beings appear to me in rapidly changing ways: often as if from nowhere and in any case as capable of continually surprising me. What other kind of looking is as well suited for dealing with such surprise? Let us consider two cases in point, in the first of which I glance at the other while in the second there is a mutual exchange of glances. Each bears on what Nancy designates as the "being singular plural" that is characteristic of human relationships.

Case 1. I am now on a bus in Wuppertal, and I glance at the person who has just seated himself opposite me. My discernment of certain basic features is immediate: "heavyset," "has been working all day," "probably Turkish," "middle-aged," "melancholy dark eyes," "hands roughly textured," and so on. These overtly stereotypical traits constitute my apperception of my traveling companion as an individual who embodies a certain generic image: "a Turkish worker in Germany."[30] I also grasp him as someone who is not just a representative of a class or race or generation. I realize this not *after* my grasp of this man's typicality (for we have to do with the cut of the instant in the glance, not with the amassing that occurs in prolonged perceptual looking), but *at the same time:* I see right away his very singularity, his utter uniqueness, his difference from every stereotype (including those he seems to manifest so transparently). In other words, I take in at once both his exemplification of certain social and cultural, age and gender categories *and* his being himself, being the singular

---

29. See Aristotle, *Politics*, 1327a1–1327a2). The phrase "speed and politics" refers to Paul Virilio, *Speed and Politics* (New York: Semiotext, 1986).

30. These traits, though pertaining to the individual before me, do not constitute him as singular; at the most, they help to bring out the singular by way of sheer contrast. Here I depart from Nancy, who claims that "the typical traits (ethnic, cultural, social, generational, and so forth), whose particular patterns constitute another level of singularity, do not abolish singular differences" (ibid., p. 8). I do not regard typical traits as *themselves singular,* but I agree with Nancy that the typical traits may serve to "bring [the singular differences] into relief" (ibid.). Cf. also p. 32 for Nancy's distinction between singular, individual, and particular.

human being he is.[31] This latter status is not a matter of being an "exception" in Kierkegaard's sense—for that presumes the standard or system over against which one is exceptional—nor is it a question of existential individualization (as that would require the introduction of yet other categories such as "authenticity," "resoluteness," and so forth). It is a matter, instead, of a singularity that is the very correlate of my glance itself. Like this glance and in it, it flashes forth suddenly and rises to meet it—again, not wholly unlike the Platonic model whereby the outgoing visual ray (*opsis*) and the incoming daylight meet to create a momentary middle ground where vision can arise.[32]

The immediate effect is not only the apperception of strangeness in the other (stressed by Nancy) or his destitution or need (as Levinas would emphasize), but also the clear sense that the other is so radically singular as to be *a being apart*— apart from me, apart from the categories he himself embodies, indeed apart from himself (in the end, he knows himself no better than I know myself). Kierkegaard had already said that "existence separates" and Nietzsche that "we knowers are unknown to ourselves," and it is this sheer separation that is caught in the glimmer of the glance.[33] This is not to say that I always experience such apartness as an explicit theme but rather that my glance feels its force in one way or another (for example, as alienation, or mystery, or plain puzzlement). The passenger opposite me is apart from me, and I know this in a glance.

Case 2. The same man on the same bus now looks back at me: he glances in the immediate wake of my glance. We "exchange glances" as one says in ordinary English, without pausing to ask what this means. What is happening here? Certainly no literal exchange—which is strictly speaking impossible, since each one's own glance is inalienable; stemming from him or her alone, it cannot be substituted for another's glance. Instead, there is a virtually simultaneous *engagement* of two looks, as each glance takes its clue from the other; I am aware that the other is sending (and sometimes shooting) a glance at me, and my own glance is undeterred and uninhibited: it looks right into the other's look, it looks at its source.[34] As I look straight into the other's eye, the other looks into mine: "When you see the [other's] eye you see something going out from it. You see the

---

31. I do not say "singular person," for that would be to introduce yet another genus, the legal person or the person of strict self-identity.

32. See my discussion of the *Timaeus* in chap. 5. I am mindful of Nancy's critique of *milieu:* "From one singular to another, there is contiguity but not continuity . . . there is no intermediate and mediating 'milieu'. Meaning is not a milieu in which we are immersed. There is no *milieu*" (*Being Singular Plural,* p. 5; his italics). What works as a model for sheer vision may not work in interpersonal relations, where the idea of *milieu* connotes compromise.

33. The Kierkegaard quote is from *Concluding Unscientific Postscript,* ed. and tr. H. V. Hong and E. H. Hong (Princeton, N.J.: Princeton University Press, 1992), p. 107; the Nietzsche citation is from *The Gay Science,* tr. W. Kaufman (New York: Vintage, 1974), p. 186. Nancy is aware of this dimension: "All of being is in touch with all of being, but the law of touching is separation" (ibid., p. 5). On this point, see Jacques Derrida, *Le toucher* (in *Le toucher, Jean-Luc Nancy* [Paris: Galilée, 1998]).

34. This source is termed "origin" by Nancy: see ibid., esp. pp. 10 ff.

look in the eye."[35] This look is directed at my look, and mine at it. It is a situation of "transference" in Freud's sense (that is, *Übertragung:* literally "carrying over"), or of what Nancy calls the "crossing-through" of two looks, immediate and direct even if conveying the strange and the unknown.[36] What is transferred, though, is *not* one's own (or the other's) personal identity; nor is it a matter of mutual recognition in a life-and-death struggle, as in Hegel, much less a sadomasochistic episode (as in Sartre). Nothing that determinate, nothing that dramatic or momentous, happens in the transferential crossing-over; there is only the felt sense that this other, whom I have grasped in my glance, is returning the favor (or I his)—the favor of noticing me as I notice him, each seeing the other as an utterly singular being: so singular that no name is yet pronounced, nor is there any gesture of the lived body other than the bare shifting and focusing of the look.

Still more than this is at stake, however. In an exchange of glances, the participants constitute a momentary community of two, a visual dyad that entails no further commitment beyond being in each other's face, thereby creating a two-way with-structure: me-with-you, you-with-me, both of us held together in the glance. From this nothing further follows—nothing but everything! Nothing in particular: no indicated or even adumbrated action, nothing one *must* do (unless the other person is in visible distress to which one feels called to respond). But everything also happens: a basic form of community arises, that of the "first-person plural" in which "*we others* are charged with [the] truth."[37] For in this moment I and the other know ourselves as (in) the truth of being with-one-another. More radically still: we know ourselves as othered by each other—othered by the other's mere glance. For we are other to each other as we look at one another in the same shared act of vision: an act of "intervision" in Jankélévitch's suggestive word.[38]

Here the glance is once more in the vanguard position, not now as a scout who sees what lies ahead as a determinate danger or good but as what is already ahead of itself and is thus to this extent realized *now,* in this instant of simultaneous looking in which each looker is co-essential to the emergent community created by both. Instead of the one-sided noncommunity of the in-itself for-us, here is a two-sided show. Each glance crosses through and over the other, being

35. Ludwig Wittgenstein, *Zettel,* tr. G. E. M. Anscombe and G. H. von Wright (Berkeley: University of California Press, 1976), p. 40. I have cited this in the coda to part 2.

36. "The alterity of the other is its being-origin. Conversely, the originarity of the origin is its being-other, but it is a being-other *than* every being *for* and *in crossing through (à travers)* all being" (*Being Singular Plural,* p. 11).

37. "From now on, *we, we others* are charged with this truth—it is more *ours* than ever—the truth of this paradoxical 'first-person plural' which makes sense of the world as the spacing and intertwining of so many worlds (earths, skies, histories) that there is a taking place of meaning, or the crossing-through [*passages*] of presence"(ibid., p. 5; his italics).

38. See Vladimir Jankélévitch, *Philosophie Première: Introduction à une philosophie du "presque"* (Paris: Presses Universitaires de France, 1954), pp. 71–76. I return to the notion of *entrevision* in the concluding thoughts.

both for itself (*it* looks out) and for the other (who looks *back*). Thus is effected a conspiracy of looks in which silence is not a contingent feature but part of the action itself. A strange moment indeed—yet the very basis of the strangeness of the other. That moment when we may not be looking the other *in the eye*, but we nevertheless see the other *with the eye*, in the beam of its glance and in the gleam of its light. In Wittgenstein's words again, "The ear receives; the eye looks. (It casts glances, it flashes, radiates, gleams)."[39]

There is spacing here—and timing too. We locate each other in a crossfire of glancings caught in the between which they co-constitute. This happens in that special simultaneity that only the interplay of glances can achieve so effortlessly and yet so efficaciously. Just now, just here: the two together at once.

VI

And what does such interhuman glancing yield? Beyond the creation of the mini-community just outlined, it yields these four things: (i) the *indefeasibility* of the other's status as a sovereign source of looking, an absolute beginning, an "origin" in Nancy's sense of something that is both unique and multiple: unique as event, multiple in that more than one entity participates in its coming-to-be; (ii) the *instantaneity* of this event, its nondurational temporality, its suspension of time's flow in a *Querschnitt* or transverse section (as Husserl might put it), its "cut" or *coupure* (to speak with Bachelard and Foucault), its *not taking any time to take place*. The glance skates across the surface of the riverrun of time (Joyce, *Finnegans Wake*) in an action of immediate *glissement* that leaves any effort to "time it"—to determine its duration—futile. The two glancing partners realize a "lived synchrony" that defies any "morbid geometrism" of measurement.[40] (iii) Nancy speaks of "an exposition of singularity that experience claims to communicate with."[41] It is this singularity that brings with it heterogeneity and separation. Each glance takes in the literal *ex-position* of the other glancer in the fragile field of looking, a standing-*out* in this field as a pure look from within its limits. (iv) At the same time—that is, *simultaneously*—the singularity of the other discerned by the glance also (and always) entails a plurality, a cohort of "we others": of we being other to each other in and by the glance. The intertanglement of glances, their mutual transference, is protosocial in character. It constitutes society in an inaugural moment of singular plurality—on its very surface.

If the first level of my description in this chapter showed the glance to be the

39. Wittgenstein, *Zettel*, p. 40.

40. I borrow the two phrases in double quotes from Eugene Minkowski, *Lived Time: Phenomenological and Psychopathological Studies*, tr. N. Metzel (Evanston, Ill.: University of Northwestern Press, 1970): "lived synchronism" is at pp. 65, 69–70, 337; "morbid geometrism" at pp. 277 ff.

41. Nancy, *Being Singular Plural*, p. 9.

singular and singularizing apperception of features, regions, and characters of things in the environing world, and if the second level pointed to the layout of surfaces as the proper home-ground of glances, the third level (which is last only in order of exposition; ontologically it is first on Nancy's reckoning) shows itself to be qualified by the apprehending (or rather, the co-apprehending) of inde-feasibilities, instantaneities, ex-positions, and singular pluralities in the social world. In that world, we start—and forever restart: every day, on every bus on which we sit, every sidewalk on which we walk, every dispute in which we partake—with the *socius,* the "companion" who spars with us in the bright brief world of glancing back and forth at each other.

"Spars," I say: not fights—this is not a classic struggle of recognition, nor even a dispute. It is closer to a scene of immediate two-way witnessing in which the partners deal real but fugitive blows, glancing off each other's body, yet without hurting or maiming; instead, entering more intimately into the daily round of heterogeneous multiplicity. Sparring in the arena of spontaneous looking, do-ing mock-battle in the ring of crossed-over communications that communicate nothing other than the sheer facticity of the redoubled glance. The glance gallivants and glides across the very gap between myself and the other—an intervisual *écart* that it at once acknowledges and deepens by its gentle yet forceful action.[42]

VII

My primary aim in this chapter has been to explore the affinity between the glance and singularity in two major contexts: in ordinary perception (where the glance picks out at least three special kinds of singularity) and in the intersubjec-tive realm (in which glancing opens up our bi-singular being with-one-another). But in closing let me ask: what is the relationship between these two contexts as they implicate the glance and the glance implicates them?

The bond they share is *surprise:* their capacity to disconcert us suddenly. What Nancy calls "the surprise of the event" is the basic deliverance of the merest glance, which allows us to "gain access" to things otherwise closed to us in more belabored and beholden kinds of looking such as observing and scru-tinizing, scanning and staring: in short, the pillars of oculocentrism.[43] These pillars serve to support matters of constancy and weight, in contrast with the unballasted movement of the glance—which frees us from the spirit of gravity and takes us, in a single stroke, into the lightness of being.

42. For a comparable but much more worked-out critique of the struggle of mutual recogni-tion, see Kelly Oliver, *Witnessing: Beyond Recognition* (Minneapolis: University of Minnesota Press, 2001), especially parts 1 and 2. Oliver's account of vision, set forth in part 3, parallels my own recourse to the glance, albeit on a different model—that of circulating energies.

43. On "gaining access"—i.e., to the origin—see Nancy, *Being Singular Plural*, pp. 10 ff., esp. p. 12. On surprise, see the essay entitled "The Surprise of the Event," in ibid., pp. 159–176.

"In a single stroke" (*tout d'un coup*): this is the very phrase that Nancy uses when explaining his title *Being Singular Plural*:

> Being singular plural: in a single stroke, without punctuation, without a mark of equivalence, implication, or sequence. A single, continuous-discontinuous mark tracing out the entirety of the ontological domain, being-with-itself designated as the "with" of Being, of the singular and plural, and dealing a blow (*coup*) to ontology—not only another signification but also another syntax.[44]

It is indeed the gentle blow of the glance that can unsettle the supposed certainty of ponderous doctrines of matter or spirit, starting with their apophantic syntax. This is why I have alluded to the sparring of the glance, whose outgoing beams strike and slide off the body of the other in an alleviated agonistics of instantaneous looking. I referred to the "glancing blow" earlier when I talked about the way the glance diverts itself from its object, darting away as soon as it has made contact. This is the essential liberating action: sensing the surface, whether that of the inanimate world or that of the other human body, only to fly off that same surface and to receive one's own glance back in the very next moment—literally so from a mirror surface but also, in different ways, from the less polished surfaces of the environing layout and from one's companions in the glance.

This is a matter of surprise: not just in what we quickly discover in this way but also in being taken back over by the glance we thought we had wasted on a barren world. The two basic contexts I have discussed, nonhuman and interhuman, connect not just because both proffer a distinctive surface-to-be-glanced-at, but because each surface in each context bears the blow of the glance with expressive grace—surprising us by returning that blow, that stroke or *coup*, to its place of origin: a place that is a face. This place belongs to the glancer who emits the look that comes back from the other: as a glance in exchange, a reflection in a mirror, or as a trace of our look (for example, in memory). Such a scene of continual recirculation is the scene of the glance.

Perhaps we have never noticed, or at least not paid enough philosophical attention to, this diversionary action of the glance. Yet it is of decisive significance in coming to terms with the surrounding perceptual world as well as the equally circumambient social world. If we have missed the import of the stroke of the glance, this is not just because it was so diminutive as to be unassessed but, more fatefully, because it was so rapid as to pass unappreciated. But that is just the point: it is in the instantaneous, the cut of the now, that some of the most momentous things happen, indeed that *events occur in their very capacity to surprise us*. "Being," declares Nancy, "only takes place in each instant."[45]

44. Ibid., p. 37. *Tout d'un coup* can also be translated as "suddenly," but I prefer to follow the English translators' more literal rendering. For a related statement, see p. 40: "the 'with' is the (singular plural) condition of presence in general [understood] as copresence."

45. Ibid., p. 33. Nancy adds: "The essence of Being is the shock of the instant [*le coup*]. Each time, 'Being' is always an instance [*un coup*] of Being (a lash, blow, beating, shock, knock, an

Just so. And we might add: rather than preceding all that becomes, being itself begins in the burgeoning of the glance, wherein it finds its most effective point of access, its most poignant moment of encounter, and the source of its wonder. The glance is that whereby the singularity of being—a singularity always already a plurality—is first signaled. With the glance we first move into the midst of things: which is to say, into being with-one-another as well as with the animals and plants and places of the circumambient lived world. If it is true that "the world always arises suddenly each time according to a decidedly local turn [of events],"[46] then it is also true that this arising of the world and this turning of events are accomplished to start with in the decidedly delimited action of the glance. The glance is the herald of what is coming and to come, and it occupies the premonitory position from which the ex-position of the present is to be seen and from which the future will just as surely stand out. It is in the leading position that is already in the future from which the present itself is seen to come. And all of this happens in the single stroke of the leanest and most lambent look.

---

encounter, an access)" (ibid.). The surprise, then, can be considerable even if the blow of the glance is gentle. Note that "instant" is not here used in the sense I have criticized in the previous chapter; it is closer to "stroke," where this latter term implies both blow and a passing moment of time (as in "stroke of time").

46. Ibid., p. 9. Here and in the epigram to this chapter, I have changed "appears" to "arises suddenly." The French verb is *surgit*.

8

GLANCING TIME

Whether it is a matter of inside or outside, of us or
of things, reality is mobility itself.

> —Henri Bergson, *La pensée et le mouvant*

In order to advance with a moving reality, you must
replace yourself within it.

> —Henri Bergson, *L'évolution créatrice*

Every moment of our life . . . splits itself at the same
time as it posits itself. Or rather, it consists in this
very scission.

> —Henri Bergson, *L'énergie spirituelle*

I

We spend most of our lives glancing—just glancing about, glancing around.
You are glancing at the pages of this chapter as you begin to read them; but I
would wager that you are also glancing about the room you are in, perhaps out a
window onto the larger world. The fact is that all of us are glancing all the time,
gathering the surrounding world into momentary kaleidoscopic assemblages,
from which certain forms of provisional order will fall out.

We do all this in a certain space, that of location and of orientation as explored
in a previous chapter, which addressed the question: where do I glance? But
there is also the question: *when* do I glance? For we glance in a certain time—
the time of the glance. Evidently this is a very brief time: just time enough to
attend to something. But we do not often reflect on the character of such
diminutive time: how much time does it really require, what kind of time does it
constitute—and what sort of time does it contest?

In short, how does time happen in the glance? And how does the glance
happen in time? What does the nature of time itself tell us about the glance—
and, conversely, what does the glance tell us about time? These are the primary
questions to be pursued in this chapter. We shall do so in the light of a particular
paradox: the glance puts us both in and out of time—*in* an intense momentary

time and *out of* a continuous, distended time (for example, chronometric or linear time).

In and out of *time?* Isn't the glance the epitome of an act that takes little or virtually *no time* to enact? Indeed, don't we often glance when there is not enough time for more assiduous seeing? In the absence of the kind of time in which we are able to scrutinize something—for example, the protracted time of the laboratory—we often glance instead. We take in all we can in "a thrice." There is no time here for the reflective sequence that is the luxury of experimentation in the laboratory or library: first this step, then another, then the next move, all of this within an unhurried context of having plenty of time (or at least enough to pursue the experiment). Rather than any such steadily unfolding succession, in glancing there is a sense of discontinuous darting: "Quick, said the bird, find them, find them, / Round the corner . . . human kind / Cannot bear very much reality . . . Quick now, here, now, always. Ridiculous the waste sad time / Stretching before and after."[1] A glance, much like Eliot's bird, *alights;* it does not settle down but perches precariously. It touches this or that surface, often in no particular order. Just as it moves mercurially over things that are not themselves contiguous, leaping over intermediate points, so it does not fit snugly into a gapless continuum of time. Discontinuity in place—leaping over connective edges—is paired with a discontinuity in time that is peculiar to the glance.

II

But is the fact of such double discontinuity tantamount to an absolution from time? Indeed, can any action, however fleeting, be timeless? Even the blink of the eye, which splits the extended present of perception, is temporal; the same is true for the wink, another quick action that nonetheless has its own time. Surely the glance, despite its remarkable speed, does take time. Even to last a split second is still to take up time, but what kind of time is this?

It will not do to say simply that a distinctive action such as that of the glance *takes its own time,* for time is a dimension or parameter that, by its very character, has to be able to situate other actions as well. "Time binds," as we say. But it binds differently in different instances, and our task is to determine how it does so in the case of the glance.

We might wonder, to start with, where the time of the glance is to be located in relation to McTaggart's celebrated A series and B series: the former referring to past/present/future and the latter to before/after?[2] It would seem that, at the very least, the glance demarcates what lies before and after its enactment in any

---

1. T. S. Eliot, "Burnt Norton," *Four Quartets,* stanzas I and V.

2. J. M. McTaggart, "Time," chap. 33 of Book V of his *The Nature of Existence,* vol. 2 (Cambridge: Cambridge University Press, 1927); as reprinted in R. M. Gale, *The Philosophy of Time* (New York: Humanities Press, 1978).

given circumstance. But this is trivially true of any discrete action. In glancing we are more conscious of being in (or at) the time of transition than of coming before or after any particular event. For an external observer, the positioning of someone's glance between one determinate event and another is easy to effect; but for the glancer herself, the glance is often what takes her out of the before/ after enchainment, being its momentary suspension. Such suspension is an integral aspect of the glance's liberatory power, its ability to refuse to adhere to any given situation, to eschew its enticement or entrapment. The glance can always *turn away*—this is part of its peculiar freedom—and in this diversion it departs from the temporal succession that belongs to the object or event that it began by noticing. In this basic action of the glance, the B series is not so much denied (it continues to obtain for the object or event in question) as evaded.[3]

How then does the glance relate to the A series, that is, "that series of positions which runs from the far past through the near past to the present, and then from the present through the near future to the far future, or conversely"?[4] Here the plot thickens. For we notice first of all that the glance, despite its ephemerality, implicates all three phases; it arises in the present, but only as a reflection of the immediate past of interest or desire and as foreshadowing the future of possible enactment. In being thus tri-temporal, the glance constitutes a genuine *moment* of time in contrast with an *instant* of time. The instant occurs only in the present; or more exactly, it is a constricted form of the present, constricted not just because it happens as actual only but more especially because it is so often conceived as a *point,* that is, a now-point.[5] It is the pointillism of the now, its essential isolation from other now-points, that occasions Heidegger's attempt to deconstruct it in the form of the "now-series," just as it inspires Bergson's critique of the version of Zeno's paradox to which such a conception of the now gives rise: "at each instant, [the arrow] is immobile, for it cannot have the time in which to move, that is, to occupy at least two successive positions. At a given moment, therefore, it is at rest at a given point. Immobile in each point of its trajectory, it is, during all the time in which it moves, immobile."[6] Yet the arrow moves; we can see it moving and it reaches its target after all.

3. Bergson argues that duration dissolves the rigidity inherent in the B series: duration is "a memory interior to change itself, a memory that prolongs the before in the after and prevents them from being pure snapshots (*instantanés*) that appear and disappear in a present that would be incessantly reborn" (*Durée et simultanéité: à propos de la théorie d'Einstein* [Paris: Alcan, 1922], p. 55).

4. McTaggart, op. cit., pp. 87–88.

5. I am here setting aside Bachelard's interpretation of the instant as "creative" as discussed in the introduction; instead, I am taking the instant to be a shrunken version of the present moment. Similarly, I am following Heidegger in being critical of the now as tending to be conceived as a point (a "now-point" or *Jetztpunkt,* as Husserl called it) and forming part of a series (*Jetztfolge* in Heidegger's term) rather than as a source of novelty. Instead of "the instant," I here invoke "instantaneously" as qualifying that which emerges in two beats or phases in one and the same present.

6. Henri Bergson, *Creative Evolution,* tr. A. Mitchell (Lanham, Md.: University Press of America, 1983), p. 308; translation modified. More succinctly stated: "our duration is not

The analogy between the moving arrow and the human glance is significant. Each is "shot" from a human subject, each aims at something in particular. Each is altogether mobile.[7] Moreover, arrow and glance alike gather all three temporal modalities together in their very flight: (a) each occurs in an extended, noninstantaneous present (it is this very extensity that resists analysis into the before and the after), a present that is co-extensive with the trajectory of the projectile itself; (b) each brings its own past to bear on that ongoing present, a past that gives both arrow and glance its current directionality, and in this way "our past remains present to us,"[8] constituting an inherent presence rather than becoming something separate and self-contained; and (c) each does not so much move *into* a future (for there is no already-existing future into which to move) as it begins to realize that future at the extremity of its own trajectory: the arrow, like the glance, is continually edging into its own future, that is, *at* (and *as*) the tip of the arrow or the outer limit of the glance taken at any given moment of its trajectory.

The arrow and the glance show time to be (in Deleuze's words) "a perpetual *self-distinguishing*, a distinction in the [very] process of being produced; which always resumes the distinct terms in itself, in order constantly to relaunch them."[9] In particular, they show the temporality of the A series to be diasporadic from a restless present moment that, unlike the instant-point, does not allow itself to collapse into the sheer fact that it is where it is and as it is: that way lies the onto-sclerosis of time, its *rigor temporis*. Instead, time alters—is other to itself—by always mutating into two simultaneous aspects, the past of its own

---

merely an instant that replaces another instant: for then there would never be anything but the present" (ibid., p. 4). For the arrow to exist in a point of time, that is to say, an instant that is the present, is for it to coincide with a fixed position in such a way as to be inextricably tied to it: tied to its actuality, which is distinct from the actuality of every other point-instant. But, as Bergson asserts, "the arrow *is not* ever in any point of its trajectory" (ibid., p. 308; translation modified). Bergson is here remarking that the arrow is motionless if the arrow can *ever* be located at a determinate point of its trajectory.

7. Where an instant is an "immobile section (*coupe*)" of time that requires the abstract idea of succession to string together otherwise utterly disparate points—and thus to produce a travesty of time, its punctiform homogenization—the moment of the glance is a "mobile section of duration." Each moment not merely reflects or mirrors duration, but is itself durational in its very movement; or we could say that a moment is a *cut into* duration—which keeps it durational in status—rather than something *cut out* of it. (I borrow the phrase "mobile section of duration" from Gilles Deleuze in *Cinema 2: The Time-Image*, tr. H. Tomlinson and R. Galeta [Minneapolis: University of Minnesota Press, 1989], p. 98.) For Heidegger's attempt to deconstruct the now-series, see *Being and Time*, tr. J. Macquarrie and E. Robinson, sec. 81; and for his own formulation of the A series, in which the future is given primacy, see ibid., sec. 65, esp. p. 378:, "The primary phenomenon of primordial and authentic temporality is the future" (all in italics).

8. Bergson, *Creative Evolution*, p. 5. Bergson adds: "Doubtless we think with only a small part of our past; but it is with our entire past, including our original bent of soul, that we desire, will, act. Our past thus manifests itself integrally to us by its thrust and in the form of tendencies, even though only one weak part of it is represented" (ibid.; translation modified).

9. Deleuze, *Cinema 2*, p. 82; his italics.

present and the future of that "present which passes."[10] The dissymmetry of the two aspects arises from the fact that the past is retained as virtual, a vast virtuality that bears down on the actuality of the present as its ever-augmenting other, while the future is neither virtual nor actual but *possible:* that is, noncumulative and open.

In the end, the arrow and the glance diverge. The time of the arrow's flight evaporates with the completion of its arc, whereas in human temporality that is more than merely the time of observation (on which we nevertheless covertly draw in discussing the arrow) a greater whole is always at stake, whether we wish to call this "duration" following Bergson or the "Memory of the World" after Merleau-Ponty.[11] Physical motion taken by itself, apart from any subjectivity with which it may be involved, exhibits time only to the extent that it gives a measurable instantiation of it—hence the temptation to reduce such time to instants plus a diagram of their abstract succession—but any action of human (and other) organisms takes time only within a more capacious, ever-expanding world of time.[12] Indeed, the amalgam of present, past, and future in the A series is just that larger temporal whole that Bergson names *durée réelle* and Heidegger *Zeitlichkeit*—and that, as Saint Augustine argued, is held together by human consciousness in its synthetic power. Unlike the B series that supports its own linear representation (Aristotle argued that the before and after in time are ultimately modeled on the front and the back of ordinary physical objects), the A series dissolves the very line with which one tries to represent it: on the one hand, the line constantly splits up into the dyadic directionality of past and future in a dispersed manner; on the other, the parts of time are just as continually drawn back together by consciousness, duration, or Dasein's ecstatico-horizonal temporality. In other words, the becoming of time itself continually *becomes;* it keeps on consolidating its own gains and losses in a larger whole that is at once abyssal and comprehensive. This cannot be said of the arrow, which

10. Deleuze speaks of "the hidden ground of time, that is, its differentiation into two flows, that of presents which pass and that of pasts which are preserved. Time simultaneously makes the present pass and preserves the past in itself" (ibid., p. 98).

11. On the "Memory of the World," see Maurice Merleau-Ponty, *The Visible and the Invisible*, tr. A. Lingis (Evanston, Ill.: Northwestern University Press, 1968), p. 194. Earlier, Merleau-Ponty spoke of "the world's vast Memory" (*Phenomenology of Perception*, tr. C. Smith [New York: Humanities Press, 1962], p. 62). Note that Deleuze, influenced explicitly by Bergson and tacitly by Merleau-Ponty, states that "memory is not in us; it is we who move in a Being-memory, a world-memory" (*Cinema 2*, p. 98).

12. By "ever-expanding world of time," I mean a whole to which new moments are being continually added. We feel ourselves to be interior to this whole. As Deleuze says, "It is we who are internal to time, not the other way around. . . . Time is not the interior in us, but just the opposite, the interiority in which we are, in which we move, live, and change" (*Cinema 2*, p. 82). But if this is not true of the arrow—whose time is internal to its own specific motion—it is true of every experience of time in which subjectivity is at stake: to the point where Deleuze can claim that "the only subjectivity is time, nonchronological time grasped in its foundation" (ibid.).

involves no more—and no other—time than its own physical trajectory allows and requires.

What then of the glance, so much like an arrow in its directed movement (as the Greeks were the first to insist), yet in the end a denizen of the domain of human temporality? What role does it play in this domain? And what is its own time?

III

In the dense and massive heart of human temporality, in its continual self-accretion (as witnessed in the pyramiding of the past over the present), the glance plays hooky by its very inflection and indirection. It desediments the triple determination of time found in the A series, just as it disconcerts the equally relentless before-and-aftering of time operative in the B series. For the glance upsets the assurances and continual reassurances offered by both series: that is, the continuity and implicit linearity of being positioned before and after in time as well as the evolving progression at stake in the sequence past/present/future.[13]

Glancing takes us into the midst of what Deleuze (inspired by Bergson) calls "pure ceaseless becoming," or "the Open of Becoming."[14] But it does so by unraveling the thick tissue of duration as well as by splitting up the dense series of now-points on the time line. It does all this without the detachment from a human subject that is entailed by the analogy of the arrow. The glance depends on a human subject, literally "hanging from" (de-pending) this subject as part of its permanent repertoire; yet it exceeds the immediate ambit of any given human being by being directed, "shot" at an object of interest. Unlike any arrow, however, this projection does not advance to its target in a one-way trajectory that, once completed, stays at its destination. Instead, the glance loops back onto the subject who emitted it; it *folds back on* this subject, coils over and falls back onto it. But what is the temporality of this folding-back, and how is it enacted by the glance?

13. There are two senses of whole at stake in durational time: first, the whole formed by virtual images: "memories, dreams, even worlds are only apparent relative circuits which depend on the variations of [a] Whole" (ibid., p. 81); second, the whole constituted by duration itself: "through relations, the whole is transformed or changes qualitatively. We can say of duration itself or of time, that it is the whole of relations" (Gilles Deleuze, *Cinema 1: The Movement Image,* tr. H. Tomlinson and B. Habberjam [Minneapolis: University of Minnesota Press, 1986], p. 10). For further discussion of Bergson's usage of "Whole," see his *Creative Evolution,* pp. 10–12 et seq.

14. The first phrase occurs at Deleuze, *Cinema 1,* p. 10. On the "Open," a term also employed by Heidegger, Deleuze has this to say in commenting on Bergson: "If the living being is a whole and, therefore, comparable to the whole of the universe, this is not because it is a microcosm as closed as the whole is assumed to be, but, on the contrary, because it is open upon a world and the world, the universe, is itself the Open" (ibid.).

The clearest case in point is that of *glancing at oneself in the mirror.* Here I start by looking out from myself; taking my glance with me outward, I send it before me into the mirror, where I see myself glancing at myself, catching myself in the act as it were. No sooner does this happen, however, than my glanced-at glance returns to me, and is absorbed by the very face that sent it out in the first place: it folds back over this face, rejoining it as (and at) its surface of origin—as if to acknowledge this face as its own progenitor. Yet my glance returns to me not simply as to the same self but to a self now augmented by its own looking. I see myself not as I am, *simpliciter,* but as I am in glancing, a glancing self, a self that knows itself as glancing at itself, a self that has just glanced at itself.[15]

The temporality of the scene is composed of *two beats:* an outbeat gesture of (usually circumscribed) *ecstasis* as my glance is released from my body-self, and an inbeat return of the glance to the body-self that has gained an extra layer as it were: as just-having-perceived its own image in the mirror. Nothing like this is captured by the classical model of the B series (there is no separable before and after here, since the two beats belong to the same movement or trajectory) or that of the A series (I experience my glancing into the mirror and its return as occurring in an indissoluble present, from which any significant past or future has been shorn away). Nor is the double-timing here at stake the same as that obtaining when two people toss a ball at each other at the same moment: in this latter case, one moment encompasses two trajectories proceeding in opposite directions, where in the case of the mirror two moments, closely concatenated, are required for the single trajectory of my own look: a trajectory that goes out from me and returns to me in seeming simultaneity.[16] In short, glancing at

15. Moreover, as I glance I take myself outside my self-contained self into a mirror-world that has its own spatiality and temporality. I hover in this world, no longer simply in myself nor utterly beyond myself either. There, in this spectral space, I am suspended on my own glance, the object if not the victim of the movement-images I have myself generated in time. The longer I glance—up to the point of a stare—the more unreal the situation seems to become. If there is another mirror present, my glancing image will be multiplied in disconcertingly complex ways, either by engendering a bad infinity of such images (if the mirrors are aligned with each other *en face*) or by promulgating ghostly self-spectators who glance at myself glancing at myself (if the extra mirrors are set at an oblique angle to the main mirror). Even with these complications, however, my glance, both the first glance I cast and any subsequent glance, folds back upon myself as its point of origin: I cannot escape the return look if I see my own look at all: to see myself seeing is to see myself seen. The return is built into the scene of glancing itself, every bit as much as the outgoing motion by which it begins. There is a return in staring as well, but in this case the sense of return is not limited to the instantaneous reflux as in the glance; my own face, on returning, sinks into me, slowly sedimenting itself there—to the point where it becomes one with my face. No such sedimentation occurs in the return glance, which impinges on me rather than merges with me.

16. I owe the ball-throwing example to Andrés Colapinto, who points out that in this case there are two *spatial* "beats" (i.e., two tosses, two objects thrown) in one temporal moment. On my analysis, the mirror situation entails two specifically *temporal* beats, the moment of the outgoing look and that of the incoming return look, both encompassed in a single image. These two beats or moments are phases of one basic action, whose speed is experienced as instantaneous.

myself in the mirror—a situation which we have discussed before—is a matter of a two-beat movement that defies both the prior versus posterior structure of two separate events and the tri-temporality of an event that unfolds in the fullness of time. Instead, the temporal structure is that of *twice at once*.

Nor is this situation to be assimilated to the Lacanian mirror stage. For the adult glancer (whom I have taken as paradigmatic) the issue is not that of identification or ego-formation. There is, at most, an element of *re*identification: I am reassured that I look quite like the person who last glanced at himself in the mirror. But the glance is not the narcissistic gaze that would be the adult equivalent of the child's fascination with his or her image in the mirror, an image that (on Lacanian theory) triumphs, albeit fictionally and in an alienated mode, over the fragmented body heretofore regnant in the child's life.[17]

The mirror-glance exemplifies an instantaneous redoubling whereby in one present moment of my experience I immediately and forthwith spawn a virtual image of myself. This image, as seen by myself in the mirror, is the very image of my present looking. Instead of being deferred in its formation (as is the case in other kinds of image formation: where the image is the product or result of some prior operation), this image is formed at the very moment of self-apperception. If it is a virtual image—as is every mirror image—it is not a diminished perception, as Hume thought. It is neither an image *of* a perception nor a reperception; and it is not a recollective memory either; it is a sui generis image of myself caught by myself in the act of looking. It is something of a different order from perception or recollection.[18] And this is due to the fact that its temporality is distinctively different from that which rules either of these latter acts: perception is wedded to the before and after sequence of objects and events (that is, I see X, then Y, then Z); recollection is an integral part of the temporal series of present/past/future, since by this means I have access to the episodic past.

It is revealing that Bergson has recourse to the analogy of the mirror in an article on paramnesia first published in 1908:

> Pure memory (*souvenir pur*) is to perception that which the image apperceived behind the mirror is to the object placed before it. The object [before the mirror] is touched as well as seen: it can act on us as we act on it; it is pregnant with possible actions, it is *actual*. The image is *virtual* and, although similar to the object, incapable of doing anything on the basis of that from which it is composed. Our actual existence, insofar as it unfolds in time, is thus doubled with a virtual existence, with an image in a mirror.[19]

---

17. See Jacques Lacan, "The Mirror Stage," in his *Écrits*, tr. A. Sheridan (New York: Norton, 1977), pp. 1–7.

18. Memory as recollection has virtual status for Bergson. At least this is true for what he calls "pure recollection" (*souvenir pur*), not to be confused with a concrete *souvenir-image*, which is an actuality, a psychological fact. As Bergson says, the *souvenir-image* "participates in *souvenir pur*, which it begins by materializing and [embeds in a] perception where it tends to be incarnated" (*Matière et Mémoire* (Paris: Alcan, 1921), p. 143.

19. Bergson, *L'énergie spirituelle* (Paris: Bibliothèque de Philosophie contemporaine, 1919), p. 136; his italics for "virtual" and "actual," mine for "object" and "doing." Deleuze argues,

This passage suggests that glancing into the mirror is not so contingent or so delimited as it may seem at first. Indeed, the last sentence just quoted from Bergson implies that such glancing, taken as a paradigm, may have more general implications: that somehow every act of glancing has much the same double-beat structure: the same spontaneous spawning of a virtual image that reflects back to us our initial act of looking. At stake here is the doubling of the present and its own image that is the crux of any temporality conceived outside the rigorous logic of the A and B series. Further, the becoming-virtual of the present in the spontaneous generation of its own image undoes the putative primacy of the pure present: a primacy that is undermined by the presence of an image within the domain of this same present. For sheer self-presence is contaminated by any such image, above all by one that is spun off from the present itself in an act of self-division. In a remarkable passage from the same essay, Bergson anticipates Derrida's deconstruction of the privilege of the present:

> Every moment of our life thus offers two aspects: it is actual and virtual, perception on the one hand and memory on the other. *It splits itself at the same time as it posits itself. Or rather, it consists in this very scission;* for the present instant, always moving [*en marche:* so not the immobile instant of Zeno], a limit fleeing between the immediate past that is already no longer and the immediate future that is not yet, would be reduced to a simple abstraction if it were not precisely the mobile mirror that ceaselessly reflects perception as [or into] memory.[20]

This passage, again invoking the mirror, articulates the radical thesis of "a memory of the present" that splits the present more effectively than does the blink of the eye.[21] The memory here in question is not that of recollection but a memory that clings to the present itself as to its own image—yet is not "retention" in

---

more incisively than Bergson himself, that without this virtual doubling of the present in pure memory, inactual and unconscious as it is, recollection of the past itself would never be possible: "The past would never be constituted if it *had not been* constituted first of all, at the same time that it was present. There is here, as it were, a fundamental position of time and also the most profound paradox of memory: The past is 'contemporaneous' with the present that it *has been*. . . . The past would never be constituted if it did not coexist with the present whose past it is." (Gilles Deleuze, *Bergsonism,* tr. H. Tomlinson and B. Habberjam [New York: Zone Books, 1991], pp. 58–59; his italics). Merleau-Ponty converges on this line of thought by saying that "past and present are *Ineinander,* each enveloping-enveloped" (M. Merleau-Ponty, *The Visible and the Invisible,* p. 268). More specifically still, Merleau-Ponty suggests "the idea that every perception is doubled with a counter-perception" and speaks of "chiasm my body—the things, realized by the doubling up of my body into inside and outside—and the doubling up of the things (their inside and their outside)" (both citations at ibid., p. 264). But the doubling in question is not of perception with memory but of the body with itself in terms of inside/outside dimensions. Deleuze repeats the Bergsonian gesture by alluding to the mirror in this very context: "the present is the actual image, and *its* contemporaneous past is the virtual image, the image in a mirror" (*Cinema 2,* p. 79; his italics).

20. Bergson, *L'énergie spirituelle,* p. 136; my italics. In keeping with my own preferred nomenclature, "present instant" is more aptly rendered as "present moment."

21. The phrase "un souvenir du présent" (in italics in the text) is found at ibid., p. 137. As Bergson further specifies, "it is, in the present moment, a memory of this moment" (ibid.). "Moment" here rightly replaces "instant."

Husserl's sense (that is, a "sinking back" of the present in a horizon or a "heritage" that is no image).[22] As such, it does not so much split a preexisting pure present as it is the very action by which the present always spins off a virtual image of itself—like a mirror image, though not always in a literal mirror situation. If each present moment of our lives "consists in this very scission," then these lives are irrevocably self-split. My proposal is that the glance, more than any other human act, most decisively embodies such self-sundering. If glancing at oneself in the mirror is the exemplary case of self-scission, then glancing of any kind carries division-of-self forward into the rest of our lives at "every moment."

IV

On this boldly comprehensive claim, *any* human act or action would be subject to such scissioning in its ongoing temporalization. What, then, is so special about the time of the glance? Perhaps you will grant the specialness of the glance in the mirror—where the glance literally enacts before our eyes a *dédoublement* that is otherwise invisible, inactive, impassive, even unconscious.[23] You might also concede that the mirror glance rejoins other phenomena that are self-replicative, such as the shadow that falls from the body in sunlight (or moonlight): here, too, we witness a virtual image that is straightaway and involuntarily spawned. Or to go further afield: think of those redundancies in ordinary conversation that are immediate spinoffs from the main line of discourse: "Yeah, that's right, that's it, just as you said" (as we sometimes say in agreeing with what someone else has said; and sometimes with ourselves). Or: "How are you?—How are you?" (each phrase mimicking the other as two people first exchange greetings). In each of these cases, and without any employment of a mirror, we observe a basic movement of spontaneous folding-back or self-return: the shadow rejoins my body at my feet, my remarks fold back on my own or another's discourse as if in immediate echolalia. However different they are in other respects, these experiences present themselves as parallel to the glance.

But what of the glance that does *not* see itself seeing in the mirror—that is not visibly self-schismatic? If there is something truly special about the glance in regard to time, its exemplary status in contexts other than that of the mirror must be shown.

22. Husserl adopts the language of "horizon" to describe the penumbra of the past experienced in a given "now-point." He also alludes to it as a "heritage" (*Erbe*): "the heritage of the past in the form of a series of shadings." For "the now-point with the horizon of the past," see Edmund Husserl, *Zur Phänomenologie des inneren Zeitbewusstseins (1893–1917)*, ed. R. Boehm (The Hague: Nijhoff, 1966), Husserliana X, section 10; for the passage on *Erbe*, see ibid., section 11.

23. On the "unconscious" aspect of virtual memory, see Deleuze, *Bergsonism*, pp. 55–56, 71–72, and Bergson himself in *Creative Mind*, tr. M. L. Andison (Westport, Conn.: Greenwood Press, 1946), pp. 88–89, and in *Matière et Mémoire*, pp. 152–163.

Consider the circumstance in which my glance is met and returned by yours. No mirror is present here, yet there is reciprocity: my glance engages yours, and you cast a glance back at me. Your glance may not mimic mine, but it is certainly a response to it: it takes it into account and to this extent incorporates it. Your responding glance is in significant measure my own glance returning to me, however transformed it may be because of its now being *your* glance, reflecting your beliefs, history, prejudices, and momentary whims. Altered as it may have become, my outgoing glance still folds back on itself, only now as mediated by the return of your glance as it registers and replies to mine. The reply is a *repli,* a literal "folding-back," constituting what Deleuze calls a "small internal circuit," that is, a feedback loop in which the reply is a direct vestige of the outgoing message.[24] One such circuit is constituted by the return of a virtual image to its point of origin—a return that obtains both in the mirror circumstance and in the social situation of exchanged glances: where my tacit message that "I'm interested enough in you to glance at you" is given back to me by the other person's counter-message, "And I'm interested enough in you to glance back." Different as the social situation may seem to be from the mirror experience, its temporality remains two-beat: the moment of my initial look is rejoined immediately by the moment of your return look: not as two different times in a sequence of before and after but as coexisting in one social time, in which two glances have been exchanged in a single small circuit. Whether glancing at myself in the mirror or exchanging glances with someone else, "each present goes back to itself as past"[25]—a past that is not separate from the present but an intrinsic part of it.

But what if my glance is *not* returned by the other person? What then? A certain return is still at stake, still expected at some level, even when it is not actualized. I continue to presume the other capable of responding to my glance, if not by a literal glance back then by other actions. These nonglancing responses to my glance are sometimes gesticular (for example, my glance precipitates the other's reaching out to touch me) or they may take the form of a new train of thought (for example, the other person's musing to herself: "why is this person looking at me?").[26] But in each of these vicissitudes of the glance, the

24. Deleuze, *Cinema 2,* p. 80: "The more or less broad, always relative, circuits, between the present and the past, refer back, on the one hand, to a small internal circuit between a present and *its own* past, between an actual image and *its* virtual image; on the other hand, they refer to deeper and deeper circuits which are themselves virtual, which each time mobilize the whole of the past" (my italics). The former circuit refers to the circumstance under discussion in this and the last section of the present chapter. The latter circuits implicate the durational wholes to which reference has been made earlier in this same chapter. Such wholes designate the upper and more voluminous parts of the celebrated cone of time whose primary diagram is found in chapter three of *Matter and Memory.*

25. Deleuze, *Bergsonism,* p. 59. For further on the exchange of glances, see chaps. 7 and 10, this volume.

26. Such a response can be no less powerful for being tacit, as in the case of a sullen silence that is occasioned by my glance.

same sense of time obtains: whether the other shoots back a glance at me, makes an answering gesture, or begins to think something to herself, we observe a diphasic temporal process in which my initial glance spins off a counterpart belonging to the same loop. The point is not that time itself loops back, but that within one and the same temporal event at least two distinguishable phases can be distinguished. Each phase amounts to a moment, which does not exist by itself alone but only in relation to another moment: my glance/your glance back; my glance/ your gesture; my glance/your thought. The two moments are continuous with one another in a closed internal circuit, and taken together they form a peculiar unit that evades time regarded as a pure present, whether this present is regarded as perched between a prior and a subsequent event (the B series) or as preceded by a distinct past and a future to come (the A series). They split any such simple present, com-pli-cating it by their redoubling action, showing it to fold back on itself in a movement of self-diremption.

We may go further yet: nonglancing responses can be not only gesticular or mental—these belong mostly to the interhuman world—but may include responses from nonhuman and even inanimate things at which we glance. I look at my dog, and he looks back obediently, expectantly. Even my cat registers my glance, if only in her disdainful glancing-away: a return glance need not be directed *at me* to be a fully sensitive response on the part of another animal, human or nonhuman. The boulder at which I glance does not move, much less glance back; but from it, at some level, I may anticipate a response that can be felt as such. This response does not assume any articulate, or even recognizable, form. Nonetheless it is elicited by my glance. It is as if my look leaves an imprint upon the mute object—an imprint that is altogether virtual, yet is the basis of a possible response. When Merleau-Ponty proposes that trees may see us as much as we see them, he is appealing to such a response on their part: "I *feel myself* looked at by the things."[27] What matters here is not the literal truth of this response—that is, whether trees really do look at me—but the expectation that my glance, wherever it is cast, will be returned in some way, at some level, if not in fact then as a sheer possibility. And if this is the case, we have to do once more with a two-beat temporality in which the second beat is virtual rather than

27. *The Visible and the Invisible*, p. 139; my italics. Variants on this include: "the things touch me as I touch them and touch myself" (p. 261) and "it is through the world first that I am seen or thought" (p. 274). It worth noting that by taking this late step in his thought—a step that he claims certain painters (e.g., Klee) have already taken—Merleau-Ponty is in fact drawing close to Bergson, for whom animation, visibility, etc. belong as much to the things at which we look as to ourselves. This emphasis goes contrary to Husserl's stress on the unidirectionality of intentionality, which sends its visual ray outward (i.e., being "consciousness *of* X") but does not receive it back. On this comparison, see Deleuze, *Cinema 1,* p. 60: "[for phenomenology] the intentionality of consciousness was the ray of an electric lamp. . . . For Bergson, it is completely the opposite. Things are luminous by themselves without anything illuminating them." Deleuze significantly omits Merleau-Ponty's affinity with Bergson on this very issue, including Merleau-Ponty's invocation of "rays of the world" (see *The Visible and the Invisible*, p. 218, pp. 240 ff., p. 265).

actual. The second phase is not given but anticipated, but precisely as such it constitutes a valid moment of a circuit or loop in which my glance returns—if only by projection. This is no more radical than claiming that every perception or thought spins off a virtual image of itself; the only difference is that now what is virtual includes the possible response of an inanimate being.

Both virtualities are "ideal" in that neither belongs to the stream of actual events measured by physical space or chronometric time; yet neither virtuality is of trivial significance: both belong to Becoming and to the Open—to "expanding virtualities in the deep circuits."[28] The small circuits of my immediate experience give onto the larger circuits of ceaseless becoming and absolute flux that subtend them, merging into an openness of time that is more virtual than actual. And even though these particular forms of the virtual pertain ultimately to these more capacious circuits, they can be brought back, through proper contraction, into the self-severing present thanks to a single glance that animates them. This glance, issuing from the whole of time, sparks moments that fire up the present by their dissevering power.

The temporality of the glance can be characterized as a leap that loops back. Just as we leap back into the pure past when we seek to recollect it (Bergson's metaphors are expressly saltatory in this context),[29] so the glance leaps out from our seeing eye. Such a leap constitutes the first phase of a loop that brings what we glance at— human or nonhuman—into our glancing orbit; in the second phase the glance returns in imagistic form or its equivalent. The leap out inaugurates the loop between the glancer and the glanced-at—a loop that is completed by the actual or virtual return of the glance. The one-way directedness of the outgoing glance—a directedness first posited by Brentano in his account of intentionality—is here replaced by a two-way circuit in which inflow (that is, the glance on return) is as important as outflow. This has crucial implications for the understanding of time: the perceptual or mental *Blick* under description in Husserl's *Ideas I* supports (even as it reflects) the hypothesis of a unidirectional time-line; whereas the to-the-self-returning glance exemplifies the looping-back of time that is implicit in the "all-at-once" structure of absolute flux, that deep stratum of time posited by Husserl beneath the succession of events in time but never fully legitimated by his own account of time-consciousness.[30] The out-

28. Deleuze, *Cinema 2*, p. 81.
29. Deleuze remarks that in performing a recollection of the past "we place ourselves *at once* (*d'emblée*) in the past; we leap into the past as into a proper element" (*Bergsonism*, p. 56; his italics, with specific reference to Bergson's emphatic use of *d'emblée* in chaps. 2 and 3 of *Matière et Mémoire*).
30. On the structure of the "all-at-once" (*Zugleich*) and the "before-all-at-once" (*Vor-zugleich*), see section 38 of Husserl, *Zur Phänomenologie des inneren Zeitbewusstseins*. The time line appears as the horizontal line in Husserl's celebrated diagram of time in sections 10 and 43 of the same text. On the ray of the ego, see Edmund Husserl, *Ideas Pertaining to a Pure Phenomenology and to a Phenomenological Philosophy, First Book*, tr. F. Kersten (The Hague: Nijhoff, 1982), sections 35, 37, 67 (hereafter referred to as *Ideas I*), and my discussion in chap. 9.

going glance and its incoming return also occur all at once, even if the "at once" has two beats or phases that are simultaneous with each other, or so closely convergent as not to be separable in exact chronometric units. My glance returns to me—not by delay or deferral but *right away:* so quickly that it cannot be situated in any determinately sequential temporal series.

The paradox is that the glance and its return, though skimming time's surface in their celerity, rest upon a deeper temporal base, which I have been characterizing as the "whole" of time. Bergson argues that each passing state "is borne by the fluid mass of our whole psychical existence."[31] So too is the glance, dancing as it does like a water bug on the surface of the deep. The least glance we cast, occurring in a thrice, is supported by an ongoing flux of time on which it resides even as it plays itself out in its game of return. The very first concrete example cited in *Creative Evolution* is that of "the visual perception of a motionless external object." Bergson remarks that the object may well remain the same, but "the vision I now have of it differs from that which I have just had, even if only because the one is [ever so slightly] older than the other."[32] This could well be a case of a glance, given its quickly changing character. But the brevity of its action belies its durational depth, for "it is with our entire past . . . that we desire, will, and act."[33] In other words, the return loop of the glance includes much more than its immediate circuit; it also includes by implication the entire pyramid of the glancer's past, a whole heritage of previous perceptions, thoughts, desires, and intentions.

In Bergson's own model from *Matter and Memory* the recollected past, virtual but massive, forms a cone of ever-increasing diameter. Yet, enormous as it becomes in an individual's life, it manages to insinuate itself into every discrete present, represented by the tip of the cone as it touches the plane of ongoing experience.[34] The same pyramidal structure overhangs every human action, but the glance is paradigmatic in embodying in a radically condensed format the paradox to which all experience of duration is subject: namely, that a maximum of accumulated content is expressed in the most economic means of realization. Thanks to its quick action, the glance is emblematic of this quite general condition of all durational temporality. Hobbes said famously that "thought is quick,"[35] but if so the glance is a close competitor. The quickness is not an idle feature but basic to the glance's deconstructive capacity: its ability to split and sever established temporal continuities and to dis-assemble its abiding structures. The glance punctuates—at once marks and punctures—the very durational whole which it reflects and on which it is nevertheless dependent.

31. Bergson, *Creative Evolution*, p. 3.
32. Ibid., p. 2.
33. Ibid., p. 5.
34. For this model, see *Matter and Memory*, tr. N. M. Paul and W. S. Palmer (New York: Zone Books, 1988), p. 162. When I am compelled to modify this translation, I shall refer to the French edition of this work as cited above in n. 17.
35. Thomas Hobbes, *Leviathan*, chapter 3.

The glance is of even greater significance in regard to another paradox of duration—to wit, that, despite its continual and instantaneous conversion into the elapsed past, duration is the very scene of *novelty*, the exact place of becoming ever-new. Viewed one way, duration is the ineluctable amassment of the same (for, as fully and forever past, it stays ever the same in what Merleau-Ponty would call an "existential eternity"[36]); but as a qualitative multiplicity that is ever-growing, it is always different, always in touch with the new, always a new whole, always part of a changing Open. If it is true that "we are supported by this [massive] past," it is also true that "we lean over [the] future."[37] We do not just edge into the future but actively embrace it, we go out to meet it, anticipating it by our projections; not because it already exists (as "lean over" and "embrace" and "meet" might imply, taken literally) but because our very duration is able to extend itself—to grow—in keeping with whatever is happening in it. "We are creating ourselves continually,"[38] says Bergson in *Creative Evolution*, and by this he means that our duration distends to contain the most unexpected events.

Being durational is being capable of the most radical *becoming;* here any rigid distinction between Being and Becoming dissolves. It dissolves insofar as we are capable of the kind of action that effects basic changes in what is now going on while nevertheless reflecting in some degree all that we have been. "Duration means invention," affirms Bergson, "the continual elaboration of the absolutely new"[39]—where the absolutely new signifies the strictly *unforeseeable*, "that which has never [before] been perceived, and which is at the same time simple . . . an original moment of a no less original history."[40] No one, he insists, is able to foresee how things will turn out or what their organization will be.[41] For this organization, albeit simple in its overall structure, is unique in the form it will take in a given circumstance—a form that fully emerges only in the course of the becoming of the new event itself.

Precisely in this context, glancing takes on a special significance. Beyond its action in the present it bears on what is new—that is, on the future. Indeed, it is just because the future is so unforeseeable that the glance is so very valuable. It looks out in advance of what is now happening toward what might happen; it enters the horizon of the possible before an event arises as actual and/or virtual in the present—and then becomes virtual altogether as belonging to the expired past. In this proactive capacity, it is the sentinel of the sentient being; the outpost

---

36. Merleau-Ponty relates the existential eternity of the body to the rays of the world: "Describe the world of the 'rays of the world' beyond every serial-eternitarian or ideal alternative—Posit the existential eternity—the eternal body" (*The Visible and the Invisible*, p. 265).

37. Bergson, *L'énergie spirituelle*, p. 6: "sur ce passé nous sommes appuyés, sur cet avenir nous sommes penchés."

38. Bergson, *Creative Evolution* (New York: Dover, 1998), p. 7.

39. Ibid., p. 11.

40. Ibid., p. 6.

41. No one can "foresee the simple indivisible form which gives to . . . purely abstract elements [i.e., particular causal influences] their concrete organization" (ibid.).

of the organism in its effort, its need and desire, to come to terms with the *imprévisible* before it has become literally *visible*. As in other contexts, it is here a vanguard act, situated at the forward edge of the present, attempting to discern in advance what might happen. Indeed, the glance is a primary way in which we are watchful of the incipient future, warily aware of its beginning to occur in some determinate form: its becoming to come, its coming to become. Other acts contribute as well to this circumstance (for example, touching, hearing), but the glance has a genius for sensing what is about to occur. It is like an antenna designed to feel out the form of futurity, not wholly unlike Freud's idea of the sense organs as "feelers" that probe the external world in a protentional way.[42]

Not only does the glance go out toward a possible future, it also *expects* it to happen in a certain way and in this spirit it may even *escort* it into the present. Beyond its active reaching out, the glance has its own receptivity to what is beginning to happen, attending to it as it arises: "l'attention est une attente," says Bergson.[43] We rediscover here the attentiveness of the glance on which we shall focus in chapter 9—an attentiveness that helps to usher the oncoming future into the present. The imminently happening event is anticipated, and once it starts to occur it is accepted, carried, and finally incorporated into the durational present, being welcomed there as at once actual and virtual and no longer as possible alone.[44]

---

42. "The sense organs . . . consist essentially of apparatuses for the reception of certain specific effects of stimulation [as well as] protection against excessive amounts of stimulation. . . . They may be compared with feelers which are all the time making tentative advances towards the external world and then drawing back from it" (S. Freud, *Beyond the Pleasure Principle*, vol. 18 of *The Standard Edition of the Complete Psychological Works of Sigmund Freud* [London: Hogarth Press, 1955], p. 28). I borrow the word "protentional" from Husserl, who uses it to designate the forward fringe of any act of consciousness. See *Zur Phänomenologie des inneren Zeitbewusstseins*, sections 24–26.

43. "Attention is an awaiting" (*L'énergie spirituelle*, p. 5). Husserl, Bergson's exact contemporary, arrived at a strikingly similar conclusion. In Husserl's own terms: there is an "advance consciousness" (*Vorbewusstsein*) that amounts to a protention within retention: a "self-fulfilling" with the "self-emptying" of sinking back. Otherwise put, there is future-directedness—i.e., "anticipation," as I call it here—as a basic "tendency of consciousness (*Tendenzbewusstsein*)." For this line of thought, see E. Husserl, *Die Bernauer Manuskripte über das Zeitbewusstein (1917–1918)* (The Hague: Nijhoff, 2001), Husserliana XXXIII, pp. 2 ff. I owe the translation of these terms to Parviz Mohassel, who first brought them to my attention.

44. It is actual as occurring in the present, virtual as casting itself into an image upon this very occurrence. I should also make it clear that the future does not *require* such ushering in by the glance as I here discuss. Rather, the glance is an especially effective escort for the future, which will of course take its own course by and large: "by and large" for it is also true that as having been anticipated the future will itself be altered somewhat in its eventual happening: it will be less unknown, though not necessarily less surprising (since we cannot anticipate, even in the most acute glance, its precise form of appearance). Moreover, the glance does not always welcome the oncoming event, which it may *resist*, e.g., by glancing away and choosing to ignore its very becoming-present. But such aversive action, though always possible in principle, is defensive in its motivation and thus still recognizes, albeit sub rosa, the oncoming reality

In the circumstance I have just described we witness once more the folding-back structure that has become a leitmotif of this chapter. The watchful vanguard glance goes out from the eyes to discern what might possibly happen, and in its vigilance the same glance aids the anticipated event to settle into the durational whole by folding back into it. Here too there is a two-beat rhythm of going out and returning—this time realized as an entering into the not yet having happened and as a returning of (and with) it into what is becoming the present and will become the past. As before, we experience a double moment, a diphasic occurrence, in which the two moments or phases are inseparable from each other in fact even as they are distinguishable in description.

This redoubling, here consisting of anticipating and awaiting the future, eludes the A and B series as surely as does the redoubling that occurs when the present itself, now *become,* has consolidated into a coherent unit of experience.[45] As we have seen, no sooner has that same present happened than it splits itself into the actuality of its occurrence and the virtuality of an image of itself. The same splitting continues in the avatars of glancing and its return that we have examined in various contexts. In the case before us, the anticipatory glance goes out to meet a future that is already beginning to happen and that, for this reason, is also awaited—the two phases coinciding in the event of becoming itself. This becoming is the happening of the new to which the glance has directed itself even as it ushers it into our cognizance. In this respect, it may not be "absolutely new" as Bergson claimed; but it is new enough to surprise us and even, on occasion, to be the subject of wonder.

V

Despite Bergson's own precautions against misunderstanding duration as a mere "block" of time, he nevertheless conceives of it as a special kind of whole. This wholeness, even if always incorporating the new, is in tension with an equal emphasis on duration's sheer qualitative heterogeneity: a self-othering that refuses to be totalized. As a whole, duration is all-encompassing and seamless, yet as heterogeneous it cannot be self-contained. Given this internal tension, there

---

of the event if it is indeed oncoming. Just as the glance is not the only way of escorting the future into the present, so not every glance does so; but in a significant number of cases, it does just this—with remarkable finesse.

45. The A series is eluded insofar as the future here in question is not the future as such but its oncoming edge only; it is not the full-fledged future of the unidirectional progression past/present/future. The B series is eluded to the extent that we do not have to do with events that arrange themselves in any simple sequence of before vs. after; as previously, we are dealing with phases of events rather than events themselves: the anticipation and the awaiting are not free-standing and complete mental acts but constituent features of glancing on its forward edge. A given act of glancing is indeed an event, but the features (i.e., the two phases) of which it is composed are not eventmental in status: hence they cannot be members of any B series.

is "leakage"(*échappement*) in the system.[46] Duration is perforated from within as it were, and it is my contention that the glance contributes centrally to this perforation of the durational matrix.[47]

The glance lacerates duration. Not only does it strike, as signified in "a glancing blow," but it also *cuts* and *tears* what persists. This appears most conspicuously in social scenes, where a demeaning or insulting glance can upset a carefully constructed equilibrium of forces. Whenever we "size up" a group of people as beneath our dignity and glance demeaningly toward them (or, just as tellingly, away from them), or whenever we engage in invidious judgments based on mere glances, we are cutting up the social fabric, tearing it by our very look, and in this way contesting the Bergsonian axiom that "there is [nothing but] a continuity which unfolds."[48] A glance can be disruptive in the perceptual domain as well—for example, when from boredom or indifference it skips over what is presented to it on a given surface, or conversely when we try to look aggressively *through* an object, forcing our way into an interior we can glimpse at best only translucently, for example, when we look angrily at the hood of a car that won't run, imagining that we can somehow see our way into its damaged engine. In contrast with Husserl's reassurance that "the look abides,"[49] the glance is restless, and it can question and take apart that which the social and perceptual worlds offer to us on their self-confident sleeves.

If the work of the glance is constructive in welcoming the future into the present in the manner I described in the last section as well as in numerous interpersonal circumstances (some of which we shall examine in chapter 10), it can be destructive in other regards. Such destructiveness is not to be confused with the separation-work of the intellect that neatly divides space and time into punctiform points and instants—that way lies the false homogeneity for whose inaugural deconstruction Bergson is justly celebrated.[50] Instead, the

46. This is Merleau-Ponty's term at *The Visible and the Invisible*, p. 265; which refers the reader to the *Phenomenology of Perception*, p. 189, where Merleau-Ponty refers to "forms of behavior [that] deviate from their pre-ordained direction, through a sort of *leakage* and a genius for ambiguity that might serve to define man" (his italics).

47. Other perforating forces are more particular and operate in specific contexts: e.g., priestly *ressentiment* (on Nietzsche's conception) as it poisons religious hegemonies, certain nomadic tendencies (as considered by Deleuze) that upset settled styles of living, avant-garde works of art that challenge the established order, disruptive social movements, etc. Moreover, other forms of looking besides glancing have their own perforative capacity, e.g., staring at something in such a way that we "bore a hole" in it. But the very inconspicuousness of the glance, the fact that it is so much a part of our everyday behavior, renders it all the more effective in its performative power and allows it to be active in many more contexts than is staring.

48. Bergson, *Creative Evolution*, p. 4.

49. *Ideas I*, section 122. Derrida discusses this sentence at *Speech and Phenomena*, tr. D. Allison (Evanston, Ill.: Northwestern University Press, 1973), p. 104: "Contrary to the assurance that Husserl gives us a little further on, 'the look' cannot 'abide.'"

50. The homogenization of time is first discussed by Bergson in his *Time and Free Will*, tr. F. L. Podgson (New York Dover, 2001), esp. chap. 2.

glance tears open the very cloth of duration to which it otherwise contributes so much; it detects miniscule fault-lines in the surfaces of things and places and people: weaknesses, incapacities, limits, signs of bad faith. Like David before Goliath, the glance is a slingshot that penetrates the armamentarium of continuous duration and planiform space, perforating by its sharp look "the universe [that] appears to us to form a single whole."[51] It belongs to the deep duration that subtends and supports it; yet it turns back upon this same temporal matrix and finds faults within it.

The glance is an embracing experience indeed, but it is also an insidious and disruptive force. From acts of glancing, we take in and build up whole worlds; but at other times and by other glances, we tear them down again.

VI

From the apparent innocence and seeming insouciance of the glance, we have traveled to a more considered view of its secret force, its concealed power, and its sometimes destructive edge. I have been playing off the lightness of its being, its distracting and distracted actions, its fitfulness, against the heaviness and solidity of durational becoming. I have just argued that its stealthy weapon, a mere outgoing look, accounts for its very ability to bring down giants, including such otherwise opposed philosophical giants as thick durational time and thin linear temporality, not to mention the importation of the "auxiliary space" that is responsible for the latter.[52] Have I overstated my case? Let us reconsider the matter for a final time.

I am agreeing with Bergson that the larger whole of time is indeed something like *durée réelle.* The issue becomes that of situating the punctuating power of the glance in relation to such "real duration." Given its massive presence, it would seem that this power, effective as it may be in perceptual and social situations, is in the end only a ripple on its surface.[53] This view is reinforced when we encounter Bergson's own admission that it is easy to suppose that there is "one Duration of the universe" and thus to espouse "the hypothesis of one material and universal Time."[54] Even if in the end he rejects the idea that there

51. *Durée et simultanéité,* p. 56.

52. On the importation of auxiliary space, see Bergson, *Time and Free Will,* chap. 2.

53. "A man is so much the more a 'man of action' as he can embrace in a glance a greater number of events: he who perceives successive events one by one will allow himself to be led by them; he who grasps them as a whole will dominate them"(Bergson, *Creative Evolution,* pp. 301–302). Just before, Bergson had said that "from our first glance at the world, before we even made out *bodies* in it, we distinguish *qualities*" (p. 300; his italics). The man of action is someone who tries to stabilize the inherently unstable qualities of matter by his imperious glance. Thus Bergson adds this sentence immediately after that concerning the man of action: "In short, the qualities of matter are so many stable views that we take of its instability" (p. 302).

54. For the assertion of one duration of the universe, see *Durée et simultanéité,* p. 56 (I have underlined the word "one"); and for the hypothesis of one universal Time, see ibid., p. 58.

is a single universal duration—a Duration of durations in effect—he still insists that the durational whole of each individual is indivisible and, in his own term, "absolute."[55] Hence the Bergsonian imperative: "It's no use trying to *approach* duration: *we must install ourselves within it straight away.*"[56] Would not Bergson say the same of the glance, namely, that we should install it within duration right away or, more exactly, recognize that it is always already so installed? Indeed, does not my own two-beat model of the glance, valorizing as it does the glance's influx as much as its outflow, mimic the holistic (if not monolithic) durational schema of Bergsonian metaphysics and thus prove its subordination to this schema?

It is one thing to admit that the most ordinary glance arises from and returns us to duration: this much is true of any action we undertake. But it is something else to claim that the return movement of the glance is a return to the Same, a nostalgic retreat, an Odyssean homecoming. This latter model is one of subordination and fails to capture the reverse movement of the glance, which even if originating in deep duration is not subordinate to it. On the contrary: the glance I send out returns to me bearing on its slender shoulder the world I witness by its means. This world in return—the world I get back—is able to alter the subject who first glances at it, enlarging and extending the glancer in ways that are as radically new and unforeseeable as the course of duration itself. In particular, the newness of the world taken in—and it is always new to some degree, in its form as in its matter[57]—can change the subject who first sends the glance into that world. The subtlety of the change, the fact that it is often imperceptible, makes it no less momentous in and for the ongoing history of this subject. A single glance can launch a thousand ships, inspire a myriad projects in the world at large; but every glance, upon its return, is capable of renewing (and sometimes transforming) the subject who sent it forth.

The glance can be considered as a leading instance of the "ritornello," that is, the return phrase or refrain that despite its brevity or otherwise modest aspects is essential to the operation of the overall circuit of the song or song cycle to which it belongs. The term has application beyond its origin in musical form. Deleuze and Guattari's examples of extended ritornellos include that of a "territory" that is indispensable to the larger circuit of the Earth, or (following Nietzsche) the small recurrence that proves decisive to Eternal Recurrence.[58] Just as

---

55. For the claim as to duration as "the Absolute," see Bergson, *Creative Evolution*, p. 298: "then the Absolute is revealed very near us and, in a certain measure, in us. It is of psychological and not of mathematical nor logical essence. It lives with us. Like us, but in certain aspects infinitely more concentrated and more gathered up in itself, it *endures*" (his italics).

56. Bergson, *Creative Evolution*, p. 299; my italics.

57. Even form, previously held sacrosanct by philosophers as the preserve of nonchange, is subject to change: "what is real is the continual change of form: form is only a snapshot view of a transition" (ibid., p. 302; partly in italics).

58. "[In *A Thousand Plateaus*] we tried to make the ritornello one of our main concepts, relating it to territory and the Earth, the little and the great ritornello" (Deleuze, interview

the refrain in classical harmonics reinstates a basic melodic line, so the glance returns to reaffirm the very duration that it challenges in its diphasic temporality and especially its anticipatory projection of the future.[59] The ritornello movement is one of the most effective ways in which movement of any kind—evolutionary as well as musical, cosmic as well as terrestrial—can gather force by folding back on itself, coiling over onto its own back, starting again from renewed power. All of this stands in contrast with movement that merely goes on and on, forward or backward: a matter of *phora* or transfer of motion, in contrast with *kinesis* or qualitative change.

In its own ritornello movement, the glance contributes kinetically to the rich qualitative multiplicity of duration. It illustrates with exemplary clarity the truth of Bergson's durational imperative: "In order to advance with a moving reality, *you must replace yourself within it.*"[60] The action of replacement—or *reimplacement* as I prefer to call it—is accomplished more effectively by the glance than by those more ponderous human actions such as scientific scrutiny, abstract contemplation, concentrated heeding, and the like, all of which are concerned with the attainment or discernment of abiding or determinate presence.

Otherwise put: the diminutive circuit of the glance, in its tacit and often taciturn ritornello movement, reimplaces the subject within increasingly deeper circuits of duration, within its widening gyres—ramifying into the world, the Open, the Whole. But it does not make a straightforward contribution to the larger scene of duration, the "world-whole" as Kant would call it. Even if (as a single sweeping glance) it may survey the entirety of a given perceptual field, its penetrative particularity and its singular return action act to detotalize whatever it searches out. And within the subject it undoes the inwardly embraced whole of duration that inspires Bergson to call each such Whole an "Absolute." As part of this detotalizing action, it punctures the durational subject from within just as it perforates the enduring world from without: a case of double leakage, an act of double deconstruction.

Similarly, the time of the glance, the two-sided prismatic moment in which it lives so briefly, undercuts any presumptive totality of time. There is always just enough time for the glance, and the time it takes, its moment of becoming, is situated between the infinitesimal instant and the infinity of duration. In its intermediacy (and in spite of its immediacy), the time of the glance has its own speed and spread, enabling the double beat of its operation, going out into the

---

with R. Bellour and F. Ewald in September 1988; incorporated in Deleuze, *Negotiations: 1972–1990,* tr. M. Joughin [New York: Columbia University Press, 1995], p. 137; cf. the translator's footnote 1 at ibid., p. 200). For the original discussion, see Gilles Deleuze and Félix Guattari, *A Thousand Plateaus,* tr. B. Massumi (Minneapolis: University of Minnesota Press, 1987), pp. 299–302, 310–350.

59. By "anticipatory projection"—a term with Heideggerian overtones—I mean the anticipatory and awaiting aspects of the glance as it portends the future. See Heidegger, *Being and Time,* section 67.

60. Bergson, *Creative Evolution,* p. 308. My italics.

world and returning to the subject who emits it, thereby sinking back into the durational flux that is the ultimate provenance of each subject in time.

Despite the regularity of its diphasic movement—including its continual refrain of return—the glance is never fully integrated into the temporal world of its own projective subject. Its recoil brings with it foreign times as well as places, those of others whom it has glimpsed, pieces of shrapnel from their lives that cannot be fully assimilated to one's own life.[61] For this reason, the glance is a disquieting force both in its outward course—where it first encounters the human and extrahuman other as alien—and in its return within, where the other can be incorporated in its very alienation from what belongs properly to the self. At stake here is not the return to the Same but the constitution of the Different.

But this is only to say: the constitution of ever-new becomings. It is the thesis of differentiated duration, combined with the unforeseeability of the future, that permits Bergson to reject the notion of a single Becoming and to espouse the idea of "infinitely varied" becomings, each with its own time and duration, each traveling its own course, each finding its own future, each always new to some extent. In the generation of multiple becomings, the glance has a crucial role to play: it gives shape to any particular becoming by being the primary agent of its acute ongoing engagement with the circumambient world, and by carrying the edges and surfaces of that world back into the attentive subject. When Bergson writes that "an infinite multiplicity of becomings variously colored, so to speak, passes before our eyes,"[62] he could well have been speaking of the way our glancings deliver to us a diversely populated world of variegated beings in space as well as inducing our own continually changing becomings in time.

The glance does all this thanks to its peculiarly indirect insertion into the social and perceptual worlds, its laterality, its location on the agitated edge of the restless subject. Instead of proceeding by cinematographic means—"taking snapshots of passing reality"[63]—it acts kaleidoscopically, by opening us to a qualitative disparity that it manages to arrange into more or less coherent patterns. What Bergson says of the kaleidoscopic basis of perception can be said of the glance that is its traveling body, its proxy in the scene of otherness:

> There is, between our body and other bodies, an arrangement like that of the pieces of glass that compose a kaleidoscopic picture. Our activity goes from an arrangement to a re-arrangement, each time no doubt giving the kaleidoscope a

61. Bergson writes in a passage we have considered before: "As the shrapnel, bursting before it falls to the ground, covers the explosive zone with an indivisible danger, so the arrow which goes from A to B displays with a single stroke, although over a certain extent of duration, its indivisible mobility" (ibid., p. 309).

62. Ibid., p. 305.

63. Ibid., p. 306: "We take snapshots, as it were, of the passing reality, and, as these are characteristic of the reality, we have only to string them on a becoming, abstract, uniform and invisible, situated at the back of the apparatus of knowledge, in order to imitate what there is that is characteristic in this becoming itself."

new shake, but not interesting itself in the shake, and seeing only the new picture. . . . *The cinemato-graphical character of our knowledge of things is due to the
kaleido-scopic character of our adaptation to them.*[64]

With its cutting edge composed of shards of perspective, the glance, like the
kaleidoscope, gathers the materials from which cinematographic images are
fashioned in symmetry and grace. These images, as "immobile sections," are
ultimately dependent on the "mobile sections" that are the movements of the
glance itself.[65] They are the virtual counterparts, the instantaneous offshoots, of
the animated glance. As William James remarked in commenting on Bergson,
such movements "come in drops, waves, or pulses," with the result that, as
James adds, "time itself comes in drops."[66]

   This should come as no surprise by now if it is indeed true that (as we read in
Creative Evolution) "action is discontinuous, like every pulsation of life; discontinuous, therefore, is knowledge [as well]."[67] Nor should it be surprising to
realize that this double discontinuity of action and knowledge alike is in turn
made possible by the discontinuity of the glance, at once the emblem and the
source of the qualitative multiplicity of duration and the heterogeneous newness of each becoming.[68]

   64. Ibid., p. 306; his italics.
   65. As specified in n. 7 above, the terms "mobile section" and "immobile section" of time are
those of Deleuze expanding upon Bergson: see Deleuze's *Cinema 2*, p. 98.
   66. William James, "Bergson and His Critique of Intellectualism," in *A Pluralistic Universe*
(New York: Longmans, Green, 1909), pp. 238 and 232, respectively. The previous statement
reads in full: "Sensibly, motion comes in drops, waves, or pulses; either some actual amount of
it, or none, being apprehended." Concerning the dropful nature of time, James adds: "the
times directly *felt* in the experiences of living subjects have originally no common measure"
(ibid., p. 232; his italics).
   67. Bergson, *Creative Evolution*, p. 307.
   68. An earlier version of this chapter appeared in an essay with the same title in Elizabeth
Grosz, ed., *Becomings* (Ithaca, N.Y.: Cornell University Press, 1999), pp. 79–97.

9

ATTENDING AND GLANCING

All genuine activity is carried out in the scope of attentiveness.

—Edmund Husserl, *Experience and Judgment*

. . . that still "empty" but already determinate intention which *is* attention itself.

—Maurice Merleau-Ponty,
Phenomenology of Perception

The mass of our thinking vanishes for ever, beyond hope of recovery, and psychology only gathers up a few of the crumbs that fall from the feast.

—William James, *Principles of Psychology*

I

Every time we glance we are attending to something—whatever this may be: a physical object or a person, a building or a landscape, an image or a thought. The scope of attention is vast; it covers most of what we do, so much so that inattention is the exception rather than the rule. Indeed, so extensive is the scope of attending that William James can say outright that "my experience is what I agree to attend to."[1] Every experience is attentional to some degree; if it were not, it would lack the minimal focus that makes it what John Dewey calls "*an* experience."[2]

Glancing is one of the major ways in which attending happens. To claim this is to fly in the face of the view that glancing—mere glancing—is a superficial incursion into the visual world, an isolated act. "A mere glance," we say, implying either that we did not focus on anything long enough to be able to claim that we had attended to it—or else that what we glanced at was not worthy of being

---

1. William James, *Principles of Psychology* (New York: Holt, 1890), vol. 1, p. 402; his italics.
2. John Dewey, *Art as Experience* (New York: Capricorn, 1932), chap. 3, "Having an Experience"; my italics.

attended to in the first place. Samuel Beckett sums up this dismissive view in which glancing and attending would seem to exclude each other: "One glimpse and vanished,"[3] he writes in a short prose piece entitled *Imagination Dead Imagine*. If what we capture in a glance is so quickly vanishing, how can we *attend* to it? Why should we bother? Do not attending and glancing move in very different directions, each exhibiting a very different interest: in the one case, gaining (only to release) something barely apperceived, in the other holding onto something we plan to scrutinize further?

These are not the only questions we should ask in the circumstance. May we not attend to what we glance at precisely in order to get a better grasp of what would otherwise pass us by? In this case, attending comes to the aid of the glance, supplementing its shortcomings. In other cases, the glance lights up a whole scene of future attendings by giving us a first sense of what that scene is like, guiding us into it more fully. This suggests that glancing and attending, far from being opposites, can help each other out in significant ways. More generally, what is fickle and flippant in the glance, its mercurial character, seems compensated for in the seriousness of attending; by the same token, the studied pace of attending appears to be alleviated by the glance.

But to leave the matter thus is to underestimate the scope of the acts in question. Not only is each act more complex than this quick sketch allows, but the claim of compensatory action presumes that they remain different in kind even as they complement each other. But what if glancing is itself one form of attending, even a central such form? And what if attending could not happen except by some form of glancing? We shall see that, at the very least, the two acts overlap significantly in conjoint activities of glancing in attending and of attending by glancing. More than formal complementarity is here at stake.

The model of close collaboration I shall pursue in this chapter suggests that glancing is not a superficial action of trivial import compared to the deep deliverances of attention. Nor is it the case that attending is always slow and deliberate; on the contrary, it is often shot through with momentary glances. It gains greatly from the seemingly wayward look; it is thickened, not diminished, by the intervention of glancing. But this is only because glancing itself is already much thicker, more insightful and telling, than we assume when we think of it as a form of distraction only. Distraction it may be in some significant sense; but if so, it is a distraction that adds to our knowledge of the world and does not merely detract from it.

My claim will be that attending and glancing belong together, enhance each other, and are finally conterminous acts. The glance contributes centrally to attention, being its avant-garde as it were, and is itself a form of attending. The two acts are as thick as thieves; rather than stealing from one another, however, each contributes to the other's welfare.

3. Samuel Beckett, *Imagination Dead Imagine* (London: Calder and Boyars, 1965), p. 7.

II

A first approach to the relationship between attending and glancing is provided by the *saccade*. A saccade is the leap (*saccadus* means "leap" or "jump") that our eyes take all the time, in virtually every circumstance of vision. This happens for the most part without any explicit awareness on our part. In focusing on a single object or set of objects, becoming absorbed in them, we are not conscious of the extraordinary saccadic activity our eyes are undertaking throughout. But the fact is that each eye—usually in close concert with the other—is moving rapidly, dashing from one position to another every few milliseconds. (The only moment of immobility, that of visual "fixation," normally lasts for 150 to 350 milliseconds.) Saccades are defined as "fast eye movements that are normally used to drive the eyes from one point of fixation to another as quickly as possible."[4] Not only are saccadic motions miniscule, but each of us has spent a lifetime effecting such actions: for the most part, they are "preprogrammed."[5] No wonder we do not take note of them as such. Yet they constitute an entire netherworld of vision, whose work is comparable to that described in *Faust:* "unseen the threads are knit together, and an infinite combination grows."[6] As such, saccades support the work of attention, without being ingredient in every act of attending. They also subtend actions of glancing, and while it is tempting to consider saccades as miniature glances, the truth is that they make glances possible without being themselves genuine glances. Both are eye movements, however, albeit effected at different levels of realization.

4. C. Cabiato, M. Pastomerio, R. Schmid, and T. D. Zambarbieri, "Computer Analysis of Saccadic Eye Movements," in *Eye Movements and Psychological Functions: International Views,* ed. R. Groner, C. Menz, D. F. Fisher, and R. A. Monty (Hillsdale, N.J.: Erlbaum, 1983), p. 19. Saccades can be described by parameters of amplitude, duration, and peak velocity, as well as by a time lag between stimulus presentation and the beginning of eye movements.

5. Saccades, according to one researcher, are "preprogrammed movements and the information 'where' the eyes should move next must be delivered at the oculomotor centers before the movement starts" (Burkhart Fischer, "Saccadic Reaction Time: Implications for Reading, Dyslexia, and Visual Cognition," in *Eye Movements and Visual Cognition: Sense Perception and Reading,* ed. Keith Rayner [New York: Springer-Verlag, 1992], p. 31). Psychologists have been tracking saccades for decades, ever since they became a topic of concerted research in the 1960s. They were first detected by an early American psychologist, R. Dodge, who wrote of them in two classical papers, "Visual Perception during Eye Movement," *Psychological Review* 7 (1900): 454–465, and "The Illusion of Clear Vision during Eye Movement," *Psychological Bulletin* 2 (1905): 193–199. Dodge was building on the extensive research on attention that was a focus of nineteenth-century experimental psychology and that, starting with the pioneering contributions of Gustav Fechner and Wilhelm Wundt in the period between 1850 and 1870, reached an early culmination in James's *Principles of Psychology* (first published in 1890). For an engaging account of this research that locates it in its larger cultural setting—which I have had to ignore in this chapter—see Jonathan Crary, *Suspensions of Perception: Attention, Spectacle, and Modern Culture* (Cambridge, Mass.: MIT University Press, 1999), esp. chap. 1, "Modernity and the Problem of Attention."

6. J. W. v. Goethe, *Faust: A Tragedy,* Part I, scene 4, tr. Bayard Taylor (Boston: Houghton Mifflin, 1906), p. 88.

Let us first ask: why are saccades such pervasive and universal phenomena (they occur in all able-visioned humans and higher primates)? Physiologically considered, the reason is straightforward: the area of the eye capable of high-resolution vision is restricted to the rim of the fovea (that is, the small depression in the retina); vision outside this specialized place—that is, in the "parafoveal" and peripheral regions—is imperfect and cannot achieve resolution on its own: hence the highly specialized fovea must continually shift its focus into these extra-foveal areas, especially within the central twenty degrees of the visual field. Thus if the target object is located anywhere within this central region, we can focus on it by saccadic movements alone; anything beyond this requires us to move our entire head and/or body as well as our eyes, thereby calling upon an inherent spatial framework that helps to orient us in the visual field overall.[7] The saccade is thus designed to overcome an organic restriction of our vision: without it, we would be purblind beings indeed; with it, we can range across this field and take in virtually anything that crosses our direct visual path.

Saccades are highly sensitive to visual stimuli—doubtless for evolutionary reasons[8]—and we can imagine how useful they must have been for early hominids living on the savannah: when especially alert eye movements were required to track the movements of predators. These movements must have become habitual over time. But to be habitual is still to allow for significant variation in particular cases: there is a critical moment just before a given saccade is wholly under way when its direction and speed can be altered significantly. Proof of this comes from an experiment in which the target object eliciting the saccade was made to change position suddenly 100 milliseconds after the detection of a first position: the resulting saccade visibly changed course to take account of the new position. This means that an "internal feedback" (that is, in which the two positions were compared) led to an alteration in the saccadic trajectory.[9] Per-

7. There is a local debate as to whether this framework obtains for the head vs. the eyes, or for both together: concerning this debate, see John M. Findlay, "Programming of Stimulus-Elicited Saccadic Eye Movements," in Rayner, *Eye Movements and Visual Cognition*, pp. 19 ff. On the spatial framework model itself, see Nancy Franklin and Barbara Tversky, "Searching Imagined Environments," *Journal of Experimental Psychology: General* 119 (1990): 63–77.

8. In situations of danger, it is imperative to be able to have instantaneous access to predators who suddenly appear at the periphery of the visual field (a typical saccade emerges after only 100 to 150 milliseconds of "reaction time" or "latency"). (For a study of reaction times—especially the differences between the "express saccades" that arise in about 100 milliseconds and the "fast regular saccades" that occur at about 150 milliseconds, see Fisher, "Saccadic Reaction Time," esp. pp. 31–41.) Thus, even if basic saccadic movements are in some sense preprogrammed, this does not mean they are "hard-wired." They evolved as adaptive responses to environmental dangers. Only later did they become regular in their course; yet this does not mean that they became altogether fixed. Any view that saccades are "ballistic" (i.e., cannot vary their course after onset) or that they are strictly "stereotyped" has been shown to be mistaken. "It is now clear," says John M. Findlay, "that saccades are neither completely ballistic nor totally stereotyped" ("Programming of Stimulus-Elicited Saccadic Eye Movements," p. 9).

9. Such a trajectory is mapped in the quasi-elliptical course of the eye movements in the dia-

haps we can imagine that the two positions here being continuously tracked are those of a crouching puma who is altering his posture ever so slightly as he prepares himself for a possible spring at the human being who has crossed his path in the savannah. It would be crucial to survival in this circumstance to be able to follow the puma's change of position closely and to do so with a minimal movement of one's body. The saccade provides this movement effortlessly and involuntarily.

This is not to say that saccades are merely automatic reactions. They are subject to "cognitive influences," for example, pertinent knowledge and established expectations. It can be demonstrated that if a given target is expected to appear in the right portion of the visual field, the subject's saccades will swing

---

grams just below as the eye at + follows the object as it changes from an initial position at the left to a position at the right (i.e., as marked by the two small squares), with the dots of the path indicating successive eye positions as tested every 10 milliseconds:

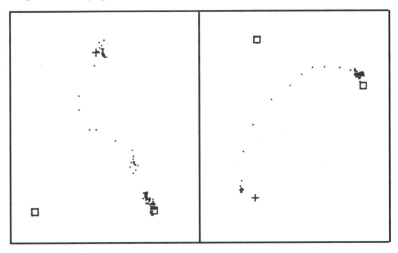

Two examples of saccadic trajectories showing pronounced curvature. The saccades were recorded in the double-step paradigm. The cross shows the initial fixation point and the two squares the successive positions of the target. The small dots represent successive visual axis positions, sampled every 10 ms. The saccades are initially directed at the first target position. The target stepped between the two positions about 100 ms before the saccade started. Reprinted by permission, from Findlay and Harris (1984), fig. 6.

Findlay concludes that "these demonstrations provide support for a model of saccade programming in which internal feedback plays a part in determining the saccade goal" (Findlay, "Programming of Stimulus-Elicited Saccadic Eye Movements," p. 9).

further right than usual.[10] Saccades exhibit other subtleties as well. They can be distinguished as to initial and final angle of orientation, along with transitional phases in between. Their temporal and spatial dimensions are established differentially, allowing still greater latitude of response in given circumstances. Of most interest is the fact that saccades respond more quickly to global than to local effects; thus it has been demonstrated that the target object's position is not encoded in a point-by-point way but in a highly distributed form.[11] Even if a particular target object does elicit or precipitate a saccade, the fact that this object operates by means of global structures and belongs to a field of collocated objects means that the saccade itself is a finely modulated action that is actively responding to a complex scene before and around it.

For this very reason, it would be a mistake to assimilate the saccade to the gaze rather than to the glance, as in this claim: "The ability to redirect the gaze within a fraction of a second to any part of the visual field [that is, as in the saccade] ranks high among the significant features of vision."[12] On the contrary, it is the *glance,* more than any other form of looking, that is implicated in the saccade. For the glance possesses the requisite speed, variability, sensitivity, and closely attuned enactment to ally itself with the saccade at every point. It is the

10. P. He and E. Knowler, "The Role of Location Probability in the Programming of Saccades: Implications for 'Center-of-Gravity' Tendencies," *Vision Research* 29 (1989): 1165–1181. For Findlay's critique of the overall position of He and Knowler, see his "Programming of Stimulus-Elicited Saccadic Eye Movements," pp. 20–21.

11. For evidence of global effects on saccades, see H. Deubel and G. Hauske, "The Programming of Visually Guided Saccades," in *Processing Structures for Perception and Action,* ed. H. Marko, G. Hauske, and F. W. Johnson (Weinheim: Verlag Chemie, 1988), pp. 67–74. Concerning distributed coding, see F. P. Ottes, J. A. M. van Gisbergen, and J. J. Eggermont, "Metrics of Saccadic Responses to Double Stimuli: Two Different Modes," *Vision Research* 24 (1984): 1169–1179. Findlay speculates that in the case of distributed and global stimuli there is "a remapping of retinal space into a representation involving very large, overlapping receptive fields" ("Programming of Stimulus-Elicited Saccadic Eye Movements," p. 14). This last statement entails that saccadic movements (which follow the mapping representation provided by "retinal space") do not merely respond to discrete and isolated "stimuli" or "targets" but are much more attuned to entire visual environments.

12. Findlay, "Programming of Stimulus-Elicited Saccadic Eye Movements," p. 8. For other comparable uses of "gaze," see Anne Sereno, "Programming Saccades: The Role of Attention," in *Eye Movements and Visual Cognition,* ed. K. Rayner p. 89; John M. Henderson, "Visual Attention and Eye Movement Control During Reading and Picture Viewing," in ibid., p. 280. An experienced researcher in the field, David LaBerge, professor of psychology at Simons Rock College, writes that "I can testify that one does not find the word 'glance' in the vast majority of research papers on attention and vision, perhaps because of the ambiguity concerning whether or not a saccade must be involved" (e-mail communication from the author, April 11, 2002). LaBerge himself defines a glance as "brief attention to a location in space" (e-mail communication from the author, April 10, 2002). I am indebted to LaBerge for his clarification of many of the issues under discussion in this chapter. For his own views on attention, see his book, *Attentional Processing: The Brain's Art of Mindfulness* (Cambridge, Mass.: Harvard University Press, 1995) as well as "Attention, Awareness, and the Triangular Circuit," *Consciousness and Cognition* 6 (1997): 149–181, and "Attention, Consciousness, and Electrical Wave Activity within the Cortical Column," *International Journal of Psychophysiology* 43 (2001): 5–24, 43, esp. 17, where the circumstance of the glance is discussed.

glance, not the gaze, that exists between reaction and decision, and it is the glance as well that is geared to global effects of complexly distributed stimuli. But is the saccade in fact a form of glancing? Or is the glance itself composed of saccades in its microstructure—thus depending on their preparatory action—while being itself, at its own level, an act of a higher order?

III

I shall concentrate on a single strand of thought that will cast light on these last two questions. This is that there is a decisive difference between attention and eye movements, including saccades as the primary such movement. We must not assume that attention requires eye movements as such. On the one hand, attention to something that appears in the central foveal region of our look requires no such movements; since the targeted object is already present in this region, we need not shift our eyes to capture it: it is already the very content of our focal looking. On the other hand, we can shift our attention away from the foveal region toward something that appears on its margins, yet *without having to undertake the corresponding eye movements*. Such movements may accompany or ensue upon this shift—and often do; but they need not. Let us take an example:

> I am focusing on the screen of my laptop as I write these words, and I continue to do so even though I find my attention being drawn to a group of three people who have just entered the café in which I am working. They enter from the door that, in relation to where I'm seated, is at the left and above the screen. I take note of them, however dimly, as appearing on the periphery of my visual field, all three in their late twenties and speaking volubly; I am aware of their movement toward the counter where coffee is ordered, still further to the left; yet my look remains fully fixated on the screen: I have not swung my eyes to make the new guests the foveated center of my regard, even though I am attending to them throughout in some significant sense.

On the basis of this quite ordinary experience, we can distinguish three modalities of visual attention:[13]

(i) *central attending:* This is the looking I do as I focus on my laptop screen; my eyes maintain a continuing position of steady regard; nevertheless, delimited saccadic movements doubtless subtend this focalized attending, even if I am not aware of them as such.

(ii) *attending-away:* Here I shift my attention, *though not my eyes*, to something that appears beyond the foveal region of this field (that is, the central

13. I leave aside consideration of other sensory modes of attention, e.g., aural, kinesthetic, etc., although these frequently accompany purely visual attention (in the above example, in the form of the newcomers' voices).

15 to 20 percent of this field). In short, I look away without *looking* away. To be able to say this latter indicates the intrinsic ambiguity of "look," which can signify focused visual attending to something in particular—as when we say we are "looking *at*" something—but which can also connote an action of being *diverted in our look:* that is, changing the position of our eyes as we *turn toward* a new object of attention.

(iii) *identifying in attending:* To look away from the first content of attention and toward something else—an action labeled "orientation" in the psychological literature—is not yet to determine what it is I am looking at. To do the latter is a further act, one that is manifestly cognitive in character. In the above example, it signified that moment in my changing attention when I recognized the new items in my visual field as "people in their twenties," "talking loudly," and so on. There was a moment, not definite enough to merit inclusion in my description, when I had not thus identified them— "detected the stimuli" in the psychological lingo. I was being drawn away from my initial and primary focus on the computer screen, but I could not say that I had yet *identified* or *recognized* them as such.[14]

And where is the glance in all this? Anywhere we wish it to be: it can figure in any of the three moments of attention I here distinguish, yet it is not necessarily present in any of them. For example, in the second moment my attending-away, instead of occurring at the edge of a persisting look, might have consisted in a sudden glancing toward the new persons in the café. Even the very first moment of attention, however, could have consisted in glances: instead of staring at my screen, I might just as well have been glancing at it from the start in a series of brief looks that were strung together coherently enough to constitute attending to my evolving text. So, too, the act of identification could take place by, or more exactly *in,* a glance—for example, as when we recognize something to be of a certain kind by glancing at it. Thus, in fact *every* stage of attending could be accompanied or accomplished by the appropriate form of glancing.

There is certainly a correlation between many acts of attention and certain eye movements, but this does not signify a strict concomitance: I can shift my eyes in a new direction while continuing to attend to something situated right before me.[15] Even if attention and eye movements are both elicited by conspicuous peripheral events, there is a "striking tendency of attention to move to the target prior to an eye movement."[16] This suggests that the active agent is attention and not eye

14. I take the terms "orientation" and "detection" from Michael I. Posner's classical article, "Orienting of Attention," *Quarterly Journal of Experimental Psychology* 32 (1980): 3–25. I owe this reference, as well as a clarifying discussion of related matters, to David LaBerge. As Posner puts it, "Since one can move attention to a potential source of signals before any input has occurred, it is clear that orienting can occur without detection" (ibid., p. 32).

15. For this circumstance, see ibid., pp. 17–18, as well as R. Klein, "Does Oculomotor Readiness Mediate Cognitive Control of Visual Attention?" in *Attention and Performance VIII*, ed. R. Nickerson (Hillsdale, N.J.: Erlbaum, 1979).

16. Posner, "Orienting of Attention," p. 19.

movements as such, whether these movements be those belonging to subtle saccades or to overt glances. "An attentional shift," writes John M. Henderson, is "necessary to initiate eye movement programming . . . prior to an eye movement, attention must be allocated to the location about to be fixated."[17]

To endorse this last claim means to subscribe to the primacy of intentionality in our lives: not just the intentionality of pure consciousness so much stressed by Brentano and Husserl but the "operative intentionality" underlined by Merleau-Ponty.[18] The presence of such concrete intentionality points to the way in which an ostensibly "mental" factor—such as "interest," in William James's term—is not only continuous with its bodily enactment but strongly calls for it in the form of physical eye movements.[19]

It follows that attention "is not intrinsically tied to the foveal structure of the visual system nor slaved to the overt movements of the eye."[20] Attention forges its own path: one that is often not predictable, much less stereotyped, in its trajectory. Except when overwhelmed by something deeply demanding such as driving for the first time or disturbing such as a trauma, for the most part we attend to what we wish: once more, "my experience is what I *agree* to attend to." There is a factor of freedom in attentional consciousness that rejoins that at stake in the glance. As Robert M. Steinman writes:

> Perhaps the most striking aspect of human oculomotor performance is its independence from stimulus variables. By this I mean that a normal human adult can look about in his visual world and attend to whatever region catches his fancy undisturbed by the distribution of light on his retina, or, in perceptual terms, the way the visual world looks at a particular moment. . . . [A human being has] considerable freedom in directing his attention to any region without regard to the color, brightness, shape, or motion of objects within it.[21]

17. John M. Henderson, "Visual Attention and Eye Movement Control during Reading and Picture Viewing," in Rayner, ed., *Eye Movements and Visual Cognition*, p. 267. It is of related interest that the same principle obtains in the case of imagined objects, where the visualized rotation of such an object requires a period of time that is roughly equivalent to the time that would be taken by actual eye movements to follow such a rotation. See the classical studies contained in Roger N. Shepard and Lynn A. Cooper, *Mental Images and their Transformations* (Cambridge, Mass.: MIT, 1982), esp. part 1, "Mental Rotation."

18. See Maurice Merleau-Ponty, preface to *Phenomenology of Perception*, tr. C. Smith (New York: Humanities Press, 1962), p. xviii.

19. James, *Principles of Psychology*, vol. 1, p. 404. Concerning interest, James says this: "Interest alone gives accent and emphasis, light and shade, background and foreground— intelligible perspective, in a word" (ibid., vol. 1, p. 402). Interest accounts for the discriminateness of experience (ibid., vol. 1, p. 403). We shall return to the factor of interest below, but it is evidently central to attention on James's account.

20. Posner, "Orienting of Attention," p. 22. Cf. p. 10: "the covert mechanisms of attention are not tied intrinsically to the fine structure of the visual system." This is not to deny that "although it has been known for some time that we can dissociate our attention from the point of fixation, most of the time our attention and our eyes are directed at the same part of the stimulus field" (Rayner, "Eye Movements and Visual Cognition: Introduction," in Rayner, ed., *Eye Movements and Visual Cognition*, p. 1).

21. Robert Steinman, "Role of Eye Movements in Maintaining a Phenomenally Clear and

No wonder we so often think of attention as a beacon light that casts its illumination forward in our experience, bringing in its wake various physical motions (including eye movements) that act it out at the level of the body. This is true, but we need to add as well that attention, however free it may be in its enactment, is often elicited by various items in the visual field: the interest that provides its usual motive force is drawn out by something that first appears in the periphery of our foveal vision. In a revealing experiment, when subjects were told on which side (right or left) of the visual field a stimulus was more likely to appear but were not informed as to whether it would be central (that is, foveal) or peripheral in status, they almost always expected it to be peripheral in location.[22] The experimenter remarked that this strong expectation "assumes that the fovea will take care of itself, even though our data say clearly that the costs in RT [reaction time] will be as great as for the periphery."[23] Expecting to attend to the peripheral position of the object prepares for the eye movements that will bring such an object into focused attention.[24]

Taking account of both aspects of attending—its sensitivity to the peripheral stimulus and its ability to change direction at will—we have a situation summed up in James's telling shorthand for attention's leading trait: "reactive spontaneity."[25] As spontaneity, attention is free-ranging and outgoing; as reactivity, it acts in terms of what is occurring in the surrounding visual field. This double virtue is exactly how we would describe the human glance, which is spontaneous in its swift shifts of direction—hence its apparent fickleness—while being closely attuned to nuanced features in the objects that present themselves to it. Whatever its degree of attunement, however, the glance is never the lackey of the objects at which it looks; its spontaneity collaborates with its reactivity but is never overcome by it. This is why Merleau-Ponty can claim for the glance a certain primacy:

> Just my glance toward the [perceptual] goal already has its own miracles. It too takes up its dwelling in being with authority and conducts itself there as in a conquered country. It is the not the object which obtains movements of accommodation and convergence from my eyes . . . I would never see anything clearly, and there would be no object for me, if I did not use my eyes in such a way as to make a view of a single object possible. . . . It is my glances themselves—

Stable World," in *Eye Movements and Psychological Processes,* ed. R. A. Monty and J. W. Senders (Hillsdale, N.J.: Erlbaum, 1976), pp. 121–122.

22. See Michael Posner, *Chronometric Explorations of Mind* (Hillsdale, N.J.: Erlbaum, 1978), fig. 7.8.

23. Posner, "Orienting Attention," pp. 8–9, commenting on his own earlier experiment.

24. At the same time, one suspects that the greater alertness to extrinsic stimuli reflects the earlier-mentioned evolutionary aspects of needing to be on the outlook for predators on the outer edges of one's visual field: a need heightened by the fact that human eyes are located exclusively on the front of the head and thus require shifts of attention (and functionally corresponding eye movements) to the margins of the field, including the orbiting of the head as a whole.

25. James, *Principles of Psychology,* vol. 1, p. 402.

their synergy, their exploration, and their prospecting—which bring the imminent object into focus.[26]

If the glance gives us the most dramatic display of the spontaneity of the look, attention is its sober counterpart. Yet unlike the saccade—which tends to follow the lead of attention—the glance, though itself normally composed of saccades, is at the vanguard of attention: it is already scouting out the situation that calls for attention.[27] We can see this in the following remarkable diagram, in which the close alliance of glance and attention, of overt and covert looking, is in evidence:

Figure 9.1. Schumacher, W., and A. Korn (1983). "Automatic Evaluation of Eye or Head Movements for Visual Information Selection." Fig. 6 in R. Groner, C. Menz, D. F. Fisher, and R. A. Monty (eds.), *Eye Movement and Psychological Functions: International Views.* Hillsdale, NJ: Lawrence Erlbaum Associates, Publishers. Reprinted with permission.

26. Merleau-Ponty, "Indirect Language and the Voices of Silence," tr. R. C. McCleary in T*he Merleau-Ponty Aesthetics Reader*, ed. G. Johnson (Evanston, Ill.: Northwestern University Press, 1993), p. 102.

27. Concerning the precedence of attention to the saccade, Posner comments: "Attention moves rapidly prior to the eye movement and returns to the original fixation as the fovea settles in at the target. . . . We had the distinct impression that we were able to return attention to fixation even as the eye was moving toward the target" ("Orienting of Attention," p. 17). I say that the glance is "normally composed" of saccades, because there are situations in which one can glance at items in a closely knit array without moving one's eyes: e.g., the Treisman search task as discussed in Anne Treisman, "Features and Objects: The Fourteenth Barlett Memorial Lecture," *Quarterly Journal of Experimental Psychology* 40A (1988): 201–237. Concerning this task, David LaBerge comments that "the attention aspect of a glance need not involve a saccade. Therefore, for the Treisman search task, attention can move quickly from one location to another without moving the eyes (the estimated 'dwell time' of attention is about 80 ms, which is much less than the 250 ms average time it takes to move the eye" (e-mail communication of April 11, 2002).

The string superimposed on the aerial photograph of farmlands represents the "scanpath" of eye movements as they swept over the lands, starting from the center of the photograph and proceeding to a water tank that lies partly concealed in the lower right-hand corner. Protuberances such as bushes and trees, along with the water tank, are the target objects of the saccadic movements that carry out the visual action as a whole. I say "as a whole," for the looking here at stake occurs in a more or less continuous pattern of scanning the visual representation by closely concatenated saccades.[28] The zigzag form of the scanpath should not mislead us: it has its own logic, since its moves ever forward from the center to its destination, with loops along the way that represent side-searches in promising areas. The fact is that we can scan effectively even when we do not move in any regular, much less rectilinear, manner. The irregularity of the scanpath does not mean that we are merely looking at random objects, or drifting aimlessly across a field.[29] The looking traces out a trajectory that, however bizarre its apparent form, takes in what matters to the interest active in attention: as we can also see in the perception of paintings, which we often scan in a zigzag fashion that manages to yield subtle structures and holistic aspects.[30] In all these

28. Strictly speaking, any eye movements that occur in the central twenty degrees of the visual field (but outside the two degrees constituted by the fovea proper) constitute scanning by saccades: "Visual perception in man and higher vertebrates with a specialized fovea requires scanning of the field of view. Within the central 20 degrees of the visual field this scanning is accomplished by saccadic eye movements" (Fischer, "Saccadic Reaction Time," p. 31). In the eye movement literature, scanning does not connote systematic line-by-line, serial scrutinizing but a looking over the visual field so as to locate something situated in that field. (Note, however, that scanning does not always involve eye movement: when a red letter V "pops out" of a group of black Vs and Ns, we can attend to this without moving our eyes. I owe this point and the example to David LaBerge (e-mail communication of April 11, 2002). Later, we shall see an instance of a "scanpath" that looks highly irregular, yet is ultimately successful in finding its target object. (See the discussion just above of figure 9.1 as discussed in W. Schumacher and A. Korn, "Automatic Evaluation of Eye or Head Movements for Visual Information Selection," *Eye Movements and Psychological Functions: International Views*, p. 37.)

29. This latter occurs only when there is such dim illumination as to make it difficult to maintain a steady eye position. On this situation, see Steinman, "Role of Eye Movements in Maintaining a Phenomenally Clear and Stable World," p. 135: "If targets are too feeble to be seen when they fall on the fovea, a good deal of voluntary control is lost and a maladaptive eye-movement pattern ensues. A feeble target, placed in the near periphery where it can be seen, will be returned to the central fovea where it disappears."

30. The same is true of the perception of ambiguous figures: see A. G. Gale and J. M. Findlay, "Eye Movement Patterns in Viewing Ambiguous Figures," in *Eye Movements and Psychological Functions: International Views*, pp. 145–168. For the case of successfully scanning paintings by quick eye movements that are highly interpretive and proceed in terms of visual hypotheses about the identity of the whole image, see E. H. Gombrich, *Art and Illusion: A Study in the Psychology of Pictorial Representation* (Princeton, N.J.: Princeton University Press, 1960), chap. 8: "Ambiguities of the Third Dimension." It is a generally established fact that such movements proceed in terms of the holistic features of the scanned item: "Saccadic response is generally directed by 'global' aspects of the visual information" (J. M. Findlay and T. I. Crawford, "The Visual Control of Saccadic Eye Movements: Evidence for Limited Plas-

cases, the saccadic eye movements exhibit minute but measurable movements of their own. These movements constitute the organic bases of glances and can be considered their operative enactors, as it were. Thanks to the mobility provided by saccades, a given glance assumes the premonitory position of staking out the visual field through which it sweeps in an act of visual attention.

But what if the "glancescan" was not directed at maps or paintings—or at any other figures inscribed on exterior surfaces—but was instead deployed within our own mind? How does the conjoint action of attending and glancing take place there?

IV

Husserl opened up an entire domain of genuinely new investigation when in his *Ideas* he began to speak of "the mental look" (*die geistige Blick*).[31] Husserl's concerns were frankly eidetic: he wanted to determine which structures inside the mind can be counted on to recur in regular ways such that *any mind*, looking into itself, would encounter these structures, for example, structures of primary and secondary memory, thinking, being emotional, and imagining. In keeping with his commitment to the intentional character of mind, these structures were regarded as accruing to acts such as heeding and judging as well as to the contents of such acts: for example, fantasied events, ideas, feelings, and so on. Taken all together, such structures constitute a highly coherent internal field of consciousness, bifurcated into act and content at every point and filled with eidetic structures whose distinguishing mark is their comparative fixity and permanence. This was in effect a major contribution to the study of attention.

Although Husserl uses the very term—*Blick*—that can signify "glance" in German, he thought of it in a generic sense of "look" that does not lend to the glance any special significance. For example, his employment of the term *Blickstrahl* (literally, "ray of the look") signifies a visual ray in that pervasive sense that first arises among the early Greeks, notably among the Atomists and with Plato.[32] Even if the gleaming that is peculiar to the glance dramatically embodies something like a visual ray—the special "look in the eye" of which Wittgenstein speaks—the ray itself is by no means confined to the glance: in fact, it characterizes every sort of looking. For Husserl, the differences between looking in general and glancing were not significant; for us, they are of critical importance.

---

ticity," in *Eye Movements and Psychological Functions: International Views*, p. 115). Indeed the global effect obtains even when it is obviously maladaptive: see ibid., pp. 125 ff.

31. Edmund Husserl, *Ideas Pertaining to a Pure Phenomenology and to a Phenomenological Philosophy, Book One: First Book: General Introduction to Pure Phenomenology*, tr. F. Kersten (The Hague: Nijhoff, 1982), sections 35–38 (hereafter referred to as *Ideas I*).

32. For further treatment of the Greek understanding of the visual ray, see chap. 5, where I take up Plato's treatment in some detail, along with a brief allusion to Husserl.

A basic distinction between looking and glancing can be understood thus: where looking arises mainly when we are engaged in perceiving things situated in the external world, glancing, though often outer-directed, can also occur wholly inside my mind. Just as there is inner attention, so there is a mental glance. This takes place in two main forms: glancing around and concerted glancing.

(i) *Glancing around* signifies "noticing" (in another of Husserl's favorite words in this context) what is going on at the level of, say, thought or emotion but in no emphatic or focused way. Our attentional powers are "on idle" (in a Wittgensteinian turn of phrase): not turned off to the point of oblivion but not directed to any particular item either. We are certainly noting what is there, but not singling out anything in particular, much less scanning the scene in any directed way.[33] An example:

> I am waking up from a nap. As I lie on the couch, I savor what is "on my mind": my sense of well-being after the rest I have just taken, a vague sense of what I'll do next: make a cup of coffee? or get right back to work? It doesn't yet matter which: no decision needs to be made right now. I follow my mind farther afield, drifting between several open possibilities: should I attend that meeting in New York, or stay writing in Chicago a few more days? Should I contact my friend in Richmond now or later on? These questions do not fully engage me; I am just cruising in the realm of mind, sampling whatever arises, not unlike Freud's "basic rule" of psychoanalysis—letting anything that occurs to me count as a valid experience, no matter how trivial it may seem.[34] But I am not taking the *next* step recommended by Freud: to interpret these meanderings with regard to how they cast light on my life. I am just accepting them as they present themselves, all of them, without categorizing, judging, acting on them, or even relating them to each other.

(ii) In *concerted glancing* the situation changes dramatically: now I start to glance intently within the field of my mental activity. I single out certain things, as if I were casting a psychical lasso around them and pulling them into the net of my active mind, there to be illuminated, either for their own sake or at least as seen in their comparative prominence (since I can continue to be aware of items that lie at the margins of the glanced-at thing, event, person, and so forth). In the state of glancing around, my attention is more or less equally distributed: here I achieve what Freud called (with reference to the analyst's receptive attitude) "evenly hovering attention." With the advent of concerted glancing, however, the visual field is no longer

---

33. Both glancing around and concerted glancing can occur in the perceptual as well as the mental domain: an example of the former is my experience of looking out of my new apartment as reported in the prologue; instances of the latter are detailed at several points in part 1: e.g., my glancing at other customers in the Café Felix. "Glancing around" covers much the same experiential territory as "looking around" as discussed in the afterword.

34. "My patients were pledged to communicate to me every idea or thought that occurred to them in connection with some particular subject" (Sigmund Freud, *The Interpretation of Dreams*, in *The Standard Edition of the Complete Psychological Works* [London: Hogarth, 1953], vol. 4, p. 100).

merely bifurcated into focal area and background (as is every field of presentation, perceptual or mental) but is more adequately characterized as heterogeneous. Husserl himself spoke of the "polythetic" character of the *Blick*, its capacity for attending to several things at once.[35] So, too, when I actively glance into my mind, I can glance at more than one item at a time and what I don't glance at does not always recede into the background in any regular way. There are degrees of the "relinquishment of attention,"[36] for example, that do not leave a level playing field for subsequent acts of glancing. But let us continue with our example:

> I am still in my postprandial reverie. Suddenly, I find myself attending to one line of thought much more than to the others: the insistent thought that I must call Delta Airlines by tomorrow if I am indeed to go to the New York meeting; otherwise, I'll have to pay a much higher fare. This thought seizes my attention as my mental glance goes rapidly to it: I not only focus on it, I begin to think it through: I *follow the thought*. My glance perdures just long enough to let this happen. Even as I am doing this, I remain aware of the other things that first came to my attention, only now as de-accentuated—still there in my mental field, yet less insistent.

Striking here is the fact that my mental glance takes on the character of *thinking*, not just of *imaging*. If the glance in the realm of ordinary, outward-directed perception is almost always visual—the only exceptions being those of transposed glancing by means of touch (for example, barely touching) or hearing (for example, overhearing) or even smelling (for example, whiffing)—in the mental realm glancing modalizes much more easily. Such glancing is still predominantly visual—as we witness in aptly named "visualizations"—but it can also rapidly change into a form of remembering, or thinking, or supposing, and so on. Each of these counts fully as glancing, and none needs to be compared to visualizing, much less reduced to it. There is no longer a core modality of glancing, a central or essential form of it. I can glance mentally any which way, and it will still figure fully as glancing. And this ease of modalization applies both to the explicit "content" of my focused glance (the Delta airline ticket) as well as to the marginal items—which can just as well be contemplated, or remembered, or supposed, and so forth. At each of these I can take a concerted glance that amounts to a displaced look.

This remarkable circumstance is philosophically significant. It challenges oculocentrism, which requires robust objects that last under my gaze in the bright light of day. Within the twilight world of the mind, the only light is that cast by the *geistige Blick* and, in particular, that of the glance that beams its psychic rays on its preferred theme or topic. These rays are no longer exclusively, much less literally, visual in character; part of their polythetic character consists in their polyaesthetic enactment: the real possibility that they can be realized in several

---

35. See *Ideas I*, sections 118–19.

36. I borrow this term from John M. Findlay: "Some process that may be termed *relinquishment of attention* is involved in the saccade" ("Programming of Stimulus-Elicited Saccadic Eye Movements," p. 23; his italics).

sensory modalities. Instead of invoking the ancient model of a visual ray, we can just as well speak of a "stream" of attention, which may take various sensory forms in keeping with the character of what is attended to (just as this latter can be entertained in a number of cognitive modalities as well). Experience here becomes radically democratic; in it the multiplicity of the mental reigns.

V

It is attention, and especially attention in and by the glance, that brings out this mental multiplicity most convincingly. But not in any strictly ordered way on which we can count, much less that we could predict! For there is often a crazy quilt motion here, not unlike the active saccadic movements of the physiological eye—but now occasioned by the heterogeneous contents we find within our mind. Yet diversity of content and the corresponding attentional moves do not mean confusion, much less that state of *Zerstreutheit* ("dispersion") cited by James as lying at the limits of attention proper.[37] For we are not in a situation of utter distraction (which would mean the loss of mind itself), but rather of complex consciousness. The complexity is due to several specific factors: elusiveness/evanescence, braidedness, availability, self-illumination.

(i) *elusiveness/evanescence.* I here refer to the phantom-like character of the objects of inner attention, as well as to their tendency to disappear almost as soon as they appear: "one glimpse and vanished." Only rarely do these mental objects have the constancy of perduring perceptual objects, the continuing identity that would make them available day in and day out. In contrast, erotic fantasies may keep insisting on reappearing; traumatic memories often return unbidden. In these two cases, we have little choice but to attend to their content since they dominate the psychic space altogether. Short of these demanding situations, however, our mental life is filled with flotsam and jetsam of a very disparate sort that calls for a special kind of multiple attention to deal with their heterogeneity. Such polyattention has to be capable of considerable nuance in its operation if it is to account for all the differences in presentation, and in particular it must be able to capture these differences before they vanish, each in its own manner. If we can count on the persistence of perceived objects—since in their case we know that we shall be able to return to an item that may have temporarily disappeared (that is, thanks to "object permanency")—we can no longer do so in the case of the inner world: even the erotic and traumatic

37. James, *Principles of Psychology,* vol. 1, p. 404: Attention "implies withdrawal from something in order to deal effectively with others, and is a condition which has a real opposite in the confused, dazed, scatter-brained state which in French is called *distraction,* and *Zerstreutheit* in German."

revenants may someday fail to return as they come under therapeutic scrutiny or dissolve with changes in our life situation. In the end, the elusiveness of what we attend to within ourselves extends to the entire *Innenwelt* itself: as Hume insisted, nothing guarantees that the inner world will stay the same from one day to the next, even from one moment to the next. It evanesces under our very (mental) eyes.

(ii) *braidedness.* Often we are directed outside ourselves, taken up with daily tasks and preoccupations. Into this busy everyday world the awareness of our mental life insinuates itself continuously yet unpredictably: not just when we are emotionally upset, but any time a thought or expectation or memory arises within. The phenomena of such inward arising and disappearing bring their own modalities of attention, often as occasioned by the unexpected—in which case, we turn toward it with a corresponding swiftness. All of this is happening even as we attend to external events around us. The result is that our experience overall has a peculiarly *braided* quality, ordinary perception being deeply intertwined with the mind's coming and going in the midst of everyday engagements. Such braidedness at once alleviates and complicates our experience in the life-world.

(iii) *availability.* This is not to say that the elusiveness and evanescence of the inner world of attention render that world inaccessible or useless to us. Pervasive as these two qualities are, they do not tell the whole truth. The inner world is not a scene that forever exceeds our grasp; it is available to us at almost any time, however imperfect its access may be and however complexly interbraided it is with the external world of perception. Only consider the fact that the inward domain of mind constitutes a world in which everything presented is just *that* thing (event, and so on)—that and no other—and that cannot be occluded by some other thing (event, and so on). If I remember a scene of massive objects, these latter *do not block* other contents lurking behind them: there is no significant sense of "behind."[38] Vaguely as a particular memory or thought may appear to us, still it is *that very thought or memory*. We deal with and respect the vagueness as such. "It is," said William James, "the re-instatement of the vague to its proper place in our mental life which I am so anxious to press on the attention."[39] Nor does it matter that we may choose to integrate the thought of memory with other mental contents, or use it in some other way (for example, as inspiration in art, and so forth). The inner world to which we attend allows us to *take it on its own terms*, without recourse to intermediary items.

38. Concerning edges, see my forthcoming essay, "Looking Around the Edge of the World," *Chōra*, 2007, where I explore the persistent ancient conviction that the earth must have edges: it must drop off somewhere.

39. James, *Principles of Psychology* (New York: Holt, 1890), vol. 1, p. 254.

(iv) Integral to the intrinsic availability of the attentional world is the fact that it is always already illuminated, indeed *self-illuminated:* lit up not by any external source of light but from a special luminescence of its own, a psychical lighting to which I have already made brief allusion. There are felt degrees of this inner light, ranging from a pellucid transparency to an extremely dim presentation. But whatever its exact extent, it is a light that is unquestionably adequate to the full content of our attention; it is not as if having *more* such light would allow us to see something we cannot otherwise see: *we see all there is to see.* Nothing is left over to see further, or to see better, even if we might *understand* it better upon reflection. The illumination here in question is neither that of the visual ray beamed outward nor that of the world's rays coming from outside the organism. This is a third form of light, one that begins and ends within the mind. There, and there alone, is it to be found. Not only does it make attention to our mind possible; it is part and parcel of mental attention itself, which as fully self-illuminating, brings with it its own powers of illumination, requiring no other source but itself.

To each of these four features of the inner attentional world there corresponds a fitting form of inwardly glancing regard.

(a) First, there is a *glancing-after* elusive and evanescent items of thought and memory, fantasy and supposition. Even as these perpetually perishing things evade any secure grasp of the sort to which we are accustomed in the external perceptual world, they call for a special kind of glancing which is designed to note that which flees any oculocentric comprehension. To glance in this way is precisely to *follow* that which eludes any simple seizure; this is a docile looking that is content to fit into the trail or track of what eludes us: say, the passing thoughts I entertained on waking up from my nap. It is to glance *after* in both senses of "after": the temporal sense of coming after an event has already transpired (i.e., its "aftermath"), and the spatial sense of occurring in the wake of what moves away from us (i.e., the "afterplace"). Much of attentional glancing has the character of following just after what has appeared in our mind. We attend by glancing-after what we have already experienced.

(b) A second sort of attentional glancing is *glancing-at* the evanescently fading. Since evanescence qualifies the uncontrollable course of our mind, its spontaneous arising or subsiding, we have no choice but to glance *at* what comes into our ken so surprisingly. As discussed in chapter 2, the "at" of glancing-at signifies a factor of directed awareness—the pinpointing of emergent phenomena, their quick discernment as they arise and move into an intimate connection with perceptual things and events, becoming interbraided with them. In contrast with (a), there is here an element of apprehension or grasp. Indeed, the "at" is none other than that of "at-tention" itself:

an *at* of concentrated attention that brings itself right up to the phenomenon (as is once again suggested in the French expression *à même*).[40] This suggests that glancing-at is a central form of glancing when it comes to attention, whether outwardly or inwardly directed, or involving their interaction. This interaction is a breeding ground for the unexpected: for example, in the experience of the walker whose expectations are confirmed or discredited at virtually every turn of the street. Likewise, to be stopped in one's course by the foiling of one's mental anticipations is to provide an occasion for an intent glancing at these anticipatory thoughts: what was I *really* expecting to find on the boulevard today before I set out? To check out my mind in this fashion is to take a concerted glance at what I was thinking.[41]

(c) I also find myself *glancing-through* the inner attentional world, and all the more so if this is a world fully available to me: without the particular obstacles that occlude the perception of things and events. In the absence of these obstacles, I sense myself gliding through the mental presentation, carried on the wings of my glance as it were. When occlusions vanish, an important source of resistance disappears, leaving me free to glance through what I think, imagine, or remember at my own pace and as I wish.

(d) A fourth form of glancing closely associated with the realm of mind may be designated as *glancing-into*. In this case, I attend to the contents of my own mind by looking into what is fully revealed in an internal self-lit realm. In this case, the ready accessibility of what I attend to calls me to witness whatever is arrayed on the surface of my own mind, set forth in the light of my own mentation. I look into a realm that is irrecusably my own. This is not to deny that my way of glancing-into is deeply formed from cultural influences and constraints, but only to emphasize that at the moment of mental regard the mental scene is irrecusably manifest. For at this moment I am aware of my own act of attention as if it were a coal miner's light, and my style of glancing follows forthwith: I glance into what announces itself as *jemeinig* (in Heidegger's expression for the fact that my own existence is "in each case mine to be").[42] By this act, I own up to what I glance into as genuinely my own—inalienably mine and self-illumined within the darkness of the larger reaches of mentality.

Glancing-after, glancing-at, glancing-through, and glancing-into: so many forms of attending to what transpires within ourselves—in that fugitive but ever-unfolding region we like to call "mind" or "psyche."

40. For the philosophical importance of this phrase, see Jean-Luc Nancy, *Being Singular Plural*, tr. R. D. Richardson and A. E. O'Byrne (Stanford: Stanford University Press, 2000), p. 3, inter alia; see the translators' note on p. 194.

41. For further discussion of the walker in the person of the flâneur, see chap. 6 above.

42. On the *jemeinig*, see Heidegger, *Being and Time*, tr. J. Macquarrie and C. Robinson (New York: Harper and Row, 1962), p. 67.

VI

I have been concentrating on the fourfold form of the glance in its internality, its mind-directedness, its intense concentration—all this in contrast with the glancing we do in the circumambient world of perception. But are we restricted to these two extremities, one mental and one perceptual? Do we not attend and glance in a third context that combines both psychical and physical features? In this context, mind and body are conterminous and no longer alienated from one another. Even though this is arguably the most basic level of human experience, many human beings have lost touch with it by insistently living in terms of pure mind or sheer body, as underscored by dualistic models of experience in the long wake of Descartes. So as not to subscribe to this kind of model in my own consideration of glancing and attending, I shall here point to an alternative model in which their relationship bears on body and mind alike: their conjunction, rather than their disparity.

The conjunction is realized in *attentiveness,* a manner of paying attention to one's current state of being as a whole. Many practices have underlined the importance of such attentiveness, ranging from yoga and Zen meditation to free association in Freudian psychoanalysis and active imagination in Jungian analytical psychology. A contemporary form of such practice of particular value for our purposes is found in the focusing technique of Eugene Gendlin. Gendlin asks the person who is engaged in focusing to get in touch with a "felt sense" of his or her life situation at the moment.[43] To do this requires an attentiveness in which the usual distinctions between body and mind, intentional object and act, ego and deep self, self and other, and so on fade in the face of their sheer continuity.

In focusing, it is a matter of becoming attentive to felt sense. The emphasis is less on what one encounters in this process—as in therapies in which discovery and insight are valorized—than on the very experience of gaining and holding attention in new and unexpected ways. These are ways that call for disciplined practice. The practice is set out in Gendlin's technique of focusing, which has six movements or "steps" in its procedure. Although these can be creatively modified—indeed, must be—to suit the occasion, they provide the framework for achieving attentiveness. In his own words:

> Take a moment just to relax . . . (5 seconds). All right—now, inside you, I would like you to pay attention to a very special part of you . . . pay attention *to that part where* you usually feel sad, glad, or scared (5 seconds). Pay attention to that area in you and see how you are now. . . . Sense how you feel. Let the answers come slowly from this sensing. When something comes, DO NOT GO INSIDE IT. Stand back, say "Yes, that's there. I can feel that, there." . . . From among what came, select one

---

43. "Focusing is part of a wider philosophy. In focussing one pays attention to a 'felt sense'. This is felt in the body, yet it has meaning. It has all the meaning one is already living with because one lives in situations with one's body. A felt sense is body *and* mind before they are split apart" (Eugene T. Gendlin, *Focusing* [New York: Everest House, 1978], p. 165; his italics).

personal problem to focus on. . . . Of course, there are many parts to that one thing you are thinking about—too many to think of each one alone. But, you can *feel* all of these things together. Pay attention there where you usually feel things, and in there you can get a sense of what *all of the problem* feels like. Let yourself feel *all of that* (1 minute). As you pay attention to the whole feeling of it, you may find that one special feeling comes up. Let yourself pay attention to that one feeling (1 minute). . . . If this one feeling changes, or moves, let it do that. Whatever it does, follow the feeling and pay attention to it (1 minute).[44]

Notable in this description is that the process of "paying attention" (a phrase here reiterated no less than six times) is not to be confused with pinpointing. Focusing is not fixating. Instead of limiting oneself to something focal about which one will likely obsess, one is encouraged to respect that to which one attends, its very surface ("DO NOT GO INSIDE IT"): rather than fastening onto it greedily, one is asked to stand back and look at it respectfully ("re-spectare" in Latin means "to look back at"). Paying attention includes paying homage to what one takes in. But one does this best by entering fully into the process of attending itself: not just for the sake of discernment or identification —which are conclusive or terminal acts—but so as to extend the process into other modalities: "Keep following one feeling. Don't let it be *just* [in] words or pictures—wait and let words or pictures come from the feeling."[45] Though they emerge in a different medium from that of inward vision, these new entities (images, words, and other associated feelings) carry forward the opening moment into subsequent events in an open-ended manner that Gendlin has come to represent typographically in the form of ". . . ," that is, "and so forth."

Most crucial is Gendlin's last remark cited above: "Whatever it does, follow the feeling and pay attention to it." Attentiveness is not a static matter; it is always evolving, following the lead of felt sense as this sense evolves in its own vagaries— not so as to incorporate it but so as to pay more nuanced and respectful attention to it. As Derrida, building on Torok and Abraham, underlines: incorporation is a form of encryptment that closes off the incorporated content within the self, burying it there in effect, whereas the entire effort of paying attention is to keep the scene as open as possible: to achieve what Heidegger calls "the openness of the Open."[46] What is held open is not just the future course of one's attentive experience—that is the point of the procedure that fosters *becoming* attentive— but the *prima materia* to which attention is paid: felt sensings that are as bodily

---

44. Gendlin, *Focusing*, p. 48; his italics (but the time indications were originally in italics). Gendlin now might put this differently: see his later model in his *Focusing-Oriented Psycho-therapy: A Manual of the Experiential Method* (New York: Guifford Press, 1996), as well as the more elaborate "TAE" (Thinking at the Edge) model now being pursued, which has more steps and substeps than the above.

45. Ibid., p. 48; his italics.

46. Martin Heidegger, "The Origin of the Work of Art," tr. A. Hofstadter in *Poetry Language Thought* (New York: Harper, 1971), p. 55; Jacques Derrida, "Fors," tr. B. Johnson, in *Georgia Review* 31 (1977): 64–116.

as they are psychical. Such sensings not only call for being noticed; they are felt to be *worth* attending to—intrinsically so—and not valuable just for their effects (symptom relief, better health, self-understanding, and so on). They are not to be considered "deep" if this means concealed under a surface; rather, the surface is such that it *yields depth*. But it does so only by means of continual attending, an unending process of glancing and reglancing at one's felt state, considering it and taking it into account.

In this circumstance, attending takes in content that cannot be considered an "object" in any usual sense—not even a mental object. We are far from an intentionalist paradigm. The circumstance is not just that of *noting* some discrete thing but of *immersing* oneself in one's own onstreaming experience, at once bodily and mental. Even in the most ordinary circumstance, we attend to nonobjects: a style, a smile, a way of being. But now we are in a domain where there are no robust materialities or discrete items; instead, we engage with diffuse feelings that are, however, definite with respect to the insight they offer into our concrete lives. In the practice of a technique such as focusing, the customary celerity of the glance is tempered with a certain patience and sensitivity that resemble traditional psychoanalytic and meditative techniques. But in contrast with Freudian and Jungian psychoanalysis, and with Zen meditation —for which the psychical is the primary emphasis—we are encouraged to be as much in touch with our body as our mind.

In the practice of focusing, we can detect two special ways in which the glance is engaged: glancing-in-depth and glancing-alongside.

Glancing-in-depth. The glancing at stake in focusing is geared to the presence of depth. We continue to glance at surfaces—this is a virtual axiom of all glancing—but now these surfaces are themselves surfaces-in-depth, nonsuperficial surfaces as it were. To glance at them in Gendlin's sense of "paying attention" is to glance into their very depth: not so as to see into their other side (there is no such side; as in the case of skin, the only side is the one we witness) but to linger for a moment in their ambience: to savor the deliverances thereon, to sense what is happening on these very surfaces. This sense is *felt* in Gendlin's strong sense of opening from vision into other sensory modalities such as touch or different media such as words; it is as if we come to terms with our own state of mind by rejoining it through attending to our felt bodily states. We glance into the depth of the surfaces of these states in order to experience more than we can experience in mind alone.

Glancing-alongside. In part, I here draw on the idiom of "going along," as when we say that we "go along with" what a friend suggests or a situation indicates; but I also mean "along" in the sense of "alongside": as when we say that we have positioned ourselves *alongside* something, taking our measure from it, aligning ourselves with it, being beside it. When we pay attention to something closely, we take ourselves into its nearness, as if we brought ourselves alongside its very surface. We do this by glancing along this surface, which is at once corporeal (as bodily feeling) and psychical (as felt from within). As a result, we begin to live on its terms rather than our own personal terms alone. We let *it* take the lead, but we can do this only because we have first taken the initiative of a disciplined attentiveness whose primary agent is the glance.

This situation contrasts with that in which glancing-at obtains: there, we are alert to sudden changes in evanescing phantoms, taking account of these changes briefly and pointedly. It also differs significantly from the glancing-after we do when we follow elusive phenomena, living in their spatiotemporal wake. Nor is it the glancing-through that glides over surfaces and between them, anxious to move on. And it is not the same as glancing-into an already-settled scene. For the scene at stake in glancing alongside and glancing-in-depth is an evolving one, albeit changing more slowly than that which characterizes the level of mental life as such, where (as Hobbes said) "thought is quick."[47] Now we have to do with changes in our state of mind, our psychic disposition, and our bodily feeling: all of these all at once. As Gendlin suggests, "If this one feeling changes, or moves, let it do that...."[48] In paying attention to it, we are following it "whatever it does"—or perhaps better, *wherever it goes*, whether into mind or body or (more to the point) their complex amalgam. We are glancing alongside it, we are glancing into its depth, and in this way we are coming to terms with "all of that"—all that makes our life worth attending to.

VII

Attention has shown itself to be a most extraordinary activity. This is most evident in its collusion with ordinary perception, but even when it becomes inner it is not a pale reflection of its role in such perception but an act in its own right. Inward attending and its appertaining modes of glancing have a life of their own. For here the glance is borne along by the mind—by its productions and presentations—and is not dependent on peripheral stimuli, as in the case of the saccades that underwrite attention shifts in the open-eyed visual realm. As Husserl first emphasized, I can attend and glance within my own mind. My inward regard moves through the diaphanous realm of minding in its several modalities of remembering, imagining, supposing, fantasying, and so on. Yet far from being something merely derivative, attention gains in power in its inner avatars. Or rather, it moves into another power than it knows elsewhere.

This power is not that of more acute vision. Unlike the case of external attention (where we can shift our eyes or head, sometimes our whole body, in order to bring the attended-to object into definite focus, so as to reach clarity and high resolution), the aim in such attention is neither acuity nor resolution. The model of the beacon light need no longer tempt us. For we are not explor-

---

47. Thomas Hobbes, *Leviathan*, ed. R. Tuck (Cambridge: Cambridge University Press, 1996), p. 27. I have had occasion to cite this quasi-axiomatic saying before.
48. Gendlin, *Focusing*, p. 48.

ing a dark region into which artificial light has to be brought but a realm that is always already illuminated with its own psychical lighting. No visual rays need to issue from our inner eyes, as if to rejoin light that comes from without. This latter model, which works so well when we are concerned with everyday perception, here loses its phenomenological pertinence. For we are in a situation of visual—or more exactly, visualized (and sometimes visionary!)—engagement in our own psychical domain.

At another level, we find attending in a third avatar. This level is at once psychical and physical. What matters here is not at-tention if this means *being alert* to what lies before us as an object or other determinate content. Instead, it is a question of *being attentive*, which arises in the form of *becoming aware*. This experience knows no definite moment of origin, nor does it have an unambiguous final point. Attentiveness, as set forth in Gendlin's work, is more of an attitude or posture, a process, than something we have already acquired. It involves body as well as mind, and both together in feeling. It is ongoing. It is also outgoing: in being attentive in this enriched manner, we treat ourselves to new vistas, different sights (and sounds and touchings) than we know in literally looking outside ourselves in external perception or inward into the psyche. The amazing thing is how vast the vistas are, considering the delimitation of the place of entry (a feeling, an image, or even a word) and the paucity of means available to us (we are not building on theory but on our own direct experience).

Moving in this third dimension, we find ourselves in a new region, no longer entirely inward nor altogether outward. In order to enter this new dimension, we have to reconsider our direction and to adopt different steps that take us to a new path. This happens by rethinking attention in the generous guise of attentiveness, attending in the open-ended form of paying attention to what is happening to us in body as well as in mind. Just as the narrow range of pinpointed attention gives way to the broad action of attentiveness, so a constricted conception of mind as consisting in a bilateral structure of act/content yields to an open vista of mind in touch with body. This prospect, constituting the scene of attentiveness, is at once reactive and spontaneous, interested and disinterested, stemming from the self yet coming from what is other in us, and it grants to attention an amplitude that it cannot know in external perception alone or in inner contemplation alone. The world of attentiveness is not, however, *another world*. It is the life-world of ongoing experience—a world with two closely coordinated aspects or parameters, those of mind and body as these come together in feeling. At virtually every moment, we are free to turn to this world—to take it in by glancing it in.

If attending to the external environment finds its organic substructure in the saccadic movements of our foveated eyes—micromovements at once necessary and slight—attending to mind no longer directly depends upon this physiological basis of ordinary perception. Its self-enlivened enactment takes place in a genuinely psychical field that I can finally, and first of all, call "my own." But this can occur only if I am willing to suspend the very differences between interior and exterior, physical and psychical, self and other to which I am otherwise committed in the course of my existence in the life-world of daily experience. I enter into this perpetually new-found world not only by the special practices at stake in meditation or focusing, active imagination or free association—these intensify and specify the glancing I do all the time—but also by the many glances I cast ever so casually and yet ever so definitively into its midst: into which *I glance my way.* I select from a set of at least six forms of glancing that are available to me in virtually every human circumstance: not only glancing-at and glancing-through, glancing-after and glancing-into (these four forms arise mainly in psychical experience), but also glancing alongside and glancing-in-depth (most active in an expanded attentiveness). The diversity of these forms of glancing—and others cited elsewhere in this book—reflects the remarkable variety of ways we can attend by glancing. By their very indirection and collective interaction we find out the many directions our polymorphous experiencing can assume.

VIII

William James, in his classic account of attention in chapter 11 of the *Principles of Psychology,* remarks almost casually that "Attention, implying a degree of *reactive spontaneity,* would seem to break through the circle of pure receptivity which constitutes 'experience.'"[49] James's phrase "reactive spontaneity" has already caught our eye. But what does it really signify?

To begin with, we might think of what James himself calls "the varieties of attention"[50] under this dual rubric. Under "reactive," we could place such things as apprehending, just barely noticing, taking note, picking up, detecting, and so on.[51] Under "spontaneous," we might put such attentional phenomena as heeding, seizing upon, taking into account, coming to terms with, and reaching out to what exceeds our current grasp. Each of these latter seems to be increasingly active or effortful. Thus we would have before us a neat typology of some ten specific acts, half of them ranged under "reactive" and half under "spontaneous."

Yet we should not suppose that James's suggestive phrase signifies the existence of two great kinds of attending that divide the field in a decisive manner, which would be comparable to the division between internal and external attention that I traced out in earlier parts of this chapter. Instead, we have something closer to a single continuum with two poles, around one of which cluster phenomena of being guided to what has *already* (and usually *just already*) drawn our attention, the other of which gathers more active forms of searching for

---

49. James, *Principles of Psychology,* vol. 1, p. 380; my italics.

50. Ibid., p. 393.

51. The first two members of this series, i.e., apprehending and just barely noticing, would seem to fall within "the circle of pure receptivity" which James considers attention to challenge in principle, even though he himself includes "passive, reflex, non-voluntary, effortless" traits as characterizing one whole variety of attending (most typically in the immediate sensory attending of childhood).

what *will* or *would* draw our attention—not wholly unlike the "retentional" and "protentional" horizons of time-consciousness on Husserl's model of time-consciousness. The very phrase "reactive spontaneity" is best respected by keeping the two words *together*—as if to say that attention is somehow always *reactively spontaneous* or *spontaneously reactive*, albeit in different degrees or ways. But what does this really mean? And how is it related to glancing?

Let us examine a case in point. Looking out from a rented house in Williamstown, Massachusetts, across the road and through the snow, my glance settles suddenly on a gray-green house opposite mine. I had not intended to look at this building (no particular effort is involved in the looking), nor do I have any special interest in it (it is not a highly motivated looking). Instead, my attention has wandered from the furnishings of my near sphere (that is, the table on which I am working), has swept outward through sliding glass doors, moving over the snow-laden lawn and over the narrow asphalt road, and crept up the hill across from me until meeting the house at its crest—wherein it suddenly terminates.

There are several noteworthy features in this otherwise quite ordinary experience. One is that I did not become aware of my looking itself, its spatial arc and temporal duration, until my glance reached the house as its outer limit. The consciousness of this glancing was retroactive as it were; only at the end of the experience did I gain an explicit awareness that I had been looking in the way I did. During the glancing itself—here in a frankly external form that can also be designated as "looking"—I was certainly taking time and traversing perceived space, but I was not aware of it as such: I was simply traveling through the spatiotemporal field in front of me at my own pace; I was in the act but not conscious of the act itself. Once reaching the house, my look seemed to look back at its own trajectory, almost as if I were seeing it *from the house,* though I know that this could not be the case.[52]

The stoppage of my look at the house is itself peculiar.[53] The house was not so much a barrier to further looking—I could certainly have looked around it to note the distant mountains on its right side; or I could have actively imagined what the other side of the house looks like—as a conclusion to my looking, inducing a distinct moment of pausing as well as a certain momentary satisfaction: as if to say that my act of attending to the landscape in front of me had reached a saturation point. In no way forbidding further acts of attending by means of additional glances, nevertheless the house as a focal finale ended this one episode of attentional looking, giving to it a cap and a sense of fitting closure.

All of this, let me be clear, was a decidedly minor act in the course of my perceptual day. The clock time taken by this act of attentional consciousness was probably no more than four or five seconds, though I was hardly timing the

---

52. This curious self-retraversal of the external glance arises in situations in which a certain felt distance has first been spanned by an initial glance. It is peculiar to this kind of glance, yet not a necessary feature of it.

53. On perceptual stoppage, see Eugene Gendlin, *A Process Model* (n.d.). Unpublished manuscript available at http://www.focusing.org/process.html.

experience as I had it. Nor was there anything momentous in the content I took in: the landscape was more like a still life than anything dramatically developed. In short, the attending I did was as innocuous as it was swiftly realized. Nevertheless, it tells us something essential about attending and its close alliance with glancing.

About attending, it indicates that the act often arises spontaneously, that is, for no apparent reason, and yet in response to something in the circumambient world that draws it out (in this case, the immediate landscape). A fine balance is immediately struck between the reactive and the spontaneous; or rather, both are in play: I was at once drawn to look out at the house (this is the reactive element), yet not compelled to do so (I did so spontaneously). Further, this act of attention need have no definitely marked beginning or endpoint. It can arise in the course of events so smoothly as not even to be noticed in its emergence; and even if it ends abruptly, momentarily staunching the attentional stream, it need not stand out from that stream in any conspicuous, much less lasting, way. No wonder, then, that in cases such as this attending does not announce itself as anything extraordinary. It is so immanent to the experiential flow as not to call for any special scrutiny. Hence, in the ordinary course of things, we rarely attend to attending itself. Hence, too, James's temptation to eliminate it as a significant act in its own right:

> Attention may have to go, like many a faculty once deemed essential, like many a verbal phantom, like many an idol of the tribe. It may be an excrescence on Psychology. No need of it to drag ideas before consciousness or fix them, when we see how perfectly they drag and fix each other there.[54]

In the end, James hesitates to apply Occam's razor to the entire phenomenon; he would like to believe that "the voluntary effort to attend" is of great value, since it "would deepen and prolong the stay in consciousness of innumerable ideas which else would fade more quickly away. The delay thus gained might not be more than a second in duration—but that second might be *critical*."[55] For in that second I may discover something of central importance that really makes a difference in my current conduct: say, a glimpse of smoke emerging from the upstairs bedroom of that same gray-green house, occasioning a call to the fire department on my part. (But notice that even this discovery does not call for concerted attention; my look need only pause just long enough to detect the fire.[56])

And the looking? What are we to say of this? First of all, it occurs here in the

54. James, *Principles of Psychology*, vol. 1, p. 428.

55. The first words are from ibid., p. 428, the second from p. 419 (his italics). He adds: "for in the constant rising and falling of considerations in the mind, where two associated systems of them are nearly in equilibrium it is often a matter of but a second more or less of attention at the outset, whether one system shall gain force to occupy the field and develop itself, and exclude the other, or be excluded itself by the other. When developed, it may make us act; and that act may seal our doom" (ibid., p. 429).

56. James refers to the gaining of time for critical "ideas"; but his point obtains equally for perceptions.

guise of glancing, itself a paradigm of spontaneous seeing. I was, after all, just looking through the window as the episode got under way; and just looking, as we have observed, is equivalent to glancing around in a perceptual modality. But the same look, modest as its origin was, sustained my attending all the way across the road and up the hill to the house where it found its terminus. Here glancing acts as the phenomenal "bearer" (*Träger*), the literal "porter" of my attending, displaying the wares of virtual perception to which I may attend.

But the glancing enacted here was more than merely instrumental; it gave to the attending a characteristic visual arc that was at once swift and comprehensive, focused and discerning. The way of the glance is mercurial yet insightful, momentary yet capable of covering much ground. As such, it is the natural ally of attention, its silent Hermetic partner. In the perception of the world around us, the glance often leads the way, charting out the pathways of attention. These pathways are not independent tracks or trails to be followed *later* by attentional acts; instead, they blaze the trail of attending itself, being its forward fringe: at once the harbinger of the action and part of the action itself. The very insubstantiality of the glance, its mereness and playfulness, aids it immensely in this trailblazing behavior. The glance beckons us to attend; it summons us to pay attention; but it is also integral to attending itself. It is at once the vehicle of attending, escorting it into existence, as well as a primary means of attending itself. My glance took me to the gray-green house in the first place, and in so doing it allowed me to see the house itself more clearly—to pause at its surface so as to attend to it more completely.

IX

My experience in Williamstown was monothetic in that the attending and the glancing alike were enacted entirely in perceptual terms. Earlier, I considered cases in which both acts were mental in status: for example, in following my first thoughts upon waking from a nap. In such cases as these latter, we attend and glance with the aid of "the mind's eye." But still other avatars are possible, namely, those in which perceptual and mental activities both contribute to one coherent experience. These cases, which are more numerous than we might think, demonstrate that truth dwells not just "in the inner man" (Saint Augustine), nor exclusively outside us in the perceptual realm, but in complex combinations of both regions. If phenomenology teaches us that the domain within is at least as rich and multifarious as the domain without—that both are genuine *fields*—we also need to recognize that the two fields are capable of significant alliance.[57]

57. This is not to deny that each kind of field has its own peculiar structures, its own unique specificity: its *Eigenheit* in Husserl's early term. The axiomatic statement is this: "Every mental process belonging to the stream which can be reached by our reflective regard has an *essence of*

We saw one form of this alliance at play in Gendlin's technique of focusing, where the mental and bodily/perceptual components were indistinguishable in felt experience. Another such alliance is that in which these components are distinguishable even if ultimately inseparable. A case in point is described by Husserl:

> [Consider] a free turning of "regard"—not precisely or only of the physical, but rather of the "*mental regard*" [*geistigen Blickes*]—from the sheet of paper regarded at first [perceptually], to the objects already previously appearing, therefore attended to "implicitly" before the turning of the regard [*Blickwendung*] but which become explicitly attended to (either "attentively perceived" or "incidentally heeded") *after* the regard is turned to them.[58]

What Husserl seems to have in mind here is something close to what I shall term "adumbration": from within an experience of ordinary perceiving (which has its own dialectic of attention and glancing), we can effect a change in the *order of attention,* moving from one kind of "regard," that of ordinary perceptual looking (as directed at a focal thing) to another, specifically marginal attending. With respect to what we are now actively perceiving, the latter is merely "implicit," that is to say, it is implicated by the perception but will not become explicit until we turn our perceptual look toward it completely; until that action, we have to do with a moment of lateral noticing. At first, in its adumbrated (literally, "shadowed forth") state, it is something we have "in mind": it comes along with my present perception but is not focally given in it, I am aware of it but it has not been spelled out in explicit perceptual terms. Until this latter happens, its status is that of "preperception,"[59] that is, a holding in mind until a direct perception of it arises.

Husserl here presents us with a complex case in which straightforward attending by means of ordinary perception is accompanied by mental glancing, with both being succeeded by the actual perception of what was marginally noticed: the one giving rise to the other in a tightly knit sequence in which we are barely aware of the transition from one act to the next. Abetted by the fact that we are dealing in all three phases with the same object (or set of objects), the effect is that of a virtually seamless series, i.e., perceiving/holding in mind/ perceiving. In this way we witness a genuine continuity between mental and perceptual attending. Not only does this continuity contest the classical dichotomy between "impressions" and "ideas" enshrined by Hume, but it also calls into question my own working distinction between attending that is "external" (that is, perceptual) and that which is "inner" (that is, mental). It also suggests that mental attending is not restricted to introspective acts; it can assume forms that are capable of joining forces with external attending as an active partner of the latter. But in every case, the action of the *Blick* is essentially the same:

---

its own [*ein eigenes Wesen*] which can be seized upon intuitively, a 'content' which allows of being considered *by itself in its ownness*" (Husserl, *Ideas I,* section 34, p. 69; his italics).

58. Ibid., p. 71; his italics. Translation modified.

59. James cites this term from G. H. Lewes at *Principles of Psychology,* p. 416.

"advertence" (*Zuwendung*) to the object, whether this object is perceived or adumbrated, imagined or remembered.[60]

Another concrete instance of the alliance between perceptual and nonperceptual elements is this: I am in conversation with Richard V., someone I have known from early childhood. I grasp his face, indeed his whole body, as he speaks; I explicitly advert, in my perception of him, to those aspects that he is presenting to me directly—aspects that are auditory and kinesthetic as well as visual. Staying with this initial presentation, I find myself anticipating his next conversational move in a spontaneous and effortless way. I have a distinct if implicit preperceptual sense of the way his lips will move, how his head will pivot ever so slightly, and how his arms will move forward in an expressive gesture in which his hands will also be involved. Since these various micromovements have not yet happened, I cannot be said to *perceive* them as of yet. Indeed, a sudden new turn of thought on his part may send the ensuing perceptual presentation in a very different direction from what I was anticipating. But just as possible is a scenario in which my imaginative anticipation coordinates closely with what I come to see subsequently—an anticipation based in large part on my previous acquaintance with my friend. A first glance, the perceptual look proper, is immediately succeeded by another glance, properly mental (*geistige*), which links the opening perceptual glance with a later such glance that fastens fully onto what I have glimpsed adumbratively in the first glance. The mental glance is a veritable mediatrix between the two explicitly perceptual advertences:

ADVERTENCE 1

1st perceptual glance: explicit perception of my friend speaking

ADVERTENCE 2

Preperceptual, imaginative/memorial adumbration of my perception of this friend's next move

ADVERTENCE 3

2nd perceptual glance: arising from adumbration of my friend's next move

Two caveats are here in order. First, in the actuality of continuing experience, the succession of advertences is much subtler and swifter than the above dia-

---

60. James might well support this non-dichotomizing move: his categories of interest and effort apply equally well to perceptual and to "intellectual" attending.

gram, with its high degree of segmented spatialization, would suggest. Rather than an "objective succession" (in Kant's phrase), we have to do with a flux of phases that is closer to what Bergson would designate as a "heterogeneous multiplicity" in which the several phases (that is, acts of advertence) overlap rather than neatly and simply succeed each other, one by one. The actual situation is more like this:

Second, the mental glance as the middle term (that is, "advertence #2) is not exclusively forward-looking: it is also, and equally, backward-tending: postperceptual as well as preperceptual, "retentional" as much as "protentional." Part of the close dovetailing effected by the mediation of the mental glance (advertence #2) is its continuation, or at least its reflection, of the just-preceding phase (advertence #1) on which it builds even as (and precisely insofar as) it looks ahead to the next phase (advertence #3) by way of anticipation. The term "adumbration" (itself modeled on Husserl's *Abschattung*, "profile") captures the bi-directionality here at stake: the intermediate *geistige Blick* at once incorporates what it has just seen and projects what is about to happen.

X

On still other occasions, there is an even more distinct alternation between acts of perceptual attention and those of mental attention—where the latter do not adumbrate the former but signify a genuinely inward glance into our own mental field. Another example from recent experience:

> Gina asks me if I had truly sent a letter of recommendation on her behalf to the director of the Collegium Phaenomenologicum concerning her participation in this summer's meeting at the Collegium: "Ed, are you sure you sent it?" I search my memory, at first drawing a blank, but then, suddenly, a vague but unmistakable memory image arises before my mind's eye: myself putting *two* letters of recommendation into a single envelope to be sent to David Wood, the director of the Collegium. Since I know I mailed only two such letters, one for Gina and another for Rita, and since it would make sense to mail them together (though I had not distinctly remembered this), I take this to prove the point and I exclaim: "Gina, you can relax now. I must have sent it."

This glance into my memory represents an instance of primary mental attending; no detail of my immediate local environment was part of the attended-to content, nor was it even relevant (I was now in a different geographical location from that in which I wrote the letters). Instead, there emerged, from a nebulous mental field, a pertinent item that satisfied my search for confirmation: the long envelope into which my phantomic hands were seen as placing the two letters in question. A mere mental glance sufficed to answer Gina's pressing question. Strikingly, the confirming item, albeit vaguely presented, allowed for a "singling out and seizing," as in perception proper, yet without any "experiential background" of the sort that figured in my own earlier example of fully perceptual attending wherein I knew the gray-green house at which I glanced to be surrounded with a ring of mountains, even though I was not adverting to them as such.[61]

Thus the absence of a distinctive background constitutes a first difference from advertence in ordinary perception. The second is the absence of a continuously traversable space over which my glance moved. In the case of Gina's letter, my look shot straight to the relevant remembered episode, without crossing any discernible or felt space. The image of stuffing an envelope arose as if from nowhere, and its appearance was an all-or-nothing matter. There is no traversal here of a single stretch of time or space, indeed no sense of approach at all, in contrast with my perception of the house in Williamstown. All that was present were the envelope and the ghostly fingers inserting letters into it: that and nothing more, with the result that there was only one thing to attend to, one content of my mental glance. This exemplified a certain psychical economy in which nothing was wasted, nor was there anything unexpected: hence it was well suited to answer Gina's inquiry.

Consider a second example of mixed modes—"braided" in my nomenclature —but one that is more anticipatory than remembered:

> It is evening in New York. I have just looked out my window toward Harlem, which is lighting up rapidly as the sun sets. I find myself thinking of my upcoming trip to California next week on Jet Blue. This will be my first trip on this airline, and my first-ever flight into the Oakland airport. I imagine myself flying in over Berkeley, and seeing the runway (through the window) to be rough and full of holes; then my mental look leaps to renting a car at this same airport, something I seem able to do in one quick instant; another leap takes me onto Highway 880 heading north to 80, on my way to my sister's town of Vallejo: I envisage myself both inside a nondescript rental car *and* looking onto the roadway as if from high above it. . . . I return to looking out the window at Harlem bejeweled now that darkness has set in more fully.

This example is hardly unusual; I would wager that many human beings imaginatively project an oncoming future event in some comparably complex but sketchy way. But it is unusual indeed when compared to the kind of attending we do when we are in the midst of the perceptual field and looking into it or

---

61. The terms "singling out and seizing" (*herausfassen*) and "experiential background" (*Erfahrungshintergrund*) are Husserl's: see *Ideas I*, pp. 65–72.

across it. My attention now is much more saltatory; it occurs by leaps, with little to connect the incidents on which it focused except for the fact that they were part of my journey to California. First one event (flying over Berkeley), then another (landing on the runway), then another (renting the car), then still another (being on Highway 880)—so many events, each distinct and self-enclosed, but with no linking events or places. My mental glance jumps effortlessly from one to the next, lingering neither between events nor on any single event: even renting the car, often a tedious time-consuming matter in practical reality, is imagined in a thrice.

This example shares two features with previous instances in this and the last section. First of all, in each of these four cases mental attending occurs in a moment of pause between two acts of overt perceptual looking; such attending is literally inter-mittent. Second, it occurs effortlessly even though it represents an entire change of level: that is, from perceptual to pre- or postperceptual, and from this latter back to perceptual. But in the two examples given in this section this interstitial attending is not merely escorted and supported by a mental glance but more radically occurs *as* this kind of glance. One glimpse and seen! Just one distinct *geistige Blick* suffices, and this happens in an instant or moment, an *Augenblick* in the expressive German term (which, as we have seen before, means literally, "blink of the eye" or "quick look"). To attend to the remembered envelope-stuffing or to the projected view over Berkeley/renting the car/beginning to drive *is* to glance at these things; and conversely, to glance at them *is* to attend to them. Either way of putting it works; the two acts fully overlap.

In neither of these last two cases is there what James calls reality's "whole sting and excitement,"[62] its resistance, its having-to-be the way it looks. Whereas the explicitly perceptual glance encounters gradients of adversity as it makes its way across a preexisting and lasting landscape, the expressly mental look moves frictionlessly through a diaphanous medium that offers virtually no resistance: hence the saltatory character of the last example. Not that this medium is *un*real, for example, hallucinatory or delusional; it is perfectly genuine as a mode of consciousness that, in and by itself, does not mislead us; but it lacks the bite of the real that is reflected in the German word for "actuality": *Wirklichkeit* (*wirklich*, from *wirken*, connotes having a felt effect, working on us, thanks to its edge or bite). It is as if the sting of the real had been removed—suspended in an act of spontaneous *epoché*—allowing us to go right to the attentional thing or event itself, at which we are able to glance freely and uninhibited by the constraints of the actually perceived world around us, entering an inner world wherein the requirement of continuous traversal in space and time has been lifted.

---

62. "The whole feeling of reality, the whole sting and excitement of our voluntary life, depends on our sense that in it things are *really being decided* from one moment to another" (James, *Principles of Psychology*, vol. 1, p. 429; his italics).

XI

So far we have considered four situations in which attention and glance coexist and collaborate: one in which both figure as fully perceptual in status (wherein the glance carries attention to its material target, at once facilitating and focusing attentional consciousness); another, in which both attending and glancing occur by means of the mind's eye, whether in imagining or remembering; a third, wherein the mental glance intervenes to supplement ordinary perceptual attention by an adumbrative action that links perceptions more closely together; finally, a circumstance in which we consult something introspectively as a separate act located between two (or more) perceptions that braids them together.

Of course, in living experience the matter is rarely so neat and clear as this cursory typology suggests. Gendlin's technique of focusing shows us a situation in which the corporeal and the psychical conjoin in the expression of feeling: an expression that is an act of attention to our current state of being through a recognitory glance at that state. Moreover, just as we cannot always parse out what is spontaneous from what is reactive in a given instance of attending, so we cannot easily sort out the precise form of collaboration between attending and glancing, their distinct contributions to a collocation complicated further by the fact that each can occur in a perceptual or a mental manner. The truth is that this collaboration is more of a cascade of roiling waters than a smooth stream. This is not even to consider that perception itself is not the simple, "basic act" that Husserl envisioned at the time of *Logical Investigations;* in its object-obsession, perception must be distinguished from what both Erwin Straus and Merleau-Ponty call "sensing," which concerns the pre-objective and qualitative aspects of experience and is not to be confused with "sensation" (which is held to occur in atomized formats).[63] Several of my examples have privileged perceptual attention (for example, as in the case of the house to which I attended across the snowy lawn) or its mentalistic equivalent (the envelope I recalled upon my student's question); but a factor of sensing was never far away: the house was grasped as *gray-green,* the envelope as *white:* that is, in terms of distinct colors even if the objects they qualify were not altogether complete or definite. Many acts of attention combine perceiving with sensing—as when I attend to something I perceive, taking full account of my current bodily or emotional state: for instance, suddenly seeing a long-lost friend with special delight. By the same token, what I have been calling "mental" attending is not monological either; we

63. On sensing vs. perceiving, see Erwin Straus, *The Primary World of the Senses,* tr. J. Needleman (Glencoe, Ill.: Free Press, 1963), pp. 317 ff.; and Merleau-Ponty, *Phenomenology of Perception,* preface, et seq. Eugene Gendlin in effect develops a model of sensing in his *Experiencing and the Creation of Meaning: A Philosophical and Psychology Approach to the Subjective* (New York: Free Press, 1962). Regarding perception as the "basic act," see Edmund Husserl, *Logical Investigations,* tr. J. N. Findlay (New York: Humanities, 1970), vol. 2, Investigations V and VI.

have already seen two variations of it in the instances of memorial recapture and anticipatory projection; doubtless still other forms of "presentification" (*Vergegenwärtigung*) are also possible, for example, by means of signs or symbols as they collaborate with imagining and remembering—each of which in turn has its own distinctive modalities (such as primary versus secondary memory, imageful versus imageless imagining).

Of still greater import is the question as to whether attending is to be considered one kind of act—that is, attending as such—or several in kind. Husserl, in a late text, argues for two basic sorts of attending, doxic and nondoxic. The first bears on what is taken to exist (though also modalized as perhaps existing, supposedly existing, probably existing, and so on), and it characteristically awakens an interest in its object's presence and fate. The second does not concern itself with existing things but with sheer possibilities and the like.[64] James recognizes at least six forms of attention: sensorial, intellectual, immediate, derived (that is, by way of association), effortless or passive, and active or voluntary.[65] Despite this proliferation of types, both Husserl and James single out a central, pervasive feature of all attending, a core action as it were. For Husserl, this is "tending-toward in realization" (*vollziehend Tendieren*).[66] James says similarly that attention is "the taking possession by the mind, in clear and vivid form, of one out of what seem several simultaneously possible objects or trains of thought. Focalization, concentration, of consciousness are of its essence."[67] Moreover, for James interest is also of capital importance: that to which I do not attend is what holds no interest for me.[68] The convergence of these generic claims is as striking as their differences: though James underlines active possessing in contrast to Husserl's milder notion of tending-toward (a close cousin of advertence), each agrees that attention has to do with concentration on a single object or train of thought.

There are two difficulties with this convergent, otherwise reasonable position. First, we can attend to whole complexes of objects and not single objects alone: attention, as we have seen, can be "polythetic" as well as single-minded. Second, concentration as such is not unique to attention, since many other intentional acts involve some factor of concentration. The truth is that any effort to come up with an overall definition of attention either overlooks significant phenomena (for example, polycentered foci) or is so general as to be threatened with vapidity: it may well cover all known cases, but only in the most diffuse manner. Yet

---

64. See Edmund Husserl, *Experience and Judgment*, tr. J. S. Churchill and K. Ameriks (Evanston, Ill.: Northwestern University Press, 1973), sections 18–20.

65. James, *Principles of Psychology*, vol. 1, pp. 393–394.

66. Husserl, *Experience and Judgment*, p. 80.

67. James, *Principles of Psychology*, vol. 1, pp. 381–382. Compare F. H. Bradley: "We may call attention a state which implies domination or chief tenancy of consciousness. Or we may compare it to the focusing of an optical instrument. . . ." ("Is There Any Special Activity of Attention?" in *Collected Essays* [Oxford: Clarendon Press, 1935], vol. 1, p. 182).

68. See James, *Principles of Psychology*, vol. 1, pp. 380, 393.

when we go to the other extreme by underlining differences between acts of attending, we discover a hornet's nest of disparate ways to attend. Does this mean that there is no "special activity of attention" in F. H. Bradley's phrase, or perhaps that it is a will-o'-the-wisp, falling through our analytical fingers whenever we try to pin it down? Slippery it may be, but I would opt for a model of family resemblance whereby "attention" names an open-ended collection whose members are similar to each other without, however, sharing a single common trait. Bradley's assessment is thus on target: there is not "any *one* special activity [of attention] at all, but various activities [which], if they lead to one result, are called attending."[69] In the last several sections, I been arguing for at least three major such activities, each of which realizes attending in its own distinctive way: perceiving, introspecting, and adumbrating.

Granting then the diversity of attending, what of glancing? This, too, is multiple in format, and all the more certainly so when it colludes with attending. Not only do we glance with our organic eyes, we glance mentally with the mind's eye in a quasi-optical way. Each of these in turn can be a voluntary or a spontaneous act. Moreover, we glance in such a way as to discern or pick out, or else to determine what surrounds something. So far the parallel with attention, especially with its perceptual forms, is close. But consider that we sometimes glance in such a sweeping way as to forgo any particular focus—we just *glance across* something, for example, refusing to settle on any particular detail. And we also *glance around*, casually and intermittently, with no plan or purpose, just letting our look land wherever it may. In these cases, only fragmentary glimpses are afforded—a side of this, the color of that: wisps of looks rather than full-fledged scrutinies, "passing glances" instead of invested gazes, glances askance instead of steady stares. Yet these bare glancings-around and glancings-across make up the glance-world as much as the brief but concerted glancings-at or glancings-toward that so often fill out, or confirm, outright perceptual looking (such as when we take a quick "second look" to be sure of someone's identity). The more casual forms of glancing are desultory by their very character, and they can be quite unsettling in what they suddenly bring to light—often seemingly from nowhere. These forms can obtain in inward as well as external vision. When these passing modes of glancing are added to more focused forms, we have an entire family of types and subtypes, occupying a house with many floors and ad hoc additions whose occupants are very diverse yet still related to each other as members of a quite expansive genus.

Given the evident complexity of attention as well as the array of ways in which we glance, we cannot claim that the two actions are equivalent in some basic manner, or even parallel in their operations, much less that they are constant companions. Their relationship is much like that of the glance and the saccade: often occurring together, yet not necessarily so. We can think of attending and glancing as forming a double helix, circling around each other, sometimes criss-

69. Bradley, "Is There Any Special Activity of Attention?" p. 181. My italics.

crossing in moments of close collaboration, and sometimes acting apart. At the moments of intersection, they can be virtually indistinguishable—as when my mental glance at that remembered envelope was at the same time my attending to it. At other times, I can glance without attending at all, for example, in a sweeping glance that scans a scene without taking note of any particular thing in it. Or I can attend without glancing, as when I am engaged in a prolonged scrutiny of something, say, a specimen at the end of a microscope through which I am looking studiously; or when I am mulling over a memory. In such cases of comparative independence, the gyres widen. But they never move into entirely different orbits having no relation whatsoever to each other, as if they were utterly disparate actions.

Whenever I glance, the possibility of attending to what my glance takes in lurks nearby; almost always when I attend to something, I have been led there by a glance, or I can glance at it now that I am attending to it, and I can always glance away at something else. Or else my attending occurs precisely in and by glancing: the one act is the accomplishment of the other. Whichever is the case on any given occasion, attention and glance engage one another in a veritable *pas de deux*, a two-step dance in which neither partner takes the lead every time. An odd couple, oddly balanced in their very imbalance, even in their unevenness, complementary even as they differ, conjoint in their very disjointedness.

Attending and glancing constitute a pair composed of odd *and* even, same *and* different, like *and* unlike. This is not Plato's *ariostos dyas* ("indefinite dyad")— not anything metaphysically based or biased—but something epistemically and descriptively significant as integral phases of an ongoing experience, intrinsic to its alertness and readiness, scope and range. Indispensable parts of our vision of the world—of our vision *in* the world, of the world-on-view—these two inconstant but indispensable companions are everywhere commingling in minding and perceiving, both being essential to the manifestness of everything we see wherever and however we look.

Part 4

Praxis of the Glance

We delved deeply into the human subject in the previous part of this book—into this subject's temporality, inherent singularizing powers, and acts of attending—after having made a foray outward from the enclosure of this subject in part 2, where we explored certain cultural, historical, and social dimensions of the glancing person. In this final part, we shall take up further aspects of the human subject's concrete life in the place-world. This time the focus will be on particular forms of action in which glancing figures formatively even if not always conspicuously. In effect, we will be returning to our point of departure in part 1, where everyday modes of glancing practice were at stake—for example, in the public space of the Café Felix and in getting oriented in Ann Arbor, Michigan. Indeed, throughout this book, the issue has been how glancing forms part of daily life; but where earlier the focus was on its insertion into unsorted ongoing actions of this life—reading, writing, driving, walking, talking—now we will look more closely at three particular areas, each of which has its own format, rules, inspiration, and goals: the ethical dimension of humans, ethics in the natural environment, and art. Each of these latter constitutes its own domain of operation, with its own distinctive goals and rules. Nevertheless, in all three realms we will witness the glance in its outgoing intentionality, its movement away from the interiority of the glancer in a decided thrust into exteriority.

"Exteriority" is Emmanuel Levinas's term for the ethical relation among human beings as they are in face-to-face proximity to each other. Such proximity is not to be confused with literal closeness: according to Levinas, in the ethical relation human subjects are in a situation of profound separation in which each is infinitely transcendent to others, standing over against those others in a "height" that brooks no measurement. The practice of ethics is the assumption of responsibility for the Other (capitalized so as to indicate the sheer transcendence of the other human being) without any prospect of genuine reciprocation. Ethical actions are one-way: they go from me to the Other grasped in his or her destitution and need. In other words, such actions go *out of me:* out of my egological enclosure, out from my narcissistic satisfaction in material possessions and comfortable dwelling, and in every case they go *toward the Other.* This happens by my actions, by my praxis rather than by the invocation of a principle to respect the Other or any intention to have benevolent intentions toward him or her. The ethical consists thus in *acting out,* not in the usual pejorative sense of this term, but in the sense of addressing the Other's distress from within my own unmitigated responsibility.

The Levinasian paradigm, here only schematically presented, will be very much at issue in the first and second chapters of this concluding part. I employ it as exemplary of an effort to de-subjectify the ethical domain and to insist that ethics itself is a matter of practice, of doing instead of intending or recommending doing. This clears the space for demonstrating that the glance is a constituent part of such practice. If the ethical entails acting concretely—as thinkers as diverse as Aristotle and Levinas have emphasized—my contention will be that the glance, the very vanguard of so much human action, is an integral part of ethical action. And it remains at the literal forefront of such action when the realm of concern is no longer the human as such but the nonhuman in the comprehensive sense of the natural environment as a whole (a whole that exceeds the human even as it includes it).

We shall explore the ethical in its human and nonhuman reaches (chapters 10 and 11) and move from there to a treatment of the aesthetic (chapter 12). Practice is primary both in the creation of art and in its enjoyment, each being a form of embodied activity. My emphasis will be on the production and appreciation of images in the visual arts, specifically painting and photography. We shall see that the glance figures centrally into the activity, the very praxis, of these arts: even more so than we might at first imagine. It is the cutting edge of the practice whereby such images are created in the first place and then taken in by others. This happens so spontaneously and with such rare recourse to abstract principle that it deserves to be tracked in its own right—something that is rarely performed in the manner of the detailed analysis offered here.

It might seem that in moving from ethics to aesthetics as I do in this last part I am trying to link two disciplines usually held far apart (with certain notable exceptions such as Plato and Kant, who closely ally the beautiful with the good). But this is not my express intention, and in any case the disciplinary difference is not the difference that will matter in my account. Rather, we shall be concerned with two particular extroversions of praxis:

(i) from enacting the ethical in the human domain to redressing undue damage to the natural environment;
(ii) from spontaneously generating inner images to creating and crafting images that are perceivable by others as they inhabit certain visual artworks.

The first movement is from the delimited sphere of the human to the open-ended region of natural entities of many kinds, and the second is from the psychical to the physical. It is thus a matter of actions of glancing in two domains that can be said to *bear out* what might otherwise have been *kept within.* Thinking this way, we cannot restrict ethics to the domain of "the moral law within" (in Kant's celebrated phrase) or art to the realm of inner imagination or inspiration. Escorted upon the wings of the glance, we shall venture in this part to go from the robust human Other in the opening chapter to the encompassing world of nature in the next chapter, and finally (in the last chapter) to the art world of painted and photographed images. Overall, the movement is from person to nature to image: from other human beings as ethically compelling to the natural world that surrounds us, and from these two compelling realms to what entices us by its formal beauty and sublime upsurge. We shall pass through the human to the nonhuman, and end with painted and photographed images of both. We move in this way from what is massively *given,* namely, other humans and wild nature, to what is *fabricated*—that is, the creation of artifacts that are considered artworks.

In this way, we shall make a journey through three levels of being: the interhuman domain, the natural environment, and the artistic image. In each case, the glance plays a distinctive role, that of being the pilot of the pertinent praxis, leading the action onward and outward. In the case of ethical action, the glance goes out to meet the Other on the Other's own terms: it glances out to let the Other take the lead.[1] Here it is essential to the interstitial actions of the face-to-face relationship, being the pre-discursive yet highly expressive medium of the first contact with the Other. It is also the basis of the acknowledgment of the other person as a singular being who is at the same time a member of the human species: the Other as a singular universal. Nothing better than a glance is able to discern this special status of the Other so quickly and definitively in ethical encounters. Further, as the field of the glance is broadened so as to include the "other-than-human" (in David Abram's phrase),[2] it shows itself uniquely capable of discerning disturbances in the natural world, whether they exist in a nascent or a developed state, and to respond to these troubles by inducing appropriate interventions. In the case of the artistic image—which I shall construe as an "image-thing" that is not confined to the mental image—the glance projects itself (that is, "throws itself before itself") into the space of the possible or the actual. It is as if the artist's glancing eye strayed from its accustomed source in the head and traveled down the brush to the canvas, there to trace out the lines and to create the colors of what *might be the case;* while the photographer's wandering eye goes out through the camera into a scene that is *certainly the case.* In either instance, the glance leads the way, and in both it sediments itself into a painted or photographed image that in turn solicits the spectator's glance back at the created work.

In this last part, then, we shall be dealing with three forms of praxis, each imbued and informed by the human glance: the action of acknowledging the Other as a singular human subject, the action of noticing and responding to environmental distress, and the action of creating and appreciating the artistic image. I am not claiming that the glance constitutes *all* of the actions called for in these diverse situations; other actions are required as well, whether these be of further discernment by a different kind of looking (for example, intense scrutiny) or of follow-up in another sensory modality (for example, touching or hearing). But I am maintaining that in every such situation the glance is decid-edly active in its uniquely premonitory power and alert foresight: in the brief moment of its issuance, it adumbrates and guides more complete and more concretely effective actions. Slender as its contribution may seem at first blush, on closer inspection it looms large—much larger than it does in those many theories that privilege perception over apperception, principle over action, and more generally interiority over exteriority.

1. Or so it is on the Levinasian model that I shall take to hold true of the interhuman world, though requiring substantial revision when it comes to the natural world.

2. See David Abrams, *The Spell of the Sensuous* (New York: Pantheon, 1998), passim.

10

THE ETHICS OF THE GLANCE

> In a wee wooden schoolhouse, something put it into
> the boys' and girls' heads to buy gorgeous visiting
> cards—ten cents a package—and exchange. The ex-
> change was merry, till one girl, a tall newcomer, re-
> fused my card—refused it peremptorily, with a
> glance. Then it dawned upon me with a certain sud-
> denness that I was different from the others; or like,
> mayhap, in heart and life and longing, but shut out
> from their world by a vast veil.

—W. E. B. Du Bois, *The Souls of Black Folk*

> Ethics is an optics.

—Emmanuel Levinas, *Totality and Infinity*

I

How can anything so light-headed and playful as a glance contribute to something as ponderous and serious as ethics? Is not the glance the epitome of the
superficial in human experience, concerning itself with the sheer surface of
things, the merely phenomenal—if not the epiphenomenal—rather than with
the noumenal, wherein the ethical is supposed to find its foundation on a Kantian model? What can the glance have to do with the idea of the good or the
intuition of the right? Given its waywardness, how can it relate to what is a
matter of principle, of imperatives and rules, normativities and values? What
does the glance—so easily lured into any trivial pursuit—have to do with pure
practical reason, which writes its own rationally sanctioned laws in stone and
speaks portentously with the spirit of gravity?

Despite these plausible doubts, I shall persist in pursuing this unlikely topic.
To begin with, consider a fairly frequent experience that already suggests that
the glance may occupy a special place in the ethical domain. I refer to the
sudden perception of someone as ethically exemplary. When I witness on the
evening news a person diving without hesitation into icy waters to save people
whose plane has crashed in a Washington, D.C., river, I see, immediately arrayed before me, an inspiring instance of human heroism. In the same spirit, I

can tell from a glance at Frank Hurley's haunting photographs of the ill-starred Shackleton expedition to Antarctica that extraordinary moral strength was at play in this saga of impacted polar ice. The same goes for many other less dramatic actions, which wear their ethically exemplary status on their sleeves: the other night the manager of a restaurant in downtown Chicago told me he wasn't charging me for dinner, saying that he just "felt good that day."

The striking thing about exemplary actions—and this is true of those that are aesthetically or politically as well as ethically exemplary—is that a mere glance is almost always enough to persuade us of the inherent value of those actions. In part, this is because they are not mere tokens of a type that would invite comparisons with other actions fitting under the same type; they bristle with the type itself: they embody the very essence of being or doing good, creating beauty, or acting in a politically efficacious way. Think of films of Picasso or Matisse painting; or photographs of Gandhi practicing *satyagruha*. Since the type is here present in the token itself, I can grasp it in the bare appearance of the latter. This stands in contrast with all those cases in which I must *infer* what is right to do, or beautiful to create, or politically efficacious to enact: either by putting an individual instance under a preexisting rule, or by collecting many such instances to reach for a general law of the good or the right or the beautiful. Precisely because of the immediacy of its apprehension, I am all the more likely to want to undertake the same kind of action myself: the exemplary, grasped in a glance, is always exemplary *for me,* carrying with it the message that I, this mere passing witness, can do these things myself. The ethical force derives not just from what I observe but from that which, having been glimpsed, I internalize in such a way as to bring about change within myself.[1]

"In the deadly crush of an air-raid shelter the glances of two strangers suddenly meet for a second in astonishing and unrelated mutuality; when the All Clear sounds it is forgotten; and yet it did happen, in a realm which existed only for that moment."[2] Martin Buber, who relates this incident from his World War II experience, remarks that something intensely significant has here happened "even in the tiniest and most transient events which scarcely enter consciousness."[3] In a mere exchange of glances, something important between human beings has transpired—important for ethical engagement and important for a phenomenology of the ethical itself.

---

1. The same obtains for others who are comparably moved by the exemplary action and, ideally, for myself-with-others in an act of communal recognition of the exemplary. I owe this observation to Emily Lee.

2. Martin Buber, *Between Man and Man,* tr. R. G. Smith (London: Kegan Paul, 1947), p. 204.

3. Ibid.

II

My overall strategy is to present various concrete instances of the glance as it figures formatively in ethical situations. Several of these situations come from life on city streets; others from the natural environment will be treated in the next chapter. These are very different contexts, yet they share one thing in common: the unsuspected power of the glance in ethically demanding circumstances.

As it happens, I began writing on the glance on Martin Luther King Jr. Day. All that King did—all the changes he instituted—came from his concrete perceptions that injustice was being done in very specific ways: ways so specific that they could be gleaned in a glance. Just walking onto a bus in the Deep South in the 1950s showed in an instant the reality of Jim Crow seating policies; the same was true of segregated classrooms, restaurants, theaters, and businesses—and of the bathrooms and water fountains found in each of these institutions. As we say revealingly, "a moment's notice sufficed" to see the pervasiveness and tenacity of such segregationist practices. A glance was quite enough. Enough to ignite outrage for all who had eyes to see. Not that it hadn't been seen before: above all, by numerous blacks living in the southern states. But given a certain readiness in the social and political environment, the particularly powerful look of a moral leader such as Martin Luther King Jr. could detect right away what was wrong and how to go about remedying it. In order to enlist others in this action (notably those who did not live in the South), he had to encourage them to take in what was awry about segregationist practices: he had to get them to look, too. Change came from the massive coordination of all these onlookers—all those who took the time, the intense moment, to look evil in the face, and to take certain decisive actions—until the very laws of the land were changed in response to a vast canvas of interwoven glances.

Of course, gaining civil rights for blacks was a massive historical event with many determinants, among which the immediate confrontation with evil was only one ingredient. Yet have we ever fully pondered how crucial this confrontational moment may be? Sartre spotted much the same moment early in the French Revolution when tiny groups of three or more citizens gathered on street corners to form the critical "groups in fusion" that, linking up with other such groups, helped to make the Revolution as a whole happen. But this moment—which is the moment of the glance: the concerned citizens exchanged glances even more rapidly and knowingly than they exchanged heated words—is itself swept up and lost in the larger movement of *The Critique of Dialectical Reason,* the book in which the very idea of such groups in fusion was first set forth in 1960, presaging the social movements of the decade to come.

In the same vein, a minor but no less revealing episode from later in that decade comes to mind. It was 1967 and I was a graduate student in Chicago. I was walking back from the El to my apartment on Hudson Street when I suddenly noticed a man beating a woman across the street, striking her head repeatedly against a car. I saw this at a glance, I felt it was wrong, I walked right over to the scene—and my merely heading toward the couple in such a concerted way distracted the man sufficiently so that the woman could flee. He was trying with his glances back at me to figure out what kind of a threat I posed. Rash behavior on my part? Probably. I could have made things *worse* for the woman, and endangered myself to boot. But my point is not about appropriate behavior or its actual consequences. It is about the glance that precipitates conduct, wise or not. Not just *at* a glance but still more importantly *in* the glance, I saw injustice occurring; I saw immediately that things were not right in that street scene; what I did about it can be debated, but my bodily action ensued directly upon the initiatory moment of the glance.

Emmanuel Levinas might well have held that this Chicago street scene is an instance of his own notion of justice as requiring a "third" (*le tiers:* curiously, the same term used by Sartre in his description of a group in fusion, in which each member is a third in relation to the other two). As he says in a 1981 conversation with Philippe Nemo, "How is justice possible? I answer that it is the fact of the multiplicity of human beings, the presence of the third beside the Other, which is the condition for laws and institutes justice."[4] Justice implies judgment, and judgment (as we know from Kant) is a synthesis of concepts, that is, another kind of thirdness. On that Chicago street, I was the third who judged the couple to be engaged in a damaging circumstance that was manifestly unjust (given that the greater physical strength of the man was being employed to hurt the woman in a truly dangerous way; even if she had provoked his anger, his response was manifestly unjust in its excess).

Levinas distinguishes stringently between a situation of justice—in which equality of treatment is always at stake—and the ethical as such. In the ethical, there is no third person who judges; indeed, there is no judgment as of yet, nor even any concepts at play. Instead, there is "the ethical relation," which is not mediated by any concept or judgment. The concrete form taken by the ethical relation is that of the face-to-face, in which my face confronts another's, each in an essential "nudity" that implies not lack of clothing but the absence of any justifying apparatus whereby either I or the Other could arrogate worldly power over the other. On the contrary, the Other appeals to me in his or her distress or trouble—commanding me in effect to help him or her. This means that I am not "for myself" (as Sartre had insisted in *Being and Nothingness*) but "for the other" (in Levinas's phrase) and thus ready to substitute myself for that other— as I was doing unreflectively and spontaneously on Hudson Street: putting myself in the place of the woman as the potential target of her male friend's wrath. (Fortunately, he decided that I was not worth the trouble to mess with; but by that time, the woman had disappeared.)

---

4. Emmanuel Levinas, *Éthique et infini: dialogues avec Philippe Nemo* (Paris: Fayard, 1982), p. 94; English translation by Richard A. Cohen, *Ethics and Infinity* (Pittsburgh: Duquesne University Press, 1995). I have modified this translation somewhat here as well as in subsequent citations.

In the ethical relation of being face to face with the Other taken as both transcendent and infinite in regard to myself, I am in "proximity" with him or her—where such proximity is not a matter of spatial nearness or literal distance but of genuine intimacy. Here I should like to ask Levinas: is not the glance, mine to the Other, the Other's to me, part of this intimacy, and thus essential to the ethical relation?

III

Let us grant, then, that the glance may play an important role in the very first moment of an ethical encounter. In this role, it sets the stage for considered ethical thought and reflection. Not that these things happen in some simple sequence. Often, they happen together, all at once. No sooner did I see that woman in difficulty than I began to act; here there was no separate moment of reflection. Had I not glanced at what was going on, I would not have acted; but once I glanced, action arose. In a case such as this, ethical action is not precipitated by taking thought but by noticing a situation of distress: a compelling call for action is first grasped in the moment of the glance.[5]

Beyond its special virtue as the opening moment of ethical action, its first move as it were, what are the specific contributions of the glance in ethical life? Here I shall single out only a few aspects of what is in fact a very complex circumstance:

(i) The glance provides direct *access* to the Other: to his or her mood, thought, interest, attitude at the moment: what the Other *feels* right now. This is crucial for ethics, since (as Max Scheler has argued) ethical values are conveyed by emotions as their "bearers" (*Träger*): to get a glimpse of a particular emotion is to get a sense of what ethical issue is at stake.[6]

(ii) The glance also captures a sense of *less manifest aspects* of the Other, say, the darker thoughts (beyond the physical fear) of that woman who was being pummeled; here something is "intimated" as we say. Here the glance exercises its insinuative power, its ability to find the subtler aspects of the manifest phenomenon—all the while staying on the apperceived surface and without any interpretive activity on my part. Here, indeed, the depths are on the surface.

(iii) This is not to mention certain telltale *signs* that the glance picks up instantly and that may be pertinent to ethical activity: class, gender, race, way of

---

5. It may also be *heard,* as in a cry of distress; but then we have to do with the auditory equivalent of the glance—for which there is, significantly, no exact word in European languages: the power, even the linguistic power, is accorded to the glance. This is not, I think, a simple case of oculocentrism.

6. This is not to say that my take is infallible; it is to grasp it better that I get a good, if not a sure, hold on the other's feeling.

dressing (betokening niche within class), even educational level; these are external indicators of the Other's identity, history, and present milieu; they are often (I don't say always) evident in a glance, and they have everything to do with my ethically tempered behavior.

(iv) There may also be an *exchange of glances* that is extremely relevant to ethical matters; in this dense dialectic, which we have considered before in chapters 5 and 6, the Other shows himself by returning my glance; and it is the engagement itself, its duration and quality and direction, that becomes significant for ethical thought and action alike. (Strangely, for all his emphasis on the importance of the face-to-face relation, Levinas does not attend to the *interchange* of glances—a curious lacuna that can only be explained by his focus on the first-person experience of the ethical actor: I in relation to You in your destitution.)

In these four ways—of which I here give only cursory indications—the glance can be said to *give witness* to the Other: to testify to that Other's compelling and demanding presence in the ethical field. The witness given by the glance is to the *place of the Other.* By "place" I do not mean merely location but something far more complex, namely, the situation of the Other vis-à-vis myself—a situation that Levinas designates expressly as "ultimate."[7] It is ultimate because there is no further court of appeal in the ethical relation (again in contrast with justice, construed as a matter of lawyers and courts, judges and concepts). Rather than comment on the situation, much less pass judgment on it, in the ethical relation I am there primarily to witness to the suffering of the Other. I say "witness *to*" and not just "witness," for here it is not a matter of sheer observation (which would unduly objectify the situation) but of being there *for the Other,* assuming responsibility for his or her suffering. To be there for the Other in this testimonial sense is accomplished in the brief moment occupied by the glance. To glance at the Other is to give witness to that Other—immediately and unconditionally, without any compensatory action (for example, a reward or even an acknowledgment) being expected or required.[8]

At the same time, and by the same bare glance, I *welcome* the Other: the Other, who, no matter how fortunate in worldly ways, is nevertheless always in need of feeling welcome—indeed, of *being* welcome. For all his stress on welcoming (in many ways it is the inaugural ethical move), Levinas does not tell us

7. "The face to face remains an ultimate situation" (Emmanuel Levinas, *Totality and Infinity,* tr. A. Lingis [Pittsburgh: Duquesne University Press, 1969], p. 81).

8. This is not to deny that there can be a significant response to my glance: e.g., a glance returned in kind, or another action to which my glance gives rise (such as aggressive behavior on the part of someone who is offended by being glanced at). But at the ethical level, I cannot exact any given response to my glance: I send it to the Other not as part of any bargain between us but as a pure gift. I shall take up further complexities of witnessing in the concluding thoughts.

anything about how this is concretely accomplished, except to say that it occurs in intimacy and especially in feminine gentleness.[9] But this intimacy and gentleness, and their many successors in every subsequent act of welcoming, surely include the glance as a constituent part of their operation: in welcoming the Other into one's domestic domain, the glance is a minimal but powerful opening moment. I welcome the Other in first sending out my mere glance to that Other—who, meeting it and taking it in, feels welcomed by it. (Such welcoming is the converse of the threatening that is also a resident power of the glance, as we know from the animal kingdom as well as from dangerous public situations.)

In spite of his explicit recognition of the centrality of witnessing to, and welcoming of, the Other in the ethical relation—they are in effect its double pillars—Levinas does not spell out the exact ways by which these are accomplished. I submit that they are realized in the fourfold way I have just outlined—the way of the glance. The glance fills the void left by Levinas's failure to consider the precise means by which witnessing and welcoming occur. It is the missing member of any description of the ethical relation that would claim completeness.

IV

Levinas's conspicuous neglect of the glance should not surprise us. It arises from his critique of perception as a form of knowledge. Ethics, however, is not a matter of knowledge; no amount of knowledge of the Other will help one to become ethical in relation to that Other. Instead, the ethical is a matter of desire, and desire bears on what transcends the known or knowable.[10] If this is the case, then any approach to the Other as an object of knowledge, as something thematically or synoptically grasped, is bound to miss the ethical mark:

> I do not know if one can speak of a "phenomenology" of the face. . . . By the same token, I wonder if one can speak of a look (*un regard*) turned toward the face, for the look is knowledge, perception. I think, rather, that the access to the face is ethical straight off.[11]

9. On welcoming, see *Totality and Infinity*, pp. 155–158. Strictly speaking, welcoming is part of dwelling and habitation, and is thus not yet ethical; yet the Other does figure here in the form of the "thou": "The Other who welcomes in intimacy is not the *you* [*vous*] of the face that reveals itself in a dimension of height [i.e., of command from on high], but precisely the *thou* [*tu*] of familiarity: a language without teaching, a silent language, an understanding without words, an expression in secret" (*Totality and Infinity*, p. 155). For further on welcoming, especially in terms of feminine gentleness, see ibid., pp. 154–155.

10. "Ethical witnessing is a revelation that is not [a matter of] knowledge" (Levinas, *Éthique et infini*, p. 114). He adds that "the relation to the Infinite is not [a form of] knowledge, but of Desire" (ibid., p. 97).

11. Ibid., p. 89. Compare this statement: the Infinite "does not appear, since it is not thematized, at least not originally" (ibid., p. 112).

Levinas adds that "the best way to encounter the Other is not even to notice the color of his eyes"—or, for that matter, his nose, forehead, or chin.[12] Any such perceived features of the face take us down the garden path of the knowable and the representable, and thus away from the true path of ethics, for "the Infinite does not show itself."[13]

This is a moment of double crisis. On the one hand, Levinas here departs from phenomenology—his discipline of origin—while, on the other hand, he denies any relevance of perception to the ethical relation as this is embodied in the face-to-face encounter. In short, he rejects a phenomenology of perception as playing any significant role in ethics. I wish to show, on the contrary, that such a phenomenology (and thus in effect *all* phenomenology, as Derrida argues in *Speech and Phenomena:* "phenomenology . . . is always phenomenology of perception"[14]) remains not just relevant to ethics but essential to it, both in its delimited human format and in a more extended ethics of the environment.

Despite his outright denial of any place for perception in general (and thus for the glance as the vanguard act of perception), Levinas ends by allowing a place for one form of perception. In a conversation with Philippe Nemo, published in English under the title *Ethics and Infinity,* Levinas begins by speaking of the face as "a signification without a context," as "uncontainable" within the bounds of perception, as a "rupture" with perception, and so on.[15] Indeed, "one can say that the face is not 'seen' (*vu*)."[16] Having claimed this, however, Levinas says suddenly that "there is in the *appearance* of the face a commandment, as if a master spoke to me."[17] Can there be an "appearance" (*apparition*) without a *perception* of some sort? A *nonperceived appearance* makes no sense at all; and if this is so, then surely perception is, after all, an ingredient in the relation to the face.

That Levinas himself is not entirely averse to this conclusion is indicated by two further remarks:

—"the relation with the face can certainly be dominated by perception, but that which is specifically face is that which cannot be reduced to it";[18]

12. See ibid., p. 89. I am grateful to Peter Atterton of the philosophy department at San Diego State University for drawing my attention to this and related passages on the problematic perception of the face.

13. Ibid., p.113. He adds: "It is by this witnessing, whose truth is not that of representation or of perception, that the revelation of the Infinite is produced" (ibid.).

14. Jacques Derrida, *Speech and Phenomena*, tr. D. Allison (Evanston, Ill.: Northwestern University Press, 1967), p. 104.

15. Levinas, *Éthique et infini*, pp. 90, 91. Elsewhere, Levinas ties perception to the tendency to be comprehensive and synoptic: "The experience of morality does not proceed from [eschatological] vision—it consummates this vision; ethics is an optics. But it is a 'vision' without image, bereft of the synoptic and totalizing capability, a relation or an intentionality of a wholly different type" (*Totality and Infinity*, p. 23; Levinas underlines "consummates").

16. Levinas, *Éthique et infini*, p. 91.

17. Ibid., 93; my italics.

18. Ibid., p. 91.

—"access to the face is not of the order of perception pure and simple, of [an] intentionality that aims at adequation."[19]

In the first statement, Levinas admits the very great difficulty of separating out perception from the ethical relation to the face; by saying that the relation cannot be *reduced* to perception, he nonetheless insinuates that perception remains the natural conduit for this relation, that in which it comes clothed even if in the end the relation must doff the clothing itself. And by speaking of "perception pure and simple" in the second statement, he implies that there is a mode of perception that is *not* pure and simple and that might therefore be at stake in the ethical relation with the Other's face.

What, then, would this impure and nonsimple perception be? Presumably it would be the very thing designated as "apparition" elsewhere. Reverting to a term I first used in chapter 7, let us call it *apperception,* a term I have borrowed from Leibniz: a form of "minute perception" that underlies and in any case undoes the otherwise inveterate tendency of full-blown perception to objectify —to be a matter of knowledge, of comprehension and thematization. In our relation with the Other, apperception is always already at work. I would like to suggest that its primary avatar is precisely the glance, which in its mobile entrainment on the surfaces of things does not consolidate into robust perception. Indeed, the glance deconsolidates obdurate perceptual objects with their determinate edges and sides, definite volumes and weights, and so on. It does so by its darting playfulness, its irreverent attitude toward the solid and the settled. In this way, it makes possible the nuanced apperceptive interplay of which it is the active agent.[20]

V

On city streets, human beings do a great deal of glancing about. To be on these streets is to be in a veritable Glance-orama, with everyone glancing every which way and all over the place. We glance at buildings, cars, the sky. We glance distractedly into thin air. But we glance above all at each other—and even in very

19. Ibid., p. 102.
20. Like sensibility—as the vanguard of sensibility itself—the glance "establishes a relation with a pure quality without support" (*Totality and Infinity,* p. 136; cf. also p. 137: "I enjoy this world of things as pure elements, as qualities without support, without substance"). The glance is also pre-representational—again like sensibility and enjoyment: "sensibility is therefore to be described not as a moment of representation, but as the instance of enjoyment" (ibid., p. 136). The same is true of the glance, which does not represent but only grasps. It grasps not things but part-objects; thus the fact that the glance is pre-representational goes hand in hand with its evasion of things (and thus sides of things): if "things have a name and an identity" (ibid., p. 139), then they also have the status of something represented. (Cf. ibid., pp. 138–140 for this linkage.)

diverse ways, indirectly as well as directly, lewdly and reassuringly, furtively and straightforwardly.

We first explored the thematics of urban looking in chapters 1 and especially 6. Now I wish to focus on the specifically interpersonal aspects of the street glance. In this ordinary—and yet quite extraordinary—glancing there is an unsuspected ethical significance: a significance arising from the mere fact that people glance at each other as they pass each other by in the busy course of everyday life. How can this possibly be?

Consider what these passing glancers, these "slipping glimpsters,"[21] are really doing. They are not just noting the existence of others, or satisfying some idle curiosity in the manner of the classical nineteenth-century flâneur, or getting some good aerobic exercise as might be an aim more recently. They may be doing these things too, but they are also, and more momentously, *acknowledging each other.* This is not merely to recognize the sheer fact of others' existence, but their being *as persons*—their personhood no less. It is to see the person in the face of the other: in that peculiarly potent sur-face in which the person expresses himself or herself and comes to gestural and visual and vocal articulation.[22]

The key here is the *passing glance,* in which there is eye contact with the other on the street, even if this contact lasts only a few seconds. The effect is that of catching the other out of the corner of our eye. In casting such a glance, our interest is not in becoming better acquainted or in learning anything in particular about the other. Having no utilitarian purpose, the point of the passing glance is to acknowledge the other's being and, if the other returns the glance, to have one's own being acknowledged as well. This involves a dialectic of the singular and the universal. In a passing glance at you in the street, I affirm your being as a singular fact: I am looking *just at you* and *at no one else.* At the same time, I also affirm something much more expansive in scope: I also affirm you as a member of the human race, as (fully and truly) *another human being.* The singular you whom I recognize by my mere glance is not the autobiographically unique you—*that* I may know nothing about, since you are very likely to be a stranger to me on the modern metropolitan street—but a singularity that manifests the universal of being human in just *this* place and at *this* time and with *this* flesh. My glance in effect salutes Everyone in You, and conversely You in Everyone.[23]

This remarkable, yet frequently encountered, circumstance exemplifies the strange logic of the glance: something quite exiguous, seemingly trivial, shows

21. Willem de Kooning spoke of himself as a "slipping glimpster." See Phillip Leider, "Vermeer and Hopper," *Art in America,* March 2001.

22. This is not to deny that the glancing person also apperceives the full body of others seen in the street. Certainly so. But the part of the body that bears the main ethical brunt is the face, wherein the ethical personhood of the Other appears in its most concentrated format.

23. On the strong but tacit collusion between the singular and the universal, see Gilles Deleuze, *Difference and Repetition,* tr. P. Patton (New York: Columbia University Press, 1994), esp. pp. 1–5, 189–213, 276–284. We here return to a theme broached in chapter 1 and extended in chapter 7.

itself to be immensely significant in its scope and effect. Once more, a narrow defile opens onto a vast vista. This is the very opposite of the Law of Diminishing Returns, or any comparable entropic phenomenon of enforced exhaustion. It is, rather, a Law of Diminutive Support, by which an undramatic and ordinary act gives rise to a quite unusual and important encounter with the being of the other. Such a Law holds for many phenomena of the glance, whose brevity belies its effectuality in the visual world.[24]

In the case before us, a meager look assures us of our being human: we are upheld in the look of the other. Remember Buber: "In the deadly crush of an air-raid shelter the glances of two strangers suddenly meet for a second in astonishing and unrelated mutuality . . . in a realm which existed only for that moment." The import of this moment exceeds what we might first imagine. We can grasp this import from imagining a circumstance in which others never offered any such confirmation: this would be a disturbing place indeed.[25] Others' passing looks at me do not prove my existence—this is not necessary, such proof being already supplied by consciousness (as Descartes would argue) or my body (as Merleau-Ponty would insist)—but they do act to *acknowledge* it. Without the confirming glances of others cast at me en passant, I would be less than myself: I would be adrift in a Sargasso Sea of anonymous generality in which my very identity, as well as my singularity, would be dissolved in a swirl of indifference.

To be adrift in a sea of strangers who do not pay attention to me even in this minimal form is to experience anomie of an especially acute sort. I might begin to wonder: Is there something wrong with me? Am I the singular I take myself to be? I certainly would not be so in the eyes of others—I would have lost my social being. It's one thing for these others not to speak to me: this is too much to expect if I have recently come to the city or am in a district where I'm not known. But for them not even to glance at me! This seemingly trivial loss of visual support is in fact a quite serious matter. The others, on whom I count for at least momentary confirmation, might as well have annihilated me.[26] But I can

24. We shall return to the Law of Diminutive Support in the concluding thoughts.

25. This is the situation in the Nazi extermination camps, to which I return in the concluding thoughts to this book.

26. To be confirmed by others in this way is the intersubjective equivalent of glancing at oneself in the mirror, as we so frequently do without suspecting the larger stakes. Here, too, I am supported by a mere look back—in this case, the literal reflection of my own looking at myself. This look, stemming from me in the most spontaneous way, is captured in the mirror, held there in such a way as to acquire a momentary existence of its own. It is as if it had become, for a brief second, the look of another—hence our sense sometimes that it is the look of someone we do not know: can this be me, we ask ourselves? This is an alienated look that seems to leap back at me from its place in the mirror, a dis-placed place that is no longer my own. Developmentally, this is the moment of Lacan's celebrated "mirror stage," in which the emerging ego is built from its false identification with its own image, a merely fictitious and alienated version of a self that until then had been wholly fragmented and uncoordinated. Such identification is based on a fundamental *méconnaissance,* a failure of self-acknowledgment. For I am identifying with a petrified image of myself, a self who is in fact another: once again in

be restored to life by the merest passing glance, which acknowledges me to be the singular being that I am for myself and for the other—and the other is for me when I glance back.

Not that this mutual confirmation always happens. Sometimes the glance, even the passing glance, is lacking, and this in a quite quotidian context. I set out for a stroll near my apartment in Rogers Park, and cannot help but notice the rarity of any significant glancing happening in the street. Not only are looks averted; I do not even encounter the other looking straight through me. Indeed, I am confronted with *no look at all,* no noticeable glance either given or received. The street on which I am living seems swept clean of the glance: the Glance-orama is empty. No longer do I need to imagine this limit-situation: it is happening on the very street on which I live.

I begin to suspect that I'm not even worth a glance! For I am here experiencing not just a paucity of glances exchanged but a situation of *no glance at all:* a no-looker in short! It feels as if I am being given a lesson in HOW NOT TO GLANCE! Or shall we call it "the art of glancing away"—so radically far away that I cannot even catch the first glimmering of a glance, much less any effective follow-through.

Admittedly, this circumstance stems from a quite specific historical moment in a quite specific place. On other streets, in other cities and at other times, I find a great deal more glancing going on. All is not lost in the glance-world. Nevertheless, there is today in almost any city of the Western world a sizable reduction of the glance's public presence, compared not just to the great boulevards of a century ago but also to the small-town sidewalks that were a central feature of life in the Midwest during my youth: there, people not only looked at each other with open eyes but often stopped to talk as well: indeed, they *lingered* to talk, glancing at each other all the while.

I do not wish to wax nostalgic. Times have changed; but, short of the desperation of my experience in north Chicago, one will usually find in American cities a modicum of glancing going on: enough, at least, to say that walkers are acknowledging each other's presence by their casual looks. Fully reciprocated glancing in public may be less conspicuously and openly pursued than it once was, but the role of glances exchanged on city streets has not fallen altogether fallow.

Rimbaud's famous phrase (very much on Lacan's mind), "je est un autre." I am an other because I do not recognize that I am in fact identifying with my own awkward, uncoordinated bodily self. For adequate acknowledgment to occur, I would have to realize that this mirror image is in fact *me,* albeit a me that is slightly distorted (e.g., in terms of right/left reversal) and more steadily presented than I experience myself by myself without a mirror. Short of this acknowledgment, my ego has gotten off to a false start; it is formed in a "fictional direction" (Jacques Lacan, "The Mirror Stage as Formative of the Function of the I," in *Écrits: A Selection,* tr. A. Sheridan [New York: Norton, 1977], p. 2). The importance of this bare recognition, however fraught with egological danger it may be, is again indicated by the shock I would experience if I glanced into a mirror only to see *no image of myself* there at all. I would be quite literally—visually—*wiped out* by this experience, self-blinded as it were.

This bare remnant is more important than it may seem at first. A failure to look at the other person, albeit just in passing, is in effect a failure to affirm that other as a fellow member of the species. I would go so far as to say that there is an *obligation* to acknowledge the other by one's mere look: quite apart from, and well before, any obligation to say or do other things. We owe it to our fellow beings—before we owe them anything else—to affirm their presence before us and with us. A glance at another person in the street (or anywhere else, for that matter) is the *first* sign of respect for that person. This is why the withholding of the glance can be so puzzling and so painful. The reclusion of the look amounts to an exclusion of the unacknowledged person from the sphere of the human: it is as if the unacknowledged other did not belong to the Kingdom of Ends, as if You were not an integral and organic part of Everyone. There is much more at stake in the glance than meets the eye of the beholder.

A brief example illustrates this. A woman of my acquaintance lives in a "dangerous" neighborhood in south Chicago. When she is out walking on the street, she sometimes passes by groups of young men gathered at a street corner. Instead of looking the other way in the hope that others will not notice her, she makes sure that she looks at each member of the group: not defiantly but just to acknowledge their being there. At one level, she takes this to be an ethical obligation; at another, it is quite effective in a much more practical way: those at whom she looks realize she is not cringing before them, or trying desperately to bargain for her safety (both ploys might invite the very trouble she is trying to avoid). Her forthright look encourages young men to regard her as a person who shares a common humanity rather than as someone who is an object of prey. Her glancing in such a circumstance encourages others to respect her: to look back in a move of counteraffirmation (where "respect" means literally to look back via its Latin root, *respecere*).[27]

This is not all. Acknowledging another human being by way of the glance means taking in this other not only as being a (singular) member of a (universal)

---

27. My informant is Ginger Costello, who does what I here report not just from the standpoint of the most effective strategy but because of an obligation she feels to acknowledge everyone she meets, including potentially harmful figures in her urban environment. My point in citing this example is not that this tactic always works or that it is always appropriate. In other circumstances, it might well be ill-advised and even disastrous. But for the glance to play such an affirmative role as it does in Ginger's ambiguous situation is nevertheless revealing of its persuasive power and ethical force. This is not, of course, the only role it can play in such a setting; another woman, in a comparable scene, will choose to look away in an effort to avoid suggesting that she is interested in an erotic engagement. Such averting of the glance is an always available option, and may be preferable or even necessary at times. But this is not to exclude the rightness of the acknowledging glance at other times. Just as my passing glance at the other is not always liberatory—it may be merely curious or lecherous—so it need not always seek to recognize the other in his or her singularity cum universality. But the latter does occur, and occurs emphatically, on many occasions. It is to this often-neglected event, in its considerable ethical significance, that I wish to point. (This last line of consideration is a response to an observation made by Emily Lee.)

species but as someone who is able to become something other than he has been so far. Just by recognizing the other as other in the glance, I in effect release this other to become the person he wants to be before and with others. This is a version of what W. B. Yeats calls "the brightening glance" that transfigures what it sees.[28] My mere glance sanctions the other to become still more other—still more singular than ever, still more his own person (though not more universal: there are no degrees of universality), and above all still more the way he wishes to present himself to me as the agent who glances at him. Under my glance, he may be seen as a tough guy, or as a compassionate being, or as someone indifferent to others. Taking him in as he is, I as glancer encourage him as glanced at to become other to himself—or just more or less of himself—as he sees fit. Just as my glancing is freely undertaken as it directs itself to him, so his response is an affair of freedom in the domain of public appearance: my being-for-others precipitates his being-for-me.[29]

The converse of this is the fixated and fixating stare that confines the other to how the other is grasped on just this occasion, as if it were definitive for all future occasions: as if the other could not become other to himself. The stare—a species of the gaze—reduces the other to a perceptual particular with no powers of self-transformation. It embodies the spirit of gravity, which delimits, pins down, and finally bogs down. It fixes on the other just as he or she *is*. The glance that acknowledges affirms the other as other, a matter of *being* (that is, being a singular member of humanity) and of *becoming:* it alleviates the other's self-presentation like a grace note, allowing this other to realize a self-othering that is curtailed under the regime of the gaze. Supporting the being and the becoming of the person rather than contributing to his or her static perception, the glance shows itself to be indispensable in the interaction with others that constitutes the very medium of the ethical realm.

28. See W. B. Yeats, "Amongst School Children." I am grateful to Richard Kearney for this reference and for suggesting the line of thought that is developed in this section of the chapter.

29. "Being-for-others" is Sartre's term for the way in which I acquit myself in the presence of others: how I act in this presence by means of my bodily behavior (including my "look"). See Jean-Paul Sartre, *Being and Nothingness: An Essay in Phenomenological Ontology,* tr. Hazel Barnes (New York: Washington Square Press, 1992), part 3. As Sartre shows so lucidly, the way I choose to present myself to others under their look—which for him takes the primary form of the gaze—includes the real possibility of appearing to them in a guise that is alien to my true self: i.e., in the bad faith of a fixed role (e.g., as a "waiter" or a "pedophile"). This is just as true of the situation in which I am glanced at by the other: to become other to myself under the other's glance may mean becoming something alien to myself, that is, a false self that misrepresents my self as a creature of my "basic project." This *via negativa* is an uneliminable possibility in the circumstance of spontaneous glancing in the street. My point in the above discussion is not that my glance necessarily brings out the *better* self of the other—e.g., a more responsible, more sensitive self—but that it allows the other to present himself in a way that differs from previous such presentations. His "becoming other to himself" can be for better or for worse; whichever is the case, my glance does not inhibit such becoming but actively supports it— unlike the gaze, which delimits the freedom of self-presentation even if it cannot eliminate it entirely. (This clarification is in response to an objection raised by Andrés Colapinto.)

VI

An appreciative but skeptical reader of an earlier draft of this chapter had this to say: "No conscious reflection [is needed in] the glance . . . [because] a life-time of character formation, of the development of conscience, previous experiences of manifest injustice, parental or other examples, the moral imperatives of religion—all these and more must have operated in the choice before you [on Hudson Street]. To be sure, the glance was enough to move you, but only because it exposed a moral nerve, so to speak. Another man [that is, with another kind of moral nerve, or with little such nerve at all] would have [stayed] on the other side of the street, like the Pharisee in Jesus's parable of the good Samaritan."[30] My friend adds: "A glance at a virgin forest may rejoice a man's heart for different reasons, one of which might be the chance of making a fortune in cutting it down. Think of the first viewers of the great redwoods! Maybe a glance of awe and thanksgiving, but as likely a calculation of board-feet. No, without 'the moral law within,' there is no [respect for the] landscape. The glance is the trigger, not the powder or the gunsight."

My friend makes a forceful point, and it is best to confront it squarely before drawing any further conclusions as to the ethicality of the glance. He is certainly right to insist that the glance that is sensitive to ethically charged situations cannot be naive—a matter of a chance encounter or some arbitrary whim. It must be a glance that knows what it is doing: not consciously, much less reflectively, but nevertheless effectively. It must *know its way about* in an ethically challenging circumstance.[31] It must have discernment of an ethical sort if it is to be a glance that instigates effective action instead of merely noting this circumstance. But how does this happen? What enables the glance to be so adroit in the ethical realm—and so maladroit in the case of the entrepreneur with board-feet eyes?

It is undeniably true that without an extensive, or at least intensive, moral education no glance (or any other ethically relevant action) could be consistently insightful, much less effective. It is a matter of a "knowing look," not of a naive look that has no idea what it is looking at or what the stakes are. One is not born with a knowing look; it arises from the very sorts of experience mentioned by my friend: the exemplary actions of others, religious injunctions, the cultivation of conscience, and so on. All of these make up our ethical *Bildung*—the history of the formation of our character. The difficult question becomes how such *Bildung*, which arises from the long haul of one's whole life, finds its way into something so merely momentary and passing as a glance: how it seeps into the extremities of one's active body, one's eye (and sometimes one's arm or leg), informing them with its practical wisdom.

30. Letter from Stanley A. Leavy, M.D., June 25, 1999.
31. This is not to say, however, that the glance contains anything like propositional knowledge; if it involves knowing-how, this does not mean that it also possesses knowing-that (i.e., knowing that something is the case).

What Aristotle calls "habit" (*hexis*) is the crucial formative factor. By means of the slow acquisition of the right habitual actions—learned from example as well as precept—one's "customary body" literally incorporates what is ethical, which sediments itself into the appropriate sinews of one's "momentary body."[32] One comes to act as one is formed. One does not have to reflect on what one has already become. Instead of thinking on it, one acts on it: that is already enough. If it is true that (as Heidegger affirms) thinking is carried out by the hands,[33] it is equally true that ethics is borne by the eyes. Far from inhibiting the glance—as might seem to ensue from its sedimented status—ethics inhabits it.

Rather than viewing character as a model in which ethically informed character is self-contained—confined to pure practical reason (as in Kant) or to the superego (as in Freud)—we ought to think of it as suffusing the entire person, and I mean the entire body of the person. Suffusing it right down to the toes of the feet (which propel one to cross the street or to stay on the same side), the fingertips (which tell us just where to direct our arms vis-à-vis other tangible bodies), and the outer edges of our eyes (with which we glance about). Nor is it a matter of a complemental series in which we could say simply, "The more of X, the less of Y, and vice versa." It is not as if the more (or better) our *Bildung*, the less the body needs to be involved: as if we could simply know something by thinking it. On the contrary: the more I acquire a certain *Bildung*, the more the body will figure: indeed, the more it will be required. The glance is not a reflective action, but it does *reflect* my moral background, bringing it to bear on any given occasion, just as a mirror might refract a ray of light onto an object toward which it is tilted. The whole ray finds its way onto the surface of the whole object, just as the entirety of one's ethical *habitus* comes to be concentrated in a single glance that falls onto an ethically challenging situation.[34]

Hence we cannot separate the trigger from the gunpowder or the gunsight—in my friend's suggestive analogy. Moreover, the trigger is an integral part of the circumstance of firing a gun. It is mechanical in nature, but it is not blind in its activation. The finger that releases it is an educated organ; it is as much a thinking finger as the glance is the activity of a knowing eye. The gunsight

---

32. The terms "customary body" and "momentary body" are Merleau-Ponty's: see his *Phenomenology of Perception*, tr. C. Smith (New York: Humanities, 1962), pp. 142–147.

33. Martin Heidegger, *What Is Called Thinking?*, tr. J. Glenn Gray (New York: Harper, 1968), pp. 16: "Every motion of the hand in every one of its works carries itself through the element of thinking. . . . All the work of the hand is rooted in thinking." The original inspiration for Heidegger's statement is found in Aristotle, especially in his statement: "there is an analogy between the soul and the hand; for, as the hand is the instrument of instruments, so the intellect [i.e., the highest form of soul] is the form of forms" (*De Anima*, 432a).

34. I am using *habitus* in Bourdieu's sense, which locates it between nature and culture as their dynamic intermediary. See Pierre Bourdieu, *Outline of a Theory of Practice*, tr. R. Nice (Cambridge: Cambridge University Press, 1977), pp. 72–85. For my own treatment of this area of research, see "Habitual Body and Memory in Merleau-Ponty," *Man and World* (fall 1984) as well as "The Ghost of Embodiment: Is the Body a Natural or a Cultural Entity?" in Donn Welton, ed., *Body and Flesh* (London: Blackwell, 1998).

through which the marksman looks is not limited to the scope on the barrel of the gun but extends to his index finger, which has its own form of directedness. And the gunpowder that will explode when that action is taken is remarkably analogous to the habitual mass of inculcated responses: these, too, will be instantly released when the appropriate bodily action is undertaken—when the hand touches what needs to be felt, the foot steps forward forthrightly, and the eye glances discerningly.

The glance is indeed an instigator of ethical action, but it is a far more complex precipitating event than it presents itself as being. It instigates by being the delegated agent of a lifetime of ethical learning and practice. For nothing, not even the bare glance, is a mere mindless trigger in matters of morals. It is not that everything ethical is predetermined—hardly so!—but there is a decided proclivity to act in certain ways rather than others. This does not mean, however, that the glance is a mere creature of this proclivity; it often leads the way, scouting out new circumstances in which to enact new versions of one's deep ethical habitualness. It may be driven by its habitual past, but it directs itself to unanticipated targets in the present. So, too, releasing the trigger of a gun is a matter of practice, but the timing of the release and the choice of the target are up to the subject who shoots the gun—the same subject who also glances toward the same target. What is overdetermined in one regard is self-determining in another.

The ever-lengthening shadow of one's ethical *Bildung*, far from precluding a diversity of responses in various circumstances, enables it. The Pharisee and the redwood leveler are not simply unethical; they did not fail to see, much less to glance; but they see and glance differently from the Good Samaritan and the environmentalist. They look in accordance with their own *habitus* even as they exercise freedom in how to realize it and to what purpose on a given occasion. We can criticize the intention and effect of this *habitus*—that is part of the task of ethical reflection—but we should not be dismayed, or even surprised, by such disparate responses: in fact, we should expect them in a world that does not impose exactly the same stringent moral codes on all its human inhabitants and that allows to each a modicum of freedom in the visual realm.

One result is certain. Neither the direction of the glance nor its customary speed is undermined by the formative influence of *Bildung;* if anything, both are reinforced. It is just because one has so fully incorporated the pertinent principles and exemplary instances that one can glance so freely and tellingly in such a brief span of time. In this case, a complemental relationship does obtain: the more deeply embodied the ethical upbringing, the less time one needs for reflecting on a new problematic situation—or even for deciding what to do in that situation.[35]

---

35. This is not to claim that time for reflection and decision is of any lesser value; in certain circumstances, such time can be invaluable, indeed required: especially in those circumstances in which a glance does not suffice to figure out what one must do.

We can now understand better why the glance has been so long neglected in ethical theory. The contrast between the *longue durée* of one's ethical formation and the alacrity of the glance has led philosophers to assume that the glance cannot be of any real significance for ethical action: how can something so literally momentary be of genuine moment for ethically challenging circumstances? The glance is something of a Trojan Horse in the city of Ethics: only because it is so seemingly innocuous is it admitted into the fortified walls, only to show itself to be capable of decisive action therein: an action founded as much on disciplined habit as on imaginative vision.

The glance is not an automatic enactment of "the moral law within"; it is itself an active agent of that law, its free-ranging deputy in the visual world. The glance not only acts "in the eyes of the law"; *it is the very eye of the law,* its sensitive sentinel. It bears the moral law in incarnate form into the seen world— not just recognizing it there (as when an ethical imperative is taken up) but also helping to realize it in ever-more effective ways. These ways reflect the positive ambiguity of the glance itself: free and yet informed, unprecedented within a history of precedents, habitual as well as innovative, determined from within and exploratory without, a matter both of being and of becoming. "The glance," writes another correspondent, "is not simply a product of one's background, but also the opening through which (or because of which) one starts on the road to becoming and hence gaining new backgrounds."[36]

VII

Six final comments are in order:

1. If the glance is to play an important part in ethics—as I have been proposing —then it is at once more nuanced and more powerful than we are apt to admit if we are doing ethics in a traditional manner. It must be more *nuanced* if it is to contribute to determining what is good or right to do in certain circumstances: first by noticing disruptions in a given scene (a crucial moment, to be further explored in the next chapter) and then by instigating action to deal with these incongruities. This action, of which it is the precipitator, brings to bear a history of previous looking: a history that is culturally informed and socially instructed. Thanks to both of these moments, the glance possesses a discernment of its own, at once apperceptive and informed. Because of the continuing influence of one's perceptual and apperceptual *Bildung,* the glance is not effected by a guileless eye but is a matter of an educated look: a look that is no less spontaneous for having such a rich background of previous lookings. (This includes the very real

36. Emily Lee, e-mail letter of July 14, 2003. Lee adds: "While you want to uphold that the information from a glance is a result of the culture, history, and moral background of a person . . . you [also] want to hold out that the glance is yet still that which impels action, or I guess the initial action, that which starts the momentum of becoming in some ways" (ibid.).

possibility of a *mis*educated look that sees only with bigoted eyes—that, instead of acknowledging the other as an intrinsically valuable being immediately, and in the glance itself, reduces that other to a shrunken, stereotypical image of that being: Black, Jew, Muslim, Southern Baptist, thereby losing all nuance. This was the experience of W. E. B. Du Bois in the formative experience he reports in the epigraph to this chapter.[37])

Another strand of the subtlety of the glance stems from its status as an apperception that does not require whole, stable objects as its specific content; escorted by "petite perceptions," it penetrates into the interstices of robust perceptual objects—things and persons and places— so as to grasp their subtly wrought infrastructures.

The glance must also be more *powerful* than we are likely to suppose. If it is to make a difference in ethical life, it cannot be a mere registration of difference, much less the bare registration of fact. It has to be sufficiently forceful to effect the active witnessing and welcoming I first ascribed to it, to acknowledge other persons on the street, and (as we shall see in the next chapter) to respond to environmental imperatives. The basis of this power lies in the glance's ability to apperceive its object instantaneously and to size it up—to see it for what it is and to grasp its significance right away: as when I sense without hesitation whether I am welcome or not as I enter a social gathering. In large measure, this is a function of its culturally encoded state (again: the better grounded at a habitual level, the swifter its action can be); but it is also a matter of the glance's free variation of its previous history—a variation evident in its impatience, its refusal to linger, its saltatory swings from one item to another, its crazy zigzag course. In the end, the nuance and the power of the glance join forces in one and the same operation, that of a living look that charters its own course even as it embodies what courses it (and other glances of other persons) have taken in the past.

2. The nuanced power of the glance is sufficient to support another ethically relevant dimension of glancing, its *subversiveness*. Despite the embedding of character and culture in its very manner of looking, the glance does not simply enact commonly affirmed norms and values—as if there were no other choice. A stare is more likely to repeat unquestioned attitudes: Patricia Williams speaks of "an impassive stare that passes right through all that which is me . . . [and] is deeply humiliating."[38] The glance, in contrast, is under no compunction to

37. A contemporary example of the miseducated, socially tendentious glance: Paget Henry, now professor of Sociology and Africana Studies at Brown University, was stepping onto an elevator when he was a graduate student at CUNY. He was late for class and in a rush. A white woman on the elevator went into a panic, assuming he was a dangerous presence; she called the university police, who questioned Henry and asked him to prove that he was enrolled in the course to which he was late. His only "crime" was the misfortune he shared with W. E. B. Du Bois: being black (from a conversation with Paget Henry, Providence, Rhode Island, July 2003).

38. Patricia Williams, *The Alchemy of Race and Rights* (Cambridge, Mass.: Harvard University Press, 1991), p. 222. The full passage is this: "My parents were always telling me to look up

conform to ethical conventionalities, but may question them and even act to undermine them. By a mere flicker of the eye, a modulation of its gleam, a redirection of its look, the glance may make clear its disdain for accepted normativities and its desire for something quite different. We say that "he has a certain devilish look in his eye," and we speak tellingly of the glance as "arch," "skeptical," "sardonic," "withering"—all of which betray a subject's subversion of social norms.[39] No longer a matter of the glance's apperceptive outreach to the world, these acrid attitudes are given off by the glance, exuded from it as it were, rather than serving as ways of taking in the surrounding world. These attitudes exhibit the glance as lance: as cutting down to size or cutting through social pretentiousness, general hypocrisy, and rank presumption. In their very corrosiveness, they point to new directions of ethical conduct that go beyond familiar forms of behavior, adumbrating these directions if not explicitly articulating them. Freely chosen, they show the subject in his or her subversiveness: not only knowing how to glance (this latter is a matter of skill, tact, and personal history) but also *where* to look beyond expected destinations: where one wishes value to be placed and actions to be done, no matter what the prevailing norms. This is anywhere you wish to go by your mobile look. One thinks of the way in which young monks are trained in the more rigorous Zen monasteries in Japan. There, the leanest look of the head monk tells all: what should be done; in what style to do it; in what spirit; and with what state of mind. In the same training, however, space is made for hilarity and freely ranging attention—for glancing wildly and widely, with eyes open and alert. In this way and for this moment, the seriousness of the practice overall, its spirit of gravity, is alleviated.

3. Pondering these larger reaches of the glance, it becomes clear that we cannot regard it as something merely propaedeutic that precedes ethical action. Instead, it is *part of the action itself.* As we shall explore further in chapter 11, it goes right to the imperative to act that calls out to it by its intensity; not only does it detect this imperative; as a form of vigilance, it already belongs to the action the imperative calls for: it is the premonitory phase of such action. The inherent

---

at the world; to look straight at people, particularly white people; not to let them stare me down; to hold my ground; to insist on the right to my presence no matter what. They told me that in this culture you have to look people in the eye because that's how you tell them you're their equal. . . . What was hardest was not just that white people saw me . . . but that they looked through me, as if I were transparent . . . [by] an impassive stare that passes right through all that which is me . . . [and] is deeply humiliating" (ibid.). Looking people in the eye, a form of gazing, is a concrete modality of acknowledging others' presence as singular in their universality. Just as the glance can be put to socially deleterious uses (e.g., as in the childhood experience of Du Bois), so the gaze can contribute to socially constructive purposes. But when the gaze becomes a stare, this latter outcome is no longer likely.

39. This is not to deny that each of these qualities may also inhere in a glance—and even more so, a stare—that merely reflects these same norms. Part of the mercuriality of the glance is its very bivalence in this regard, its ability to mimic as well as undermine stable social conventions.

activism of the glance is no less evident in glancing at others in such a way as to acknowledge them as fellow human beings. Here the acknowledgment is the action itself: which is to say that it is inherently performative in character: by the sheer act of glancing the other is acknowledged. In neither case—whether the glance picks up an imperative or affirms others as singular in their universality— does the glance merely precede the ethically pertinent action; it inaugurates it and may also accomplish it. In my Hudson Street experience, my glance uncovered a compelling circumstance, and was itself noticed by those at whom it was aimed; like my initial apprehending, their glances back at me were already forms of acting—acting differently than they would have done had they gone undetected by my look. The point is not just that the glance leads to a different outcome in such a circumstance but that it is itself part of the difference it makes.[40]

4. All of this points to an expanded descriptivism in ethics. I have been pursuing the glance as an exemplary "peri-phenomenon" into some rather unaccustomed corners—as unaccustomed for ethics as for the study of human perception. When we put ethics entirely under the heading of the prescriptive, the unaccustomed appears as the merely bizarre: for then there is no meaningful connection between what ought to be the case according to ethical theory and what is in fact the case when ethics is enacted: there is no room for the glance in the abyss that separates the "ought" from the "is." But if we stay descriptive— which is not the same as staying altogether factual, much less statistical—there will be room for the glance. Room enough not just to bear on the ethical but to bear out the ethical itself: to illuminate it in new ways, one of which is that it often takes place in a glance or by an exchange of glances.

5. Ironically, despite my stated reservations, Levinas is right in one basic regard. Construed as an integral part of ethical action, the glance is indeed not just another perceptual act. Its ethical efficacity does not consist in its being a mode of perception per se; if anything, it is an apperception; and in any case, it has shown itself to be more actional than observational. But this does not mean—and here I again depart from Levinas—that the glance does not involve some form of knowledge (that is, in the guise of a tacit *Bildung* that sediments itself into the discernment of a given glance) or that it is not synoptic (a single sweeping glance can be quite comprehensive). It can be both of these things and yet still remain enactive in character (for example, as the agent of witnessing and welcoming, of acknowledging and recognizing)—just as the fact that it takes only a moment to perform does not undermine its effectiveness in ethical situations.

---

40. It will be noted that in this last example I am using "glance" both in a first- and a third-person sense: sometimes it is *my* glance that is at stake: i.e., when I detected the troubled couple; sometimes it is this same glance insofar as it is *taken as looking* by others, i.e., by this same couple as they spotted me looking at them. Either way, my point remains that the glance is not a merely preliminary, pre-actional event but belongs to the action itself.

The glance cuts to the quick of these situations; it belongs to what Levinas pointedly calls the "ethical relation" and is not a separate, much less an autonomous, act: it is an act *within* the enactment of the ethical relation itself.

6. This is not to say that the glance is *all* of this relation or that it makes up the whole of its enactment—nor even that it is the only factor of the quick at work in ethics (the mind, not to mention memory, can be equally dexterous and swift). But the quicksilver action of the glance allows it to get to the heart of the ethical matter. It comes to this heart in a single moment of disclosure. This is not the moment of *kairos*—the time of dramatic decision that turns time itself around— but the modest moment of apperception that can, despite its delimitation, make a decisive difference in how we live out the ethical dimension of our lives.

Strange indeed how such a slight action can make such a momentous difference! If so, it is because the Law of Diminutive Support remains in force. "Even in the tiniest and most transient events which scarcely enter consciousness" (in Buber's words once again), something ethically quite significant can happen. It can happen in a glance: as when we glance at others whom we pass in the street. Little as the glance may look to be—it presents itself as the slenderest reed in the life of vision—it proves to matter a lot in the ethical realm.[41]

41. An earlier version of this essay has appeared in M. B. Matuštík and W. L. McBride, eds., *Calvin O. Schrag and the Task of Philosophy after Postmodernity* (Evanston, Ill.: Northwestern University Press, 2002), pp. 91–115.

11

THE NATURAL ENVIRONMENT
IN A GLANCE

Direct strokes [Nature] never gave us power
to make; all our blows glance; all our hits are
accidents.

—Ralph Waldo Emerson, "Experience"

Everything that happens and everything that is said
happens or is said at the surface.

—Gilles Deleuze, *The Logic of Sense*

Can things have a face?

—Emmanuel Levinas, "Is Ontology
Fundamental?"

We can be ethical only in relation to something we
can see, feel, understand, love, or otherwise have
faith in.

—Aldo Leopold, "The Land Ethic"

I

Ethical action often takes its rise from noticing that something is out of joint in our immediately surrounding world. Much as analytical reflection starts from what John Dewey called a "problematic situation," so ethical consideration is born from a sense of incongruity, a failure of fit. Such was the case when I spotted the quarreling couple on Hudson Street. Something distinctly out of line, which I grasped in a glance, alerted me to the trouble: the pitched voices, the violent movement of the woman's body being forced against the car. Without these melodramatic signs, I would have continued walking on my side of the street. So, too, when I am in the midst of the natural world far from any city, I will pay attention to things that stand out by their conspicuous character—and that signal to me that all is not right with the environment I behold: say, a pipeline cutting across the tundra in Alaska. I see in a glance the disjunctive character of the circumstance. Absent the sense that something is awry in some important way, I will not be motivated to do anything about it. Without my intervention (or that of others equally alerted), the scene is likely to remain noxious, troublesome, and subject to extension or repetition. Not that notice alone is enough; effective ethical action calls for the mobilization of various pertinent resources: it calls for follow-through. But the first moment of bare apperception is indispensable; without this, nothing will happen, nothing will ensue.

In this chapter I shall examine the role of the glance in apprehending and responding to environmental distress. This will build on the outcome of the previous chapter by extending our considerations to a new set of circumstances, those pertaining to the natural environment. The focus will be on a question only noted in passing in the last chapter: namely, *where* is the source of the moral imperative, that is, the place where we first find the call that moves us to ethical action? Without such imperativeness, such a "sense of oughtness" (in Wes Jackson's phrase),[1] we would not be moved to act in the first place. Ethics would be merely customary action: what most of us do for the most part. But to act ethically requires a sanction that is not reducible to commonalities of behavior or to established norms of conduct. Since this sanction is not determinable by sociological analysis—it exceeds, and may go quite contrary to, what most people think is right on a given occasion—it must be found somewhere else. But where is this?

Just as Heidegger posed the leading question, "Where is the work of art?" in his celebrated "The Origin of the Work of Art,"[2] so we must ask the same kind of locatory question in the realm of ethics: where is the source of an ethical imperative? Here, too, the Where precedes the What of determinate content—that is, what one should do in order to be ethical—as well as the How of how to apply the What: how to make it work, and ideally to last, in a given circumstance. Even if it is true that the What and the How rank high in the order of ethical *conduct*— we must know what to do and how to do it if we are to get anywhere at all in the moral life—it is in the Where that the source of the compelling power of the ethical is to be found.[3]

1. Wes Jackson, presentation at the conference, "Prairie Phenomenology," Emporia State University, Emporia, Kansas, June 2001.

2. "Wo aber ist das Kunstwerk?" Martin Heidegger, "The Origin of the Work of Art," in *Poetry Language Thought*, tr. A. Hofstadter (New York: Harper, 1971), p. 17: "Where and how does art occur?"

3. In the history of Western ethics, there have been at least four coherent proposals as to where the source of the ethical is to be found. This source has been located in the Good, God, the spiritual self, and (more recently and thanks to Levinas) the human face. These in turn divide into two sets of answers: either the source of the ethical lies in something transcendent to the human—in the Good, as the ultimate object of knowledge, or in God as the final metaphysical or theological force—or in something intrinsically human: whether this be the spiritual self or the face. In contrast with God, the Good, and the deep self, the face has the advantage of being visible and thus directly accessible. As Levinas puts it in an early essay: "It is

II

Levinas's signal achievement was to have located the force of the ethical in a feature of the actuality of the human subject, in its presence here and now in the ethical relation. This feature, as we have seen, is found in the face—from which emanates the Other's call to me to be responsible for him or her. The face is the pivotal place, the source, of ethical commitment: for in it is mirrored the Other's destitution and distress in the most expressive way. In the case of the extra-human natural world the question becomes: is there a comparable site of ought-ness that solicits ethical comportment on my part? Without a forceful solicita-tion from the environment, I would not be drawn to *do* anything ethically efficacious regarding the problematic situations into which it can fall. Human beings rarely act directly from purely abstract principles, not from Kant's cate-gorical imperative in its three formulations and not even from the Ten Com-mandments! But where can we find in the other-than-human world the impera-tiveness that being ethical requires? Is there anything like a face that commands us in the presence of nature—that conveys to us with comparable intensity the damage and destruction that may afflict the natural world?

It is quite remarkable that Levinas, who says very little about an ethics of the environment, raises this very question. He asks: "Can things have a face?"[4] He rejects the idea that such a face would be merely "relative to an environing plenitude."[5] A genuine face must be grasped on its own terms, not those of a surrounding context.[6] In such a context, especially the seemingly endless con-text of the natural world, it might seem difficult to locate anything with the special poignancy, much less the ethical authority, of a face. It appears that either there is nothing like a face in the environment—with the result that we have lost the primary locus of oughtness—or the face is everywhere we look: in which case, its meaning would be so diluted as to risk losing any ethical urgency.

---

above all a question of finding the place from where human beings cease to concern us exclusively on the basis of the horizon of Being [as in Heidegger]. . . . The human existent (*l'étant*) as such (and not as an incarnation of universal being) can only exist in a relation where it is invoked. The human existent is the human being, and it is as a fellow being (*prochain*) that human being is accessible. As a face" ("L'Ontologie est-elle fondamentale?" *La revue de métaphysique et de morale* [1951]: p. 20). Significant in this statement is Levinas's express effort to find a "place from where" (*la place d'où*) ethics can become possible without having to rely on the encompassing horizon of Being at stake in *Being and Time*, yet still be fully "accessible" to human beings in the course of everyday life. The point of access is found in the face—the face of the other, my "fellow being" or "neighbor" (as *prochain* may also be trans-lated). The face allows ethics to find its fulcrum in something quite focused and singular.

4. "L'Ontologie est-elle fondamentale?" p. 22. But Levinas immediately diverts this question into whether the question of whether "art is an activity that lends faces to things," perhaps through "the impersonal allure of rhythm" (ibid.).

5. Ibid.

6. The German word for "environment" (*Umgebung*) underlines the idea of something surrounding us, since *um-* signifies "around."

This is the kind of dilemma into which Levinas puts us: either the face is strictly human (and then no ethics of the larger environment is possible) or it is part of an immense, nonethical totality called "life" or "nature."[7] Otherwise said: ethics is human or does not exist at all. This rigid choice gets us nowhere when we want to consider right and good action in the other-than-human world.

In confronting this dilemma, it is tempting to give up any search for a literal human face but still to look for something human or humanlike in the environment as the hook onto which to put the hat of ethics. After all, Levinas is not advocating the ethical primacy of the literal, physical face that would be the object of ordinary perception. Could we not say that the whole natural world is like an immense body, the "world's body" (in John Crowe Ransom's memorable phrase), and that it is therefore the analogue of our lived body? This is an intriguing idea—Levinas himself sometimes holds the whole body to be equivalent to the face[8]—and yet this formulation involves the fatal flaw of anthropocentrism. The world's body thus conceived is dependent on the human body, and to generalize the latter over the entire environment is to indulge in an unself-critical humanism, making man indeed "the measure of all things." It is also to invite the insoluble problems occasioned by the analogizing at play in any such generalization, whereby we effect a "pairing" (in Husserl's term) between our body and natural objects. Just as this act of *Paarung* is notoriously inadequate as a model of how we know other human beings to be similar to ourselves, so it is futile when it (or any other kind of analogical inference) is invoked to explain how the world as a whole is similar to our own body.[9]

Our task is clear: we need to find what answers to the face in the natural world—a sense of face that is neither a literal face nor its mere analogue. To avoid humanism and anthropocentrism, we need to find in the natural environment not an actual face but its equivalent: what can play a comparable role of announcing trouble and invoking action—despite all the manifest differences between what is human and what is other-than-human. More focused and par-

---

7. "The living being (*le vivant*) in totality exists as a totality, as if it occupied the center of being and were its source. . . ." (Levinas, "Le Moi et la totalité," in *Entre Nous: Essais sur le penser—à-l'autre* [Paris: Grasset, 1991], p. 23). "Totality" for Levinas is precisely what cannot hold or sustain, much less present, the ethical relation. It is the fit object equally of abstract natural or social science—or, more fatefully, of war.

8. As Levinas remarks to Nemo: "I analyze the inter-human relation as if, in proximity to the Other—beyond the image I make of the other person [i.e., in perception]—his face, that which is expressive in the Other (and *the whole human body is, in this sense, more or less, face*), were that which orders me to serve him" (Emmanuel Levinas, *Éthique et infini: dialogues avec Philippe Nemo* [Paris: Fayard, 1982], p. 104; my translation and my italics); in the original text, Levinas underlines "orders"; see the English translation, *Ethics and Infinity: Conversations with Philippe Nemo*, tr. R. A. Cohen [Pittsburgh: Duquesne University Press, 1985, p. 97).

9. By this reference to "pairing" I am referring to Husserl's celebrated Fifth *Cartesian Meditation*, where the model of grasping other human beings through "analogical apperception" is proposed (see Edmund Husserl, *Cartesian Meditations*, tr. D. Cairns [The Hague: Nijhoff, 1960], esp. sections 50–51).

ticular than anything like the world's body, this has to have the urgency and force to act as the crux of ethical commitment: at once its origin and its point of application. And it must be something that we can take in at a glance.

This may seem a tall order. But consider that when we find the environment to be "hurting" we act toward it as if it were extending its face to us—appealing to us. I look at a tree dying from a parasitic vine and empathize with its strangled state: not because this is any state that I know myself and am projecting onto it but because I can read the strangulation right off in the parched yellowed leaves of the tree and in its overall lean and dry appearance. I see it dying before my very eyes. Its threatened state is evident in a glance, and I find myself wanting to cut out the vine that is choking it to death. In another instance, I encounter the dead body of a seagull washed up with the tide, its body covered with dark oil from a spill that occurred nearby a few days ago. I take at once—I cannot help but see—this unfortunate creature as the victim of the spill that resulted from human ineptitude. Not only the bird's demise but its recent suffering is written all over its body, the grimace of its face, its contorted legs: all this I take in at a glance. My imagination, spurred on by this quick apperception, supplies the rest: how the gull must have swooped down to catch an underwater prey and suddenly found itself floundering in the water with heavy oil spread on its feathers.

Unlike the case of the parasite, in which one natural entity has encroached upon the well-being of another, I see clearly and without hesitation that the suffering of the seagull (itself a strangulation of sorts) has a distinctly human origin, one that could have been avoided with enough caution or foresight. This inference follows directly upon the apprehension of the bird's pathetic final state. The bird's already-decaying body appeals to me as might a human face in distress: can you help to prevent this from happening ever again? The fact that one organism is dead and the other still alive does not matter here; what matters is the fact that I find myself in a situation of urgent appeal. The two beings in distress, human and bird, convey to me much the same sense of urgency. This is so despite the fact that they belong to different orders of the natural world—orders that fatefully intersect in the case of the seagull—while the strangulated tree, though not the victim of any human depredation, belongs to a third such order. Throughout, there is either a face (as in the human case of an actual suffering face) or something operating with the acute appeal of a face (as with the tree and the bird) in circumstances that catch my glance and call for appropriate action.

III

Let us back up and start again—this time by looking at a larger framework that does not borrow any of its basic traits from human beings, not even by implication. I refer to the environing *world* and, more particularly, to what I like to call the *place-world*. It is axiomatic that *every* entity of any environment, human or nonhuman, belongs in some significant measure to the natural world, and it inheres in this world by way of the particular place it inhabits. Thinking in terms of the place-world avoids invidious searching among species for priority in the ethical realm, since all natural entities, including unspeciated ones, are part of the place-world. Every entity, living or not, belongs to this world, which takes the form of a concrete, complicated nexus of places.[10]

A clue to this last line of consideration is found in the following thought-experiment. Faced with the choice as to whether we should destroy a single member of a species or its habitat, we would almost always decide to save the habitat even if it meant sacrificing the animal.[11] The greatest value accrues not just to the larger whole but to the particular place-world in which certain animals flourish. Or to put the same point somewhat differently: whereas we value human beings primarily for what they are in each individual case (we can be face-to-face with only *one* Other at a time), we value nonhuman animals not only for themselves (this we certainly do as well, as we know from the case of beloved pets) but also for their being denizens of the place-world they inhabit. The source of the ethical commitment to recognize and support them that they inspire in us stems in significant measure from our appreciation of the places to which they belong as co-inhabitants of the same region or territory.[12]

Another clue, this time from the history of language: *ethos,* the Greek word that lies at the origin of the word "ethics" and that signified collective character in Attic Greek, first of all meant (in Homer's time) "animal habitat," for example, the place where wild horses go when they settle down at night. There is, then, an ancient link between ethics and place in the West—a link that remains in force, however confusedly, when we speak of a "place-based morality" or "situation ethics." We neglect this same link when we make ethics into a matter of procedure or rule, law or principle: all of which are indifferent to the place in which they are enacted. The fact is that the ethical happens in concrete places, including human habitats.

Even if it is granted that place-worlds are the ultimate locus of ethical action in the environmental field, something more specific to anchor the ethicalness of the environmental imperative is required: namely, what Lacan called a *point de*

10. Many of these places are peculiar to particular species (e.g., the red fox) or to material things (e.g., granite); but some are shared by numerous species: e.g., the ocean, the air, the coastline.

11. I say "almost always," for an exception might arise in the case of the last known member of a given species. Even so, we might hesitate, especially if preserving the habitat were a way of saving the animal and its offspring. The Southwestern Center for Biodiversity is noted for its efforts to maintain bioniches as a way of supporting species threatened with extinction.

12. John Findlay once remarked in conversation that animals—especially dogs—should be regarded as "associate members of the kingdom of ends." This bon mot got it halfway right. Animals are associate members of the kingdom of the living (as we revealingly call it, echoing Kant's "Kingdom of Ends"). More generally, all natural entities, including human beings, are associate members of the place-worlds to which they commonly belong. (I put "place-world" in the plural to indicate that a given entity may belong to more than one place-world, as we see in complex natural environments such as rain forests or borderline ecosystems.)

capiton, a "button tie" or stitch that pins down a button to cloth or other material.[13] Some such focal point, a concrete crux, is needed as well in the field of the environment if we are to pin down the source of an environment's summoning power. Where can this be?

If we meditate upon the place-world and look for its most characteristic unit of presentation, we soon reach the *landscape* by means of which the place-world appears. Construing "landscape" to include cityscape, seascape, plainscape, mountainscape, skyscape, and so on—any form of "placescape"—we find that it has two primary features: "layout" and "surface." *Layout* is J. J. Gibson's term for any coherent congeries of surfaces in the environment; it is "the persisting arrangement of surfaces relative to one another and to the ground."[14] It is the way in which various visual (and other) phenomena co-constitute an environment in its very extendedness. Layout also connotes the way in which a given environment provides opportunities to its inhabitants—opportunities that Gibson terms "affordances," remarking that "different layouts [offer] different affordances for animals."[15] The place-world, then, delivers itself to us in terms of particular landscapes, and these in turn occur as layouts in our perceptual field—extended regions in which natural entities are not only located but afforded the chance to do various things, whether this be to build houses, pursue prey, or just to "vegetate" and stay put.

Still more specifically, the layout of the place-world, that is to say, the whole environment, is composed of *surfaces*, a topic to which we here return in the wake of our treatment in chapters 2 and 7. Not only is layout a matter of the arrangement of surfaces in relation to each other, but the very *ground* to which each of these surfaces relates is itself a surface: it is "the basic persisting surface of the environment."[16] Indeed, "environment" itself, the most encompassing term of all, is in effect a concatenation of surfaces, since the "substances" of which it is composed present themselves only through surfaces, and the "medium" of the environment is imperceptible except in terms of particular surfaces (for example, the boundary between a field and a forest, the edge of the wind as it moves across a stand of wheat; the submerged face of a continent and the

13. See Jacques Lacan, "The Subversion of the Subject and the Dialectic of Desire," in *Écrits,* tr. B. Fink (New York: Norton, 2002), p. 291: the *point de capiton* is that "by which the signifier stops the otherwise indefinite sliding of signification"(see the translator's note in ibid., p. 351). In psychoanalytic practice, a symptom plays this pivotal role, for in it are condensed the repressed and repressing forces whose compromised conjunction constitutes a nodal point in the psychic field.

14. J. J. Gibson, *The Ecological Approach to Visual Perception* (Hillsdale, N.J.: Erlbaum, 1986), p. 307.

15. Ibid. I would add: not just for animals but for all natural things in a given environment, where "environment" (in Gibson's own description) "consists of a medium, substances, and the surfaces that separate the substances from the medium" (ibid.).

16. Ibid. Cf. p. 10: "The literal basis of the terrestrial environment is the ground, *the underlying surface of support* that tends to be on the average flat—that is to say, a plane—and also level, or perpendicular to gravity" (my italics; Gibson underlines "basis").

ocean that surrounds it). Insofar as a surface is where a given thing and its medium (for example, its atmosphere) meet,[17] it is the indispensable mediatrix between everything of import in the environment; it is never absent from the particular combinations of entities that make up the surrounding world. Everywhere we look, feel, and sense, we are confronted by surfaces: by their phenomenal properties (for example, shape, color, size, and so on), their intersection, and finally their layout. They are the constituent units of every immediately surrounding world (*Umwelt*): "Animals," observes Gibson, "perceive surfaces and their properties, since animal behavior must be controlled by what the surfaces and their substances afford."[18] Surfaces are equally important for plants and stones, which are even more fully determined, indeed dominated, by the surfaces they proffer to the world. In their capacity to present entities within a given environment, surfaces furnish the means by which the landscapes of the place-world are given specificity and shape. If it is true that (as Kant held) nature makes itself specific for our understanding, it does so in terms of the surfaces that are essential to material things—things whose concatenation creates the landscape layouts that make up any given place-world.[19]

IV

Gibson says suggestively in a late essay on surfaces that "the perception of the [surface] properties of the persisting substances of the habitat is necessary if we are to know what they afford, what they are good for."[20] This points toward the ethical, which directs us to be and do good in terms of what the surfaces of our immediate environment afford—what they are "good for."[21] Although we are surrounded by surfaces,[22] we rarely pause to take note of what is special about them, especially not with regard to their role in ethical life. Yet if the glance

17. In the formula that I have cited in chap. 7, a surface is "the interface between a substance and [a] medium." (J. J. Gibson, "What Is Involved in Surface Perception?" in J. J. Gibson, *Reasons for Realism: Selected Essays of James J. Gibson,* ed. E. Reed and R. Jones [Hillsdale, N.J.: Erlbaum, 1982], p. 111).

18. Ibid., p. 112.

19. See Immanuel Kant, *Critique of Judgment,* tr. W. Pluhar (Indianapolis: Hackett, 1987), p. 25: "nature makes its universal laws specific in accordance with the principle of purposiveness for our cognitive power."

20. Gibson, "What Is Involved in Surface Perception?" p. 110.

21. The phrase "good for" signifies not the ethical as such but one way *toward* it: a decidedly instrumental way that is far from a Levinasian, Platonic, or Kantian assessment of "the good." Kant says, for example, "We call something (viz., if it is something useful) *good for* [this or that] if we like it only as a means. But we call something *intrinsically good* if we like it for its own sake" (Immanuel Kant, *Critique of Judgment,* p. 48; his italics). Restricted as its scope may be, however, the instrumental signifies that the realm of nature, taken as the realm of the "good for," is not value-free.

22. "Animals [including human animals]," says Gibson, "see their environment chiefly [as] illuminated surfaces" ("Ecological Optics," in *Reasons for Realism,* p. 75).

indeed plays a central role in ethics, including an ethics of the environment, then the perception of surfaces will be central in this life. For surfaces are precisely where glances alight: we glance at appealing or threatening, beckoning or off-putting surfaces. But what is it about surfaces that makes them so well suited for presenting ethical imperatives that bear on the environment? Two things mainly: expressivity and elementarity.

At one level of analysis, surfaces show themselves to be eminently capable of *expressivity*, which is indispensable to those imperatives that call to us and engender action. It is not just the face, or the whole body, that is expressive but the surfaces of bodies and things, nonhuman as well as human. This is due to the fact that surfaces are capable of the kinds of variation that are important to expressivity. I think here of variations in pliability, elasticity, contour, extended-ness, coloration, texture, and so forth: all of which, once coordinated, contribute to expressivity in a given instance.[23] It is just because of this multiplicity of co-variant factors that the full range of expressivity is possible, whether it is dis-played in a face or in the layout of a landscape. All the more so when it is a question—as it always *is* a question in an environmental setting—of several surfaces interacting at once. Then we perceive their continual reconfiguration as surfaces meet and mingle, overlap and occlude each other, thereby increasing exponentially the possibilities for expressivity. By emphasizing surface rather than something supposedly substantial underneath a surface—for example, a human self under the skin of its own body—expressivity is no longer attached exclusively to human beings, much less to their literal faces. This allows us to speak straightforwardly, and without outright anthropocentrism, of a landscape as being "haunting" or "melancholy," "joyous" or "happy."[24]

At a second level, a given surface is able to hold together and present these diverse aspects precisely because of its own *elementarity*. The elemental is a form of materiality that is so basic and indeterminate that it cannot be "possessed" in terms of determinate features or traits.[25] The elemental is also notable for its comparative simplicity. Consider the surface of a mirror or that of a windowpane. Their very smoothness, their lack of qualitative complication, their transparency or sheer reflecting power allow them to hold within their frame very complex

23. Conditions for being indicative are characteristically both more austere—e.g., as in the case of being a bare sign—*and* more sophisticated: to grasp an indicative sign is to have to understand the larger context within which it functions.

24. On expressivity in the landscape, see the pioneering essay by Otto Baensch, "Art and Feeling" in *Reflections on Art: A Source Book of Writings by Artists, Critics, and Philosophers*, ed. S. Langer (New York: Oxford, 1961), pp. 10–36. For a concept of expression whose scope is equal to this expanded notion of expressivity, see Walter Benjamin, "Über Sprache Überhaupt und Über die Sprache des Menschens," in *Gesammelte Schriften* (Frankfurt am Main: Suhr-kamp, 1991), vol. 2.

25. As Levinas says, "Every relation or possession is situated within the non-possessable which envelops or contains without being able to be contained or enveloped. We shall call it the elemental" (*Totality and Infinity*, p. 131). Levinas also emphasizes the indeterminate character of the elemental at ibid., p. 132.

images and scenes. This suggests an inverse law of "ecological optics": the less complicated the surface, the more complex and configurated the contents it can set forth, *on* the surface in the case of the mirror, *through* the surface in the case of the windowpane. In their very simplicity, such surfaces gather items for display. Examples of these surfaces in the natural environment include flat prairie lands (against which variegated grasses and wildflowers stand out) or the perceived sky (on which intensely different cloud formations are set forth) or even the open sea (which, as we have seen, holds together very different stretches of water). In such cases, the elemental as land or sky or water acts as an indeterminate ground that may have its own patterns but nevertheless allows more complex configurations to emerge upon their surfaces. Because of their comparative consistency as grounds—a consistency that reinforces their simplicity—these elemental surfaces are capable of supporting things (other surfaces, layouts, whole landscapes) that are vastly different in content and scope and type.

Given that surfaces of the natural world facilitate expressiveness while their very elementarity enhances the conveyance of environmental complexity, we have on hand a ready basis for that which can catalyze ethical action bearing on the environment. This is *the direct presentation of environmental distress.* When I glimpse the dumping of waste in a swamp or the ruination of soil on a farm from overgrazing, I am witnessing distress in the environment.[26]

When surfaces express environmental distress, the natural order of things is not just complicated but significantly undermined. We witness an *opus contra naturam.* By this, I do not mean merely a "freak of nature"—though this can be environmentally telling too, as in the case of birth defects caused by water pollution—but any feature of the layout that goes contrary to the natural order. Rather, I mean any object or event that interrupts normal cycles of growth and decay, for example, by causing abortive growth or premature decay. Then, instead of a layout that presents itself as coherent and unproblematic—as exhibiting a natural cycle of being and well-being—we are confronted with manifest disarray. We sense that something is rotten in the state of nature: something awry or upset, incoherent or inconsistent.

What I have just called "distress" refers to any kind of environmental disorder that is registered—expressively—on the surfaces of the layout constituted by a given group of natural entities. This is not to deny that certain forms of damage are invisible in early stages (for example, Dutch elm disease before it is manifest;

---

26. The disorder in the environment may be more subtle, of course—in which case, of course, a trained ecologist may be required to detect it. This is especially important in the case of early warning signs of environmental distress, say, the perception of the larvae of what will become an insect destructive of trees once it is fully developed. It has been pointed out to me by a veteran ecologist that rather than seeing such educated perception as merely a matter of specialization, it in fact approximates to what many human beings would be capable of were they to live more fully in the natural environment—as was the case for many millennia before the advent of city-based inhabitation (e-mail remark of L. L. Woolbright, Siena College, Albany, New York, February 18, 2000).

the deadzone in the Gulf of Mexico before it became toxic to fish and sea plants). Sometimes disruption of the surface can be healthy, as when forest fires lead to culling of old stock and the growth of new trees. Such cases notwithstanding, however, there is a great deal we can trust in our perception of environmental disorder: for the most part, we can draw on our "perceptual faith" (Merleau-Ponty), and count on our "animal faith" (Santayana).[27] The signs of such disorder are telling us something; they are expressing a wound to the ecosystem, a tear in its fabric, an illness in the landscape. To those who had eyes to see, the baneful effects of nineteenth-century industrialism in England and America were manifest in the country as well as in the city—as acute observers such as Blake and Dickens, Thomas Cole and Thoreau all saw so poignantly.

These ecologists of perception not only decried the destruction that was billowing in the air and poisoning the ground: they saw it in a glance. So we, too, at the beginning of this new millennium can glimpse the initial effects of global warming not just in the massive losses of sea otters and seals in the Pacific Ocean but in such expressive elemental phenomena as changing weather patterns, whose persistently hotter surfaces we feel in our skins. When I sense dis-ease in the environment, I attend to where it is located, in what place and layout, and especially on which surfaces of these latter—including the surfaces of my own body. This is why the glance is so aptly invoked in this very circumstance: its pointed penetrating power allows it to go straight to where the problem is, like a hawk zeroing in on its prey. Or like a lance launched at its pinpointed target: *Ort*, the German word for "place," derives ultimately from "tip of a spear": the glance, like a lance, is typically thrown at its target (as the French say, glancing means to "throw a blow of the eye": *jeter un coup d'oeil*). The target in landscape apperception takes the form of a particular layout of places in the environment, a set of surfaces that betray the state of its health.

Analogues to this situation abound: the practiced medical doctor knows by a mere glance what her patient is suffering from, the painter knows by the briefest of looks what has to be added or subtracted from his work, the poet to her text, the cook to the dish being prepared. The person familiar with his or her local environment—the farmer, the gardener, the landscape architect—can tell with similar swiftness if this environment is in trouble, and even if it is only starting to head for difficulty. The place-world shows itself in its surfaces, as existing within its own normative parameters, geomorphic or evolutionary, agricultural or wild—or else as exceeding or undermining these parameters, as ill at ease with itself. The glance takes all this in without needing a separate act of judgment or reflection. A bare apperception, a mere moment of attention, is enough: *a glance suffices.*[28]

27. On perceptual faith, see Maurice Merleau-Ponty, *The Visible and the Invisible*, tr. A. Lingis (Evanston, Ill.: Northwestern University Press, 1968), pp. 50 ff.; on animal faith, see George Santayana, *Skepticism and Animal Faith* (New York: Scribners, 1923).

28. Here the glance is strangely the counterpart of the earth, which as Levinas says also

V

A glance suffices not just to see distress and disorder. It also picks up the imperative to do something about these dissonances. Here we take the crucial step from being *noticeable* to being *compelling*. Certain surfaces of the environment are noticeably in trouble, and we see this at a glance; but what about the ethical demand that we find a way to resolve the trouble? How can anything as insistent as this demand arise from mere surfaces and the layouts they make up? We might grant that our glance takes in many environmental problems quickly and accurately. But does it suffice to grasp the *imperative* to remedy the earth's maladies?

It does, but only if we single out one more factor in the distressed surfaces we notice. To be expressive and to be an elemental foil to the complexities of the environment are both essential to presenting difficulties happening in a given place. But a certain *intensity* is also required: an intensity *on* and *of* the very surfaces that draw our attention in the first place. A pleasant and healthy landscape lacks intensity; it lulls us into the pleasure of the beautiful. Only when a landscape is troubled does intensity emerge in our apperception of it: an intensity that calls out for our intervention, indeed demands it. Qualitative intensity is a matter of tension. In Kant's notion of the sublime, for example, there is an intensity lacking in the beautiful; this intensity stems from a tension between imagination and reason. In environmental distress, a different but equally powerful tension arises: a tension between the natural order of things and its disruption. This tension engenders an intensity that asks us to act and not just to spectate. From within this intensity we grasp an imperative for action without engaging in reflective thought processes such as induction or deduction: we grasp it in a glance.

Is this the same glance as that by which we take in the trouble? Not necessarily. Sometimes I need to take a second look—a second glance. This is especially the case if my first glance is overwhelmed by the damage I witness, stunning my senses as it were; then I need to glance again, on the rebound as it were, if I am to catch the imperative to do something about it. Often, however, it is indeed with the same look that I see environmental distress as well as the call to rectify it. Let me cite a case in point.

I once beheld the devastation wrought upon an entire slope of a giant mountain as I hiked up Cottonwood Canyon in the Crazy Mountains in central Montana. My companion confirmed that there had indeed been extensive clear-

---

suffices in its own way: "The earth upon which I find myself and from which I welcome sensible objects or make my way to them suffices for me. The earth which upholds me does so without my troubling myself about knowing what upholds the earth" (*Totality and Infinity*, p. 137). This last sentence could well be a statement about elemental surfaces, about whose support we also do not usually concern ourselves; even the ground to which they ultimately relate is itself, as Gibson avers, a surface of its own. Both glance and earth are creatures of surfaces, albeit each in its own way.

cutting up there for some time. In fact, he and others had filed suit against the United States Forest Service for their having allowed the sale of the land, without adequate preliminary inspection, to the logging company that had effected the depredations I was now witnessing. From my bare glance at this scene of destruction, I sensed the need for some such concerted legal action, along with still more ambitious moves to have most of the Crazies permanently protected from logging. Nor did I need to have further evidence: the decisive and compelling evidence was before me, etched in the distress of the land: the sawed-off tree trunks jutted from the soil like so many ugly protuberances and the soil itself was a mass of mud in the absence of the protection of the trees; nor had any new trees been planted to palliate the situation. The contrast with healthy growth on nearby slopes was painful and telling: the landscape was telling me a story of extensive environmental damage and announcing the imperative not to let this happen again. Whole stands of ancient conifers had lost their rightful place in an aboriginal biotic life-world—with only burnt-out stumps remaining in an infernal scene of devastation that suggested war had been waged here. As indeed it had: a war against the natural world and its own cycles of growth, death, and regeneration.

The imperative to take ecological action in Cottonwood Canyon was at one with my grasp of the intense disruption of the scene there, its shattered surfaces speaking dramatically to my bare apperception. The elemental expressivity of these surfaces possessed an intensity that made action no subject of idle speculation but something that had to be done if more such savagery was to be avoided.

The clear-cut mountain slope I beheld was like a festering wound; it was a scene of concentrated affliction. It presented itself not unlike a *symptom* that draws attention to itself even if the person it affects has no idea what it can mean. As Freud said of a symptom in the context of psychoanalysis: "if one did not see it before one every day one would never bring oneself to believe in it."[29] Despite its cryptic origins and opaque meaning, the symptom is overt: it is on the agenda all the time. It is so painful and puzzling as to dominate a life. A symptom is literally *in*-tensive, infecting the subject even as it conceals its origins from this same subject. A symptom is also "overdetermined"; it has at least several causes; it is part of a larger trans-subjective context. To understand a symptom—and to relieve the patient's suffering from it—is to advert to a more encompassing set of factors than are manifest in the symptom itself.

Just so the clear-cut forest in central Montana was symptomatic on both counts. On the one hand, it compelled attention on the basis of its sheer disarray: not just the wraith-like remains of cut-down trees but crudely constructed access roads that crisscrossed the landscape like so many razor slashes on its upturned face. My glance was drawn into the heart of this darkness. This is the

29. Sigmund Freud, *Introductory Lectures on Psychoanalysis*, tr. J. Strachey, in J. Strachey, ed., *Standard Edition of the Complete Psychological Works* (London: Hogarth, 1963), vol. 15, p. 259.

moment of pain that calls for alleviation by the appropriate action: a pain that belongs equally (but very differently) to the land and to me as its beholder. On the other hand, the same symptomatic suffering brings with it a profound puzzlement: Why this destruction? Why here? Why now? Why at all? If I were to pursue this puzzlement, I would have to look to the larger picture. I would become an ecoanalyst of sorts, someone who investigates the genealogy of the situation—not just its causes but also its reasons. I would consider history, social and political forces, and even metaphysics.[30] In this way, I would move away from the apperception of the immediate environmental trauma; I would engage in reflection and other cognitive and judgmental operations: my glance, which inaugurated the entire experience, would no longer suffice. Its lambent lightness, combined with its compelling disclosure, is now replaced by carefully considered thought processes. An environmental imperative, taken in at a glance, has precipitated reflective and responsible analysis of the situation.

I have been driven to the idea of symptom in an effort to understand the peculiar intensity embedded in my experience of the clear-cut demise of an entire mountainside in the middle of Montana—an intensity that not only appalled and angered me but that called out for action of the sort that my friend, more forthright and knowledgeable than I, had already undertaken: where I grasped the injunction on my first exposure to the destruction, he had acted on it in effective ways. But both of us started from the dismaying experience of a damaged landscape whose imperativeness was located *in the environment*—in the layout of the landscape, its very surfaces, and not in "the moral law within." The felt intensity that came from the tension between a scene of devastation and nondisrupted parts of the same landscape was there for all to see. A disturbed and symptomatic place-world drew our chagrined glances to itself compellingly —even if the larger causality lay elsewhere in the home offices of the great paper companies of the Northwest and across the nation in the endless and mindless consumption of paper on the part of millions of ordinary American citizens.

VI

I have been suggesting that intensity is the thin red line that links glance, surface, and responsiveness to environmental disorder. It heightens the compellingness of environmental imperatives. But we still have to grasp more exactly in what such intensity consists. Granting that it cannot be measured by extensive magnitude (that is, sheer quantity), it nonetheless appears on surfaces that

---

30. I say metaphysics, because if Heidegger is right the Age of Technology is a certain era of Western metaphysical thought in which the earth has come to be regarded as "standing reserve" in a massive enframing action that regards the earth as nothing but a resource to be exploited. See Martin Heidegger, "The Question Concerning Technology," in *The Question Concerning Technology and Other Essays,* tr. W. Lovitt (New York: Harper, 1977), pp. 3–35.

possess such magnitude. This means that it reflects the primary and especially the secondary qualities of extended surfaces.[31] Nevertheless, the intensity with which an environmental problem expresses itself is not just a matter of "too much," even if excess as such can be a valuable warning sign: for example, sewage streaming into the marshland. In the presence of such undeniable givens, one stares the problem itself in the face; but even here what one grasps is the *qualitative* configuration of something having quantitative dimensions: one sees the discoloration of the marshland water caused by the leakage of the sewage: quantity manifests itself as quality. Moreover, one reads the problematic situation on its surface, and is a direct witness to the distress: a glance is quite enough to take in the qualitatively distorted surfaces of the damaged marsh.

The appropriate response to an environmental imperative aims (in Deleuze's suggestive phrase) to "liberate the singularities of the surface."[32] For if "the accomplished action [in this case, the detrimental action] is projected on a surface"[33]—there for all to read at a glance—the remedial action must also bear on that same diseased surface: for example, the surface of the earth in the case of Cottonwood Canyon. Its task is to re-endow it with distinctive and singular potentialities of health so as to counter the damage of environmental disruption and to rectify it: if not to return it to a pristine state (for such damage is often irreversible), then to reinstate a significant measure of biotic well-being: for example, by planting new growth in the wake of the clear-cutting. Just as the sense of eco-dystrophy arises from a glance cast upon a distressed surface, so the action called for must also deal with this same surface—with what Deleuze and Guattari call the "planomenon."[34] The intensity of the distress is addressed by the concertedness and effectiveness of the action taken in relation to the surface on which this distress appears.

To say that the intensity of environmental disruption is qualitative is important as a corrective to geomorphic or econometric models of ecological disorder, models that stay within the realm of extensive magnitude. It keeps the situation in the phenomenological register—in the realm of first-person experience

31. As Deleuze puts it, "we know intensity only as already developed within an extensity, and as covered over by qualities" (Gilles Deleuze, *Difference and Repetition,* tr. P. Patton [New York: Columbia University Press, 1995], p. 223). See also this statement: "intensity itself is subordinated to the qualities which fill extensity. . . . Intensity is difference, but this difference tends to deny or to cancel itself out in extensity and underneath quality" (ibid.). I am arguing, however, that in the case of environmental trauma, the qualitative aspect is *not* buried beneath the quantitative dimensions but appears precisely in or through them.

32. Gilles Deleuze, *The Logic of Sense,* tr. M. Lester with C. Stivale, ed. C. V. Boundas (New York: Columbia University Press, 1990), p. 141.

33. Ibid., p. 207.

34. G. Deleuze and F. Guattari, *A Thousand Plateaus,* tr. B. Massumi (Minneapolis: University of Minnesota Press, 1987), p. 70: "The plane of consistency, or planomenon, is in no way an undifferentiated aggregate of unformed matters, but neither is it a chaos of formed matters of every kind." At p. 252 the authors assimilate the planomenon to the "Rhizosphere"—hence to a non-arborescent, non-striated, immanent form of becoming.

where the disruption is first noticed and where any imperative for change must first announce itself. Contributing to this experience is the fact that the alarming character of the disturbed environmental surface often takes the form of presenting *contrary qualities* on that surface: for example, in the way in which the blatantly artificial colors of industrial sludge contrast with the mellow hues of the marshlands into which they have seeped. The metallic colors of the sludge seem to subvert the earth tones of the wet land; they constitute a different spectral scene, one whose lines of force move contrary to those of the natural world. All of this occurs on the sheer surface of what is visible, where the drama, the clash of the tension, is manifest.[35]

The surfaces of a given natural environment are especially well suited to display this clash. For they provide ongoing bases for comparison among the qualities that specify their content. In particular, they act as common grounds for detecting the contrariness that I am here singling out as indicative of environmental turbulence. The clash of colors just mentioned is rendered more noticeable because all the colors, artificial as well as natural, are situated on the same overall apperceived surface, that of a given marshland. They contrast more vividly insofar as they share the same connective texture, that of the perceived marshland as a whole. So, too, the clear-cut area of Cottonwood Canyon stands out in contrast with the still-forested areas because both kinds of areas, hale as well as damaged, are part of the same continuous surface of the canyon to which they belong. The contrary qualities that signal environmental distress show themselves in a shared layout of surfaces, and it is this layout that yields itself to a glance.

VII

Thanks to the intensity registered on the complex and sometimes conflictual surfaces of the environment, there is room, after all, for the face, allowing us to return to our point of departure in this chapter. There I had argued that a face, or its equivalent, is integral to an ethics of the environment. Why this is so has been suggested in the course of exploring the factors of expressivity, elementarity, and intensity. It is first of all in a human face that these three factors conspire. Nothing else, no other part of the human body, can play this role so convincingly: no wonder that Levinas chose the face-to-face as the original scene of the ethical relation. For much the same reasons, a face is an effective vehicle of imperativeness. When we venture out into the natural environment, however, we do not encounter anything just like a human face. But we do find centers of intensity and expressive surfaces, all set within the element of the earth. These constitute the equivalent of a face if not a face itself. Yet this is the

---

35. "From all points of view, whether of quantity, quality, relation, or modality, contraries appear connected at the surface as much as in depth" (Deleuze, *The Logic of Sense*, p. 175).

case only if the face is no longer considered something strictly human, something that is revealed in an existential encounter—in an ethical "relation" that is
interhuman only. If the equivalent of a face is to play a role in an ecological
ethics, it must be dehumanized or, more exactly, seen as other-than-human from
the start. How can this be? Where, as what, is it to be found?

Here we can borrow a clue from Deleuze and Guattari's *A Thousand Plateaus,* where the authors take the extra step from the human to the nonhuman
that Levinas failed to make after he raised the crucial question of whether things
have faces.[36] Agreeing with him that the whole body needs to be facialized—"not
only the mouth but also the breast, hand, the entire body, even the tool, are
'facialized' "[37]—they add the crucial rider that facialization does not stop at the
limits of the body: it extends to the full environment, the layout of the landscape
in which that body is implaced. What they call the "faciality" machine, that is,
"the social production of [the] face,"[38] is such that it "performs the facialization
of the entire body *and all its surroundings and objects, and the landscapifica-
tion of all worlds and milieus.*"[39] The result is what the authors call a "face-
landscape," in which landscape is facial and a face landscapelike. Just because
the face is no longer exclusively human—thereby sidestepping the dual pitfalls
of analogy and anthropocentrism—we can conjoin it to landscape in a very close
alliance in which the human being can no longer claim priority over the nonhuman world.

This is an especially important move, given that normally the face epitomizes
the human and is broadly thought to be the very site of expressivity. A critique of
humanism must include a questioning of the primacy of the literal human face,
wherein a human being is contained in an all too confined and precious compass. But what if the face belongs in the first place to the landscape and not to
the human being? Then we need not invoke projection or analogy to explain
metaphorical expressions such as "the face of the world."[40] Nor need we fear an
insidious anthropocentrism that lurks in most accounts of the natural environment. Still more importantly for our purposes, we would have located a place of
ethical intensity that is in no way constricted to the head of the human being
(and thus to speech as emanating from this same head). Precisely as "deter-

---

36. As I have noted, Levinas raises this question in his 1951 essay, "L'Ontologie est-elle
fondamentale?" But by the time he published *Totality and Infinity* in 1961, his answer was
resolutely negative: "things have no face" (*Totality and Infinity,* p. 140).

37. Deleuze and Guattari, *A Thousand Plateaus,* pp. 174–175. Cf. also pp. 170, 181. The
authors do not refer explicitly to Levinas in these passages.

38. Ibid., p. 181. Because of this social origin of the face, "the face is not a universal" (ibid.,
p. 176).

39. Ibid., p. 181; my italics.

40. Thus we must be wary of a claim that "the human face is the face of the world itself" (Emmanuel Levinas, "Phenomenon and Enigma," in *Collected Philosophical Papers,* tr.
A. Lingis [Dordrecht: Nijhof, 1987], p. 69). Such a statement implies that the world's face
is nothing but the massive projection of the human face: just the view I am here opposing.

ritorialized," that is, taken out of its humanized role, the face becomes coeval with landscape and allows us to imagine a different basis for an ethics of the environment:

> Now the face has a correlate of great importance: the landscape, which is not just a milieu but a deterritorialized world. There are a number of face-landscape correlations. . . . What face has not called upon the landscapes it amalgamated, sea and hill; what landscape has not evoked the face that would have completed it, providing an unexpected complement for its lines and traits?[41]

In this way of putting it, we cannot really say which comes first in the matter of the face, the front of the human head or the other-than-human landscape. Deleuze and Guattari do not merely reverse the priority of human and nonhuman, they suggest that any priority between them is undeterminable. That suffices for an ethics of the environment that valorizes the way in which a human glance is capable of dealing with something wholly different in kind or status, namely, the natural world and its vicissitudes. This glance, streaming from our all-too-human face, apperceives what is right and wrong with an environment to which it belongs ultimately but which presents itself in a manner that cannot be assimilated to human speech. If I have spoken of a "call" issued from a troubled environment, this is not to say that it has an actual voice, or can be assimilated to language in any rigorous way. It means, rather, that the glance is capable of picking up distress directly from a facialized landscape, that is to say, from its expressive surfaces and elemental intensities.

Just as earlier I had to denaturalize the glance (that is, by reclassifying it as apperception) to make it consonant with the human face as conceived by Levinas, so Deleuze and Guattari similarly recommend that we withdraw the face from its fate as part of an anatomical head to be placed among other natural organs of the human animal. The human head is only relatively different from the heads of other mammals. But the face, like its glance, is something of a different order: to understand it requires a radical withdrawal from the usual paradigms of organicity and sensory perception; and this withdrawal is made possible by the very traits that Levinas ascribes to it: its ability to bear and express meaning (its "signifyingness") as well as its status as a subject (its "subjectification"): both of which make it incommensurate with natural phenomena, enigmatic in relation to them, and thus absolutely deterritorialized.

If we follow this line of thought, it becomes less peculiar to assimilate the face to the landscape as proposed by the authors of *A Thousand Plateaus*. For the landscape is not itself a natural entity, a summative whole of discrete physical parts. It is a "detotalized totality" (Sartre) that can harbor distinctly unnatural phenomena such as faciality—which is the equivalent of a face but no literal face at all. Moreover, it is in a landscape that the equivalent of a face shows itself—

41. *A Thousand Plateaus*, pp. 172–173. See all of chap. 7, "Year Zero: Faciality," esp. pp. 181, 190.

shows itself to be amenable and settled, distressed and disrupted, or else an uneasy mixture of both. And we apperceive all of this in a special act of attending that, being no mere act of ordinary perception, detects its wellness or illness in the time of the glance.[42]

VIII

In this chapter I have been proposing a prolegomenon to an ethics of the environment, keeping in mind that "pro-legomenon" means in its root "before the saying is said" (before the *dire* is *dit* as Levinas might like to put it). Before anything is said—either among interlocutors engaged in earnest ethical discourse or in an individual's invocation of a categorical imperative—there is the moment of ethical engagement in and by the glance. Already in the last chapter, I noted how often and how effectively the glance serves to initiate this first phase of the ethical encounter. Its ability to go straight to the heart of the matter, to size up a problematic situation quickly, and to see possible lines of remedial action: all these powers of the glance help us to discern the compelling character of the circumstance—that which calls for responsiveness on our part. Traditional ethical theory has rarely if ever made room for this initiatory moment of the glance, concentrating as it has on reason and rules, persons and norms, sanctions and justifications.

Traditional ethical theory has also neglected the natural environment and its special set of problems and needs. I have been arguing that here, too, the glance is of crucial consequence in alerting human subjects to things that need to be done in order to address environmental damage and distress. I act accordingly not because I always know exactly what to do, or because I am in a seigniorial position in which I can lord my human wisdom over that of a paltry natural world. This world has its own wisdom and its own force, and my task is to read the signs of both rather than to impose on it my own preferences. When I act in environmental exigencies, it is not out of a presumed stewardship over the earth, much less from supposing that I am its patron. I act to assist in circumstances where the environment has come into a conflictual circumstance that offers no solutions on its own terms—other than disease and death. Whether the conflict

42. Despite the convergence I have just suggested, Levinas finally diverges from Deleuze and Guattari: for Levinas, the face is incongruous with natural phenomena because it is transcendent to them—at once ethical, religious, and metaphysical ("ethics," adds Levinas tellingly, is "the spiritual optics" [*Totality and Infinity*, p. 78])—whereas for Deleuze and Guattari it is discontinuous with such phenomena for the very different reason that they are held to be social constructs. The authors of *A Thousand Plateaus* insist that the correlate of the face is not the natural world or "milieu" but *landscape*, but this is only because landscape is itself a social construct in their view. For my own view of landscape as an inclusive whole that is at once non-natural and yet not socially constructed, see my *Representing Place: Landscape Painting and Maps* (Minneapolis: University of Minnesota Press, 2002), chap. 1 and glossary.

(which I have characterized as a clash or contrast between a currently degenerate state and certain norms of growth and life) is due to the predation of human beings or other animals, or whether it is self-inflicted (as in the case of parasites or microbes out of control) does not matter. What matters is that I apperceive trouble in the making, and intervene to bring the ailing circumstance to a more salubrious stage.

In view of the fact that we are literally surrounded by environmental layouts at all times (the natural world encroaches into the city in many guises),[43] the sweeping glance is of particular value. Its comprehensive character—its gift for *taking in so much in so little time*—is aptly deployed vis-à-vis difficulties in the environment. It spots problems as they emerge, including those that are not altogether obvious. This is not to say that it spots every emerging problem, or that it is infallible. Moreover, there are important differences between the trained eye of the ecologist and the first-time hiker in the local woods: the former has a clear advantage in identifying problematicities and in knowing how to address them in the most effective way. But the comparatively naked and naive eye is not to be discounted. It has its own swift insights and can for the most part be trusted. This is why I have been presuming no specialized knowledge on the part of the glancer in the midst of the natural context. This glancer is able to recognize environmental trouble and trauma without elaborate training: as in my first impressions of Cottonwood Canyon, or in witnessing a tree strangled by a parasite, or noting the mixture of sludge and seawater in a marsh. Thanks to its native acumen, even the most untutored glance can pick up the kind of inconsistency that heralds environmental distress, and it can also divine what has to be done to alleviate it. For this reason, both in human affairs and in the other-than-human world, the glance can be considered the leading edge of the ethical: that which opens the ethical relation in both worlds, indeed gets it under way.

This is to take a significant step beyond Levinas and any others (among them, Kant and Sartre) who would want to confine the ethical to the interhuman domain. I took this step by searching for the equivalent of the human face in this domain: not its precise analogue (which would require the presence of resembling features) but something that serves as the compelling source of imperativeness. Hence my recourse to the idea of a facialized landscape—so long as this notion of Deleuze and Guattari's does not imply the projection of the face onto the surrounding world but rather the existence of something that plays a role equivalent to the role of the human face: above all, that of being a compelling source that issues a "call to action,"[44] whether this action is taken by human beings or by other creatures (as when elephants assist each other's mourning). I have maintained, moreover, that this call has to come from *somewhere* that is

---

43. On the irrepressible incursion of the wild into the urban, see the remarkable essay by Christina Maile, "Sewing and Weeds," *On Site Review* (spring 2002).
44. This is the title of a section of Levinas's "Phenomenon and Enigma."

located (even if not simply located) in the place-world: in the layout of its landscape. Without this concrete location, it would be situated in the thin air of ethical discourse and metaphysical principle, wherein it lacks the "sting of the real" as William James called it: the visual bite of the poignant scene that makes a disturbed circumstance come to our attention in the first place. Such a scene is the equivalent of the human face, but it arises in an other-than-human context and it is not the mere projection of such a face.

The intense point, the compelling source that conveys "the sense of ought-ness," is something I apprehend by the glance in its vanguard role. This sense is to be seen on the surfaces of the environment: surfaces that constitute its ac-cessibility, its very perceptibility. We need to endorse Gibson's axiom (first cited in chapter 7) that "the surface is where most of the action is"[45]—not only the apperceptive action but the ethical action as well. If the telltale symptom of environmental disturbance appears anywhere, it must appear on the surface of things—not in some hidden depth (however differently this latter is interpreted by the environmental scientist and the metaphysician). It must be there to be seen at a glance. And what do we then see? We see distress, which can be variously construed as incongruity, discordance, contrast, clash, contrariness, tension—but above all as intensity. Following Kant and Deleuze, intensity must here be interpreted as qualitative, thus as something we feel as well as apper-ceive. Differential in character, it presents itself by degrees—building to a point where it not only draws our attention but *requires* it. And when we do attend to it (often by a series of concerted glances), we find something compelling us, telling us, to act so as to alter the disturbed circumstance: to "set it right."[46]

In the end, the natural world does indeed present the equivalent of a face to us—but only as belonging to the layout of expressive surfaces inherent in a given landscape. The natural world turns a face to us from within its many surfaces: not the infinite and transcendent enigmatic face of the Other of such high valency for Levinas but an immanent, intense faciality of its own, one in which we can discern distress without having to make it analogous to human suffering. *That*

---

45. Gibson, *The Ecological Approach to Visual Perception*, p. 23.

46. Emily Lee points out plausibly that not all complicated and confusing environments are in need of assistance; what appears chaotic or disequilibriated to us may be its "natural" state; and in such cases, it would be mistaken to try to set them right: in their visual complexity, they are already wholesome enough and not the victims of depredation or disease (Emily Lee, e-mail communication, August 2003). This is certainly true. My ignorance or inexperience may prevent me from acknowledging such a state: as when I mistake the violence of certain animals who prey on weaker animals for an undesirable and correctable condition, not realizing that in the larger scheme of things this violence has its proper place. To this I can only respond that not every glance is adequate to the scene it witnesses; as with any other form of the look, it can be misled by appearances; and it certainly does not always know the more encompassing order of the natural world. Admitting this, however, is not tantamount to denying the extraordinary insightfulness and swift rightness of a given glance: two virtues that bring the glance imme-diately into the ambience of the ethical, where it can play a surprisingly central role along the lines I have been sketching in this and the last chapter.

face is the face of a nonhuman nonsubject—a landscape whose singularity belongs properly to the natural realm. Skeptics will respond: what guarantees that I
(or anyone else) will respond sensitively to this intensity? What of all those who
do not respond, either from self-interest (the logging companies, the paper
companies, the chemical companies) or from cynicism or indifference? Does not
response to environmental detrimentality require a certain education or sophistication? Is this not a social or political matter rather than an ethical one? These
are questions that can also be posed to a Levinasian model of ethical relation, in
which a high level of responsiveness is no less presumed. And I would have to
give a Levinasian answer as well: even if human subjects fail to pick up the ethical
command, even if they are oblivious to its force, this does not mean that they are
not *subject to its call to responsible action*. As Levinas remarks:

> The tie with the Other is realized only as responsibility, whether this [respon-
> sibility] be accepted or refused, whether one knows how to assume it or not, or
> whether one can or cannot do something concrete for the Other. To say: here I am
> (*me voici*). To do something for the Other. To give. . . . [This is what] the face [of
> the Other] orders and commands me.[47]

In other words, I may not feel the force of an ethical imperative at a given
moment, but it subsists in its demand upon me nonetheless: its hold on me
transcends my response to it. This holds for the natural environment no less
than for the human realm. Much the same injunctive priority obtains for other
very different models of an ethics of the environment: say, the Buddhist doctrine
of the interdependency of all natural beings, or Hans Jonas's point that I am
responsible for future generations, according to which I should act as if all
beings are interdependent and I am accountable to my successors on earth.
Even if I am not consciously aware of any such imperatives, much less acting to
endorse them, I am *no less under their sway*.

True, a certain kind of education or benevolent influence from enlightened
others will help make me aware of these injunctions—and thus more likely to
embrace them and to act accordingly. Whether embracing them or not, however, I am still in the presence of intense commands to respond. My failure to do
so stems not just from self-interest or indifference or lack of ecological enlightenment but also from a deeper failure, which is not my own alone: that is, the
failure to link vision meaningfully with the lived world around me, ultimately
due (in the West) to the detached Cartesian eye that bespeaks a massive cultural
disconnection between human beings and their environments.[48] In a Cartesian

---

47. Levinas, *Éthique et infini*, pp. 101–104. The expression "Here I am" is traced back by
Levinas to the Old Testament: "To the voice that calls from the burning bush, Moses answers
'Here I am', but does not dare to lift up his eyes" ("Phenomenon and Enigma," p. 68).

48. I owe this point to David Michael Levin, in conversation. See his books, *The Opening of
Vision: Nihilism and the Postmodern Situation* (New York: Routledge, 1988) and *The Philoso-
pher's Gaze: Modernity and the Shadows of Enlightenment* (Berkeley: University of California
Press, 1999).

culture, ruled by rigidly compartmentalizing norms, the glance often falls short; it may barely notice, if notice at all, the signs of environmental trouble; such glancing will fall from the ecological surface without taking in the expressive intensities of that surface, quickly sliding off the glabrous back of the place-world. This situation, all too common in the wake of Cartesian thought, is not so much unethical or immoral as, shall we say, *a-ethical:* the message is missed by blinkered human subjects who fail to respond, even though they still stand under the imperative to be responsive. The intensity of disturbance is there, but they are not able to say *me voici:* here I am for you, I will make some difference, I will do something to save your symptomatic skin, something to put you back in the right place, to resituate your afflicted layout in a more hale and halcyon world. And I need to say all of this nonpatronizingly, bearing in mind that I myself belong to the same natural world I am here called to address.

If there is indeed an ethical relation between human beings, there is also an equally (if differently configured) ethical relation among all members of the natural environment—to which Levinas's challenging ethical theory remains relevant even as it requires revision and expansion. In both kinds of relation, we stand "encumbered":[49] enjoined to witness, called to action. And if glancing is important in the first case—more important than Levinas allows—it is just as crucial in the second. In both cases, glancing can make the difference between indifference and concern. Uncaring people look away even before they glance; or if they do glance, their look careens off the scarified face of the human as well as the other-than-human world, failing to detect the state of distress in either case. A more alert and more attuned glance captures at once the distress and the imperative to act on it.

Unless we can catch the discordance and the pain, the affliction and the destruction, we shall be in no position to do something that makes a real difference to other human beings in the despair of destitution, much less to any entity who is part of a dangerous or damaged environment. But if we can acknowledge such despair and danger and damage—if we can catch it in the delicate net of our darting glance—we can begin to own up to our unending responsibility to support and enhance the well-being of all entities, human as well as nonhuman, who live and move and have their being in the place-worlds they share.[50]

49. "As soon as the Other looks at me (*me regarde*), I am responsible for him, without having to *take* responsibility for him; this responsibility *encumbers* me" (Levinas, *Éthique et infini,* p. 102; his italics). I am maintaining that I first learn of such responsibility through my own action of glancing at this Other—and at the natural environment. But a failure to glance does not absolve me from this responsibility, which bears upon me even in my most unapperceptive state.

50. Earlier versions of this essay have appeared in *Research for Phenomenology,* special issue on Environmental Philosophy, 2001, and in B. V. Foltz and R. Frodeman, eds., *Nature Revisited: Environmental Philosophy in a New Key* (Bloomington: Indiana University Press, 2004).

12

GLANCING AT THE IMAGE IN PHOTOGRAPHY AND PAINTING

> . . . to give the image of what we see, forgetting everything that has appeared before our time.
>
> —Paul Cézanne, cited in B. Dorival,
> *Paul Cézanne*

> . . . what still must be done in order to restore the encounter between [the artist's] glance and the things which solicit it. . . .
>
> —Maurice Merleau-Ponty,
> "Indirect Language and the Voices of Silence"

> I am thinking of aesthetics as the equivalent of *aperçus,* which seems to have been the original meaning. This has not been systematized.
>
> —Wallace Stevens, letter to John Crowe
> Ransom, 1944

I

What do we glance at? Above all, surfaces: those of things, people, events, even of the fleeting phenomena of our inner life. But we can equally well say that *images* are what we glance at. Even when we are glancing at persons or things—those seemingly most substantial presences in our immediate environment—we are looking at them in their being as images: how they present themselves, how they appear to us: how they come forward to meet us on their own terms. These terms are those of sheer phenomena, where the word "phenomenon" signifies *"that which shows itself in itself,* the manifest."[1] The factor of showing is crucial; it connotes coming to appearance, becoming evident, manifesting—where the manifestation is not of something else but of the phe-

---

1. Martin Heidegger, *Being and Time,* tr. C. Robinson and J. Macquarrie (New York: Harper, 1962), p. 52; his italics.

nomenon itself, the thing itself (whether this "thing" is an object, a person, or an event). When this happens (and it is never *not* happening in human experience), an image comes forth: not separately from the thing, as if it were a distinctly different presence, a second thing or a phantasmal replica of a first thing, but more exactly *as the thing itself.*

What kind of a thing is this? Not the thing as substance: which would imply hidden parts or invisible levels, the *je ne sais quoi* of which Locke spoke. Instead, it is the thing as it gives itself up entirely to the realm of appearance—the thing as showing itself "in itself," where this means showing itself not from concealed depths but *from (and on) its very surface:* there and nowhere else. This is at once altogether ordinary and quite extraordinary. Ordinary insofar as it is what happens regularly, day in and night out; extraordinary inasmuch as it defies the commonsensical assumption that substance and property, thing and appearance are irremediably opposed.[2] It also goes contrary to the presumption that "images" are merely mental phenomena, psychic phantoms whose exclusive source is a confabulative imagination. Either way, images are regarded as secondary phenomena that are extraneous to things: not things themselves but something lesser than things. As such, they lack the dignity and force of thinghood; factitious, they are merely fabricated or imagined.

Once we set aside these prejudicial views—all belonging to the "natural attitude" (in Husserl's term)—we realize that in spontaneous daily experience we take material things (and persons and events) as coextensive with the images we have of them. Far from being independent entities, we experience things as coming-to-presence in these images, as already having come-to-image as soon as we perceive them. We experience the thing *as and in its image:* as nowhere else, nothing else. Even if we were to grant that physical things can exist on their own when we are not perceiving them—contrary to Berkeley's thesis of subjective idealism—nevertheless insofar as we are perceiving them (that is, in what I have called "external attention") we grasp them as images: where "image" signifies their very appearance, their way of showing themselves at and through their surfaces of presentation. This is why Bergson can claim that whenever I perceive I am in effect saying: "Here I am in the presence of images . . . images perceived when my senses are opened to them, unperceived when they are closed."[3] To be "in the presence of images" is to be in the presence of things

2. Image as the appearance of the thing itself does not tolerate any difference between the thing and its coming-forth as image. This contrasts with the sense of appearing invoked by Heidegger: "Appearance, as the appearance 'of something', does *not* mean showing-itself; it means rather the announcing-itself by [*von*] something which does not show itself, but which announces itself through something which does show itself" (ibid., p. 52; his italics). It is the virtue of image as I am discussing it to undermine the difference between something that does not show itself and that which announces it: in short, between thing and appearance—a distinction that can be traced back to Descartes in the early modern era.

3. Henri Bergson, *Matter and Memory,* tr. N. M. Paul and W. S. Palmer (New York: Zone, 1988), p. 17.

themselves, that is to say, things as they present themselves to us by way of their surfaces, and this is so whether these surfaces are perceived or imagined or remembered. And if this is so, then we can no longer maintain that images are merely secondary features of things, much less always imaginary in status.[4]

As Blanchot writes: "The image must cease to be second in relation to a supposedly prior object and must demand a certain primacy. . . . There is no longer any original but an eternal twinkling in which the absence of any origin is dispersed in the flash of detour and return."[5] This suggests in turn that there is an elective affinity between *image* and *glance,* which is the close ally of the twinkle (as in "the twinkling of an eye"[6]) and the flash (as in the "flash of recognition" in Benjamin). It is this affinity that I shall explore in this new chapter, but before doing this I want to clarify further the idea that the image is primary.

The primacy of the image is easier to grasp in the case of memory than in perception, where "things" seem to resist their designation as "images" on the basis of their sheer materiality, their "coefficient of resistance" (in Bachelard's phrase). When I recall something in sensory form, that is, with a certain qualitative specificity, I bring an image to mind; although I know it to be such, I do not hesitate to consider it as the thing itself: "Aunt Leone's face," "the public swimming pool in Abilene," "the ancient elms in my grandparents' front yard," and so forth. In each of these cases, the remembered thing has become an image, and I do not concern myself with any residual difference between this image and the thing in its original format (in each of these cases, a physical person or object). This difference becomes an issue only when questions of evidence and truth are at stake. But if I am faithful to the experience of remembering, I find that the image and the thing coincide: I remember Aunt Leone in my very image of her face, looking distinctively dignified in a certain way; and if I compare that face with my long-deceased mother's face, I am only extending the remembered realm to include more content of a properly imagistic sort.

But the same convergence between appearing-as-image and existing-as-thing occurs in perception itself. Even as I look at the computer screen in front of me, for example, I do not focus on it as a piece of synthetic material studded with

---

4. Of course, sometimes images *are* imaginary, that is, when they are the proper contents of an act of imagining; but the scope of the term is much broader than this, as we realize when we say such things as "getting an image of you," "the president wants to project an image of defiance," "I need to get a better image of that"—not to mention photographic, filmic, and video images, none of which need be imaginary in their manifest content.

5. Maurice Blanchot, "Le rire des dieux," *Nouvelle Revue Française* (July 1965); cited by Gilles Deleuze, *Difference and Repetition,* tr. P. Patton (New York: Columbia University Press, 1994), p. 319, n. 28.

6. The reference is to Saint Paul, 1 Cor. 15, 51–52: "In a moment, in the twinkling of an eye, we shall all be transformed" (*Revised Standard Edition* translation). On this theme, see David L. Miller, "Through a Looking-Glass—The World as Enigma," in R. Ritsema, ed., *Human and Cosmic Mirroring* (Ascona, Switzerland: Insel Verlag, 1986), esp. p. 401: "The twinkle changes things." I return to the twinkle in relation to the glance in the concluding thoughts.

innumerable pixels and illuminated from a light hidden within it. Instead, I take it to be something that gives itself without remainder—as just *this screen*. If it is a thing, it is a "phantom-thing"(*Phantomding*) as Husserl called it—neither merely fantastic nor sheerly substantial but something more consistent than a fantasy and more purely phenomenal than any entrenched substance. It is, as I prefer to term it, an "image-thing."

Image-things are not isolated entities. They co-inhabit and cohere with other such purely apparent entities to form entire "image-worlds."[7] These are worlds in which we live for the most part, as anyone can attest who has walked the streets of a great city and found it to be a gradually unfolding whole as one block gives way to another seemingly without end. Here our perambulatory experience is that of an ongoing world of images that envelop and re-envelop us as we walk. As we move into and through this image-world, we have the sense of entering into an unbounded region that opens to and for us as we keep walking. It is just such a sense of continually flowing appearances that the *flâneur* savors and that Benjamin tracked so closely. Even were we to reach the city limit suddenly and step into the surrounding countryside, we would only find ourselves reincluded once more, now in a closely concatenated image-world whose contents are rural rather than urban. There is not just *one* image-world but many, and these many are not separate realms: however different they may be in terms of specific content, they exist in tandem and may overlap significantly, with only rare exceptions.[8]

Image-worlds may not be separate, but they are often distinct from one another; and they are distinct either by virtue of their contents (for example, one city block in contrast with another) or because of being enframed. Frame here means a boundary that sets apart contents that, however similar in character, can be considered to belong to different places or regions: hedgerows in England versus those in New England, picket fences in Kentucky in comparison with those in Kansas, cobbled streets in London in contrast with those in the West Village of Manhattan. The frames at stake in such instances reflect specificities of agricultural or urban history, along with changing architectural styles and the differential fates of various populations. In their historical and material mutability, these frames differ decisively from another kind of frame, that which not only surrounds something and helps to establish it as distinct geographically or

7. This term first appears with Eugen Fink (in the form of *Bildwelt*) and reemerges in Susan Sontag's discussion of photography: "While real people are out there killing themselves or other real people, the photographer stays behind his or her camera, creating a tiny element of another world: the image-world that bids to outlast us all" (*On Photography* [New York: Anchor, 1977], p. 11). For Fink's treatment of *Bildwelt*, see his *Studien zur Phänomenologie* (The Hague: Nijhoff, 1966), pp. 73–78.

8. Notable exceptions are such extreme places of privation as a Nazi concentration camp such as Buchenwald (which, though only a few kilometers from the highly cultivated city of Weimar, constituted a world apart), in which the fiendish world within was experienced as almost entirely discontinuous with the world without.

historically but also acts to define the thing itself, being intrinsic to its phenomenal being: that is, how it presents itself. Take, for example, the large velvet curtain on a theater stage: this not only marks the opening and closing of acts of a given play—a purely functional significance—but it is essential to theater as it is performed in a given period of its history. Without its presence, a dramatic production would not be recognized as fully theatrical in that period but as something quite different—an aberrant genre at best, perhaps something not theatrical at all. This example makes it clear that frame in this second sense cannot be reduced to a physical surrounder or defined exclusively by its merely functional identity; frame is now something that acts to present a distinctive *kind of thing*, whether the kind in question is an artistic genre or style (for example, a way of presenting theatrical productions), a whole manner of thinking or acting, or even a certain way to be (culturally, personally, and so forth).

In this spirit, I shall examine two image-worlds in this chapter, each of which derives a major part of its character and effect from having a certain kind of frame in the expanded sense just discussed. These are the worlds of painting and photography. Not only does each of these worlds employ certain characteristic forms of physical framing for its images: there are no paintings without frames of some sort (even the absence of a material frame is experienced as a frame) and the same holds true for photographs; but, more significantly, works in these worlds come framed in ways that exceed their physical formats: for example, those frames provided by their distinctive styles.[9] Moreover, how a given world is framed at both levels influences the way we glance at its contents. Each such world, suitably enframed, solicits the glance in its own unique way—and the glance, in turn, enters into the nuances of the image-world in question. We shall discover a delicate dialectic between the glance and the images within which it moves in the worlds of painting and photography.[10]

This dialectic should not surprise us. There are far-reaching affinities between the action of the glance and the allure of the image. These lie at the basis of my opening contention that the image can be considered the specific content of the glance, its proper object. For instance, if an image can be defined as "a sudden salience on the surface of the psyche,"[11] a glance is precisely that act which picks out such a salience on this (and others kinds of) surface and thrives upon it. It is clear that there is a shared tendency to concentrate on the surface of a given phenomenon, the image being the very appearance of that surface and the glance characteristically landing on it. In both cases, there is a concern with the inaptly named "secondary qualities" (color, texture, and so forth) that bedeck surfaces. The glance is attracted to the gleam or glitter of a surface rather

9. For a more detailed discussion of framing in the case of painting, see my *Representing Place: Landscape Painting and Maps* (Minneapolis: University of Minnesota Press, 2002), Interlude: "Material Conditions of Representing Place in Landscape Paintings."

10. I wish to thank Andrés Colapinto for specific suggestions as to the formulation of this last paragraph.

11. Gaston Bachelard, *The Poetics of Space*, tr. M. Jolas (New York: Orion, 1964), p. xi.

than to any depth below it, and the image, rather than being a denizen of depth, is precisely a creature of the surface of any given appearance. Glance and image alike are both characterized by evanescence and each is concerned with what is unique in the phenomenal presentation—with what shows itself in a sudden and surprising manner.

Image and glance form their own "indefinite dyad" in Plato's recurrently useful term—a dyad we last observed in the case of attending and glancing. In such a dyad, two otherwise disparate items show themselves to have profound and often less than apparent connections. Images and the glances that take them in seem to rejoice in each other's company: not unlike an odd couple whose successful relationship confounds everyone's most reasonable (and thus all too cautious) expectations.

II

As the very plurality of image-worlds implies, images come in many stripes— at least as many as there are kinds of glance. Just one type of image alone shows itself to have several subtypes: mental images, for example, include memory images, fantasy images, hallucinations, even certain passing thoughts that take imagistic form (for example, Galton's "number-forms," by which many people unconsciously give a distinctive shape to the series of natural numbers, say, from one to twenty).[12] Each of these mental images calls for its own sort of inner glance: we might linger over a memory image and return to it frequently, whereas a fantasy that flashes before us is satisfied with a single, momentary mental glance. Nor is it only a matter of the comparative duration of the glance: subtle differences in aspect, quality, and directedness distinguish these modes of inward glancing from each other. As we saw in the discussion of such glancing in chapter 9, the way we glance in meditation differs significantly from the way we glance when pursuing a psychological practice such as focusing. The images by which we present ourselves to ourselves in mental life are as various as that life itself—a life teeming with inner witnessing of many kinds.

When we look around the life-world we inhabit in ways that are not exclusively mental, we realize that images in Bergson's expanded sense proliferate and thereby call for different ways of looking at them. Some of these images are not satisfied with a single glance: they invite, instead, prolonged scrutiny, as when we carefully examine a piece of furniture we are thinking of buying, or when we become "lost" in gazing at a monumental landscape such as the Grand Canyon seen from its south side. In other situations, we become engaged in an alternating pattern of glancing and more concerted looking—for example, gazing or some other kind of concerted perceptual looking—in a manner I have termed "braided." Or we can be wholly taken up in glancing at the images

12. See Francis Galton, *Inquiries into Human Faculty* (London: Dent, 1907), pp. 60 ff.

constituted by things and events and people in the surrounding world: glancing upward at an ever-changing cloud pattern, glancing anxiously at faces in a crowd to see if we can spot the person we hope to meet, and so on. It is evident that there is an enormous range of situations in which images of many kinds, construed as sheer appearances, call out our glance.

The truth is that *each time my glance goes out to meet the visual allure or challenge of such situations, it seeks an image.* Even in the midst of the most settled or robust perceptual scene—filled with material particulars that have altogether determinate dimensions of volume, weight, and so forth—my glance reaches out to these particulars in their imagistic being, their sheer surface, their very visuality. It seeks out, and flourishes in, the presence of such things construed in their presentational being, their phantomic features, their aesthetic aura. In this context, the glance can be construed as operating along a continuum that stretches between two extremes: the self-standing Thing, with intrinsic features of extension, depth, and so on, and the Image with traits that are much more informal and qualitative. For the most part, the glance delves into the many intermediary items that combine aspects of both poles: it concerns itself with image-things. These are hybrid entities that refuse to be considered either Images or Things in any straightforward or exclusive way. Among these entities are those possessing a pictorial character: paintings, photographs, movies, television, DVDs, videos. The manifest content of each of these image-things is distinctly picture-like.

The pictoriality possessed by these image-things means at least two things, each of which reflects one of the two poles between which it is situated. On the one hand, there is reference to some reality beyond itself, either by way of direct indication (as when photographs are used for purposes of personal identification: "so that is how Thad Hoffman looked in those days!") or by means of allusion (as when certain paintings by Camille Pissarro convey to us the atmosphere of Paris in the late nineteenth century). In this case, the material thing or person is signified, overtly or by allusion; it is *represented*, though the mode of representation can vary significantly—ranging from rigorous "re-presentation" (that is, reduplication) to "*re*presentation" (that is, an imaginative departure from sheer repetition, whether by way of distortion, transformation, supplementation, and so forth).[13] On the other hand, the picture draws attention to itself as an image—to certain pictorial properties presented in their own right and for their own sake. This is most marked in the case of paintings, which, whatever their identificatory or representational value, are appreciated and judged on the basis of their intrinsic aesthetic attractiveness: a Pissarro painting may well represent the Boulevard Montparnasse, but it is also beautiful in its sheer painterly surface.

13. For discussion of these terms, see Casey, *Representing Place: Landscape Painting and Maps*, chap. 10 and glossary.

This double aspect of pictoriality, its literal ambiguity, is also found in some significant measure in photographs (even family photographs are often judged by aesthetic criteria), videos and DVDs (especially those that have some redeeming artistic merit), and movies and television (including documentaries that are prized as well for their informational value).

One can speculate that the prominence of the frame—which encompasses so many visual artworks[14]—itself reflects a picture's ambiguous position between Image and Thing. A frame acts to contain the ambiguity by demarcating a quasi-autonomous space, a coherent and delimited context, in which the pictorial can prosper on its own terms. No matter how effective the frame may be in a given case, however, the ambiguity remains to some degree. Indeed, such ambiguity is part of the prowess possessed by artworks in which the pictorial figures; a frame encourages the viewer to accept the ambiguity of being a pictorial image-thing and to find in it an aesthetic virtue rather than a defect. The pictorial work figures both as image and as thing, and we are encouraged to admire it on both counts at once.

Wittgenstein remarks that "we *regard* the photograph, the picture on our wall, as the object itself (the man, landscape, and so on) depicted there."[15] Here Wittgenstein suggests that in our ordinary unreflective experience of a photograph we take the physical photograph *as* that which it depicts ("the object itself"). Nevertheless, by his underlining of the verb "regard" he is admitting that there is still a discernible distinction to be made between the picture and its represented content—a distinction that will reassert itself after this experiential moment of merged levels. The ambiguity is only momentarily overcome, for upon a moment's reflection we realize that the photograph remains a hybrid, both image and thing. But how can one and the same entity be both at once?

Recall here my opening move in this chapter, where I argued that everything, insofar as it can be considered something sheerly apparent or phenomenal—showing itself in itself—is already on its way to being an image: a self-presenting image of the thing itself. True, it never becomes entirely or simply such an image, or it would cease to be a thing—it would become other than itself, e.g., a sheer sign. But when it becomes an image-thing, it demonstrates that the image-potential of each thing is powerfully present in the thing itself. And if this is so, pictorial image-things such as photographs and movies, paintings and videos only serve to realize this potential more effectively than would a nonpictorial material thing itself: their pictoriality accentuates the image component and lets it stand forth more saliently. Otherwise said, the image-thing allows the thing to become expressly an image: to step forward into an explicitly imagistic format, as if to say: "This is not just X but an image of Y!" The thing as image—true of *all*

14. Not all visual artworks are enframed: sculpture is a notable exception.
15. Ludwig Wittgenstein, cited by Susan Sontag, *On Photography*, p. 198; his italics.

things we experience in their sheer appearing—is now a pictorial image: an image-thing that is an image-of-something. We have in effect two hybrids for the price of one.

It may be so effective—this double transformation of thing into image-thing and of image-thing into pictorial image-thing—that we may come to believe not only that the picture *is* the represented object (this is the point of Wittgenstein's observation) but even that it exceeds the object in terms of its comparative reality. For it is at once a physical thing *and* a thing that counts as a picture: a more versatile kind of thing than the object depicted in it. As Susan Sontag puts it:

> the force of photographic images comes from their being material realities in their own right, richly informative deposits left in the wake of whatever emitted them, potent means for turning the tables on reality—for turning *it* into a shadow. Images are more real than anyone could have supposed.[16]

On this assessment, the image as picture exceeds the thing of which it is the image—a decidedly anti-Platonic move. It is a move so radical that Sontag, for all her audacity, cannot sustain it herself, and she falls back on more familiar claims in the course of her classic book *On Photography:* photographs become mere "semblances," they convert experience into images, and they "do not seem to be statements about the world so much as pieces of it, miniatures of reality that anyone can make or acquire."[17] I take this apparent inconsistency ("miniature" implies being less than an original reality by way of condensation) not as a logical flaw but as a sign of the ambiguity inherent in the photographic image itself: it is a reality in its own right if we emphasize its material surface and what appears on it, but it is also a semblance insofar as we wish to underline its purely pictorial powers. It is both *image* and *image-of,* at once true to its origin as an *imago* that captures and holds a prior reality within its own thinghood—as in an *"imago dei,"* an icon that itself contains divine power—and a reinstatement of reality, something that refers to a reality that is outside itself.

The issue is not that of playing epistemic games in which image and reality are competitors or rivals (games in which there are no real victors) but to realize that photographs—along with paintings, movies, videos, DVDs, and television, as well as images on the Internet—possess a genuinely productive polyvalence: they are at once images and things, image-things and pictorial image-things such that no decision has to be made in favor of any of these various terms. Such polyvalence is a source of inspiration for painters, filmmakers, photographers, and video artists. Even if this complex source is rarely made explicit, much less a matter of coherent argument, visual artists thrive on the very fact that they are not forced to choose between thing or image-thing or pictorial image-thing.

16. Sontag, *On Photography,* p. 180; her italics.
17. Ibid., p. 4. The claim concerning semblance is at p. 24: photographs give us "a semblance of knowledge, a semblance of wisdom." The idea that photographs are matters of "converting experience into an image" is articulated on p. 9.

The challenge for us comes down to this: how are we to deal with this polyvalence? In particular, how are we to be inspired by its power rather than become suspicious of its indeterminacy?

It is precisely in this impasse that the glance comes to our aid. For among human visual capacities the glance is uniquely able to cope with the complexity of the pictorial image. To be equal to such an image and to work creatively with it calls for a triple-take that only a glance in its celerity can accomplish. When I glance at a pictorial image, I am able to take it in as a thing in its own right *and* as its own image *and* as depicting other things and reflecting their influence; I take note of all three aspects in a triple-timing in which I honor the immediacy of the thing itself—its frontal presence to me right now—as well as the pictoriality that conveys me to other presences having their own time (a time that can be simultaneous with the image, as in "real time" television programming, or an anterior time that has already expired, or a future time of pure projection). In a sweep of my glance I apprehend what is now appearing along with what has appeared (for example, the historic subject of a photograph) or what may appear in some possible future (the content of a projective pictorial image-thing). I do all this within the basic two-beat temporality of the glance that was discussed in chapter 8: now, however, I glance out onto something that is composed of more than one level before I glance back. The extra level, that provided by pictoriality, takes me into other times than that of my own present looking.

In glancing at entities intermediate between Thing and Image, I capture the image-thing in its paradoxicality, its status as both thinglike and picturelike. I bring two otherwise disparate epicenters together: the Image as the pictorial surface at which I glance and the Thing whose depth comes forward in this same surface. Glancing at this surface and glancing into its depth, which are separate acts in other contexts (for example, that of concerted attention), here become two phases of a single action that bears out the Wittgensteinian axiom that the depths are to be found on the surface: being presented there, such depths can be *seen* and not merely inferred or posited.

Glancing has a gift for dealing with just such a circumstance, since it leaps between levels so alertly and adroitly. In so doing, it bears witness to the complexity of the situation, laying down a legacy of respect for the ambiguous and polyvalent that is essential in artistic creativity. Such creativity prospers in the presence of the image-thing in its pictoriality, which furnishes a *materia prima* for imaginative artistic work. Rather than being an occasion for deciding what is ultimately real—as when philosophers pit thing against image—the glance thrives upon the indeterminacy and hybridity of the painting or photograph, video or film. As we shall see, this also holds true for the spectator of such works. Both artist and spectator profit from the paradoxicality of the pictorial, the former from the challenge of dealing with primary material that is as imagistic as it is thinglike—and that is pictorial in building on both—and the latter from grasping with nuance the results of coping with this very challenge.

III

In this section, I take up the case of still photography, where the interplay of the glance and the image figures in several significant ways. I leave aside the role of the glance vis-à-vis other kinds of photographic images, notably those that *move* (in cinema, video, DVD, and television), and thus draw upon the glance's extraordinary ability to parse an image that is not only complex but constantly (and often instantaneously) changing.

"The street has allowed me to educate and nourish my look."[18] This statement of Walker Evans poignantly conveys his conviction that the photographic image should reveal the rude reality of the everyday world. It should bring what is at our fingertips and under our feet directly to our attention. It should, in short, "frame the real."[19] Evans was a master of such direct framing of reality, whether this was mostly material (as in his close-ups of debris on city streets) or social (as in his celebrated photographs of Alabama sharecroppers during the Depression) or scenes from daily life (as in the New York subway portraits he made with a concealed camera in the late 1930s). For example:

Figure 12.1. Walker Evans, "Chicago," 1946. © Walker Evans Archive, The Metropolitan Museum of Art.

Figure 12.2. Walker Evans, "New York," 1938–1941. © Walker Evans Archive, The Metropolitan Museum of Art.

18. "La rue m'a permis d'éduquer, de nourrir mon regard. De combler la soif du regard," Walker Evans, cited in *Walker Evans: La soif du regard* (Paris: Seuil, 1993), p. 2. See also the statement from an interview with Leslie Katz: "Quand on est juene, on fréquente les musées. . . . Puis la rue devient votre musée, car ce dernier vous porte désormais tout" (cited in ibid., p. 296, n. 2).

19. "Cadrer le réel" (Gilles Mora, introduction to ibid., p. 12).

It is as if Evans realized in his lifework the formula pronounced by Sontag: "Photographs really are experience captured."[20] But if so, the experience that counts is everyday experience in its very mundanity—not the extraordinary moments of interpersonal intimacy witnessed by Henri Cartier-Bresson, the drama of war as displayed by Robert Capa, or the monumentality of nature so movingly depicted by Ansel Adams. It is not surprising that Evans has been seen as an important precursor of Pop Art, especially of Andy Warhol (who once borrowed the title *Let Us Now Praise Famous Men* from the 1941 volume written by James Agee and illustrated by Evans).[21] What matters for our purposes is that even when an artist seeks to set forth images of an unbleached reality—a reality that (in Evans's own words) manifests "a purity, a rigor, an immediacy, a clarity that obtain in the absence of any pretension to art"[22]—he cannot do this outright. Intervening variables, such as framing, texture, perspective, comparative brightness, and so on, complicate any effort to give a full transcription of the real, yet they are altogether necessary to the conveyance of the real itself.

The truth is that Evans's photographs, though complicating any simple realism of the everyday, still deeply reflect it, and if they are not direct depictions of the mundane world they are at the very least *haunted by it:* much as Evans's own morose look haunts this early self-portrait:

Figure 12.3. Walker Evans, "Self portrait," circa 1929. © Walker Evans Archive, The Metropolitan Museum of Art.

20. Sontag, *On Photography,* p. 4.

21. Wim Wenders testifies that "Je crois Walker Evans a fait plus de choses pour développer un sens et une sensibilité à l'égard du pop art que Robert Indiana ou Andy Warhol. Il n'a peut-être pas été le premier à voir tout le potentiel plastique du paysage américain; mais il a été sûrement le premier à donner à ce paysage américain une forme adéquate" (cited in *Walker Evans: Le soif du regard,* p. 13, n. 3).

22. Walker Evans, lecture at Yale University, March 11, 1964, in *Walker Evans at Work,* ed. John T. Hill (New York: Harper and Row, 1982), p. 238.

Here is Evans looking at us with a mixture of open expectation (especially evident in his alert left eye) and withdrawn reserve (as is conveyed by his lowering right eye). His look haunts our look. Is it a gaze or a glance? At its origin (that is, at the time of its being photographed), it was likely to have been a glance, for it captures a momentary look in the reproductive eye of the camera. But it consolidates this look, freezing it forever in a photographic image, and thereby converts it into the equivalent of a gaze. If a glance can wither and set us back, only a gaze can haunt: it alone has the staying power to be felt as a haunting presence. This is all the more the case in a look that is photographed: this look, originally a glance, becomes a gaze by virtue of the quasi-permanence of the photographic medium.

Such haunting is not limited to photographic portraits, much less to self-portraits of the sort we observe just above. It characterizes many, if not all, photographs, including those in which no human look, no glance or gaze, is involved. If photographs indeed capture reality in some strong sense, they do so in such a way as to haunt those of us who look at them: Why else do they move us so much? In what does such haunting consist? In part, it signifies the lingering of a thing or event, person or occasion—first, in the physical photograph that is in effect its material record; then, in our perception of this same photograph: survival to the second power! It is the second sense of lingering that is most significant; unlike the evanescent images of inner attention or the fleeting images of cinema or video, the photographic image as perceived (and then remembered) possesses a steady availability that allows it to submit easily, time and again, to our attentive return to it: we need only open an album or book of photos to gain access once more to an image contained therein. Thanks to the physicality of the photograph, its status as a persisting thing, the image it conveys is easily reanimated in our perception and memory of it; and this image is in turn depictive of a certain past reality. A photograph is a pictorial image-thing, a triplex artwork whose effect is reinforced by virtue of its being at once image and thing and picture.

A photograph gains its full haunting power from the fact that its image is continually recoverable. Even if we never re-perceive a given physical photograph, we know that its imagistic-pictorial content is available to us in an album or an archive, a book or a museum: each of which *maintains* it as perceptible for ourselves and others. Wherever we may be, the image is *there*, supported by an appropriate material thing to which (were we so inclined) we can gain access in principle. We sense Walker Evans to be still gazing at us from his self-portrait—in whichever format it may assume. Indeed, it looks at us even as we look away: this is the core of its hauntingness. The merest memory, or just chancing upon the cover of the book *Walker Evans: La soif du regard* in a Parisian bookstore, confirms this. Whatever the status of our relationship to the particular material "analogon" in which his look appears—that is, whether this analogon is now in front of us, or merely remembered—we are assured that

Evans will be seen as looking out through it.[23] He will be haunting us so long as at least one material analogon supporting that look still exists.

Even in the case of photographs in which no face, human or otherwise, appears, we often experience the subject matter of the work as addressing itself to us: sometimes accusingly or angrily, sometimes gently or humorously, some-times indifferently. But in every case there is a sense that the depicted "object" or "event" is *looking out toward us as its current viewers.* The exterocentric aspect of such photographs lends to them not just a life of their own but also a distinct sense of their own identity, even their own mass. This identity and mass, phantom-like and belonging exclusively to the image, is another basis of their haunting us. This is true of the least photographic image—whereas it holds only for certain paintings and movies. Just as Klee experienced himself as looked at by trees in a forest,[24] so we may sense ourselves as somehow witnessed by the trees or flowers or animals that figure into photographs: we become the objects of their enigmatic but directed look. And when this happens, we feel haunted by them.

The photographic image—which conveys the looks of human beings or non-human things—*perdures* in and through the physical photograph that presents it. This does not guarantee the survival of the image, but it does mean that it will be preserved in an accessible format until that format itself perishes.[25] The format belongs to the material analogon as the bearer, the *Träger*, of the image, and the life of the image is tied to its fate: once the bearer ceases to exist, so does the image that depends on it for its presentation.[26] But so long as the analogon or

23. I am using "analogon" in Sartre's sense of the term as developed in the final section of his *Psychology of Imagination*, "The Work of Art." See Jean-Paul Sartre, *The Psychology of Imagination*, tr. B. Frechtman (New York: Washington Square Press, 1966), pp. 246–253. I employ it here to underline the fact that the conveyance of a given image can take many specific material forms, each of which is analogous to the others insofar as all of them present the same imagistic content: each bears and manifests this same content. I am not here con-cerned with the special problems that this term raises. For a discussion of these problems, see my essay "Sartre on Imagination" in *The Philosophy of Jean-Paul Sartre*, ed. P. A. Schilpp, Library of Living Philosophers series (Carbondale, Ill.: University of Illinois Press, 1981).

24. For Klee's observation, see the citation in Merleau-Ponty, "Eye and Mind," tr. C. Dal-lery, in J. Edie, ed., *The Primacy of Perception* (Evanston, Ill.: Northwestern University Press, 1964), p. 167.

25. This format functions as a frame for the image, which requires spatial delimitation to be effective as identifiable and locatable.

26. As Sontag comments, "a photograph is not only like its subject, a home to the subject. It is part of, *an extension of, that subject*" (*On Photography*, p. 155; my italics). Being an "exten-sion" of its "subject"—i.e., what I am here calling the "image"—the photograph's fate as a physical bearer of the subject will affect the subject itself: the demise of one is tantamount to the death of the other. Then the only survival is in the memory of someone who has seen the photograph—or in a retake of this same photograph in another photograph. (I am using "bearer" in the sense first introduced by Max Scheler in his theory of values, which require material *Trägern* to present them in concrete perceptual and historical contexts.)

bearer lasts, the image perdures to haunt those who perceive it *through* its
format. The image comes to us in and by the bearer's format, and it stays with us,
haunting us, in that same format.

Another aspect of the perduring power of photographs relates to the hand
more than to the eye. I refer to their comparative handiness, their literal manip-
ulability: the fact that they typically fit easily into one's own hand. This is especially the case with snapshots, whose comparatively diminutive size allows them
to reside comfortably in the palm of the hand; but it is also true for albums or
books of photographs, which are produced so as to be held by one hand while
the other turns the pages. This is not just a matter of convenience or convention;
the literally "handy" size invites palpation on the spectator's part in actions of
holding, turning, and so on. The result is a special form of intimacy, implying
that a given photographic image is minimally *mine*—at least mine to admire,
manipulate, play with, and more. Even if the image itself is of someone else,
even of a complete stranger, I still regard it as entering my life-world. When I
look at images of drifters from the American West as photographed by Richard
Avedon—people whom I have never met and who look back at me from their
very strangeness—I still experience them as momentarily part of my world (and
sometimes I in theirs), and in any case as ingredient in the intimacy of my act of
looking at them.[27] The intimacy is all the more intense if the images are of
friends or family members—for example, in a "family album," wherein I am able
to become reacquainted with people I know well from familiar settings. Even
when I am asked to look at an album of photographs from the past of someone I
have just met, however, I feel invited into an intimate world in which I am
momentarily included.[28]

This last discussion suggests that a factor of narcissism may be endemic in the
experience of photographic images: the pleasure we take in them is not only that
of the acquisition or possession of the real[29] but also of *bringing their imagistic
content into our present world* (or, alternately, of letting ourselves be taken into
their world). No matter how different the photographic image-world is from our
own, a brief moment of glancing at it is enough to incorporate it into our current
life-world—or conversely, letting ourselves join its image-world. We do this even

27. The fact that certain of Avedon's photographs are markedly outsize—e.g., circa 6′ × 4′—
does not diminish the effect of intimacy but, on the contrary, brings these images, closer to
literal life-size, *right into my face*. I feel as if I could reach out and embrace them with my
arms. (I refer to the Richard Avedon show at the Metropolitan Museum, New York City,
summer–fall 2002.)

28. Lily R., whom I had known for only a few weeks as the daughter of a friend, suddenly
showed me albums from her childhood: I felt pleased and privileged to be invited into this
otherwise private world, of which I was a willing witness, even though I knew nothing of this
world except what the photographic images conveyed to me on this occasion.

29. Such acquisition is emphasized by Sontag: e.g., *On Photography*, p. 155: a photograph is
"a potent means of acquiring [the subject of the photograph], of gaining control over it."

when the depicted world is freakish and monstrous (as in many of Diane Arbus's photographs) or if it is undeniably violent, as in Capa's celebrated *Falling Soldier:*

Figure 12.4. Robert Capa, "The Falling Soldier," 1936. Magnum Photos.

This is what, after all, the "in-" of "intimate" implies: bringing *in,* making part of what is already *here,* in the home-world of our own looking. It is this very world that is haunted by photographic images and that is inhabited by them in their handy availability: they come to populate this world, filling it up momentarily with images whose literal content may be located worlds apart—but that have come to join the circle of our narcissistic looking, in our hands and under our eyes. No wonder we are so curious about seeing further images, so greedy to see new things one after another—as often happens when we "leaf through" an album of new photographs: a glance at one image suffices as we rush to the next, only to glance at it in turn, and so on. Such glancing betrays a visual greediness that is a symptom of the glancer's nascent narcissism: a wish to bring the images of things, if not the things themselves, into the glancer's own world, there to savor the sanctity of visual immersion.

Underlying the narcissistic enclosure is a primary vector of photographic images: *from the world beyond us into the world in us.*[30] This inwardizing

30. As I have indicated just above, the contrary movement is also possible: the viewer's incorporation into the world on view; but I take this to be secondary to the main thrust of the circumstance, which is from the image that haunts (whether by way of attraction or repulsion) to the inner sanctum of the viewer.

direction occurs with minimal knowledge of what is happening in the process: "photographed images do not seem to be statements about the world so much as pieces of it."[31] Being pieces of it, they come to us from without: as if they were gifts of the image-world to which they belong originally. This contrasts with paintings, which appear to reverse the directionality: paintings seem to induce a flow *from ourselves out to the world beyond:* the image-world as set forth in the work. The work takes us into that world—even though the same work issues from the subjectivity of the artist, and is often laden with his (implicit or explicit) painterly aims and interpretations, theories of space, figuration, perspective, and more, all of which mediate the image long before it reaches us as spectators. In this respect Plato had a definite point to make: paintings come to us several times removed from the real.

In contrast, photographic images *present themselves* as coming to us directly from their world of origin, with a minimum of cognitive machinery attached to them: this is why they are experienced as gratuitous offerings from another place, with few if any conditions for their viewing other than certain visual curiosity on our part.

"Look at me," photographs seem to say, "and do so without concern for school or style or epoch or author." The implication is that the subject matter of the photograph is always worth looking at—as it virtually always seems to be. The novelty of the image, however slight it may be, is enough to attract our attention, and "the hunger for looking" (*la soif du regard*) (Evans), always a factor in a life that is otherwise "image-poor,"[32] is drawn to the depicted topic of the photograph, as if to merge with it secretly, forming a silent pact. To the self-aggrandizing tendency of my own primary visual narcissism—the desperate wish to make everything seen become *part of me*—there is added the countertendency of my wanting to be *part of it:* to rejoin the image that stems from the preexistent world of other humans, animals, and things, a world I valorize precisely as worthy of my joining it. These two tendencies cross in the place of the image, which supports and enhances both in an intensified chiasmatic field of force. If the primary vector of the photograph is from the world to the self, this self nevertheless wants by counterthrust to rejoin the world that is the source of the image—wants to belong to its show, its ostensible originality, whether from a need to rejoin the viewer's roots or from a mere sense of curiosity, and however momentary and transitory this rejoining may be.

"Momentary and transitory": what kind of time are we dealing with here? In particular, what kind of *moment*? Is it the case of a "frozen moment," as is often said of photographs. Arnold Newman claims as much: "[In photography] subject

---

31. Sontag, *On Photography,* p. 4.

32. This is Heidegger's descriptive term: *bildarm.* See his statement: "Das wort des Deukeus ist biedarm und ohne Reiz" (Martin Heidegger, *Vorträge und Aufsätze* [Pfullingen: Neske, 1954], p. 229).

matter that exists in a continuum of time and space is reduced to a frozen moment arbitrarily restricted to a particular area."[33] Let us, however, resist the language of "frozen," a notion that is foreign to the flow of time: Cartier-Bresson remarks that "the world is movement," and if this is so nothing, not even the most portentous photograph of the moment of death (as in Capa's *Falling Soldier,* fig. 12.4) can undo the liveliness of temporal development. Cartier-Bresson himself famously maintained that the proper designation for the temporality of photography is the "decisive moment." But his discussion of the term exhibits its considerable ambiguity. "Sometimes you light upon the picture in seconds," he remarks, but "it might also require hours or days."[34] To what, then, does the decisive moment belong? To the action of the photographer—that is, the moment in which the lens is definitively engaged: the "click" of the apparatus—or to the subject matter of the photograph: *its* decisive moment, as it were? Or *our own* decisive moment of viewing? Whose moment is it? Where is it located? How are we to find it?

The decisive moment is the moment of the look. The fact that this moment is manifold—that it is differently embodied and situated—only makes its role all the more crucial. First of all, there is the look that belongs to the subject matter that is being photographed: in the case of human beings, this ranges from the briefest of cursory glances (for example, William Klein's *Mère et Fille,*[35] in which mother and daughter are both shown looking aside, glancing at something off the margin of the photo that has caught their attention momentarily) to the most pensive and prolonged gaze (for example, in many of Avedon's straight-on portraits in which the photographic subject, eminent or unknown, seems to look right into our soul; or in Newman's *Woman on Porch, West Palm Beach,*[36] in which a black woman is looking despairingly off her porch into a very uncertain future). Sometimes, a "collective look" is at stake—as in many of Klein's dense and crowded photographs taken in the midst of crowds: for example, *Thanksgiving Day Parade, 1959,*[37] in which four people are caught glancing, two in one direction and two in the other. Many other variations are possible, but in every case what matters is that the subject matter is *caught looking,* whether glancing or gazing: these are all photographs *of the look,* whatever its exact modality.[38]

33. Arnold Newman, "Afterword," in Arnold Newman, *Five Decades* (New York: Harcourt Brace Jovanovich, 1986), p. 123.

34. Henri Cartier-Bresson, "The Decisive Moment," a 1952 essay, in Henri Cartier-Bresson, *The Mind's Eye: Writings on Photography and Photographers* (Millerton, N.Y.: Aperture, 1999), p. 24. Of the decisive moment itself, Cartier-Bresson says this: "Of all the means of expression, photography is the only one that fixes forever the precise and transitory instant" (ibid., p. 27).

35. *Mère et Fille* (Paris 1953), in *William Klein* (Paris: Nathan, 1999), plate 43.

36. *Woman on Porch, West Palm Beach* (1940–1941), plate 7 in Newman, *Five Decades.*

37. This is plate 6 in *William Klein.*

38. I argued above that a photograph of an ostensible gaze may well be, in its original circumstance, that of a glance—which, being fixed in the medium, presents itself as that of a

A very different matter is the look that is entailed by the mechanics of the camera and of photographic reproduction. Now the decisive moment belongs to the apparatus and the technology, including the film and the development process. The looking occurs in the preparatory period of finding an enticing subject matter, beginning to focus on it (and, connected with this, getting the right lens and light setting, and so forth), and then pressing on the lever that opens and closes the lens. This last action involves an intimate collaboration between hand and eye—as does the sorting out of prints that will be developed. Together, taking the photograph and sorting out the results constitute the critical moments of "selection": "there is the selection we make when we look through the view-finder at the subject; and there is the one we make after the film has been developed and printed."[39] Human looking may intervene at each phase of selection: in looking through the viewfinder to choose the image we wish to take, and in looking over the developed images.[40] The result is an extraordinary collusion of the mechanical and the organic: the eye of the camera both mimics and supports the human eye that guides and sustains it. But the photographic image that is produced does what the living eye cannot do at all: it preserves a moment in time so as to present its content to others who will see it in future viewings with their own very different eyes.

Something else contributing to the moment of the look, making it still more pronounced, is the framing integral to the photographic image. This framing delimits and surrounds the image that has emerged from the process just described, and it takes both implicit and explicit forms. On the one hand, the edge of the physical film acts as an implicit frame that serves as the outer limit of the image. This is a frame inherent in the materiality of the medium itself, and it operates negatively: no photographic image can exceed what the limit of the film allows: the image is here conditioned by the materiality of the thing. On the other hand, there are two explicit framings that act in a positive manner. First, the finished photograph can be set within a physical frame of

---

gaze. Here I leave open the question of whether photographs of inanimate things can be said to capture *their* looking in a sense affine with Klee's claim of being viewed by the trees in a forest. (My colleague Robert Harvey points out to me that the French word *témoin*, "witness," applies to inanimate objects such as tables and trees, walls and windows, etc.) More generally, my point is not that all photographs exhibit explicit images of glances or gazes but that a disproportionate subset present such images or their equivalent—where the latter phrase refers to cases of haunting without the explicit presence of a glance or gaze.

39. Cartier-Bresson, *The Mind's Eye: Writings on Photography and Photographers*, p. 25. He adds: "After developing and printing, you must go about separating the pictures which, though they are all right, aren't the strongest" (ibid.).

40. The look here at stake is once again gazing as well as glancing: glancing when the photographer looks quickly through the lens (or at the developed prints) and gazing when he or she takes our time in framing the shot before actually shooting it (or when pondering the resulting prints).

paper, wood, or metal, as part of its public presentation. Second, it can have an internal frame: this is explored by Klein in his later work under the heading of "contact peints," whereby he sets a photograph within a boldly painted swash of primary colors, with the result incorporated into a single enormous print.[41] In effect, a photographic image is here set within a painted image, and if the entire print is in turn framed in a traditional way, the result is a double enframement.

Figure 12.5. William Klein, "Seven Members of the Club Allegro Fortissimo," Paris 1990. With kind permission of William Klein.

Each basic form of framing—implicit as well as explicit—acts to make a given photograph more look-worthy. As was already evident in my opening remarks, a frame is not just a decorative border but also gives to my look a coherent and contained place of attachment, a visual anchor. It is the spatial limit of what I see, and as such it both guides and localizes my act of looking. Also contributing

41. For a discussion of this process, see Christian Caujolle, "Note sur les contacts peints," in *William Klein*, opposite to plate 57. Klein sometimes refers to the resulting print as a "page"—another framed entity.

to this delimitation are such contextual factors as whether we see a photograph hung by itself in a show, or as part of a book of photographs; of influence as well is the actual size of the physical photograph.[42] However the framing is carried out, the effect is to delimit my look as well as to lure it: both at once. Acting in accordance with the framing of the photographic image, my look is drawn out, joins forces with the artwork, and witnesses its world.

We here encounter a situation in which the moment of the look combines with the moment of the image: the two moments becoming one in an intensely visual experience. We, the viewers of the photographic image, look at a work that possesses, by a complex combination of material constraints, its own visual allure. The viewer has the sense of being an interloper into an already constituted image-world—peeping into it, as it were—and yet also of being welcome in that same world. As I look into this world by means of the photographic image, I sense that its occupants are inviting me to join them. They seem to regard me, the onlooker, as a companion of their own looking. This looking, captured by the mechanical look of the camera, is twofold: they have "looks" as sheer appearances ("how they look") and they look out from where they stand. As I see them in the photographic image, both kinds of look float among their original occurrence, their selection for photographic reproduction, the creation of the physical print, and my present viewing. One set of looks is relayed by another—and then by still others: looking multiplies in a veritable mirror-game of indefinite reflection. Whether the actual looking of the subjects who were photographed takes the form of glances or gazes—and whether these subjects are human or not—they remain beholden to the interlocking series of subsequent lookings that belong to the lens of a camera and to the retinas of human spectators. Both the camera and the spectators (including the photographer as the first spectator) take note of them and thereby take their measure: even as they are preserved by a mechanical coup d'oeil, they are reanimated by the visitation of viewers, all this taking place within factors of frame and format.

In this way, the double look of the subject matter (its appearance as well as its own mode of looking) finds itself surrounded by two other forms of looking in a situation schematizable thus:

camera's LOOK // LOOKS/LOOKING (of subject matter) // viewers' LOOKS

42. As I have already remarked in the case of Avedon's large photographic prints, the larger the photograph the more we feel invited to enter its domain. This last effect was strikingly true of the large Klein photographs that were part of the major exposition "Paris/Klein" at the Musée européen de la photographie in Paris, France, May 2002. Here the viewer had the distinct sense of *being included* in the photograph, e.g., "Grande Arche de la Défense," in which four or five large heads were prominently featured from within a few feet of distance: I felt that my head, too, could well be part of this group—indeed, that it was so in a virtual manner.

Instead of a simple causal sequence (that is, existing subject matter/fact of being photographed/act of being seen), this schema suggests that the double look of the subject matter is held between two other sorts of look—held open for re-enlivening by these latter. This is not a matter of conscious alliance, as happens between two human subjects looking at each other. Instead, it is a matter of a tacit connivance whereby the subject matter lends its double looks to the photographer and the spectator—who are in turn complicit through the intermediary of the image as it appears on the photographic print. In this manner there arises a synergistic bonding between otherwise quite distinct entities and events: human and nonhuman members of the perceptual world, an optical machine, and the discerning look of the visually curious (both photographer and spectator). Such synergy may help to explain the compelling power of much photography as well as its ability to haunt us. Our draw to it, our hunger for it, is not just for the sake of the images it conveys, much less for the particular referents depicted in these images. We are drawn by the conniving of the elements, becoming participants in the process. Our looks link up with those of others: human, nonhuman, and mechanical. All of these looks intersect—they inter-look—in that pictorial image-thing we call a "photograph."

And the place of the glance in all this? It is present throughout the nexus of looking I have just outlined—sometimes as the single most pertinent act and sometimes as a confederate of the gaze. In the first case, for example, it is the dominant factor in the activity of the photographer, whose practiced eye is adept at noticing what is eminently photographable in a given setting. The decisive moment is here that of his or her glance as it darts to an emergent event or striking thing, seeing it instantly as "to be taken." Such a glance is skillful in identifying what is unusual or unique, rare or remarkable, beautiful or sublime. No sooner is such a scene spotted in a glance than the photographer's ready hand brings the camera into position, making whatever adjustments for light and distance may be required, and presses the shutter release for the shot—all of this within a matter of seconds. The lens of the camera, blinking open for a fraction of a second, enacts its own mechanical glance that mimics the photographer's initiatory glance. It is doubtless for this reason that the French call a photograph an *instantanée,* that is, a snapshot, since it is the direct result of a mechanized movement that is as quick as the blink of an eye. We witness here a close collusion between the eye of the photographer and the eye of the camera: each glances outward, taking in what is salient in the immediate surroundings.

What is taken in, once again, has its own modes of looking: of *looking like* (that is, appearing as similar in its sheer surface) and of *taking looks* (looking out from this same surface). The latter often assumes the form of a glance. We see this dramatically when crowds of humans are photographed without their being aware of it: individuals in such crowds are characteristically glancing every which way, as we see in this scene of people at a public funeral:

Figure 12.6. William Klein, "The Funeral of Thorez, Duclos' Predecessor," 1964.
With kind permission of William Klein.

But we have seen that still portraits also capture a glance that issues from the subject toward the photographer and, through the latter's agency and position, toward us as viewers of the finished photograph. But the glances of people in crowds and those of single persons posing before a camera share the stage with gazes that are captured by the same camera action, as when it depicts persons who are ruminating or staring at others. Such gazes are often interlarded with glances; but the camera lens is democratic enough to record both: its glance takes in glance and gaze alike. And it also takes in the gazes and glances (or their equivalent) on the part of nonhuman entities—of animals and plants, rocks and soil. The breadth of modes of looking here at stake only reflects the fact that the image-worlds of photography are finally coextensive with the entire perceived world and its highly varied subjects. The gaze and glance are associate members of this world, each as valid as each is different from the other.

The picture changes yet again when we consider the viewers of the presented photographic image—the audience, the public, the spectators of photographic work. In their case, the glance takes literal priority: it is what responds *first* to photographs that attract it. It "takes notice" of them in a manner that is parallel to that of the photographer whose eye was attracted in the first place to a certain subject matter. Now that this subject matter has been incorporated into a photographic print, it can catch the eye of the spectator—often for much the same reason as it struck the photographer: something conspicuous stands out, something is telling, something speaks to the viewer. This same viewer responds with a glance that is itself telling: it tells of interest, emotion, or history in the life of the spectator. One glance, that of the photographer, calls for another, that of the spectator, instituting a dialectic of looks that is especially characteristic of photography, which has a genius for eliciting and valorizing the glance of the photographer and that of the spectator alike.

This is not to deny that the spectator who has taken sudden notice of a photograph may come to gaze at the same image that announced itself in a glance. This happens when this first look, instead of passing on to other images, concerns itself with a given image, lingering on its surface appearance and savoring it as such. As a result, the glance gives way to the gaze in a form of partnership that subdues any residual competitiveness between the two kinds of looking. In the same fraternal spirit, the gaze cedes place to the glance in turn when, rifling through the pages of a photograph album or walking through an exhibition of photographs, a new image solicits a new glance. This confederacy of glance and gaze differs from that of the perceived world in which the subject matter of a given photograph resides: in that world, gazing and glancing belong indifferently to any and all, and succession or transition between them is not an issue. The disparateness of that open visual world both as to source and type of look contrasts with the comparatively domesticated world of spectatorship, in which the very activity of looking at photographs has its own decorum and habitus—its own history. In the accustomed terms of that history, especially as it has developed in the Western world since the invention of the *camera obscura* in the late sixteenth century, there is an established rhythm of glancing cum gazing in a virtual pas de deux of the human look.

However, there is nothing fixed or final about such a two-step dance of vision. As photography itself evolved from still photography to the "moving pictures" of early cinema—and now to cinema and television and DVD—the eye of the beholder has come to assume different rhythms. These rhythms often favor the glance, which keeps up with rapidly changing images better than does the gaze—except where the images are of a single thing or person seen from a stationary standpoint, thereby inducing a steady looking that is more akin to the gaze than to the glance. But when the cinematic screen itself becomes multiple, or presents multiple images on the same screen, the glance alone is equal to the task of tracking the disjointed display: in following a multichannel film like Julie Talen's remarkable *Pretend* (2003), the seated spectator has little choice but to glance constantly back and forth between the scenes that unfold separately in different "windows" that open across the same screen. In such a situation, it is as if the glance were reasserting its priority in matters of the look—just as it does whenever the viewer is herself in motion, glancing around her as she walks through a variegated landscape (including the cultural landscape of an art museum).[43]

IV

I turn now to painting, where the image reaches an apogee of sorts—as is indicated in the German usage of *Bild* to mean both "image" and "painting." At the very least, *a painting brings its content into an image.*[44] When we enjoy a painting, we savor the image it gives us far more than that which it represents (indicates, signifies, stands for). This is as true for "representational" paintings as it is for frankly nonrepresentational works. John Constable's *Wivenhoe Park* is a painting of a particular estate in the English countryside, and is in fact an accurate "representation" of the estate and its splendid country house. But when we regard it as a *painting*, we are not concerned with issues of verisimilitude (which might be the focus of a historian of art, a biographer of Constable, or an architectural historian) but rather we are concerned with how effectively it works as an artistic presentation. That is to say: *as an image,* as something having attractive aesthetic qualities that work on their own to invite our glance in the first place and to encourage subsequent glances to keep coming back to it.

The liaison between image and glance is close indeed in the case of painting, which is a haven for their interplay at many levels. We can posit a general rule that *paintings occur as images to which the glance gives primary access.* In the realm of painting, the glance moves to the image and the image comes to the glance: one cannot exist without the other, each inspires the other, both benefit from their intimate interaction. The image-glance bond holds even more forthrightly for paintings than for photographs. Why is this? It stems from the fact that when we view paintings we are only rarely concerned with the identity of

43. Julie Talen remarks that the important distinction is that "between still and moving images; still photographs and still paintings to my mind get the same kind of look. The traveling of one's eye over a work—which I believe you call glance—the motion you're speaking of occurs in the eye, rather than in the object being view. I developed my [J. T.'s] glimpseculture idea based on the amount of moving images which confront us in our contemporary home and landscape—that's the culture part—and the navigation of those landscapes is where my idea of glimpsing comes in, the biological basis of the glimpse being something based on peripheral vision—that is, something in motion that makes you turn and look. It is related to but not the same as your glance . . . ." (e-mail communication of March 25, 2005). In fact, I agree with much of what Talen here says about "glimpse," which for me is a variety of glance (see the afterword to this book). Glancing and glimpsing both involve my eye's "traveling," whether the visual content I note is still or moving, and whether my body is in motion or not. For more on Talen's work as a gifted creator of multichannel film and its theory, see her website: www.glimpseculture.com.

44. By "painting" I include not only acrylic and oil painting on canvas or paper but watercolor, gouache, and egg tempera, along with the many forms of etching (copper plate, drypoint, etc.), printmaking (monoprint, etc.), and sketching (in ink, pencil, crayon, etc.).

their subject matter or the place of their origin. Freed from issues of identity or origin, we are led to focus on the character and configuration of a painting's surface for its own sake, rather than on what the objects or events depicted on this surface betoken. We are asked to concentrate on the imagistic component of the triadic complex of thing-image-picture.

Consideration of the surface also matters in the perception of photography that we take to be art; but in a photograph there is always an issue, however indirect or muted, of an original entity or event that exists somewhere other than the photographic surface itself. Even such abstract photographic images as Man Ray's "rayograms" still tempt us to ask: from what exact things did these images stem and by what processes of transformation? Indeed, the more abstract the photographic image the more we are tempted to ask: *what* did the photographer take as his point of origin? *From which* objects did he begin, however much he managed to distort their image? These same questions can certainly be asked of certain paintings: did Delft really look the way Vermeer depicted it in his celebrated *View of Delft*? But we can just as easily avoid such questions and admire the painting in its own right; indeed, raising such questions tends to interfere with aesthetic appreciation. In photography, posing these questions is not just more tempting but appropriate and expectable: the issue of origins is always on the agenda. Not surprisingly: the photographic image conveys the event of origin itself—its own origin in a certain specific setting.

If we are led to consider what speaks to us in a painting, this is only rarely an identifiable object or person, however moving or famous they may be, but rather an amorphous and impersonal force: a force that can be designated as Earth and World (Heidegger), or as the Visible and the Invisible (Merleau-Ponty). These forces are not objects or persons and thus cannot be represented as such; they are, rather, directions or tendencies or dimensions that manifest themselves in the painterly image: in the very surface that presents this image. For the image of the artwork occurs in, and as, this surface manifestation.

At this manifest image, this pure phenomenal presence, we are invited to glance. Not just to note, much less to observe, though sometimes to gaze. But what forms does glancing take here? I shall discuss this question in two parts, one concerning the glance of the artist and the other that of the viewer, before coming to a more general assessment.

1. *Glancing on the part of the artist:* This is a rarely considered aspect of visual art, yet it is basic to the production of such art: how else is a painter going to accomplish an artwork except by various modes of looking and re-looking? Picasso has underlined the importance of the artist's own experiences of looking in those engravings and paintings in which he represents himself peering into a studio scene—depicting himself as artist-looking-at-a-model and sometimes as leering at this same scene from behind a curtain: looking at himself looking. This redoubled representation of vision stands in for his own intense engagement in the artistic process. Every painter (or draftsman) participates in such looking; to eliminate it, as Descartes suggests we should, is to block the genesis of visual art

at its very origin.[45] The only question is how we are to describe it. I shall attempt to do so in terms of four moments in the creation of painting: moments in which looking, and more especially glancing, figures prominently.

(a) *drawing from a model.* Picasso did not focus idly on this particular situation: it is exemplary of the intimate interaction that often obtains between the artist and his/her subject matter. The nudity of a human model underscores the erotic dimension of the painter's look, whose attraction to exposed flesh as intrinsically desirable is only a more overt version of the attraction of the artist's eye to anything beautiful in the immediate environment, including flowers, decorative patterns on wallpaper, views from windows, and so on—as we see still more graphically in Matisse's love for interiors, for anything from rugs to fishbowls, colorful sofas to doors opening onto verandas. To each of these parts of the studio the artist's omnivorous, shifting glance is drawn, but it is especially attracted to a model as a visual cynosure whose nudity exemplifies the power of the look to "lay bare." The glance is drawn into a special dialectic of the look, going back and forth rapidly between model and medium (canvas, paper, and others). Each of these epicenters of the scene of creation is visually enticing, and in the end the artist does not have to decide between them: his task is to be equal to both, in the one case by the glancing of the eye, in the other by the responsive action of the hand.[46]

But more than a mere cooperation of eye and hand is at play here (we have already observed their complementary action in the case of the photographer); rather, the eye is active *at every stage.* For the artist looks both at the model and at the lines or strokes he/she is making, and then back again at the model, and so on in an open series of drawing after glancing and of glancing after drawing, and sometimes the two at once: stroke-by-glance, glance-by-stroke. In the end, no straightforward sequence prevails in the circumstance, which ranges from realized drawing while glancing to prolonged looking at the model without drawing at all and to continual drawing without looking back at the model. In these latter two instances, the glance is replaced by the gaze; but any such gaze gives way to

45. "The blind, says Descartes, 'see with their hands'. The Cartesian concept of vision is modeled after the sense of touch" (Merleau-Ponty, "Eye and Mind," p. 170). By devalorizing vision as such, Descartes in effect replaces seeing at a distance—a species of "action at a distance"—with the requirement of direct contact, for which touch is paradigmatic. The archetypal form of art becomes etching, i.e., a strictly linear art in which the artist in effect traces and retraces the outlines of an object, as if by a phantom hand rather than by an appreciative eye. See ibid., pp. 169–173.

46. "The eye is an instrument that moves itself, a means which invents its own ends; it is *that which* has been moved by some impact of the world, which it then restores to the visible through the offices of an agile hand" (Merleau-Ponty, "Eye and Mind," p. 165; his italics). Expanding on this thought, Merleau-Ponty remarks that "what is designated by the terms *glance, hand,* and in general *body* is a system of systems destined for the inspection of a world" ("Indirect Language and the Voices of Silence," tr. R. McCleary, in G. Johnson, ed., *The Merleau-Ponty Aesthetics Reader: Philosophy and Painting* [Evanston, Ill.: Northwestern University Press, 1993], p. 103; his italics).

the glance as soon as it dissolves—as it always does. I may scrutinize the model at length, but in the end I will glance back at my evolving sketch, and then glance again at the model to determine where I have gone wrong so far. A process of visual "checking" obtains as I look back and forth in view of what I have created and with an eye toward what I aim to achieve. Indeed, the glance is involved in an ongoing game of rectifying visual mistakes, both my own misapprehensions of the subject matter (that is, flawed vision) and my misbegotten drawn or painted image (that is, flawed technique). The *va-et-vient* that here takes place so spontaneously is such as to glimpse *one in view of the other:* the emerging artwork in relation to the seen model, the model as set forth in the work. The result is a dense intermingling of glancing and drawing that is closely comparable to what happens in full-scale painting:

> The eye sees the world, sees what inadequacies [*manques*] keep the world from being a painting, sees what keeps a painting from being itself, sees—on the palette —the colors awaited by the painting, and sees, once it is done, the painting that answers to all these inadequacies just as it sees the paintings of others as other answers to other inadequacies.[47]

Merleau-Ponty here expands the scope of the intimate visual relationship between artist and model, but the principle remains the same whether one is confined to the studio or moves out into the open landscape: *the glance acts to supply deficiencies in the image,* whether the image be that constituted by the artwork (the sketch or painting) or that inhering in the perceived world itself (the model, the still life, the landscape).

(b) *the artist before the landscape.* The enclosure of the studio—symbolized by, but by no means limited to, the artist sketching the model in that confined space—gives way to the open expansiveness of the landscape. The array and diversity of this landscape are so considerable that only a sweeping glance can take it in. As in Kant's description of the colossal—before which the human subject stands in awe, unable to grasp its full dimensions even by the use of imagination—so before an open landscape vista the artist confronts a vastness to which he or she must somehow try to make himself/herself equal. The glance comes forward in this perceptual impasse to fill in the gaps with alacrity and grace: not by producing fictitious material, which would be the proper work of a productive imagination; nor by any mode of conceptual synthesis (as on a more or less Hegelian model); but by seeing in the outspread landscape a world-whole in which the viewing and the viewed become compresent if not coextensive: no longer a passive witness, I make myself adequate to the scene by glancing it out.

The genius of the glance allows it to penetrate into the depths of the lived world around me, whether these depths be those of a human face, the body of a model, or the recession in a natural landscape. This happens by a characteristic leaping action that suspends and then surpasses provisional perceptual limits.

47. Merleau-Ponty, "Eye and Mind," p. 165.

My leaping look goes through the trees before me—penetrating even their densest branches—so as to move beyond into another group of trees in the middle distance. No sooner have I glimpsed the latter, however, than I have moved on to a different level, this time to the fields that lie on the far side of these trees, and thence, in another leap of vision, into the far sphere of the scene, its outlying parts, and finally its horizon. All of this happens in one continuous outflowing of the look, in a smooth sequence that can, at any moment, reverse its directionality and return to the middle and near realms of the same scene. This is a look that respects perceptual gaps: rather than filling them in prematurely or ignoring them by some habitual maneuver, it moves around them—as when I simply accept the fact that I cannot see the backside of the trees I have started looking at: the visual lacuna presents itself as integral to the coherent image of the total scene itself, not as a sheer absence but as a lack within the larger whole that my eager glance takes in.

Now this inherent power of the leaping look, spontaneously enacted by every sighted person, is employed by the landscape painter to remarkable effect. Painting outside in *plein air* (or, alternatively, sketching there and painting later in the studio), she or he brings a comprehensive glance to bear on the work in progress, incorporating what it captures in this looking into the painted work as if by perceptual transfusion. There is once again a two-step procedure at play: not that of glancing-at and glancing-down as in the near sphere of the studio, but of glancing-out and glancing-back: looking out into the far sphere of the landscape world and bringing back what it sees into the evolving work held literally at arm's-length. The aim is to see if the work can somehow be made commensurate with the landscape vista—where "com-mensurate" means "measured together," the work together with the vista and vice versa, the painter serving as their congenial mediatrix.

Renoir, stationed before the sea at Cassis, painted a scene of bathers at an inland stream. He glanced out at the blue of the ocean and took it back into the progressing work, even though its explicit subject matter was located somewhere else. His look took in the material essence of water and transferred it to another circumstance. He was not *representing* the seascape but providing an emblematic *resemblance* of it in another setting; he was capturing "the same or, if one prefers, a *similar* thing, but according to an efficacious similarity which is the parent, the genesis, the metamorphosis of Being in [the artist's] vision."[48] The agent of this metamorphosis was his mere glance, which leavened the dense spatiality of the seascape; only something as quick and subtle as a glance could penetrate the massive solidity of the sea and bear it elsewhere. The sea, as Merleau-Ponty adds, "contains all sorts of shapes of being and, by the way it has

48. Ibid., p. 166; his italics. Merleau-Ponty cites Giacometti: "What interests me in all paintings is resemblance—that is, what is resemblance for me: something which makes me discover more of the world" (cited in ibid., p. 165). With this "more of the world" the glance has everything to do.

of joining the encounter with one's glance, evokes a series of possible variants and teaches, over and beyond itself, a general way of expressing being."[49]

Otherwise said: the "world's instant" that Cézanne sought to paint is the moment of the glance, which darts back and forth between painter and land or sea.[50] By glancing out and back, the painter establishes resemblances between the scene by which he or she is surrounded and the artwork that is its displaced icon.

(c) *abstract painting.* But what about paintings whose contents are wholly imaginary—which contain no recognizable figures or landscape features? What is the role of glancing here? The matter is complex. Consider first of all the fact that we continually construct our own imaginaries in the form of fantasies, reveries, waking dreams, and so on. The abstract artist can be considered someone who is particularly skilled at such inward imagining, or its equivalent,[51] being able to generate images of shapes and colors and movements that are nowhere located in current or past actualities of space or time. These autogenously generated images need not be entirely explicit, yet their vagueness renders them no less important in the process of painting. Once more, it is a question of the value of the vague—in the Jamesian sense to which I referred earlier in this book. The fact is that the painter can take inspiration and gain insight from the most abstract or the vaguest of images: the conjunction of *Einsicht* ("insight") and *Einfall* ("sudden inspiration") obtains even when images are not recognizable in their exact identity or precise origin.[52] The abstract artist takes off from such images as productively as does the representational realist who depends upon close observation of the external environment. The very nebulousness of these images leaves the artist all the more free to employ them as he/she wishes.

The crucial difference from the two previous circumstances of glancing is that now there can be no such thing as checking, much less comparing, abstract or vague images with the emerging work, much less with an aboriginal model. By the time any such checking is completed, the image itself will have vanished.

---

49. "Indirect Language and the Voices of Silence," p. 93. Merleau-Ponty adds: "Renoir can paint women bathing and a freshwater brook while he is by the sea at Cassis because he only asks the sea—which alone can teach what he asks—for its way of interpreting the liquid element, of exhibiting it, and of making it interact with itself" (ibid.).

50. "A minute in the world's life passes! to paint it in reality! and forget everything for that. To become that minute, be the sensitive place" (Paul Cézanne, cited in B. Dorival, *Paul Cézanne,* tr. H. H. A. Thackthwaite [London, 1948], in ibid., p. 169, n. 17).

51. I say "or its equivalent," for I am not claiming that the abstract artist needs to consult his or her inner imaginary as such; the issue is not introspection per se, but the consultation of a realm that has no precise analogue in external perception.

52. For a discerning treatment of the affinity of these terms in the experience (*Erfahrung*) of the "new," see Laszlo Tengelyi, "Vom Erlebnis zum Erfahrung," *Antrittsvorlesung,* Dept. of Philosophy, Universität Wuppertal, June 11, 2002: "Denn woher stammt das echte Wissen, wenn nicht aus dem Einfall und der Einsicht? Jeder Einfall und jede Einsicht bleibt aber—in einem gewissen Sinne des Wortes—eine Erfahrung" (Ms., p. 18; cf. also p. 13).

More importantly, such checking is beside the point; what matters is that the emerging image is *exfoliated in the artwork:* precisely as in Kandinsky's aptly named series of *Improvisations* and *Compositions.* Take, for instance, this example from the latter series:

Figure 12.7. Wassily Kandinsky, "Two Ovals (Composition #218)," 1919.
© 2006 Artists Rights Society (ARS), New York / ADAGP, Paris.

Notice that no single shape in this painting can be traced back to a known thing or event, even though there are bare intimations of such "things" as clouds, stars, mountains, fish, castles, and even (in the central black circle) a child or clown. All is fantastic, and yet all coheres in this composition, which is as comprehensive as any landscape and yet as intimate and intense as any studio scene. It can be construed as a phantasmagoria of glancing—an entire imaginary world in which lines of flight suggest visual rays emanating from a heterogeneous set of glances.

(d) *glancing amid parts of the evolving work.* In this case the glance is cast not between separately stationed items (whether perceptual or imaginal) but *amid* what the artist himself has brought forth in earlier moments. His or her look moves back and forth not between a model (or a landscape view or a mental image) and the work, but within the work itself—laterally, on its own plane as it were. Now the glance glides "onward and outward"[53] across the picture plane

53. "All goes onward and outward . . . and nothing collapses" (Walt Whitman, "Song of Myself").

that hovers over the material surface of the artwork as if it were an epiphenome-nal expression of it. Glancing here moves among parts of this plane as if they were parts of an Indian rug of complex design that attract attention in many ways at once, though always on *its* terms: in its peculiar medium and according to its dimensions. This immanent glancing activity becomes especially evident when later revisions are made to a given artwork: the artist intently looking back and forth among earlier efforts and later layers, so that the improvisations of one stage can be integrated with the considered composition of a later moment, the provisional or peremptory becoming more definitive in the final palimpsest. This process may be as radical as de Kooning's practice of scraping off all the paint he had applied during one day of work, so that he could start the next day almost clean ("almost," since there remained a congeries of pale traces), or it can be as gentle as that of Dan Rice ruminating on a work over a period of twenty years, adding to it only a very occasional stroke or a patch of new color.[54] In each case, glancing is essential to the revision, which could not proceed without it, even though it proceeds at a different pace and in a different path from artist to artist and even from work to work of the same artist.[55]

2. *Glancing on the part of the spectator.* And the viewer's experience in all this? It is one thing to appreciate the artist's glance—integral as it is to the creation of a visual work of art, especially in its more intense phases when time is at a premium ("nothing is created without a sense of urgency,"[56] says Lacan)—but what about the spectator's role? Given the comparative leisure in which most artworks are viewed (for example, in galleries and museums that encour-age patient looking), will not gazing now be favored over glancing? And in any case, is not close inspection a more responsible approach to a painting than a mere glance at it? And yet here too glancing shows itself to be remarkably active, and in ways we may not have suspected before reflecting on it. In fact, the spectator's glance is essential to coming to know a given work, which depends on it to be re-enlivened. It is at play throughout the experience of visual art. How shall we account for this pervasive activity? In answering this question, I shall examine three basic circumstances of varying scope: glancing at a single work, glancing in a larger setting, and the relation between the body and the glance in the experience of visual works.

(a) *glancing at a single work.* Despite the inducement to view carefully those

54. For a comparative treatment of de Kooning and Rice, see my *Earth-Mapping: Artists Reshaping Landscape* (Minneapolis: University of Minnesota Press, 2005), chaps. 7 and 8.

55. This is not to deny that in the process of painting glancing is often interlaced with gazing, the two forming a densely configured dialectic; but in this dialectic the glance almost always takes the lead: a glance at part of a painting on which I'm working precipitates a closer look in the form of a gaze; but the gaze in turn gives rise to further glancing when I attempt to incorporate what I have learned from gazing into concrete changes in the evolving work—changes that themselves call forth further glances.

56. Jacques Lacan, "The Function and Field of Speech and Language in Psychoanalysis," in his *Ecrits,* tr. A. Sheridan (New York: Norton, 1977), p. 54.

paintings that are hung on walls for our perceptual delectation, our actual looking is rarely sustained or systematic in character. Perhaps only art historians or
critics, or those who restore paintings, look at them with concerted scrutiny, and
even then mainly because they are searching for something in particular—some
theme on which they are writing, some development in the history of the genre,
or else some damage to the work that calls for repair. Otherwise, looking at a
painting consists largely in discontinuous glances that dart to different portions
of its image—with no definite algorithm of movement or program of expectations. E. H. Gombrich was among the first to remark expressly on the saltatory
nature of viewing visual artworks, whereby our eye leaps every which way, often
without our realizing that this is happening. As we know from earlier discussions
in chapter 9, saccadic swings of the eye are measured in milliseconds and
millimeters. These ocular leaps have the effect of disseminating our perception
over very diverse parts of the picture plane—first touching one part, then another, and so on in no apparent order. This is not to say that the glances are
chaotic, but it is to assert that they exhibit a distinctive freedom of eye movement that is basic to viewing paintings: a freedom that belongs to that minimal
(but rarely compromised) freedom of the glance that we have encountered in
other contexts—a freedom of in-determination that is at once difficult to detect
and yet integral to the enactment of human experience.

   This freedom of the glance is evident even when viewing a painting as familiar
and seemingly straightforward as, say, Leonardo da Vinci's *Mona Lisa*. One
might think that the darkly winsome subject's celebrated enigmatic gaze would
elicit a comparable gazing on my part. And it is true that I am inclined to look
rather intently into her face as if to fathom the source of her mysteriously serene
smile. Her gaze calls for mine in that moment. But in the very next moment, my
own look moves on . . . and on . . . and on. It moves from her eyes and smile—the
almost obligatory epicenters of our first act of attention—to other parts of her
face, to her cheeks and nose and hair. From there it jumps to her soft shoulders
and then, suddenly, back to the landscape behind the whole torso; once in the
landscape, it vacillates further, pausing for a moment on a single tree, then
another, finally moving to the horizon and up into the sky. Nothing forces me to
follow this course, though much has encouraged it. I start with the *Mona Lisa's*
own look and smile because these are visually compelling and so well known in
Renaissance painting; from this point on, however, I am enticed by the slightest
of clues—the tender texture of her cheeks; her soft, dark hair; the distant landscape that beckons from its very indistinctness. At no moment, not even the very
first, *must* my glance go anywhere in particular; in every instance it is gently
guided as it wanders freely from one point to another in this pictorial paradise.
Thanks to the painting's guidance—which I am free to accept or refuse—the
result is an experience that is literally "heterotopic," that is, filled with differently qualified and situated *topoi* or places, each of which elicits my glance
without demanding it. In this regard, we may say with Merleau-Ponty that such

a painting offers me "a series of appropriately mixed, instantaneous glimpses"[57] of its subject matter.

Let us consider a very different painting, Klee's *Legend of the Nile,* a colorful and lively work composed with pastel on cotton cloth that is in turn glued onto burlap.

Figure 12.8. Paul Klee, "Legend of the Nile," 1937.
© 2006 Artists Rights Society (ARS), New York / VG Bild-Kunst, Bonn.

Both the colors (blues, lavenders, Hooker greens, yellow ochres) and the lines are diverse: especially the lines, which range from contours of recognizable objects to wholly abstract shapes. Whereas the colors display an implicit pattern that underlies the pictorial surface and give it a certain directionality (for example, the blues and lavenders that descend diagonally from the left), the lines are distributed rather randomly over this same surface—with the notable exception of the boat in the center of the work. My look is drawn first to the boat, thanks to its central position and its readable sense, but from there it splays out in virtually any direction as it follows the lead of the lines: we can easily glance toward any of the four corners of the painting or at any point between them. Nothing compels me to travel one way rather than another, with the result that I experience a version of what the medievals called "liberty of indifference": my glance can

57. "The painting itself would offer to my eyes almost the same thing offered them by real movements: a series of appropriately mixed, instantaneous glimpses. . . ." (Merleau-Ponty, "Eye and Mind," p. 185).

equally well go in any direction, in-determinately so. Perhaps Klee meant to suggest that the Egyptian journey to the Other Side could land us anywhere—or nowhere: coming from the (already ambiguous) voyage of life, we cannot be sure where we shall end, just as the glance that follows the uncertain signs of this mysterious trip has no assured terminus. But even if Klee had no such intention in mind, we can at least say that the desultory path of a rocking boat calls for an equally desultory glance: as the boat goes we know-not-where in the under-world, the glance it inspires roams freely over the picture plane on which this underworld is presented.

Another painting of Klee's from a year later teaches a different lesson about glancing within the confines of a single painting:

Figure 12.9. Paul Klee, "Heroic Roses," 1938.
© 2006 Artists Rights Society (ARS), New York / VG Bild-Kunst, Bonn.

Here the linear element is no longer piecemeal and disparate but has become dominant: it lures the eye forcefully along its path, starting from the lower left, encircling the major rose, continuing around the smaller rose to the left and going upward again to encompass the still smaller rose at the top. Around this axial line are gathered lesser lines, some continuous, some fragmentary but none of them visually demanding: they belong to a dense *Hintergrund* that (very probably) signifies the dark forces of Nazi Germany swirling through Europe at the time. From these forces, the roses stand out both by their pronounced contours and their aspiring and hopeful color. Even more than in the case of the *Mona Lisa,* our eye is guided to start with. But once we make the major loop around the three roses, we can let our look range openly in the indistinct environs, where no proper sequence is indicated and no particular object is featured. The highly structured vortical movement traced out by the roses (especially the central rose) is replaced by a de-centered and outgoing lateral motion. The powerful linear factor comes close to freezing the glance and turning it into a gaze—particularly at the dead center of the large rose—and yet this never quite happens, as our look is flung out from the linearity itself and into the margins of the work. The comparative dimness of these margins and their outlying position act as a condensed emblem of the periphery of the human look itself. The glance inhabits this periphery as if it were its native ground: even in the most ordinary perceptual experience, our glancing is often most at home in the outer regions of the scene at stake—there where fewer direct demands are made, there where the focally glanced-at gives way to the marginally glimpsed.

In all three instances just considered, the glance exhibits its gift for discernment and its versatility even within the most constricted conditions. Whether these constrictions are those of fame and familiarity (for example, the *Mona Lisa*), cultural overdetermination (as in *The Legend of the Nile:* beyond the central image and quasi hieroglyphs, the very title imposes certain geographic and narratological limits), or purely formal elements (for example, the emphatic lines in *Heroic Roses*), the glance of the viewer, naive or sophisticated, finds ways to evade undue fixation—just as it does when it is confronted by the literal limits of a physical frame.

(b) *glancing in a larger setting.* We glance not only *at* given artworks but also *within* the settings in which these same works are exhibited. I refer to such things as the wall space between paintings in an exhibition or museum, the particular rooms or halls in which they are hung, and finally the entire building that houses them. Each of these settings acts to contain a given work, which is often surrounded several times over in a series of ever-more encompassing containments. What is the effect of these encirclements on the viewer's glance? Is it cut off or stymied—as the very idea of "containment" seems to suggest—or does something else quite different happen?

I shall address these questions by means of a brief narrative of a recent visit of mine to the Künstlermuseum in Düsseldorf, Germany. This recently opened museum (part of the Museum Kunst Palast) consists in a series of buildings linked internally on three floors. It presents works from very diverse periods of the history of Western art—medieval, Renaissance, early and late modern, and contemporary. What is most striking is the method of exhibition: instead of following the usual chronological order (often in concert with national and regional origins), in this museum the artworks are juxtaposed by *theme* in each major room: for example, "Melancholy," "Man and Nature," "Exotica," and so forth. For the visitor who is used to traditional criteria of presentation, the effect is at first confusing, even bewildering: Max Ernst's *Colombes bleues et roses*

(1926)—an open and frankly experimental collage—is set next to a traditional mid-nineteenth-century landscape by Arnold Böcklin, *Landscaft in den pontinischen Sümpfen* (1851), while a tightly organized *Stilleben Ecce Homo* by Gaspar Pieter Verbruggen (1635–1687) is only a few feet from Konstantan Lange's striking *Isolatorköpfe* (1991). *Las Vegas* (1999) by Thomas Struth—a large and detailed painting of a Vegas hotel with a recreated medieval castle in its courtyard—hangs chock-a-block with Pieter Lastman's *Jonas und der Walfisch* (1621). Not only are dates of creation, artists, and places of origin vastly different but their material media and physical sizes are also remarkably various: all within the same room or group of contiguous rooms.

I was particularly struck by the juxtaposition, in one corner of a long corridor, of an enormous Gerhard Richter work, *Vermalung Nr. 329* (1972), with a tiny painting by Paul Klee, *Purpuraster* (1919). The fact that both were in oil and that each employed similar coloration (deep purples and mauves) did not lessen the almost jarring contrast between them. At first, I did not recognize the diminutive painting as a Klee: I had been so overwhelmed by the sheer size and force of the painting by Richter that I could not attribute the smaller work to any painter I knew: it seemed an insignificant minor effort, placed there mischievously by the curator to showcase its gigantic partner. My first glance thus misled me; only when my companion identified it as a painting by Klee did I look again, indeed several times, and saw that she was right: who else but Klee could paint a "purple aster" in such a charmingly abstract way? This realization allowed me to glance back at the Richter and to see it, too, in a new light. No longer seen simply as huge and dominating, it took on a different aspect in my return look. I saw it as a continuation of Klee's earlier effort to move to pure color and minimal identifiable form in an abstract painting that, rather than proffering an image of something easily recognizable such as a particular flower (as he had done in the case of "Heroic Roses"), was *itself the image,* or rather an *image-thing* composed of vibrant color, conveyed by dynamic brushstrokes that create a sustaining texture in the work itself. Richter had carried on Klee's modest but radical gesture, only on a much more monumental scale.

When I glanced further to my left in the same space, I spotted Johan Wilhelm Schirmer's *Zypressen* (circa 1840), an avowedly representational image of cypress trees in a landscape. Suddenly, I realized that I was confronted, in this single corner of the Künstlermuseum, with three coherent stages of the painted image, all rendered in oil but otherwise very different: a conventional beaux-arts work (Schirmer), a wisp of representation on its way to abstraction (Klee: the wisp consisting in the title, *Purpuraster*), and full abstraction (Richter). What at first appeared merely bizarre and without order in my first viewing of these works assumed, after several interrelated looks, a much more meaningful ordering.

In this process of discovery, the glance played a crucial role, and it did so by moving back and forth between the works in question. This proceeded in two stages: a first was strictly dyadic as I took in the Richter and Klee and looked between them alone; in a second stage, I began to glance among a trio of works that now included the Schirmer work. I took this last step even though the Schirmer was separated from the Klee and Richter by an open hallway over which my glance had to leap; but leap it did, and gladly so! In a thrice, it overcame vast discrepancies in style and period and size. Not to mention the picture frames that otherwise set them apart: the elaborate, traditional frame around the Schirmer landscape, the elegant but simple frame of Klee's tiny work, and the thin metallic strip around Richter's outsize piece. Not that I did not notice all these differences: I certainly did so; but across that highly differentiated field my glance moved freely, uninhibited by the complexities of the actual setting. My sweeping glance was at liberty to assimilate and contrast what I saw in terms of color, subject matter, medium, treatment, artistic style, form of framing, and even the apparent intention of the artist.

This situation contrasts with that to which Merleau-Ponty points in his description of physical things that stand out independently of each other in a given environment: these things are "upright, insistent, flaying our glance with their edges, each thing claiming an absolute presence which is not compossible with the absolute presence of the other things."[58] Visual artworks are absolute presences in their own right; they have their own way of being self-sufficient and freestanding; indeed, they have their own worlds.[59] At the same time, however, they configurate with each other in a shared spatial scene, for example, a place-of-exhibition; when this latter happens, the animating agent is the glance, which weaves them together spontaneously in a common tissue. Such animation and weaving require that glancing overcome modes of containment and separation that would otherwise keep artworks apart from each other in space and time. The glance moves freely in and through the heterogeneous setting of the works so as to constitute, however briefly, a place-world composed of their concatenated compresence. The coordinator of this setting, its directive visual genius, is the glance of the spectator: this glance, darting as fast as Mercury, is the connection-maker in a situation otherwise marked mainly by disparity and discontinuity.

(c) *the glance and the body.* Let us stay within the museum setting, where the eye is almost always moving. But so is the body! Even in the comparatively static instances so far examined, there was bodily movement going on. On the one hand, my head was pivoting as it followed my glance into different parts of a given painting, even an inconspicuous work such as Klee's *Purpuraster,* and all the more so when I swung my whole head to the left to see the Richter and then

58. Merleau-Ponty, "The Philosopher and His Shadow," *Signs,* tr. R. C. McCleary (Evanston, Ill.: Northwestern University Press, 1964), p. 181. Merleau-Ponty admits, however, that even in the case of ordinary perception things have absolute presence "all together by virtue of a configurational meaning (*un sens de configuration*) which is in no way indicated by [a] 'theoretical meaning' " (ibid.).

59. I am thinking here of Dufrenne's notion of "the world of the work"; see his *Phenomenology of Aesthetic Experience,* tr. E. S. Casey et al. (Evanston, Ill.: Northwestern University Press, 1973), chap. 5, "Aesthetic Object and World."

the Schirmer paintings. On the other hand, *within* my organic body there were also virtual movements, quasi performances of my body: I am thinking of such spontaneous imaginative actions as projecting myself into a work, imagining myself painting it otherwise, and so on. I was quite conscious of such actions in the case of the Richter painting: its large and capacious space, combined with its swirling dark colors, invited me into its midst and made me feel that I was not simply standing over here, in my literal viewing place, but also located over there, in the painting itself. Such virtual bodily movements are by no means trivial, even if they are sometimes hard to detect; Collingwood argues that they are essential to the appreciation of all auditory and visual art; and if this is true, they, along with the saccadic eye movements that accompany the glance, call into question any model of the purely passive viewer or listener: the literal "spectator."[60]

Leaving aside the virtual body, let us consider three situations that call for overt bodily movement: going through, going around, and going between:

(i) *going through*. By this I mean the body's explicit motions of going from room to room in an exhibition or museum. These motions can be tentative and exploratory (as when we are just "checking out" a place) or else they can be regulated by a plan to see each successive space in a certain order (as when we follow out the chronological development of a certain artist or school of art: just what the Düsseldorf museum discourages). On the first model, the glancing that accompanies my bodily movement is probative: it looks ahead or to the side in a discontinuous manner, on the lookout for items of special interest. In one case at the Künstlermuseum, I walked into a long rectilinear room and seeing nothing of special note on a first sweeping glance, my eye was caught by three smaller side rooms that led off from this larger room and, more particularly, by individual works therein: an enormous photograph of a nursing mother in one room, a scattered Joseph Beuys work in another, and several small etchings in the third room. In each case, my roving glance took the lead, acting like a miner's light attached to my head, and the rest of my body followed forth as if it were the eye's obedient servant. This is a common pattern of glancing-while-moving, interrupted only by fatigue or being distracted by particular sights. I go *through* the exhibition space, guided by the glance and propelled by willing feet. But this also obtains when I follow the second pattern mentioned: seeing artworks in succession as part of a definite plan—in which case, my glance is less adventuresome, less likely to leap over intermediate spaces, yet no less effective in leading my body to undertake certain motions in pursuit of the plan.

(ii) *going around*. Once in a given space, whether I get there by careful intention or by happy accident, I tend to take up a distinctive bodily activity of walking around that space. Even here, such movement is not necessarily successive; I was first attracted by the very large photograph of the nursing mother, but

60. For Collingwood's account of such unobservable but important movements, see R. G. Collingwood, *Principles of Art* (Oxford: Oxford University Press, 1938), pp. 147 ff.

once inside the small room in which it hung I was immediately lured away by other works on either side of it. I looked at two of these on the right of the photograph, then three others on its left, then glanced back again at the right wall to see still others. I certainly was glancing *around* this gallery space, and I eventually took in everything there. But I did so in no fixed order. Or more exactly, *the order my body followed was that ordained by the glance,* which made up its own order as it led my circumambulation. No other order mattered, not even that established by the explicit theme of the space I was in. I went around the room in question, my body obliging my glance all the while.

(iii) *going between.* Gallerygoers will sometimes sally back and forth between two or more works, in a spirit of comparison. Confronted with the celebrated *Haystacks* painted by Monet, hanging together on one wall at the Art Institute of Chicago, I at first stood in one place and scanned the series as a whole by simply moving my head from right to left and back again. Shortly later, however, I found myself walking back and forth before the same Monet paintings, pausing longer at certain ones. In this way I moved *between* these luminous works, and I did so with my whole body—perhaps presuming at some less than conscious level that my very movement would serve to unify these works more completely than when I took them in from a static position. What mattered most was the way my actual bodily movement put me in an advantageous position to look more closely at given works (and then, on this basis, to compare them with each other). In this case, I reached an equilibrium between glance and bodily movement—a two-way directionality in which my glancing was no longer the primary guide (as it is in going through and going around) but wherein my body cleared the space for glancing itself. Such glancing can be that of looking intently at a single work—the situation as discussed above at (a)—or it can be contrastive, as when I glance back and forth between several works, for example, comparing the exact hue of the haystack shadows in two of the paintings now before me. Such glancing need not follow my walking but may actively lead it or else accompany it.

It becomes evident that in the presence of artworks on exhibition *glance and body realize a close collaboration in which either one can take the lead, depending on the exact circumstance.* Sometimes, especially when it is a question of looking through or around a comparatively roomy exhibition or museum space, the glance puts itself in the advance position, that of the literal *avant-garde*—in which case, the rest of the body follows its lead, catching up with it as it were. Sometimes, the body gets there first—gets to a favorable viewing place from where it can see the paintings it wants to see—and only then is the activity of free glancing pursued. But in still other circumstances, *the two actions are concurrent,* each being simultaneous with the other.

Beyond glance, body, and artwork, there is the particular *place* in which these three factors become conterminous. In the foregoing pages, I have been employing terms like "room," "exhibition space," "position" [of the viewer's body], and "space." But comparative lack of place-talk does not mean that we have to do here with a merely subordinate dimension. On the contrary: place is the most deeply co-ordinative element of all in the foursome composed of glance, body, artwork, and place. Place acts to orient the other three, that is to say, *situates* them. This happens, for example, at each of the levels I have just distinguished in the relationship between glance and body. When I simply stand and look, moving my head minimally and resorting at most to virtual/imaginative corporeal gestures, I still must have a *place-to-stand:* that is, what is conventionally called "position."[61] This is *where my body is* during the time of looking; without it, I would be wholly unsituated, held in abeyance as it were, as if I were *nowhere* from where to glance significantly at an artwork. If I then move a few steps to see the same work better, or another work with which I pair it in my vision, these steps must occur *somewhere* in particular: typically, in a small space (for example, a side room at the Künstlermuseum) that supports comparative or contrastive looking. This is a place that locates me between individual works. Only when I turn my steps into something more like a stride in looking around—entering the next-wider circle, as it were—does the place widen in keeping with the space swept out by my walking. Now I am able to circumambulate freely among whatever works are presented in a given exhibition space, a place that may be more or less capacious depending on the architecture of the museum I am in.

Moreover, as I circulate in the building at large, I go through a much more extensive space that is built up from the particular places that are its rooms or galleries (as well as the corridors and stairways that link these latter). This is more like an entire region than a particular place—an "art-space," as it could be called. In this more commodious arena, my body perambulates (literally, "walks through"), moving freely whether in an experimental or a programmatic manner. I am in a whole place-world in which my moving body and my roving glance, collaborating continuously, attain a freedom of action that is at once the concrete condition of viewing individual artworks and the practical limit of doing so.

V

In closing, I shall compare gazing and glancing in paintings and photographs, the two primary visual artworks under discussion in this chapter. The gaze remains distinctively different from the glance in all of the major ways first identified in chapter 4 and detailed in the afterword. But such differences between the two acts in no way preclude their collaboration with each other. At one extreme, this takes the form of a momentary merging—as we saw in the case of the meditative practice examined in chapter 9. In other contexts, it assumes the guise of an active dialectic. We have witnessed this latter at several points in

---

61. My own use of "position" is different: I take it to be the fixed point in an implicit grid of space, i.e., part of what I call generically "site." See the entries under these two designations in the glossary of my *Representing Place: Landscape Painting and Maps.*

the current chapter: above all, when the artist or spectator oscillates between gazing and glancing. The painter may scrutinize his or her subject matter as part of becoming better acquainted with it, and a close look at an evolving work may alternate with bare glances at it: Turner was known to gaze at a painting he thought he had finished on the eve of its exhibition, and even if he found flaws he felt compelled to remedy them on the spot—even if this meant sneaking into the gallery late at night to make the changes! (The corrective strokes, we can be sure, depended as much on glances as the initial perception occurred in the form of a slow and critical gaze.) So, too, the viewer is someone who moves between careful gazing at certain works—those that "arrest his attention"—and spontaneous glancing at others; or, in another familiar scenario, engages in both activities vis-à-vis a single work. The actions of the living-moving body, interleaving with the specificities of place, subtend this close cooperation and render it more effective. The texture of the perceived surface of a photograph or painting, sustaining both glances and gazes, contributes further to their creative intertanglement.[62]

Beyond these relations between gaze and glance there is a further twist in their dialectic. We may glance or gaze at paintings and photographs alike, but *the photograph is more likely to induce a gaze than is a painting.* Why is this? It is mainly because photographs open a window onto a perceptual reality that has been caught at the moment of its taking: we are given direct and privileged access to a state of affairs that has now vanished, either from our own life or that of others. (This is doubtless another basis of the haunting presence of photographic images.) That state of affairs, conveyed in the instant and the light of its occurring, has been preserved by the image itself: the camera "records the moment when the camera's shutter admits light—a moment that, once past, remains perpetually present in the photograph as a surface of reflected light."[63] What has been

62. This is not to overlook certain complexities of surface such as we find in William Klein's "contacts peints," in which the photographic image proper (i.e., the "planche-contact" or photographic plate) is merged with a painterly motif (i.e., the swashes of bright primary colors that Klein adds to the plate): e.g., in his *Danse à Brooklyn, New York* (1955) as reproduced in *William Klein,* Photo Poche. Here Klein creates a single surface that is at once painterly and photographic. The fact is that we glance differently if the image at which we glance is differently related to the surface of which it is part. When the image is at one with this surface, we take in the surface *as* the artwork—and, for this very reason, we identify with it more closely. When the image is painted *on* the surface—whether this be canvas or burlap, wood or steel— the glance cannot help but see it as different from the surface, *discerning* it there as it were. In this case, the image seems to hover over the surface, and even if it physically adheres to it is still distinguishable from it. What is unusual about Klein's "contacts peints" is that he has managed to make of superimposed painterly and photographic images—normally quite distinct in character and presentation—a total image situated on a single coherent surface at which we are free to glance or gaze as we wish. The discernment of levels has been replaced by the perception of a continuously self-constituting surface that is the artwork itself. I shall return to Klein's innovation just below.

63. Julian Robson, curator of the Speed Art Museum, commentary on the show of Richard Ross's photographs entitled "Gathering Light" (exhibition at the Santa Barbara Art Museum,

photographed realizes a very special sort of survival in the photographic image, at once accurate and fragile. Accurate, because this image is the transcription, via an entire technological apparatus, of the original state of affairs: it is the reproduction of what the eye of the camera, its mechanized glance, once saw. Fragile, insofar as the image subsists first in a negative (or digital image) and then in a print, both of which are vulnerable to damage and loss; once these no longer exist, the only record of the original situation is lost with them.

The photographic image not only indicates to us that something has happened but the fact that it—the event (including its constituents: for example, the still life, the face, the crowd)—has been uniquely preserved in this image. And in no other: even when the German photographer Barbara Probst takes simultaneous shots of the same event, each resulting image captures a unique aspect of this event: so unique that on first viewing a set of her photographs of the same event (for example, herself walking in Grand Central Station; herself on top of a building on Eighth Avenue in New York) the impression seems to be of different events, even of different persons. Only close inspection reveals their convergence in one person and a single event. Each image suffices for itself, stands on its own, as a reliable (if not complete) replica of the event it conveys to our admiring or curious eye.[64]

No wonder, then, that we are tempted to gaze at the photographic image: it is as if our intent and prolonged look were acting to support the circumstance. Partly to *witness*, after the fact, the event that has been photographed: or more exactly, to be the co-witness, along with the camera and the photographer, of this event. Partly to *continue*, in our own peculiar, organic way, the highly mechanical process by which the event was first preserved as an image. *Bewahrung* ("preservation"), as Heidegger reminds us, calls for a *Wahrer* or *Wächter*, a guardian of the truth (*das Wahre*) contained in the preservation itself.[65] In the case of photography, this guardian is myself as viewer, who by merely looking carries on the initial work of the photograph. The sheer preservation effected by the latter calls for guardianship on the part of its viewers. Such guardianship, whose primary activity occurs as witnessing,[66] is most effectively realized by a steady, supportive look—in short, a gaze.

June–July 2003). Robson adds that "the photograph is an object that melds the present and the past, representing an expired moment that is [now] visually extant: each photograph turns light's presence not only into a temporal trace but also into a historical record."

64. I take this example from Barbara Probst's *Exposure No. 5, New York City, 545 Eighth Ave., 20.12.00*, as exhibited in the show *Heute bis Jetzt: Zeitgenössiche fotografie aus Düsseldorf, Teil 2* at the Museum Kunst Palast, Düsseldorf, summer 2002.

65. On human beings—regarded as Da-sein—as the guardians of truth, see Martin Heidegger, *Contributions to Philosophy (From Enowning)*, tr. P. Emad and K. Maly (Bloomington: Indiana University Press, 1999), sections 5, 6 (cf. *Beiträge zur Philosophie* [Frankfurt: Klostermann, 1989], pp. 17, 23).

66. It remains, however, that witnessing itself is often composed of a series of closely concatenated glances: see my essay on witnessing in the Holocaust (unpublished paper, Paris, May 2002) and the concluding thoughts to this book.

The gaze, in contrast with the glance, is capable of prolonging itself for a considerable stretch of time: indeed indefinitely, as we see in the looks of the two lovers photographed by Nina Schmitz, *Love Story No. 37*[67]—lovers who gaze out at us without any discernible temporal limit. Their compelling look, embodied in a lasting image, calls for our continual witnessing, much as does Walker Evans's self-portrait (fig. 12.3). This look, preserved in the materiality of the photographic medium, asks us to be its guardians by viewing and reviewing it.

Since a painting makes no pretense to preserve an original event—the rare exceptions being paintings of historical happenings (for example, *Washington Crossing the Delaware*)—our own look is not solicited in any comparable enterprise of ongoing witnessing. On the contrary: the characteristic reworking of the painterly image, its susceptibility to constant revision (of which the example of Turner furnishes a striking instance), means that there is no issue here of carrying forward a unique and instantaneous grasp of an event. Even if there was an original moment of perception that inspired the artist, the task of the painting is rarely to capture it as such, much less to preserve it. The truth of that moment lies not in its explicit reproduction—sustained by empathic gazing on the part of future viewers—but in its transformation in paint. Paint of any kind, even water-based, introduces a certain thickness, an added layer of matter shaped by the agencies of eye and hand acting in concert: a layer that has its own consistency and depth. As a consequence, the marks of accuracy and fragility that are so characteristic of photographic images no longer obtain; instead, we become concerned with other issues that cluster around what Arthur Danto calls "the transfiguration of the commonplace."[68]

The transfiguring occurs first of all in, or rather on, the painted surface (paper, canvas, board, and so on), and is only then picked up and carried further by the viewer's perception. Change is at issue throughout—the artist laboring to transform his or her experience of the surrounding world. "Nature is on the inside,"[69] as Cézanne said, meaning that it has to be incorporated in the artist before reemerging as a painting. The glance, acting in concert with the hand, is well suited to effect this reemergence, darting as it does to actual and possible forms the realized work may take. It allows the painter to pursue freely what he or she has glimpsed within or apperceived without.

By the time the spectator's eye encounters a finished painting, its original vision has been worked and re-worked, thickened to the point that it is no longer anything like a direct transcription of an occurrence, however inspirational a given event may have been in its genesis: say, the bombing of Guernica in the

67. Schmitz's photograph is part of the same exhibition, *Heute bis Jetzt,* cited above in n. 64.

68. See Arthur Danto, *The Transfiguration of the Commonplace* (Cambridge: Harvard University Press, 1981).

69. Cited by Merleau-Ponty, "Eye and Mind," p. 164. As a result, the image in painting is "the inside of the outside and the outside of the inside" (Merleau-Ponty, ibid.).

case of Picasso's painting of the same name. Rather than an instantaneous replay of any such event (as is the reportorial photograph), even the most realistic painting reaches us as a late-flowering product of countless interventions on the part of the artist, all of which are closely tied to the glance: touches, manipulations, strokings, scratchings, and more. (These latter are graphically evident in the generation of *Guernica*.[70]) These moves are provisional but they are not mere posturings; they provide texture to the artwork—to the point where one could claim that paintings are textural creations, conjointly brought forth by deft hand and eye motions that build up a veritable tissue of colors, lines, and figures. Viewed in this light, Richter's *Vermalung Nr. 329* is an epitome of painting itself: its image is the very image of sheer texturality, exuding delight in the thickness of paint applied to itself, layer upon layer being laid down on top of canvas.[71]

At such a transfigured work, the spectator is invited primarily to glance. Since it does not purport to preserve any prior event—not even the event of the artist's vigorous gestures that created it: at the most, it *embodies* these latter, as in Jackson Pollock's action paintings—I as viewer am not being asked to contribute to its continuation, to prop up its material fragility, to ratify its accuracy. These latter aims are better served by the gaze. Instead, I have the luxury of sheer looking, whose emblematic form is the glance. The glance prospers precisely in the face of a fait accompli, from being in front of a finished work—off whose worked-through surface it can bounce and play. Not having the burden of maintaining by witnessing, my glance plays with/in the thick surface of the work itself, on which singular depths reside. Nor am I bound to any past moment of happening; nothing like the imperative instant of the shot, "the moment when the camera's shutter admits light," is here at stake. Instead of prolonging the duration of any such moment, I am free to extend the temporality of the work into an open future. "If creations [such as paintings] are not a possession," concludes Merleau-Ponty, "it is not only that, like all things, they pass away; it is also that they have almost all their life before them."[72] And if this is so, it is very much thanks to the free play of the glance, which rejoins the equally free play of the imagination. Each of these unhindered acts, glance and imagination alike, move freely in a way that depends on a prior materiality, whether in the form of a manifold of sensibility or an accomplished painting: the impassivity of the latter releases the freedom of the former. But when the material factor is less insistent or obtrusive—as is manifestly the case with the photograph per se—we are

70. For a close study of the generation of this painting, see Rudolf Arnheim, *Picasso's Guernica: The Genesis of a Painting* (Berkeley: University of California Press, 1962).

71. Another way of putting the difference here under discussion is in terms of comparative finality. In the case of a photograph, our look is tempted to stay with it as a final state of things: the image is fixed forever, both by its content and its moment of origin. A painting, in contrast, gives us no comparably fixed or final view—not even the most representational painting does so—so that we are not tempted to grasp it in a gaze that answers to it by its own fixity, much less its finality; rather, we glance at it in its contingent historicity and readiness for revision.

72. Merleau-Ponty, "Eye and Mind," p. 190.

called upon to contribute more concretely and directly to the work itself: a contribution that, in the visual realm, characteristically takes the form of gazing.

This is not to say that there is always and everywhere an absolute distinction to be made between photographic and painterly images. There are many combinatory, intermediate cases. These include the fact that most paintings now reach us by way of the "imaginary museum" (Malraux) provided by photographic reproduction. The majority of paintings we know have first come to us by way of their photographic image in albums, art history books, photographs taken by friends and family members, and so on. This is only poetic justice—as if to confirm the fears of certain nineteenth-century painters who thought that the superior representational means offered by photography would put them out of business![73]

To make matters worse, some photographs, viewed at a certain distance, appear to be realistic paintings, especially those that convey the color and texture of their originals in convincing detail.[74] And the converse can happen as well: paintings can closely resemble photographs, as in the hyperrealism of Eve Ingalls or Richard Estes; such artists as these, and many others, do not hesitate to base their paintings on actual photographs.[75] William Klein, in the "contacts peints" to which I alluded earlier, actively combines painting (in the form of brushed-in primary colors) with photography (in actual photographic images of people and events that are framed by these same bold strokes of color). In each of these hybrid instances, we are called upon not just to discern differences between the two kinds of image but to valorize their very ambiguity and sometimes their indiscernibility. Which means in effect that we are asked both to gaze and to glance in another pas de deux that rejoins as well as reinforces the two-step of body and glance. These are moments when any pretension to offer an eidetic analysis of gaze and glance in strictly separate terms breaks down, for now they have become inseparable in fact even if distinguishable in principle.

The existence of such internecine cases means that painterly and photographic images possess something that sets them apart from other kinds of image such as the auditory or the haptic. This is their *planar presentation:* the fact that each form of image is given in a "picture plane" or pictorial surface that is for the most part flat, smooth, and perpendicular to the viewer. Apparent exceptions are all variations on this planiform perpendicularity: for example,

73. For a discussion of this situation, see E. H. Gombrich, *Art and Illusion: A Study in the Psychology of Pictorial Representation* (Princeton, N.J.: Princeton University Press, 1960), pp. 30–33, 56–58 as well as Greg Horowitz's dissenting view whereby nineteenth-century realism was already breaking down from its own internal problems, so that the reference to the superior technology of photography was only a ploy to divert attention from more serious issues: Greg Horowitz, unpublished talk at a meeting on art at Northwestern University organized by David Michael Kleinberg-Levin: April 2002.

74. I here think of the work of Hannes Norberg, who photographs the play of light and shadow in compositions that look very like painted verandas. In other cases, a photograph can resemble a print, e.g., in the case of Elger Esser.

75. For a discussion of Eve Ingalls's work, see my *Earth-Mapping: Artists Reshaping Landscape* (Minneapolis: University of Minnesota Press, 2005), chap. 5.

paintings that are done in an impasto manner (such as the abstractions of Hans Hoffman), tilted slightly (certain works by Marcel Duchamp), literally torn and holey (Frank Stella), or composed of juxtaposed fabrics (Alberto Mori). Similarly for the photographic image: the colossal *Stammbaum* (that is, "Genealogical Tree") by Claudia van Koolwijk in a recent Düssseldorf photograph show towers over the viewer and takes up an entire wall (circa sixty-feet high). Viewing it from the museum floor, one feels that it bends over at the top (this is an effect of hyperbolic space perception); but it remains a set of flat images on a flat wall, the images linked by an esoteric script that establishes and traces the genealogical tree. Enormous and complex as this composite work is, it remains an exercise in the planiformity of the image—and in this respect is still deeply linked to painting, despite all the manifest differences. The same work embodies the perpendicularity of the pictorial image as presented to the viewer, who is very much aware of being located on the floor as he or she looks up at the work: that is to say, situated on a horizontal plane at right angles to the massively vertical wallwork. In this circumstance, the upright posture of the viewer colludes with the colossal pictoriality of the image-thing.

Both the planar and the perpendicular contribute powerfully to the effective presentation of the painterly or photographic image. Each aspect or dimension is essential to making this image something sheerly phenomenal—a matter of pure show: as being what it is by appearing as it does. Fully considered, each is an image-thing in its own right: a *thing* whose being is found wholly in its self-presentation, that is, in its also being an *image*. What could be more self-presentational than an image whose primary predicates are those of being a flattened-out presentation, having a smooth surface, and possessing a vertical stature? These features vie with sheer luminosity as bases for making an image *manifest*—for making it not just accessible to our perception but perspicuously so.[76] This is so whether the image purports to be pictorial or not. Such features ensure that, whatever complications may arise in the production of a given image (for example, by way of experimentation with new materials, the intrusion of unforeseen effects, the artist's lack of energy or will, an adequate amount of wall space, and so on), it will present itself finally as *one image*—one painting, one photograph—and this image will be as worthy of our glance as it is of our gaze. It will solicit at least one of these two ways of looking, and sometimes both in tandem, but always as a phenomenal presence, an image-thing to which we can entrust our ongoing vision.

This chapter ends at a quite different point than we reached in the first two chapters of this part. There, we found in the discussion of the ethical domain

---

76. Sometimes, of course, the sheer luminosity of light and atmosphere contribute directly to the phenomenal image, as in many plein-air photographs or in the school of painting aptly called "Luminism." See the discussion of the latter in Barbara Novak, *Nature and Culture: American Landscape and Painting, 1825–1875* (New York: Oxford University Press, 1995) and in my *Representing Place: Landscape Painting and Maps*, chaps. 2 and 3.

that there is no complementary or cooperative relationship between the glance and the gaze such as we have just seen in the case of painting and (even more so) photography. In ethical action, whether it bears on the human or the other-than-human, the glance takes a more decided priority. It takes the lead in such action by its power to grasp what needs to be done right away in a situation of ethical duress. In this situation, immersion in the gaze risks losing the moment of truth in which action has to be undertaken. It takes us off the ethical track by landing us in a very different enterprise, that in which observation and scrutiny are of predominant value. Ethics becomes contemplative rather than a matter of praxis; it ceases to be ethical action and is instead a form of scrutiny or thought. There may be a place for gazing in ethical inquiry and ethical theory—where issues of assessment and outcome, balance and symmetry are more likely to be at stake. But it arrests the action of being ethical in the concrete and specific ways that matter most when it is a question of initiating the conduct that is called for by a given situation.

Nor does the gaze mix well with the glance in ethical action, in which there is rarely the leisure to engage in both forms of vision. The painter can afford to pause and look over her painting with a reflective gaze before returning to it in a sally of glances. To go from glance to gaze, or back again, is also a frequent option for the spectator who may contemplate a painting from afar but glances at it close-up. But any such alternation of visual acts is a liability in demanding ethical circumstances, where apposite and swift judgments are not only prized but called for.

If the glance is of special but not exclusive value in the visual arts, it is indispensable to ethical actions of the sorts I have discussed in chapters 10 and 11. We could get nowhere without it: we could not even get off the ground. The knowing glance tells us where to go and what we need to do in order to begin to be ethical; it indicates the first moves we should make; and it keeps alive a factor of spontaneity throughout, allowing crucial adjustments and redirections to be undertaken at short notice. It also leavens the ethical enterprise by preventing it from falling into that spirit of gravity from which so much ethical theory and practice alike suffer. It is the gaze that imports such a spirit into a praxis that needs to be maximally sensitive to the nuances of human and nonhuman distress; it deadens this praxis and leads it astray, substituting scrutiny for action by focusing on objecthood rather than on the surfaces that express the disturbance to which such action responds.

Art begins from surfaces as well, but it links up right away with material things and natural landscapes—to which it attempts to do aesthetic justice. In doing so, it draws upon the full gamut of human visual resources, among which the glance and the gaze are preeminent modalities. Recourse to them is therefore not diversionary but directive, and it is not surprising that the artist as well as the spectator of visual art employs both, even if not always in equal degree or in parallel practice. We have seen that the two acts are more evenly distributed in the creation and experience of photography than in the pursuit of painting.

Photography favors engagement in both acts—the glance in the original "shot," the gaze in the finished print—whereas in painting the glance tends to prevail both at the level of creation and spectation. Painting is typically a matter of a continual activation of the eye as the painted image evolves from the gestures of the artist's hand into the finished work that is savored by the glance of the spectator.

What matters, however, is not the glance's prevalence as such but that we recognize the importance of the glance to every visual art, including those I have not here been able to discuss: cinema, video, DVD, television, and much installation art. It is toward this recognition, too rarely granted, that my remarks on photography and painting are meant to contribute. In this regard, my treatment of art rejoins my earlier discussion of ethics, where the role of the glance has been even more completely neglected. It is time to underline the place of the glance in ethics as well as in art—in neither of which has its active ingredience yet received adequate acknowledgment.

CONCLUDING THOUGHTS

CATCHING SIGHT OF SURPRISE

Among the maxims on Lord Naoshige's wall, there
was this one: "Matters of great concern should be
treated lightly." Master Ittei commented, "Matters
of small concern should be treated seriously."

> —From the "Hagakure," as cited in *Ghost Dog:*
> *Way of the Samurai*, director Jim Jarmusch

Je ne cherche pas, je trouve.

> —Pablo Picasso

I

Why such a big book on such a small topic? Why have I taken so seriously a
matter of apparently minor concern, the mere human glance? You, my reader,
may well have asked yourself these very questions. When I started writing on the
glance, friends said to me, "Given the topic, this will *have to be a short book*! It
would be absurd to write a tome on the topic!" I may not have written a tome,
but I have put together something close to a treatise. This is not simply because
any topic of human interest invites endless description. More especially, it is
because the glance's own delicate operation, along with the subtlety of its insertion into many settings, call for close-up descriptions. To come down to its scale
of enactment is to engage in a detailed account; only such an account can begin
to capture what happens within its subtle substructures. If "matters of great
concern"—matters that call for the Spirit of Gravity—should be treated lightly,
"matters of small concern," which elicit the Lightness of Being, should be
treated seriously.

There is another reason why the present account has become so surprisingly
lengthy. This bears on the very nature of the glance itself, which exhibits what
I shall call the law of indefinite multiplicity. I employ "multiplicity" here in
Bergson's and Deleuze's positive sense of the heterogeneous—not as applied to
durational time or to rhizomatic Becoming (that is, their respective concerns)

but to the way in which the glance has shown itself apt to proliferate into innumerable avatars without ever reaching a lower limit, an infima species. At the same time, its analysis does not start from a single standard form—an ideal Glance—that is then divided and collected into a coherent assemblage of species. With both ends of the eidetic spectrum wide open, we have no choice but to start in medias res, as I did in part 1 of this book, where I tracked an open-ended variety of ways of glancing in contrast with gazing. This variety includes the glance's gift for collaborating with other basic intentional acts—most notably, with attention and perception, as these were studied in part 3—and sometimes with particular practices, as we found in part 4, where the role of the glance in aesthetic and ethical domains was explored. Moreover, in part 2 I studied two very different historical settings for the enactment of the glance—that is, ancient Athens and late-nineteenth-century Paris—where much the same proliferation was to be observed. In everything we look at, we see the multiplicity of the act, its resourceful adaptive powers, its penchant for finding new expressive extensions in every time and place in which it occurs.

One concrete sign of this indefinitely multiple character of the glance is the frequency with which I have been driven to describe it by means of hyphenated expressions such as glancing-at, glancing-around, glancing-into, glancing-back, glancing-through (and doubtless others not even mentioned in this book: for example, glancing-under, glancing-over). In contrast with the triplex structures that I have noted in my earlier investigations of place—for example, "right over there," reflecting the triaxial character of the human body as the primary agent of implacement—these dyadic terms reflect the ways in which a visual subject modalizes its glance in very specific ways. If the glance is an instantiation of the look (in addition to the gaze, the blink, the wink, and so on), these hyphenated terms represent how glancing itself happens in singular ways that are appropriate for certain settings and not for others, its ramification into diverse contexts.

Three cautionary points are in order. First, there is no core act of the glance that is qualified by these various adverbial or prepositional terms—as if there were a "basic act" (as Husserl called perception) entitled "the glance" that stays the same through a series of qualifications into "away," "into," "through," "around," and so forth. The various directions specified by these adverbs and prepositions so deeply restructure the glance in each instance as to constitute the equivalent of a new act. Second, no strict summation of such acts is possible. Tempting as it may be to draw up a definitive list—especially at this concluding moment of the book—no such compilation of kinds of glancing is called for. The modalities multiply without end: if a putative totality has emerged in the course of this book, it is nonetheless "detotalized" (in Sartre's expression). Third, just as there is no realizable totalization of such acts, so there is no least or minimal glance, the glance *tout court*—not even as an asymptote or ideal limit to which all acts of glancing aspire or toward which they tend. There is neither an upper nor a lower bound to the ways we can glance. This is why we have encountered such proliferation—and why this book itself has grown beyond expected limits.

There is always and only glancing this way, then that way, then some other way. Such various ways of glancing form a loose assemblage, a *Versammlung* as Heidegger would call it in his term for an action of informal gathering.[1]

It follows that there is no need, indeed no realistic possibility, of *defining* the glance. This ever-fertile activity fiercely resists being circumscribed in language. Just as it is not limited to a certain number of acts or forms of acts—not even those I sketch in the afterword—so it cannot be captured in so many words. It evades definition even as it bedevils description. Even referring to "the glance" is misleading insofar as it implies that it is some single, bare act. At every step, I have had to qualify it as "mercurial," "daring," "quicksilver," "quick-sighted," etc.—each of which points to its malleability and speed, which defy easy verbal formulation. Not only is glancing elusive but it is enormously versatile, able to change forms continually like Proteus. Taking on so many shapes in so many settings, glancing is a primary shape-shifting power in the realm of human vision.

The polyvalent power of glancing is such that it also serves as a tacit model for nonvisual acts and experiences. Thus, we speak of "a glancing touch," "a glancing remark"—not to mention a "glancing blow," one of the original meanings of the word itself. When we talk of "grazing the earth" with our hands or feet, we are evoking the haptic equivalent of the glance. This last example reminds us that there is a close relationship between touching and glancing: a glance can "caress" a surface, while lightly touching something is like glancing at it. Robert Lowell says that "the eye goes out to the light and touches it."[2] Hearing, too, is drawn into the expanded orbit of glancing: I can catch the gist of a conversation that is taking place nearby, cocking my ear to hear much as I direct my eye to glance at what is occurring in the same conversation at a visual level. Indeed, we are continually immersed in intersensorial situations wherein the glance (or its close analogue) is found in other sensory processes (and they in it). Far from belonging to sight alone, the glance takes us to the heart of such polysensory settings.

Just as Levinas extends what counts as "face" to parts of the lived body other than the frontal surface of the head (face is found in any expressive bodily gesture, he observes),[3] so the glance lends itself to forms of human comportment that have nothing to do with looking as such. This interfusion or transfer of felt sense suggests that we are here dealing with an overall action that characterizes both the glance and its many affiliated and parallel acts. This action is that of *skimming a sensuous surface.* Whether touching a tabletop lightly with a finger or glancing at it, or catching a phrase in a conversation taking place nearby, I do

1. A concrete case of such assemblage is found in the group of "gl-" words associated with the glance: glitter, glimmer, gleam, glide, *glissement*, etc.

2. As reported by Eve Ingalls; conversation, June 2002.

3. See Emmanuel Levinas, *Ethics and Infinity: Conversations with Philippe Nemo*, tr. R. Cohen (Pittsburgh: Duquesne University Press, 1995), p. 97: "the whole human body is in [a] sense more or less face."

not linger on the touched or seen surface of the table or the verbal surface of the words. After gliding over these surfaces, my touch or look or hearing moves on to other surfaces, perhaps those of a chair or rug or the clothes of the people who are talking. I skim such surfaces much as a stone skips over a body of water when I throw it.

The surfaces over which we thus leap are *periphenomena:* appearances whose paradigm is neither perception (with its emphasis on the directly given and robustly materialized object) nor thought (a cognitive operation with tenuous ties to bodily expression). The basic action is that of grazing against, or coming alongside, a surface only to move quickly onto another surface, whether the moving is accomplished by the eye or the ear, the hand or arm or leg. Periphenomena have been conspicuously neglected by philosophers, with only rare exceptions; one of them is Hume's description of imagination as "a gentle force."[4] For the most part, philosophers (including Hume when he discusses perception) prefer to concentrate on full-bodied things and events that are more than mere surfaces; they valorize persistent *phenomena.* In the *Critique of Pure Reason,* Kant focuses on just this: "phenomena" in their lawlikeness and in their continuity with noumenal depths of which they are the determinate appearances.

In contrast, the study of glancing leads us to emphasize the importance of surfaces as such. Such surfaces realize a special kind of phenomenality—"periphenomenality." I speak of *peri*phenomena in order to indicate that such appearances are situated *around* the perceptual field, *on* its margins or *in* its crevices. They elude direct grasp or stable seeing—in short, the gaze—but precisely as such they are the rightful contents of the glance and its nonvisual equivalents. (In this context, I prefer "periphenomena" to "epiphenomena," a term whose prefix signifies what lies *on top of* phenomena.) In the case of the glance and its polysensory extensions, we have to do with surface appearances that arrange themselves in the apperceptual field, not being coextensive with this field but punctuating it in the guise of images and traces that are located anywhere—anywhere except at the very center, the steady cynosure, of vision. Periphenomena are fugitive presences that our glance (or its analogue) skims for their surface features. As such, they constitute a periphenomenal whole that, though inhabiting the phenomenal world (they do not reside in some separate, invisible realm), adds a luminescent dimension to this latter world, that of everyday sensing. It is to the luminescence, the gleam and the glitter, that our glances are first attracted, and it is the same shimmering surfaces that deftly guide subsequent glancings.

---

4. For Hume's description of imagination as "that gentle force, which commonly prevails," which I have cited in chap. 9, see *A Treatise of Human Nature,* ed. L. A. Selby-Bigge (Oxford: Clarendon Press, 1967), p. 10. See William Earle's call for a new enterprise of "periphenomenology" in his book, *The Autobiographical Consciousness: A Philosophical Inquiry into Existence* (Chicago: Quadrangle, 1972).

II

Despite the ease of its transferability to other sensory domains and its own unending proliferation—both being factors of aggrandizement—the most striking single lesson we learn from a study of the glance is the Logic of the Less: the Lesser Logic, as it were.[5] In whatever context we have considered the glance, we see it as possessing powers of discernment and of specific effect in circumstances where its unprepossessing presence would not seem to make a telling difference. Yet as Master Ittei intimates in the above epigraph, from very little much can come, and in the case of glancing it comes with unexpected force. For example, taking a glance at an artwork tells me at once what it is like: what style it is in, what medium it is made of, even what artist has created it (and often at what stage of his career). Just by glancing at other humans, moreover, I instantly recognize them to be the singular beings they are—singular to the paradoxical point of being universal. And if the same glance moves out into the natural environment, it takes in much that is telling beyond the human world.

The More that issues from the Less of the glancing look is not a matter of better discernment alone. It is a matter of concrete consequences. If I regard humans as singular cum universal, I treat them differently than were I to see them as merely different from each other; to take a work of art as having a certain style is in turn to respond to it in quite particular ways—to keep looking at it if it is a style I like, or to withdraw my look rapidly if not; and if I espy undue environmental damage, I may be led to appropriate action in an effort to ameliorate the situation. None of these consequences is necessary; but each of them is preceded by a glance that precipitates their enactment—that *releases* them from the confinement of the not-noticed. After they have arisen, further glances may influence the exact form taken by these consequences: say, suggesting the comportment I should take toward someone I see being beaten (for example, striding toward the perpetrator rather than calling the police), or regarding the fate of trees savaged on a mountain slope (for instance, formally complaining to the Forest Service for letting this destruction happen), or concerning an artwork that attracts me (for example, beginning to paint in this style myself).

It follows that the glance is at once highly differentiating in its discernment and quite differentiated in its effects. This double virtue also belongs to the Logic of the Less. On the one hand, the glance is remarkably discriminating as we have come to see from its close alliance with acts of attention. It is often the basis for detecting the "just noticeable difference" (JND) that was the focus of so much early experimental work on perceptual thresholds.[6] This is the minimal

5. "Lesser Logic" refers to Hegel's shorter version of his *Encyclopedia of Philosophical Sciences.* I have discussed a comparable phenomenon earlier under the heading of "the Law of Diminutive Support": see chap. 10, section V.

6. A classical formulation of the just-noticeable difference is this: "any stimulus escapes notice when it falls below a certain point . . . stimulus differences cannot be noticed below that threshold" (Gustav Fechner, *Elements of Psychophysics,* tr. H. Adler [New York: Holt, Rine-

difference of detection that can make a major difference in perceptual judgment. Without the bare apprehension of a JND, we would see two colors (or two values of the same color) as the same and would not judge them to be different. On the other hand, the glance gives rise to very nuanced effects—not just any effects, but *this very* effect, one that is quite appropriate in the circumstance. The nuance is often expressed by an adverb: I strode toward the assailant on Hudson Street in Chicago "defiantly," my friend in Montana took legal action "deftly," and I may come to paint "concertedly" when I am influenced by a certain painting done in a particular style. In all such cases, and on both sides of the distinction between discernment and response, *the nuance captured by a glance makes a decisive difference.*[7]

Such nuance is to be contrasted with the blunter reaches of the glance in its dismissive and disdainful modalities: the withering look, the glance that puts down, the glance that classifies stereotypically, the glance that refuses to look. These avatars of the glance, though not prominent in my account, emerge in the shadow of the more prospective and productive dimensions of glancing on which I have placed primary emphasis. In their case, nuance is lost by engaging in a forced and often diremptive choice: this person I now perceive is regarded as black or white (in racial terms that depend wholly on skin color), male or female (overlooking the possibility of transgendered people), or this environment is simply healthy or sick (not paying enough attention to transitional states of nature, such as after a forest fire). True, my glance is frequently drawn to glaring differences: say, between burnt-out stumps and intact trees untouched by the fire. But this is not the same as submitting to a fixed binary choice between sickness and health: the symptom catches my glancing eye, but the form of the choice comes from elsewhere (for example, from preexisting knowledge of what constitutes a "healthy" or a "sick" environment). Or when I glance contemptuously at someone I take to be of "lower" class or race or gender—even more drastically, when I refuse to look at this person at all (as in the Musselmänner of the extermination camps: at whom no one was willing to look[8])—I have already made a choice between what is worth looking at and what is not. I have decided in advance where, and how, and when to glance in terms of a much too simplified notion of what I should devote my glances to. I have abandoned the nuance of the glance to the rigors of righteousness—or to the comfort of complacency.

---

hart, 1966; original ed., 1860], p. 208). Jonathan Crary, who quotes this passage, discusses its importance for the understanding of attention in the context of nineteenth-century experimental psychology: see Jonathan Crary, *Suspensions of Perception: Attention, Spectacle, and Modern Culture* (Cambridge, Mass.: MIT Press, 1999), p. 26.

7. It was to underline the importance of such nuance that I discussed the distinction between "apperception" and "perception" in chaps. 7, 10, and 11; only apperception, belonging properly to glancing, appreciates the subtleties of nuanced differences among the contents of ordinary perceptions.

8. I deal with these matters further in my unpublished essay, "Witnessing (in) the Holocaust: The Suppression of the Glance in Dire Circumstances," 2002.

Despite their very perversity and destructiveness, these darker modalities of the glance still follow the logic of the less. For here too we see the same movement from something diminutive in origin to something major in outcome. The least glance can wither, and have devastating consequences for an entire lifetime, as we saw in the case of the incident that was so formative for W. E. B. Du Bois: a single, scornful glance of nonacceptance from a white playmate placed him immediately in the infernal category of "nigger," engendering a "second consciousness" that was never to leave him. Not to be recognized as fully human—as a singular specimen of a common species—was enough to suggest that he belonged to another, inferior race: to impose upon him a fixed persona that was foreign to the free being he knew himself to be. After the trauma of receiving this early hostile glance, he remained free to act on the basis of this persona or to reframe himself otherwise: say, as a singular subject despite the negative judgment implicit in the other's look. Either way, however, he had to take the dismissive glance of his playmate into account: whether by accepting its verdict of racial inferiority or by contesting and resisting it. What began as a look casually cast on a playground in New England ended by shaping a lifetime of conflicted response.[9]

The lower limit of the glance can be so extreme as to be virtually a null point yet still have a powerful effect. Thus, even when someone is *not* glanced at, with the implication that this person is beneath notice, the consequences can be incalculable, as in this incident from Toni Morrison's *The Bluest Eye:*

> She pulls off her shoe and takes out the three pennies. The gray head of Mr. Yacobowski looms up over the counter. He urges his eyes out of his thoughts to encounter her. Blue eyes. Blear-dropped. Slowly, like Indian summer moving imperceptibly toward fall, he looks toward her. Somewhere between retina and object, between vision and view, his eyes draw back, hesitate, and hover. At some fixed point in time and space he senses that he need not waste the effort of a glance. He does not see her, because for him there is nothing to see. How can a fifty-two-year-old white immigrant Storekeeper with the taste of potatoes and beer in his mouth, his mind honed on the doe-eyed Virgin Mary, his sensibilities blunted by a permanent awareness of loss, *see* a little black girl? Nothing in his life even suggested that the feat was possible, not to say desirable or necessary.[10]

Here the very absence of a glance is altogether telling: it tells us that someone who enters a person's range of view is judged not to deserve "the effort of a glance"—an effort that is itself so diminutive as to be all the more noteworthy for not being enacted. As a result of this nonaction, the black girl is not acknowledged in her singularity and thus not in her common humanity either. From the

---

9. I am not claiming that this traumatic glance was the only determinant in Dubois's struggles with his personal and racial identity; but I am maintaining that it precipitated these struggles and that, by its decisive tenor, it crystallized them in one stroke.

10. Toni Morrison, *The Bluest Eye* (New York: Plume, 1994), p. 48. I owe this citation to Barrie Karp.

bare beginning of a possible perception, a least notice, comes a quite consequential failure to look and thus to see.

In the end, it is difficult to say which is more devastating: to be judged inferior
by a withering glance, or to be held not worthy of any glance at all.

Besides these deleterious "deficient modes" (Heidegger), the Logic of the
Less takes various basic shapes, among them these four:

(i) *seeing more from less:* Not only in glancing but in all forms of visual perception we find ourselves in the extraordinary situation of being able to see a
great deal from a quite restricted viewpoint. It is not accidental that I have
made allusion more than once to Freud's metaphor of the "narrow defile,"
where "the finest prospects open up on every side."[11] This is paradigmatic
for all seeing, and not only for the "sudden discovery"[12] that is at stake in
Freud's own use of this metaphor. For we always *look out from a very
delimited position* as we perceive the world around us: we see from the
delimited region of our two eyes—enclosed as they are in our skulls, and set
just beneath our foreheads—and the restriction is reinforced by the fact
that our heads only take up part of our bodies, themselves very finite
organisms in a larger surrounding world. The fact that both the eyes and
the heads in which they are located *orbit* underlines the very circumstance
to which I here point: for the orbiting is an action that optimizes information intake in an otherwise highly constricted circumstance. It allows us to
see more—much more than were our head rigidly attached to our body, as
with certain insects. Our closely coordinated eyes, acting as monitors
perched on a lived and mobile body, enable us to reach far and wide into
the visual environment. Picking up an enormous amount of "information in
the light" (in Gibson's telling phrase),[13] they deliver to us prospects on
every side of our moving bodies. Looking out from within a very compressed position in the head, our eyes lead us into the larger world of what
is seen. A concrete exemplification of this fact is found in Marcel Duchamp's late work, *Étant donnés* (1946–1966), in which the viewer is invited to look through a pinhole, from beyond which an entire landscape
unfolds, centered on a naked woman lying spread-eagle on her back in the
near distance. This arresting artwork underscores the fact that the position
and movement of the eyes are highly circumscribed, yet their potential
scope is considerable. Seen from this context, the glance is only a particularly striking instance of the more general rule that we see a great deal
on the basis of delimited physical and physiological means.

11. Sigmund Freud, *The Interpretation of Dreams*, tr. J. Strachey in *Standard Edition of the
Complete Psychological Works* (London: Hogarth Press, 1953), vol. 4, p. 122.
12. "We find ourselves in the full daylight of a sudden discovery" (ibid.)—i.e., the discovery
of the wish-fulfilling basis of dreams.
13. See J. J. Gibson, *The Ecological Approach to Visual Perception* (Hillsdale, N.J.: Erlbaum,
1986), chap. 5, "The Ambient Optic Array." Gibson emphasizes the importance of the head's
orbiting motions at ibid., pp. 203–222.

(ii) *getting there from here:* Every journey begins with the least step, and all movement through space requires that our lived body, guided by vision as just described, and supplemented by other perceptual means (such as hearing, touching, and various synaesthetic combinations) initiates and sustains its actions by incremental units. These units can be diminishingly small, and yet when concatenated they take us to our goal. This brings us to Zeno's question: how can such units, especially if they are increasingly diminished in extent (in the Zenonian format each unit is half of the preceding), get us to a designated goal having a definite position in world-space? Won't they always bring us short of this goal? In fact, we reach our goal despite this theoretical problem. As Bergson says, we do so because it is a matter of "motion within duration" rather than of punctiform positions within a static space: the former is qualitatively different from the latter and is "indivisible" despite Zeno's effort to divide it into ever-decreasing steps that are more appropriate to the tortoise than to Achilles, who moves in and with duration and not simply across space.[14] His movement takes place in another order than that of homogeneous space: it occurs in the order of heterogeneous qualitative becoming; Zeno's paradox would obtain only if homogeneous space were the exclusive basis for all motion, whereas it is in fact only the basis for measuring relative positions in space (for example, coming halfway to the goal). On the alternative description, Achilles's body moves decisively to its goal even if his steps are quite modest in measured extent. And that is just the point: a series of movements, however diminutive or delayed or distracted, will eventually take us to our destination if we are headed in the right direction. Given enough time and patience, ingenuity and luck, we will get from our current place in the near sphere to the most remote place in the far sphere. We will get from Here to There—from this very particular place to the most capacious region: say, from County Cork, Ireland, to New York, the path of my Irish forebears. From the delimited domain of being just here we are able, taking the right steps (whether by sailing over the sea or walking on the land), to arrive somewhere that is at once far from here and open-ended in comparison. From the intense actuality of the Less we reach the extensive reality of the More.

(iii) *getting more from less:* If we move beyond the lived body proper—still very much at stake in (i) and (ii)—we enter the vast realm of *return:* that is, of receiving back from our efforts far more than we put into them. Sometimes this occurs in a negative modality: "a stitch in time saves nine" in the familiar adage of preventive practical wisdom; but it also takes on a much

---

14. The phrase "motion within duration" occurs in Henri Bergson, *Time and Free Will: An Essay on the Immediate Data of Consciousness,* tr. F. L. Pogson (New York: Dover, 2001), p. 114: "Why resort to a metaphysical hypothesis, however ingenious, about the nature of space, time, and motion, when immediate intuition shows us motion within duration, and duration outside space?" Achilles moves in and through duration—his moving is part of its becoming—and not in "indefinitely divisible [hence measurable] space" (ibid.).

more positive twist in other instances. According to Chomskian linguistics, a determinate set of syntactical rules is capable of generating an infinite number of coherent sentences.[15] In the logic of the gift as developed by Derrida in the wake of Marcel Mauss, we encounter another instance of the Logic of the Less: of getting more from less, where (contra Chomsky) "more" is not quantifiable. In this case, the more means more than something equivalent to my gift: I cannot foresee, and must not expect, that what I get back from giving someone something is equivalent to my gift in value, quality, kind, extent, and so on.[16] On Derrida's acute assessment, I need to offer my gift—always delimited by its very nature (here is the "less")—in such a way that I not anticipate any return gift at all; indeed I must not even consciously consider my gift *as a gift* (for that is to enter into the circle of possible reciprocity).[17] The gift I make leads to something more than a gift in return—where "more" does not mean something more valuable but rather *other* than I had counted on: recall here how Plato interprets "different" as "other" in the *Sophist*. This is consistent with the analysis given in (ii), where we saw the purely quantitative cede place to the qualitative in the realm of movement: from one kind of action to another wholly different kind. Similarly, the more that we get by giving is not to be measured in determinate units of value but only in nonquantifiable terms, such that even if the donor gets nothing back from the donnee, the more of sheer generosity (that is, giving with no intention of being rewarded or even recognized) has occurred. We get more not by giving less but by disregarding the gift as gift—seeing it and its outcome as something other than we are taught to think in the conventional wisdom of getting more from more (for example, the larger the gift, the more it is appreciated).

(iv) *becoming more from less:* "Becoming" has shown itself to be crucial in the understanding of the bodily movement by which we get from one place to another. But it is of more general application in Lesser Logic, and this in several respects. First, there is the open potentiality of any process of organic or

15. "It is this which so strikes Chomsky—how the child is able to arrive at so much from so little" (Oliver Sacks, *Seeing Voices: A Journey into the World of the Deaf* [Berkeley: University of California Press, 1989], p. 81).

16. A gift, says Derrida, is "annulled each time there is restitution or countergift" (Jacques Derrida, *Given Time I: Counterfeit Money*, tr. Peggy Kamuf [Chicago: University of Chicago Press, 1992], p. 12). Derrida here questions the association of the return gift with the discharge of indebtedness or the maintaining of reciprocity. Instead: "There is gift, if there is any, only in what interrupts the system as well as the symbol, in a partition without return . . . *it is necessary* that the donnee not give back, amortize, reimburse, acquit himself, enter into a contract . . . the donor ought not count on restitution" (ibid., p. 13; his italics).

17. "The gift must not even appear or signify, consciously or unconsciously, *as* gift for the donors . . . [for then] it would be engaged in a symbolic, sacrificial, or economic structure that would annul the gift in the ritual circle of the debt. . . . The simple intention to give [already] . . . suffices to make a return payment to oneself" (ibid., p. 23; his italics).

social becoming. This is particularly evident in evolution: from a quite limited gene pool, shared significantly with many lower organisms, humans and other advanced species have evolved in ways and to an extent that could not have been fully foreseen. Second, a premium or surcharge may accrue upon a given event or occasion in equally unforeseeable ways; an event that at first seems comparatively insignificant or trivial assumes a special valence and force that have significant and even fateful consequences: for example, a third-party candidate who takes votes away from a certain favored candidate, who then loses the election to another candidate of less merit. Third, an "augmentation of being" (in Gadamer's phrase) can arise in circumstances as diverse as art and health, education and psychotherapy, love and hatred. In each case, the strictures of a first circumstance are suspended or trespassed—in any case, transcended—in the course of time, in ways that cannot be anticipated. Thus, the least watercolor sketch by an eccentric and obscure artist from Aix-en-Provence becomes formative of a new conception of painting worldwide; or what begins as mere attraction or infatuation becomes an enduring love, or else simple hatred turns into rage; physical exercise leads to a new sense of physical well-being that exceeds any measurable medical benefits; learning a new language opens up whole new worlds; and so forth. In every such instance, there is an augmentation in being— being creative, being in love, being healthy, being hateful—in the course of becoming. Or rather, the very process of becoming, conceived as a heterogeneous multiplicity or a flux of force, gives rise to an augmented being.

I am here pointing to four basic ways by which More derives from Less in quite diverse domains. This helps us to see that glancing is to be seen as an instance of a far more general pattern. But it is not just an indifferent instance— one among others. It is itself a leading exemplar of the pattern, a privileged way by which the Logic of the Less occurs daily, indeed minute by minute, second to second. In the dynamic field of this Logic, it steals the march on other acts—not surprisingly, considering that our ingression into the life-world is so often initiated by a glance and then is sustained by other glances. We glance out into this world before looking carefully into it or before acting in it in some more focused or deliberate way. In this regard, the glance plays a probative role—trying out something in advance of adopting more elaborate procedures. It enacts an "experimental logic" in Dewey's phrase, and it proceeds by what Pierce called "abduction"—that is, the projection of hypotheses prior to definitive experiences.[18] The glance is, again in Deleuze and Guattari's suggestive term, a "probe-head."[19] What is special about the glance in this context is its abductive outreach

18. See John Dewey, *Essays in Experimental Logic* (New York: Dover, 1916); on abduction, see Charles S. Peirce in *The Essential Peirce: Selected Philosophical Writings 1893–1913,* ed. N. Houser et al. (Bloomington: Indiana University Press, 1998), p. 95.
19. On the probe-head, see Gilles Deleuze and Félix Guattari, *A Thousand Plateaus,* tr.

in the midst of the continual experimentation that the life of vision requires. This is an outreach that is notably sparse in its means and economic in its operation. Little is wasted in the domain of the glance, and much is gained at very little human or physical cost to the glancer. This makes glancing at once exemplary and extraordinary: exemplary for other acts that instantiate the Logic of the Less, extraordinary in that it is so often itself in the literal avant-garde of these other acts, probing the early edges of the still-to-come. It is at once *out there* in the visual field and *in here* in the act of vision itself: it leaps ahead of the perceiving subject, and yet it does so only from a position of assured proximity to this subject, being an integral part of her or his visual repertoire. Thanks to the closely paired features of the out-there and the in-here, the glance sets a precedent for that part of visual experience that is at once innovative and outgoing—that refuses to stay put or settle down, that makes a virtue of being continually wayward. Glancing is a "way out" feature of vision in two senses: its beam goes way out into the scene it witnesses and it is a way out for the subject to savor this scene in the brevity of a moment. All stems from the glance's being so deeply set within the seeing subject. Here, too, the depths are on the surface.

Glancing does all this without forcing itself on the rest of vision, much less by compelling it to happen. As we have seen at many reprises, the enactment of the glance is as light as it is nuanced. Indeed, its subtlety enhances its pilot position, enabling its fine visual rays to find their way through dense media and into coarse substances. In this respect, the glance is exemplary for other, kindred phenomena: style (such as in painting, dancing, fashion in clothing, hairstyle, and so on); gestures of many kinds (where slight modulations can make a great deal of difference); or the exact form of writing (in which the kind of print, along with various typographical conventions, play a formative role). In all these cases, the glance counts less for its probative powers than for the finesse with which it takes us into the intimate infrastructures of things regarded as periphenomena, taking its genius for nuance to ever-new levels of discernment. The operative principle is this: subtle itself, it can interleave itself dexterously into the most intricate structures of that which it takes in so deftly.[20]

The delicate force of the glance—a force allowing it to be at once a source of augmented effects and of gentle insinuations—comes from its being next to nothing in its own slender being: "presque rien" in Jankélévitch's poignant phrase.[21] No wonder an act so "nearly nothing," so negligible in periphenomenal

---

B. Massumi (Minneapolis: University of Minnesota Press, 1987), p. 190: probe-heads "dismantle the strata in their wake, break through the walls of significance, pour out of the holes of subjectivity, fell trees in favor of veritable rhizomes, and steer the flows down lines of positive deterritorialization or creative flight." I owe this suggestion to Manuel de Landa at the conference "Becomings," University of Richmond, April 1997.

20. The persistence of the visual model in the history of thinking about perception may well reflect the fact that such rays act as material analogues of the subtlety of the glance in its ingressive and outgoing operations.

21. See Vladimir Jankélévitch, *Philosophie Premiére: Introduction à une Philosophie du 'presque'* (Paris: Presses Universitaires de France, 1954).

presence, has been so often neglected! Apparently ineffectual in its actions and consequences, it would seem to ask for disregard—and dis-regarded it has been! And yet behind the history of neglect lies another level of truth: only an act situated in such proximity to the vanishing point of our experience—to the "null-point of orientation" in Husserl's phrase[22]—could play such an effective ingressive role in human life. The glance is not nothing (for then it would have no power or force of its own), but it is also not a simple something either: something stable or stationary, much less substantial. Nor is it situated halfway in between something and nothing, as if it were a *via media* between the robustness of perceptual particulars and the vanishingness of thought—in a middle position akin to that of human existence on Descartes's view: that is, situated midway between God and nothing.[23] It is, rather, almost nothing—*next to nothing*, a few degrees to its right as it were, rendering it likely to be overlooked yet (for this very reason) all the more potent in its fine-fingered forays. This makes its operation analogous to guerilla warfare, in which a scattered and all but invisible force can be quite effective; or to nomadic existence, in which there is no clinging to a central place of habitation but rather continual circulation between places each of which is more or less off-center—or, more exactly, for which there is no definite geographical center in the first place.[24]

So too the trajectory of the glance is almost always that of moving from the center of a scene toward its periphery in a perpetual agitated motion that is nevertheless capable of making a significant discovery that eludes even the most conscientious gaze. This is the converse of the circumstance in Poe's short story "The Purloined Letter," wherein the police officers fail to detect what stares them in the face: the sought-after letter dangling straight down from the chimney. The letter evaded the officers' concerted gazes, blind as they were to the obvious. Had they only trusted their ability to glance around the room spontaneously in an overall sweeping action, they would have discovered the letter much sooner. Instead of following the logic of 1 versus 0 (i.e., the letter is *either* here *or* there), they should have trusted in the alternative logic of 1 versus 1.2 or 1.7— according to which the letter is *somewhere* in the room in any of several possible locations, including the most obvious. This would have been to respect the indirection of a logic of a lesser order, in which effects exceed their known causes, and insight is augmented beyond the definite deliverances of a strictly perceptual

22. The "Null der Orientierung" is equivalent to the "absolute Here" (*absolutes Hier*) of my lived body: "worldly things" perceived around me "are oriented with respect to here and there, right and left, etc., whereby a firm null-point of orientation persists, so to speak, as absolute here" (Edmund Husserl, "The World of the Living Present and the Constitution of the Surrounding World External to the Organism," tr. F. A. Elliston and L. Langsdorf, in P. McCormick and F. A. Elliston, eds., *Husserl: Shorter Works* [Notre Dame, Ind.: University of Notre Dame Press, 1981]; p. 250).

23. Compare Descartes's claim concerning human existence as lying halfway between God and nothing: see René Descartes, *Meditations on First Philosophy*, Meditation II.

24. For a much more complete description of nomadic existence in contrast with a fixed and central "state apparatus," see *A Thousand Plateaus*, tr. B. Massumi (Minneapolis: University of Minnesota Press, 1987), chap. 12, "Nomadology."

analysis. The apperception of the nomadic glance augments the perception of the sedentary gaze thanks to a vagrant operation that may seem next to nothing in its unpredictable flights and sudden lateral leaps. Such leaps and flights across periphenomenal space may be difficult to track, but they are nonetheless often quite consequential in their outcome: we get to the goal of 1 more effectively from its decimal diversions than from going straight from 0 to 1 or back again.

The guerilla movements of the glance resemble the blink of the eye by which they are often accompanied. The eye blinks as if to say that unmediated presence is too much to take in and must be closed out, however briefly. It gets to this same presence when the eye opens suddenly to encounter what had eluded perception in the unblinking stare: it sees somewhere within the visual field what had seemed just a moment ago nowhere present in the field itself. But it only gets to this from a periphery to which the glance first moves, jumping to the edge of the field before settling on any particular part of this same field. The jump, the *saltus,* occurs so rapidly that it is virtually untrackable: it is *presque rien.*[25]

III

From the Nearly Nothing to the Not is a short but important step. Given my extensive claims for the glance in this book—its largely unsuspected scope, its many forms and modalities, its agile alliances with other acts—it behooves us to determine what the glance is *not,* what its effective *limits* are. We need to consider not just the powers of the glance but its delimitations as well. I shall address these latter under three headings: epistemic, ethical, and aesthetic.

(a) *epistemic.* A given glance is not always correct or valid in its claims, implicit or explicit; it is as subject to error as any other act of cognition, and in certain regards even more so: for example, in its hasty appraisal, being unable or unwilling to persist in the inquiry it has itself opened up, and so on. Each of these represents what Aristotle might call "a defect of a virtue," for each represents a vulnerability that comes from being directed to surfaces—itself a primary strength of the glance, which has a decided gift for discerning surface qualities. But this very gift, fueling its characteristic preoccupation with periphenomena, has a definite downside that can be characterized as *epistemic impatience.* The moment in which my glance alights constitutes a cut in time wherein much happens that would not seem to be possible otherwise: in that moment, the glance realizes its special skill in discerning and distinguishing. But in that same

25. Concerning the unsuspected importance of the blink, see Malcolm Gladwell, *Blink: The Power of Thinking without Thinking* (New York: Little, Brown, 2005). Gladwell's analysis does not concentrate on visual blinking, however. He says expressly that his book "is not just a celebration of the glance" (ibid., p. 14). It is in fact an exploration of how often human beings make right decisions and judgments in a matter of seconds, whether or not these actions are accompanied by glances as such, much less based on them.

moment, the glance can go astray; it can literally mis-take what it sees, mis-apprehending it: seeing X not as Y (which it in fact is) but as Z (which it is not). The apperceptive grasp, equally adept at noting the detailed substructures of individual things as well as the major features of entire landscapes, can fall quickly into misapperception; it can misidentify the very thing it takes us to so quickly: It's not Charles, it's Jim! Nothing can prevent such misapprehension, just as nothing can guarantee the truth of the very apprehension that is effected in the glance. Greater knowledge as well as increased experience can render error less likely in the circumstance, yet never can it eliminate the sudden intrusion of errors into the glancing act. Examples of such errors include these:

(i) I look at a marsh that seems healthy at first glance, only to discover later that toxic wastes have recently been poured surreptitiously into it and are only beginning to take a toll, though this is not yet visible and cannot be known except by chemical analysis at this early point; in this case, appearances, the very surfaces themselves, mislead me into false confidence and, very likely, false inferences ("this marsh is OK and does not require further attention").

(ii) Conversely, I mistakenly judge from a glance that a swamp that has been polluted and that still looks sick is hopelessly corrupted; whereas in fact it is on its way to recovery through purification techniques whose full effects are not yet visible to the naked eye; glancing in good faith, I have been taken in by the appearances of the marsh.

(iii) I mistake the gender identity of someone I have just met, and learn the true identity only from a later conversation. I saw this person up close when I was first introduced—I cannot blame my mistake upon distance or other obscuring factors—and yet I took "him" to be a man and the gay partner of my friend David; but I find out subsequently that "he" is in fact a woman who is transgendered (breasts reduced, testosterone taken to induce growth of body hair, and so forth). In the brief moment of meeting, I overlooked certain telling signs such as "his" high-pitched voice, a certain way of smiling, even the look of "his" eyes, which came across as "male"; my glance was taken up by certain surfaces of this human subject rather than attending to others, and thereby I was taken in just in the way in which this person (and his/her partner) wished me to be: I was not deceived (such was certainly not the intent of anyone in this circumstance), but I was literally misled, that is, led to misidentify the gender of the person in question.[26]

(iv) I encounter a group of youths engaged in what appears to me to be violent behavior, and I consider intervening on the basis of my glance—much as I

---

26. This example serves at once to complicate and clarify the instance I cited in the introduction, where I claimed that disambiguation of gender is always possible in principle for glancing; I hold to this claim, even if (as the example just cited shows) a *given* glance can be mistaken.

did in Chicago in the example I discussed in chapter 10. Resisting my first impulse, I soon realize that these youths are practicing a form of martial art in which no one is being harmed—and which may even prevent harm if applied effectively on the right occasion.

Do such examples (each a variation on experiences described earlier) mean that I cannot trust in the glance—that it is an unreliable kind of looking? That would be an exaggerated inference. The situation is in fact more complex than this, for we must distinguish two epistemic levels of special import for the glance. On the first, I do correctly make out the sheer appearances and movements I see, however briefly and inadvertently I witness them; on the second, these same phenomena show themselves to signify something different from what I first take them to be. Let us call the first level that of *bare apperception;* here my powers of discernment and judgment are intact and trustworthy: I am right to think (and to say) "this marsh *looks* sick (or healthy)"; "this person *looks like* a man"; "these kids *seem* to be doing something violent." But on the second level, that of *a more careful and complete apprehension,* I am wrong to think or say these things, as subsequent experience teaches me. Here we may take a clue from the poet: "Let be be finale of seem."[27] The realm of seeming—the proper domain of the glance—must be brought to further finality when it comes to rendering true judgments: that is to say, judgments that are not only true-for-now (as is the tacit deliverance of every glance) but also true-for-other-times and, at the limit, true-for-all-times. Sometimes, of course, the two levels of experience and judgment coincide: what my glance takes to be the case really is the case: the clear-cut trees in Cottonwood Canyon really do disfigure the environment and are the victims of aggressive and acquisitive instincts. But in cases such as those cited just above, I have to practice patience, given that my first judgment, though true at the level of bare apperception, is not true of the full phenomenon that is revealed in a more extensive apprehension. My first judgment is *true to* the appearances, my second is *true about* the phenomenon itself. The former is apperceptively adequate but epistemically inadequate; the latter, building on the immediate results of apperception, is epistemically adequate—that is, as true as it can be of the whole circumstance when my glance comes to be supplemented by other acts (full-fledged perceptions, knowledge of various kinds, memories, the deliverance of theory, and so on). While the second level is necessary to the more complete picture, the first remains of indisputable value in its own right—and is itself an integral component of the second: there is no apprehension without apperception, whereas there can be apperception without apprehension.[28]

27. Wallace Stevens, "The Emperor of Ice Cream," in *Harmonium* (New York: Alfred A. Knopf, 1923).

28. Two clarifications are here in order. On the one hand, while the first level, that of bare apperception, is enacted exclusively by the glance and certain other forms of apperceptual

(b) *ethical.* The issue in ethics is *action* rather than *truth.* Hence the delimitations of the glance are in this case located in the area of failed or lacking doing rather than of mis-knowing. *Practical* knowing is indeed at stake—knowing how to act effectively in view of certain ethical principles—but not the theoretical knowing that is a properly epistemic concern. (If the latter is involved at all, it is to facilitate such preliminary steps as identification, disambiguation, and clarification.)

As with the epistemology of the glance, so its employment in ethical contexts occurs at two levels: that of immediate ethical insight, the sense of what is "good" or "evil"; and that of justified ethical practice, the active implementation of this insight in light of certain moral principles. It is one thing to grasp, without any hesitation, that something wrong is happening, an insight that may be accompanied by an impulse to intervene, as I did on Hudson Street in Chicago; but it is quite another to determine exactly what I should do about this primary grasping of the situation: "do" not just as an impulsive action but as a matter of principle. When I read the poverty in someone's circumstance directly from their emaciated physical state or from some other telling sign, I see what has happened to this afflicted person in a glance; but this apperception, reliable as it is and inspiring me to alleviate the other's distress (for example, by offering him or her the food I would otherwise consume myself), still does not tell me what action I ought to take to alleviate the dreadful situation in a more sustained way. Only considerable knowledge about the origins and effects of poverty and my own reflection on what to do about this particular poverty-stricken circumstance will lead to truly apposite intervention on my part; but by the time I take this last step, I may no longer be glancing, for I am then more invested in acting than in looking. Or we should say: acting *in the wake of* looking. For I need to have seen in the first place, witnessed with my own eyes (or, failing that, by a photograph of the destitution) the poverty itself as the alarming "problematic situation" (Dewey) that calls for my response. And it is most often by a glance that the primary detection of the problem (for example, wound, wrong, distress) occurs. Without that, my action will not be motivated by the personal concern that is essential to effective follow-through, nor can it build on the first-hand experience of an affliction. Once more, then, the apperceptive level proves to be essential to the next level: in this case, not to a more adequate or complete apprehension (an epistemic ideal) but to a better informed and more reflective response in the form of a considered action. Let me sketch a recent case in point:

---

awareness such as fleeting attention, the second level, that of appreciation, is performed by a multiplicity of acts (e.g., perception, memory, imagination, etc.). On the other hand, the two levels could be characterized as having two corresponding kinds of certainty: i.e., "naive certainty" (in Husserl's phrase) and increasing certainty. Note that Dewey also distinguishes between mere "certitude" and "certainty" (see John Dewey, *The Quest for Certainty* [New York: Putnam, 1960].)

> I am on a subway train in New York, the C line going downtown, and I suddenly see an unkempt person enter the car I'm on; he sets up a crude wooden table and proceeds to harangue his fellow passengers after first offering (in vain) the table for sale; he is clearly distressed, indeed quite disturbed, as becomes evident in the course of his ranting. Everyone on the car sees (and hears) this in a thrice; but no one, including myself, offers to help him, or even to talk to him; taking stock of this inaction—after at least four subway stops—he lurches out of the car with his portable table, still more enraged than when he first entered the car.

Here a disturbed individual caught the momentary attention of a captive audience: his desperation was evident in a glance at his disheveled appearance and distraught look, as well as in the briefest listening to his harangue (that is, the auditory equivalent of the glance). Included in this first apperception was a distinct sense not just of his troubled mental state but of the injustice of its very occurrence; whatever its source—his heated talk about the Gulf War made one suspect that his troubles stemmed from military service there—it was clear to all who noticed him that this person had been neglected if not outright mistreated by American institutions at large. All of this was evident in the merest glance. What was *not* yet evident was what to do about his suffering: how to address and alleviate it, even to eliminate it. I considered talking to him, but rejected this with the conveniently dismissive thoughts that "this may make matters worse" and "he won't listen to me anyway." I failed my glance by my abject inaction.

Other thoughts also arose from my bare glance (for example, about how to offer better psychiatric care to veterans), but none could be deemed definitive: without more knowledge of this man's exact circumstance and an appeal to certain general ethical principles (especially those that bear on human beings in distress), it was difficult to determine what should be done from what I had glimpsed in the opening moments of my encounter with him. The apperception of his suffering was unequivocal in what it announced to me: here is a human being in serious trouble. This moment of witnessing, based on nothing but a glance, sparked my ethical dilemma; it led to reflection on what was right to do. Yet no actual decision, much less any concrete action, was forthcoming in the circumstance, which was left in limbo as the man, muttering to himself, left the subway car in defiant anger. I had failed not only my glance but the man himself and his life situation.

A discrepancy between immediate ethical apperception and considered ethical action had opened up; and my glance, though calling for such consideration, was not able by itself alone to select the most effective and principled intervention, much less to carry it out in the circumstance. At the most, it might *suggest* what to do next, indicating certain lines of action rather than others. Also, the more often I find myself in comparable situations—and the more often I reflect on them in a principled way—the greater the likelihood that from a glance I can move swiftly to the right action: the three phases of apperception/reflection/action will then exist in closer proximity. (Apperception belongs to what I have been calling the first level; reflection and action to the second level.) But these

phases are always distinguishable in principle, and they will often be significantly separated in time from each other. It is the rare bodhisattva who acts
directly on what he or she sees: acts forthrightly in acting rightly, without any
recourse to subsequent reflection. For the most part—and certainly for myself
in the circumstance I have just described—a glance is necessary but not sufficient. I need to have it, but I also need more: time to reflect and time to act that
exceed the moment of the glance itself. Otherwise put: with the exception of
saints and other ethical adepts, a glance *as a glance* cannot determine definitively what to do, and how to do it, in any fully justified way. It can grasp the
other as a singular being who is in distress—who calls for my intervention. But it
cannot undertake the deliberative processes that justify this intervention. For
that, the invocation of moral rules (such as maxims and imperatives) as well as
more complete experiences of like situations (such as those stemming from the
plight of veterans of the first Gulf War)—along with the further act of subsuming
the latter under the former—are required before reflectively justifiable, right
action is to be taken. We encounter here another limit, this time a specifically
ethical limit, to the power and scope of the glance.

(c) *aesthetic.* Although a single glance is quite enough to take in the imagistic
component—the bare appearance—of a visual artwork, it does not suffice for
certain further actions I might wish to take in relation to it. Such actions include
passing critical judgment on the work, discussing it with others, writing about it,
or undertaking a comparable or related artwork myself. I have argued in chapter
12 for the indispensability of the immediate apperception of art, as giving us our
first inroad into aesthetic experience. This inroad is invaluable, and in any case
sets the stage for what is to come, whether in the form of conversation, writing, or
the creation of further images. In particular, my glance takes me to the aesthetic
surface—just there, right there. This is already a lot, for "there" signifies *there on
the surface;* however differently configured the aesthetic surface may be, it is on
it that the most pertinent and productive aesthetic action takes place. This holds
both for the artist and the spectator: for the artist, who sees in the evolving
surface of the artwork the crucial cues for further creation on his or her part; for
the spectator, who sees in the same surface the complex plane of aesthetic
qualities that make up his or her appreciation of the artwork. Neither knowing
(theoretically) nor acting (practically) but *creating* and *appreciating* are here at
stake: creating for the artist, appreciating for the spectator (and for the critic,
who takes spectatorship to another, still more articulate level)—and often both at
once for the artist who wishes to learn from his or others' previous work. Such
creating and/or appreciating constitute acts that carry forward the contribution
of the first glance, which cannot by itself alone assume full responsibility for
complete creation or full appreciation. Further glances may accompany both of
these acts, often in a decisive way—as when a painter can tell at a glance that the
changes she has just made are not the right ones. The more practiced the painter,
the more will a bare glance indicate what is to be done next. This is the correlate
of the spectator's sense that he likes, or dislikes, a painting on first seeing it; but

this sense, too, can evolve into a more nuanced looking that involves more glances in the process of checking to see if his emerging appreciation is justified by features on the actually proffered surface of the artwork. Nevertheless, both for the artist and the spectator, these later glances occur in more complex contexts whose contents eclipse what any single glance can deliver. The members of such a series (and the series itself as a whole) do not count for themselves alone, but only as part of the history of creation or appreciation that is by then fully under way. In its primal occurrence, a sole glance, however significant it may be, does not suffice—not once different levels of accomplishment are taken into consideration. This glance may well precipitate the onset of these levels, and other glances sustain their continuing development: early and late, glances remain integral to the genesis of creation and appreciation. But this does not mean we can count on them to bring these two experiences to completion. A concrete case in point will bring out this contrast.

Anselm Kiefer's enormous (circa 75″ × 221″) painting entitled *Bohemia Lies by the Sea* (1996), owned by the Metropolitan Museum, is a massive, complex work that invokes a battlefield in World War II—here named Bohemia, a vaguely defined geographical entity in middle Europe that in geographical fact is near no sea. The painting presents flat fields that stretch toward an ominously dark horizon, fields that are filled with pink poppies seeming to symbolize dreams, death, and military veterans: there is a sinister suggestion of the aftermath of war in the form of shallow graves, splatterings of blood, and various indeterminate shapes that may well be corpses left to rot in the open air. The thickly applied media include oil, shellac, emulsion, charcoal, and powdered paint, mixed together in an impasto solution that hangs heavily on the canvas underneath—so heavily that one has the sense that the entire surface of the painting may someday fall clattering to the hard museum floor. The combination of weight and precariousness underscores the mood of the painting itself, at once somber and threatening. The powerfully convergent perspective— whereby the fields and the country road in the middle move toward the high horizon—contributes further to the fateful feeling of the scene, eerily beautiful and yet teeming with death. There is an ironic sense that somewhere over the horizon is the sea of the title if not of the actual landscape: Bohemia is said by Shakespeare in *The Winter's Tale* to border the sea. Ingeborg Bachmann, with the Shakespeare reference in mind, wrote a poem, "Böhmen liegt am Meer," which Kiefer appropriates as the title of his painting, inscribing these four words both on the road and on the horizon. In her poem, Bachmann describes Bohemia as "on one beautiful day released to the sea and now lying on the water,"[29]

29. These lines are cited in a discussion of Kiefer's painting to be found on the website of the Metropolitan Museum (http://www.metmuseum.org/). At the same location, this interpretation of Bachmann's lines is offered: Bachmann is "longing for utopia while recognizing that it can never be found—just as the original Bohemia, landlocked in central Europe, can never lie by the sea." I am indebted to Tanja Staehler for bringing this discussion to my attention.

but Kiefer's painting considerably darkens this utopian reading of the Shakespearean theme. The viewer's look is drawn ineluctably toward the grim horizon as toward his or her own death, "the bourne from which no soul returns" (*Hamlet*). The glance adheres to the painting's stark surface as to its own *Doppelgänger*, a ghostly (and ghastly) double.

At the level of apperception, the viewer's glance is wholly attuned to the dystopian image presented by (and as and on) the surface of this painting—the two together (glance/surface) constituting the appearance of the artwork as a sheer periphenomenal thing. But the same glance reaches a limit if we ask it to be the exclusive basis of the creation of the work or of its full appreciation, including a judgment as to its aesthetic value—or, for that matter, as a basis for a particular political action we might wish to take at its instigation (for example, to combat fascistic dictatorship in its newer avatars).[30] Particular glances of Anselm Kiefer's doubtless guided him in the creation of the work itself, but only in close collusion with his hand, and both in deference to the extraordinarily dense medium of the work as a whole. The actual creation also drew upon matters far from vision as such—infusions from memory and emotion, world literature and recent history, all contributing to the portrayal of military violence. Even more so, an art critic's judgment as to the merit of the work as a whole exceeds the ambit of the glance, both by virtue of being in writing and by reaching out to other viewers who make up what Kant called the *sensus communis,* the community of all those who will apprize the work.[31]

This is not to say that there is a simple succession from glancing to these other modalities of human experience. On the contrary, there is an engaged dialectic among glance, hand, emotion, memory, history, poetry, and criticism: each calling for the others, all intertangling in the evolution of the massive imbroglio that is the painting itself as it stands face to face with its spectators and critics—and the artist himself as he steps back to contemplate his own work. Moreover, in the artistic process, glancing often gives way to other activities in which it plays a minor or peripheral role—and is even more fully surpassed if questions of re-

---

30. Even when a glance is the inspiration for a given work (as in certain of de Kooning's paintings of the early 1960s, as mentioned in the introduction), or when the work is said to be expressly about glancing as such—as in Ellsworth Kelly's series *La Colombe* from the 1950s ("much of this work," said Kelly, "is a response to a 'flash' or glimpse of something seen in the world: a shadow, shape, or architectural detail" [cited on the identifying plaque of *La Colombe III* at the San Francisco Museum of Modern Art])—still the *realization* of such works involves much besides glances: the distribution and thickness of the paint, the size of the work, the composition, etc. Nevertheless, the handling of these latter is often interlarded with glances and glance-like gestures.

31. On the *sensus communis,* see Immanuel Kant, *Critique of Judgment,* tr. W. S. Pluhar (Indianapolis: Hackett, 1987), section 40 ("On Taste as a Kind of *Sensus Communis*"). Kant insists that in judging works of art we "compare our judgment not so much with the actual as rather with the merely possible judgments of others, and [thus] put ourselves in the position of everyone else" (ibid., p. 160). The *sensus communis* is thus a tacit community that, on particular occasions, is actualized in commonly held judgments.

sponsible political action, involving still another sense of community, are raised by the same artwork. The glance shows itself to be at once indispensable in the actual creation and appreciation of a painting such as Kiefer's—there can be no such creation or appreciation without the enactment of glancing in some form— and yet to be only one among several factors in a full assessment of an artwork and to play a diminished role in particular contexts such as aesthetic judgment and the political activism that is inspired by art.[32]

IV

Despite the limitations to which I have just been pointing in three different domains—exhibiting what the glance cannot do in and of itself—it retains a very special power, that of being *telling*. Earlier in these concluding thoughts, I said casually that "taking a glance at an artwork tells me at once what it is like." Not only artworks but many other things are the targets of the telling glance. For the glance does not just take in passively or lead actively to certain concrete effects, it also *tells us important things about what we have glanced at.* "Telling" is a fundamental but rarely analyzed act that is basic to human (and doubtless animal) being-in-the-world. When I tell that something is so, I determine that *it is the case:* I recognize that it exists, that it is a certain kind of thing, that it is configured in a particular way, that it might change in certain respects, and so on. Any or all of these things are at stake in a "telling look"—of which a "telling glance" is an exemplary instance.

The telling glance embodies a certain kind of intimate knowledge. When a telling glance occurs, it belongs to someone who knows something special about the person or thing at which he or she is looking: enough, in any case, for a given glance to be able to *tell* that what it takes in is significant or not. Moreover, if I witness such a glance on the part of someone else, it signals to me that the glancer has such knowledge, for it is on this basis I can see that his or her glance is indeed telling. A telling glance is therefore a two-way phenomenon: it bespeaks the insight of a given glance, that is, what it grasps in the moment of looking, and it also expresses the way such a glance appears to others who witness it.

This is not to confuse a telling with a *knowing* glance. The latter wears its heart on its sleeve since it presents to the looked-at person the clear sense that the looker is in possession of a certain claim to a knowledge that is not only intimate or special (that is, as the basis of the significance the glance finds in

---

32. Kant himself points to such limitation in his remark that in estimating the magnitude of something "the imagination selects as the [unit] a magnitude that we can take in in one glance, such as a foot or a rod [in contrast with a vast unit such as the earth's diameter]," which "the imagination can apprehend but *cannot comprehend* in one intuition" (ibid., pp. 110–111; my italics). In other words, the actively imaginative glance can apperceive but cannot definitively judge what it takes in with one look.

what it looks at) but is instead stereotypical and thus all too predictable. The artist Kara Walker puts it this way in a poetic fragment about being viewed as an African American:

> but when I gits my Affikir up
> Then I know that whatever personality I may
> possess is simply the collage effect of
> too many meaningful documentaries.
> . . . and plenty of knowing glances.[33]

Here the glance is knowing as "knowing best" and stubbornly persisting within a certain set of fixed beliefs that influence concrete perceptual judgments: for example, the belief that African Americans belong to an inferior race. It is this kind of knowing glance—that knows yet does not know—that besieged W. E. B. Du Bois and that each of us enacts whenever we look at another human being in a presumptuously all-knowing manner. It is a close cousin of the withering glance; both ways of glancing claim to know enough to pass judgment by the action of the glance itself—in contrast with genuine ethical or aesthetic judgment, which we have seen to call for another level from that of the immediate glance itself. The difference is that the withering glance seeks actively to diminish the well-being of the person at which it is cast, while the knowing glance is content to feel certain in its peremptory judgment.

The telling glance looks otherwise than the knowing or withering look. Since its knowledge is intimate—at once tacit and personal[34]—it is less vulnerable to stereotypical constraints (no glance is wholly invulnerable to these constraints). It goes to the heart of the matter: to that part of the surface of what we glance at that is most "telling," that is to say, most significant for the existence or fate of that whose surface it is. Whereas the knowing glance and the withering look stay at the familiar externalities of any surface, its superficial marks of recognition ("African American woman artist," "black boy," "WASP," "geek," and so on), the telling glance dissolves these carapaces of personal identity by uncovering the free radicality of the person. In particular, it picks out the singularity of the subject at which it looks—a singularity to which I shall return at the end of these concluding thoughts. It is at once inquisitive and recognitive, interrogative and open, spontaneous and affirmative.

Another aspect of the telling glance concerns its dual virtue of being both receptive and expressive. To tell in a glance is at once to take note of what inhabits the apperceptual field *and* to give expression to what the viewing subject thinks and feels as he or she looks into that field. In both senses, *the glance*

---

33. Kara Walker, poetic inscription accompanying an image in her exhibition, "Excavated from the Black Heart of a Negress (excerpt)," Studio Museum of Harlem, July 16–September 28, 2003.

34. I refer here to Michael Polanyi's ideas of "tacit knowledge" as this is developed in his books *The Tacit Dimension* (New York: Doubleday, 1966) and especially *Personal Knowledge* (Chicago: University of Chicago Press, 1974).

tells. It discerns the import of the thing and environing world at which it looks, but it also expresses how the glancing subject is responding to the proffered surfaces of this world. It does all this pre-discursively, without recourse to language, even if some parts of language can be considered glance-like.[35] It does it in a glance.

This is not to say that the glance that tells—and that can be seen as telling—tells everything. The glance takes in a lot, can be quite expressive of the glancing subject, and may lead to important actions, but it does not tell all. It tells many of the most definitive and pertinent things in any given context or setting—especially those things that bear on human and personal being—but it finally has its own limits. About certain features of the other-than-human world, or the future, or the traumatic past, it cannot tell for certain. The glance stands on the cusp of the future and arises from the residuum of the past, but it is never the master of either—only the eager apprentice. Rarely the central action, glancing accompanies virtually all human actions. Its own action consists in clinging to the edges of things, including those very diverse things that belong to the animal, plant, and geological worlds.

It ensues that although we must claim much more for the glance than is ordinarily allowed—notably, its tellingness—we can do so only within certain inherent limits (including those of tellingness itself). We must acknowledge its unique talents and virtues even as we recognize its shortcomings and defects.

V

Let us now turn to an undeniably positive power of glancing, its inherent *freedom.* It can be gathered from scattered remarks I have made in this book that such freedom is not located in any simple choice between distinct options, much less in a Sartrian "original choice" of my character or destiny.[36] The glance's freedom lies elsewhere, and we can best approach it by first dealing with a certain basic problem. Starkly stated, the problem is this: how can we reconcile the fact that I am normally free to glance where I wish and how I wish—without agenda or schedule—with the fact that any act of glancing is nevertheless highly informed by various kinds of experience and knowledge that have been incorporated into the act of glancing itself? Otherwise put: How can glancing be at once spontaneous in its operation *and* reflective of the glancer's own history? Not only is this a problem, it is an antinomy in Kant's formal sense: each of these two propositions obtains separately, yet taken together they are incompatible with each other. It is

---

35. I here respond to a line of thought suggested by Andrés Colapinto, who also asks: "Could we even think of *speaking* (as conversation) as having a 'glance' component to it . . . a 'being-ahead-of-itself'?" (e-mail communication of August 2003).

36. On original choice, see Jean-Paul Sartre, *Being and Nothingness,* tr. H. Barnes (New York: Washington Square Press, 1972), part 4, chap. 1, esp. p. 595: "our being is precisely our original choice."

true that I am (for the most part) free to glance how and where I want, and yet it is also true that my glance bears a legacy of prejudice (that is, in the literal sense of the "pre-judgment" that is most manifestly at work in the knowing or withering glance but that pervades all glancing to some degree). But can both of these truths coexist? It would seem not to be so. As Sartre proclaims, "two solutions and only two are possible: either man is wholly determined . . . or else man is wholly free."[37] We have already encountered a version of this dilemma in my treatment of the ethics of the glance—where I noted the tension between the instantaneous decision to intervene in a conflictual situation and the early influences from family upbringing, religious doctrines, and so on that went into my decision itself. The considerations raised by the friend I cited there are again relevant: how can I be certain that I am not acting entirely, or mostly, from such influences or doctrines and not from an autogenous freedom that I might want to claim (and that express my sense of myself as free at the time)? In my friend's vivid image: is not the finger that presses the trigger of the gun (that is, his equivalent of the glance) the creature of decades of continually reinforced habits?

In response to this last line of thought, it must be said that both sides of the antinomy are indeed true—and that, in the end, each is compatible with the other despite appearances to the contrary. My friend is right to underline the import of prior experiences for current actions and decisions, given that these experiences sediment themselves into my present bodily movements—right down my fingertips, indeed into the retinas of my eyes. Just as my glance inserts itself continually and diversely into its visual surroundings, so my personal history insinuates itself into many parts of my customary or habitual body, including its glancing behaviors. This personal history includes not only previous bodily actions but also various ideas and emotions, memories and thoughts that have been formative of my development as a human being. All of these effects (along with those of language, culture, my class, my race, my gender, my sexual preference) are indeed massively influential upon me in the present. But this is not to say that they *determine altogether* what I now do. To have such effects, to leave such a legacy is not the same as determining each and every action I undertake in the light of these effects and in the shadow of this legacy. There remains a margin of freedom available to me: to be predetermined in such ways is not tantamount to being determined *totaliter*. But what kind of freedom is this, and how is it compatible with such prior determination?

Just as it is not the positive freedom of the autonomous self, so it is not just the negative freedom of being free only in relation to certain constraints: that is, simply being *free from* these constraints. The latter way of regarding freedom, first formally proposed by Hobbes, puts the primary power in the existing determinants. Instead of rejecting the Hobbesian model by recourse to an internal noumenal power situated within the rational subject—as on Kant's classical doctrine of "pure practical reason"—we would do better to look for a middle-

37. Ibid., p. 571.

range freedom of *in*determination that does not require the positing of any such metaphysical deep self in the manner of Kant or of Bergson and yet that is not the mere creature of prior determinations.

The freedom here at stake may not be limited to acts of glancing (it is also found, for example, in making gestures of many kinds), but it does characterize these acts; it is a freedom that, even if rarely recognized as such, is nevertheless crucial in the engendering of personal identity and creative work, social interaction and political engagement. This is a freedom that is sensitive to what the world calls for on any given occasion, yet is not merely reactive to this call nor predictably responsive. Instead, it advances the position of the glancer, taking him or her forward in and through the vicissitudes of looking. By using words like "advances" and "forward," I mean that this freedom takes the glancer into the unfolding experiential world, putting him or her in the very midst of this world, from its near spheres to its horizon. It opens out rather than closes in. Situated between autonomy and determinism, such freedom has the effect of locating the glancing subject to whom it belongs in the middle of things, literally in medias res, while also enabling this glancer to turn away from the demands of the moment and to direct his or her attention elsewhere—anywhere in the visual field. The freedom of glancing is at once phenomenal (that is, allowing the subject to deal with specific matters close at hand) and periphenomenal (letting this same subject's eye follow the surfaces of things ad libitum). It delivers the detail of nearby events even as it picks up what is happening in the far sphere. It is the freedom of moving the look in and out of a given situation, and back and forth across its many surfaces.

This same advertive and deflective power, the polymorphic power of the glance—its literal "in-determination," as I have called it in the opening remarks to part 2—is not only compatible with various pre-determinations of habit, custom, and knowledge; *it requires them* in order to thrive, and it contributes to them in turn by altering the course of the existing self: giving the self *Lebensraum*, elbow room so to speak by disclosing vistas not otherwise accessible ("I can go over there now," "that way is possible"). Ultimately, my style of glancing (for example, boldly, timidly, furtively, guardedly, and so on), though having important cultural determinants, is freely pursued and just as freely modified. In glancing as elsewhere, "Le style c'est l'homme même." My glancing style belongs to my personal identity: it is part of who I am and how I am known to be by others.

The antinomy of freedom and determinism can be resolved not only because there are two levels of analysis to be distinguished within one and the same action, but more significantly because one level, that of freedom, cannot be fully enacted without the ingredient of the other, that of existing determinations by way of prior experience and cultural influence. And the reverse holds as well: I could not be effectively determined without having a factor of freedom *within which* determinations themselves are enacted and become effective, or else are modified or even rejected. The two sides of the antinomy, rather than warring with each other and canceling each other out, end by supporting and sustaining one another. The more informed my glance—short of its being overdetermined by routine, stereotyping, and so on—the more freely I can guide it to new things and situations and therefore to new surfaces in an ever-augmenting periphenomenal world.

Glancing is not only free itself as an act in its own right; it also frees things, situations, and surfaces themselves to be openly viewed. It lets them be by respecting what it sees. Just as glancing freely enacted suspends the ego of the glancer, it allows what it views to come into its own singularity. The freedom of in-determination is not merely indeterminate, nor is it simply amorphous. Just as it stems from actual determinants, it has real effects: it alters the way the world looks, just as it changes the way the subject looks at the world.

VI

The discussion of freedom has allowed us to savor a major positive feature of the glance. Another positive trait is found in its role as *mediatrix*. This is not to say "mediator," for that implies a compromise between opposed terms in which the terms themselves are diluted in their original force. Rather, a mediatrix is a connection-maker that not only respects but also strengthens the terms brought into relationship. Hermes is such a figure: he puts disparate things in touch, not just the gods with one another, but humans with gods (and vice versa). Wherever he is to be found, a matrix of newly related terms emerges. We may imagine that the word "mediatrix" combines "medium" and "matrix" in a single word that signifies a Hermetic prowess that, far from merely reconciling existing differences, brings forth new directions and powers from newfound connections.

The glance is a genuine mediatrix, thanks to its capacity to link very different things in one sweep of the eye, while itself stealing away from view (echoing another aspect of Hermes: his secretiveness, symbolized in classical sculpture by his holding a finger to his lips). The glance connects edges and surfaces and whole things: people who come face to face, animals encountered in domestic space or in wilderness, basic elements (water, air, earth, fire), and much more. In every case, the glance acts like a lasso that encircles such things, drawing them into its ambit, only to release them again. Not only does it shoot across a certain space to snare its targets, but it helps to constitute this space itself, opening new pathways by which subsequent looks are carried to their intended objects. These pathways bear the trace or imprint of which I have spoken in part 3, and they have the special property of being traversable in two directions by the gleam of my glance as it moves out of me ("Out of myself, but wanting to go beyond that . . . ,"[38] says Rumi) and, only a moment later, is sent back to me along the very pathway it has itself opened up.

Moving back and forth across these multiple trajectories, the glance detects what fills out its circumambience; it "picks up information" there. But its path-

---

38. Rumi, "What I See in Your Eyes," from *The Glance: Songs of Soul-Meeting*, tr. Coleman Barks (New York: Penguin Compass, 1999), p. 52. I owe this reference to Irene Klaver.

making also thickens the space itself by engaging in actions of acknowledgment and recognition, discernment and singularization. Whether as bare appercep- tion or as creative augmentation, the glance makes denser what would otherwise be thin and diaphanous. Its pathways are not just added to a preexisting space: they complicate and intensify this space, creating a field or, better, an interplace wherein connections are made, things happen, and advent arises. The open ground thus brought into being is not a neutral, meaningless medium but a ground for the advent of meaning itself. As Merleau-Ponty says:

> We propose . . . to consider the order of culture or meaning an original order of *advent*, which should not be derived from that of mere events . . . or treated as simply the effect of extraordinary conjunctions. It is characteristic of the human gesture to signify beyond its simple existence in fact, to inaugurate a meaning. . . . Each [such gesture] is both a beginning and a continuation which . . . points to a [further] continuation or recommencement. . . . Advent is a promise of events.[39]

In this light, a glance can be considered the eye's gesture toward the advent of meaning in the visual world—toward a "coming-to" (as "ad-vent" literally means) that signifies something more than bare existence or mere contiguity or conjunction. Going beyond the level of spatiotemporal location (where its pin- pointing powers are at play), it opens onto a level of meaning or visual signifi- cance (such as historicity of structure or presentation of sense) that promises further insights in subsequent acts of glancing and eventual acts of informed judgment. This, too, is thickening: enriching the present with meaning and with what is to come.[40]

In short, *the action is in the interaction,* and the glance as a mediatrix puts us into the midst of things and events, creating from their momentary interfusion an advent of meaning that exceeds their "simple presence."[41] The glance con- nects the otherwise unconnected across a space common to the glancer and the glanced-at; it brings them together in a place they share that is more than simple location. It is a genuine interplace in the literal sense of this term: a place of the between as well as a space between places. As such, it is a scene of what Jankélévitch calls *entrevision,* "intervision," literally "seeing between."[42] Link- ing things in the visual field is the specific work of the glance, whose probative force transforms what it apperceives into a meaningful spectacle.

This means that the glance as mediatrix is *part of the action itself.* It is not in a purely spectatorial position, as an oculocentric interpretation would maintain.

39. M. Merleau-Ponty, "Indirect Language and the Voices of Silence," tr. R. McCleary and reprinted from *Signs* in G. A. Johnson, ed., *The Merleau-Ponty Aesthetics Reader: Philosophy and Painting* (Evanston, Ill.: Northwestern University Press, 1993), pp. 105–106; his italics.

40. On the emergence of visual significance, see especially Rudolf Arnheim, *Visual Thinking* (Berkeley: University of California Press, 1969).

41. "Its value exceeds its simple presence" ("Indirect Language and the Voices of Silence," p. 105). What Merleau-Ponty here says of "gesture" is all the more true of the glance.

42. See Vladimir Jankélévitch, *Philosophie Première: Introduction à une philosophie du "presque,"* pp. 71–76.

As actively visuocentric, it is engaged in its own outgoing venture—its *adventure* —as a full participant in the crisscrossing betweenness of the visual world. Only in this fashion can it create common ground and realize a new level of vision, an altered state of seeing that envisions new forms of meaning.

Such a basic transformation occurs, for example, when my glance interacts with another's: "Suddenly a gleam appeared, a little bit below and out in front of its eyes; its glance is raised and comes to fasten on the very things I am seeing."[43] Merleau-Ponty is here speaking of another person, whose glance I am myself seeing; I cannot but be struck by its forwardness as it rushes out of the other's eyes and attaches itself to some particular thing in a visual environment I share with this other. Our glances intersect at a crossroads of looking where two pathways meet: Hermes was also the god of crossroads.

In this particular circumstance, my glance not only notices the other's but rejoins it as both of our looks converge on a commonly beheld item while in each other's company. The result is a complex dialectic of glances that, even short of direct exchange with each other (which has its own complexity, such as when two lovers glance at each other[44]), engage in a conjoint action of crossed looks that takes place in its own shared space, that constituted by simultaneous glancing. In this delicate and sometimes fateful drama, two pathways are opened across the same visual space, one of which (the other's) is directed entirely onto the thing seen and the other (my own) onto this same thing as well as onto the other's looking at it, my own glance here crossing the other's. And when more than two people engage in glancing at something in common, other combinations, bringing still further complications, emerge. This is not the place to trace out the ramifying interpersonal matrix of such glancing—nor that of the different kinds of complexity that ensue when other animals and inanimate objects are also involved. Suffice it to say that in every such instance Hermetic connections occur, supervenient space emerges, advent of meaning arises, and the plot of intervision thickens—all of this thanks to the glance as mediatrix.

VII

Another attribute of Hermes is his celebrated *speed*. This, too, accrues to the glance and is a third of its major positive features. But speed in what sense? Clearly, we are not speaking of measurable velocity: who could clock a glance?

---

43. Merleau-Ponty, "The Philosopher and His Shadow," tr. R. McCleary, in *Signs* (Evanston, Ill.: Northwestern University Press, 1964), p. 169. This statement should be set beside that of Wittgenstein on the gleam that issues from the eye as cited earlier in chap. 7: *Zettel*, tr. G. E. M. Anscombe and G. H. von Wright (Berkeley: University of California Press, 1976), p. 40.

44. Popular songs do not fail to refer to this circumstance: "He won't leave my sight for a glance" (line from "The Music That Makes me Dance," as sung by Shirley Horne in the album *You Won't Forget Me*); "Strangers in the night / exchanging glances" (from the song "Strangers in the Night"); "You and your glance make this love" (song from *Finian's Rainbow*).

Nor are we speaking of the extremities of speed—either zero or infinite speed. These alternatives belong to the ancient conception of the perfect cosmic circle, which can be considered to be wholly at rest or moving at a literally in-finite speed (that is, a speed that cannot be computed by any finite number).[45] But the conception of time as "the moving image of eternity" (in the formula of the *Timaeus*), according to which time returns upon itself as it completes a circular route, does not obtain for the glance, which if anything traces out a more elliptical path whose two epicenters are provided by the eye and the glanced-at thing or person.

The epicenters themselves, temporally rather than spatially regarded, embody the two beats of the time of the glance under discussion in chapter 8. These beats are not the successive tick-tock members of a classical A series of before and after in which each would have a separate status; nor do they represent anything like the past/present/future phases of the B series. Instead, they are quasi-simultaneous moments of time: so close to simultaneous that we cannot separate them in experience even if we can distinguish them in theory. They are overlapping: no sooner does my glance go out than it is returned to me in some form—mimetically in the case of a mirror, as a response (a gesture or a glance back) in the case of other humans who take in my glance, and as a trace in the instance of inanimate objects. In each case, the glancer has the impression of a virtually immediate return of his or her look, as if it leapt back from the target just as it reaches this target.

The interleaving of the outbound and the return trajectories of the glance is so intimate that we are not even aware of them as distinct phases of the same experience: I look at myself in the mirror and my image comes back to me, with such dazzling speed that one would be hard put to classify the circumstance as involving duration. Instead of unfolding—the *déroulement* with which Bergson characterizes duration[46]—time here happens with a kind of *absolute speed* that is not to be confused with infinite speed. Absolute speed is not simply a lot of speed, not even a very great lot of it (as with infinite speed, which is still measurable in principle even if no number can be affixed to it). It is, rather, speed that happens *all at once, totum simul.* It happens not just in a highly compressed state (as "simultaneous" and "instantaneous" both signify) but with sudden effect as an event that takes place "at a single stroke" (*tout d'un coup*). The absolute speed of the glance is that of an advent, a quickened event that occurs in a flash, not unlike lightning—whose flash also occurs with intense

---

45. It is this circumstance to which Derrida alludes when he employs the phrase "at the zero or infinite speed of the circle" (Jacques Derrida, *Given Time I: Counterfeit Money*, p. 24). He is discussing the idea of the gift as belonging to a circular exchange that evokes the ancient paradigm.

46. On *déroulement,* which can also mean "spreading out," see (among many other passages), *Time and Free Will*, p. 73–74: "we shall now have to inquire what the multiplicity of our inner states becomes, what form duration assumes, when the space in which it unfolds (*déroule*) is eliminated."

speed. This flash or stroke of happening is comparable to the moment of sudden awakening to which Benjamin pointed, or to the *Augenblick* that combines time with eternity in a single event on Kierkegaard's conception.

We are not talking of the speed of light—which has a numerical value, however vast—even if light is a material condition of the glance itself. It is a matter, rather, of *the absolute speed of advenition*. Advenition or "coming-to," which is a progenitor of coming-to-be, occurs in a flash. This flash need not be as dramatic as a stroke of lightning. It can be as inconspicuous as the twinkling of an eye. In contrast with the blink that closes the eyes, a twinkle is not terminated by a moment of closure. Where closure ends an event—hence allows for its possible measurement—nonclosure lets time emerge as ab-solute: not to be dissolved in numbers or minutes, not to be counted as such but rather allowed to happen: just to be, or rather to be as becoming. In the twinkling of an eye, with absolute speed, an event comes to be as an advent; it becomes, all at once and in a single stroke, something more than a mere happening.

The Biblical phrase "in the twinkling of an eye" (*en rhipó opthalmou*) comes paired with the equally significant phrase "in a moment" (*en atomé*) to yield the celebrated claim of the New Testament: "In a moment, in the twinkling of an eye, we shall all be transformed" (1 Corinthians 15, 51–52; *Revised Standard Edition* translation).[47] The moment of transformation is that of the advenition of the divine into the human realm, resulting in an instantaneous transformation of the latter. But advenitions also arise between human beings in certain epiphanic moments: for example, that of the "face to face" in Levinas's sense of the primal moment of ethical encounter. In the advenition of the glance, something transformative occurs: "the twinkle changes things."[48] Something advenes within the ordinary world of perception and interpersonal communication, giving to the glancer the advantage of a special leverage upon the seen world. This is the visual equivalent of the Archimedian principle: "give me [the right place] and I will move the whole world." Just so: the world is seen anew in the twinkling of an eye, and in the intense illumination of this epiphanic moment the seeing subject is also renewed. One transformation not only calls for the other actively but induces it—immediately, without delay. Both transformations occur at the same time: in the moment of the glance that is enacted with absolute speed.

Am I advocating a dromocentrism of the glance? "Dromocentrism," a coinage of Paul Virilio's, means being obsessed with speed—the fascination, and the fate, of Western civilization according to Virilio.[49] Whatever the ultimate truth of

---

47. For a remarkable treatment of this dictum, see David L. Miller, "Through the Looking-Glass—The World as Enigma," in R. Ritsema, ed., *Spiegelung in Mensch und Cosmos* (Ascona, Switzerland: Insel Verlag, 1986), pp. 401 ff. I have invoked this same dictum and Miller's treatment in chap. 12.

48. Miller, ibid., p. 401.

49. Paul Virilio, *Speed and Politics,* tr. M. Polizzotti (New York: Semiotexte, 1986), as well as "La Dromoscopie et la lumière de la vitesse," *Critiques* (1978).

Virilio's claim, there is an undeniable dromocentric dimension of the glance, a "good dromocentrism" that is allied with the visuocentrism which I contrasted with oculocentrism at the beginning of chapter 5. Just as the glance is irrecusably visuocentric (it is oculocentric only when appropriated for determinate scientific, social, or political purposes), so it does indeed prize speed. Not speed for its own sake (the target of Virilio's caustic critique) but for the sake of the change that the luminescence of the look can bring. Or let us say: for the *enantiodromia* it effects—in Heraclitus's word for "sudden reversal into the opposite" (where "sudden" translates as *dromia*, itself derived from *dromein*, "to run").

In the twinkling of an eye, in the absolute speed of the glance, a transformation of self and world alike takes place, a sudden reversal occurs, and all is different. This is what the transformative speed of the glance delivers. The change wrought by this speed is subtle but sweeping.[50] It is just here that the habituality of the glance, its inherent tacit knowledge, is suspended if not overcome; for at this moment the glance, despite its sedimented history, is capable of bringing about the radically new, what is coming and to come, what is visually extraordinary standing out from the dense ground of its becoming.

A brief dromocentric corollary is this: the glance takes us *out of the sighted subject with utmost alacrity: lurchingly, leapingly.* This, too, is a Hermetic property: Hermes holds his right index finger to his lips not just to signify silence and secrecy but to symbolize the radical consequences of something (sound, air, gesture, look, and so on) escaping from the body of the subject. There is a saltatory movement out of the subject of which the glance is a leading instance— literally so, since the glance leads out from the face of the subject so spontaneously. It is always already beyond the subject from which it stems. Here its absolute speed joins forces with its outer-directed intentionality: its outward-boundness, its ardent attraction to the outer reaches of vision.

But just as the glance goes out to meet the world by this its primary intentionality, so it also brings the world back in: it brings back not just its own image or imprint but everything else that it encounters and experiences—people and animals, trees and sky, sea and earth. It brings them all back, albeit in fragmentary and schematic glimpses, bare profiles made up of edges, blurred horizons and indeterminate middle distances. If the sallying forth of the glance is notable for its economically realized outward thrust—its lean "operative intentionality" (in Eugen Fink's term)—the contents brought back by this same glance are comparatively massive: they include "all the living relationships of experience, as the fisherman's net draws up from the depths of the ocean quivering fish and seaweed."[51] Thus the glance takes us out of ourselves—precipitously, suddenly,

---

50. "Sweeping" is another meaning of *rhipé*, and it is certainly striking that we speak unself-consciously of a "sweeping glance." Still further senses of *rhipé* include swinging and rushing— the former suggesting the swinging back and forth in the glance's two-beat rhythm, the latter the rapidity of the glance. I owe this clarification to Eric Casey.

51. M. Merleau-Ponty, *Phenomenology of Perception*, tr. C. Wilson (New York: Routledge, 1989), p. xv. See comparable passages in Sören Kierkegaard, *Either/Or*, tr. H. V. Hong and E. H. Hong (Princeton, N.J.: Princeton University Press, 1987), vol. 1, pp. 92, 325.

as if borne on the back of an anonymously issued visual ray—yet it also brings us back in by bringing *more than ourselves into ourselves.* In this way, the new is continually incorporated into our midst. The affirmation inherent in the glance, its parsimonious penetrative force, comes paired with an incorporative countermovement. The glance takes us out into the world, but it also brings that world back into us. It brings us up long and short at once: short in the moment of projection, long in the haul garnered and internalized. It takes back in even as it leaps out. The absolute speed of its emission is matched only by the *longue durée* of what it captures and incorporates in the twinkling of an eye.

VIII

To glance is to be open to *surprise,* a last and quite significant positive trait of glancing to which I have pointed several times earlier in this book. To glance is to enter an Open where surprise is not only possible but highly probable. Why else would we glance unless we were willing to be surprised? (This is so even when we are fearful, furtively glancing at just what we fear the most.) Were we not willing to be surprised, we would restrict the circle of vision to what is already fully known—or known well enough to exclude surprise. Rather than looking *out,* we would look *in:* either inside the perimeter of the familiar or within ourselves, where we think we know the way. The characteristic vector of the glance is outward. Which is just what Husserl's chosen term *Blickstrahl* connotes: the eye's ray moves from the retina into the world—a world full of surprise, whether on the streets of Paris or in a mall in Fairfield, California.

Despite the many ways in which it occurs, in glancing we move into an arena of open possibility where, as Heraclitus put it, "Unless you expect the unexpected you will never find [truth], for it is hard to discover and hard to attain."[52] It is the unexpected, or at least the not fully known, that we take in with the glance: to this reverse directionality from the world to us there corresponds the *Weltstrahlen* posited in Husserl's later writings (though already present in Greek theories of vision as intromissionist). By our glance we are drawn—or, alternately, we draw ourselves—into a region where many things can happen and thus where we can count on being surprised: where we will have to take in what we did not expect to encounter. If a mere glance can take in so much, this is only because we have risked something to begin with: nothing ventured, nothing gained. The venture, the adventure, of the glance is to go out into the domain of the unfamiliar, whether hoped for or feared, and to witness what happens there—come what may.

To venture out in this way is to be *curious* as to what lies outside of direct vision. In contrast with Heidegger's caustic and dismissive analysis of curiosity as

---

52. Heraclitus, Fragment #18 (Diels), translation of P. Wheelwright in his *Heraclitus* (New York: Atheneum, 1968), p. 20.

on a par with gossip—both being for him forms of everyday fallenness—the curiosity at stake in the glance is a constructive epistemic matter.[53] It is not a matter of being cognitively "nosy" or seeking the new for the sheer sake of the new, that is, a matter of mere "idle curiosity." The glancer is genuinely curious as to what may be the case around her, and wants to find out even at the expense of being disappointed or shocked by what meets the glance. In the *Republic*, Plato speaks of being overcome by spirit, by *thumos*, when a person is impelled to look at a corpse on the roadside even though his reason tells him not to. (The morbid, as well as the erotic, are virtually irresistible objects of the glance.) On the other hand, the curiosity in question is not to be assimilated to *wonder*, that prototypical philosophical emotion.[54] Wonder implies a sense of awe or mystery that is missing in the curiosity appropriate to the glance. Wonder may be induced by glancing, especially in "the now of recognizability" as specified by Walter Benjamin, but once aroused from what is sudden and surprising it calls for a slow, contemplative looking that is more akin to the gaze than to the glance and that includes an element of longing: *pothos* and *thaumazein* are closely affine in early Greek thinking. The longing is to know the ultimate truth of the way things *are*— the metaphysical truth of being, as Aristotle holds—whereas glancing is content to know the truth of what happens on the surface of things: that is, what is first in the order of seeming rather than first in the order of being. The glancer reverses the counsel of Stevens's "Emperor of Ice Cream": not "let be be finale of seem" but rather "let seem be the content of be."

The active curiosity of glancing is expressed in the basic desire to know *what is going on in my circumambient world*. To enact this curiosity in a glance I cannot be altogether apprehensive—or else I will close myself to what the glance reveals. I must be willing to expose myself to what my glance itself exposes. I must be, in every sense of the word, *open-eyed* to what I do not yet know for sure is the case—to what is concealed from the glance as it starts to send its ray outward. And it is just because the world conceals so much of itself—gives itself only by partial profiles, as Husserl says—that the glance is drawn to discover what I do not yet know about my physical or social surroundings, my layout. I take in the world at a glance only because the world itself withdraws so radically from full revelation. It does not give itself all at once, but for this very reason the glance is inspired to light on appearances that do present themselves all at once, here and now—even if these appearances, and the fact of their being apperceived together, cannot claim to deliver the ultimate truth of things.

The price of this gift of the world's seeming—its presenting itself in and by

53. For Heidegger's analysis of curiosity, see *Being and Time*, tr. J. Macquarrie and E. Robinson (New York: Harper and Row, 1962), section 36, pp. 214–219.

54. In Aristotle's words: "It is owing to their wonder that men both now begin and at first began to philosophize" (Aristotle, *Metaphysics* A, 982b 12–982b13; in the W. D. Ross translation as revised by J. Barnes; as cited in J. L. Ackrill, ed., *A New Aristotle Reader* [Princeton, N.J.: Princeton University Press, 1982], p. 258).

its exposed surfaces—is comparatively small. The price is simply surprise. To glance into the world is to let oneself be surprised by the world. "Surprise" is regarded by theorists of emotion as one of the seven basic emotions (happiness, fear, anger, sadness, disgust/contempt, and interest being the other ones).[55] According to one leading researcher, the aim of surprise, especially in its primitive form of "startle," is "to help prepare the individual to deal effectively with [a] new or sudden event and with the consequences of this event."[56] Beyond its sheer utility, however, surprise is the cognitive or emotional *response* to the discovery of the unexpected, and it is the constant companion of glancing. To glance is to expose oneself to surprise, and it is to do so in the mode of the *sudden*.

As I noted in chapter 8, the importance of the sudden was brought back to late modern attention by Kierkegaard, for whom it represented the exception to the Hegelian System, that which forever evades this System—in which nothing happens suddenly but only according to the slow labor of the negative.[57] The sudden interrupts and disrupts the Juggernaut of continual dialectical synthesis. Like the instant, it is a factor of discontinuity. Hence its disconcerting character: human beings generally, and not only logocrats such as Hegel, prefer the continuous and predictable. But they also know that all is not continuous and predictable. Thus they glance out around themselves in order to anticipate the sudden before it arrives wholly unbidden, blindsiding them.

The sudden cuts into the customary, arriving seemingly from nowhere. To meet it halfway, rather than being its mere victim, is to beat it at its own game. Thus we go out to meet the sudden—most effectively, *in a glance*, often defined as "a hurried [or quick] look."[58] Our glance's characteristic celerity, its dartingness, equals that of the sudden it is prepared to confront: one swiftness calls for another. This is why it is never too soon to glance, and the sooner the better. The more quickly we glance the more adequate we are to the world's waywardness, its quirky happening, its effervescent eventfulness. In the face of this cosmic uncertainty, we are saved by a glance—by the almost nothing that matters greatly in the scheme of things.

Kierkegaard, speaking out of the temporocentrism that kept him tied to Hegel despite his animadversions against the System, considered the sudden

55. On the seven basic emotions, see Paul Ekman, ed., *Emotion in the Human Face* (New York: Cambridge, 1982; 2d ed.), esp. chap. 3.

56. Carroll Izard, *Human Emotions* (New York: Plenum 1977), p. 281. I owe this reference and that in the previous footnote to Jenefer Robinson, "Startle," *Journal of Philosophy* 92 (Feb. 1995): pp. 53–74. Robinson makes it clear that startle is also closely related to fear: startle is "a developmentally early form of two emotions in particular, namely, fear and surprise" (p. 57).

57. Sören Kierkegaard, "Interlude," *Philosophical Fragments* (tr. D. Swenson and H. Hong (Princeton, N.J.: Princeton University Press, 1962), pp. 89–110.

58. "Hurried look" is from the *Oxford English Dictionary;* "brief look" is given in the *American Heritage Dictionary.*

to be a temporal category—thus allied exclusively with the present moment (*Augenblick*). But if the sudden is a truly radical interruption *of time itself*, then it cannot be just another temporal notion—something to be swallowed and surpassed by the Saturnian succession of time. On the contrary, to be sudden is to resist temporal, indeed causal, analysis: to appear, not just from nowhere but more particularly from *nowhen*. At the same time, the sudden accrues more closely to place than to time. This is a lesson we learned from Walter Benjamin, who traced the sudden and the surprising alike as they arose in city life in late-nineteenth-century Paris.

Typically, we experience the sudden as attaching to a given scene of action: "the forest is aflame!" we say, pinning the sudden on a patch of fuming woods that constitutes a concrete place. Although we can certainly have sudden thoughts or memories, the suddenness at stake in the glance characteristically has material exemplification—and thus a place in which to appear (as well as edged surfaces in which to be manifest). This follows from the fact that we glance from here to there, that is, from one place to another. This transplacement happens in an *Augenblick*, literally "look of the eyes" and not merely in a "moment" as the German word is often translated into English; and this is a look that happens immediately (as *augenblicklich* colloquially connotes), "in the blink of an eye." The action of the glance is an immediate look (outward) of the eyes—a look that is attuned to the sudden way the world of places, the place-world, emerges differently from what we had expected, thereby surprising us.[59]

It is not just because of time-consciousness, then, that we must "admit the other into the self-identity of the *Augenblick;* nonpresence and nonevidence . . . into the *blink of an instant*."[60] These words of Derrida's—intended to deconstruct Husserl's phrase "*im selben Augenblick*" ("at the same time," "simultaneously") as employed in the latter's *Logical Investigations*—could well apply to the glance. For it is by the glance that what is other than what we had expected is allowed to interrupt our self-certainty and self-presence—that the nonpresent and the nonevident enter into us as avid lifelong lookers.

The glance allows us to savor the world as a surprising affair—as something that happens suddenly, somewhere. It lets us see the world on a slender sleeve of seeming whose surface surprises us in the sudden unexpectedness of its appearings. It lets us see so much in so little—so much surface, so little time and space. If the poetic image is, according to Bachelard, "a sudden salience on the surface of the psyche,"[61] the content of the glance is an equally sudden salience on the surface of things and places. The source of this content is the world that, surprising us, is itself surprised in a glance.

59. For discussion of several points in this paragraph, and for reflections on the importance of the bodily "here," I am grateful to Irene Klaver in conversation.

60. Jacques Derrida, *Speech and Phenomena*, tr. D. Allison (Evanston, Ill.: Northwestern University Press, 1973), p. 65; his italics.

61. Gaston Bachelard, *The Poetics of Space*, tr. M. Jolas (New York: Orion, 1964), p. xi.

IX

This brings us to an ability of the glance that is closely correlated with the primary powers I have singled out: namely, its capacity for *undoing divisive dyads* of various sorts—especially traditional binaries that pit one metaphysical term or set of terms over against another. This may seem paradoxical, given my emphasis just above on the two-way, in-and-out movement of the glance, and earlier on its two-beat and two-space character. But the paradox is only apparent, for it overlooks the connective strength of glancing and its laying out of the shared ground of intimate relationship between disparate items. Here we return to the first of the Hermetic virtues—linkage across shared space. Indeed, the glance can be said to be the apperceptual equivalent of the imagination conceived as "the link of links"(Bruno). It is thanks to its chiasmatic power of crossing-over in the midst of a common space that the glance comes into its own, and it does so by disowning dichotomies that threaten to divide this space into incompatible oppositions.

I have in mind such binary pairs as mind versus matter, self versus other, spirit versus soul, sky versus earth. Each of these dyads suggests a forced choice between one or the other of the two terms, rather than their mutual affirmation or complex collocation. But it is the latter that is the direction of promise. In Derrida's elegant formulation: it is a matter of "neither/nor, that is, *simultaneously* either or."[62] Instead of exclusionary choices, or third options, we should recognize the choice between members of a given dyad as something "undecidable" that vacillates between extremes, choosing neither alone ("neither/nor") while respecting both ("*simultaneously* either *or*").[63] This is not only *like* the glance; it describes its own operative intentionality of moving fitfully but forcefully between distinguishable terms—between points on a surface in acts of apperceptive transfer that affirm the entire field of vision in its periphenomenal displays. Not only across this field but within it—along the fault lines on its surface—the glance adroitly connects the disconnected, solders the split, undoes the dichotomized. As David L. Miller says pointedly:

> How can there be divisive dualisms—heaven over against hell, divine over against human, male over against female, reality over against representations—when there is a twinkle in the perspectival eye, a riffling-ruffling-rippling (*rhipó*) perspective of the human and the cosmic, when everything is a mirror: mirrors mirroring mirrors, up and down and in and out? And everything *is* a mirror when it is reflected upon, for in the reflections the world twinkles back at us.[64]

Miller here anticipates my emphasis in chapters 7 and 8 on the importance of the mirror for understanding the dynamics of the glance in its ritornelle move-

---

62. Jacques Derrida, *Positions,* tr. A. Bass (Chicago: University of Chicago Press, 1981), p. 43; his italics.

63. On the logic of undecidability, see ibid., pp. 42 ff.

64. Miller, "Through a Looking-Glass—the World as Enigma," pp. 401–402; his italics.

ment. But more than mirroring is at stake: it is the sense that the world at which we glance somehow looks back at us. This sense, which we have encountered several times in the course of this book, is given express formulation by Lacan: "the pre-existence of a look—I see only from one point, but in my existence I am looked at from all sides."[65] If things themselves and not only mirror images return my glance—if there is a more complex order of visual exchange happening than is captured in any model of one-way looking—then the traditional dyad that puts the human on one side and everything nonhuman on the other is no longer viable. For glancing will occur in many circumstances in which such a dyadicity will not obtain. In these circumstances of lively intervision—wherein looks crisscross every which way—the glance will be a primary animator, catalyzing the most diverse and unlikely collaborations between otherwise divisive dyads. No longer to be regarded as minor or marginal in status, it will be recognized as the major mediatrix in the world of vision: a world that is taken in at a glance.

X

Let me make it clear that I am not attributing to nonhuman things such as trees or rocks any inherent visual apparatus comparable to that operative in human vision. To do this would be to engage in ungrounded speculation that verges on a projected panpsychism. Instead, I am referring to the felt *sense* that such things—and thus the world they compose together—somehow stand in witness of human beings and their lookings: the sense that humans (most notably, artists and mystics but ordinary people as well) are being looked at even as they look at these same things. A nonparanoid visual interaction is felt that amounts to an asymmetrical reciprocity: rather than an explicit give-and-take in which one look responds to another in a dialectical exchange, there is immersion in a shared space traversed by various kinds of witnessing. I need not hold that a certain tree is expressly looking at me to believe that I am in its presence and am

65. Jacques Lacan, *The Four Fundamental Concepts of Psychoanalysis*, tr. A. Sheridan (New York: Norton, 1977), p. 72. I have changed "gaze" to the more neutral verb "look," since the French term, *le regard*, can mean either gaze or glance. For Lacan's revised discussion of the mirror—beyond his earlier "mirror stage"—see ibid., pp. 80 ff., in which the situation of "seeing myself seeing" is analyzed. In "Eye and Mind" Merleau-Ponty cites André Marchand on the forest looking at me rather than the reverse—"it was not I who was looking at the forest . . . I felt that the trees were looking at me" ("Eye and Mind," tr. M. B. Smith in *The Merleau-Ponty Aesthetics Reader*, p. 129)—and he elaborates on this theme in *The Visible and the Invisible*, tr. A. Lingis (Evanston, Ill.: Northwestern University Press, 1968), chap. 4, esp. pp. 154–155: "As soon as I see, it is necessary that the vision . . . be doubled with a complementary vision or with another vision: myself seen from without . . . he who sees cannot possess the visible unless he is possessed by it, unless he *is of it,* unless, by principle, according to what is required by the articulation of the look with the things, he is one of the visibles, capable, by a singular reversal, of seeing them. . . ." (his italics).

being witnessed by it in some sense—a sense that may well escape analysis in any standard philosophical or scientific paradigms and for which adequate models are lacking. My glance not only testifies to this circumstance of felt intervision; it is an active participant in it, engaging it in the first place and sustaining it in later phases.

I here underline the event of intervision not because it is new in this book—we have encountered it before, most notably in chapters 5 and 6—nor because it is the exclusive agent of connection in the intervisual environment just described (doubtless gazes and other kinds of look also contribute) but because it brings home strikingly the ability of the glance to overcome binary oppositions. This ability is expressed in inspired mercurial movements across differences of many kinds: differences among human beings, humans and nonhumans, different parts of the visual field as well as the different kinds of things populating that field: inanimate as well as animate, those with smooth surfaces and those with rough. Its interstitial action is dramatically evident in the situation just discussed, where a sense of common witnessing is shared by virtually all denizens of a given scene, however heterogeneous each may be to the others. Where it was duration that holds together such qualitative multiplicity on Bergson's temporocentrist view, I am maintaining that the glance—which lives on the outermost edges of duration, that is, in the moment and as activating the all-at-once—accomplishes something quite comparable in the realm of things and places. The glance reunites disparate things as well as parts of entire place-worlds, and in so doing overcomes divisive differences as effectively as does *durée réelle* on Bergson's reading.

For example, in moving rapidly between sky and earth—those two primal sectors of the environing world of nature—the glance conveys to us a sense of a coherent landscape scene that, despite its regional differences, is still *one* world of vision. Were this not so, the natural world would fall apart, and painters would be deprived of a major basis for their work: even when they emphasize visual discrepancies between earth and sky, they do so only insofar as the latter require each other. Not only the painter but each of us standing in the open landscape holds together heaven and earth just by glancing between them.[66]

Or take mind versus matter, the very paradigm of dichotomy in modern philosophy. Regarded as different in basic substance—as Descartes argues—they are irreconcilable, being linked only in the most artificial of ways (for example, through the positing of a pineal gland between them). Yet every hour of every day my mind quite spontaneously links up with matter, and one of the most pervasive ways this happens is by means of the merest glance. When something draws my eye, and I glance at it, I do so as a body/mind complex: one

66. "The upward glance (*das Aufschauen*) passes aloft toward the sky, and yet it remains below on the earth. [It] spans the between of earth and sky. This between is measured out for the dwelling of man" (Martin Heidegger, ". . . Poetically Man Dwells . . . ," in *Poetry, Language, Thought*, tr. A. Hofstadter [New York: Harper, 1971], p. 220).

and the same act is at once bodily (as in the physical movement of my eyes) and mental (in the form of my consciousness of this movement and of any passing thoughts I might have at the time). Nothing is easier to effect than this unrehearsed interinvolvement between mind and matter, even if nothing is less valorized in modern philosophy that takes its lead from Descartes. Yet in everyday visual experience we move back and forth between the mental and the physical with every glance we take. They emerge as two aspects of the same situation rather than two substances set apart from each other.

In the case of spirit and soul, another dyad cited above, the glance also anneals the otherwise oppositional; but it does so now as a distinctive mental glance of the sort that we took up in chapter 9. For it is by looking within myself, by swinging from one pole ("spirit") to another ("soul"), that I reconnect what would be diremptively different without the intermediation of the glance, linking a soulful mood (for example, melancholy) to a spirited state (for example, elation) if only to observe how their differences co-inhere in my own psychic being. The differences remain, but they are linked at their edges by the mental glance that moves between them.[67] This last case instructs us that the deconstruction effected by the glance need not be a dissolution of differences (including dyadic ones) but can be their maintenance in the common space created by actual and virtual trajectories of an act of glancing —a space that, far from being a neutral and placid preexisting medium, is a cat's cradle of pathways blazed by these trajectories themselves.

Much the same obtains in the case of the final pair of opposed terms I mentioned, that of self and other. Here the role of the glance is even more actively intermediatory, since it is by the darting back and forth of glances between two or more human beings—their *interglancing*, as it were—that an elementary sense of community, a "proto-community" as I have called it, arises. Whatever our otherwise divisive differences (that is, of color, age, gender, comparative experience, and so forth), we know each other in such moments as beings of the same delimited but significant stripe: as human glancers who possess a certain equipoise (if not actual equality) in that very activity. At such moments, it is as if we were announcing to each other wordlessly: "at least both of us are engaged in the same common activity of glancing." Each glances in and out in relation to the other; an immediate reciprocity is established by the simple interchange of looks, since each glancer possesses the same basic freedom of indetermination to glance at the other and to glance back when glanced at. (It is just this freely chosen dialectic of glances that is not possible between human and nonhuman beings.) At the same time, this exchange does not act to deny, much less to dissolve, the differences that such interglancing itself brings to our attention. The differences remain, only now they have been apperceived and

___

67. For further discussion of the relationship between the soulful and the spirited, see the foreword to my *Spirit and Soul: Essays in Philosophical Psychology*, 2nd ed. (Putnam, Conn.: Spring Publications, 2004).

acknowledged—and by all parties. With the important exceptions of knowing and withering glances (and of failing to glance at all), the interplay of human glances is telling: it tells us much about interhuman differences from within the momentary bond created by mutual glancing itself. It does not tell us what to do about these differences—that is another phase of ongoing experience—but it does bring them to our shared attention, and is the essential beginning of concerted action taken together in a shared future.

XI

I spoke above of "the world of vision" rather than "the visual world" (that is, the perceived world as such). The world at a glance is the world of vision, and in this concluding section I shall draw some larger lessons when vision is considered the more encompassing term, of which ordinary visual perception is an important part even if not the whole story. The whole story includes the properly apperceptual as well as the perceptual levels of visual experience. It is all too easy to consider the glance a mere modality of ordinary perception. This is especially tempting when we reduce glancing to noting or detecting—merely apprehending—certain distinct features of a given perceptual layout. The glance certainly does these things too, and I don't want to gainsay their significance in the realm of daily practice. It is even likely that glancing itself was first evolved to cope with difficulties and dangers posed by lurking predators and hostile humans in the realm of everyday perception; it was an efficient vehicle of the alertness that was required to survive in the forest or on the savannah. Glancing extends the range of perceptual awareness greatly: once it is operative, human perception is no longer confined to the determinate deliverances of the gaze and its many avatars (for example, scrutinizing, concentrated looking, and so on). These latter help to cope with robust objects in the perceptual field that call for close inspection under a watchful eye. But such standardized forms of straightforward visual perception are less able to handle the unexpected appearance of things emerging suddenly on the periphery of the visual field: the snake that darts from a tree limb sharply to one's left, the suspicious sound behind one's back, the enemy hidden behind a bush. For these situations of sheer surprise, another way of seeing had to evolve, one that could size up right away the extent of the threat.[68]

68. "If an animal has eyes at all it swivels its head around and it goes from place to place. The single, frozen field of view provides only impoverished information about the world. The visual system did not evolve for this. The evidence suggests that visual awareness is in fact panoramic and does in fact persist during long acts of locomotion" (Gibson, *The Ecological Approach to Visual Perception*, p. 2). Just so, but on my reading it is due primarily to the glance that the requisite panoramic vista is gained as the head rotates on the moving body. It is the glance that breaks up "the single, frozen field of view" by its aptitude for darting all over this field with that alacrity I have underlined earlier in these concluding thoughts.

Whatever its roots in such exigencies—in circumstances of survival and adaptation—the glance underwent other vicissitudes in later phases of human history. Still useful at the level of inspection and prospection, which are concerned with full-bodied things (persons, objects, events), it has become active at another level that I have called "apperception" in an effort to capture the nuanced manner by which it ferrets out subtleties that escape ordinary perception. If glancing still has to do with such perception, it is in terms of what Leibniz termed "petites perceptions," which are too spontaneous and too minute to measure by the usual units of what is often called pleonastically "sensory perception." The redoubling involved in this latter term—as if most of perception were not already sensory—underscores the fact that ordinary perception employs established sensory channels to reach perceived objects, for example, gazing, handling, smelling, hearing, tasting.

In contrast, the glance enacts a mode of apperceptual awareness that is literally sub-standard, since it privileges a more indirect and less possessive approach to things seen. Its proper contents are not well-rounded, fully palpable physical things—apples, trees, human bodies, streetlights—even though it does convey to us aspects of these things: the glimmer on the apple's skin, the peculiar shade of green in the leaves of that tree, the special contour of the other's body, the way the streetlight gleams at night. These contents are often considered "ephemera" when compared to their sturdier counterparts—lightweight next-to-nothings, mere epiphenomena, phantoms of the perceptual opera. I prefer to call them *image-things* in the term I have adapted from Bergson's *Matière et Mémoire*. "Me voici en présence d'images": this curt announcement on the opening page of this great book opens up a new world, not only in art (as I have emphasized in chapter 12) and not only as perceived (as Bergson himself interpreted the claim).[69] This is the world of vision—the world of the glance. It is a world composed of less than complete and less than fully extended things, and it includes such insubstantial things as imprints and traces, shadows and horizons. Rather than physical substances or *res extensa,* the glance gives us the surfaces of things—in particular, the shimmering of colors on these same surfaces and their disappearance at an edge—just as it gives us the unique person in someone's face and bodily contour, the "silhouette" rather than the mass of the material body subtending that face or body.[70] In its psychical extension (that is, as the "mental glance"), it also gives us passing thoughts and memories, glimmerings of mentation rather than discrete ideas. In every case, the glance gives us not full-fledged

69. The sentence I quote is translated as "Here I am in the presence of images" (Henri Bergson, *Matter and Memory,* tr. N. M. Paul and W. S. Palmer [New York: Zone, 1988], p. 17). The sentence continues: "images [are] perceived when my senses are opened to them, unperceived when they are closed" (ibid.).

70. " 'People' are silhouettes that are both imprecise and singularized, faint outlines of voices, patterns of comportment, sketches of affects. . . ." (Nancy, *Being Singular Plural,* tr. R. D. Richardson and A. O'Byrne [Stanford: Stanford University Press, 2000], p. 7).

events but advents. Instead of perceptual phenomena, it gives us apperceptual periphenomena.[71] Among these latter are such diverse things as phantom limbs, "voices" I seem to hear but for which there is no auditory basis, and the sense that someone (whom I cannot see) is now looking at me and from a definite direction: the look boring into the back of my neck.[72]

The world at a glance is a luminous, periphenomenal whole of image-things that are specified by surfaces and edges, contours and faces, memories and thoughts, colors and happenings: none of which are simply located in time or space. This is not to say that they are located outside space and time, in some parapsychological or mystical realm. Just as the image-things are not mental—if this means contained in the mind, or still more problematically in the brain: when I glance into my stream of consciousness I see things that exceed this stream itself (for example, Uncle Ralph's face, a quadratic equation)—so their periphenomenal presence is not noumenal either, although it may be numinous in its presentation. "Noumenal" (Kant's term) signifies something transcendent to the perceptual world and (in the context of ethics or religion) spiritual as well. It is not in this direction that the glance points primarily. Its world is at once extra-mental—outside mind as an enclosed realm of its own, *res cogitans*—and yet neither material nor noumenal (the only two options allowed by Kant). It is a detotalized totality of image-things that are glimpsed by an apperceptual act that proceeds *from* the outgoing, seeing subject *to* a replete but nonrigid world.

71. As with Leibniz, I consider mental glancing to be apperceptual, i.e., as a special form of "inner apperception"—without this latter term implying the existence of a separate mind.

72. The first two examples here mentioned are periphenomena of other, nonvisual senses. For the last-cited phenomenon, see Rupert Sheldrake, *The Sense of Being Stared At (and Other aspects of the Extended Mind)* (New York: Crown, 2003), especially chap. 8, which documents cases of feeling that one is being stared at from behind or afar, yet without being able to perceive the actual source of the stare. Sheldrake claims that 70 to 90 percent of his correspondents have had this distinct feeling: "People not only sense they are being looked at, but also detect where the gaze is coming from" (p. 126). Given Sheldrake's explanation of this curious phenomenon—i.e., that each person is surrounded by a "perceptual field" that is sensitive to the least incursion from another person's attention—it follows that a glance can have the same effect as a gaze and that the stare in particular is not requisite for the way in which a given look can leave an immediate imprint on this field. See esp. p. 211: "When someone stares at another person from behind, the projection of the starer's attention means that his field of vision extends out to touch the person he is staring at. His image of that person is projected onto that person through his perceptual field. Meanwhile, the person stared at also has a field all around herself. I suggest that the starer's field of vision interacts with the field surrounding the person stared at. One field is influenced by another field." Could we not substitute "glance" for "stare" and "glancer" for "starer" in each occurrence in this statement and still affirm Sheldrake's basic point? Note that Sheldrake is here committing himself to the ancient idea of "extramission," whereby light—or in his vocabulary an "image"—issues from the eye of the beholder in the equivalent of a visual ray; but see also ibid., pp. 206–211, where he endorses "intromission" as well: both being required in a full account of looking. This combined view, significantly similar to that of Plato, returns us to the debate I reconstructed in chap. 5.

About things in this world, we could not say what Husserl says in echoing Descartes: "the rigid body is the normal body."[73] Rather, the things at which we glance are changing and fluid—as we saw in the ever-altering intensities of green I witnessed from my Wuppertal apartment as described in chapter 7. The appearances we apperceive are not fixed attributes or permanent properties of things but moving figures dancing on surfaces, forms mutating under our very eyes, a world in continual transformation rather than a sum of established items. The latter can be listed and totalized, whereas the image-things at which we glance—and by means of which we glance—can be captured only in a periphenomenological description. No wonder: their presence to us is not secure and stable, regulated by consistencies or constancies, but constitute a scene of demi-presences that twinkle like so many "stars of our life."[74] They look gently back to us as we glance boldly out toward them. It is by such precarious looking, always subject to surprise, that we gain a new world—the world at a glance.

In glancing, then, we win a world by being "beside ourselves"—in a phrase from Plato's *Ion* that is meant to describe poetic transport but that fits just as well the circumstance of glancing.[75] Not only the human subject but the world itself is beside itself in the glance. The glancing subject leaps away from his or her physical substantiality and psychological subjectivity—becoming other to these modes of particularity—while the world, in being glimpsed in a glance, leaves its fixed format as a settled scene of perceived substances in order to become a world-whole of transitory but telling image-things. In both metamorphoses, the gain is as great as the effort is easy.

Neither transmutation can happen without the instigation and contribution of the other—never by itself alone. The world of vision does not come forward from itself alone, as on a naive or direct realist account. Nor does my glance shoot forth into an apperceptual void. I glance at what attracts or repels me—what surprises me—but this glanced-at image-thing belongs to a world that has made itself available to me at a periphenomenal level: it has given me not just the assurance that it is really there but the "affordance" that makes it accessible at a level distinct, though inseparable, from the level that offers epistemic certainty (that is, the level of "animal faith" or "Urdoxa").[76] Just as the level of

---

73. Husserl, "The World of the Living Present and the Constitution of the Surrounding World External to the Organism," p. 239.

74. "Say that the things are structures, frameworks, the stars of our life: not before us, laid out as perspective spectacles, but gravitating around us" (Maurice Merleau-Ponty, *The Visible and the Invisible*, tr. A. Lingis [Evanston, Ill.: Northwestern University Press, 1969], p. 220).

75. "For what they say is true, for a poet is a light and winged thing, and holy, and never able to compose until he has become inspired, and is beside himself, and reason is no longer in him" (Plato, *Ion* 534b2–534b4; Lane Cooper translation). Compare Jean-Luc Nancy's claim that a singularity is an imminence that is always "*beside,* always beside. ('Beside himself', as the saying goes. . . ." (Nancy, *Being Singular Plural*, p. 7; his italics).

76. I take "affordance" in the sense of Gibson, *The Ecological Approach to Visual Perception,* pp. 127–143. "Animal faith" is the expression of George Santayana in his *Skepticism and*

apperception could not arise without an existing level of perception, so the action of the glance cannot take place without a world that does *not* yield to the glance: a world of hard particulars and obdurate things that resists being glimpsed. Glimpsing itself is not "an abnormal kind of vision," much less "a poor sort of awareness."[77] Understood as belonging to normal apperception with an accent on *what* is caught in a glance, glimpsing is an active modality of vision itself and yields very rich contents indeed. We catch a glimpse of the apperceived world every time we glance at it.

Al-Ghazálí, in his *Niches of Light,* claims that the glance "ascends to the highest heavens" and "descends down into the confines of the earth."[78] These words, meant to praise the power of the glance, are not to be dismissed as exaggerated. For the heavens come down to the earth, and the earth rises upward, in the discerning eye of the glance, which opens up a middle realm between both. This is the interplace of connections and crossroads, traversals and transitions, for which the glance is the guiding genius, thanks to the absolute speed of its Hermetic being.[79] It is an *intermonde* in which visuocentrism is appropriate and right. What is lacking in terms of the magisterial presence of high verticality—sky or god or Other—or in the rude earth down here below (soil or root or rock) is made up for in the flight of the glance as it moves from one

---

Animal Faith (New York: Dover, 1955), and I take "Urdoxa" from Edmund Husserl, *Ideas Pertaining to a Pure Phenomeonology and to a Phenomenological Philosophy, First Book,* tr. F. Kersten (The Hague: Nijhoff, 1982), sections 104, 113.

77. Gibson, from whom I borrow these phrases, is here commenting ironically on a model of perception that is based on the camera as producing a set of discrete reproductive images of the robust world: "The artificially produced *glimpse* is an abnormal kind of vision, not the simplest kind on which normal vision is based. It is a poor sort of awareness. But it has seemed to be fundamental for hitherto persuasive reasons: it results from an *image;* it comes from a *stimulus;* it is a *sensory input;* it is what the nerve *transmits.* But if this is so, how could the series of glimpses be integrated? How could the sequence, as I put it, be converted into a scene" (Gibson, *The Ecological Approach to Visual Perception,* p. 304; his italics). My suggestion is that the spontaneous glance is not only normal but also a rich form of awareness that is indeed fundamental in its ability to integrate a given visual scene in a nonreproductive manner. It proceeds by images of a very different kind from those produced by a camera—image-things that convey the scene itself and not only the sequence of its viewings.

78. Al-Ghazálí, *The Niche of Lights,* tr. D. Buchman (Provo, Utah: Brigham Young University Press, 1998), p. 6. Despite this claim, Al-Ghazálí exudes a deep skepticism toward mere "eye service" (ibid., p. 46) that is "veiled from God by the sheer darkness that is in [the glancer's] own souls"(ibid.). Al-Ghazálí's remarkable work, most notable for its imaginative treatment of the light of vision and of visual perception, is marred by an insistence on the degenerate status of such eye service in comparison with the true vision of a higher reason. On my view, the glance itself renders such a comparison otiose, since its ability to merge "the highest heavens" and "the confines of the earth" in the periphenomenal world of vision has its own dignity and force that do not pale in the presence of reason. On the contrary, it is a premonition of the synthetic power of reason itself.

79. On interplace, see my *Getting Back into Place: Toward a Renewed Understanding of the Place-World* (Bloomington: Indiana University Press, 1993), pp. 154 ff.

region of this world of vision to another, forging it into a coherent world-whole that is not a strict totality of determinate presences.

The world of vision is not infinite; it is more of the character of place than of space. "The world always appears each time according to a decidedly local turn,"[80] says Nancy, and this is above all true of the world in which we glance. The glance can range far, but it does not pretend to extend to the end of space as does the abstractive intellect in the ambition of pure mind. The glance goes out to the horizon and back, it looms over the local landscape in its comprehensive sweep, but it does not seek to find or construct a world of infinite space. It is content with the multilocalism of its nomadic course, swinging from one place to another within a given landscape or region. It is at once localizing—picking out places in the swing of its trajectory—and local itself, that is, stemming from the spontaneous eye movements of the body-subject.

The same glance, adhering to the same world, is also singular and singularizing. It is the glance of a singular subject, at once eccentric and idiosyncratic, and it actively singularizes what it glimpses in its lambent look, playing over the surfaces of the things and places and persons at which it is directed. It seeks the singularities of these surfaces, and in so doing it makes both the world they constitute and the subject whose world it is into singular entities. "It is a question of practicing singularities," adds Nancy as if responding to Deleuze's dictum that we must "liberate the singularities of the surface."[81] Both pronouncements come to much the same thing, since it is only by such liberating practice that the pursuit of singularity is to be achieved and the freely glancing subject is to come forth.

This subject always glances at more than one surface; like the butterfly on the glacier, her or his glance flits from surface to surface, with every surface being "that which gives itself and shows itself only in the plural."[82] In contrast with the gaze, which focuses on one identical thing at a time,[83] one particular, one instance of a general—when it is not staring into infinite space—the glance is at once pluralistic and localized. It chases from here to there, up and down, backward and forward in "quick, flicking, facile"[84] motions that trace out the rims of

---

80. Nancy, *Being Singular Plural*, p. 9.

81. The Nancy citation is from "Eulogy for the Mêlée" in *Being Singular Plural*, p. 156; the Deleuze quotation is from *The Logic of Sense*, tr. M. Lester with C. Stivale, ed. C. V. Boundas (New York: Columbia University Press, 1900), p. 141. The Deleuze citation is given in chap. 11, where it guides my discussion of the glance in the environment.

82. Nancy, *Being Singular Plural*, p. 156: "It is a question of practicing singularities, that is, *that which gives itself and shows itself only in the plural*. The Latin *singuli* means 'one by one', and is a word that exists only in the plural" (my italics).

83. When Nancy adds that "it is precisely not a question of playing one identity off another" (ibid.), he could well be speaking of the glance in contrast with the gaze.

84. Oliver Sacks, "The Mind's Eye: What the Blind See," *New Yorker*, July 28, 2003, p. 57: The blind can realize "a deep attentiveness, a slow, almost prehensile attention, a sensuous, intimate being at one with the world which sight, with its quick, flicking, facile quality, continually distracts us from."

things and lay down pathways through the place-world that transfigure it into a glance-world. From its premonitory position, it looks out and around an idio-local scene of its own shaping.

With ciliated attentiveness, the seeing subject "casts a glance" and thereby gets a sense of what the world of vision is like. This sense is finally the sense that is made of the primal domain of visual perception by drawing this all-too-solid phenomenal realm into something periphenomenal but edged, ephemeral yet effective, apperceptive as well as perceptive. This happens in the gentle blow of an interanimating action—an action accomplished in the single stroke that displays the world at a glance.

* * *

To end with two episodes: one from a domain of human innocence, the other from a scene of dark portent.

My grandchildren are playing in the backyard of their home in Denver. I have been inside the house, not paying attention to them. I walk out of the door onto the back porch, and suddenly I spot them "making glue" (that is, incorporating sugar into water until it congeals) with great glee, laughing, mocking each other, being whimsical and a little out of control. I see all this in a single moment: I see their unbounded joy in a glance that itself becomes joyous in witnessing this high-spirited spectacle.

Only three days later I am in Manhattan, walking in Central Park. At Cherry Hill I come upon an open-air exhibit entitled "Eyes Wide Open" whose placard announces "The Human Costs of the Iraq War." Before me are 976 pairs of boots—one pair for each deceased American serviceman—along with more than 1,000 pairs of ordinary shoes that stand in for the many thousands of Iraqi civilians killed since the war began. I am stunned. In one glance, I take in this whole sad spectacle; I see all the empty shoes arranged in rows in one ever-widening circle. I understand right away the grim significance of this scene. The tragedy of war comes home to me in the moment of my looking. I see the world of war, and of this current war in particular, in a glance.

Two episodes, very different in tenor, nevertheless convey the same lesson: I see the world, felicitous or tragic, in a glance.

AFTERWORD

FAMILIES OF THE GLANCE AND THE GAZE

> To arrive at the "purity" of the gaze is not difficult,
> it is impossible.
>
> —Walter Benjamin, "Paris, the Capital of
> the Nineteenth Century"

I

In the course of this book, it has become clear that the glance is no single, simple act. It consists of a family of closely related acts. We have already encountered another such family, namely, that of the gaze. In chapter 4, I briefly explored members of the gaze family: contemplating, scrutinizing, scanning, staring, and glaring. In this afterword, I shall provide a comparable analysis of leading members of the glance family, while also supplementing the earlier discussion of the gaze. In the case of the glance, I shall focus on looking around, glimpsing, and peeking/peeping as distinctive *modes* of glancing, that is to say, ways in which glancing is concretely realized on given occasions. Such modes are to be contrasted both with *modalities* and *kinds*. Modalities are the detailed ways in which modes themselves are enacted. They are often designated by quite specific prepositional phrases: hence "peer into," "peek at," "view of," and so on. Kinds are the cardinal sorts of visual perception, two such kinds being precisely glancing and gazing. Indeed, they are two of the major means by which human beings (and doubtless other animals) look at each other and their environments.

With this trilevel model in mind, let me suggest the following schema of gazing and glancing:

KINDS	GAZING	GLANCING
MODES	Contemplating; Scrutinizing; Scanning; Staring; Glaring	Looking around; Glimpsing; Peeking/Peeping;
MODALITIES	Scanning over, through; Staring at; Glaring at	Peeking at, out; Peeping into, through; Glimpsing of

An important caveat: by setting forth this trichotomous classification, I do not mean to imply that visual perception occurs in a tidy manner. The existence of eidetic differences and formal schemata does not mean that the acts in question are *experienced* with a comparable distinctness. Above all, the lines between certain of the modes are apt to blur—just as they do in the case of species in the natural world. An especially intense case of peeping, for instance, is difficult to distinguish from certain acts of staring—even though the former is, strictly speaking, a form of glancing and the latter is a mode of gazing. Similarly, within one and the same kind, we shall see how close peeking can be to glimpsing, or for that matter staring to glaring, and scrutinizing to scanning. There is family resemblance and thus overlap at every level, including that of modality (for example, between peeking at and peeping into).

The fact is that we cannot maintain strict borders between the various members of any given mode or modality, between entire modes and modalities, or even between whole kinds: glancing and gazing themselves are capable of close cooperation if not outright merging, as we have seen toward the close of chapter 4 and again in chapters 5 and 12. Indeed, kinds have their own modalizations, as is evident in such locutions as "glancing through" or "gazing intently." Everywhere we look, we find fluid boundaries, allowing us to move freely both horizontally (that is, between various modes of a given kind) and vertically (that is, between kinds and modalities).[1] For this very reason, in later parts of this book I do not adhere altogether stringently to the distinctions I make in this afterword; nor have I made explicit reference to some of them. Nevertheless, pointing to these distinctions is of value at a more formal level, precisely in contrast with the amorphousness that inheres in concrete descriptions. The immersion of experience profits from the clarity of eidetic analysis, while such analysis requires in turn the rough edges of enactment: in the end, each calls for, indeed enriches, the other.

1. On the distinction between borders and boundaries, see my forthcoming essay "Borders and Boundaries: Edging into the Environment."

II

Let us first take up certain primary modes of glancing:

looking around. Here we engage in a comparatively comprehensive vista of the perceived world; we take in whatever lies before us and to our sides. Such looking is open-ended and is the least restricted of the four forms of glancing here under consideration. In looking around, I do not stay focused on just one feature of a thing. My glance travels from one item of interest to another, always remaining on the surface and (unlike the gaze) never seeking to delve into depths distinct from this surface. Looking around is a highly receptive action in which we are content with noticing whatever comes to our attention. Despite its interest in taking in as much as possible, looking around has nothing desperate or greedy about it; it occurs with a certain equanimity. Gazing is not necessarily voracious either; but it almost always arises from an attempt to understand or master some entity, to find out something about it. This helps to explain why philosophers from Thales onward have been so drawn to gazing as a paradigm of looking; it is a way of coming to grasp the world more comprehensively. In looking around by glancing, however, I look just in order to see, not from an ulterior motive of acquiring reliable or systematic knowledge. At the most, I *witness the way the world is* at a given moment; I am open to the world without any pretense of gaining access to the depths of the world itself.

glimpsing. To glimpse something is to catch a passing sight of it, typically something at the edge of a perceptual scene: what is "over there" somewhere, peripheral to the primary interest of the scene. I glimpse what is either marginal or momentary, or both. Thus far, glimpsing shares a great deal with other modes of glancing. But in glimpsing proper, the emphasis falls on the content, that is, on *what* I glimpse. Other glancing modes are typically characterized by reference to aspects of their enactment: that is, *how* I am glancing in a given circumstance, its active aspect as it were: "he is glancing knowingly," "they exchanged meaningful glances," "she glanced suspiciously," and so on. Glimpsing is a more passive or receptive activity; it is comparable to barely noting what is unfolding before me.

In keeping with this stance of taking in, only rarely do we add adverbs or adjectives to descriptions of glimpsing; they occur only in such generic locutions as "I barely glimpsed her," or "I caught a passing glimpse of him." In these latter cases, however, the effect is not just to draw attention to the action of glimpsing itself but, more particularly, to its content: to barely glimpse someone is to perceive very little of that person; to catch a passing glimpse is to receive only a very transitory impression of that someone.

It is notable that we say "a glimpse *of* X" but never a "glance of X." The "of" is that of the objective genitive: by glimpsing, I apperceive some aspect of the object I perceive, I bring myself into the vicinity of this aspect, I situate myself there, my attention is *in* that which I glimpse and is no longer fully invested in the act itself. On the other hand, I say that I have "a glance *at* Y." The "at" signifies a directed looking that occurs in a moment of special intensity. This moment stands out from a continuing engagement with the object or its general setting, from which I prescind to glance at just *this* object or only *that* feature of it: both before and after such attentive glancing-at, I may still be perceiving the object at which I glance, for example, in a prolonged gaze. In glimpsing, I do not have to curtail this basic perceiving; I am departing from it momentarily in order to focus momentarily on an aspect of what I see: I am "catching a glimpse" of it.

There is no such thing as steady glimpsing—glimpsing that is slowly paced and self-possessed and devoted to the careful perception of traits. For this reason, glimpsing only rarely belongs to a project of getting to know something better or more intimately. Other forms of glancing may more readily find a place in such a project: for example, when I glance intermittently at certain things in a laboratory to check out what is happening to details in the course of an experiment; or when I glance at the evening news on television to get a sense of what is happening in the Middle East. These acts of glancing can contribute centrally to the pursuit of my ongoing interests: not surprisingly, since they often proceed from a subject who is more or less reliably anchored in the world: indeed, this very stability is what allows the subject to glance around freely and to engage in various forms of this activity. But no such basic stability is presupposed in glimpsing, which I can very well do in rapidly changing circumstances, as when I am lost driving in a new city and look out of the car window to get a sense of where I am. I get this sense by getting a glimpse. Of course, I can also glance in this last situation, for example, by just looking around; but if I do, the implication is that I am less desperate, less deeply lost: I am looking on idly as it were, rather than trying to get a glimpse of, a quick visual fix on, my immediate surroundings. "To get a glimpse" is the critical phrase here. "Get"—a verb which we rarely use in conjunction with gazing or other modes of glancing—bespeaks possessing or holding onto. But in the case of the glimpse, my look only holds onto parts of objects—or, more exactly, it gives us *partial takes* that cannot pretend to be either complete or comprehensive, much less definitive.

peeking/peeping. Like glimpsing, both peeking and peeping have to do with getting a partial view of something; each takes special satisfaction in gaining such a view: hence my pairing of them. But each is distinguished by occurring in context of a certain obstruction of full sight and represents an effort to get around that obstruction. No such effort is called for in looking around or glimpsing, which arise in unobstructed circumstances: there is nothing easier than to look around or to get a glimpse of something, whereas peeking and peering both call for a certain concerted action.

Peeking is located at one extreme end of the spectrum of glancing modes. It contrasts especially with looking around, the least constricted member of this spectrum as well as the most leisurely. Peeking is content with a less than complete survey. Indeed, I feel lucky to have at least *this* much: the modest deliverance of a single peek. I take in only that aspect or part of the object that addresses my immediate visual desire: that alone suffices, nothing else is required. In a manner more playful than glimpsing or looking around, my look darts over or around the surface of things, leaping freely between them. Obstacles, though present, are not difficult to overcome: as when I "take a peek" at a present given to me before the agreed-upon time to open it has come, peeling off the wrapping paper with a certain glee.

Peeping, in contrast, is a more concerted venture in vision. To peep is to look into a situation intently, with a decided focus on the object of one's interest. Peeping takes a decided extra effort that is occasioned by the circumstance of looking, which is typically more obstructed than in peeking: for example, looking in the dark as with a Peeping Tom. While we peek at something *despite* an intervening impediment—we peek from *behind* or *around* it most characterisistically—we peep at something *through* an obstacle such as a keyhole or a chink in the wall. Thus, both by its intentness of looking at a particular kind of thing (often something sexual, but occasionally something macabre: for example, a corpse by the road) and by its momentary struggle with obstructive conditions, peeping is less playful than peeking. It is also more covert: we can peek in the presence of others, but peeping is usually done stealthily and solo: incognito, in a way that others cannot easily detect. I make myself as unnoticeable as possible. Just as I peep through impediments to gain more lucid looking, so in the act itself I make myself less than lucid to others. As Sartre remarks, in peeping I attempt to make myself *nothing*, to make myself invisible; I suspend my being-for-others in order to identify myself entirely with my look: my consciousness is wholly at one with what I am peeping at, as if I had left my body behind me as an inert mass.[2]

Other differences between peeking and peeping exist. Peeping prolonged becomes gazing, as with the Peeping Tom who stares continuously at his visual target. Peeking, in contrast, is always in motion, continually changing its intended object: I peek at this, then that, then something else again. It is telling that peeping is more often an activity of adults than of children; it requires a certain focused intensity. Its aim is altogether determinate: for example, to peep at that woman undressing at night through her bedroom window. The peeper seeks a definite object of desire. There is absorption in this object, not for its sake but for the peeper's own visual pleasure.

Peeping is often a last-ditch strategy: we peep when we can no longer see something in the unobstructed light of day, or when such seeing is not socially sanctioned.[3] It thus takes a certain amount of scheming to peep, whereas we peek at whim. Walking along Main Street in Stonington, I peek into the window of a bookshop. I have no serious intent to buy books or to search for a particular book. This happens in public: I do not mind being seen peeking. But if I were espied peeping at the woman in the window, I would be mortified. In contrast

2. For Sartre's analysis of looking through a peephole, see *Being and Nothingness*, tr. H. Barnes (New York: Washington Square Press, 1972), pp. 347–354

3. I am here ignoring the other, wholly nonvisual sense of "peep," which is to emit short, high-pitched sounds, as when chicks peep.

with the playfulness of peeking, peeping works hard to achieve its goal. In peeping, I seek both to overcome physical barriers to, and to suspend social strictures on, my vision. I succeed insofar as I "cause [the object I seek] to appear slightly" (*Oxford English Dictionary*) across these barriers and strictures. Such bare appearing, minimal as it may be, is what I covet in peeping, which is more possessive than any other form of glancing. If the peeping yields no determinate content—only a blur or a perceptual phantom, the woman who, instead of undressing, moves quickly to another room—I am subject to a special frustration of desire. This frustration is a sign of my concerted intentionality: to peep is to look with a definite sense of purpose. No wonder that peeping is often characterized by a certain "eye-strain" (for example, from continual squinting) whereby I try to have an unimpeded look at something I ardently desire to see. To this end, I put myself in a position from which I can bring into clear focus what I seek to see: I make myself a subject whose very being is dependent on such clarification. I am at one with my look—in contrast with peeking, in which I retain my consciously felt personal identity throughout a series of attentional diversions.

For the gaze and looking around, the more encompassing the vista the better; but when it comes to peeping and peeking—and to glimpsing—a less comprehensive visual grasp suffices. Indeed, less is truly more in these latter cases. The peek takes to an extreme what is already the case with the glimpse and the peep (and what is actively avoided in the gaze and looking around): a delimitation of vision. In peeking, however, the delimitation is openly embraced. I am content with the partial content I receive: indeed, glad to have it, as when I get pleasure in the very act of unwrapping a present. This is an active pleasure taken in fleeting appearances. There is something innocent and childlike in such pleasure, which contrasts with the more concerted intentionality of peeping—and, all the more so, that of gazing. These latter fasten on the object of the look as if it were a definitive gain—hence their tendency to linger on this object—whereas the peek never stays put.

Nevertheless, we speak of "taking a peek," where this suggests an element of active volition, a certain seeking to look. But the desire to see is not here the wish to concentrate on any one thing to the exclusion of others. I may *begin* by wanting to peek at a particular thing, but if I don't find it or if I am prevented from seeing it I am not as disappointed as I would be in peeping. There is nothing like a "peep show" here: in the latter, I am bent on seeing something freakish or lascivious, and I am willing to pay money to have a view: I seek an expected pleasure, and when this doesn't occur I am frustrated.[4] When peeking

---

4. Hence the frequent recourse to technological assistance in the case of peeping: the *Rear Window* phenomenon. One peeps through binoculars as well as through actual windows in order to be the silent witness of a visual spectacle of the other in erotic display (or, as in the case of the film, the revelation of violence). Peeping at this other amounts to an intensified albeit displaced possession of him or her.

uncovers something unexpected, I am merely amused: for example, when a Chihuahua appears in the window at which I am looking. In peekaboo, for example, the child peeks to find an object that has disappeared momentarily— and upon whose sudden reappearance there is a triumphant exclamation of "boo," a verbal expression for delight at the return itself.

Peeking, then, is a highly channeled mode of seeing that thrives from its very restrictedness by transforming such seeing into a scene of light-hearted looking. There is scopic desire in it, but the desire is not as insistent as in peeping. At play is a gentle wish to gain a delimited view of a person or thing: or more likely, just parts of these latter. If there is something somewhat desperate—anxious, voracious—in the act of peeping, peeking is in contrast more relaxed, more open to the vicissitudes of looking. In the one, I am intent on viewing just one object, almost always erotic; in the other, I am able to enjoy a succession of objects— thanks to my pleasure in merely circulating among them.[5]

III

As mentioned earlier, it is a curious linguistic fact (and such a fact is, in J. L. Austin's counsel, the "first word," even if not the last, in any given philosophical discussion)[6] that we speak of "a glance at," "a peep at," and "a peek at." In contrast, we talk about having a "view of" something just as we speak of getting a "glimpse of" it. These are not idle idioms. They bespeak a thin red line that runs through the family of modes of glancing I am here exploring. The *at* at stake in peeping and peeking alike bespeaks a directed form of attentiveness—one that attempts to go straight to the heart of the matter. It is in this spirit that we speak of a "penetrating glance" or a "revealing peek" or an "arousing act of peeping," even if what we glance and peek and peep at may be quite different things. Signified as well by the "at" employed in designating these three acts is a sense of getting near to, coming close-up: we glance in general so as to bring our look to the very surface of what we see, we peep so as to gain a view of something voyeuristically desired, and we peek in order to pick up what is currently un-available in vision in the near sphere.

In instructive contrast, the "of" embedded in "view of" and "glimpse of" bespeaks a diminished concern with such proximal adhesion to perceptual par-ticulars; it points, instead, to a situation of gaining sight of something—whether this sight be commanding and panoramic or merely partial and passing. What we see need not be near by; it can be remotely situated so long as we have a vista

---

5. I allude to the poem of Wallace Stevens, "The Pleasures of Merely Circulating."

6. "Certainly, then, ordinary language is *not* the last word: in principle it can everywhere be supplemented and improved upon and superseded. Only remember, it is the *first* word" (J. L. Austin, "A Plea for Excuses," in *Philosophical Papers*, 2nd ed. (Oxford: Oxford University Press, 1970), p. 185; his italics.

on it. The *of* adumbrates an openness to whatever is on display in the overall layout of surfaces, apperceived at virtually any distance.[7]

It is important to note I am not claiming that the members of the glance family I am here discussing are on an indifferent par with each other. Despite their manifest differences, glimpsing and looking around are more frequently pursued modes of glancing, which often alternates between just glimpsing something outright and viewing it in a more extended manner (as the action of looking around implies). If peeking and peeping are less frequently enacted, this is because they entail a concerted desire to see in spite of attenuations of, or hindrances to, seeing itself. That is why I have discussed them next to each other as closely related members of a quasi pair: "peeking/peeping" signifies in effect "peeking and/or peeping."

These various members of the glance family dispose themselves on an axis that runs from more comprehensive and open on the left to more focused and closed at the right of the following diagram:

{ looking around // glimpsing][peeking // peeping }

This quite schematic picture has the advantage of showing the full spectrum of acts here at issue. Belonging to the same overall set, these modes of glancing exhibit affinities with each other—beyond the correlations between the members of the two pairs I have analyzed in section II above. For example, glimpsing and peeking converge when to *get a glimpse* of something and to *have a peek* at it are alternative, or alternating, inroads into a given scene. When I am a member of a dense crowd at a parade and catch sight of a certain personage who is being driven past in a limousine, I may *peek* between other members of the crowd who stand before me and thereby catch a *glimpse* of the personage herself. The main difference is that I can glimpse something without any express intention to do so, whereas I always peek with a desire to look, however mild or muted this may be.

By the same token, looking around and peeping, for all their evident differences, have an affinity with each other as well. Each is concerned to optimize the scene of looking, to gain a better view of things. Looking around is paradigmatically panoramic; it attempts to take in all that can be seen within the current visual horizon. When we peep, we do not seek a more comprehensive view but

7. There is, however, an important difference between these two cases. The view we gain in looking around has little if any possessiveness toward what it sees; it is mainly the registration of a panoramic sweep of co-presented items. A glimpse of something, however, implies that we have gained a perception we might have otherwise lacked; here the "of" indicates that what we glimpse now *belongs* to our look; however diminished it may be in extent (typically, it is a mere patch of something), in being glimpsed it has nevertheless become part of our perceptual repertoire, an item we have seized from oblivion—something we now *know*, however imperfectly and partially.

we do attempt to improve our current view, sometimes against considerable odds (for example, the darkness of nighttime, a closed door). In contrast, neither glimpsing nor peeking aims at bettering our view; they are content with taking in what is presented to us at the moment.

Each mode of glancing helps us to attain a unique aspect of what is seen. In glimpsing, I catch sight of something en passant, retrieving it for my look as it were; in peeping, I make a special effort to look at something across physical or social obstacles; in peeking, I glance delicately but deliberately at something despite its being closed off to me momentarily; and in looking around, I let my glance fall upon an open scene arrayed with diverse contents.

The larger lesson here is not just the sheer multiplicity of modes and modalities of glancing—their internal complexity, their intrigue or plot—but the protean character of the act itself, its shape-shifting power. Such variety of means reflects in turn the way in which the visual world is continually changing course and altering form. In this respect, glancing is paradigmatic of visual experience as a whole—and shows itself not to be the marginal act it is so often assumed to be. The latter assumption stems from the temptation to consider glancing as subordinate to a supposedly more reliable or substantive act such as gazing. Its very marginalization, however, signals the threat that glancing poses to more staid and static models of visual perception in which strict borders are erected between traditionally distinct levels: for example, between "sensation" and "perception," or between "perception" and "judgment." The merest glance, in any of its four primary modes, moves effortlessly between these levels, and thereby deconstructs any fixed differences between them.

The ability of glancing to dissolve epistemic borders exhibits the agitated energy of the glance in its scopic appetite—its desire to notice everything within its range, to take it all in, and to evade anything that blocks its way. Even if only certain glances are truly comprehensive, every glance carries with it the same telos: to see as far and as wide as possible. We may take it as axiomatic that *the glance moves on,* being only momentarily satisfied with what it delivers in a given glimpse or peek, peep, or look around. This deliverance is *just enough but not more.* An important part of the glance's restlessness has to do with its not yet having a comprehensive enough view on any given occasion: comprehensive enough to afford the glancer the sense that she has fully witnessed the visual world into which she looks so fleetingly yet so intensely. Even so, glancing is a gift, and takes us to the apperceived world in ways that no other perceptual power can realize. The modality of "glancing into" articulates this gift: the "into" signifies the gently penetrating quality of the glance as well as its potential inclusiveness: getting into all that it can possibly see once it has connected with the surfaces of the surrounding world.

We touch here on one of the primary virtues of the glance: its nimble evasion of established encrustations along with its tendency to gather together in one look as much of the layout of surfaces as it possibly can. The result is a "detotalized totality" (in Sartre's phrase): a totality qua comprehensive outlook, yet nonsummative thanks to its incisive and saltatory actions. This paradoxical combination of traits is precisely what makes the glance so uniquely diverse among ways of looking. As looking around, it seeks to be comprehensive; as peeping, it aims at a maximally clear view in obstructed circumstances; as peeking, it takes us lightheartedly where we want to go on a given visual occasion; as glimpsing, it thrives in partial views. This range of modes of looking, far from undermining the glance, strengthens it and makes it more adaptive to disparate settings. By now it is clear that there is no such thing as "glancing proper," a single right or even central way to glance: integral to its power is the ability of any glance to change its mode or modality at the blink of an eye, yielding a remarkable potpourri of ways in which we look at the visual world—of which the four modes and eleven modalities I have here identified are exemplary but not exhaustive instances.

IV

So, too, there is no gazing proper—only a basic kind of vision with at least five different modes: contemplating, scrutinizing, scanning, staring, and glaring. Much as in the case of the various modes of glancing, these latter can be arranged with respect to their comparative comprehensiveness, as in this figure:

{ contemplating // scanning // scrutinizing][staring // glaring }

As in the case of looking around, the second and third modes on the left aim at comprehensiveness, while the three others pursue more restrictive ends. I scan a scene as a whole as systematically as I can, "line by line" as it were, whereas I scrutinize the same scene to discern what I am looking for in more detail. Staring and glaring are still less interested in the full field before them, being ways of concentrating on delimited matters at hand. Where we routinely say "stare at" and "glare at," as if pointing to more focused forms of looking, the English verbs "scrutinize" and "scan" take no associated prepositions—the implication being that both directly confront the open field they survey, though in scrutiny I single out a particular part of this field. In contemplation, I also focus on something special albeit in a more receptive way.

It remains the case that gazing in each of its modes and associated modalities is more open-eyed than any single form of glancing; only looking around approaches such openness, though its noncommittal character contrasts strikingly with the more concerted character of scanning and scrutinizing. In gazing, I engage myself in continuing concentration on my perceptual field and its contents, seeking their respective depths. In glancing, I pursue a more discontinuous and desultory approach, staying with the apperceived surfaces of this same field. Each kind of looking is informative, indeed essential, with regard to our acquaintance with the visual world; but each is informative and essential in very different ways.

INDEX

EDWARD S. CASEY is Distinguished Professor of Philosophy at SUNY–Stony Brook. He is author of a number of books, including *Getting Back into Place* (1993), *Imagining* (1976; 2000), and *Remembering* (1987; 2000), all with Indiana University Press. *The World at a Glance* is the first of two volumes; the second is entitled *The World on Edge*.